UNDERSTANDING TAXATION OF BUSINESS ENTITIES

UNDERSTANDING TAXATION OF BUSINESS ENTITIES

Walter D. Schwidetzky
Professor of Law
University of Baltimore School of Law

Fred B. Brown
Associate Professor of Law
University of Baltimore School of Law

ISBN: 978-0-7698-6904-9

Library of Congress Cataloging-in-Publication Data
Schwidetzky, Walter D., 1952- author.
Understanding taxation of business entities / Walter D. Schwidetzky, Professor of Law, University of Baltimore School of Law; Fred B. Brown, Associate Professor of Law, University of Baltimore School of Law.
pages cm
Includes index.
ISBN 978-0-7698-6904-9 (softbound)
1. Business enterprises--Taxation--Law and legislation--United States. I. Brown, Fred B., author. II. Title.
KF6450.S39 2015
343.7306'7--dc23
2014044146

NOTE TO USERS
To ensure that you are using the latest materials available in this area, please be sure to periodically check the LexisNexis Law School web site for downloadable updates and supplements at www.lexisnexis.com/lawschool.

Editorial Offices
630 Central Ave., New Providence, NJ 07974 (908) 464-6800
201 Mission St., San Francisco, CA 94105-1831 (415) 908-3200
www.lexisnexis.com

MATTHEW◊BENDER

DEDICATION

To my parents, wife, and children, who have supported me in so many ways.

Fred Brown*

To my grandmothers Mary Augusta Jones and Suzanne Schwidetzky, both of whom attended university around 1900, and one of whom came from a working class background. There were feminist pioneers decades before the word "feminist" entered our vocabulary.

Walter Schwidetzky

---

* I am very grateful to Stacey Morris for her excellent research assistance.

PREFACE

This book is an overreaction to a problem that I experienced in teaching business entity taxation. I could not find a single-volume supplemental text to recommend to students that I felt fully met their needs. From my own experience in teaching the course, I know that there are some areas a professor covers in detail, others that are just skimmed over, and still others that are somewhere in between. Fred Brown and I wanted a book that is user-friendly and that would allow students to opt for just a broad overview or dive into the material in more detail. At the same time, we wanted a "twofer," a text that would be valuable to students who take separate courses in corporate and partnership taxation. Students would be spared the cost of buying two different texts. Further, it is common for professors teaching one subject to refer to the other. For example, if an owner contributes property to a corporation subject to debt that exceeds the owner's basis, the corporate tax rules typically have a different answer from the partnership tax rules. Having a single-volume text makes it easy for a student to get up to speed in both areas. Since we could not find what we wanted, we wrote what we wanted. We hope you find our effort helpful.

Walter Schwidetzky
Fred Brown

TABLE OF CONTENTS

TABLE OF CONTENTS

TABLE OF CONTENTS

TABLE OF CONTENTS

TABLE OF CONTENTS

TABLE OF CONTENTS

TABLE OF CONTENTS

TABLE OF CONTENTS

TABLE OF CONTENTS

TABLE OF CONTENTS

TABLE OF CONTENTS

TABLE OF CONTENTS

TABLE OF CONTENTS

TABLE OF CONTENTS

TABLE OF CONTENTS

TABLE OF CONTENTS

TABLE OF CONTENTS

TABLE OF CONTENTS

TABLE OF CONTENTS

TABLE OF CONTENTS

TABLE OF CONTENTS

TABLE OF CONTENTS

Chapter 1

INTRODUCTION

A. Overview

Welcome to business entity taxation! We intend this book to supplement casebooks used in law school courses on partnership, corporate, or business entity taxation (i.e., a course that covers both partnership and corporate taxation). Business entity taxation is, of course, very important for the tax specialist, but it is also important for business law practitioners. It is not possible to be an effective business lawyer without knowing something about business taxation.

The book is broken into a part on partnership taxation and a part on corporate taxation. The part on corporate taxation is broken into two subparts, one on C corporation taxation and one on S corporation taxation. We have broken each chapter into two sections, a "Basic Overview" and a "Detailed Analysis." There are two main reasons for this approach. The Basic Overview can help you ease into the material. It gives you the big picture, before diving into the Detailed Analysis. Further, it is not possible in a law school business entity taxation course to cover it all in detail in the 2-4 credits that are typically available. Necessarily, your professor will need to go over some topics lightly. For those topics, reading the Basic Overview alone may be sufficient for your needs. For each type of business tax entity, we will go through its life cycle, formation, operations, and liquidation, along with reorganizations and divisions for corporations.

Virtually all substantive business entity law is state law. Each state has its own law that determines such issues as formation, operation, and liquidation of the various business entities. The state law business entity choices have expanded dramatically since the mid-1990s: Sole proprietorships, general partnerships, limited liability partnerships (LLPs — general partnerships with a liability shield), limited partnerships (LPs), limited liability limited partnerships (LLLPs — limited partnerships with an extra liability shield protecting the general partner from liability — exists in a minority of states), limited liability companies (LLCs), and corporations. The details of these entities we will leave to other law school courses.

A preliminary tax policy issue for business entities is whether they should be treated as an "aggregate" of their owners or as separate taxpayers. This dichotomy is often referred to as "aggregate" versus "entity" taxation. Pure aggregate taxation means that the entity is ignored and the owners are seen as the only relevant taxpayers. Pure entity taxation ignores the owners and only looks at the entity. We do not have pure aggregate taxation, but for both tax partnerships and S corporations the entity is not normally taxed, all income and expenses flow through and are taken into account by the owners. It is not pure aggregate taxation, because much of what goes on at the entity level determines how income and expenses flow through. For example, for both partnerships and S corporations, income and expenses are characterized (as ordinary or capital) at the entity level, not the owner level. We do have pure entity taxation for C corporations, which are treated as taxpayers entirely separate from their shareholders.

Of course, the core business entity tax rules are contained in the Internal Revenue Code of 1986, as amended (the *"Code"* or *"I.R.C."*). Often as important as the Code itself are the regulations promulgated by the Department of the Treasury interpreting and implementing the Code (the *"Regulations"* or *"Treas. Reg."*). Partnerships are covered by Subchapter K of the Code. As you may now already guess, the first letter in C corporation and S corporation refers to the subchapter in which the relevant tax law is (at least to a large extent) located. C corporations are covered by Subchapter C, S corporations by Subchapter S (though much of Subchapter C remains relevant). As may not be apparent, the designation of C or S corporation is purely a federal tax designation. Taxpayers form corporations at the state level. A corporation will be taxed as a C corporation unless it elects (and qualifies) to be an S corporation. An LLC may also elect to be taxed as a C corporation (very rare) or an S corporation (fairly common). The income of a C corporation is subject to two levels of tax. One is at the corporate level on its taxable income (i.e., the entity tax). But if the C corporation distributes dividends to the shareholders, those dividends are taxed to the shareholders. To simplify a little, dividends are for the most part post-tax income of the C corporation, so the same income is being taxed twice, once at the corporation level and once at the shareholder level. As a consequence, you will often hear professors and practitioners refer to the "double taxation" of C corporations. Of course, owners prefer one level of tax to two, so C corporations are usually avoided by closely held businesses. As we will discuss below, widely held businesses usually cannot avoid C corporation status. While in the case of C corporation dividends there is an owner-level tax, this is not an example of aggregate taxation. Nothing going on at the owner level determines the taxable nature of a dividend (though the shareholder-level tax rates can vary and are usually lower than ordinary income tax rates).

While there are many different types of state law entities, the tax code only recognizes three types: partnerships, S corporations, and C corporations. Of course, a taxpayer can conduct business without using a business entity, i.e., as a sole proprietor. But taxpayers rarely operate as state law sole proprietors due to the lack of a liability shield. Typically, one-owner businesses form an LLC or a corporation to conduct the business (they cannot form a partnership, which definitionally requires at least two owners). How are these myriad state law entities, some with one owner, some with many, funneled into the federal tax system? We discuss that next.

B. The Classification of Domestic Business Entities for Tax Purposes

I.R.C. § 7701 defines a partnership to include a syndicate, group, pool, joint venture, or other unincorporated organization, through or by means of which any business, financial operation, or venture is carried on, and which is not, under the

Code, a trust or estate or a corporation;[1] and the term "partner" includes a member in such a syndicate, group, pool, joint venture, or organization.[2] It defines a corporation to include associations, joint-stock companies, and insurance companies.[3] We are willing to bet these definitions did not do much for you.

The Regulations happily come to the rescue. The portion of the Regulations dealing with entity classification is commonly called the "check-the-box" Regulations, because the Regulations provide an election to change the tax treatment of some types of entities by "checking the box" and filing the appropriate form. That said, it would make more sense to call them the "don't-check-the-box" Regulations because usually parties will prefer the default rules to the alternative election.[4]

If a business entity has only one owner, the entity will be automatically treated as a corporation for federal income tax purposes if formed as a state-law corporation.[5] If the one-owner entity is not formed as a state-law corporation, then it generally will be treated as a disregarded entity for tax purposes, unless it elects to be treated as a corporation.[6] A disregarded entity is one that is ignored for federal income tax purposes. For example, if a state law LLC has a single owner, under the default rule the LLC is ignored for federal income tax purposes. If the sole owner is an individual, the owner is taxed as if she were operating as a sole proprietor.[7] The owner may, however, check the box and have the LLC taxed as a C corporation or, if she qualifies, as an S corporation.[8]

If a domestic business entity has more than one owner, the entity may not be a disregarded entity. Thus, the entity must either be a corporation or a partnership. Under the check-the-box Regulations, a business entity with more than one owner is treated as a corporation for federal income tax purposes if it is formed as a state-law corporation.[9] If the more-than-one-owner entity is not formed as a state-law corporation, then it generally is treated as a partnership for tax purposes, unless it elects to be treated as a C- or S corporation.[10] In most cases, partnership classification is preferred.

Whether an entity has more than one owner is determined under federal tax principles, rather than solely under state law. For example, a domestic LLC with more than one member for state law purposes may be a disregarded entity if one of its members is itself a disregarded entity owned by the other member.[11]

---

[1] I.R.C. § 7701(a)(2).

[2] *Id.*

[3] I.R.C. § 7701(a)(3).

[4] Treas. Reg. § 301.7701-2.

[5] Treas. Reg. § 301.7701-2(b)(1).

[6] Treas. Reg. § 301.7701-2(b)(1), -3(b)(1).

[7] *See* Treas. Reg. § 301.7701-2(a).

[8] Treas. Reg. § 301.7701-3(a).

[9] Treas. Reg. § 301.7701-2(b)(1).

[10] Treas. Reg. § 301.7701-2(b)(1), -3(b)(1).

[11] Rev. Rul. 2004-77, 2004-2 C.B. 119.

Similarly, an LLC with two members for state law purposes was treated as a disregarded entity where one of the members had no economic rights in the venture.[12]

As we noted above, most of the time taxpayers will not want to elect out of the default rules, but when they do it usually will be to elect to be taxed as an S corporation. Practitioners often prefer a state-law LLC to a state-law corporation because the former has more modern statutory architecture. If they want the advantages of the S corporation taxation rules, they often form an LLC rather that a state-law corporation and elect S corporation status. It would be very rare for an LLC to elect C corporation status due to the onus of double taxation.

One exception to the general rule that domestic business entities with more than one owner may not be treated as disregarded entities is a spousal partnership. I.R.C. § 761(f) provides that a husband and wife who operate a joint venture may elect not to treat the joint venture as a partnership; in other words, they may treat it as a disregarded entity. In order to qualify, both spouses must materially participate in the business of the entity, and they must file a joint return. Rev. Proc. 2002-69[13] also allows spousal partnerships to be disregarded in community property states without regard to the material participation standard.

C.   The Classification of non-U.S. Business Entities for Tax Purposes

The check-the-box Regulations provide a list of non-U.S. entities that will be treated as C corporations[14] and are not eligible to elect to be treated otherwise.[15] The preamble to the originally proposed version of the check-the-box Regulations indicates that it was the intent to give per se corporation treatment to entities that would have unavoidably been classified as corporations under the prior entity classification Regulations.[16] A number of foreign entities are thus automatically classified as corporations for federal tax purposes. An example is the German Aktiengesellschaft.

If a non-U.S. business entity is not per se classified as a C corporation under the check-the-box Regulations, then the default classification will depend upon whether liability of all of the owners is limited. If the liability of all owners is limited, as is typically the case, the default classification for a non-U.S. business entity is as a C

---

[12] PLR 199911033 (March 22, 1999).

[13] 2002-2 C.B. 831.

[14] Foreign entities that are automatically classified as corporations cannot elect to be S corporations because an S corporation must be a domestic corporation. *See* Chapter 24.

[15] Treas. Reg. § 301.7701-2(b)(8).

[16] Notice of Prop. Rulemaking, 61 F.R. 93, 21989 (May 13, 1996). Under the prior entity classification Regulations, an entity was classified as an association taxable as a corporation if it had more than two of the following four factors: (i) centralized management, (ii) perpetual life, (iii) free transferability of interests and (iv) limitation of liability. Treas. Reg. § 301.7701-2 prior to amendment by T.D. 8697, 61 F.R. 244, 66584 (Dec. 18, 1996). *See also* Kintner v. United States, 107 F. Supp. 976 (D. MT 1952). Many of the *per se* corporations are usually publicly held.

corporation.[17] If the liability of any owner of the entity is not limited, the default classification of the entity is either as a disregarded entity, if the entity has only one owner, or as a partnership, if the entity has more than one owner.[18] In either case, however, the foreign entity can elect out of its default status. Thus, if the default status is that of a C corporation, it can elect disregarded entity or partnership status depending on the number of owners, and vice versa.[19] (Under I.R.C. § 1361(b)(1), a foreign entity cannot qualify as an S corporation.)

D. Publicly Traded Entities

The overwhelming majority of publicly traded entities are formed as state law corporations. Due to the large number of shareholders, they cannot qualify as S corporations (which, generally, have a 100-shareholder limit).[20] Nonetheless, publicly traded state law limited partnerships and even LLCs exist. If a business entity would otherwise be treated as a tax partnership, but its interests are publicly traded on an established securities market or are readily tradable on a secondary market (or the substantial equivalent), then, in general, the entity is treated as a C corporation for federal income tax purposes.[21] However, the state law partnership or LLC is still treated as a tax partnership if at least 90% of the gross income of the partnership for each taxable year after 1987 is comprised of passive types of income.[22] To be specific, passive income includes interest, dividends, real property rents, gain from the sale or disposition of real property, income and gain derived from the exploration, development, mining or production, processing, refining, transportation (including pipelines transporting gas, oil, or products thereof) or the marketing of any mineral or natural resources (including fertilizer, geothermal energy and timber), gain from the sale or disposition of a capital asset (or property used in a trade or business) held for the production of income described in this sentence and, for certain partnerships, income and gain from commodities (not treated as inventory) or futures, forwards and options with respect to commodities.[23]

---

[17] Treas. Reg. § 301.7701-3(b)(2)(B).

[18] Treas. Reg. § 301.7701-3(b)(2).

[19] Treas. Reg. § 301.7701-3(a).

[20] *See* Chapter 24.

[21] I.R.C. § 7704(a), (b).

[22] I.R.C. § 7704(c).

[23] I.R.C. § 7704(d). The 90% of gross income exception does not apply to any partnership which would be described in I.R.C. § 851(a) (relating to regulated investment companies) if the partnership were a domestic corporation. However, to the extent provided in Regulations, the regulated investment company exception to the 90% of gross income exception will not apply to any partnership which has as a principal activity the buying and selling of commodities (not treated as inventory) or options, futures, or forward contracts with respect to commodities. To date, no Regulations have been promulgated that provide for the commodity trading exception. The qualification of commodities-type income for the 90% of gross income exception only applies to partnerships that have as a principal activity the buying and selling of commodities (not treated as inventory) or options, futures or forward contracts with respect to commodities.

E. Taxes Doing the Driving

As will become more apparent as you work your way through the book, the "choice of entity decision" is heavily tax driven. Partnership taxation is more flexible than other areas, leading to a preference for tax partnerships. LLCs are usually the most flexible state law entity. As a consequence, typically the maximum flexibility is achieved using an LLC taxed as a partnership. This dynamic makes LLCs the "entity of choice," i.e., the entity most practitioners usually prefer. So does that mean partnership taxation is the most important area of tax law? Don't rush to this judgment. It depends on the nature of the lawyer's practice. For a lawyer who mostly represents closely held businesses, partnership and S corporation taxation tends to be the focus, for those who represent widely held corporations, C corporation taxation comes to the fore. But all business tax lawyers need to know something about all areas of business taxation. So the answer to the question we posed might be "it is all important."

F. State Taxation

Note that this text is solely about the federal tax rules. States have independent taxing jurisdiction. While states commonly follow the federal lead, they do not always. Several states, for example, assess some kind of entity level tax on LLCs (which usually does not occur at the federal level).

And now, onward "into the breach!"[24]

---

[24] 'Cry God for Harry, England, and Saint George!' speech of Shakespeare's Henry V, Act III, 1598.

PART I:
PARTNERSHIPS

Chapter 2

DEFINING PARTNERSHIPS AND PARTNERS FOR TAX PURPOSES

BASIC OVERVIEW

Before we can discuss how the partnership rules work, you first need to know whether a partnership and/or a partner exists for tax purposes. State law and the parties' nomenclature are not controlling. It does not make any difference whether an entity is or is not a partnership for state law purposes. Persons who do not call themselves partners can be held to be partners in a partnership, and persons who do call themselves partners may be held not to be. That is true even if the parties are acting in good faith.

Many times, the existence of a business entity will be apparent. If a partnership or a limited liability company (an "*LLC*") is formed under a U.S. domestic state law with a valid business or financial purpose on other than a transitory basis, there is likely to be little question that a business entity exists. Controversies may develop, however, as to whether the entity has been formed for a valid business or financial purpose and whether the entity has been formed other than on a transitory basis.[1] For example, in *Andantech L.L.C. v. Commissioner*,[2] a Wyoming LLC was disregarded by the Tax Court because the LLC was not formed for the purpose of carrying on a business, but rather for the sole purpose of tax avoidance. (See Detailed Discussion.)

On the other hand, it is also possible to create a business entity for U.S. federal income tax purposes without creating an entity for state law purposes. Treas. Reg. § 301.7701-1(a)(2) provides that a "joint venture or other contractual arrangement may create a separate entity for federal tax purposes if the participants carry on a trade, business, financial operation, or venture and divide the profits therefrom." A continuing question arises as to whether "other contractual arrangements" create a business entity for tax purposes. By the way, the term *joint venture* is synonymous with *partnership* for almost all purposes. Sometimes practitioners will use the term *joint venture* instead of *partnership* when the partnership is for a single deal. The tax rules are the same.

---

[1] See, e.g., Commissioner v. Tower, 327 U.S. 280 (1946); ASA Investerings Partnership v. Commissioner, 201 F.3d 505 (D.C. Cir. 2000).

[2] 2002 T.C.M. (RIA) ¶ 2002-097, *aff'd* 331 F.3d 972 (D.C. Cir. 2003).

Once it is determined that a domestic business entity[3] has been formed, the entity must be classified as a disregarded entity, a partnership or a corporation.[4] We discuss these rules in detail in the introduction to the text and do not review them again here.

Simply knowing whether or not you have a business entity and knowing the check-the-box Regulations is usually enough, but alas, not always. You also need to understand the legal definition of a tax partnership. I.R.C. §§ 761(a) and 7701(a)(2) define a partnership as a syndicate, group, pool, joint venture, or other unincorporated organization, through or by means of which any business, financial operation, or venture is carried on, and which is not a trust or estate or a corporation. The definition is quite broad, and, as mentioned above, the definition may cause some undertakings that are not business entities for state law purposes to be treated as partnerships for federal tax purposes. However, not every joint undertaking gives rise to a partnership for federal tax purposes. The definition may also be applied to cause an entity treated as a business entity for state law purposes to be disregarded as an entity for federal tax purposes.[5]

Rather than using the rather amorphous Code definition, it is often said that a partnership exists when the parties join together in the present conduct of an enterprise and share the profits or losses of the enterprise.[6] However, not all profit-sharing arrangements result in the creation of a partnership for tax purposes. For example, a lender does not become a partner with the lender, just because the loan document provides that the lender will pay the borrower a percentage of the revenues of a venture. If, however, the lender has a substantial voice in the operation of the venture, a partnership for tax purposes could be created, even if for state law purposes the lender/borrow relationship is respected.[7] Where a purported lender was not obligated to be paid in all events but only had a right to be paid out of 50% of the net profits of the venture, the lender was treated as a partner for tax purposes.[8]

The owner of a business may agree to compensate a hired manager or key employee with a percentage of the income of the business, or a broker may be retained to sell property for a commission based on the net or gross sales price without creating a partnership for tax purposes.[9] In *Estate of Smith*,[10] an investment manager characterized the contracts with its customers as joint venture agreements. Although the agreements gave the investment manager a percentage of the profits, the court found that the investment manager had no

---

[3] In this context, a "domestic" business entity means created or organized in the United States or under the laws of the United States or of any state. I.R.C § 7701(a)(4).

[4] Treas. Reg. § 301.7701-2.

[5] Reinberg v. Commissioner, 90 T.C. 116 (1988); Bussing v. Commissioner, 88 T.C. 449 (1987).

[6] Commissioner v. Tower, 327 U.S. 280 (1946).

[7] Commissioner v. Williams, 256 F.2d 152 (5th Cir. 1958). *See also* Astoria Marine Construction Co. v. Commissioner, 1945 Tax Ct. Memo LEXIS 275.

[8] Hartman v. Commissioner, 1958 T.C.M. (PH) ¶ 58,206.

[9] Comtek Expositions, Inc. v. Commissioner, 2003 T.C.M. (RIA) ¶ 2003-135.

[10] 313 F.2d 724 (8th Cir. 1963).

economic interest in the capital or commodities purchased, no right to withdraw funds, and no right to a distribution on termination of the relationship. Under these circumstances, where the parties did not display an intent to create a partnership, no partnership was created for tax purposes.

A "working interest" in an oil and gas lease is often held to be an interest in a partnership. The working interest is the one empowered to drill and develop the well. Passive investors such as limited partners may be involved as well. In *Bentex Oil Corporation v. Commissioner*,[11] where each part owner of a working interest in an oil and gas lease was responsible for their proportionate share of the expenses of the exploration and production, the co-owners could separately commit or not commit to any exploration and the co-owners took their proportionate share of the production in kind and sold it separately, the court held that there was "no doubt" that the arrangement was a partnership.[12]

Rents may be based upon a percentage of the gross receipts of a tenant without causing the rents or the lease to be recharacterized.[13] But as was the case with lenders and borrowers, if the "landlord" has too much control over the business of the "tenant," a partnership may be created.[14]

A mere co-ownership of property does not create a partnership for federal income tax purposes.[15] A co-ownership of property that is maintained, kept in repair, and rented or leased does not constitute a business entity for tax purposes absent other activities of the co-owners.[16] However, co-owners may also be partners if they or their agents carry on sufficient business activity. Determining when co-owners have crossed the line and become partners can be a very slippery affair. In Revenue Ruling 75-374,[17] two parties each owned an undivided one-half interest in an apartment building. A management company retained by the co-owners managed the building. Customary tenant services, such as heat, air conditioning, trash removal, unattended parking, and maintenance of public areas, were provided at no extra charge. Additional services were provided by the management company for a separate charge. The IRS ruled that the customary services were not extensive enough to cause the co-ownership to be treated as a partnership. The revenue ruling indicates that if the two co-owners had provided noncustomary services such as valet parking, they would have been treated as partners.

Even if a partnership is found to exist, not every purported partner's status as a partner may be respected. For example, if a purported partner's only interest is a

---

[11] 20 T.C. 565 (1953).

[12] It may also be significant that the co-owners of the lease filed partnership returns for three years. Working interests in oil and gas leases are also often viewed as partnerships for state law purposes. *See, e.g.*, Wagner Supply Co. v. Bateman, 18 S.W.2d 1052 (Texas 1929).

[13] *See* H.R. Conf. Rep. No. 100-495, 947, Omnibus Budget Reconciliation Act of 1987, P.L. 100-203, 1987 U.S.C.C. & A.N. 2313-1693.

[14] Campise v. Commissioner, 1980 T.C.M. (PH) ¶ 80,130.

[15] *See* Estate of Appleby v. Commissioner, 41 B.T.A. 18 (1940), *aff'd* 123 F.2d 700 (2d Cir. 1941).

[16] Treas. Reg. § 301.7701-1(a)(2).

[17] 1975-2 C.B. 261; see Treas. Reg. § 301.7701-1(a)(2).

fixed return with a fixed maturity date, which is insulated from the success or losses of the venture, the "partner" may in substance be a lender.[18]

Even if otherwise a partnership, it is possible to elect out of subchapter K of the Code (which contains most of the partnership tax provisions). We review these rules in our Detailed Discussion.

DETAILED DISCUSSION

§ 2.01   THE EXISTENCE OF A BUSINESS ENTITY

The portion of the Regulations dealing with entity classification is commonly called the "check-the-box" Regulations, because the Regulations provide an election to change the tax treatment of some types of entities by "checking the box" and filing the appropriate form. They probably should be called the "don't-check-the-box" Regulations, because usually taxpayers will prefer the default rules to the alternative election. Under the check-the-box Regulations, one must first have determined that a business entity exists before one can conclude that a partnership exists.[19] We discuss the check-box-regulations in detail in the introduction to the text and do not review them again here.

Most of the time, the existence of a business entity will be apparent. If a partnership or a limited liability company (an "LLC") is formed under a U.S. domestic state law with a valid business or financial purpose on other than a transitory basis, there is likely to be little question that a business entity exists. Controversies may develop, however, as to whether the entity has been formed for a valid business or financial purpose and whether the entity has been formed other than on a transitory basis.[20]

For example, in *Andantech L.L.C. v. Commissioner*,[21] a Wyoming LLC was disregarded by the Tax Court because the LLC was not formed for the purpose of carrying on a business. In *Andantech*, the LLC was formed to enter into a series of sale-leaseback transactions with a lessor of computer equipment subject to existing leases.[22] The LLC then entered into a series of transactions in which income was theoretically accelerated into a year in which tax indifferent partners[23] were allocated the income by the LLC. In a later year, a loss was recognized by the LLC, which was allocated to the U.S. taxable partners. In disregarding the LLC, the court concluded in the alternative that (i) a valid business activity does not include

---

[18] ASA Investerings Partnership v. Commissioner, 1998 T.C.M. (RIA) ¶ 98,305, *aff'd* 201 F.3d 505 (D.C. Cir. 2000).

[19] Treas. Reg. § 301.7701-2.

[20] *See, e.g.*, Commissioner v. Tower, 327 U.S. 280 (1946); ASA Investerings Partnership v. Commissioner, 201 F.3d 505 (D.C. Cir. 2000).

[21] 2002 T.C.M. (RIA) ¶ 2002-097, *aff'd* 331 F.3d 972 (D.C. Cir. 2003).

[22] A sale-leaseback transaction is a transaction in which the owner of property sells the property to a buyer and then leases the property back.

[23] Tax indifferent partners are partners that are either not subject to U.S. tax on the type of income allocated to them or which have so many net operating losses or tax credits that they have a very low effective tax rate.

an activity whose sole purpose is tax avoidance and (ii) the structure should be collapsed together as transitory under the step-transaction doctrine. Under either approach, the LLC could be disregarded because it was not formed by persons for the purpose of carrying on a trade or business or sharing in the profit or loss from the transaction.[24]

On the other hand, it is also possible to create a business entity for U.S. federal income tax purposes without creating an entity for state law purposes. Treas. Reg. § 301.7701-1(a)(2) provides that a "joint venture or other contractual arrangement may create a separate entity for federal tax purposes if the participants carry on a trade, business, financial operation, or venture and divide the profits therefrom." A continuing question arises as to whether "other contractual arrangements" create a business entity for tax purposes.

§ 2.02   CLASSIFYING PARTNERSHIPS FOR TAX PURPOSES

A.   The Nature of Partnerships

I.R.C. §§ 761(a) and 7701(a)(2) define a partnership quite broadly as a syndicate, group, pool, joint venture, or other unincorporated organization, through or by means of which any business, financial operation, or venture is carried on, and which is not a trust or estate or a corporation. In order for a federal tax partnership to exist, the parties must, in good faith and with a business purpose, intend to join together in the present conduct of an enterprise and share in the profits or losses of the enterprise. For these purposes, whether the entity exists or does not exist under state law does not determine whether or not it exists for federal income tax purposes.[25] The existence of a valid partnership depends on all of the facts, including the agreement of the parties, the conduct of the parties in execution of its provisions, their statements, the testimony of disinterested persons, the relationship of the parties, their respective abilities and capital contributions, the actual control of income and the purposes for which it is used, and any other facts throwing light on the parties' true intent (the factors just listed are known as the "*Culbertson factors*").[26]

None of the *Culbertson* factors or the factors developed in other cases are conclusive of the existence of a partnership. In *Culbertson*, the U.S. Supreme Court rejected the notion that there exists a set of specific criteria for determining whether or not a partnership exists for tax purposes. Instead, all of the facts must be considered to determine whether the parties "intended to join together in the present conduct of the enterprise."[27]

---

[24] *Andantech* at 541.

[25] Commissioner v. Tower, 327 U.S. 280 (1946).

[26] Commissioner v. Culbertson, 337 U.S. 733 (1949); ASA Investerings Partnership v. Commissioner, 201 F.3d 505 (D.C. Cir. 2000), cert. denied 531 U.S. 871 (2000).

[27] 337 U.S. at 742.

Although the Regulations concerning the classification of entities have changed radically since the time of *Culbertson*, court decisions are still relevant for the purposes of (i) determining whether a relationship that is not formed as an entity for state law purposes should be treated as a business entity for Federal tax purposes and (ii) determining whether an entity formed under state law should be ignored as a business entity for Federal tax purposes.

§ 2.03 DISTINGUISHING PARTNERSHIPS FROM OTHER CONTRACTUAL ARRANGEMENTS

It is often said that a partnership exists when the parties join together in the present conduct of an enterprise and share the profits or losses of the enterprise.[28] But not all profit-sharing arrangements result in the creation of a partnership for tax purposes.

A. Distinguishing Partnerships from Loans

Agreeing to pay a party lending funds a percentage of the revenues of a venture should not result in a tax partnership without further evidence of the intent to create a partnership.[29] In *Williams*, a spouse made no contribution to the capital of a venture, assumed no risk and provided no services. The promise by the spouse operating the venture to pay her half of the profits did not transform the loan into a partnership interest. Similarly, subject to some limitations, when a portion of the interest on an instrument that would otherwise be characterized as debt is based upon the appreciation of the value of property of the borrower, the shared appreciation aspect does not automatically cause the loan to be recharacterized as an equity instrument.[30]

On the other hand, where a purported lender is not obligated to be paid in all events but only has a right to be paid out of 50% of the net profits of the venture, the lender was treated as a partner for tax purposes.[31] Further, the greater the right a lender has to participate in a business, the greater the risk is that it will be held to be a partner.

B. Distinguishing Partnerships from Service Agreements

The owner of a business may agree to compensate a hired manager or key employee with a percentage of the income of the business, or a broker may be retained to sell property for a commission based on the net or gross sales price, in

---

[28] Commissioner v. Tower, 327 U.S. 280 (1946).

[29] Commissioner v. Williams, 256 F.2d 152 (5th Cir. 1958). *See also* Astoria Marine Construction Co. v. Commissioner, 1945 T.C.M. (PH) ¶ 45,083.

[30] Rev. Rul. 83-51, 1983-1 C.B. 48. In one case, *Farley Realty Corp. v. Commissioner*, 279 F.2d 701 (2nd Cir. 1960), the court held that the appreciation rights could be treated separately from the remaining instrument treating part of the instrument as debt and part as equity. Rev. Rul. 83-51 appears to be a concession that the holding of *Farley Realty Corp.* is not the general rule.

[31] Hartman v. Commissioner, 1958 T.C.M. (PH) ¶ 58,206.

both cases without creating a partnership for tax purposes.[32]

In *Estate of Smith*,[33] an investment manager characterized the contracts with its customers as joint venture agreements. Although the agreements gave the investment manager a percentage of the profits, the court found that the investment manager had no economic interest in the capital or commodities purchased, no right to withdraw funds, and no right to a distribution on termination of the relationship. Under these circumstances, where the parties did not display an intent to create a partnership, no partnership was created for tax purposes. On the other hand, in *Podell v. Commissioner*,[34] the taxpayer entered into an agreement with another for the purchase, renovation, and sale of real estate. In the hopes of obtaining long-term capital gain treatment upon the sale of the property, the taxpayer argued no partnership had been created. But given the taxpayer's participation and profits rights, the court concluded that he was, indeed, a partner.

C.   Distinguishing Partnerships from Leases

A working interest in an oil and gas lease is the interest vested with developing the well. There may be other owners with passive interests who have no right to participate in the development of the well. Perhaps unsurprisingly, in *Bentex Oil Corporation v. Commissioner*,[35] where each part owner of a working interest in an oil and gas lease was responsible for their proportionate share of the expenses of the exploration and production, the co-owners could separately commit or not commit to any exploration and the co-owners took their proportionate share of the production in kind and sold it separately, the court held that there was "no doubt" that the arrangement was a partnership.[36]

In contrast, non-energy related leaseholds do not have the same presumption of partnership status. For example, where a landlord and tenant under a crop-share lease split the cost of seed, fertilizer, limestone, herbicides, insecticides, soil tests and grain drying and the rent paid was 50% of farm production, no tax partnership was created when the parties did not intend to create a partnership, neither held itself out as a partner, and neither undertook the other's expenses or responsibilities.[37]

---

[32] Comtek Expositions, Inc. v. Commissioner, 2003 T.C.M. (RIA) ¶ 2003-135.

[33] 313 F.2d 724 (8th Cir. 1963).

[34] 55 T.C. 429 (1970).

[35] 20 T.C. 565 (1953).

[36] It may also be significant that the co-owners of the lease filed partnership returns for three years. Working interests in oil and gas leases are also often viewed as partnerships for state law purposes. *See, e.g.*, Wagner Supply Co. v. Bateman, 18 S.W.2d 1052 (Texas 1929).

[37] Harlan E. Moore Charitable Trust v. U.S., 812 F. Supp. 130 (DC IL 1993), *aff'd* 9 F.3d 623 (7th Cir. 1993), *acq.* 1994-2 C.B. 1. The language of both the trial court and the appellate court suggests that the intent was to create a special rule for sharecropping, rather than create a general rule for interpreting leases.

Rents may be based upon a percentage of the gross receipts of a tenant without causing the rents or the lease to be recharacterized.[38]

D.   Distinguishing Partnerships from Co-Ownerships

A mere co-ownership of property does not create a partnership for Federal income tax purposes.[39] A co-ownership of property that is maintained, kept in repair, and rented or leased does not constitute a business entity for tax purposes absent other activities of the co-owners.[40] However, co-owners may also be partners if they or their agents carry on sufficient business activity. The distinction between mere co-owners and co-owners who are partners for income tax purposes lies in the degree of business activity of the co-owners or their agents.[41] For example, a separate entity exists for Federal income tax purposes if co-owners of an apartment building lease space and in addition provide services to the occupants either directly or through an agent.[42]

However, in Revenue Ruling 75-374,[43] two parties each owned an undivided one-half interest in an apartment building. A management company retained by the co-owners managed the building. Customary tenant services, such as heat, air conditioning, trash removal, unattended parking, and maintenance of public areas, were provided at no extra charge. Additional services were provided by the management company for a separate charge. The IRS ruled that the customary services were not extensive enough to cause the co-ownership to be treated as a partnership. In addition, because the management company was not an agent of the owners and the owners did not share in the fee for non-customary services, the non-customary services did not cause the co-ownership to be treated as a partnership. Had the converse been the case, likely a partnership would have been created.

In *Bergford v. Commissioner*,[44] 78 investors purchased "co-ownership" interests in computer equipment subject to a seven-year net lease. The co-owners authorized the manager to arrange financing and refinancing, purchase and lease the equipment, collect rents and apply those rents to the notes used to finance the equipment, prepare statements, and advance funds to participants on an interest-free basis to meet cash flow. Under some circumstances, the manager could decide to sell the property. Based upon the authority given to the manager, the court held that the co-ownership was a partnership for tax purposes.

---

[38] *See* H.R. Conf. Rep. No. 100-495, 947, Omnibus Budget Reconciliation Act of 1987, P.L. 100-203, 1987 U.S.C.C. & A.N. 2313-1693.

[39] *See* Estate of Appleby v. Commissioner, 41 B.T.A. 18 (1940), *aff'd* 123 F.2d 700 (2d Cir. 1941).

[40] Treas. Reg. § 301.7701-1(a)(2).

[41] Cusick v. Commissioner, 1998 T.C.M. (RIA) ¶ 98,286.

[42] Treas. Reg. § 301.7701-1(a)(2).

[43] 1975-2 C.B. 261.

[44] 12 F.3d 166 (9th Cir. 1993).

Similarly, the sharing of the output of the venture may be the equivalent of sharing in the profits of the venture, creating a partnership for tax purposes.[45] In the famous case *Madison Gas & Electric Co.*, three utility companies joined together to build and operate a nuclear power plant. The Tax Court held that the venture was a partnership because the parties had joined together to produce a common product with economies of scale and take the product in kind. The fact that they received distributions in the form of electricity rather than cash did not change the outcome.

To provide some clarity in one aspect of the distinction between partnerships and other co-ownerships, the IRS promulgated Revenue Procedure 2002-22,[46] under which taxpayers who are co-owners of real estate may apply for a ruling that the co-ownership does not constitute a partnership for Federal tax purposes. To qualify for a ruling, a taxpayer must satisfy a number of technical requirements, including the following:

Each of the co-owners must hold title to the property (either directly or through a disregarded entity) as a tenant in common under local law.

The number of co-owners must be limited to no more than 35 persons.

The co-owners must retain the right to approve, by unanimous vote, the hiring of any manager, the sale or other disposition of the property, any leases of a portion or all of the property or the creation or modification of a blanket lien.

In general, each co-owner must have the right to transfer, partition and encumber the co-owner's undivided interest in the property without the agreement or approval of any person.

Each co-owner must share in all revenues generated by the property and all costs associated with the property in proportion to the co-owner's undivided interest in the property.

All leasing arrangements must be bona fide leases for Federal tax purposes.

§ 2.04   DETERMINING WHO IS A PARTNER

The *Culbertson* factors again become relevant in determining who are the partners in a venture once it is determined that a partnership exists.

If a purported partner's only interest is a fixed return with a fixed maturity date, which is insulated from the success or losses of the venture, the "partner" may in substance be a lender.[47] But where a purported lender is only payable out of 50% of the net profits of the venture, the "lender" is in substance a partner.[48]

---

[45] Madison Gas & Electric Co. v. Commissioner, 72 T.C. 521 (1979).

[46] 2002-1 C.B. 733.

[47] ASA Investerings Partnership v. Commissioner, 1998 T.C.M. (RIA) ¶ 98,305, *aff'd* 201 F.3d 505 (D.C. Cir. 2000).

[48] Hartman v. Commissioner, 1958 T.C.M. (PH) ¶ 58,206.

A person is recognized as a partner if the person owns a capital interest in a partnership in which capital is a material income-producing factor, whether or not her interest was derived by purchase or gift from any other person.[49] Whether or not ownership of the partnership interest has been transferred will be determined by all the facts and circumstances including: (i) the degree of direct or indirect control retained by the transferor, (ii) the ability of the transferee to participate in management, (iii) the right of the transferee to receive distributions of the income of the venture, (iv) the participation of the transferee in the conduct of the business of the venture, (v) the age and competence of the transferee and (vi) whether the transferee is motivated by tax avoidance.[50]

In January of 2003, the Treasury released proposed Regulations[51] to add a new Prop. Treas. Reg. § 1.761-3 that would provide tests to determine whether a noncompensatory option should be treated as an interest in a partnership. These options are beyond the scope of this text.

§ 2.05   ELECTING OUT OF SUBCHAPTER K

The members of an unincorporated organization may elect to have the organization excluded from the application of Subchapter K.[52] An unincorporated organization may only make this election if it is availed of for (i) investment purposes only and not for the active conduct of a business, (ii) for the joint production, extraction, or use of property, but not for the purpose of selling services or property produced or extracted, or (iii) by dealers in securities for a short period for the purposes of underwriting, selling or distributing a particular issue of securities.[53]

Further, for investors in investment property to elect out of Subchapter K (i) they must own the property as co-owners, (ii) the co-owners must reserve the right to separately take or dispose of their shares of any property acquired or retained and (iii) the co-owners must not actively conduct a business or irrevocably authorize some person or persons to purchase, sell or exchange the investment property. The Regulations allow, however, a delegation of the right to purchase, sell or exchange the property for a period of not more than one year.[54]

Where the participants engage in the joint production, extraction or use of property, the participants may elect out of Subchapter K if (i) they own the property as co-owners, either in fee, under lease or under another form of contract granting

---

[49] I.R.C. § 704(e)(1).

[50] Treas. Reg. § 1.704-1(e)(2).

[51] REG-103580-02, 68 CFR 2930 (Jan. 22, 2003).

[52] Subchapter K includes I.R.C. §§ 701-777.

[53] I.R.C. § 761(a).

[54] Treas. Reg. § 1.761-2(a)(2)(iii). It should be noted that it is the position of the IRS that an entity that is recognized for state law purposes does not constitute a co-ownership that may make an election out of Subchapter K if it is, Rev. Rul. 2004-86, 2004-2 C.B. 191, This Ruling concluded that beneficiaries of a trust classified as a partnership for Federal income tax purposes could not elect out of Subchapter K under I.R.C. § 761 because the assets were not owned by the beneficiaries as co-owners under state law.

exclusive operating rights, (ii) the co-owners reserve the right separately to take in kind or dispose of their shares of any property produced, extracted or used and (iii) they do not jointly sell services or the property, produced or extracted, although each participant may separately delegate authority to sell for periods of not more than one year.[55]

The election may be made explicitly by a statement attached to Form 1065 not later than the time for filing the return (including extensions),[56] or the election can be made implicitly if all parties consistently treat the co-ownership as not being a partnership.[57] An implicit election is indicated if either one of the following facts is true: (i) at the time of the formation of the organization, there is an agreement among the members that the organization will be excluded from Subchapter K beginning with the first taxable year of the organization; or (ii) the members of the organization owning substantially all of the capital interests report their respective shares of the items of income, deductions and credits of the organization on their respective returns in a manner consistent with the exclusion of the organization from Subchapter K beginning with the first taxable year of the organization.[58]

If a valid election out of Subchapter K is made, the co-ownership is not generally treated as a partnership for purposes of Subchapter K, but the definitional provisions of I.R.C. § 7701 and the check-the-box Regulations still generally apply for the purposes of the remainder of the Code.[59] In other words, the election out of Subchapter K does not change the nature of the partnership, and it can still be considered to be a partnership for non-Subchapter K Code sections.[60]

---

[55] Treas. Reg. § 1.761-2(a)(3).

[56] Treas. Reg. § 1.761-2(b).

[57] Treas. Reg. § 1.761-2(b)(2)(ii).

[58] *Id.*

[59] Bryant v. Commissioner, 46 T.C. 848 (1966), *aff'd* 399 F.2d 800 (5th Cir. 1968); Rev. Rul. 65-118, 1965-1 C.B. 30.

[60] *See* Bryant v. Commissioner, 46 T.C. 848 (1966), *aff'd* 399 F.2d 800 (5th Cir. 1968).

Chapter 3

FORMATION OF THE PARTNERSHIP

BASIC OVERVIEW

The first thing to remember is something you learned in your basic tax course. When taxpayers exchange properties, the general rule is that each exchanging party recognizes the gain or loss inherent in his exchanged property. Under this general rule, any gains are income. The losses are generally only going to be deductible if the underlying property is a business or investment asset. As you also learned in your basic tax course, there are exceptions to this general rule. You likely learned that no gain or loss is normally recognized under I.R.C. § 1041 on the exchange of property between spouses or under I.R.C. § 1031 on the exchange of real estate held for business or investment purposes.

There is also an exception in the partnership context. A partnership interest, of course, constitutes property. Generally, under I.R.C. § 721(a), no gain or loss is recognized when property is exchanged for a partnership interest by (i) the transferring partner, (ii) the recipient partnership, or (iii) any of its partners. Several points are worth noting. First, it does not matter whether the property is contributed to a newly formed partnership or an existing partnership. Second, there is no requirement, such as the one in I.R.C. § 351(a) (dealing with transfers to corporations) that the transferring partner(s) receive any specific percentage ownership in the partnership.[1]

The next question is what constitutes property for this purpose. Cash and pretty much anything that qualifies as a property interest under property law qualifies. All tangible property, including inventory, qualifies. Some examples of qualifying intangible property include contractual rights and third-party promissory notes. What about accounts receivable? An account receivable is, generally, a right to be paid for services performed. A lawyer who performs legal services (not covered by a retainer) sends a bill to his client. That bill is an account receivable. You might wonder whether accounts receivable should constitute property. Shouldn't the assignment of income doctrine trump and require the income to be taxed to the contributing partner? It is a good question, but generally accounts receivable constitute property. As we will see, I.R.C. § 704(c) makes sure the income is taxed to the correct person when the accounts receivable is paid. As you may already suspect, certain types of intangible property interests can raise tricky issues. We go into more detail in the Detailed Discussion.

---

[1] Treas. Reg. § 1.721-1(a).

Perhaps the most important, commonly contributed item that does not qualify as property is a partner's services[2] — more on this shortly.

Notwithstanding the general rule of I.R.C. § 721(a), I.R.C. § 721(b) provides that gain (but not loss) is recognized on a transfer of a property to a partnership that would be treated as an "investment company." Generally, a partnership will be an investment company if 80% of its assets consist of stocks and securities held for investment and the contribution diversifies the transferor's interest.[3]

There are many nonrecognition sections of the Code that provide for tax-free treatment of the receipt of certain kinds of property, but which also contain a separate provision governing the receipt of property not entitled to be received tax-free, commonly called "boot."[4] Generally, gain (but not loss) has to be recognized to the extent of the boot received.

I.R.C. § 721 does not contain a comparable provision. Rather, the normal rules regarding partnership distributions are applied to determine the tax consequences of the distribution. Thus, if a contributing partner receives money as part of the contribution transaction, the money reduces her basis in the partnership interest. A partner recognizes gain to the extent that a distribution of money exceeds her basis in the partnership interest.[5] It is treated as gain recognized from the sale of a partnership interest, not the contributed property.

I.R.C. § 722 provides that the contributing partner's basis for a partnership interest acquired by a contribution of property to the partnership is the amount of money and the adjusted basis of other property contributed by the contributing partner.[6] Sometimes this is called taking a "substituted basis" as the basis of the contributed property (plus any money) becomes the basis of the partnership interest. I.R.C. § 723 provides that the partnership takes the same basis in contributed property as the contributing partner had. This is often called a "carryover basis."

The length of time a taxpayer holds property, cleverly called the holding period, can in many cases be of great importance. If a taxpayer holds a capital asset over one year, any gain on the sale is subject to favorable long-term capital gains tax rates.[7] If a taxpayer holds trade or business property more than one year, she can qualify for the favorable rules of I.R.C. § 1231. To the extent a partner contributes a capital or I.R.C. § 1231 asset to the partnership, her holding period in the partnership interest "tacks" on to the holding period of the contributed asset. Thus, if the partner contributes a capital asset with a nine-month holding period, the partnership interest received for it in the exchange has a nine-month holding period. If that capital asset has more than a one-year holding period (how much

---

[2] Treas. Reg. § 1.721-1(b)(1). *See* § 8.08.

[3] *See* I.R.C. § 351(e)(1) and Treas. Reg. § 1.351-1(c).

[4] *See* I.R.C. § 351(b), 356(a)(1) and 1031(b).

[5] *See* I.R.C. §§ 733, 731(a)(1).

[6] In the case of a taxable transfer to an investment company under I.R.C. § 721(b), the basis is increased by the amount of gain recognized by the contributing partner. I.R.C. § 722.

[7] I.R.C. § 1(h).

more is of no tax significance), the partnership interest has a more than a one-year holding period. I.R.C. § 1223(1). The partnership's holding period in the property received technically always tacks, but is only relevant, in the main, for capital and I.R.C. § 1231 assets. I.R.C. § 1223(2).

In many instances, in addition to contributing property to the partnership, the partnership will either assume liabilities of the contributor, or will acquire the contributed property subject to liabilities. For example, a taxpayer may contribute real property that is subject to a mortgage to a partnership in exchange for a partnership interest, with the partnership either assuming the mortgage debt or merely taking the real property subject to the mortgage.

Generally, if the partnership takes on the liabilities of a partner, that partner's share of those liabilities decreases and the other partners' share of liabilities increases. To use a simplified example, assume A, B, and C are equal partners in the ABC general partnership. A contributes property subject to a $900 liability. Net, A's liabilities decrease by the two-thirds that in a sense are taken on by B and C, i.e., by $600. B and C's liabilities increase by that same $600, or $300 each. A bit more on the relevant rules: Under I.R.C. § 752(b), any decrease in a partner's individual liabilities by reason of the assumption by the partnership of those individual liabilities is treated as a cash distribution to the partner by the partnership. That distribution reduces the contributing partner's basis in his partnership interest (by $600 for A in our example) under I.R.C. § 733. If the deemed distribution exceeds basis, the partner has gain to the extent of the excess under I.R.C. § 731(a)(1). Even though there has been no actual sale of the partnership interest, the gain is considered to arise from the sale of the partnership interest (not the contributed property), which means the gain will almost invariably be capital gain. If there is an increase in a partner's share of partnership liabilities ($300 each for B and C in our example), under I.R.C. § 752(a), the increase is treated as a contribution of money by the partner to the partnership, which increases that partner's basis in the partnership interest under I.R.C. § 722.

If a partner holds ordinary income property, the taxpayer might seek to obtain capital gain treatment upon its sale by first contributing the property to a partnership. Conceivably, the partnership could hold the asset as a capital asset and, assuming the holding period exceeded one year, have favorably taxed long-term capital gain on the sale. Alternatively, if a taxpayer holds a capital asset that has a built-in loss, the taxpayer might attempt to obtain ordinary loss treatment by transferring it to a partnership that would hold the property as an ordinary income asset. To prevent partnerships from being used in this fashion, I.R.C. § 724 was enacted.

I.R.C. § 724(a) provides that if a partner contributes property to a partnership that was an "unrealized receivable" in the contributing partner's hands, any gain or loss recognized by the partnership on the disposition of that property is treated as ordinary income or ordinary loss, as applicable. For this purpose, the term "unrealized receivable" has the meaning given that term in I.R.C. § 751(c).[8]

---

[8] I.R.C. § 724(b)(1).

Generally, an unrealized receivable is what is more commonly called an account receivable from the performance of services or the sale goods by cash basis taxpayers. For example, if an attorney bills for his services, the bill is an account receivable. An account receivable is always an ordinary income asset to the person who generated it, and I.R.C. § 724(a) ensures that it stays that way in the hands of the partnership, irrespective of how long the partnership holds it.

I.R.C. § 724(b) provides that if a partner contributes property that constituted an inventory item in her hands (and, thus, also an ordinary income asset), then any gain or loss recognized by the partnership on the disposition of the inventory property during a five-year period beginning on the date of the contribution is treated as ordinary income or ordinary loss, as applicable. After that, the asset is characterized in the hands of the partnership (for which it may not constitute an inventory item).

I.R.C. § 724(c) provides that if the property contributed by the partner was a capital asset in the hands of the contributing partner with a loss inherent in it, then any loss recognized by the partnership on the disposition of the property during the five-year period beginning on the date of the contribution is treated as a loss from the sale of a capital asset up to the loss inherent in the asset on contribution. Any loss in excess of that amount, and any loss after the five-year period, is characterized at the partnership level.

When parties form a partnership, they unsurprisingly incur "organizational expenses." I.R.C. § 709 covers their tax treatment. Examples of organizational expenses are legal fees for the partnership agreement, accounting fees to set up an accounting system, and filing fees.[9] Under I.R.C. § 709(b), if the partnership elects, it may deduct up to $5,000 of organizational expenses incurred by it, reduced on a dollar-for-dollar basis by organizational expenses in excess of $50,000.[10] Any amount in excess of what may be immediately deducted may be amortized over 180 months beginning with the month in which the partnership begins business. If the partnership is liquidated before the end of that 180-month period, the expenses that have not as yet been amortized may be deducted as a loss to the extent provided in I.R.C. § 165.[11]

"Start-up expenses" are different than organizational expenses. Start-up expenses are expenses incurred in determining whether to begin a business. Examples are marketing studies costs and investigatory expenses. I.R.C. § 195(b) provides rules for the deduction and amortization of start-up expenses, which are identical to the rules for organizational expenses.

---

[9] *Id.*

[10] This deduction is phased out for partnerships whose organizational expenses exceed $50,000. I.R.C. § 709(b)(1)(A).

[11] I.R.C. § 709(b)(2).

DETAILED DISCUSSION

§ 3.01   TRANSFER OF PROPERTY TO PARTNERSHIP

When the current scheme of partnership taxation was introduced in the Internal Revenue Code of 1954, partnerships were mostly used for small businesses and professional practices. Subchapter K was drafted to make it easy for taxpayers to go in and out of partnerships without incurring taxation. That same framework continues in effect today, with some limitations and modifications, although partnerships (in particular limited liability companies taxed as partnerships) are used for sophisticated, large businesses and often as part of tax shelters.

A.   General Rules

The general rule is straightforward: Under I.R.C. § 721(a), no gain or loss is recognized by (i) the transferring partner, (ii) the recipient partnership, or (iii) any of its partners, when property is contributed to a partnership in exchange for an interest in the partnership. Two points are worth noting. First, it does not matter whether the property is contributed to a newly formed partnership or an existing partnership. Second, there is no requirement, such as exists in I.R.C. § 351(a) (dealing with transfers of corporations) that the transferring partner(s) receive any specific percentage ownership in the partnership.[12]

B.   What Constitutes Property

I.R.C. § 721(a) only applies to contributions of "property" to a partnership. The question becomes, therefore, what constitutes property for this purpose. The answer is that almost anything that can be cognized as property or an interest in property qualifies.

1.   Cash

It is clear that cash is property for purposes of I.R.C. § 721, although that is of little consequence to the contributing partner, since he could not have a gain or loss upon the contribution of cash (other than a currency exchange gain or loss if a foreign currency were involved). It is relevant for purposes of the partnership, however, because in the absence of I.R.C. § 721(a), a partnership receiving cash could have taxable income.

2.   Contract Rights

In general, contract rights are considered property for purposes of I.R.C. § 721(a).

---

[12] Treas. Reg. § 1.721-1(a).

a.   Promissory Notes

i.   Contributor's Promissory Note

If a partner contributes her own promissory note to the partnership (i.e., a promissory note of which the partner is the maker and the partnership is the payee), it is likely that the transaction will be considered a "nothing," that is, likely this will not be seen as a transfer of property. That said, there is no definitive law on this issue. An alternative view that would not change the bottom line would be to view the transaction as a contribution of zero basis property. There are authorities that have taken this position in the context of transfers to corporations covered by I.R.C. § 351.[13]

When the partner makes payments on the promissory note, it likely will be considered a capital contribution made by the partner at the time the payments are made.

ii.   Third-Party Promissory Note

Here what is usually meant is a promissory note that arose when the contributing partner lent money to a third party and received a promissory note in return. If that note is contributed to the partnership, it constitutes property for purposes of I.R.C. § 721(a).

iii.   Installment Note

An installment note (sometimes called an installment obligation) arises when someone sells property and "carries back" the financing. The buyer thus pays the seller for the property over time (with interest). For qualifying property, I.R.C. § 453 provides that the seller recognizes gain proportionately as the payments are made. Treas. Reg. § 1.721-1(a) makes clear that the contribution of an installment obligation constitutes a contribution of property for purposes of I.R.C. § 721(a).[14] The partnership will step into the shoes of the contributing partner, recognizing gain as payments on the installment obligation are made.[15] This is contrary to the general rule that a disposition of an installment obligation results in recognition of gain or loss.[16]

If the installment note is an obligation of the partnership to which it is transferred (i.e., the partnership was the purchaser in the installment sale and the contributing partner was the seller), the result is likely different. As a result of the partnership, following the contribution, being both the obligor and the obligee, the installment obligation ceases to exist by virtue of the doctrine of merger. In this situation, the installment obligation is likely to be considered to have been

---

[13] *See, e.g.*, Rev. Rul. 80-235, 1980-2 C.B. 229 and Rev. Rule. 68-629, 1968-2 C.B. 154.

[14] Similarly, Treas. Reg. § 1.453-9(c)(2).

[15] Under I.R.C. § 704(c), however, the gain recognized at the partnership level will be allocated solely to the contributing partner.

[16] I.R.C. § 453B(a).

"satisfied" for purposes of I.R.C. § 453B(a).[17] Under I.R.C. § 453B(a)(2), if an installment obligation is satisfied, gain or loss is recognized and measured by the difference between the basis of the installment obligation and the fair market value of the obligation.[18]

iv.   Partnership's Indebtedness to the Partner

If a partnership is indebted to a person, whether they are already a partner or not, and the indebtedness is canceled in exchange for a partnership interest, does I.R.C. § 721(a) apply? Had the partnership repaid the indebtedness and then the obligee turned around and contributed the cash received, it is clear that no gain or loss would be recognized by either the partnership or the person acquiring the partnership interest, assuming the separateness of those steps is respected. Should the result be different if instead of paying the debt and then making a cash contribution, the indebtedness is simply canceled in exchange for a partnership interest? The answer is generally no, but keep reading.

If the partnership's indebtedness is canceled by virtue of the partnership issuing a profits interest or capital interest in the partnership to the creditor, I.R.C § 108(e)(8) provides that the partnership is treated as having satisfied the indebtedness with an amount of money equal to the fair market value of the interest issued. Thus, if the fair market value of the interest issued is less than the amount of the indebtedness canceled, the partnership recognizes cancellation of indebtedness income (commonly called "COD"). I.R.C. § 108(e)(8)(B) further provides that if any cancellation of indebtedness income is recognized by reason of the partnership issuing a capital interest or profits interest in exchange for debt, the discharge of indebtedness income must be allocated to the partners who were partners immediately before the discharge (i.e., the cancellation of indebtedness income cannot be allocated to the former creditor if he was not yet a partner).[19]

We discuss capital accounts in detail in Chapter 6. Generally, a partner is entitled to be paid a positive balance in her capital account upon liquidation of the partnership interest. If the partnership is sufficiently solvent and the contributor receives a capital account credit equal to the face amount of the indebtedness, it would not appear that there should be any cancellation of indebtedness income because the contributor has in fact received a capital interest with a value equal to the debt discharged. If, however, the partnership is not sufficiently solvent to pay the capital account balance, the contributing party does not receive a capital account credit in connection with the contribution of the indebtedness, or receives a capital account less than the face amount of the indebtedness, then a facts and

---

[17] I.R.C. § 453B(f)(1) provides that if an installment obligation is cancelled or otherwise becomes unenforceable, the obligation is treated as if it was disposed of in a transaction other than a sale or exchange. *See also* Jack Ammann Photogrametric Engineers, Inc. v. Commissioner, 341 F.2d 466 (5th Cir. 1965).

[18] If the obligor and obligee are related persons (within the meaning of I.R.C. § 453(f)(1)), the fair market value of the obligation is deemed to be not less than its face amount. I.R.C. § 453B(f)(2).

[19] Prop. Treas. Reg. § 1.108-8(b)(2) provides a safe harbor for determining the fair market value of the partnership interest issued by the partnership to a creditor in exchange for debt.

circumstances test applies, and cancellation of indebtedness income may arise.[20] Regardless of whether or not the partnership has cancellation of indebtedness income, by reason of the liabilities of the partnership decreasing as a result of the cancellation of the debt, there will be a deemed distribution to the existing partners of the partnership.[21]

The discussion above has been limited to the partnership's side of the transaction. It is also necessary to consider the effect on the contributing partner. Generally, the contribution of the partnership's debt should be treated as a contribution of property on which no gain or loss is recognized by virtue of I.R.C. § 721(a). If, however, the indebtedness is the result of services performed by the contributor for the partnership, or goods sold by the contributor to the partnership, additional issues come into play. In the case of services rendered, if the contributor has not previously included the amount in income and the contributor receives a capital account credit, then the contributor should have services income to the extent of the capital account credit. If the provider of the services does not receive a capital account credit for forgiving the debt, then the transaction should be viewed the same as if a profits interest was issued for services, with the result that no income should be recognized by the contributor.

b.   Option to Acquire Property and Letters of Intent

An option typically constitutes property.[22]

Generally, a letter of intent is a nonenforceable statement (commonly in a letter, thus the name) of the general terms of a deal to which the parties have agreed. While typically not enforceable, laying out the general outlines of the deal is obviously helpful in drawing up the formal agreement. Letters of intent have been held to be property for I.R.C. § 721(a) purposes.[23]

3. Services

It is clear that services (whether performed or to be performed) do not constitute property for purposes of I.R.C. § 721(a).[24] Thus, if a partner receives a capital interest in the partnership for services, the value of that interest will be income. Proposed Regulations would also tax the issuance of profits interests to the service provider in some circumstances. See Chapter 9 for the exciting details.

---

[20] Unless the debt was owed proportionately to each of the partners and each of the partners made the capital contribution, there would be a change in the economics which would have to be explored. For example, if the partner canceling the debt as a capital contribution was related to the other partners, there may be gift issues involved.

[21] *See* I.R.C. § 752(b).

[22] The IRS has proposed a regulation dealing with contributing contracts. Under the proposed regulation, if a partner contributes a contract to a partnership and the partnership subsequently acquires property pursuant to that contract, the acquired property is treated as section 704(c) property with the same amount of built-in gain or built-in loss as the contract. Prop. Treas. Reg. § 1.704-3(8)(iii). This would imply that the contract could be contributed to the partnership without the recognition of gain.

[23] U.S. v. Stafford, 727 F.2d 1043 (11th Cir. 1984).

[24] Treas. Reg. § 1.721-1(b)(1). *See* § 8.08.

4. Right to Use Property

The term "property" as used in I.R.C. § 721(a) must be distinguished from the right to use that property. For example, a partner owning a computer may allow the partnership to use the computer, although the partner would continue to own the computer. Treas. Reg. § 1.721-1(a) clearly distinguishes between a contribution of property and merely allowing the partnership to use property. If a partner receives a capital account and profits interest in exchange for agreeing to allow the partnership to use the computer, the value of the partnership interest received by the partner should generally be taxable (i.e., rental income). The situation is effectively the same as if the partnership cash to the partner to lease the computer which the partner then contributed back to the partnership.[25]

5. Recapture Property

Upon the disposition of certain depreciable property and mineral property, taxpayers generally are required to recognize as ordinary income (i.e., recapture as ordinary income) any gain up to the amount of the depreciation, intangible drilling and development costs, exploration expenditures and mine development expenditures previously deducted.[26] I.R.C. § 721(a) shields the contributing partner from having to recognize recapture gain when this type of property is contributed to the partnership, but the recapture "taint" stays with the property, meaning that the partnership may recognize ordinary income when it disposes of the property.[27]

6. Inventory and Unrealized Receivables

It is clear that inventory and accounts receivable constitute property that is covered by the nonrecognition provisions of I.R.C. § 721(a). Note that the assignment of income doctrine does not trump I.R.C. § 721(a), but also note that the income inherent in the inventory or receivables will be taxed to the contributing partner when recognized by the partnership. [28] See Chapter 6.

7. Recapitalizations

Often partnerships have different classes of interest. In a limited partnership, there are always at least two classes, the general partner and the limited partner interests. In many more complex partnership arrangements, there are often a variety of classes, each of which has different rights and preferences. If a partner changes the class of interest they own (e.g., the general partner becomes a limited partner, or a Class A Member of an LLC becomes a Class C Member), or if the partnership recapitalizes and issues different classes of interest to its existing

---

[25] A carved out oil payment has been held to be "property" for purposes of I.R.C. § 351 in *H.B. Zachry Co. v. Commissioner*, 49 T.C. 73 (1967), *appeal dismissed* (5th Cir. 1968), as has a nonexclusive patent license in *E.I. Dupont de Nemours & Co. v. United States*, 471 F.2d 1211 (Ct. Cl. 1973); see Treas. Reg. § 1.707-1(a).

[26] *See* I.R.C. §§ 1245 and 1254.

[27] *See* I.R.C. §§ 1245(b)(3), 1250(d)(3) and 1254(b)(1).

[28] *See* Rev. Rul. 80-198, 1980-2 C.B. 113, involving transfers of unrealized receivables to a corporation in a transaction governed by I.R.C. § 351; also see I.R.C. § 724.

partners in exchange for the classes they previously held, an issue arises as to whether these transactions are taxable transactions in which the transferring partner recognizes gain or loss. These transactions might well be treated as exchanges under I.R.C. § 1001, which could result in gain and possibly loss being recognized as no statute clearly exempts gain and loss recognition.

In Revenue Ruling 84-52,[29] a general partnership proposed to convert to a limited partnership. Two of the four partners would become general partners and the other two partners would become limited partners. The Ruling holds that although two of the partners have changed their general partner interests in the general partnership for limited partner interests in the limited partnership, no gain or loss will be recognized by the partners by virtue of I.R.C. § 721.[30] Otherwise there is little authority in the area.

C.   "Contribution"

I.R.C. § 721(a) only applies to a "contribution" of property to a partnership in exchange for a partnership interest. As we will discuss, a partner can interact with the partner as a third party and, for example, sell property to the partnership. Of course, I.R.C. § 721(a) does not then apply.

D.   Effect on Depreciable Assets

As indicated above, no depreciation recapture is recognized if depreciable assets are contributed by a partner to a partnership. Although generally a new taxpayer begins a new depreciation schedule with respect to property acquired, in the case of a contribution of depreciable property to a partnership to which I.R.C. § 721 applies, the partnership steps into the shoes of the contributing partner and the partnership continues to depreciate the property in the same manner as the contributing partner would have depreciated the property.[31]

E.   Stock of Corporate Partners

If a corporation transfers its own stock to a partnership in exchange for a partnership interest, it is clear that the stock is treated as property for purposes of I.R.C. § 721. Trickier questions are the corporation's basis for its partnership interest and the partnership's basis for the corporate stock, as well as the manner in which I.R.C. § 704(c) operates in this situation.

---

[29] 1984-1 C.B. 157.

[30] The IRS has held in a number of Private Rulings that a conversion of a general partnership to a limited liability company was a transaction to which I.R.C. § 721 applied. *See, e.g.* PLR 9809003 (Feb. 27, 1998) and PLR 9841030 (Oct. 23, 1998); a comparable result was also reached for LLCs. *See* PLR 200345007 (Nov. 7, 2003).

[31] I.R.C. § 168(i)(7) and Prop. Treas. Reg. § 1.168-4(d)(5).

F. Disregarded Entity Becoming Partnership

As a result of the check-the-box Regulations,[32] an entity that has a single member (typically an LLC) is treated as a disregarded entity. What happens if the single-member entity gets a new member, with the result that the entity is now treated as a partnership (assuming it has not elected to be taxed as a corporation)? The answer to this question was provided in Rev. Rul. 99-5.[33]

That Ruling discussed two situations. In one situation, a new member made a capital contribution to the LLC. In the other situation, the new member became a member by purchasing a portion of the interest in the LLC previously owned by the single member. Rev. Rul. 99-5 holds that in the first situation the single member is deemed to have contributed all of the assets of the LLC to a newly formed partnership, simultaneously with the capital contribution made by the new member. The deemed capital contribution made by the former single member is treated the same as if an actual capital contribution had been made to a partnership in exchange for a partnership interest, with the result that I.R.C. § 721(a) applies to the transaction.

In contrast, in the second situation, the transaction is treated as if the former single member sold a portion of the assets owned by the LLC, subject to the liability of the LLC, to the purchaser and then both the former single member and the new member made capital contributions to a newly formed partnership. In this situation, although the deemed capital contribution made by the former single member to the partnership is subject to the provisions of I.R.C. § 721(a), gain or loss is recognized by the former single member on the deemed sale of the assets of the LLC. This conclusion makes sense, because in the second situation, the former single member has the cash from the new member, whereas in the first situation it is the LLC that has the cash from the new member.

In addition, there will be a difference in the partnership's basis for its assets. In the first situation, the partnership has a carryover of the former single member's basis in the assets of the LLC, while in the second situation the partnership has a basis equal to the former single member's basis for the assets deemed contributed by the former single member, and a carryover of the new member's basis for the assets deemed purchased by the new member (which will reflect fair market value).

§ 3.02 EFFECT OF RECEIPT OF "BOOT"

There are many nonrecognition sections of the Code that provide for tax-free treatment of the receipt of certain kinds of property, but that also contain a separate provision governing the receipt of property not entitled to be received tax-free, commonly called "boot." Generally, gain (but not loss) has to be recognized to the extent of the boot received.

I.R.C. § 721 does not contain a comparable provision. Rather, the normal rules regarding partnership distributions are applied to determine the tax consequences

---

[32] Treas. Reg. §§ 301.7701-2, 3 and 4.

[33] 1999-1 C.B. 434.

of the distribution. Generally, the distributions will not be taxable to the recipient partner, except to the extent an actual or deemed distribution of money exceeds the partner's outside basis in the partnership interest. Under I.R.C. § 731(a)(1), the partner will have gain to that extent. The gain will be treated as gain from the sale of the partnership interest, i.e., typically capital gain.

§ 3.03   EFFECT OF LIABILITIES

In many instances, in addition to contributing property to the partnership, the partnership will either assume liabilities of the contributor, or will acquire the contributed property subject to liabilities. For example, a taxpayer may contribute real property that is subject to a mortgage to a partnership in exchange for a partnership interest, with the partnership either assuming the mortgage debt or merely taking the real property subject to the mortgage.

Subchapter K does not have a counterpart to I.R.C. § 357(c) (which provides that a contributing shareholder, in what is otherwise a nonrecognition transaction under I.R.C. § 351, recognizes gain to the extent the liabilities assumed by the corporation exceed the shareholder's basis for the property contributed). Subchapter K does, however, have a significant scheme for dealing with liabilities.

Under I.R.C. § 752(b), any decrease in a partner's individual liabilities by reason of the assumption by the partnership of those individual liabilities is treated as a cash distribution to the partner by the partnership. Pursuant to I.R.C. § 752(c), if property is subject to a liability, it is considered to be the liability of the owner of the property. Under I.R.C. § 752(a), if there is an increase in a partner's share of partnership liabilities, the increase is treated as a contribution of money by the partners to the partnership.

Thus, if a partner transfers property to a partnership and the partnership assumes any of the partners' liabilities, or acquires the contributed property subject to liabilities, the amount of the liabilities is treated as a distribution to the contributing partner. Because the contributing partner is a partner of the partnership, however, by virtue of the partnership having additional liabilities, in most instances the contributing partner will have an increase in that partner's share of the liabilities of the partnership. The regulations make clear that if, as a result of a single transaction, a partner incurs both an increase in the partner's share of the partnership's liabilities and a decrease in the partner's share of the partner's individual liabilities, only the net decrease is treated as a distribution from the partnership.[34] Thus, for example, assume A contributes property to a general partnership subject to a liability of $10,000 in exchange for a 40% partnership interest, and that under the rules of I.R.C. § 752, 40% of the liabilities are assigned to A after the contribution. A share of individual liabilities will drop by $10,000, his share of partnership liabilities will go up by $4,000, for a net decrease in his share of these liabilities of $6,000. I.R.C. § 752(b) treats this net drop as a distribution of $6,000 to A. If that deemed distribution exceeds A's basis in the partnership interest, A will have gain to that extent under I.R.C. § 731(a)(1). Even though no actual sale

---

[34] Treas. Reg. § 1.752-1(f).

of the partnership interest will have taken place, the gain will be treated as gain from the sale of the partnership interest, meaning almost invariably it will be capital gain.

§ 3.04   BASIS OF PARTNERSHIP INTEREST TO PARTNER

I.R.C. § 722 provides that the contributing partner's basis for a partnership interest acquired by a contribution of property to the partnership is the amount of money and the adjusted basis of other property contributed by the contributing partner.[35] This is often referred to as a "substituted basis." As indicated above, if a partnership assumes the liabilities of the contributing partner, or acquires the contributed property subject to indebtedness, the net amount of the indebtedness of which a contributing partner is relieved is deemed a cash distribution to the contributing partner, which would reduce the contributing partner's basis for his or her partnership interest.[36]

§ 3.05   HOLDING PERIOD OF PARTNERSHIP INTEREST

I.R.C. § 1223 governs holding periods. Under I.R.C. § 1223(1), if the property contributed to the partnership is a capital asset or a section 1231 asset, then the partner's holding period of the partnership interest includes the period during which the partner held the contributed property. This is known as taking a "tacked" holding period. Thus, if the partner contributes a capital asset with a nine-month holding period, the partnership interest received for it in the exchange has a nine-month holding period. If that capital asset has more than a one-year holding period (how much more is of no tax significance), the partnership interest has a more than one-year holding period. I.R.C. § 1223(1).

If the partner contributes both qualifying and nonqualifying property to the partnership, then she will take a split holding period for the partnership interest, with part tacking, and part not, based on the relative fair market values of the contributed property.[37] For example, assume a partner contributes $5,000 in cash and a capital asset having a basis of $14,000 and a fair market value of $10,000. Because, by fair market value, one-third of the taxpayer's interest was received for the contribution of cash, one-third of the taxpayer's holding period in the partnership interest begins the day after the contribution. The taxpayer has a holding period for two-thirds of the partnership interest, which includes the period during which the taxpayer held the capital asset.[38]

While the result reached in the regulations seems appropriate in connection with initial contributions to partnerships, in the case of ongoing capital contributions, it reaches results that were surprising to most practitioners. For example, assume that partner A has held a 10% partnership interest in partnership ABC for a

---

[35] In the case of a taxable transfer to an investment company under I.R.C. § 721(b), the basis is increased by the amount of gain recognized by the contributing partner. I.R.C. § 722.

[36] Treas. Reg. § 1.722-1, example 1.

[37] Treas. Reg. § 1.1223-3(b)(1).

[38] Treas. Reg. § 1.1223-3(f), example 1.

number of years. Partnership ABC requires additional capital and each of the partners makes a pro rata capital contribution to the partnership, with A contributing $5,000. If at the time A made the capital contribution, the fair market value of A's partnership interest (immediately prior to the contribution) was $45,000 and A, within one year of the date of the making of the $5,000 capital contribution, were to sell the partnership interest, 10% ($5,000 ÷ $50,000) of the gain realized would be treated as short-term gain.

To ameliorate, to some extent, this harsh result, Treas. Reg. § 1.1223-3(b)(2) provides that if a partner makes cash contributions to the partnership and receives distributions from the partnership during the one-year period ending on the date of the sale or exchange of a partnership interest, the partner may reduce the cash contributions made during the year by cash distributions received. Furthermore, for this purpose, deemed capital contributions resulting from an increase in a partner's share of partnership liabilities, and deemed distributions resulting from a decrease in a partner's interest in partnership liabilities, are generally disregarded.[39]

If a partner with both a short- and long-term holding period in his partnership interest sells all of the partner's partnership interest, the capital gain or loss is divided between long-term and short-term holding periods in the same proportions as the holding period of the partnership interest is divided. If a partner sells less than all of the partner's partnership interest, the capital gain or loss is divided in the same way it would have been if the entire partnership interest had been sold.[40]

§ 3.06 PARTNERSHIP'S BASIS FOR CONTRIBUTED PROPERTY

The partnership's basis for property contributed to the partnership by a partner is the contributing partner's adjusted basis for the property contributed (increased by the amount of gain recognized in the case of transfers to investment companies).[41] This is often referred to as a "carryover" basis. This basis is not affected by changes to the contributing partner's basis in the partnership interest received in exchange for the contributed property, such as would result, for example, from a net relief of liabilities.

§ 3.07 PARTNERSHIP'S HOLDING PERIOD FOR PROPERTY RECEIVED

The partnership's holding period for the contributed assets is determined under the general rules of I.R.C. § 1223. Under I.R.C. § 1223(2), the partnership's holding period always tacks to that of the contributing partner. But keep in mind that holding periods are normally only relevant for properties that are capital and I.R.C. § 1231 assets in the hands of the partnership.

---

[39] Treas. Reg. § 1.1223-3(b)(3).

[40] Treas. Reg. § 1.1223-3(f)(c).

[41] I.R.C. § 723.

§ 3.08   CHARACTER OF GAIN OR LOSS FROM SALE OF CONTRIBUTED PROPERTY

If a partner holds ordinary income property, he might seek to obtain capital gain treatment upon its sale by first contributing the property to a partnership that would hold the property as a capital asset, rather than as an ordinary income asset. Alternatively, if a taxpayer holds a capital asset that has a built-in loss, the taxpayer might attempt to obtain ordinary loss treatment by transferring it to a partnership that would hold the property as an ordinary income asset. To prevent partnerships from being used in such a fashion, I.R.C. § 724 was enacted.

A.   Contributions of Ordinary Income Assets

1.   Unrealized Receivables

If a partner contributes property to a partnership that was an unrealized receivable in the contributing partner's hands, any gain or loss recognized by the partnership on the disposition of that property is treated as ordinary income or (very rarely) ordinary loss.[42] For this purpose, the term "unrealized receivable" has the meaning given in I.R.C. § 751(c) (except that any reference therein to the partnership refers to the contributing partner).[43] Under I.R.C. § 751(c), the term "unrealized receivable" includes, to the extent not previously included in income, any rights to payment for (i) goods delivered (or to be delivered) to the extent the proceeds would not be treated as amounts received from the sale or exchange of a capital asset, or (ii) services rendered or to be rendered.

2.   Inventory Items

If a partner contributes property that constituted an inventory item in his hands, then any gain or loss recognized by the partnership on the disposition of that property during a five-year period beginning on the date of the contribution is treated as ordinary income or ordinary loss.[44] For this purpose, the term "inventory item" has the meaning given in I.R.C. § 751(b) (except that references to the partnership instead refer to the contributing partner).[45] I.R.C. § 751(b) defines the term "inventory item" to mean (i) property described in I.R.C. § 1221(a)(1) (the standard definition), or (ii) any other property which on its sale or exchange would be considered property other than a capital asset and other than property described in section 1231.[46]

---

[42] I.R.C. § 724(a).

[43] I.R.C. § 724(b)(1).

[44] I.R.C. § 724(b).

[45] I.R.C. § 724(b)(2).

[46] For this purpose, I.R.C. § 1231 is applied without regard to any holding period provided in that section. I.R.C. § 724(d)(2).

B. Contributions of Capital Loss Property

If the property contributed by the partner is a capital asset in the hands of the contributing partner, then any loss recognized by the partnership on the disposition of the property during the five-year period beginning on the date of the contribution is treated as a loss from the sale of a capital asset to the extent that the contributing partner's adjusted basis for the property at the time of the contribution exceeds the fair market value of the property at that time. In other words, only the loss inherent on contribution is classified by I.R.C. § 724. Any loss beyond that amount is classified exclusively at the partnership level. [47]

§ 3.09 ORGANIZATION AND SELLING EXPENSES

A. Selling Expenses

No deduction is allowed to a partnership or a partner for the costs incurred to sell interests in a partnership.[48] These expenses include brokerage fees, registration fees, legal fees of the underwriters, securities advice (including advice concerning tax disclosures in offering documents), printing costs, etc.[49]

B. Organizational Expenses

Expenses of organizing the partnership generally are nondeductible, but there is an election available to amortize organization expenses.[50] To qualify as an organization expense, the expense must be (i) incident to the creation of the partnership, (ii) properly chargeable to capital accounts, and (iii) of a character that if incurred in connection with the creation of a partnership having an ascertainable life, would be amortizable over that life.[51] In order to be incurred incident to the creation of the partnership, the expense must be incurred during the period beginning a reasonable time before the partnership begins business and ending with the due date for the partnership tax return for the partnership's taxable year (without extension) during which the partnership begins business.[52] The Regulations give as examples of organization expenses, legal fees relating directly to the organization of the partnership, such as negotiation and preparation of the partnership agreement, accounting fees for services incident to the organization of the partnership, and filing fees.[53] Temp. Treas. Reg. § 1.709-1T(a)(3) makes clear that if the election is not made to amortize organizational expenses (a rarity), no deduction of capitalized selling expenses is allowable in the year in which the partnership liquidates.

---

[47] I.R.C. § 724(c) to I.R.C. § 724(d)(3)(A).

[48] I.R.C. § 709(a).

[49] Treas. Reg. § 1.709-2(b).

[50] I.R.C. § 709(b).

[51] Treas. Reg. § 1.709-2(a).

[52] *Id.*

[53] *Id.*

If the I.R.C. § 709 election is made, then under I.R.C. § 709 (b)(1), the partnership may deduct up to $5,000 of organization expenses incurred by it, reduced on a dollar-for-dollar basis by organizational expenses in excess of $50,000. Any amount not deducted may be amortized over a period of not less than 180 months beginning with the month in which the partnership begins business. If the partnership is liquidated before the end of the 180-month period, the expenses that have not as yet been amortized may be deducted as a loss to the extent provided in I.R.C. § 165.[54]

Temp. Treas. Reg. § 1.709-1T(a)(2) provides that the partnership is deemed to have made the election to amortize organizational expenses under I.R.C. § 709(b) for the taxable year in which the partnership begins business. If the partnership does not wish to make this election (fat chance), it may do so by clearly electing to capitalize its organizational expenditures on a timely filed return for the taxable year in which the partnership begins business.

C. Start-Up Expenses

Start-up expenses of a partnership are nondeductible, but there is an election available to amortize start-up expenses under I.R.C. § 195.

I.R.C. § 195(c) provides the definitions of the terms "start-up costs" and "beginning of trade or business." Start-up costs are costs for creating an active trade or business or investigating the creation or acquisition of an active trade or business. Start-up costs include any amounts paid or incurred in connection with any activity engaged in for profit or for the production of income before the trade or business begins, in anticipation of the activity becoming an active trade or business. The expenditures must be of such a nature that they would be deductible if they had been incurred in the operation of an existing business. Examples are marketing studies and expenses incurred to investigate the possibility of starting a business.

When an active trade or business is purchased, start-up costs do not include costs incurred in the attempt to actually purchase a specific business. These are capital expenses and are not amortizable under I.R.C. § 195.

I.R.C. § 195(b) provides rules for the deduction and amortization of start-up expenses that are identical to the rules for organizational expenses. As in the case of organizational expenditures, Temp. Treas. Reg. § 1.195-1T(b) provides that a taxpayer is deemed to have made the election under I.R.C. § 195(b) to amortize start-up expenditures for the taxable year in which the active trade or business to which the expenditures relates begins. If the taxpayer does not wish to have the election apply (another fat chance), the taxpayer may do so by clearly electing to capitalize its start-up expenditures. Note, if the taxpayer does not enter the business, I.R.C. § 195 would not provide for a deduction. In this event, a loss deduction may be allowable under I.R.C. § 165(c)(2), if the taxpayer can demonstrate that the transaction was entered into for profit.

---

[54] I.R.C. § 709(b)(2); however, a technical termination under I.R.C. § 708(b) will not trigger the unamortized expenses. Prop. Treas. Reg. § 1.708-1(b)(6).

If a partnership disposes of its trade or business before the end of the amortization period, any unamortized start-up expenses may be deducted to the extent allowed under I.R.C. § 162.[55] If a partnership that has elected to amortize start-up expenditures under I.R.C. § 195(b) terminates in a transaction or series of transactions described in I.R.C. § 708(b)(1)(B), the termination is not treated as resulting in a disposition of the partnership's trade or business for the purposes of I.R.C. § 195(b)(2).[56] Instead, the new partnership must continue to amortize the remaining unamortized expenditures of the terminating partnership over the remaining portion of the amortization period of the terminating partnership.[57]

---

[55] I.R.C. § 195(b)(2).

[56] Treas. Reg. § 1.195-2(a).

[57] Treas. Reg. § 1.708-1(b)(6).

Chapter 4

OUTSIDE BASIS AND ALLOCATION OF LIABILITIES

BASIC OVERVIEW

First of all, you need to learn two terms: *inside basis* and *outside basis*. Inside basis is the basis that the partnership has in its assets (they being "inside," as it were, the partnership). Outside basis is the basis a partner has in the partnership interest (because the partner stands, in a sense, "outside" of the partnership). This Chapter discusses the relevance of a partner's outside basis and the manner of computing that basis. As we will see, partnership liabilities are particularly important in this regard.

Outside basis plays a large role in the life of a partner. If a partner sells her partnership interest, gain or loss is measured by the difference between the amount realized and the outside basis. Partnership losses flow through to the partners. Under I.R.C. § 704(d), a partner may only deduct the partner's allocable share of partnership losses to the extent of the partner's outside basis at the end of the taxable year in which the loss is incurred. I.R.C. § 731(a) provides that if a partnership distributes cash to a partner and the amount of the cash exceeds the partner's outside basis immediately before the distribution, then gain will be recognized. There are numerous other examples.

I.R.C. § 705 sets forth the general rules for determining outside basis. The general philosophy of I.R.C. § 705(a) is that a partner's basis for her partnership interest should reflect the partner's share of the economic activity of the partnership from the time the taxpayer acquired the partnership interest. Thus, a partner's outside basis is increased by the partner's "distributive" share of partnership taxable income and is decreased by distributions received by the partner and the partner's "distributive" share of partnership losses. "Distributive" is the term used I.R.C. § 705 and is in some ways unfortunate. It has nothing to do with distributions. What is meant is the partner's allocable share of income and loss. In addition, if a partner makes any capital contributions to the partnership subsequent to becoming a partner, the outside basis is increased as provided in I.R.C. § 722.

The adjustments provided for in I.R.C. §§ 705(a)(1)(A) and 705(a)(2)(A) are necessary to ensure the single level of tax that is at the heart of Subchapter K of the Code. If taxable income were recognized by a partnership, the partners paid tax on that partnership income and the basis of their partnership interest were *not* increased, then at some earlier point the distributions made by the partnership would exceed the partner's outside basis and there would be a second level of tax at the partner level. The adjustment provided for in I.R.C. § 705(a)(1)(A) prevent this from happening. Likewise, the adjustment provided for in I.R.C. § 705(a)(2)(A) prevents a partner from claiming a double loss.

I.R.C. § 705(a)(1)(B) provides that a partner's outside basis is increased by the amount of tax-exempt income. I.R.C. § 705(a)(2)(B) provides that a partner's outside basis is reduced by expenditures of the partnership that are not deductible in computing its taxable income and not properly chargeable to capital accounts. Examples are tax penalties, bribes. I.R.C. § 705(a)(2) provides that a partner's outside basis is decreased by distributions by the partnership as provided in I.R.C. § 733. I.R.C. § 733 provides that in the case of a nonliquidating distribution by a partnership to a partner, the outside basis is reduced by the amount of any money distributed and the adjusted basis of property other than money distributed.

There is one rule in tax that has no exceptions: A taxpayer cannot have a negative basis in anything. I.R.C. §§ 705(a)(2), 705(a)(3) and 733, when referring to reductions in a partner's outside basis, contain the parenthetical phrase "but not below zero." This, when combined with the prohibition on a partner claiming losses in excess of the partner's outside basis contained in I.R.C. § 704(d) and the limitation on the basis of distributed property contained in I.R.C. § 732(a)(2), prevents a partner from ever having a negative outside basis.

I.R.C. § 752(a) provides that an increase in a partner's share of partnership liabilities is treated as a contribution of money by the partner to the partnership. This is a unique characteristic of partnership taxation that has resulted in entities taxable as partnerships often being the preferred vehicle. The ability of a partner to include partnership liabilities in her outside basis enables the partner to claim deductions flowing through the partnership in excess of the amount contributed by the partner to the partnership. By contrast, shareholders in an S corporation may not increase their stock bases by corporate debt.

To illustrate, assume AB partnership has two equal partners, A and B. The partnership purchases an office building for $1,000,000, paying $200,000 in cash and borrowing $800,000 on a mortgage loan. A and B will each see their shares of partnership liabilities increase by $400,000, and thus each will be considered to have made a $400,000 cash contribution to the partnership with a corresponding outside basis increase. To round out the statutory scheme, I.R.C. § 752(b) provides that a decrease in a partner's share of a partnership's liabilities is treated as a distribution of money to that partner. In the example, if the partnership sold the office building, A and B's share of liabilities would drop by $400,000, and each would be considered to have received a distribution of $400,000 of cash with a corresponding outside basis decrease. Lastly, I.R.C. § 752(d) provides, in effect, that if a partner sells his partnership interest, his amount realized includes any liabilities associated with his partnership interest.

The Regulations have a very different scheme for allocating recourse and nonrecourse partnership liabilities. Treas. Reg. § 1.752-1(a)(1) provides that a liability is a recourse liability of a partnership to the extent that any partner bears the "economic risk of loss" for that liability. Treas. Reg. § 1.752-2(b)(1) provides, in effect, that a partner bears the economic risk of loss to the extent of the partner's bottom line, unprotected obligation to make payment on the debt after taking into account all facts and circumstances, including a partner's right of reimbursement on the debt. For example, assume A is a 60% partner and B is a 40% partner in a traditional general partnership formed under the Revised Uniform Partnership Act ("RUPA") that is not a limited liability partnership ("LLP"). Under RUPA, each partner is jointly and severally liable for all of the debts of the partnership. Assume the partnership owes $1,000 of recourse debt. If, hypothetically, the creditor collected the entire amount of the debt from A, A would be entitled to be reimbursed for 40% of it from B. It is normally assumed that B will fulfill his obligations. Accordingly, A's economic risk of loss on the debt is 60% of $1,000 or $600. B has the economic risk of loss for the other 40%.

What if a partner contributes property subject to recourse debt? Assume partners A and B form an equal general partnership that is not an LLP. A contributes $600 and B contributes property with a fair market value of $1,000, an adjusted basis of $500, and subject to a recourse debt of $400. As equal partners, A and B now should be equally liable for the debt. Note that in this example, A's share of the debt initially was 0 and then went up by $200. That $200 increase is treated as a contribution of money by A under I.R.C. § 752(a) to the partnership with a corresponding outside basis increase under I.R.C. § 722. On the other hand, B's share of the debt initially was $400 and dropped to $200. That $200 drop is treated as a distribution of money to B under I.R.C. § 752(b) with a corresponding outside basis decrease under I.R.C. § 733. Thus, B's partnership basis is now $400-$200 = $200. What if B's tax basis in the property had only been $100? In that event, his outside basis would drop to zero ($100-$200 = 0 as tax basis cannot be negative). The excess of the deemed distribution over basis, i.e., $100, is treated as gain under I.R.C. § 731(a)(1). Note that I.R.C. § 731(a)(1) treats this as gain from the sale of a partnership interest, making it almost invariably capital gain. Note that B's holding period in the partnership interest now can become very important. If B has a holding period of one year or less, the capital gain is short-term capital gain taxed at ordinary income rates. If B's holding period exceeds one year, the gain is favorably taxed long term capital gain.

Treas. Reg. § 1.752-2(c)(1) provides a general rule that a partner also bears the economic risk of loss for a partnership liability to the extent the partner has made a nonrecourse loan to the partnership and the economic risk of loss with respect to the loan is not borne by another partner. It is not uncommon for banks that make nonrecourse loans to receive, in addition to interest, a small percentage of profits. To facilitate these loans to partnerships, the Regulations contain an exception to the general rule. The nonrecourse loan will not be treated as recourse if the partner's interest in each item of partnership income, gain, loss, etc. for every taxable year is 10% or less, and that partner makes a loan to the partnership that constitutes qualified nonrecourse financing within the meaning of I.R.C. § 465(b). To oversimplify a bit, this is nonrecourse debt borrowed from a commercial lender that is secured by real estate. Similarly, in the case of a partner having less than a 10% interest in each item of partnership income, gain, loss, etc., a guaranty by that partner of a loan that otherwise would be qualified nonrecourse financing if the guarantor had made the loan to the partnership is not treated as recourse debt.[1]

---

[1] Treas. Reg. § 1.752-2(d)(2).

The definition of a nonrecourse liability is very simple. It is any liability that is not a recourse liability (i.e., one for which no partner bears the economic risk of loss aside from the exception discussed above).[2] Typically, nonrecourse liabilities are secured by one or more assets of the partnership, such as a mortgage on real property. In the case of entities taxed as partnerships where no owner has personal liabilities for the obligations of the entity (such as LLCs, LLPs, or limited liability limited partnerships), it is possible for an obligation of the entity to be a nonrecourse liability even though the obligation by its terms does not so state.[3] In such a case, liabilities can be allocated among the partnership's property in any reasonable manner so long as the debt allocated to a particular property does not exceed the property's fair market value.[4]

Nonrecourse liabilities are allocated based upon a three-tier formula (sometimes called a "stacking rule") set forth in Treas. Reg. § 1.752-3(a). Nonrecourse liabilities are allocated in the following order of priority:

(i)   First allocated to the partners are nonrecourse liabilities equal to their respective shares of partnership "minimum gain." Minimum gain is the amount by which nonrecourse liabilities exceed the "book value" of property, i.e., its fair market value on acquisition less, generally, depreciation deductions. Don't quite get that? Don't worry, we will be coming back to this topic. Just focus on the next two rules for now.

(ii) Second, to oversimplify a bit, a nonrecourse liability is allocated to the partner who contributed the property to the partnership to the extent the nonrecourse liability exceeds the property's tax basis.

To fully understand this, you need to read (and spend a lot of time absorbing) Chapter 5. To get you by for now, we offer the following example:

Assume partners A and B form an equal partnership. A contributes $600 and B contributes property to the partnership with a fair market value of $1,000, a tax basis of $100, and subject to a nonrecourse debt of $400. There is no minimum gain here, as minimum gain only exists to the extent the nonrecourse debt exceeds book value. Here book value is $1,000. Under the second tier of the allocations, however, $300 of the nonrecourse debt is allocated to partner B (i.e., the amount by which the nonrecourse debt exceeds tax basis, $400 - $100 = $300).

(iii) Third, there is allocated to the partners their share of the balance of the nonrecourse liabilities in accordance with the partners' shares of partnership profits. In the above example, the final $100 of debt ($400 - $300 allocated to B) is allocated $50 to A and $50 to B as they are equal partners.

Note that in this example, A's share of the debt initially was 0 and then increased by $50. That $50 increase is treated as a contribution of money by A under I.R.C. § 752(a) to the partnership with a corresponding outside basis increase under I.R.C. § 722. On the other hand, B's share of the debt initially was $400 and

[2] Treas. Reg. § 1.752-1(a)(2).

[3] PLR 200120020 (May 18, 2001).

[4] PLR 200340024 (April 10, 2003).

dropped to $350 ($300 under rule 2 plus $50 under rule 3). That $50 drop is treated as a distribution of money to B under I.R.C. § 752(b) with a corresponding outside basis decrease under I.R.C. § 733. Note unlike in our example with recourse debt, it is not possible for B to have gain on the contribution of property subject to nonrecourse debt. As B's tax basis in the property goes down, his debt allocation under rule 2 goes up. Thus, if B's basis in the property were zero, he would be allocated all $400 of the debt under rule 2.

DETAILED DISCUSSION

§ 4.01   INTRODUCTION

This chapter will focus on a partner's basis for the partner's partnership interest, as opposed to the partnership's basis for its assets. A partner's basis for the partner's partnership interest is typically referred to as the "outside basis," whereas a partnership's basis for its assets is referred to as the partnership's "inside basis." This Chapter will discuss the relevance of a partner's outside basis and how it is computed. A significant portion of this Chapter will be devoted to the effect of partnership liabilities on a partner's outside basis.

§ 4.02   GENERAL RULES FOR COMPUTING BASIS

A.   Adjustments to Basis of Partnership Interest — Generally

I.R.C. § 705 sets forth the general rules for determining a partner's outside basis. The general philosophy of I.R.C. § 705(a) is that a partner's outside basis should reflect the partner's share of the economic activity of the partnership from the time the taxpayer acquired the partnership interest. Thus, a partner's outside basis will be increased by the partner's "distributive" share of partnership taxable income and is decreased by distributions received by the partner and the partner's "distributive" share of partnership losses. "Distributive" is the term used I.R.C. § 705 and is in some ways unfortunate. It has nothing to do with distributions. What is meant is the partner's allocable share of income and loss. In addition, if a partner makes any capital contributions to the partnership subsequent to the dates the person became a partner, the partner's outside basis will be increased as provided in I.R.C. § 722.

The adjustments provided for in I.R.C. §§ 705(a)(1)(A) and 705(a)(2)(A) are necessary to ensure the single level of tax that is at the heart of Subchapter K of the Code. If taxable income were recognized by a partnership, the partners paid tax on that partnership income and the outside basis did *not* increase, then at some point the distributions made by the partnership would exceed the partner's outside basis and there would be a second level of tax at the partner level. The adjustments provided for in I.R.C. § 705(a)(1)(A) prevent this from happening. Likewise, the adjustments provided for in I.R.C. § 705(a)(2)(A) prevent a partner from claiming a double loss.

B.   Special Adjustments

1.   Tax-Exempt Income

I.R.C. § 705(a)(1)(B) provides that a partner's outside basis is increased by the distributive share of tax-exempt income. This adjustment is necessary so that what is otherwise tax-exempt income does not become taxable when it is distributed to a partner. If the partner's outside basis is not increased by the amount of the tax-exempt income recognized by the partnership, then when that income is distributed (or ultimately at liquidation), the partner would receive distributions in excess of the partner's outside basis, resulting in the partner being taxed on what is intended to be tax-exempt income. Rather than the income being tax exempt, it would be merely tax deferred.

2.   Natural Resources Property

Let us warn you, there is little chance this will get much coverage in your course, unless you live in an oil and gas or mining state, and even then it is doubtful.

I.R.C. § 705(a)(1)(C) provides that a partner's outside basis is increased by the excess of the deductions for depletion over the basis of the property subject to depletion. This provision is only applicable to partnerships engaged in natural resources businesses and then only if percentage depletion is used (which allows for an indirect deduction for the cost of acquiring natural resources based on the percentage of income earned), rather than cost depletion (which works much like the regular depreciation rules, permitting the taxpayer to recover actual acquisition costs of natural resources over time).[5] This adjustment is necessary because if an adjustment were not made, the benefit of percentage depletion would ultimately be lost. It also eliminates a disparity between inside basis and outside basis, which would otherwise occur because the partnership's basis for its assets is not reduced by excess depletion.

Another special rule relating to natural resources is provided in the case of depletion with respect to oil and gas properties. Under I.R.C. § 613(a)(c)(7)(D), percentage depletion with respect to oil and gas properties is determined separately by each partner, not by the partnership. In recognition of this fact, I.R.C. § 705(a)(3) provides that a partner's outside basis is decreased by the amount of the partner's deduction for depletion with respect to oil and gas property to the extent the deduction does not exceed the partner's proportionate share of the adjusted basis of the property allocated to that partner under I.R.C. § 613A(c)(7)(D).

The Regulations provide that a partner's outside basis is also adjusted to reflect any gain or loss to the partner resulting from the disposition by the partnership of an oil and gas property.[6]

---

[5] With the percentage depletion method, deductions for depletion may be claimed even though the amount of the depletion deductions in the aggregate exceed the taxpayer's basis for the property.

[6] Treas. Reg. § 1.705-1(a)(5).

3. Nondeductible Expenditures

I.R.C. § 705(a)(2)(B) provides that a partner's outside basis is reduced by expenditures of the partnership that are not deductible in computing its taxable income and not properly chargeable to capital accounts. The purpose of this section of the Code is to prevent a taxpayer from having an unintended loss from nondeductible expenditures, much like the increase in basis for tax-exempt income is intended to avoid inappropriate income recognition. There is little guidance concerning the specific items that are covered by I.R.C. § 705(a)(2)(B). It is likely that this section of the Code includes losses disallowed under I.R.C. §§ 267(a)(1) or 707(b)[7], life insurance premiums that are not deductible by virtue of I.R.C. § 264, the interest expense disallowed under I.R.C. § 265, bribes, and penalties. It is unclear whether amounts paid to promote the sale of partnership interests by the partnership that are rendered nondeductible by I.R.C. § 709 are included within the provisions of I.R.C. § 705(a)(2)(B), but it would appear that they should be included.

Under I.R.C. § 702(a)(4), charitable contributions made by a partnership are separately taken into account by the partners. The IRS has held that if a partnership makes a charitable contribution of property, each partner's outside basis is decreased by the partner's share of the partnership's basis for the property contributed.[8]

4. Distributions

I.R.C. § 705(a)(2) provides that a partner's outside basis is decreased by distributions by the partnership as provided in I.R.C. § 733. I.R.C. § 733 provides that in the case of a nonliquidating distribution by a partnership to a partner, the outside basis is reduced by the amount of any money distributed and the adjusted basis of property other than money distributed. See Chapter 7 for more details.

C. No Negative Basis

I.R.C. §§ 705(a)(2), 705(a)(3) and 733, when referring to reductions in a partner's outside basis, contain the parenthetical phrase "(but not below zero)." These provisions, when combined with other code sections discussed elsewhere in this text, prevent a partner from ever having a negative outside basis.

D. Time for Computing Basis

As can be seen from the above, because of the various adjustments that must be taken into account by a partner in determining the partner's outside basis, if a partner were continually required to determine the outside basis, it would be extremely burdensome. To avoid this, Treas. Reg. § 1.705-1(a)(1) provides that a partner must determine the outside basis "only when necessary for the determination of his tax liability or that of any other person." That Regulation further provides that ordinarily the determination need only be made at the end of

---

[7] Rev. Rul. 96-10, 1996-1 C.B. 138.

[8] Rev. Rul. 96-11, 1996-1 C.B. 140.

a partnership taxable year. To avoid having to determine a partner's outside basis mid-year when distributions are made by a partnership during the year, Treas. Reg. § 1.731-1(a)(1)(ii) provides that advances or drawings against the partner's share of income are treated as current distributions made on the last day of the partnership's taxable year.[9]

E. Ordering Rules

In addition to knowing when computations must be made of a partner's outside basis, it is also important to know the order in which the adjustments are made when they are made at the same time. It is clear that allocations of income are made to partners prior to distributions reducing the outside basis.[10] In determining the applicability of the loss limitation rule of I.R.C. § 704(d), the partner's outside basis is first increased under I.R.C. § 705(a)(1) and then decreased under I.R.C. § 705(a)(2) (other than with respect to losses of the taxable year and losses previously disallowed).[11] This makes it less likely that a gain need be recognized under I.R.C. § 731(a)(1).

§ 4.03 EFFECT OF PARTNERSHIP LIABILITIES

A. General Rules

I.R.C. § 752(a) provides that an increase in a partner's share of partnership liabilities is treated as a contribution of money by the partner to the partnership. This is a unique characteristic of partnership taxation that has resulted in entities taxable as partnerships often being the preferred vehicle. The ability of a partner to include partnership liabilities in the outside basis enables the partner to claim deductions flowing through the partnership in excess of the amount contributed by the partner to the partnership, notwithstanding the limitation of I.R.C. § 704(d). The ability to increase a partner's outside basis by his share of the liabilities of the partnership is one of the major distinguishing characteristics between a partnership and an S corporation (where corporate liabilities do not increase stock bases).

The theoretical purpose of allowing a partner to increase the outside basis is to put the partner in the same place the partner would have been in had the partner directly conducted the activity being conducted by the partnership as an individual, rather than through a partnership.[12] In effect, this is the use of the aggregate theory of partnerships.

To illustrate, if an individual purchased an office building for $1,000,000, paying $200,000 in cash and borrowing $800,000 on a mortgage loan, the individual would

---

[9] In Rev. Rul. 94-4, 1994-1 C.B. 195, it was held that a deemed distribution of money under I.R.C. § 752(b) resulting from a decrease in a partner's share of partnership liabilities is treated as a distribution on the last day of the partnerships taxable year pursuant to Treas. Reg. § 1.731-1(a)(1)(ii).

[10] Treas. Reg. § 1.731-1(a)(1)(ii).

[11] *See* Rev. Rul. 66-94, 66-1 C.B. 166.

[12] *See* Crane v. Commissioner, 331 U.S. 1 (1947); Commissioner v. Tufts, 461 U.S. 300 (1983).

have a $1,000,000 basis for the office building. The individual would be permitted to depreciate the entire cost of the office building, even though the individual only paid $200,000 out of pocket. If instead of that individual purchasing the office building, that individual and another individual formed a partnership to purchase the office building, the partnership's basis for the office building would also be $1,000,000. If the individuals were not permitted to increase their bases for their partnership interests by the amount of the mortgage loan, however, because of the loss limitation of I.R.C. § 704(d), the losses that could be claimed by the partners would be limited to $200,000. To remedy this situation, I.R.C. § 752(a) allows the partners to increase the bases of their partnership interests by the $800,000 mortgage loan, thereby permitting them to claim losses of up to $1,000,000. That said, the rules of I.R.C. § 752(a) apply to all partnership liabilities, not just those included in the basis of partnership assets.

I.R.C. § 752(c) provides that for purposes of I.R.C. § 752, a liability to which property is subject is considered as a liability of the owner of the property to the extent of the fair market value of the property. The effect of this provision is that partners can increase their outside bases not only for recourse indebtedness of the partnership, but also for nonrecourse indebtedness of the partnership.

To deal with the converse circumstance, I.R.C. § 752(b) provides that a decrease in a partner's share of a partnership's liabilities is treated as a distribution to that partner, reducing a partner's outside basis; if the reduction exceeds the partnership's outside basis, the partner has gain under I.R.C. § 731(a)(1). Lastly, I.R.C. § 752(d) provides that in the case of a sale or exchange of a partnership interest, liabilities are to be treated in the same manner as liabilities in connection with the sale of property other than a partnership interest;[13] i.e., liabilities associated with a partner's partnership interest are included in the selling partner's amount realized.

As can be seen above, the statutory provisions dealing with liabilities in partnerships are fairly simple, consisting of four subsections, each of which is one sentence long. Notwithstanding the brevity of the Code provisions, the regulations implementing this Code provision are extremely lengthy and complex.

B.   Definition of Recourse and Nonrecourse Liabilities

The Regulations have a very different scheme for allocating recourse liabilities of a partnership from that applicable to the allocation of nonrecourse liabilities of a partnership. For that reason, it is extremely important to know whether a liability is a recourse liability or a nonrecourse liability for purposes of the Regulations. In 2014, Treasury proposed new I.R.C. § 752 Regulations that would significantly change the rules. As they are still in proposed form, we do not discuss them.

---

[13] Generally, when a taxpayer sells property, liabilities assumed by the purchaser, as well as liabilities to which the property sold is subject, are treated as part of the amount realized.

1. Definition of Recourse Liability

Treas. Reg. § 1.752-1(a)(1) provides that a "liability is a recourse liability of a partnership to the extent that any partner or related person bears the economic risk of loss for that liability under § 1.752-2." Ultimately, economic risk of loss looks to a partner's unprotected, bottom line obligation on a debt. Keep that in mind as we go over the details. Treas. Reg. § 1.752-2(b)(1) provides that a partner or related person bears the economic risk of loss with respect to a liability if (i) the partnership constructively liquidated, (ii) as a result of the constructive liquidation, the partner or related person would be obligated to make a payment to any person because the liability became due and payable, and (iii) the partner or related person would not be entitled to reimbursement from another partner or a related person to another partner.

In a constructive liquidation, the following events are deemed to have occurred simultaneously (this is sometimes called "the nuclear bomb test"):

(i)   all of the partnership's liabilities become payable in full;

(ii)   all of the partnership's assets, including cash, have a value of zero, other than property contributed by a partner to secure a partnership liability;

(iii)   the partnership disposes of all of its property in a fully taxable transaction for no consideration other than the release of liability with respect to nonrecourse liabilities;

(iv)   all items of income, gain, loss, etc. are allocated among the partners; and

(v)   the partnership liquidates.[14]

As indicated above, in the constructive liquidation, property is generally considered to be sold for no consideration, and thus generating losses that are allocated to the partners. These hypothetical losses could create hypothetical negative capital accounts that partners would have an obligation to restore, helping to determine partners' economic risk of loss. There is an exception to the zero consideration rule for property subject to nonrecourse debt. In that case, the property subject to that debt is treated as sold for an amount equal to the amount of the subject nonrecourse liability, and gain or loss is recognized depending upon the partnership's basis for the asset subject to the debt.[15]

In determining the extent to which a partner has an obligation to make a payment, all of the facts and circumstances are taken into account. This includes all statutory and contractual obligations, and includes obligations imposed by the partnership agreement, as well as those imposed outside of the partnership agreement. Examples of items taken into account are guarantees, indemnifications, reimbursement agreements, obligations to make capital contributions to restore deficit capital accounts upon liquidation, and obligations imposed by state law.[16] Even if a partner is obligated to make a payment, the partner's obligation to make the payment is reduced to the extent that the partner or a person related to the

---

[14] Treas. Reg. § 1.752-2(b)(1).

[15] Treas. Reg. § 1.752-2(b)(2).

[16] Treas. Reg. § 1.752-2(b)(3).

partner is entitled to reimbursement from another partner or a person related to another partner.[17] In determining whether a person has a payment obligation, it is assumed that all partners and related persons who have obligations to make payment actually perform those obligations, notwithstanding their net worth, unless there was a plan to "circumvent or avoid the obligation."[18] Notwithstanding this general rule, if the partner is a disregarded entity[19] (typically a single-member LLC), then different rules apply. In this case, the payment obligation is only taken into account to the extent of the net value of the disregarded entity as of the date on which the determination of the partner's share of partnership liabilities is determined.[20] If the owner of the disregarded entity is required to make a payment with respect to an obligation, however, then this rule does not apply.[21] The net value of a disregarded entity is equal to the fair market value of all of the assets of the disregarded entity that may be subject to creditor's claims under local law (excluding the disregarded entity's interest in the partnership in question), less obligations of the disregarded entity.[22]

Treas. Reg. § 1.752-2(c)(1) provides a general rule that a partner also bears the economic risk of loss for a partnership liability to the extent the partner or related person has made a nonrecourse loan to the partnership and the economic risk of loss with respect to that loan is not borne by another partner. In order to facilitate financial institutions making loans to partnerships in which they are a partner, the Regulations contain a *de minimis* exception to this rule. Thus, if the partner's interest in each item of partnership income, gain, loss, etc. for every taxable year is 10% or less, and that partner or a person related to that partner makes a loan to the partnership that constitutes qualified nonrecourse financing within the meaning of I.R.C. § 465(b) (determined without regard to the type of activity financed), then the partner is not deemed to bear the economic risk of loss.[23] Generally, qualified nonrecourse financing means (1) financing by a person regularly engaged in the business of lending who is not a related person, or from a government or guaranteed by a governmental agency, (2) that is secured by real property, (3) and with respect to which no person is personally liable for repayment and that is not convertible debt.[24]

---

[17] Treas. Reg. § 1.752-2(b)(5).

[18] Treas. Reg. § 1.752-2(b)(6) This general rule is subject to one exception for partners for state law purposes that are disregarded entities for tax purposes. In such a situation, a partner is treated as capable of performing its obligations only to the extent of the net value of the assets of the disregarded entity. Treas. Reg. § 1.752-2(k).

[19] A disregarded entity is generally a business entity other than a corporation which has a single owner. A disregarded entity is treated as a sole proprietorship if it is owned by an individual and as a division if it is owned by another entity. Treas. Reg. §§ 301.7701-2(c)(2) and 301.7701-3(b)(1)(ii). Also see

---

[20] Prop. Treas. Reg. § 1.752-2(k)(1).

[21] *Id.*

[22] Prop. Treas. Reg. § 1.752-2(k)(2).

[23] Treas. Reg. § 1.752-2(d)(1).

[24] I.R.C. § 465(b)(6)(A).

Essentially the same rule applies to guarantees. In the case of a partner having less than a 10% interest in each item of partnership income, gain, loss, etc., a guaranty by that partner is deemed not to give the partner any economic risk of loss, and thus leaves the loan nonrecourse, provided it would be qualified nonrecourse financing if the guarantor had made the loan to the partnership.[25]

As indicated above, in determining whether a partner bears the economic risk of loss for a partnership liability, it is necessary to take into account the obligations of a "related person." The term "related person" means a partner and a person who bears a relationship to that partner that is specified in I.R.C. §§ 267(b) or 707(b)(1), except that (i) 80% is substituted for 50%, (ii) brothers and sisters are excluded, and (iii) I.R.C. §§ 267(e)(1) and 267(f)(1)(A) are disregarded.[26]

2. Assumption of Liability

As indicated above, a partner's assumption of a partnership liability is treated as a contribution of money by that partner to the partnership and the assumption by a partnership of an individual partner's liability is treated as a distribution of money to that partner. A person is treated as assuming a liability only if (i) the assuming person is personally obligated to pay the liability and (ii) the creditor knows of the assumption and can directly enforce the partner's (or related persons) obligation and no other partner or related person to another partner would bear the economic risk of loss for the liability immediately after the assumption.[27] This comes close to saying that the parties have to have a novation of the loan to have a recognized assumption. But there is a large exception to the general rule. In the case of property contributed by a partner to a partnership, or distributed by a partnership to a partner, which is subject to a liability, the transferee is treated as having assumed the liability regardless, even if none of the regular assumption rules are met. This is only true to the extent the liability does not exceed the fair market value of the property at the time of the contribution or distribution.[28]

3. Definition of Nonrecourse Liability

The definition of a nonrecourse liability is very simple. It is any liability that is not a recourse liability (i.e., one for which no partner or related person bears the economic risk of loss, recalling under the "10% rule" discussed above the creditor or guarantor is deemed not have any economic risk of loss).[29] Typically, nonrecourse liabilities are secured by one or more assets of the partnership, such as a mortgage on real property. In the case of entities where no owner has personal liabilities for the obligations of the entity (such as limited liability companies or limited liability limited partnerships), it is possible for an obligation of the entity to be a nonrecourse liability even though the obligation by its terms does not so state.[30] In

---

[25] Treas. Reg. § 1.752-2(d)(2).

[26] Treas. Reg. § 1.752-4(b)(1).

[27] Treas. Reg. § 1.752-1(d).

[28] Treas. Reg. § 1.752-1(e).

[29] Treas. Reg. § 1.752-1(a)(2).

[30] PLR 200120020 (May 18, 2001).

this case, liabilities can be allocated among the partnership's property in any reasonable manner so long as the debt allocated to a particular property does not exceed the property's fair market value.[31] As this rule suggests, for most purposes in tax law nonrecourse debt must be associated with property even if it is not under state law.

4. Bifurcated Liability

It is possible for a liability to be both a recourse liability and a nonrecourse liability. For example, a partnership may borrow $800,000 from a bank to purchase some property. The property acts as security for the loan, but the loan is otherwise nonrecourse to the partnership. If one of the partners guarantees $300,000 of the mortgage debt, the liability will be bifurcated into a $300,000 recourse liability and a $500,000 nonrecourse liability, and the liability will be allocated accordingly.[32]

C. Allocation of Recourse Liabilities: Examples

Here are some recourse liability examples:

Example (1). Assume that A and B are equal partners in a general partnership that is not a limited liability partnership. Each of the partners contributes $10,000 to the partnership and the partnership borrows $80,000 to purchase a $100,000 building.

Because A and B are general partners, by statute, A and B have an obligation to satisfy the liability. This being the case, the liability is a recourse liability. In determining the manner in which this $80,000 recourse liability is allocated among the partners, the constructive liquidation rule is applied. Under this rule, if the partnership had no assets and an $80,000 liability, each of the partners would be obligated to contribute one-half of that amount to satisfy the liability. Thus, A and B would each bear the economic risk of loss for $40,000 of the $80,000 obligation.

Example (2). Same facts as in Example 1, except that the partnership is a limited partnership, A is a general partner, and B is a limited partner.

Because A is a general partner, A, by statute, has an obligation to satisfy the liability whereas B, as a limited partner, does not have that obligation. Thus, the liability is a recourse liability. Because A would be required to fully satisfy the liability if the partnership had no other assets, all of the $80,000 liability is allocated to A.

Example (3). Same facts as in Example 2, except that B, the limited partner, is the guarantor of the $80,000 liability.

The liability is still a recourse liability because both A and B now have payment obligations. How the liability will be allocated depends upon whether B would be subrogated to the rights of the lender against the partnership. If B would be subrogated to the rights of the creditor (as is typically the case under guaranty

---

[31] PLR 200340024 (April 10, 2003).

[32] Treas. Reg. § 1.752-1(i).

law), then B would have a right to be paid by A if B made payment on the guaranty, with the result that B would not be considered to bear the economic risk of loss. Thus, all of the liability would be allocated to A. If, on the other hand, B, upon making payment on the guaranty would not be subrogated to the right of the creditor (because, typically, he waived those rights as part of the guaranty), then B would not have a right over/against A and the entire liability would be allocated to B.

Example (4). Same facts as in Example 1, except that partnership losses are allocated 75% to A and 25% to B and under the terms of the partnership agreement a partner with a deficit balance in their capital account is obligated to restore that deficit to the partnership.

The liability is still a recourse liability. If the partnership sold all of its assets for no consideration, the partnership would have a $100,000 loss. This loss would be allocated $75,000 to A and $25,000 to B, resulting in A having a deficit capital account of $65,0000, and B having a deficit capital account of $15,000. Because both A and B would have an obligation to restore their respective negative capital accounts, they share the liability in proportion to their negative capital accounts (i.e., $65,000 to A and $15,000 to B).

Example (5). Same facts as Example 1, except that instead of a general partnership, a limited liability company taxable as a partnership is the borrowing entity.

Because, in the case of limited liability company, the members are not obligated to satisfy the obligations of the limited liability company, no member of the limited liability company bears the economic risk of loss. This being the case, the liability is now a nonrecourse liability.

In determining the extent to which a partner or related person bears the economic risk of loss, it is necessary to take into account when the payment obligation is required to be satisfied. If the obligation to make a payment is not required to be satisfied within a reasonable time after the liability becomes due, or the obligation to make a contribution to the partnership is not required to be satisfied before the later of (i) the end of the year in which the partnership interest is liquidated, or (ii) 90 days after the liquidation, then the liability is only taken into account to the extent of its value.[33] This rule is meant to prevent partners from gaming the system, by technically having the economic risk of loss on a debt, but at such a remote time as to make the obligation to pay the debt of little real import.

D. Allocation of Nonrecourse Liabilities

Nonrecourse liabilities are allocated based upon a three-tier formula set forth in Treas. Reg. § 1.752-3(a). This is sometimes called a "stacking rule." Nonrecourse liabilities are allocated in the following order of priority:

(i)   First, there is allocated to the partners their respective shares of partnership "minimum gain." Minimum gain is determined in accordance

---

[33] Treas. Reg. § 1.752-2(g)(1).

with the rules of Treas. Reg. § 1.704-2(d)(1) and a partner's share of minimum gain is determined in accordance with Treas. Reg. § 1.704-2(g)(1). See Chapter 6 for the exciting details. Generally, minimum gain exists to the extent nonrecourse debt exceeds the book value of the property securing that debt. Book value is generally the fair market value of property when it is acquired by the partnership. Book value (like tax basis) can, for example, be reduced by partnership depreciation deductions and increased by additional investments in the property. The Regulations provide a method for allocating minimum gain among the partners. This will make more sense to you once you have mastered Chapter 6, but we give you a gentle example at the end of the rules.

(ii)   Second, to simplify a little, in the case of property contributed to the partnership that is subject to nonrecourse debt, the amount by which nonrecourse debt exceeds the tax basis of the property is allocated to the contributing partner.[34]

Can we give you an example? Sure:

Assume partner A contributes property to a partnership with a fair market value of $1000, a tax basis of $100, and subject to a nonrecourse debt of $400. There is no minimum gain here, as minimum gain only exists to the extent the nonrecourse debt exceeds "book value." Here book value is $1000. Under the second tier of the allocations, however, $300 of the nonrecourse debt is allocated to partner A (i.e., the amount by which the nonrecourse debt exceeds tax basis, $400 – $100 = $300). We give another, more detailed example of the operation of this tier below.

(iii)   Third, there is allocated to the partners their share of the balance of the nonrecourse liabilities (referred to as "excess nonrecourse liabilities") in accordance with the partners' shares of partnership profits.

The partners' interest in profits is determined by taking into account all of the facts and circumstances relating to the partners' interests in the partnership. The Regulations allow the partnership agreement to specify the partners' interest in partnership profits for purpose of allocating excess nonrecourse liabilities so long as the interests are reasonably consistent with allocations that have substantial economic effect of some other significant item of partnership income or gain.[35] See Chapter 6 again.

The Regulations also permit excess nonrecourse liabilities to be allocated among the partners in accordance with the manner in which it is expected that nonrecourse deductions will be allocated. In addition, the Regulations permit excess nonrecourse liabilities to first be allocated to a partner to the extent of the built-in gain that is allocable to the partner under I.R.C. § 704(c)(2), or property for which reverse § 704(c) allocations are applicable, to the extent that gain exceeds the gain allocated to them in the second tier. To the extent the excess nonrecourse liabilities are not fully allocated under the previous sentence, then the balance of

---

[34]   Treas. Reg. § 1.752-3(b)(1).

[35]   Treas. Reg. § 1.752-3(a)(3).

the excess nonrecourse liabilities must be allocated using one of the other methods in Treas. Reg. § 1.752-3(a)(3).[36] Don't even try to understand that until you have read Chapter 6.

A nonrecourse debt example:

Example. A and B form a limited liability company, A contributing $10,000 and B contributing $190,000. The LLC obtains an $800,000 interest only loan and purchases a $1,000,000 building. The Operating Agreement provides that losses are allocated entirely to B, that income is allocated entirely to B until such time as the allocations of income are equal to prior allocations of loss, and thereafter income is allocated 40% to A and 60% to B. The Operating Agreement provides that excess nonrecourse liabilities are allocated 40% to A and 60% to B. During each of its first ten years of operations, the LLC has a $25,000 loss, all of which is attributable to the depreciation of the building.

During the first eight years, the basis of the property would be equal to or greater than the amount of the nonrecourse liability. This being the case, there is no minimum gain. Based upon the provisions of the Operating Agreement, the excess nonrecourse liabilities would be shared 40% by A and 60% by B.

At the end of year nine, however, the LLC's basis for the building would have been reduced to $775,000, resulting in $25,000 of minimum gain. Assume that A's share of the minimum gain is $1,250 and that B's share of the minimum gain is $23,750. At the end of year nine, $311,250 of the nonrecourse liability is allocated to A [$1,250 + 40% x ($800,000 - $25,000)], and $488,750 of the liability is allocated to B [$23,750 + 60% x ($800,000 - $25,000)]. It may not look like it, but that is all fourth grade math.

E. Contributions and Distributions of Encumbered Property

As noted above, an increase in a partner's share of partnership liabilities is treated as a contribution of money by the partner to the partnership, and a decrease in a partner's share of partnership liabilities is treated as a distribution of money to that partner. If a partner contributes property to a partnership and the partnership assumes liabilities of the contributing partner, or if the property contributed is subject to a liability, there may be both deemed money distributions to the partner, as well as deemed money contributions by the partner. Similarly, if a partnership distributes property to a partner and a partner assumes a partnership liability, or the property distributed is subject to debt, there can be deemed money contributions and distributions.

Treas. Reg. § 1.752-1(f) provides that where the same transaction produces both an increase and decrease in a partner's share of partnership liabilities, only the net increase is treated as a contribution of money by the partner and only the net decrease is treated as a distribution of money to the partner. The effect of this netting rule can be demonstrated by the following example.

---

[36] Id.

Example. A contributes real property with a fair market value of $1,000,000, subject to an $800,000 recourse liability, to a general partnership in exchange for a 25% interest in the partnership. A's basis for the real property is $700,000.

Assume under state law that each of the partners of the partnership is required to make a payment in proportion to their interests upon a constructive liquidation. A's share of the liability post-contribution is thus $200,000. Because A's personal liabilities decrease by $800,000 on the contribution of the real property subject to the debt, but increase by $200,000 as a result of A's share of the partnership liability, there is a deemed distribution to A of $600,000. This deemed distribution reduces A's $700,000 outside basis to $100,000. This is true, even though the amount of the liability to which the contributed property was subject was in excess of A's basis for the property at the time of the contribution. Had A made a similar contribution to a corporation, by virtue of I.R.C. § 357(c), A would have recognized gain. But note that if A's basis in the real property had been $500,000, A would have had gain of $100,000 under I.R.C. § 731(a)(1) on the distribution.

When a property that is subject to nonrecourse liability is contributed to a partnership, the allocation of that liability is far more complicated. The IRS has addressed this situation, however, in Rev. Rul. 95-41.[37] In that Revenue Ruling, A contributed depreciable property with a fair market value of $10,000 to a partnership in exchange for a 50% interest in the partnership. The property was subject to a nonrecourse liability of $6,000, and A's basis for the property was $4,000. The Revenue Ruling first notes that as a result of the contribution, A's individual liabilities decrease by $6,000. It was then necessary to run through the Regulation's three-tier allocation scheme to determine A's share of the partnership's nonrecourse liability.

Minimum gain exists if the debt exceeds the property's book value. Here the debt is $6,000, the book value of the property is its fair market value or $10,000. Thus there is no minimum gain and no allocation under the first tier. Under the second tier allocation, if the property was disposed of for an amount equal to the amount of the liability, a $2,000 gain would be recognized ($6,000 - $4,000). The manner in which the liability is allocated under the second tier is dependent upon the method used for purposes of I.R.C. § 704(c). See Chapter 6. If either the traditional method or the traditional method with curative allocations (whatever they are) is used, $2,000 of the nonrecourse liability would be allocated to A under the second tier.

The excess nonrecourse liabilities are allocated under the third tier and, as indicated above, there are a variety of means in which that allocation could occur. Because the amount of the section 704(c) gain was $4,000, and only $2,000 of that gain was allocated under the second tier, the partners could agree to allocate an additional $2,000 of the liability to A and allocate the balance of the liability one-half to each of A and B.

---

[37] 1995-1 C. B. 132.

F. Tiered Partnerships

It is not uncommon for a partnership to own an interest in another partnership. This is referred to as tiered partnerships. The partnership that is the partner in another partnership is referred to as the "upper-tier partnership," and the partnership having a partnership as a partner is referred to as the "lower-tier partnership." Where there are tiered partnerships, it is necessary to know how the liabilities of the lower-tier partnership will be shared by the partners of the upper-tier partnership.

The general rule is that the upper-tier partnership's share of the liabilities of the lower-tier partnership is treated as a liability of the upper-tier partnership.[38] Thus, the normal rules may then be applied with respect to how the deemed liability of the upper-tier partnership is to be allocated.

In determining the upper-tier partnership's share of a recourse liability of the lower-tier partnership, there is taken into account (i) the economic risk of loss that the upper-tier partnership bears with respect to the liability, plus (ii) any other amount of the liability with respect to which the partners of the upper-tier partnership bear the economic risk of loss.[39]

G. Sales of Partnership Interests

As indicated above, I.R.C. § 752(d) provides that in the case of a sale or exchange of a partnership interest, liabilities are treated in the same fashion as in the case of an exchange not involving a partnership interest. Outside of the partnership context, if a taxpayer sells property and the purchaser assumes a liability of the seller, or takes the property subject to a liability, the amount of the liability is part of the amount realized for purposes of computing gain or loss from the sale. Although a transfer of a partnership interest may not directly result in the selling partner's liabilities being formally assumed, and the partnership interest itself may not be subject to liabilities, nevertheless the liabilities of the partnership must be taken into account. This is the purpose of I.R.C. § 752(d). Assume a 25% partner of a partnership has an outside basis of $20,000 and her basis includes her 25% share of the $100,000 liabilities of the partnership (i.e., $25,000). If she sells her partnership interest for $15,000, the gain or loss recognized by the partner is not simply the difference between her outside basis and the amount of cash received. The amount realized in this situation includes her $25,000 share of the partnership's liabilities. Thus, the amount realized is $40,000 ($15,000 + $25,000) and a gain in the amount of $20,000 ($40,000 - $20,000) is recognized.

---

[38] Treas. Reg. § 1.752-4(a).

[39] Treas. Reg. § 1.752-2(i).

H. Anti-Abuse Rule

Treas. Reg. § 1.752-7 is designed to prevent the acceleration or duplication of loss through the assumption of certain types of obligations.[40] Prior to the promulgation of Treas. Reg. § 1.752-7, taxpayers would transfer assets to a partnership and have the partnership assume a contingent liability (such as a potential environmental liability). The taxpayer would take the position that the assumed liability was not a liability for purposes of I.R.C. § 752 and, therefore, the taxpayer was not required to reduce the basis of the taxpayer's partnership interest. The taxpayer would then sell the partnership interest to a third party for an amount that was significantly less than the taxpayer's basis (because the purchaser would take the liability into account) and claim a loss. When the liability was paid, the partnership would claim a deduction. Thus, the same liability would produce a double deduction.[41] The Regulations are complex and beyond the scope of this effort.

---

[40] Treas. Reg. § 1.752-7(a).

[41] *See* Notice 2000-44, 2002-2 C.B. 255.

Chapter 5

OPERATION OF THE PARTNERSHIP: CALCULATION OF PARTNERSHIP TAXABLE INCOME

BASIC OVERVIEW

An entity treated as a partnership for federal tax purposes is not itself taxable. Rather, the income and deductions flow through to the partners. I.R.C. § 702(a) requires that each partner, in determining his income tax, take into account his "distributive" share of various partnership items.[1] "Distributive" share is an awkward term as it has nothing to do with distributions. What is meant is a partner's allocable share. More on this shortly.

Notwithstanding the fact that the partnership is not taxed, it must still compute taxable income. The basis adjustments of I.R.C. § 705 are keyed, in part, to partnership taxable income or loss. I.R.C. § 703 (a) provides that the taxable income or loss of a partnership is computed in the same manner as in the case of an individual, with certain stated exceptions. The first exception is that those items described in I.R.C. § 702(a)(1) through (7) are separately stated (to be discussed below). The second exception is that deductions only relevant to individuals, such as the personal exemption, are not allowed (as are some other deductions for technical reasons). To round out the statutory scheme, I.R.C. § 702(b) generally provides that the character of any item of income, gain, loss, deduction, or credit is determined at the partnership level. Thus — whether, say, an item would or would not be a long-term capital gain to a partner is normally not relevant. The only question is whether it qualifies for long-term capital gain treatment to the partnership. The partnership gives each partnership a "K-1" showing that partner's share of the various partnership items.

I.R.C. § 702(a) requires any item that can have a variable effect on a partner to be stated separately on the K-1. For example, long-term capital gains can affect different partners differently, depending upon whether they have other capital gains and losses and what kind of capital gains and losses are involved. While I.R.C. § 702(a)(1)-(6) specifies a number of items that must be stated separately, even items not listed must be stated separately if they could have a variable effect on partners.[2] (As a group, these items are often called "separately stated items" or "variable effect items.") The items specified in I.R.C. § 702(a) are long-term gains

---

[1] A partner is required to include his distributive share of the partnership's income even in situations in which there are disputes among the partners and the income of the partnership are being held in escrow. Burke v. Commissioner, T.C. Memo 2005-297, *aff'd* 485 F.3d (1st Cir. 2007).

[2] I.R.C. § 702(a)(7), Treas. Reg. § 1.702-1(a)(8).

and losses, short-terms gains and losses, section 1231 gains or losses, charitable contributions, dividend income, and foreign taxes paid. An example of an unlisted item that must be stated separately is investment interest, as under I.R.C. § 163(d) individuals may only deduct investment interest to the extent they have net investment income.

After taking into account all of the items required to be separately stated, the remaining items are lumped together (e.g., gross income less most typical business expenses) as a "bottom line" income or loss and passed through to the partners as a single number on the K-1. As noted above, partnerships are required to calculate taxable income even though they pay not tax, so all items that go into partnership taxable income are recombined from the separately and nonseparately stated items.

There are many elections that a taxpayer must make in order to determine the taxpayer's taxable income or loss. I.R.C. § 703(b) provides that most elections required to be made in computing the taxable income of the partnership are made at the partnership level rather than at the partner level.

I.R.C. § 704(d) provides that a partner's share of the partnership's loss (including capital loss) is allowed only to the extent of the partner's outside basis at the end of the partnership's taxable year in which the loss has occurred. Any loss that is disallowed by reason of the foregoing provision is carried over and may be deducted when the partner's basis for his partnership interest is positive.[3] Under I.R.C. § 752(a), a partner is able to increase the partner's basis for the partnership interest by the partner's share of the partnership's liabilities. The ability of a partner to include partnership liabilities in her basis for her partnership interest enables a partner to claim deductions passed through from the partnership in excess of the amount contributed by the partner to the partnership.

A loss that is not disallowed by I.R.C. § 704(d) must next be analyzed under the at risk rules of I.R.C. § 465, and then under the passive loss rules of I.R.C. § 469. We will go into depth on these complex areas in the Detailed Discussion. Suffice it for now that there are significant limitations on the deduction of losses attributable to nonrecourse debt or activities in which the partner does not materially participate.

I.R.C. § 706(b) generally requires that a partnership have a taxable year that is determined by reference to the taxable year of its partners. There is a three-tier system for determining the partnership's taxable year. First, if there is a "majority interest taxable year", i.e., if partners holding a majority of interests in the partnership are on the same tax year, then that tax year must be used by the partnership. If there is not a majority interest taxable year, then the partnership must use the taxable year of all of the "principal partners," provided the principal partners are on the same tax year. A principal partner is one who holds a five percent or greater interest in the partnership. If the principal partners are not on the same tax year, then a taxable year must be used that produces the least

---

[3] I.R.C § 704(d); Treas. Reg. § 1.704-1(d)(1).

aggregate deferral of income.[4] See Detailed Discussion for what that means.

Notwithstanding what we just said, I.R.C. § 706(b)(1)(C) provides that a partnership may have a taxable year other than one of the ones we just described, if it is established to the satisfaction of the IRS that there is a business purpose for such taxable year. For example, a ski resort might have a business purpose for a tax year ending at the end of the ski season.

DETAILED DISCUSSION

§ 5.01   PASS-THROUGH NATURE OF PARTNERSHIP

An entity treated as a partnership for federal tax purposes is not itself taxable. Rather, the partners are taxed on the economic activity that occurs at the partnership level.[5] Thus, it is important to understand how the economic activity that occurs at the partnership level affects the partners.

A.   Generally

I.R.C. § 702(a) requires that each partner, in determining his income tax, take into account his "distributive" share of various partnership items.[6] "Distributive" share is an awkward term as it has nothing to do with distributions. What is meant is a partner's allocable share. I.R.C. § 702(a) contains a list of seven items that are to be taken into account separately, with the balance of the taxable income or loss of the partnership, excluding these separately stated items, included as a single number (the so called bottom-line allocation). We will come back to this shortly. Each partner is given a "K-1" showing his share of the various partnership items.

B.   Taxable Income of the Partnership

Notwithstanding the fact that the partnership is not a taxable entity, it must still compute its taxable income or loss. I.R.C. § 703(a) provides that the taxable income or loss of a partnership is computed in the same manner as in the case of an individual, with certain stated exceptions. The first exception is that those items described in I.R.C. § 702(a)(1) through (7) are separately stated — more on this below. The second exception is a list of six types of deductions that are not to be taken into account by the partnership.[7] These exceptions are (i) the personal exemption provided for in I.R.C. § 151, (ii) the deduction for foreign taxes paid, (iii) the deduction for charitable contributions provided in I.R.C. § 170, (iv) the net operating loss deduction provided for in I.R.C. § 172, (v) the additional itemized deductions allowed individuals in I.R.C. §§ 211 through 223, and (vi) the deduction for depletion with respect to oil and gas wells provided for in I.R.C. § 611.

---

[4] Treas. Reg. § 1.706-1(b)(2)(i)(c).

[5] I.R.C. § 701.

[6] A partner is required to include his distributive share of the partnership's income even in situations in which there are disputes among the partners and the income of the partnership are being held in escrow. Burke v. Commissioner, T.C. Memo 2005-297, *aff'd* 485 F.3d (1st Cir. 2007).

[7] I.R.C. § 703(a)(2).

To round out the statutory scheme, I.R.C. § 702(b) provides that the character of any item of income, gain, loss, deduction, or credit with respect to the items required to be separately stated on the K-1 pursuant to I.R.C. § 702(a)(1) through (7) is to be treated as if such item were realized directly from the source from which it was realized by the partnership, i.e., it is characterized at the partnership level. Indeed, the Regulations provide that any item that could affect different partner differently must be stated separately on the K-1. As a group, these items are sometimes called "variable effect" or "separately stated" items. An example of an item not listed in the statute that must be stated separately is investment interest, which under I.R.C. § 163(d) may only be deducted to the extent of net investment income.

C. Separately Stated Items

1. Gains and Losses from Sales

I.R.C. § 702(a)(1) through (3) require that three types of gains or losses from sales or exchanges be separately stated: Long-term gains and losses, short-terms gains and losses, and section 1231 gains or losses. Under the Regulations, rather than being required to include the partner's distributive share of each long-term capital gain or loss or each short-term capital gain or loss, the long-term capital gains and losses and short term capital gains and losses are netted at the partnership level and the netted amount flows through.[8] Similar rules are provided for section 1231 gains or 1231 losses.[9] Although a net section 1231 gain is treated as a long-term capital gain,[10] even if a partnership has a net section 1231 gain and "regular" capital gains, these amounts are not combined.[11] This is because if a partner has other section 1231 gains or losses, the section 1231 gains or losses passing through from the partnership need to be combined with those other section 1231 gains or losses of the partner to determine whether the partner has a net section 1231 gain or a net section 1231 loss (which would be treated as an ordinary loss). Since the Regulations were promulgated, Congress has adopted different long-term capital gain rates for collectables (typically 28%), "unrecaptured section 1250 gain" (typically 25%), and "adjusted net capital gain" (typically 15%). See I.R.C. 1(h). Presumably, net long-term capital gain from each of these categories must flow through separately.

2. Charitable Contributions

I.R.C. § 702(a)(4) require that the partners' shares of the charitable contributions of the partnership be separately taken into account by the partners. The partners and not the partnership take the deduction. The Regulations indicate that each class of charitable contribution (e.g., cash contributions, property contributions to public

---

[8] Treas. Reg. § 1.702-1(a)(1), (2).

[9] Treas. Reg. § 1.702-1(a)(3).

[10] I.R.C. § 1231(a)(1).

[11] *Id.*

charity, property contributions to private foundations, etc.) be separately stated.[12] This is necessary because there are different limitations under I.R.C. § 170 for different types of charitable contributions.

3. Dividend Income

I.R.C. § 702(a)(5) provides that dividend income must be separately stated. This separate statement of dividend income is necessary because currently certain dividends are taxed at preferential rates.[13] In addition, corporations are often allowed a dividends received deduction with respect to the receipt of certain dividends.[14]

4. Foreign Taxes Paid

I.R.C. § 702(a)(6) requires that foreign taxes paid by a partnership be separately stated. This is because foreign taxes paid may be treated as either a deduction under I.R.C. § 164, or as a credit under I.R.C. § 901(a).

5. Other Items

I.R.C. § 702(a)(7) authorizes the IRS to promulgate regulations that can require the separate statement of items other than those provided for in I.R.C. § 702(a)(1) through (6). As noted above, the IRS has exercised this authority. The Regulations provide some specific items that must be stated separately.[15] But, as indicated above, Treas. Reg. § 1.702-1(a)(8)(ii) contains a catch-all and requires that each partner take into account separately the partner's distributive share of any partnership item which, if separately taken into account by any partner, would result in an income tax liability for that partner, or for any other person, different from that which would result if that partner did not take the item into account separately. In other words, any item that can have a variable effect on the partners must be stated separately.

D. Bottom Line Profit or Loss

After taking into account all of the items required to be separately stated, the remaining items of the partnership (i.e., items that do not have to be stated separately) are netted and the "bottom line" profit or loss flows through to the partners as a single number. For example, most ordinary and necessary business expenses do not have to be stated separately. They would be netted against partnership domestic gross income when calculating bottom line profit or loss.

---

[12] Treas. Reg. § 1.702-1(a)(4).

[13] I.R.C. § 1(h)(11).

[14] I.R.C. § 243.

[15] See Treas. Reg. § 1.702-1(a)(8).

§ 5.02 ELECTIONS

There are many elections which a taxpayer must make in order to determine the taxpayer's taxable income or loss. I.R.C. § 703(b) provides that elections required to be made in computing the taxable income of the partnership are made at the partnership level rather than at the partner level.[16] Some elections potentially have application both at the partnership level and at the partner level. For example, I.R.C. § 179 permits taxpayers to elect to treat the cost of section 179 property[17] as an expense not chargeable to a capital account. I.R.C. § 179(b)(1) has a dollar limit of the maximum amount of aggregate cost of section 179 property that may be taken into account in a single year.[18] I.R.C. § 179(b)(2) phases out the benefit of I.R.C. § 179 if the aggregate cost of section 179 property exceeds certain thresholds.[19]

Treas. Reg. § 1.179-2(b)(3)(i) provides that in applying the dollar limitation of I.R.C. § 179(b)(1), a partner's share of I.R.C. § 179 expense allocated to the partner is aggregated with any non-partnership I.R.C. § 179 expenses of the partner. However, the same paragraph states that the cost of I.R.C. § 179 property placed in service by the partnership is ignored for purposes of determining the phase-out thresholds.

A partnership elects its own accounting methods. Generally, there is no requirement that the accounting method chosen by the partnership be the same as that of its partners. Thus, a partnership may use the cash receipts and disbursements method of accounting, even though the partners use the accrual method, and vice versa.[20] There are, however, restrictions on the ability of a partnership to use the cash method.

A. C Corporation is Partner

Under I.R.C. § 448(a)(1), a C corporation generally may not use the cash method. In order to prevent C corporations from doing indirectly that which they cannot do directly, I.R.C. § 448(a)(2) provides that a partnership that has a C corporation as a partner may not use the cash method. There are a number of exceptions, including for certain service corporations, corporations with modest assets, and farming businesses.[21] Further, I.R.C. § 448(a)(3) provides that a tax shelter, as defined in I.R.C. § 461(i)(3), may not use the cash method.

---

[16] Exceptions are made with respect to the elections under I.R.C. §§ 108(b)(5) and 108(c)(3), 617 and 901.

[17] Section 179 property is tangible property to which I.R.C. § 168 applies, certain software, which is used in an active trade or business. I.R.C. § 179(d)(1).

[18] The maximum varies depending upon the calendar year in which the expenditures are incurred.

[19] Like the maximums of I.R.C. § 179(b)(1), the thresholds for the reductions in the maximums varies depending upon the calendar year.

[20] Fong v. Commissioner, 1984 T.C.M. (RIA) ¶ 84,402, aff'd 816 F.2d. 684 (9th Cir. 1987), cert. denied 484 U.S. 854 (1987).

[21] See I.R.C. §§ 447 and 448.

§ 5.03   CHARACTERIZATION

As indicated above, I.R.C. § 702(b) provides that separately stated items under I.R.C. §§ 702(a)(1) through 702(a)(7) should be determined as if they were realized directly from the source from which the partnership realized the item, or incurred in the same manner as it was incurred by the partnership. Although this language is not a model of clarity, it is clear that they are characterized at the partnership level.[22] We have avoided until now talking about bottom line income or loss. While it is curious that it is not covered by I.R.C. § 702(b), bottom line income or loss is always ordinary income or loss (typically arising from a trade or business), and would be, irrespective if it were incurred by the partnership or any partner.

A.   I.R.C. § 724

In order to prevent partners and their partnerships from playing games with the general characterization rules, Congress enacted I.R.C. §§ 724. Under I.R.C. § 724(a), if a partner contributes unrealized receivables to a partnership, any gain or loss recognized by the partnership on the disposition on the unrealized receivables is treated as ordinary income or ordinary loss. I.R.C. § 751(c) generally defines unrealized receivables as accounts receivable from the sale of goods or the performance of services (i.e., receivables that generate ordinary income — or, rarely, ordinary loss — on collection). Under I.R.C. § 724(b), if a partner contributes inventory to a partnership, it stays inventory in the hands of the partnership for five years. Finally, I.R.C. § 724(c) provides that if property that was a capital asset in the hands of a partner is contributed to the partnership, any loss recognized by the partnership on the disposition of such property, within five years of its contribution, is treated as a capital loss to the extent of the loss inherent in the property on contribution. Any loss the partnership realizes in excess of that initial loss is characterized at the partnership level. These rules are designed to prevent the partnership level characterization rule from being used to convert ordinary income to capital gain, or a capital loss to an ordinary loss.

B.   Holding Period

It is clear that the determination of whether there is a long-term or short-term holding period for properties sold by a partnership is determined by reference to the partnership's holding period, not the holding period of a partner for the partnership interest.[23]

C.   Hobby Loss Rules

I.R.C. § 183(a) limits the deductions that can be taken by an individual or an S corporation if the activity is not engaged in for profit. Although the Code, by its terms, only applies to individuals and S corporations, the authorities are uniform in holding that I.R.C. § 183 applies to partnerships as well and that the determination

---

[22] *See* United States v. Basye, 410 U.S. 441 (1973).

[23] Rev. Rul. 68-79, 1968-1 C.B. 216.

of whether the activity was engaged in for profit is determined at the partnership level, not the partner level.[24]

D. Discharge of Indebtedness Income

If a partnership's debt is forgiven, the partnership will recognize discharge of indebtedness income. I.R.C. § 108(d)(6), however, provides that in the case of a partnership, I.R.C. §§ 108(a), (b), (c) and (g) are applied at the partner level. Thus, discharge of indebtedness income must be separately passed through to each of the partners, and is not a part of the bottom line profit or loss.

Under I.R.C. § 108(a)(1), gross income does not include discharge indebtedness income if the discharge occurs in bankruptcy, when a taxpayer is insolvent (to the extent of the insolvency), when the indebtedness discharged is qualified farm indebtedness or when the indebtedness discharged is qualified real property business indebtedness. Thus, even if the partnership is in bankruptcy or insolvent, if the partner is not in bankruptcy or is solvent, those exclusions will not be available to the partner. Under I.R.C. § 108(b), if discharge of indebtedness income is not included in income by reason of one of the exceptions contained in I.R.C. § 108(a), then the taxpayer is required to reduce the taxpayer's tax attributes as provided in I.R.C. § 108(b)(2). As a result of the provisions of I.R.C. § 108(d)(6), the attribute reduction required by I.R.C. § 108(b)(2) will be made at the partner level, not the partnership level.

If the partnership's indebtedness is canceled by virtue of the partnership issuing a profits interest or capital interest in the partnership to the creditor, I.R.C § 108(e)(8) provides that the partnership is treated as having satisfied the indebtedness with an amount of money equal to the fair market value of the interest issued. Thus, if the fair market value of the interest issued is less than the amount of the indebtedness canceled, the partnership will recognize discharge of indebtedness income. I.R.C. § 108(e)(8)(B) further provides that if any discharge of indebtedness income is recognized by reason of the partnership issuing a capital interest or profits interest in exchange for debt, the discharge of indebtedness income must be allocated to the partners who were partners immediately before the discharge (i.e., the discharge of indebtedness income cannot be allocated to the former creditor who is now a partner).

§ 5.04 LOSS LIMITATION RULES

There are three sets of loss limitation rules that a partner has to contend with: I.R.C. § 704(d) (basis limitation rules), I.R.C. § 465 (at risk rules) and I.R.C. § 469 (passive loss rules). They are applied in that order. Only to the extent a loss "survives" I.R.C. § 704(d), is it analyzed under I.R.C. § 465, and only to the extent it survives I.R.C. § 465, is it analyzed under I.R.C. § 469. Further, for example, an allocable loss that is less than the partner's basis in her partnership interest will reduce that basis, even if it is in turn disallowed by I.R.C. § 465. Similarly, a loss that

---

[24] *See* Polakof v. Commissioner, 820 F.2d 321 (9th Cir. 1987); Tallal v. Commissioner, 778 F.2d 275 (5th Cir. 1985); Brannen v. Commissioner, 722 F.2d. 695 (11th Cir. 1984).

is allowed under I.R.C. § 465 will reduce a partner's amount at risk, even if it is in turn disallowed under I.R.C. § 469. Thus the loss disallowance rules operate on parallel tracks, with the proviso that is has to be allowed on one track before it moves to the next.

A. Basis Limitation

I.R.C. § 704(d) provides that a partner's share of the partnership's loss (including capital loss) is allowed only to the extent of the partner's basis in his partnership interest at the end of the partnership's taxable year in which the loss has occurred. Any loss that is disallowed by reason of the foregoing provision is carried forward indefinitely and may be deducted when the partner's basis for his partnership interest is positive.[25]

Under I.R.C. § 752(a), a partner is able to increase the partner's basis for the partnership interest by the partner's share of the partnership's liabilities. The ability of a partner to include partnership liabilities in her basis for her partnership interest enables a partner to claim deductions passed through from the partnership in excess of the amount contributed by the partner to the partnership, notwithstanding the limitation of I.R.C. § 704(d).

In determining a partner's basis for his partnership interest, basis is first increased by those items referred to in I.R.C. § 705(a)(1), and then decreased by the items referred to I.R.C. § 705(a)(2) (other than the loss for the taxable year and losses previously disallowed under I.R.C. § 704(d)).[26] If the partner's distributive share of items of loss specified in I.R.C. §§ 702(a)(1), (2), (3), (7) and (8) exceed the partner's basis for her partnership interest, the limitation on losses provided for in I.R.C. § 704(d) must be allocated to the partner's distributive share of each of such losses. This allocation is determined by taking the proportion that each loss bears to the total of all such losses.[27] It should be noted that the items referred to in I.R.C. §§ 702(a)(4) (charitable contributions) and 702(a)(6) (foreign taxes) are not referred to in Treas. Reg. § 1.704-1(b)(2). This raises the question of whether such items are subject to the loss limitation rule of I.R.C. § 704(d). It appears that charitable contributions are not subject to the limitation of I.R.C. § 704(d), even though a partner must reduce her basis for her partnership interest by her distributive share of the partnership's charitable contributions under I.R.C. § 705(a)(2)(B).[28] Although there does not appear to be any authority on point, it appears that foreign taxes paid by the partnership would be treated in the same fashion as charitable contributions (i.e., not subject to the I.R.C. § 704(d) limitation).

---

[25] I.R.C § 704(d); Treas. Reg. § 1.704-1(d)(1).

[26] Treas. Reg. § 1.704-1(d)(2).

[27] *Id.*

[28] PLR 8405084 (Nov. 3, 1983).

B.   At Risk Rules

1.   Limitations on Losses to Amount at Risk

Under I.R.C. § 465(b), an individual and certain closely held C corporations may only deduct losses from an activity to the extent they are "at risk" with respect to the activity at the end of the taxable year. While I.R.C. § 465(c)(1) lists five specific activities to which the at risk limitation rules apply, I.R.C. § 465(c)(3) provides that the activities to which the at risk limitation applies includes any activity engaged in by the taxpayer in carrying on a trade of business or for the production of income. Thus, the at risk limitation effectively applies to all such activities.

2.   Calculations of Amount at Risk

Under I.R.C. § 465(b), a taxpayer is generally at risk regarding an activity with respect to (i) the amount of money and adjusted basis of property contributed by the taxpayer to the activity, and (ii) amounts borrowed for use in the activity to the extent that the taxpayer is unprotected personally liable for repayment, and (iii) amounts borrowed for which the taxpayer has pledged property, other than property used in the activity, as security for the borrowed amount (to the extent of the net fair market value of the pledged property).[29]

Notwithstanding the provisions for I.R.C. § 465(b)(2), a taxpayer is not considered to be at risk with respect to borrowed amounts if the amount is borrowed from a person who has an interest in the activity or from a person related to a person who has an interest in the activity.[30] For this purpose, a related person means one who bears a relationship to a person specified in either I.R.C. §§ 267(b) or 707(b)(1), but substituting "10%" for "50%".[31] A person is also a related person if they are engaged in trades or businesses under common control within the meaning of I.R.C. §§ 52(a) or 52(b).[32]

The taxpayer's at risk amount with respect to an activity is reduced to the extent the taxpayer claims a loss from the activity which is not disallowed under the at risk rules.[33] The taxpayer's amount of risk is also decreased by cash and the basis of property withdrawn from the activity, but is increased by the taxpayer's share of income from the activity.[34]

In Hubert Enterprises, Inc. v. Commissioner,[35] the Tax Court held that a deficit restoration obligation contained in an operating agreement of a limited liability company taxed as a partnership did not result in the members being at risk with respect to the recourse liabilities of the limited liability company because (i) the

---

[29] I.R.C. § 465(b)(2).

[30] I.R.C. § 465(d)(3)(A).

[31] I.R.C. § 465(d)(3)(C).

[32] I.R.C. § 465(d)(3(C)(ii).

[33] I.R.C. § 465(b)(5).

[34] Prop. Treas. Reg. § 1.465-41, example 2.

[35] TC Memo 2008-46.

deficit restoration obligation would only be effective if the limited liability company liquidated, and even then there was no assurance that the amount of the deficit restoration obligation would be equal to the amount of the unpaid recourse debt, (ii) under the terms of the operating agreement, the amount paid under the deficit restoration obligation could be paid to members with positive capital account balances, rather than to creditors, and (iii) the creditors had no enforceable right to collect any unpaid debt directly from the member by reason of the deficit restoration obligation.

3. Nonrecourse Financing

Notwithstanding the general rule set forth above, I.R.C. § 465(b)(4) contains an overriding principle that a taxpayer is not considered at risk with respect to amounts protected against loss through nonrecourse financing, guarantees, stop loss agreements or other similar arrangement. Thus, generally, a partner is only at risk to the extent of his bottom-line liability on a recourse debt. There is, however, an exception to the general rule in the case of qualified nonrecourse financing. Under I.R.C. § 465(b)(6), a taxpayer engaged in the activity of holding real property is considered at risk with respect to the taxpayer's share of any qualified nonrecourse financing that is secured by real property used in that activity.

The term "qualified non-recourse financing" generally means nonconvertible, nonrecourse debt that is borrowed with respect to the activity of holding real property and that is (i) borrowed from a government or instrumentality thereof, (ii) guaranteed by a government, or (more likely) (iii) borrowed from a person regularly engaged in the business of lending money who is neither a person related to the taxpayer, a person from whom the taxpayer acquired the property (or related persons to such person), nor a person who receives a fee with respect to the taxpayer's investment in the property (or related person to such person).[36] There is an exception to the rule prohibiting loans from related persons. Funds borrowed from related persons will be taken into account if the related person financing is commercially reasonable and on substantially the same terms as loans involving unrelated persons.[37]

Pursuant to I.R.C. § 465(b)(6)(C), if the qualified nonrecourse financing is incurred by a partnership, a partner's share of the partnership's qualified nonrecourse financing is determined on the basis of the partner's share of liabilities of the partnership incurred in connection with such financing determined under I.R.C. § 752.

4. Carryover of Disallowed Losses

If the taxpayer is prohibited from taking a loss by reason of the applicability of the at risk limitation, the amount disallowed may be carried forward indefinitely, but the deductibility of such loss is still subject to the at risk limitation in any

---

[36] I.R.C. § 465(b)(6)(B).

[37] I.R.C. § 465(b)(6)(D)(ii).

subsequent year.[38]

5. Applicability to Partnerships

The at risk rules are applied at the partner level, not the partnership level. While I.R.C. § 465(a)(1) refers to the amount the taxpayer is at risk at the close of the taxable year, where the activity is engaged in through a partnership, it is the close of the taxable year of the partnership which governs, not that of the partner.[39] This rule could make a difference where the partner and the partnership have different taxable years.

6. Disposition of Activity or Partnership Interest

If a partner disposes of all or a portion of the partner's partnership interest, or if a partnership engaged in an activity to which the at risk rules apply disposes of an activity, any gain resulting from such disposition is treated as income from the activity.[40] Thus, if a partner has previously had losses disallowed by reason of the at risk limitation, those losses are generally allowed in the year of the disposition of the activity or the partnership interest in the partnership conducting the activity to the extent of those gains.

There is a special rule with respect to certain carryover basis transactions. If (i) a partner transfers the partner's interest in a partnership, (ii) the basis of the transferee is determined in whole or in part by reference to the basis of the transferor, (iii) the transferor has suspended losses by virtue of I.R.C. § 465(a) at the time of the transfer, and (iv) at the close of the taxable year in which the transfer occurs the amount of the transferor's loss from the activity is in excess of the transferor's amount at risk in the activity, the excess is added to the transferor's basis in the activity.[41] This rule is applied solely for the purpose of determining the basis of the property in the hands of the transferee (typically a carryover basis).

There is another special rule that is applicable to transfers of partnership interest that is basically the flipside of the one just covered. If (i) a partner transfers a partner's entire interest in the partnership, (ii) the basis of the transferee is determined in whole or part by reference to the basis of the transferor, and (iii) the transferor has an amount at risk which *is in excess* of losses from the activity (i.e., the at risk rules have not suspended a loss), then at the close of the transferor's taxable year in which the transfer occurs, the transferor's amount at risk in the activity is added to the transferee's amount at risk.[42] In addition, in the case of a gift of a partnership interest, the transferee's amount at risk is increased by the amount that the donee's basis is increased under I.R.C. § 1015(d) (relating to gift tax paid by the transferor).[43]

---

[38] I.R.C. § 465(a)(2).

[39] Prop. Treas. Reg. § 1.465-1(a).

[40] Prop. Treas. Reg. §§ 1.465-66(a); 465-12(a).

[41] Prop. Treas. Reg. § 1.465-67.

[42] Prop. Treas. Reg. § 1.465-68.

[43] Prop. Treas. Reg. § 1.465-68(b).

C. Passive Loss Limitation

1. Loss Disallowance Rule

Even if a partner's losses from a partnership are not limited by the basis limitation or the at risk limitation rules, the partner's share of the partnership's losses may be disallowed under the passive loss rules. In the case of individuals, estates, trusts, closely held C corporations and personal service corporations, I.R.C. § 469(a) disallows the deduction of a passive activity loss or the claiming of a passive activity credit. Any loss or credit disallowed by virtue of I.R.C. § 469(a) is treated as a deduction or credit applicable to the activity in the next taxable year (i.e., the disallowed loss or credit is carried over).[44]

2. Passive Activity

Big Picture: Generally, a partner's passive losses are only deductible from that partner's passive income. The devil, as usual in tax, is in the details. I.R.C. § 469(d)(1) defines the term "passive activity loss" to be something of a misnomer: The amount by which the aggregate losses from all passive activities of the taxable year exceed the aggregate income from all passive activities for such year. Because this amount is typically disallowed, a better term would be "disallowed passive activity loss" or, perhaps, "passive activity loss carryforward." The key to getting a handle on I.R.C. § 469 is understanding what constitutes a passive activity. I.R.C. § 469(c)(1) defines the term "passive activity" to mean any activity that involves the conduct of a trade or business and in which the taxpayer does not materially participate. There are a number of special rules applicable to rental activities and working interests in oil and gas property.[45]

It would be easy to end-run the passive loss rules if "portfolio income" counted as passive income. Consequently, even though it is passive in nature, gross income from interest, dividends, annuities or royalties not derived in the ordinary course of a trade or business, and gain or loss attributable to the disposition of property producing this income is not treated as passive income. Similarly, expenses, which are clearly and directly applicable to such gross income are not taken into account either.[46]

3. Material Participation

In general, an activity is passive with regard to a partner, if he does not "materially participate" in the activity (the material participation rules operate differently — or not at all — in the case of certain rental activities and working interests in oil and gas property).[47] It is the participation of the partner, not the

---

[44] I.R.C. § 469(b).

[45] I.R.C. § 469(c)(2), (3), (7).

[46] I.R.C. § 469(e)(1)(A).

[47] I.R.C. § 469(c). Passive activities do not include working interests in oil and gas properties subject to certain requirements. I.R.C. § 469(c)(3). There is also an exception for real estate professionals, I.R.C. § 469(c)(7), and certain individuals subject to a $25,000 limitation. I.R.C. § 469(i).

partnership, which is relevant.[48] Whether a partner materially participates in an activity conducted by a partnership is determined based upon the taxable year of the partnership, not the taxable year of the partner.[49]

I.R.C. § 469(h)(1) provides that a taxpayer is treated as materially participating in an activity only if the taxpayer is involved in the operation of the activity on a regular, continuous and substantial basis. Temp. Treas. Reg. § 1.469-5T(a), however, provides that an individual is treated as materially participating in an activity if and only if one of seven tests are met. These tests are as follow:

(1) The individual participates in the activity more than 500 hours during the year.

(2) The individual's participation in the activity for the year constitutes substantially all of the participation in such activity of all individuals for such year.

(3) The individual participates in the activity for more than 100 hours during the taxable year and such participation for the year is not less than the participation in the activity of any other individual for such year.

(4) The activity is a "significant participation activity" (within the meaning of Temp. Treas. Reg. § 1.469-5T(c)) for the year and the individual's aggregate participation in all significant participation activities during such year exceeds 500 hours.

(5) The individual materially participated in the activity for any five taxable years during the immediately preceding 10 taxable years.

(6) The activity is a personal service activity and the individual materially participated in the activity for any three taxable years preceding the taxable year in question.

(7) Based on all the facts and circumstances, the individual participates in the activity on a regular, continuous and substantial basis during the year.

As you can see, it is not all that difficult to materially participate under the regulations. Indeed, well known tax attorney Richard Lipton said if you took the legislative history and stood it on its head, you would get the Regulations. One of the reasons the regulations are relatively liberal are because Treasury wanted to combat PIGs, passive income generators. The passive loss rules applied to investments made before their enactment, and those whip-sawed investors were particularly interested in finding ways to generate passive income. By making the material participation rules more liberal, it made it harder for those investors to earn passive income.

Rental activities are passive unless a heightened material participation rule is met: More than half of the personal services performed by a taxpayer must be in real property trades or businesses; further, the taxpayer must perform more than 750 hours of personal services in real property trades or businesses and materially participates (under the regular rules) in those activities. The 750-hour rule does not

---

[48] Temp. Treas. Reg. § 1.469-2T(e)(1).

[49] *Id.*

make this final requirement inevitable. If a taxpayer participates in an activity 80 hours per year and others participate more, the 80 hours will count toward the 750-hour rule, but the taxpayer will likely not materially participate in the activity in question under the regular rules.[50]

I.R.C. § 469(h)(2) provides that except as provided in Regulations, no interest in a limited partnership as a limited partner is treated as an interest with respect to which a taxpayer materially participates. The IRS originally took the position that a person would be treated as a limited partner if either (i) the person's interest is designated a limited partnership interest in the limited partnership agreement or the certificate of limited partnership or (ii) the liability of the person for obligations of the partnership is limited under state law to a determinable fixed amount. This raises a serious question as to whether a member of a limited liability company holds a limited partnership interest without regard to the amount of the member's participation in the activity. Following a series of cases the IRS lost for entities that were taxed as partnerships but were not limited partnerships under state law,[51] the IRS issued Proposed Regulations that take a different position.

Prop. Treas. Reg. § 1.469-5(e)(3) provides that for purposes of I.R.C. § 469(h)(2), an interest is treated as a limited partnership interest if (i) the entity is treated as a partnership for federal income tax purposes, and (ii) the holder of the interest does not have rights to manage the entity at all times during the relevant taxable year. Thus, a member of an LLC who has a right to participate in the management of the LLC would not be treated as a limited partner even though he has no liability for the obligations of the partnership. The Proposed Regulations further provide that an individual will not be treated as holding a limited partnership interest if that individual also holds another interest in the entity that is not treated as a limited partnership interest (e.g., a general partnership interest in a state law limited partnership). It is unclear if the terms of the operating agreement can override state law. Thus, if the operating agreement of a member-managed LLC only authorizes certain members to take action on behalf of the LLC (as sometimes happens), it is unclear if the remaining members will be treated as limited partners.

D. Disposition of Partnership Interest

I.R.C. § 469(g) provides that if during the taxable year a taxpayer disposes of the taxpayer's entire interest in any passive activity in a fully taxable transaction, the excess of (i) any loss from such activity for such taxable year, over (ii) any net income or gains for such taxable year from all other passive activities, is treated as a loss that is not from a passive activity. Thus, relevant suspended passive losses become fully deductible, with the proviso that they must first be offset against passive income before being offset active income. Naturally, there is an exception: If the person acquiring the activity is a related party within the meaning of I.R.C. § 267(b) or 707(b)(1), then the forgoing rule does not apply until the taxable year in which such interest is acquired by somebody who is not a related person. If the disposition is a result of the death of the taxpayer, then the general disposition rule

---

[50] I.R.C. § 469(c)(2),(7).

[51] *See, e.g.,* Garnett v. Commissioner, 132 T.C. No. 19 (June 30, 2009).

only applies to the extent that the losses are greater than the excess of the basis of the property in the hands of the transferee over the basis of the property in the hands of the taxpayer immediately before death. Note that, generally, under I.R.C. § 1014, a transferee from a decedent (English: heir) takes a fair market value basis in the inherited property.[52] Any suspended losses up to the step-up in basis resulting from the death of the taxpayer are not allowed as a deduction for any taxable year.[53]

Where the passive activity is conducted through a partnership and there is a sale, exchange or other disposition of the partnership interest, a ratable portion of any gain or loss from the disposition is treated as gain or loss from the disposition of an interest in each trade or business, rental or investment activity in which the partnership owns an interest.[54] The ratable portion in the case of gain applicable to an activity is generally equal to the amount of gain recognized multiplied by a fraction, the numerator of which is the gain that would have been allocable to the partner had the partnership sold its entire interest in the activity for its fair market value, and the denominator of which is the amount of gain that would have been allocable to the partner had the partnership sold all of its activities in which gain would be recognized for their fair market value.[55]

§ 5.05   TAXABLE YEAR OF PARTNERSHIP

A.   Required Taxable Years

Unless the partnership has a "business purpose tax year" (see below), I.R.C. § 706(b) generally requires that a partnership have a taxable year that is determined by reference to the taxable year of its partners. There is a three-tier system for determining the partnership's taxable year on this basis. First, if there is a "majority interest taxable year," then that must be used by the partnership. The term "majority interest taxable year" means the taxable year of one or more partners having an aggregate interest in partnership profits and capital of more than 50% (i.e., partners meeting this threshold must be on the same tax year).[56] If there is not a majority interest taxable year, then the partnership must use the taxable year of all of the "principal partners," assuming they are on the same tax year. A "principal partner" is a partner having an interest of 5% or more in partnership profits or capital. If there is no taxable year of all of the principal partners, then the partnership must be on a tax year that produces the least aggregate deferral. Treas. Reg. § 1.706-1(b)(2)(i)(c).

In a law school course you are not likely to cover this, but here are the rules anyway. Under Treas. Reg. § 1.706-1(b)(2)(i)(c), the aggregate deferral for a particular year is equal to the sum of the deferrals of each of the partners. The

---

[52] I.R.C. § 469(g)(2)(A).

[53] I.R.C. § 469(g)(2)(B).

[54] Temp. Treas. Reg. § 1.469-2T(e)(3)(ii)(A).

[55] Temp. Treas. Reg. § 1.469-2T(e)(3)(ii)(B)(1).

[56] I.R.C. § 706(b)(4)(A).

deferral for a partner is determined by multiplying the months of deferral that would be generated for a given taxable year and each partner's interest in partnership profits for that year. The partnership taxable year that produces the lowest sum when compared to the other partners' taxable years is the taxable year that results in the least aggregate deferral of income. If the calculation results in more than one taxable year qualifying as a taxable year with least aggregate deferral, the partnership may elect any of such taxable years, unless one of such years is the partnership's existing taxable year, in which case the partnership must maintain its existing taxable year.[57]

The following example, taken from Treas. Reg. § 1.706-1(b)(3)(iv), Example 1, illustrates the application of the least aggregate deferral rule. A and B each have a 50% interest in partnership profits. A has a June 30 taxable year and B has a July 31 taxable year. The determination of the taxable year that produces the least aggregate deferral is made as follows:

Test 6/30	Year End	Interest in Partnership Profits	Months of Deferral for 6/30 Year End	Interest x Deferral
Partner A	6/30	.5	0	0
Partner B	7/31	.5	1	.5
Aggregate Deferral				.5

Test 7/31	Year End	Interest in Partnership Profits	Months of Deferral for 7/31 Year End	Interest x Deferral
Partner A	6/30	.5	11	5.5
Partner B	7/31	.5	0	0
Aggregate Deferral				5.5

Thus, June 30 is the year with the least aggregate deferral.

B. Business Purpose

I.R.C. § 706(b)(1)(C) provides that a partnership may have a taxable year other than the required taxable year determined in accordance with I.R.C. § 706(b)(1)(B) if it is established to the satisfaction of the IRS that there is a business purpose for such taxable year (which does not include the deferral of income to partners). The IRS has issued a revenue procedure providing guidance regarding when a partnership has established a business purpose for a taxable year.

---

[57] Treas. Reg. § 1.706-1(b)(3)(i)

Under Rev. Proc. 2002-38,[58] a partnership can establish a "business purpose year" by satisfying a 25% gross receipts test. The 25% gross receipts tests is met if the gross receipts from sales and services for the last two months of the desired business year are more than 25% of the gross receipts from sales and services for the 12-month period ending on that date and for the two preceding 12-month periods.[59] Even if the taxpayer meets the 25% gross receipts test, the taxpayer must also establish that there is not another annual accounting period that also meets the 25% test and that produces a higher average of gross receipts than does the year requested by the taxpayer.[60]

In addition to the mathematical tests provided for in Rev. Proc. 2002-38, a partnership will be permitted to adopt a taxable year other than a required taxable year if the taxpayer can establish a business purpose for the taxable year based on all the relevant facts and circumstances.[61] For example, an ice cream stand with equal income each month, but that closes for the months of December, January, and February, would not meet the standards of Rev. Proc. 2002-38. Nonetheless, under the facts and circumstances test it could qualify for a November 30 year end.

The IRS has indicated that it will grant permission to adopt or change a taxable year under the facts and circumstances test only in rare and unusual circumstances.[62] Rev. Proc. 2002-39 indicates that reasons which will not qualify as a good business purpose include (i) administrative and convenience reasons, (ii) the use of a particular year for regulatory or financial accounting purposes, (iii) hiring patterns, (iv) the use of price list, model years or other items that change on an annual basis, (v) the use of a particular year by related entities and (vi) the use of a particular year by competitors.[63]

C. § 444 Election

Under I.R.C. § 444, a partnership may elect to have a taxable year other than a required taxable year. I.R.C. §§ 444(b)(1) limits the choices of elected taxable year to one that does not provide a deferral period longer than three months (i.e., if the required taxable year is the calendar year, then only the last day of September, October or November may be elected under I.R.C. § 444). The cost of making an election under I.R.C. § 444 is that the taxpayer is required to make the payments required by I.R.C. § 7519.[64] Although the manner of computing the payment required by I.R.C. § 7519 is rather complex,[65] the effect of the payment is that the partnership is prepaying the tax applicable to the income deferred by reason of making the election under section I.R.C. § 444. Because there is no financial benefit to an I.R.C. § 444 election, they are very uncommon. When I.R.C. § 444 was

---

[58] 2002-1 C.B. (Vol. II) 1037.

[59] Section 5.05(2)(a) of Rev. Proc. 2002-38.

[60] Section 5.05(2)(b) of Rev. Proc. 2002-38.

[61] Section 5.02(1)(b) of Rev. Proc. 2002-39, 2002-1 C.B. (Vol. II) 1046.

[62] *Id.*

[63] *Id.*

[64] I.R.C. § 444(c)(1).

[65] Treas. Reg. § 1.7519-1T(b)(vi).

enacted, Congress thought that accountants would be overwhelmed with taxpayers with 4/15 year ends and would encourage taxpayers to make the I.R.C. § 444 election. Whether or not the former has happened, the latter has not.

Chapter 6

OPERATION OF A PARTNERSHIP: ALLOCATION OF PARTNERSHIP INCOME AND LOSSES

BASIC OVERVIEW

Warning: You do not have to dig very deeply in this area before things start getting very complicated. For that reason, an unusually large amount of material is deferred to the Detailed Discussion.

As you have learned, a partnership is a flow-through entity. Income and deductions are passed through to the partners. A mechanism needs to exist, therefore, for determining what each partner's allocable share of partnership income and deductions is. I.R.C. § 704(b) and its Regulations generally allow partners a great deal of flexibility in this regard. The allocations do not necessarily need to be in proportion to the underlying ownership of the partnership interests (as is the case with S corporations).[1] Someone who is otherwise a 50% partner could be allocated 90% of depreciation deductions, for example. Or, all losses could initially be allocated to the "money partners," with subsequent income allocated to them to the same extent as losses were, and then with income allocated 50% to the money partners and 50% to the promoters. (This is sometimes called a "flip;" flips are quite common.)

I.R.C. § 704(b) provides that a partner's "distributive share of income, gain, loss, and deduction, or credit . . . shall be determined in accordance with the partner's interest in the partnership . . . if the partnership agreement does not provide for how a distributive share will be allocated *or* if the allocations do not have substantial economic effect." Thus, if an allocation *does* have substantial economic effect, it need not be in accordance with a partner's interest in the partnership. As we will learn, a partner's interest in the partnership is determined under a facts and circumstances test that is fairly vague. The Regulations, on the other hand, provide detailed and specific rules as to when allocations have substantial economic effect. These substantial economic effect rules provide a structure that is intended to be a safe harbor. If the partnership agreement complies with the rules, the partnership knows the transaction will be safe. Many practitioners will endeavor to comply with them, if possible. It used to be that practitioners viewed compliance with the substantial economic effect rules as being virtually mandatory, but in recent years practitioners have been increasingly drafting agreements to come under the partners' interest in the partnership facts and circumstances test.

---

[1] *See* I.R.C. § 1377(a); since partners can have varying interests in capital and profits, determining what the underlying ownership interest is may not be an easy task.

For an allocation to have substantial economic effect under the safe harbor, the capital accounts must be maintained in accordance with the rules in the Regulations.[2] As the concern here is with the economic rather than tax impacts, the rules for keeping capital accounts are quite different than the rules for computing tax basis.

Under the Regulations, a partner's capital account is increased by:

1. The amount of money contributed to the partnership.

2. The fair market value of property contributed to the partnership (net of liabilities secured by the property that the partnership is considered to assume or take subject to under I.R.C. § 752).[3]

3. Allocations of partnership income and gain, including tax-exempt income.

A partner's capital account is decreased by:

1. The amount of money distributed to the partner.

2. The fair market value of property distributed to the partner (net of liabilities secured by the property that the partner is considered to assume or take subject to under I.R.C. § 752).

3. Allocations of expenditures of the partnership that can neither be capitalized nor deducted in computing taxable income (e.g. penalties or bribes),

4. Allocations of partnership loss and deduction.

Note that unlike the adjusted basis in the partnership interest, a partner's capital account does not include that partner's share of liabilities. If the partnership has liabilities, a partner's basis often will exceed his capital account balance.[4] Because, subject to the at risk and passive loss rules, a partner may receive loss allocations up to his basis in the partnership interest, a partner may have a positive tax basis and a negative capital account.

For purposes of the allocation rules, what is relevant is not tax gain, loss and deduction, but "book" gain, loss and deduction. Thus, for example, in calculating depreciation for purposes of the allocation rules, we look at book depreciation, not tax depreciation. Book depreciation is based on book value, initially the fair market value of property on acquisition. If property is acquired with cash, book value and tax basis are the same. But if property is contributed to the partnership, they can be different. Rules we will discuss later in this chapter tell us how to allocate tax items — but one step at a time.

There are two parts to the substantial economic effect test. First, the allocation must have economic effect. The Regulations provide a largely mechanical test for

---

[2] Treas. Reg. § 1.704-1(b)(2)(iv)(a).

[3] The fair market value assigned to property will be regarded as correct provided that (1) such value is reasonably agreed to among the partners in arm's length negotiations and (2) the partners have sufficiently adverse interests. *See* Treas. Reg. § 1.704-1(b)(2)(iv)(h).

[4] This is not inevitably the case, however. For example, if the partner contributes property to a partnership with a fair market value that greatly exceeds its basis, the capital account may exceed the tax basis of the partnership interest even after factoring in liabilities.

determining whether or not an allocation has economic effect. Second, because it is possible to manipulate the economic effect test, the Regulations also provide that the economic effect of an allocation must be substantial. Generally, the economic effect of an allocation will be substantial if on an after-tax, present value basis, a partner's economic investment in the partnership is either enhanced or diminished as a consequence of the allocation.

Partnerships have three options under the Regulations to meet the "economic effect" test, the principal ones are the "regular" economic effect test and the "alternate" economic effect test. The regular test has three parts:

1. The partnership must keep capital accounts in accordance with the rules described above.

2. When an interest of a partner is liquidated, the partner must be paid any positive balance in his capital account.

3. If a partner has a deficit balance in his capital account, he must pay the deficit to the partnership by the end of the tax year in which his partnership interest is liquidated (or, if later, 90 days after liquidation). This last rule is sometimes called a "deficit restoration obligation" or "DRO."[5]

Assume, for example, that on January 1 of year 1 A and B invest $10,000 each in the AB partnership. The partnership purchases equipment for $20,000. Thus, the equipment's book value is also $20,000. The (book) depreciation deductions are $5,000 per year and the partnership has no debt.[6] The partnership breaks even on its operations except for depreciation deductions, and thus the partnership operates at a $5,000 loss per year. The partnership agreement allocates all of the depreciation deductions to A. At the beginning of year 1, A and B each has a capital account of $10,000. As a result of the year 1 allocation, A's capital account is reduced to $5,000 and B's remains the same.

At the beginning of year 2 the equipment is sold and the partnership is liquidated. In order to comply with the economic effect rules, the partnership must pay to each partner the balance in her capital account. We will assume the equipment has a fair market value equal to its book value, or $15,000. If that is indeed the case, the $15,000 proceeds from the sale are distributed $5,000 to A and $10,000 to B.

Now again assume that the partnership agreement provides that liquidation distributions will be made in accordance with capital account balances. A and B each contributes $10,000 to the partnership and the partnership borrows $40,000 on a recourse basis with only interest due for the first five years of the note. Note that this debt increases the tax bases of the partners' partnership interests under I.R.C. § 752, assume by $20,000 each, but does not affect capital accounts. AB purchases equipment for $60,000. The equipment generates depreciation

---

[5] Treas. Reg. § 1.704-1(b)(2)(ii)(a)-(c).

[6] We are making this number up and completely ignoring the actual rules of I.R.C. § 168, including the mid-year convention and I.R.C. § 179. Also, not that since the property was acquired for cash, tax and book items are the same.

deductions of $10,000 per year. A therefore has a beginning tax basis in the partnership interest of $30,000 and a beginning capital account of $10,000. In year 1 the partnership breaks even except for depreciation deductions on the equipment and allocates the entire $10,000 of that depreciation to A. A's basis in the partnership interest is reduced to $20,000 and her capital account is reduced to zero. Now assume that A's interest in the partnership is liquidated on January 1 of year 2 with the partnership relieving A of any obligation on the partnership liabilities. In order to comply with the economic effect rules, on liquidation the partnership must pay the partner the amount of any positive balance in her capital account. In this example, however, the capital account is zero, and thus no payment need be made to A. Note that, generally, if the partnership is in compliance with the economic effect rules, after liquidation of a partner's interest, the partner's capital account will be zero. Can you see why? In the example, A's basis prior to liquidation is $20,000. No payment is made to her. What happens to A's $20,000 share of the liability? The answer is that I.R.C. § 752(d) provides that a partner's amount realized on the disposition of a partnership interest includes any liabilities of which the partner is relieved. Thus, A's amount realized includes the $20,000 of liability relief. As A's amount realized is $20,000 and A's basis in the partnership interest is $20,000, there is no tax gain or loss to A on the liquidation.

Now let's take the example one step further. Assume that in year 2 A remains a partner in the partnership. The partnership again breaks even on partnership operations except for depreciation, and again allocates $10,000 of depreciation to A. A's basis is reduced to $10,000 and A's capital is reduced to a negative ($10,000). If A's partnership interest is liquidated on January 1 of year 3 with the partnership relieving A of any obligation on the partnership liabilities, then A is required to contribute $10,000 to the partnership to bring her capital account to zero.[7] Her basis in the partnership interest is increased to $20,000. Under I.R.C. § 752(d), the amount realized is also $20,000, for no tax gain or loss on the liquidation.

The difficulty with the regular economic effect rules is that partners are required to have an unlimited deficit restoration obligation. Especially for investors, that may not be wise. For example, assume the partners form a limited partnership and that all partners have unlimited deficit restoration obligations. An employee of the partnership, while conducting partnership business, runs over and kills a neurosurgeon with eight handicapped children. A large tort liability, in excess of insurance limits, results. The general partner is the only one liable under partnership law, and he contributes sufficient funds to the partnership to enable it to pay the liability, increasing the general partner's capital account. The payment results in a large tax loss to the partnership which (since the limited partners have unlimited deficit restoration obligations) may primarily be allocated to the limited partners. The allocation causes the limited partners to have substantial negative capital accounts. Should they have to restore those deficit capital accounts (as might happen if the general partner decided to take this opportune moment to cause the partnership to liquidate), they would in effect be paying the tort liability, something that likely was not contemplated when they entered into the

---

[7] This requirement may exist in regard to a general partnership under state law. For limited liability entities the obligation to re-contribute a negative capital account may need to be contractually created.

partnership agreement. The bottomless risk that an unlimited deficit obligation poses causes most advisors to recommend that their investor-clients not agree to such a provision.

The Regulations, recognizing this business reality, contain an alternative in Treas. Reg. § 1.704-1(b)(2)(ii)(d). Under this alternative, an allocation must meet the first two economic effect tests (keep capital accounts according to the rules and upon liquidation, pay to a partner any positive balance in his capital account). But there is no requirement that a partner have any deficit restoration obligation, though partners sometimes agree to a limited deficit restoration obligation in order to be allocated more losses. But unless the deficit capital account restoration obligation is unlimited, the rules for this alternative test must be met. The next requirement is that the partnership agreement contain a qualified income offset provision (discussed below). If this alternative test is met, an allocation will be treated as having economic effect if the allocation does not cause the partner to have a deficit capital account balance (in excess of any limited deficit restoration obligation) or increase an already existing deficit capital account balance (in excess of any limited deficit restoration obligation). A capital account can become negative for reasons other than allocations. The partnership could, for example, make a distribution to a partner that would cause a deficit capital account balance. While the IRS can force a partnership to change the way it makes allocations, it cannot control to whom a partnership makes distributions.

The IRS needed a mechanism for eliminating the deficit capital account of a partner who has no obligation to restore it (or for eliminating a deficit capital account in excess of a partner's limited deficit capital account restoration obligation). That mechanism was to require the partnership to allocate income to the partner to offset any such deficit as quickly as possible (hence the name "qualified income offset" often abbreviated "QIO"). Thus, if a QIO is triggered, the partnership must abandon its existing allocation structure and allocate income to offset the relevant negative capital accounts. This can wreak havoc with the partnerships allocation structure, and many partnership agreements provide for downstream adjustments, when possible, to get the parties back to where they would have been if no QIO had been triggered. Further, distributions are not the only events that the IRS cannot control that can cause a capital account to become negative. Certain provisions of Subchapter K can require allocations to a partner that might create a deficit capital account, so the IRS needed to account for these as well. We discuss these rules, certain anticipatory adjustments that must be made, and the formal regulatory rule in the Detailed Discussion.

For all of their complexity, the economic effect rules are not enough to get the job done. They are, in effect, mechanical rules, and like all mechanical rules, can be inappropriately manipulated. Accordingly, the Regulations provide that not only must the allocation have economic effect, that economic effect must be substantial.

Initially the Regulations provide that the economic effect of an allocation is substantial if there is a reasonable possibility that the allocation will affect substantially the dollar amounts to be received by the partners independent of tax consequences.[8] The Regulations then go on to provide that an allocation is *not* substantial if:

(1)   the after-tax economic consequences of at least one partner may, in present value terms, be enhanced compared to such consequences if the allocation were not contained in the partnership agreement, and

(2)   there is a strong likelihood that the after-tax economic consequences of no partner will, in present value terms, be substantially diminished compared to such consequences if the allocation were not contained in the partnership agreement.

Or, as one of the authors tells his students, the allocation is not substantial if on a present value, after-tax basis, someone is better off and no one is worse off than would be the case if the allocation were not present. Under these circumstances, it means that the allocation had a tax effect, but no economic effect (on an after-tax, present value basis). For there to be an economic effect, if someone is better off, some else has to be worse off. In determining whether a partner is better off or worse off, tax consequences that result from the interaction of the allocation with the partner's tax attributes that are unrelated to the partnership are taken into account. Thus, a partner's personal tax circumstances are factored in.

For example, assume taxpayers A and B are equal partners in the AB partnership. A expects to be in the 50% tax bracket over the next several years.[9] B, on the other hand, expects to be in the 15% tax bracket. Over the next several years the partnership expects to earn approximately equal amounts of tax-exempt interest and taxable dividends. A and B agree that 80% of the tax-exempt income will be allocated to A and the balance of the tax-exempt income and all of the taxable dividends will be allocated to B. The partners can make this allocation without violating any of the economic effect rules. But according to the Regulations, the economic effect of the allocation will not be substantial, because if you do the math, on a present value, after tax basis, A's position is enhanced (compared to the situation she would be in if she had received half of each type of income) and B's position is not diminished (indeed his position is also enhanced).

The Regulations provide some additional fine-tuning to the substantiality rules for what the Regulations call "shifting" and "transitory" allocations. Generally, shifting allocations occur within a single tax year, and transitory allocations occur over a period of up to five years. In either case, the economic effect of an allocation will not be substantial if there is a strong likelihood that the capital accounts of the partners will be about the same as they would have been had the allocation not been made and the allocation results in a net reduction of the partners' tax liability.

We will address shifting allocations in the Detailed Discussion. Transitory allocations, as noted, occur over a period of years. Under the Regulations, if there is a strong likelihood that (1) an "original allocation" and a later "offsetting allocation" will leave the capital accounts approximately where they would have

---

[8]   Treas. Reg. § 1.704-1(b)(2)(iii)(a).

[9]   This example is based on Treas. Reg. § 1.704-1(b)(5), example 5 which uses this now fictitious 50% tax bracket. Even today it is possible for a taxpayer to approach this tax bracket if state and Federal income tax are combined and the taxpayer lives in a state with high income taxes.

been had the allocations not occurred and (2) the tax liability of the partners will be reduced as a result of the allocations, than the economic effect of the allocations will not be substantial. The Regulations provide that if the offset happens and taxes are reduced, it will be presumed that there was a strong likelihood that this would happen unless the taxpayers can present facts and circumstances demonstrating otherwise. However, if there is a strong likelihood that the offsetting allocation will not be made "in large part" within five years of the original allocation, then the economic effect of the allocation will be substantial.[10]

For example, assume that our AB partnership has predictable, approximately equal amounts of income each year and A has an expiring net operating loss carryforward. To allow A to take greater advantage of the net operating loss carryforward, the partnership allocates all of its income in year 1 to A. It allocates all of its income in year 2 to B. Thereafter, it returns to allocating income equally between the partners. The partnership agreement complies with the economic effect rules. The economic effect of the allocation is insubstantial because there is a strong likelihood of the offset occurring and the partners' tax liability is less than it would have been without the allocation (the allocation lowers A's taxes and, except for time value of money considerations, is neutral as to B). Note that if the offset would occur more than five years after the original allocation (not that B would ever agree to that), the allocation would be allowed.[11]

As noted earlier, if the substantial economic effect test is not met, then allocations must be in accordance with the "partners' interests in the partnership." For now, recall that a partner's interest in the partnership is determined using all relevant facts and circumstances and that the kind of detailed guidance we have for the substantial economic effect test is lacking. We will come back to this topic in the Detailed Discussion.

Moving on to yet another complex area, recall that under I.R.C. § 721, no gain or loss is recognized when a partner contributes property to the partnership. The partnership takes a carryover tax basis in the property under I.R.C. § 723, and the contributing partner takes a substituted tax basis in the partnership interest under I.R.C. § 722. Yet when the partners put their deal together, the primary focus is on the economics, not the tax basis. What is of primary importance is the fair market values of contributed property. This disjuncture between tax basis and economic value gives rise to a host of complex rules.

Let's begin with an example. A contributes Land #1 to the AB partnership in which A and B have equal interests. The land has a tax basis of $ 7,000 and a fair market value of $10,000. The partnership takes a tax basis in the property of $7,000, A's tax basis in her partnership interest is increased by that amount, and no gain or loss typically is recognized to A or the partnership under I.R.C. § 721(a). Note that there is $3,000 of tax gain inherent in the property. If the partnership now sells the property for $10,000, to whom should that gain be allocated? The gain arose on A's "watch," so it would make sense for the gain to be allocated to A and indeed, I.R.C. § 704(c) so provides.

---

[10] Treas. Reg. § 1.704-1(b)(2)(iii)(c).

[11] This example is based on Treas. Reg. § 1.704-1(b)(f), example 8(ii).

In the absence of I.R.C. § 704(c), could the partnership have made a special allocation of the tax gain in A's land to B under § 704(b)? The answer is no. Recall that the land is recorded on the books of the partnership at its fair market value of $10,000 (i.e., it has a book value of $10,000). If it were sold for $10,000, there would have been no book gain or loss to allocate, and the I.R.C. § 704(b) special allocation rules apply to *book* gains and losses, not to tax gains and losses. Tax gains and losses do not affect the capital accounts and therefore their allocation cannot have substantial economic effect. How is the tax gain handled? I.R.C. § 704(c)(1)(A) provides that income, gain, loss, and deduction with respect to property contributed to the partnership by a partner is shared among the partners so as to take account of the variation between the tax basis of the property and its fair market value at the time of contribution. In the fact pattern we have been discussing, that means that $3,000 of the tax gain is allocated to A.

What if the property is sold for $12,000? The tax gain is $12,000 - $7,000 = $5,000. The book gain is $12,000 - $10,000 = $2,000. The $2,000 of book gain is allocated equally to A and B or $1,000 each. Under I.R.C. § 704(c), the tax gain is allocated $3,000 + $1,000 = $4,000 to A and $1,000 to B. Note that in this example, the tax gain equal to the book gain ($1,000 per partner) is allocated in the same manner as the book gain, and the tax gain in excess of the book gain ($3,000) is allocated to the contributing partner.[12] That makes sense. Generally, a partner should receive tax gain equal to his share of book gain. If tax gain exceeds the book gain, normally it means that the property had gain inherent in it on contribution to the partnership. That gain (here the $3,000) should be taxed to the contributing partner, and I.R.C. § 704(c) provides that it is.

Under the Regulations, I.R.C. § 704(c) property is contributed property that at the time of contribution has a book value that differs from its tax basis.[13] Note that if partners have contributed such property to the partnership, the partnership will have to keep two sets of books. One set will contain the book values of the partnership properties and the other will contain the tax values. The book items will be allocated based on the I.R.C. § 704(b) Regulations, often according to the substantial economic effect rules. The tax items, when they differ from the book items, will be allocated under the I.R.C. § 704(c) Regulations.[14] Thus, in Example 1 in which the property is sold for $12,000, the tax and book accounts are:

	A		B	
	Tax	Book	Tax	Book
Formation	$7,000	$10,000	$10,000	$10,000
Gain	$4,000	$1,000	$1,000	$1,000
Balance	$11,000	$11,000	$11,000	$11,000

---

[12] Treas. Reg. § 1.704-1(b)(1)(vi).

[13] Treas. Reg. § 1.704-3(a)(3)(i).

[14] Treas. Reg. § 1.704-1(b)(1)(vi).

As we will see in the Detailed Discussion, I.R.C. § 704(c) and its Regulations are very complex, but this is the foundation.[15] Note that after the sale, the book and tax accounts are equal. An objective of I.R.C. § 704(c) is to eliminate the disparities between the book and tax accounts. As we shall see, however, again in the Detailed Discussion, it is not always possible to do so.

While we focused on gain assets in our examples, of course losses inherent in contributed property are allocated to the contributing partner as well. Before the passage of the American Jobs Creation Act of 2004, however, it was possible for others to benefit from those losses. For example, a transferee of the contributing partner generally steps into the shoes of that partner for I.R.C. § 704(c) purposes and thus previously could have been allocated any remaining I.R.C. § 704(c) losses. The losses could have been allocated to other partners in the case of a liquidation of the entire partnership, if the contributed property was distributed to another partner, or in the case of a liquidation of the interest of the contributing partner, if the partnership continued to hold the contributed property. To address these issues Congress enacted I.R.C. § 704(c)(1)(C). It provides that if contributed property has a built-in loss, that built-in loss is taken into account only in determining the amount of items allocated to the contributing partner. In determining the amount of items allocated to other partners, the tax basis of the contributed property in the hands of the partnership is treated as being equal to its fair market value on contribution.

There are special rules for allocating deductions attributable to nonrecourse debt. Let's say a taxpayer buys an apartment building on leased land for $100,000, paying $10,000 cash and borrowing the balance of $90,000 on a nonrecourse basis. We put the apartment building on leased land to make depreciation easier to calculate. In this example, there is $100,000 of depreciable basis. Once the taxpayer has depreciated the first $10,000 of basis, she has used up her equity investment. Future depreciation deductions are attributable to the nonrecourse debt. Placing that property now in a partnership, for allocations attributable to nonrecourse debt, it is potentially the creditor that bears the ultimate economic burden, not the partners. For that reason, the allocations cannot have substantial economic effect. It is nonetheless possible, under very complex rules, to allocate deductions attributable to nonrecourse debt, which we review in the Detailed Discussion.

As you know from your basic tax course, under the assignment of income doctrine (it really should be called the nonassignment of income doctrine), one person generally may not gift income to another. Could a partnership be used to end-run the assignment of income doctrine? Is it possible, for example, for a parent to give a partnership interest to a child and for the partnership to then allocate income to the interest and thereby to the child? Under a substance over form argument you might think the answer is no, but often it is, in fact, yes. Congress preempted much of the area with I.R.C. § 704(e), which respects gifts of

---

[15] Treas. Reg. § 1.704-3(e) provides that a partnership can opt out of I.R.C. § 704(c) if there is only a "small disparity" between the book value of the property contributed by a partner in a single tax year and its tax basis. A small disparity exists if the book value of all properties contributed by one partner during the partnership's tax year does not differ from its tax basis by more than 15% and the total gross disparity does not exceed $20,000.

partnership interests as long as capital is a material income-producing factor (which it typically is in this context). We will provide a more thorough review in the Detailed Discussion.

The interest that a partner has in the partnership is not locked in stone. A partner's percentage interest in the partnership can vary during a tax year if part of his or another partner's interest is sold or redeemed, if he or another partner contributes new capital to the partnership, or if new partners enter the partnership. The starting point is I.R.C. § 706(c)(2). It provides that the taxable year of a partnership closes with respect to a partner whose entire interest in the partnership terminates, whether it be by sale, death, or liquidation.[16] The partnership then calculates that partner's share of income and deduction up to the time his partnership tax year closes. If, on the other hand, a partner disposes of part, but not all, of his interest in the partnership, whether by sale, entry of a new partner, redemption, gift, or otherwise, the partnership tax year does not close with respect to that partner.

I.R.C. § 706(d)(1) provides that if a partner's interest changes during the tax year, each partner's distributive share of partnership income or loss is determined by taking into account the partners' varying interests in the partnership during the year. Of course, as you now know, I.R.C. § 704(b) permits the partnership to make allocations other than based on strict partnership ownership percentages. But I.R.C. § 706(d) trumps, and the partnership may not make special allocations that would counteract the rules of I.R.C. § 706(d).[17] We discuss the details in the Detailed Discussion, coming up next.

DETAILED DISCUSSION

§ 6.01   INTRODUCTION

As you have learned, a partnership is a flow-through entity. Income and deductions are passed through to the partners. A mechanism needs to exist, therefore, for determining what each partner's allocable share of partnership income and deductions is. I.R.C. § 704(b) and its Regulations generally allow partners a great deal of flexibility in this regard. The allocations do not necessarily need to be in proportion to the underlying ownership of the partnership interests (as is the case with S corporations).[18] Someone who is otherwise a 50% partner could be allocated 90% of depreciation deductions, for example. Or, all losses could initially be allocated to the "money partners," with subsequent income allocated to them to the same extent as losses were, and then income allocated 50% to the money partners and 50% to the promoters. (This is sometimes called a "flip;" flips are quite common.)

---

[16] I.R.C. § 706(c)(2)(A).

[17] *See* Staff of the Joint Committee on Taxation, *General Explanation of Tax Reform Act of 1976*, 94th Cong., 2d Sess. 91-94 (1976).

[18] *See* I.R.C. § 1377(a); since partners can have varying interests in capital and profits, determining what the underlying ownership interest is may not be an easy task.

I.R.C. § 704(b) provides that a partner's "distributive share of income, gain, loss, and deduction, or credit . . . shall be determined in accordance with the partner's interest in the partnership . . . if the partnership agreement does not provide for how a distributive share will be allocated *or* if the allocations do not have substantial economic effect." Thus, if an allocation *does* have substantial economic effect, it need not be in accordance with a partner's interest in the partnership. As we will learn, a partner's interest in the partnership is determined under a fairly vague facts and circumstances test. The Regulations, on the other hand, provide detailed and specific rules as to when allocations have substantial economic effect. These substantial economic effect rules provide a structure that is intended to be a safe harbor. If the partnership agreement complies with the rules, the partnership knows the transaction is safe. Many practitioners endeavor to comply with them, if possible. It used to be that practitioners viewed compliance with the substantial economic effect rules as being virtually mandatory, but in recent years practitioners have been increasingly drafting agreements to come under the partners' interest in the partnership facts and circumstances test.

For an allocation to have substantial economic effect under the safe harbor, the capital accounts must be maintained in accordance with the rules in the Regulations.[19] As the concern here is with the economic rather than tax impacts, the rules for keeping capital accounts are quite different from the rules for computing tax basis.

Under the Regulations, a partner's capital account is increased by:

4. The amount of money contributed to the partnership.

5. The fair market value of property contributed to the partnership (net of liabilities secured by the property that the partnership is considered to assume or take subject to under I.R.C. § 752).[20]

6. Allocations of partnership income and gain, including tax-exempt income.

A partner's capital account is decreased by:

7. The amount of money distributed to the partner.

8. The fair market value of property distributed to the partner (net of liabilities secured by the property that the partner is considered to assume or take subject to under I.R.C. § 752).

9. Allocations of expenditures of the partnership that can neither be capitalized nor deducted in computing taxable income (e.g., penalties or bribes).

10. Allocations of partnership loss and deduction.

Note that unlike the adjusted basis in the partnership interest, a partner's capital account does not include that partner's share of liabilities. If the partnership has liabilities, a partner's basis often will exceed his capital account balance.[21] Because,

---

[19] Treas. Reg. § 1.704-1(b)(2)(iv)(a).

[20] The fair market value assigned to property will be regarded as correct provided that (1) such value is reasonably agreed to among the partners in arm's length negotiations and (2) the partners have sufficiently adverse interests. *See* Treas. Reg. § 1.704-1(b)(2)(iv)(h).

[21] This is not inevitably the case, however. For example, if the partner contributes property to a

subject to the at risk and passive loss rules, a partner may receive loss allocations up to his basis in the partnership interest, a partner may have a positive tax basis and a negative capital account.

The partnership also maintains "book" accounts for the properties it holds. For example, if a partner contributes property with a tax basis of $7,000 and a fair market value of $10,000, the partnership's tax basis in that property under I.R.C. § 723 is $7,000. However, the partnership's *book value* (which one of the authors — uniquely — likes to call book basis) is the full fair market value of $10,000. If a partnership makes a distribution of property for which the fair market value differs from its book value, for capital account purposes the partnership recognizes the inherent gain or loss and allocates the gain or loss to the partners. This gain or loss is recognized for capital account purposes only. There may not be any corresponding *taxable* gain or loss. For example, assume a partnership has two equal partners, A and B, and holds a property with a fair market value of $20,000 and a book value of $15,000 (ignore the tax basis and any possible tax consequences for now). It distributes the property to A. Recall that A's capital account will be reduced for the full fair market value of the property — that is, $20,000. To enable to capital accounts to properly do their job — that is, to reflect the economics of the partners' investments, the partners' capital accounts must be adjusted for the gain inherent in the distributed property. Accordingly, *for capital account purposes* (nothing need occur for tax purposes), the partnership recognizes the $5,000 of gain inherent in the property and allocates $2,500 of the gain to each partner's capital account. Thus, A's capital account will be increased by $2,500 and then decreased by $20,000.[22]

§ 6.02 SUBSTANTIAL ECONOMIC EFFECT RULES

A. Introduction

There are two parts to the substantial economic effect test. First, the allocation must have economic effect. The Regulations provide a largely mechanical test for determining whether or not an allocation has economic effect. Second, because it is possible to manipulate the economic effect test, the Regulations also provide that the economic effect of an allocation must be substantial. Generally, the economic effect of an allocation is substantial if, on an after tax, present value basis, a partner's economic investment in the partnership is either enhanced or diminished as a consequence of the allocation.

---

partnership with a fair market value that greatly exceeds its basis, the capital account may exceed the tax basis of the partnership interest even after factoring in liabilities.

[22] *See* Treas. Reg. § 1.704-1(b)(2)(iv)(e).

B. Economic Effect Rules

1. "Regular" Rules

Partnerships have three options under the Regulations to meet the "economic effect" test. The principal ones are the "regular" economic effect test and the "alternate" economic effect test. The regular test has three parts:

1. The partnership must keep capital accounts in accordance with the rules described above.

2. When an interest of a partner is liquidated, the partner must be paid any positive balance in his capital account.

3. If a partner has a deficit balance in his capital account, he must pay the deficit to the partnership by the end of the tax year in which his partnership interest is liquidated (or, if later, 90 days after liquidation). This last rule is sometimes called a "deficit restoration obligation" or "DRO."[23]

Assume, for example, that on January 1 of year 1 A and B invest $10,000 each in the AB partnership. The partnership purchases equipment for $20,000, and thus that is its book value. Again, book value rules, including book depreciation, book loss, etc., though in this example the book and tax values are the same. The depreciation deductions are $5,000 per year and the partnership has no debt.[24] The partnership breaks even on its operations except for depreciation deductions, and thus the partnership operates at a $5,000 loss per year. The partnership agreement allocates all of the depreciation deductions to A. At the beginning of year 1, A and B each have a capital account of $10,000. As a result of the year 1 allocation, A's capital account is reduced to $5,000 and B's remains the same.

At the beginning of year 2, the equipment is sold and the partnership is liquidated. In order to comply with the economic effect rules, the partnership must pay to each partner the balance in the capital accounts. We will assume the equipment has a fair market value equal to its book value, or $15,000. If that is indeed the case, the $15,000 proceeds from the sale are distributed $5,000 to A and $10,000 to B.

Now again assume that the partnership agreement provides that liquidation distributions will be made in accordance with capital account balances. A and B each contribute $10,000 to the partnership and the partnership borrows $40,000 on a recourse basis with only interest due for the first five years of the note. Note that this debt increases the tax bases of the partners' partnership interests under I.R.C. § 752, assume by $20,000 each, but does not affect capital accounts. A and B therefore each have a beginning tax basis in the partnership interest of $30,000 and a beginning capital account of $10,000. AB purchases equipment for $60,000. The equipment generates depreciation deductions of $10,000 per year. In year 1 the partnership breaks even except for depreciation deductions on the equipment and

---

[23] Treas. Reg. § 1.704-1(b)(2)(ii)(a)-(c).

[24] We are making this number up and completely ignoring the actual rules of I.R.C. § 168, including the mid-year convention and I.R.C. § 179.

allocates the entire $10,000 of that depreciation to A. A's basis is reduced to $20,000 and her capital account is reduced to zero. Now assume that A's interest in the partnership is liquidated on January 1 of year 2 with the partnership relieving A of any obligation on the partnership liabilities. In order to comply with the economic effect rules, on liquidation the partnership must pay the partner the amount of any positive balance in her capital account. In this example, however, the capital account is zero, and thus no payment need be made to A. Note that, generally, if the partnership is in compliance with the economic effect rules, after liquidation of a partner's interest, the partner's capital account will be zero. Can you see why? In the example, A's basis prior to liquidation is $20,000. No payment is made to her. What happens to A's $20,000 share of the liability? The answer is that I.R.C. § 752(d) provides that a partner's amount realized on the disposition of a partnership interest includes any liabilities of which the partner is relieved. Thus, A's amount realized includes the $20,000 of liability relief. As A's amount realized is $20,000 and A's basis in the partnership interest is $20,000, there is no tax gain or loss to A on the liquidation.

Now let's take the example one step further. Assume that in year 2 A remains a partner in the partnership. The partnership again breaks even on partnership operations except for depreciation, and again allocates $10,000 of depreciation to A. A's basis is reduced to $10,000 and A's capital is reduced to a negative ($10,000). If A's partnership interest is liquidated on January 1 of year 3 with the partnership relieving A of any obligation on the partnership liabilities, A is required to contribute $10,000 to the partnership to bring her capital account to zero.[25] Her basis is increased to $20,000. Under I.R.C. § 752(d), the amount realized is also $20,000, for no gain or loss on the liquidation.

2. Alternate Economic Effect Rules

The difficulty with the regular economic effect rules is that partners are required to have an unlimited deficit restoration obligation. Especially for investors, that may not be wise. For example, assume the partners form a limited partnership and that all partners have unlimited deficit restoration obligations. An employee of the partnership, while conducting partnership business, runs over and kills a neuro-surgeon with eight handicapped children. A large tort liability, in excess of insurance limits, results. The general partner is the only one liable under partnership law, and he contributes sufficient funds to the partnership to enable it to pay the liability, increasing the general partner's capital account. The payment results in a large tax loss to the partnership that (because the limited partners have unlimited deficit restoration obligations) may be primarily allocated to the limited partners. The allocation causes the limited partners to have substantial negative capital accounts. Should they have to restore those deficit capital accounts (as might happen if the general partner decided to take this opportune moment to cause the partnership to liquidate), they would in effect be paying the tort liability, something that likely was not contemplated when they entered into the partnership agreement. The bottomless risk that an unlimited deficit obligation causes most advisors

---

[25] This requirement may exist in regard to a general partnership under state law. For limited liability entities the obligation to re-contribute a negative capital account may need to be contractually created.

to recommend that their investor-clients not agree to such a provision.

The Regulations, recognizing this business reality, contain an alternative in Treas. Reg. § 1.704-1(b)(2)(ii)(d). Under this alternative, an allocation must meet the first two economic effect tests (keep capital accounts according to the rules and upon liquidation, pay to a partner any positive balance in his capital account). The next requirement is that the partnership agreement contain a qualified income offset provision (discussed below). If this alternative test is met, an allocation will be treated as having economic effect if allocation does not cause the partner to have a deficit capital account balance (taking certain adjustments into consideration) or increase an already existing deficit capital account balance. As we discussed above, if a partner has a negative capital account balance, economically he has taken more out of the partnership than he has put into it, thus the requirement under the regular rules that he restore any deficit on liquidation of his interest. If the partner is not going to have a deficit restoration obligation, then it makes sense that a current allocation not be allowed to cause him to have a deficit capital account. Indeed, at one time that was almost all there was to the rule. The difficulty with keeping the rule that simple is that a capital account can become negative for reasons other than allocations. The partnership could, for example, make a distribution to a partner that would cause a deficit capital account balance. While the IRS can force a partnership to change the way it makes allocations, it cannot control to whom a partnership makes distributions.

The IRS needed a mechanism for eliminating the deficit capital account of a partner who has no obligation to restore it. That mechanism was to require the partnership to allocate income to the partner to offset any such deficit. Further, distributions are not the only events that the IRS cannot control that can cause a capital account to become negative. Certain provisions of Subchapter K can require allocations to a partner that might create a deficit capital account, so the IRS needed to account for these as well. Finally, it is obviously preferable to avoid the deficit capital account to begin with. To this end, the partnership is required to reduce the capital account for certain reasonably expected future events before determining whether or not the proposed allocation will create a deficit capital account. These adjustments are only for purposes of testing whether a current allocation will cause a partner to have a negative capital account. Once this testing has been done, the adjustments for future events are backed out of the capital accounts. They are not permanent adjustments to the capital account. For example, assume a partnership wants to allocate $8,000 of depreciation to a partner, A, who does not have a deficit restoration obligation and falls within the alternate rules. A has a $15,000 balance in his capital account. Further assume that under the rules the partnership must reduce his capital account for testing purposes for a $10,000 distribution expected to be made in a future year. That would temporarily give A a $5,000 balance in his capital account, meaning that only $5,000 of the $8,000 of depreciation could be allocated to him. After that determination, the $10,000 reduction for the future distribution is removed from the capital account, restoring it to $15,000, and then it is reduced for the $5,000 of depreciation that may be allocated to A.

The regulatory rule allowing allocations where a partner does not have an unlimited deficit restoration obligation is as follows:

(1) Requirements (1) and (2) of paragraph (b)(2)(ii)(b) of this section are satisfied (i.e., the requirement to keep capital accounts in accordance with the Regulations and pay to a partner on liquidation of his interest any positive capital account balance), and

(2) The partner to whom an allocation is made is not obligated to restore the deficit balance in his capital account to the partnership (in accordance with requirement (3) of paragraph (b)(2)(ii)(b) of this section), or is obligated to restore only a limited dollar amount of such deficit balance, and

(3) The partnership agreement contains a "qualified income offset,"

such allocation will be considered to have economic effect under this paragraph (b)(2)(ii)(d) to the extent such allocation does not cause or increase a deficit balance in such partner's capital account (in excess of any limited dollar amount of such deficit balance that such partner is obligated to restore) as of the end of the partnership taxable year to which such allocation relates.

In determining the extent to which the previous sentence is satisfied, such partner's capital account also shall be reduced for —

(1) Adjustments that, as of the end of such year, reasonably are expected to be made to such partner's capital account under paragraph (b)(2)(iv)(k) of this section for depletion allowances with respect to oil and gas properties of the partnership, and

(2) Allocations of loss and deduction that, as of the end of such year, reasonably are expected to be made to such partner pursuant to section 704(e)(2), section 706(d), and paragraph (b)(2)(ii) of 1.751-1, and

(3) Distributions that, as of the end of such year, reasonably are expected to be made to such partner to the extent they exceed offsetting increases to such partner's capital account that reasonably are expected to occur during (or prior to) the partnership taxable years in which such distributions reasonably are expected to be made.[26]

A partnership agreement contains a "qualified income offset" "if, and only if, it provides that a partner who unexpectedly receives an adjustment, allocation, or distribution described in (4), (5), or (6) above, will be allocated items of income and gain (consisting of a pro rata portion of each item of partnership income, including gross income, and gain for such year) in an amount and manner sufficient to eliminate such deficit balance as quickly as possible."[27]

Thus, in the example discussed above, assuming there are no "reasonably expected" future events, if A has no deficit restoration obligation, the allocation to him is still effective because it does not cause him to have a negative capital account.[28]

---

[26] Treas. Reg. § 1.704-1(b)(2)(ii)(d).

[27] Treas. Reg. § 1.704-1(b)(2)(ii)(d).

[28] The allocation could also not increase a negative capital account she already had for some reason.

As the Regulations indicate, sometimes partners have limited deficit restoration obligations in order to be allocated more losses. They will agree to restore a deficit in their capital account up to a certain amount, but not beyond that. In this circumstance, the partnership will need to comply with the qualified income offset rules, and allocations can be made to a partner that create a negative capital account up to the fixed amount that partner is obligated to restore. Thus, if a partner has a $10,000 deficit restoration obligation, he could be given allocations that caused him to have up to a $10,000 negative capital account as long as the partnership otherwise complies with the qualified income offset rules (often called the "QIO" rules). If his negative capital account for some reason exceeded $10,000, the QIO rules would be triggered.

3. Economic Effect Equivalence

The third alternative provided in the Regulations to meet the economic effect test is the "economic effect equivalence test." Allocations made to a partner that do not otherwise have economic effect under the rules discussed above can nevertheless be deemed to have economic effect under this test. The economic effect equivalence test is met provided that a liquidation of the partnership at the end of the year in question or at the end of any future year would produce the same economic results to the partners as would occur if the formal economic effect test were met, regardless of the economic performance of the partnership.[29] For example, assume A and B contribute $75,000 and $25,000, respectively, to the AB partnership. Assume further that the partnership maintains no capital accounts (thus not complying with the economic effect rules) and the partnership agreement provides that all income, gain, loss, deduction, and credit will be allocated 75 percent to G and 25 percent to H. G and H are ultimately liable (under a state law right of contribution) for 75 percent and 25 percent, respectively, of any debts of the partnership. Although the allocations do not satisfy the requirements of the economic effect rules discussed above, the allocations have economic effect under the economic effect equivalence test.[30]

C. Substantiality

1. General Rules

For all of their complexity, the economic effect rules are not enough to get the job done. They are, in effect, mechanical rules, and like all mechanical rules can be inappropriately manipulated. Accordingly, the Regulations provide that not only must the allocation have economic effect, that economic effect must be substantial.

Initially the Regulations provide (not terribly helpfully) that the economic effect of an allocation is substantial if there is a reasonable possibility that the allocation will affect substantially the dollar amounts to be received by the partners independent of tax consequences.[31] The Regulations then get more specific and

---

[29] Treas. Reg. § 1.704-1(b)(2)(ii)(i).

[30] This example is based on Treas. Reg. § 1.704-1(b)(5), example 4(ii).

[31] Treas. Reg. § 1.704-1(b)(2)(iii)(a).

provide that an allocation is *not* substantial if:

(1)   the after-tax economic consequences of at least one partner may, in present value terms, be enhanced compared to such consequences if the allocation were not contained in the partnership agreement, and

(2)   there is a strong likelihood that the after-tax economic consequences of no partner will, in present value terms, be substantially diminished compared to such consequences if the allocation were not contained in the partnership agreement.

Or, as one of the authors tells his students, the allocation is not substantial if, on a present value, after-tax basis, someone is better off and no one is worse off than would be the case if the allocation were not present. Under these circumstances, it means that the allocation has a tax effect, but no economic impact (on a present value basis). For there to be an economic impact, if someone is better off, some else has to be worse off. In determining whether a partner is better off or worse off, tax consequences that result from the interaction of the allocation with the partner's tax attributes that are unrelated to the partnership are taken into account. Thus, a partner's nonpartnership tax attributes are taken into account for purposes of this test.

For example, assume taxpayers A and B are equal partners in the AB partnership. A expects to be in the 50% tax bracket over the next several years.[32] B, on the other hand, expects to be in the 15% tax bracket. Over the next several years the partnership expects to earn approximately equal amounts of tax-exempt interest and taxable dividends. A and B agree that 80% of the tax-exempt income will be allocated to A and the balance of the tax-exempt income and all of the taxable dividends will be allocated to B. The partners can make this allocation without violating any of the economic effect rules. But according to the Regulations, the economic effect of the allocation will not be substantial, because on a present value, after tax basis, A's position is enhanced and B's position is not diminished (indeed his position is also enhanced).

A critical question is enhanced or diminished as compared to what? In other words, how would the items be allocated if a given special allocation were not present, i.e., what are the partners' general interests in the partnership? In this example it is clear, the comparison is to the tax consequences that would result if each partner were allocated 50% of each type of income.[33] But it is sometimes quite difficult to make this assessment.

---

[32]   This example is based on Treas. Reg. § 1.704-1(b)(5), example 5 which uses this now fictitious 50% tax bracket. Even today it is possible for a taxpayer to approach this tax bracket if state and Federal income tax are combined and the taxpayer lives in a state with high income taxes.

[33]   Treas. Reg. § 1.704-1(b)(2)(iii)(a). In addition, if the partner to whom an allocation is made is a pass-through entity or a member of a consolidated group, the partnership testing an allocation must look through the pass-through partner or member of the consolidated group to the owners of the pass-through partner and the consolidated group to test the after-tax consequences. A *de minimis* rule is provided that will allow partnerships to ignore partners holding less than 10% of the partnership for the purposes of testing the substantiality rules. Treas. Reg. § 1.704-1(b)(2(iii)(d),(e).

The math on this example: Assume the partnership has $10,000 of tax-exempt income and $10,000 of taxable dividends. Under the allocation agreement, $8,000 of tax-exempt income is allocated to A. She owes no tax and so will net $8,000. The other $2,000 of tax-exempt income plus all of the taxable dividends are allocated to B. He will owe a tax of $1,500 on the taxable dividends, and so will net $10,500 ($12,000 - $1,500). As we noted, you always have to contrast a given allocation with the alternative, that is, if the allocation were not present. Determining that alternative is not always easy, but here it would be each partner receiving 50% of each type of income. If A received $5,000 of tax-exempt income and $5,000 of taxable dividends, his tax on the latter would be $2,500, for a net return of $7,500. So A's position is improved with the allocation. If B received $5,000 of tax-exempt income and $5,000 of taxable dividends, he would owe a tax on the dividends of $750, netting him $9,250. Thus, B's position is also enhanced. Because both partners improved their after-tax economic position as a result of the allocation, it means that all that was allocated were tax attributes, not economic attributes, and the economic effect of the allocation therefore cannot be substantial.[34]

2. Shifting and Transitory Allocations

The Regulations provide alternative substantiality tests for what the Regulations call "shifting" and "transitory" allocations. Generally, shifting allocations occur within a single tax year, and transitory allocations occur over a period of up to five years. In either case, the economic effect of an allocation will not be substantial if there is a strong likelihood that the capital accounts of the partners will be about the same as they would have been had the allocation not been made and the allocation results in a net reduction of the partners' tax liability.

Beginning with shifting allocations, assume our equal AB partnership now owns I.R.C. § 1231 property and capital assets, and it expects to sell each type of property in the current tax year and incur a $50,000 I.R.C. § 1231 loss and a $50,000 capital loss. The partnership agreement complies with the economic effect rules. Partner A has ordinary income of $300,000 and no I.R.C. § 1231 gains. She can therefore fully use the I.R.C. § 1231 loss, but make only limited use of the capital loss.[35] Partner B has $200,000 of ordinary income and $100,000 of I.R.C. § 1231 gains, meaning that he can fully use either type of loss and receive the same tax benefit. The partnership amends the partnership agreement and provides that for the current tax year only, all I.R.C. § 1231 losses will be allocated to A and all capital losses will be allocated to B. While the allocation will have economic effect, the economic effect will not be substantial. There is a strong likelihood (actually, an absolute certainty) that A and B will have the same capital account balances they would have had if the allocation were not contained in the partnership agreement (still a $50,000 loss each,

---

[34] See Treas. Reg. § 1.704-1(b)(5), Example 5. Some have criticized the regulatory example because A could have independently made the investments in tax-exempt securities and paid no tax, so why not allow it in a partnership?

[35] Under I.R.C. § 1231, if a taxpayer has losses in excess of gains from the sale of I.R.C. § 1231 property, the losses and gains are generally treated as ordinary losses. If I.R.C. § 1231 gains exceed I.R.C. § 1231 losses, the gains and losses are generally treated as long-term capital gains and losses. Under I.R.C. § 1211(b), capital losses are fully deductible from capital gains. Individuals may only deduct $ 3,000 of capital losses in excess of capital gains from ordinary income.

consisting of equal parts of each type of loss). Further, the total taxes of A and B are reduced as a result of the allocation (A's taxes go down, B's taxes are unaffected).[36]

Transitory allocations operate in essentially the same way as shifting allocations, except they occur over a period of years. Under the Regulations, if there is a strong likelihood that (1) an "original allocation" and a later "offsetting allocation" will leave the capital accounts approximately where they would have been had the allocations not occurred and (2) the tax liability of the partners will be reduced as a result of the allocations, then the economic effect of the allocations will not be substantial. The Regulations provide that if the offset happens and taxes are reduced, it will be presumed that there was a strong likelihood that this would happen unless the taxpayers can present facts and circumstances demonstrating otherwise. However, if there is a strong likelihood that the offsetting allocation will not be made "in large part" within five years of the original allocation, then the economic effect of the allocation will be substantial.[37]

Assume that our equal AB partnership has predictable, approximately equal amounts of income each year and A has an expiring net operating loss carryforward. To allow A to take greater advantage of the net operating loss carryforward, the partnership allocates all of its income in year 1 to A. It allocates all of its income in year 2 to B. Thereafter, it returns to allocating income equally between the partners. The partnership agreement complies with the economic effect rules. The economic effect of the allocation is insubstantial because there is a strong likelihood of the offset occurring and the partners' tax liability is less than it would have been without the allocation (the allocation lowers A's taxes and, except for time value of money considerations, is neutral as to B). Note that if the offset would occur more than five years after the original allocation (not that B would ever agree to that), the allocation would be allowed.[38]

3.   Depreciation/Recapture Gain Chargebacks

It is quite common for partnership agreements to contain provisions that provide that gain on the sale of an asset equal to the prior depreciation deductions taken shall be allocated to the partners in the same manner as the depreciation itself was allocated. Such a provision is sometimes called a "gain chargeback." You might ask whether there is a transitory allocation issue, assuming the gain is recognized within five years of the depreciation deduction. The answer is no. There cannot be a strong likelihood of the offset occurring, because the Regulations assume that a property has a fair market value equal to its book value.[39] Any gain is, given the presumption, a "surprise."

Gain chargebacks generally do not pose a problem in the case of depreciable real estate subject to straight-line depreciation, as the character of the gain does not change even if it is attributable to the fact that depreciation deductions reduced the

---

[36] This example is based on Treas. Reg. § 1.704-1(b)(5), example 6.

[37] Treas. Reg. § 1.704-1(b)(2)(iii)(c).

[38] This example is based on Treas. Reg. § 1.704-1(b)(f), example 8(ii).

[39] Treas. Reg. § 1.704-1(b)(2)(iii)(c).

basis of the property.[40] There can be a substantiality issue when the gain is from the sale of equipment or other depreciable personal property. Generally, under I.R.C. § 1245, gain equal to the depreciation deductions taken is "recaptured" as ordinary income. Any gain beyond that amount typically falls within I.R.C. § 1231. The economic effect of the allocation of recapture income cannot be substantial, as all that is being allocated is a tax attribute. In other words, whether the partnership allocates $100 of I.R.C. § 1245 gain or $100 of I.R.C. § 1231 gain, the capital account goes up by the same amount. Thus, the only difference in the allocations is the tax effect, and as we have learned, an allocation of a tax attribute fails the substantiality test. Nonetheless, the Regulations permit allocations of depreciation recapture. Specifically, the Regulations provide that a partner's share of recapture gain is the lesser of:

- the partner's share of total gain from the disposition of the property, or
- the partner's share of depreciation with respect to the property.[41]

Assume partnership AB purchases equipment for $10,000 and takes $6,000 of depreciation deductions. The depreciation deductions reduce the equipment's basis to $4,000.[42] All the depreciation deductions are properly allocated to A. Then the partnership sells the equipment for $7,000. On the sale, the partnership has $3,000 of gain, all of which constitutes I.R.C. § 1245 recapture. The partnership agreement contains a depreciation chargeback provision allocating gain equal to depreciation to the partners who were allocated the depreciation. The gain recognized by the partnership is less than the total depreciation taken. Under the partnership agreement, A is thus allocated all of the gain. In this case, A's share of the gain is the "lesser figure," and all the gain allocated to A is recapture income. Now assume the partnership sold the equipment for $13,000. Under the partnership agreement, the first $6,000 of gain is allocated to A, and the remaining $3,000 of gain is allocated equally to A and B. The total gain allocated to A from the sale is thus $7,500. In this case, the lesser figure is the depreciation allocated to A or $6,000, and that amount is recapture income. The balance of the $1,500 of gain allocated to A (and B) falls within I.R.C. § 1231.

4. Tax Credits

Partners' capital accounts are not adjusted for tax credits. Therefore, the allocation of tax credits cannot have economic effect. As we have discussed above, and will discuss below, if an allocation does not comply with the substantial economic effect safe harbor, it must be allocated in accordance with the "partners' interests in the partnership." The Regulations provide that if an allocation of a tax credit also gives rise to a valid allocation of partnership loss or deduction, then the credit may be allocated in the same proportion as the partners' respective shares of

---

[40] Straight-line depreciation is typically the only type of depreciation allowed. I.R.C. § 168(b)(3). Even if there is no character difference, there may be a capital gain tax rate differences on the gain from depreciated real property. *See* I.R.C. § 1(h)(6). *Also see* I.R.C. § 1250 and Treas. Reg. § 1.1250-1(f).

[41] Treas. Reg. § 1.1245-1(e)(2)(i). Special rules apply to depreciation recapture attributable to property contributed by a partner, *see* Treas. Reg. § 1.1245-1(e)(2)(ii).

[42] I.R.C. § 1016.

the loss or deduction.[43] For example, if the property generating the tax credit also generates a depreciation deduction, the tax credit can be allocated in the same manner as the depreciation deduction.

5. "q" Adjustments

For reasons too complex to address here, it is possible that the allocation system discussed above will not get the taxpayers to the "right" place, even if they try comply with it. Treas. Reg. § 1.704-1(b)(2)(iv)(q) provides that if guidance is lacking on how to properly maintain capital accounts, capital accounts should be made in a manner that (1) maintains equality between the aggregate governing capital accounts of the partnership and the amount of partnership capital reflected on the partnership's balance sheet, as computed for book purposes, (2) is consistent with the underlying economic arrangement of the partners, and (3) is based, wherever practicable, on Federal tax accounting principles. These adjustments are some-times called "q" adjustments.

§ 6.03 PARTNER'S INTEREST IN THE PARTNERSHIP

A. Introduction

As we have discussed, the "partners' interest in the partnership" is the fall-back position for allocating income and deduction when the partnership allocations do not meet the substantial economic effect safe harbor. This subject can be surprisingly complex, and that complexity is beyond the scope of a typical law school partnership tax course, so we will keep our discussion brief.

Many partnerships are designed in a way that the drafters know will fail the substantial economic effect test for determining partnership allocations. The drafters, thus, rely upon what they believe to be the partners' interests in the partnership to determine the partners' distributive shares. Indeed, in large transactions this may be the norm.

A partner's interest in the partnership ("PIP") and the partner's interest in any particular item of partnership income, gain, or loss are generally determined by taking into account all facts and circumstances relating to the economic arrangement of the partners. At issue is how the partners have agreed to share the economic benefit or burden (if any) corresponding to the income, gain, loss, deduction, or credit that is allocated, which sometimes can be very difficult to determine.

Any and all facts relating to the partners' underlying economic agreement will affect the determination of PIP. Treas. Reg. § 1.704-1(b)(3)(ii) provides that the following facts and circumstances are ordinarily taken into account for purposes of determining PIP:

(i) the partners' relative contributions to the partnership;

---

[43] Treas. Reg. § 1.704-1(b)(4)(ii). This rule does not apply to the "investment tax credit" to the extend it still part of the Code, which (with limited exceptions) it is not.

(ii)   the partners' interests in the economic profits and losses (if different than that in taxable income and loss);

(iii) the interests of the partners in cash flow and other non- liquidating distributions; and

(iv)   the rights of the partners to distributions of capital upon liquidation.

Although the partners' interests in the partnership have been an important consideration in determining the partners' distributive shares for 30 years, there has been less than universal agreement as to what it means. This tension may be illustrated by contrasting the comments of the two major treatises on partnership taxation. Willis, Pennell and Postlewaite conclude that "There is not a conflict between a partner's interest in the partnership and substantial economic effect. They both rely on the same overriding principle that the tax effects of partnership operations must conform to the economic effect of those operations."[44] On the other hand, McKee, Nelson & Whitmire caution that "it is far from clear that identical results would in fact be achieved under both sets of rules, and drafters of partnership agreements who stray from the safe harbor do so at their peril."[45]

Want to know more? Review the materials in those treatises.

§ 6.04   BOOK-TAX DISPARITIES — I.R.C. § 704(C) ALLOCATIONS

A.   Introduction

Under I.R.C. § 721, no gain or loss is recognized when a partner contributes property to the partnership. The partnership takes a carryover basis in the property under I.R.C. § 723 and the contributing partner takes a substituted basis in the partnership interest under I.R.C. § 722. Yet when the partners put their deal together, the primary focus is on the economics, not the tax basis. What is of primary importance is the fair market values of contributed property. This disjuncture between tax basis and economic value gave rise to a host of complex rules.

Example 1

A contributes Land #1 to the AB partnership in which A and B have equal interests. The land has a tax basis of $ 7,000 and a fair market value of $10,000. The partnership takes a tax basis in the property of $7,000, A's tax basis in her partnership interest is increased by that amount, and no gain or loss typically is recognized to A or the partnership under I.R.C. § 721(a). Note that there is $3,000 of tax gain inherent in the property. If the partnership now sells the property for $10,000, to whom should that gain be taxed? The gain arose on A's "watch," so it would make sense for the gain to be taxed to A and indeed, I.R.C. § 704(c) so provides. But for I.R.C. § 704(c), on the sale of the property, half of the tax gain would be taxed to B instead of A. Permitting that violates assignment of income

---

[44] Willis, Pennell, Postlewaite, *Partnership Taxation* ¶ 10.02[1].

[45] McKee, Nelson & Whitmire, *Federal Taxation of Partnerships and Partners* ¶ 10.02[3].

principles, though it should be noted that the shift would not be permanent.

Assume B contributed $10,000 to the partnership and thus has a $10,000 basis in his partnership interest. If $1,500 of the tax gain were taxed to B, B's tax basis would increase to $11,500. If the fair market value of B's interest does not change, upon the sale or liquidation of B's interest, B would recognize a $1,500 tax loss offsetting the prior gain. But there could be a significant time lag between the gain and the loss, and there could be a character difference as well. If the land were a lot sold by the partnership in the ordinary course of its trade or business, the gain would be ordinary income, whereas B's loss would be a capital loss. I.R.C. § 704(c) also avoids these distortions.

In the absence of I.R.C. § 704(c), could the partnership have made a special allocation of the tax gain in A's land to B under § 704(b)? The answer is no. Recall that the land is recorded on the books of the partnership at its fair market value of $10,000 (i.e., it has a book value of $10,000). If it were sold for $10,000, there would have been no book gain or loss to allocate, and the I.R.C. § 704(b) special allocation rules apply to *book* gains and losses, not to tax gains and losses. Tax gains and losses do not affect the capital accounts and therefore their allocation cannot have substantial economic effect. How is the tax gain handled? I.R.C. § 704(c)(1)(A) provides that income, gain, loss, and deduction with respect to property contributed to the partnership by a partner is shared among the partners so as to take account of the variation between the basis of the property and its fair market value at the time of contribution. In the fact pattern we have been discussing, that means that $3,000 of the tax gain is allocated to A.

What if the property is sold for $12,000? The tax gain is $12,000 - $7,000 = $5,000. The book gain is $12,000 - $10,000 = $2,000. The $2,000 of book gain is allocated equally to A and B or $1,000 each. Under I.R.C. § 704(c), the tax gain is allocated $3,000 + $1,000 = $4,000 to A and $1,000 to B. Note that in this example, the tax gain equal to the book gain ($1,000 per partner) is allocated in the same manner as the book gain, and the tax gain in excess of the book gain ($3,000) is allocated to the contributing partner.[46] That makes sense. Generally, a partner should receive tax gain equal to his share of book gain. If tax gain exceeds the book gain, it means that the property had gain inherent in it on contribution to the partnership. That gain (here the $3,000) should be taxed to the contributing partner, and I.R.C. § 704(c) provides that it is.

Under the Regulations, I.R.C. § 704(c) property is contributed property that at the time of contribution has a book value that differs from its tax basis.[47] Note that if partners have contributed such property to the partnership, the partnership will have to keep two sets of books. One set will contain the book values of the partnership properties and the other will contain the tax values. The book items are allocated based on the I.R.C. § 704(b) Regulations, often according to the substantial economic effect rules. These allocations generally reflect the economic sharing agreement of the parties. The tax items, when they differ from the book

[46] Treas. Reg. § 1.704-1(b)(1)(vi).
[47] Treas. Reg. § 1.704-3(a)(3)(i).

items, are allocated under the I.R.C. § 704(c) Regulations.[48] Thus, in Example 1 in which the property was sold for $12,000, the tax and book accounts are:

	A		B	
	Tax	Book	Tax	Book
Formation	$7,000	$10,000	$10,000	$10,000
Gain	$4,000	$1,000	$1,000	$1,000
Balance	$11,000	$11,000	$11,000	$11,000

Note that after the sale, the book and tax accounts are equal. An objective of I.R.C. § 704(c) is to eliminate the disparities between the book and tax accounts. As we shall see, however, it is not always possible to do so. I.R.C. § 704(c) and its Regulations are very complex, but this is the foundation. Be sure you understand it before proceeding further.[49]

B.   I.R.C. § 704(c) Methods of Allocation

The Regulations permit partnerships to use any "reasonable" allocation method that takes into account the variation between the adjusted tax basis of property and its fair market value at the time of contribution.[50] It provides three allocation methods that are "generally" considered reasonable, but gives itself some wriggle room, stating that even one of these methods might not be reasonable.[51] The Regulations, however, also provide that the use of a given method is "not necessarily unreasonable merely because another method would result in a higher aggregate tax liability."[52] Thus, the fact that one method gives a better tax result than another will not, for that reason alone, disqualify it. For the most part, tax practitioners stick to one of the three methods, generally feeling free to use the method that gives the best tax results. In a simple example like the one above, all three methods will yield the same answer. But, as the facts get more complex, the answers can change.

1.   The Traditional Method

Under this method, if there is built-in gain or loss, i.e., gain or loss inherent in property on contribution, it must be allocated to the contributing partner. So far that is nothing new. The traditional method used to be the only method of allocation allowed by the Regulations. As we will see, it can lead to distortions. When other methods were added that can remove the distortions, the original approach was given the moniker "traditional method."

---

[48] Treas. Reg. § 1.704-1(b)(1)(vi).

[49] Treas. Reg. § 1.704-3(e) provides that a partnership can opt out of I.R.C. § 704(c) if there is only a "small disparity" between the book value of the property contributed by a partner in a single tax year and its tax basis. A small disparity exists if the book value of all properties contributed by one partner during the partnership's tax year does not differ from its tax basis by more than 15% and the total gross disparity does not exceed $20,000.

[50] Treas. Reg. § 1.704-3(a)(1).

[51] Id.

[52] Id.

The difficulty with the traditional method is that under some circumstances it cannot eliminate the disparity between the tax and book accounts.

Example 2

Assume the same facts as in Example #1 except that the land A contributed declines in value and is sold for $8,000. The partnership incurs a $2,000 economic loss, the amount by which the land dropped in value. But because the tax basis of the property is $7,000, there is actually a tax gain of $1,000. Ideally, A should be given a $3,000 tax gain, and the partnership then given a $2,000 tax loss. That would be fair. A realized, but under I.R.C. § 721 did not recognize, $3,000 of gain when he contributed the land to the partnership. The partnership in fact suffered an economic loss of $2,000, and ideally it should be given a tax loss to match its economic loss. A would then have a net tax gain of $2,000 ($3,000 gain - $1,000 loss) and B would have a $1,000 tax loss. But under what has become known as the "ceiling rule," if the traditional method is used, these tax gains and losses cannot be created. No partner can be allocated a tax gain or loss other than that which actually is incurred. The partnership's tax basis in the land is $7,000. If it sells it for $8,000, it incurs a $1,000 tax gain. That is its "ceiling." It cannot create a greater tax gain or create any tax losses.[53] Accordingly, the tax and book accounts are:

	A		B	
	Tax	Book	Tax	Book
Formation	$7,000	$10,000	$10,000	$10,000
Gain	$1,000	($1,000)	0	($1,000)
Balance	$8,000	$9,000	$10,000	$9,000

The tax and book accounts are now out of balance, and while the partnership operates, there is no way to bring them into balance under the traditional method. Only upon liquidation could the distortions be cured. If, after the sale of the land, the partnership distributes its $18,000 to the partners, each partner is given the balance in the capital account, or $9,000. For tax purposes, A recognizes $1,000 of tax gain ($9,000 - $8,000 tax basis) and B recognizes $1,000 of tax loss ($9,000 - $10,000 tax basis). The distortions between the tax and book accounts are effectively eliminated. As we discussed above, however, the character of the gain and loss recognized on liquidation could be different from that associated with the land, and the liquidation may occur many years after the disposition of the land. Finally, if a partner dies before liquidation, his heirs take a fair market value basis as of the date of death under I.R.C. § 1014 in the inherited partnership interest, eliminating any tax gain or loss inherent in the partnership interest that existed before then. Thus, in the example above, if B dies before the partnership is liquidated, the one thing he can take with him is his unrecognized tax loss.

The distortions caused by the "ceiling rule" prompted the IRS to promulgate Regulations providing two optional alternatives. Either of these alternatives must be elected. So if no election is made, the partnership will be on the traditional method.

---

[53] *See* Treas. Reg. § 1.704-3(b)(1).

2. Traditional Method with Curative Allocations

Under this method, a partnership may make reasonable curative allocations to reduce or eliminate disparities between book and tax items of noncontributing partners. A curative allocation is an allocation of income, gain, loss, or deduction for *tax* purposes. Recall that the objective is to bring the tax accounts in line with the book accounts, so it is only appropriate to adjust the tax items. The curative allocation must be of an actually existing tax item incurred by the partnership (it can't make it up), cannot exceed the amount necessary to correct the distortion caused by the ceiling rule, and must be of the same character as the tax item limited by the ceiling rule.[54]

Example 3

Assume that in Example 2 the partnership invested the $10,000 B contributed in another parcel of land (Land #2) that it subsequently sold for a book and tax gain of $4,000. Both parcels are capital assets to the partnership with holding periods of more than one year and thus the character of the gain or loss on each is the same. The book gain from Land #2 is allocated equally, but under the curative allocation method the tax gain is allocated $3,000 to A and $1,000 to B. By being given less tax gain, B in effect receives a tax loss equal to his book loss on Land #1 and A is placed in the same position as if he had recognized his entire initial gain (($3,000) and then received a $1,000 tax loss equal to her book loss on Land #1. After the smoke clears, the book and tax accounts are equal:

	A		B	
	Tax	**Book**	**Tax**	**Book**
Formation	$7,000	$10,000	$10,000	$10,000
Sale Lane #1	$1,000	($1,000)		($1,000)
Sale Lane #2	$3,000	$2,000	$1,000	$2,000
Balance	$11,000	$11,000	$11,000	$11,000

A partnership may make a curative allocation in one tax year to offset the effect of the ceiling rule for a prior tax year if the allocations are made over a "reasonable" period, and provided for in the partnership agreement for the year of the contribution.[55] The traditional method with curative allocations tends to be used less often than the traditional method or the remedial method (discussed next). The reason for this is that the curative method is neither as taxpayer-friendly to the contributor as the traditional method nor as likely to remedy book-tax disparities as the remedial method.[56]

---

[54] *See* Treas. Reg. § 1.704-3(c); if depreciation deductions have been limited by the ceiling rule, the general limitation on character does not apply to income from the disposition of contributed property subject to the ceiling rule. For example, if allocations of depreciation deductions to a noncontributing partner have been limited by the ceiling rule, a curative allocation to the contributing partner of gain from the sale of that property can be considered reasonable. *See* Treas. Reg. § 1.704-3(c)(3)(iii)(B).

[55] Treas. Reg. § 1.704-3(c)(ii); the Regulations suggest that a property's economic life is a reasonable period.

[56] *See* Willis, Pennell, and Postlewaite, *Partnership Taxation* ¶ 10.08[3][b].

3. Remedial Method

The problem with the traditional method with curative allocations is that the partnership may not actually incur tax items that can properly offset other tax items limited by the ceiling rule. The Regulations respond by giving the partnership the option of using the remedial method. This method permits the partnership to create the offsetting tax item out of whole cloth. Again, the book accounts are unaffected. It is only tax items that can be adjusted.

Under the remedial method, the partnership first determines the partners' share of book items under I.R.C. § 704(b). The partnership then allocates the corresponding tax items recognized by the partnership, if any, using the traditional method. If the ceiling rule causes the tax item to differ from the book items, the partnership creates a remedial item of income, gain, loss, or deduction equal to the full amount of the difference and allocates it to the noncontributing partner. The partnership creates an offsetting remedial item in an identical amount and allocates it to the contributing partner.[57] The remedial allocations have the same tax attributes as the tax item limited by the ceiling rule. Thus, if the ceiling rule limited item is an item of long-term capital loss from the sale of a capital asset that was contributed to the partnership, the offset will be long-term capital gain.[58]

Example 4

The facts are the same as in Example 2 and Land #1 is a long-term capital asset to the partnership. The book accounts are unaffected. For tax purposes, the partnership creates $1,000 of long-term capital loss that it allocates to B and creates $1,000 of offsetting long-term capital gain that it allocates to A. This gives B a tax loss equal to his book loss. It places A in the same position as if she had recognized her entire initial gain ($3,000) and then received a $1,000 tax loss equal to her book loss. The tax and book accounts thus are:

	A		B	
	Tax	Book	Tax	Book
Formation	$7,000	$10,000	$10,000	$10,000
Sale Lane #1	$1,000	($1,000)		($1,000)
Remedial	$3,000		($1,000)	
Balance	$9,000	$9,000	$9,000	$9,000

4. Depreciation

The manner in which depreciation, amortization, and depletion are allocated among the partners is also governed by I.R.C. § 704(c)(1)(A). We will focus on depreciation deductions. Recall that the purpose of I.R.C. § 704(c)(1)(A) is to eliminate the disparities between book and tax accounts. Generally, a noncontributing partner should receive tax depreciation equal to that partner's share of book depreciation with the balance of the depreciation being allocated to the contributing

---

[57] Treas. Reg. § 1.704-3(d)(1).

[58] *See* Treas. Reg. § 1.704-3(d)(3).

partner. The rules are designed to help achieve that objective. This is most easily understood by way of an example.

Example 5(a)

In our ubiquitous AB partnership, in which A and B are equal partners, assume A contributes depreciable equipment with a tax basis of $6,000 and a book value of $10,000 and B contributes $10,000 cash. The equipment is depreciated using the straight-line method at the rate of 10% per year. Tax depreciation is $600 per year, and book depreciation is $1,000 per year. The book depreciation is allocated equally between the partners, or $500 each. The tax depreciation is allocated $500 to B. The balance of $100 is allocated to A.[59] The approach is logical. In a sense, B gave A $10,000 of "credit" for the equipment she contributed and should therefore receive, if possible, his full share of the tax depreciation based on that amount, that is tax depreciation equal to his share of book depreciation. This approach will also have the effect of eliminating the disparities between the tax and book accounts over time:

	A		B	
	Tax	Book	Tax	Book
Formation	$6,000	$10,000	$10,000	$10,000
Depreciation Years 1-10	$1,000	($5,000)	($5,000)	($5,000)
Balance	$5,000	$5,000	$5,000	$5,000

Now assume the property is sold at the end of year two for $9,000. Its tax basis at that time is $4,800 ($6,000 - $1,200) and its book value is $8,000 ($10,000 - $2,000). There is tax gain of $4,200 ($9,000 - $4,800) and book gain of $1,000 ($9,000 - $8,000). How are the tax and book gain allocated? Book gain is allocated equally to the partners, or $500 each. Tax gain equal to book gain is allocated in the same manner as book gain, or $500 per partner. Tax gain in excess of book gain of $3,200 ($4,200 - $1,000) is allocated entirely to A, the contributing partner. Note that if the partnership would have sold the property immediately after it was acquired, the gain that would have been allocated to A would have been $4,000. After two years, the gain allocated to A is $800 less than that. Why did it go down? Because the tax and book accounts were "caught up" by two years of "preferential" allocations of the tax depreciation to B. Each year B received $400 more depreciation than A, or $800 over two years, thus there is $800 less gain to be allocated to A under I.R.C. § 704(c)(1)(A) on the sale.

Example 5(b)

The facts are the same as in Example 5(a), except the property that A contributes has a basis of $4,000. The tax depreciation is now $400 per year. The book depreciation remains $1,000 per year. The book depreciation is again allocated equally to the two partners, or $500 each. In this case, there is not sufficient tax depreciation to give B tax depreciation equal to his book depreciation. The ceiling rule has once again reared its ugly head. If the traditional method is being used, all

---

[59] This example is based on Treas. Reg. § 1.704-3(b), example 1.

of the tax depreciation is allocated to B, and a disparity will exist on the books of the partnership:

| | A | | B | |
	Tax	Book	Tax	Book
Formation	$4,000	$10,000	$10,000	$10,000
Depreciation Years 1-10		($5,000)	($4,000)	($5,000)
Balance	$4,000	$5,000	$6,000	$5,000

If the partnership uses the remedial method, it can cure the disparity (though the cure can sometimes be complex).[60] If the partnership uses the traditional method with curative allocations, it can also cure the disparity as long as it incurs another tax item of the appropriate character that can be used as an offset.[61]

5. Other Considerations

The Regulations permit the partnership to select different methods for different properties.[62] Which method the partnership and its partners will prefer will depend on a number of considerations, including the administrative burden of complying with the latter two methods. An important consideration will be the relative tax brackets of the partners. If they are all in approximately the same tax bracket, they generally will prefer a method that will give a tax consequence that is the same as the economic consequence. When choosing between the traditional method with curative allocations and the remedial method, an important consideration will be whether the partners can live with the "phantom income" that often results from the remedial method. In the traditional method with curative allocations, there is an actual taxable transaction that is being used to eliminate the disparities, which can often mean cash is being generated that can be used to pay any additional taxes. That cash would not be generated with the remedial method, as the remedial event involves no taxable transaction.

If the partners are in different tax brackets, the analysis may change again. In Example 2, if A is in a high tax bracket and B is in a low tax bracket, and the partners are cooperative, they may prefer the traditional method, which gives A less total taxable gain.

C. New I.R.C. § 704(c)(1)(C)

As you now know, losses inherent in contributed property are generally allocated to the contributing partner. Before the passage of the American Jobs Creation Act of 2004, however, it was possible for others to benefit from those losses. For example, a transferee of the contributing partner generally steps into

---

[60] *See* Treas. Reg. § 1.704-3(d), example 1. If the remedial method is used, book depreciation may need to be computed using different periods for different portions of the book value. *See* Treas. Reg. § 1.704-3(d)(2).

[61] *See* Treas. Reg. § 1.704-3(c), example 1.

[62] Treas. Reg. § 1.704-3(a)(2).

the shoes of that partner for I.R.C. § 704(c) purposes and thus previously could have been allocated any remaining I.R.C. § 704(c) losses. (See Chapter 7.) The losses could have been allocated to other partners in the case of a liquidation of the entire partnership, if the contributed property was distributed to another partner, or in the case of a liquidation of the interest of the contributing partner if the partnership continued to hold the contributed property. To address these issues, Congress enacted I.R.C. § 704(c)(1)(C). It provides that if contributed property has a built-in loss, that built-in loss is taken into account only in determining the amount of items allocated to the contributing partner. In determining the amount of items allocated to other partners, the basis of the contributed property in the hands of the partnership is treated as being equal to its fair market value on contribution.

§ 6.05   REVERSE I.R.C. § 704(C) ALLOCATIONS

An issue similar to the one that exists for contributed property arises if a partner enters a partnership after it has been in business for a while. The partnership may have assets that for book purposes are appreciated or depreciated. That appreciation and depreciation occurred before the new partner entered the partnership and logically should be allocated to the preexisting partners. That is indeed one option. The partnership could amend the partnership agreement to provide that the preexisting book gains and losses will be allocated to the preexisting partners under I.R.C. § 704(b). Another option made available by the Regulations is to do what is called a "revaluation," often also called a "reverse I.R.C. § 704(c) allocation."[63] The book values of the assets and the partners' capital accounts are restated to fair market value as of the date the new partner enters the partnership. If that is done, depreciation, gain, and loss on the partnership property for book purposes will change and for tax purposes will remain the same. The difference between the two must be allocated following I.R.C. § 704(c) principles. It is as if a new partnership were formed, with the preexisting partners contributing the assets of the partnership and the new partner making his contribution, with I.R.C. § 704(c) then applied to get the tax gains, losses, depreciation, etc. to the right parties.

It is perhaps easiest to understand revaluations by way of an example. Assume that A and B again form the equal AB partnership.[64] A and B each contribute $10,000 and thus each has an initial capital account of $10,000. The $20,000 is invested in publicly traded securities. The securities appreciate in value to $50,000. At that time C makes a $25,000 contribution and becomes an equal one-third partner with A and B. The securities further appreciate to $59,000, and the partnership then sells them. Assume (not very realistically) that the partnership has no other activity and no other expenditures or income. The question is how to deal with the $39,000 of book and tax gain on the securities. $30,000 of that gain arose before C entered the partnership and properly belongs to A and B. The other $9,000 of gain occurred while C was a partner and belongs to all three partners. Because the $39,000 constitutes both book and tax gain, under I.R.C. § 704(b) the first

---

[63] Treas. Reg. §§ 1.704-1(b)(2)(iv)(f); 1.704-1(b)(4)(i).

[64] This example is based on Treas. Reg. § 1.704-1(b)(5), example 14.

$30,000 could be allocated equally to A and B and the remaining $9,000 could be allocated equally to A, B and C.

Alternatively, upon C's entry into the partnership, the partnership could do a reverse I.R.C. § 704(c) allocation and restate the capital accounts and book values of partnership property at fair market value. If that is done, A, B and C each will have a $25,000 capital account and the securities will have a book value of $50,000, while continuing to have a tax basis of $20,000. When the securities appreciate to $59,000 and are then sold, there will be $9,000 of book gain and $39,000 of tax gain. The book gain is allocated equally to the three partners. Under the Regulations, the tax gain must be allocated in accordance with I.R.C. § 704(c) principles. That is done by allocating tax gain equal to book gain ($9,000) equally to A, B, and C. The balance of the tax gain ($30,000) is allocated equally to A and B. Conceptually, it is as if the parties formed a partnership with A and B contributing securities with a tax basis of $20,000 and a fair market value of $50,000 and C contributing $25,000, the securities appreciating to $59,000, and then being sold.

Any of the I.R.C. § 704(c) allocation methods may be used in a revaluation. To make matters more complex, the method used for a revaluation with regard to a particular property need not be the same as the method used for that property for "regular" I.R.C. § 704(c) allocation purposes.[65] Ask your professor to give you an exam question in this regard.

Revaluations are optional[66] and are allowed only under certain circumstances. The adjustments must be based on the fair market value of partnership property on the date of the adjustment and be principally made for a non-tax business purpose:

- in connection with the contribution of money or property in exchange for a new or increased partnership interest;

- in connection with the distribution of money or property in liquidation of part or all of a partnership interest;

- In connection with the issuance of a partnership interest in exchange for services performed by someone acting in a partner capacity or in anticipation of becoming a partner; or

- under generally accepted industry accounting practices, provided substantially all of the partnership's property, excluding money, consists of securities readily tradable on an established securities market.[67]

Note that the partnership's tax bases in its assets and the partners' tax bases in their partnership interests are unaffected by a revaluation.

When would a partnership prefer a revaluation over an I.R.C. § 704(b) allocation? Revaluations are common in hedge and other investment funds holding marketable securities where partners may have the right to buy in and be bought out at some version of book value and there is a fair amount of partner turnover. By doing a

---

[65] *See* Willis, Pennell, and Postlewaite, *Partnership Taxation* ¶ 10.08[3].

[66] Though the Proposed Regulations for noncompensatory options require revaluations in some circumstances. *See* Prop. Treas. Reg. § 1.704-1(b)(2)(iv)(s)(1).

[67] *See* Treas. Reg. § 1.704-1(b)(2)(iv)(f).

revaluation, the book values are kept current for these purposes. It has been noted that applying I.R.C. § 704(c) to revaluations results "in massive complexity for the sake of theoretical purity."[68]

What if in the example the partnership did none of the above? What if it did not do a revaluation and simply allocated the $39,000 of gain equally among the three partners? While there is technically nothing to stop this, the question arises as to why the partnership and the partners would agree to this (assuming they are properly informed, not always a given). Keep in mind that if A and B shift book gain to C, they lose the concomitant capital account increase, meaning less will be distributed to them on liquidation. Therefore, not only book and tax gain are being shifted to C, but economic value as well. Why would A and B do this? Well, it might be disguised compensation to C or it might be a gift to C, and the IRS could restructure it in line with its true status.[69]

§ 6.06   ALLOCATIONS OF NONRECOURSE DEDUCTIONS

A.   Introduction

A good grasp of how nonrecourse liabilities are allocated among the partners under I.R.C. § 752 is necessary for an understanding of this area. Review Chapter 4, if necessary.

It is common for partnerships involved in the real estate industry to use nonrecourse financing. The use of nonrecourse financing involves more than just tax planning. Avoiding personal liability is preferable for obvious reasons. Lenders would, of course, prefer recourse lending, but often make nonrecourse loans to stay competitive in the lending market. A partner's share of partnership nonrecourse liabilities increases his basis in the partnership interest under I.R.C. § 752(a). Subject to the at-risk rules of I.R.C. § 465 and the passive loss rules of I.R.C. § 469, a partner may deduct his share of partnership losses to the extent of his basis in the partnership interest.[70]

The use of nonrecourse financing, however, does pose a dilemma for partnership allocations. Recall that the cornerstone of the substantial economic effect rules is that allocations have a genuine economic effect on the partners. This creates a problem for deductions generated by nonrecourse debt. These deductions are called "nonrecourse deductions."[71] We will define nonrecourse deductions more precisely below, but an example is depreciation deductions for the part of a property's basis attributable to nonrecourse debt. The partners only have an economic risk to the extent of any cash or property invested. To the extent that basis and associated deductions are generated by nonrecourse debt, in truth only the lender is at risk. If the venture fails, the partners can walk away without any personal obligation on the debt. If the deductions generated by the nonrecourse

---

[68] Willis, Pennell, and Postlewaite, *Partnership Taxation* ¶ 10.08[3].

[69] *See* Treas. Reg. § 1.704-1(b)(5), example 14(iv); Treas. Reg. § 1.704-1(b)(1)(iv).

[70] I.R.C. § 704(d), which provides that losses in excess of basis may be carried forward indefinitely.

[71] Treas. Reg. § 1.704-2(b)(1).

debt cause the partners to have negative capital accounts, a deficit restoration obligation may not be very meaningful. If all of the partners have negative capital accounts, which commonly eventually occurs when nonrecourse debt is used, there will be no one to enforce deficit restoration obligations.[72] Consequently, if property is purchased with nonrecourse debt, only allocations of deductions attributable to the equity invested by the partners can have economic effect.[73] Allocations of nonrecourse deductions (deemed to occur after the equity has been fully "used up" by depreciation and other deductions that reduce basis) cannot have economic effect.

Example 1

Assume in our AB partnership that A and B invest no funds in the partnership and the partnership borrows $200,000 on a nonrecourse basis and uses the proceeds to buy an apartment building for $200,000. No principal payments on the debt are due for five years. Capital accounts are not increased for a partner's share of loan proceeds, so the partners' beginning capital accounts are zero. If the property drops in value to $150,000, the partners could simply default on the loan and would not be obligated to make any payment to the lender. The lender bears the risk of loss on the decline in value of the property. Now assume that the AB partnership takes $20,000 in depreciation deductions on the property. If we assume that the partnership breaks even except for depreciation deductions, A and B will have negative capital accounts of $10,000 each and the partnership's basis in the property will be reduced to $180,000. In the unlikely event that A and B have deficit restoration obligations, it would not be meaningful as there would be no one to enforce it. Thus, neither A nor B have borne the economic burden of the allocation, and thus the allocations to them cannot have economic effect.

Because the allocation of nonrecourse deductions cannot have economic effect, the general rule of the Regulations is that they must be allocated in accordance with the partners' "interests in the partnership."[74] As we now know, that standard is quite vague. The use of nonrecourse debt is fairly common and there are legitimate nontax reasons for its use. It was thus incumbent on the IRS to come up with a more definite approach that would permit partners to allocate nonrecourse deductions, and indeed the Regulations provide a safe harbor. The cornerstone of the safe harbor is the fact that where there are nonrecourse deductions, there is also "minimum gain." The Supreme Court held in *Tufts v. Commissioner*[75] that if a taxpayer sells or disposes of property encumbered by nonrecourse debt, the amount realized includes the amount of that debt. Thus, at a minimum, the taxpayer must recognize gain to the extent that the encumbering nonrecourse debt exceeds the taxpayer's tax basis in the property. Indeed, on any taxable disposition of property subject to nonrecourse debt, this excess is the "minimum gain" that a

---

[72] Unless the lender could make a claim under a third party beneficiary theory. Giving the lender such a claim would be something of a stretch, since the parties normally intend no personal obligation on the part of the partners, and enforcing a deficit restoration obligation would create that obligation.

[73] If recourse debt was also used, deductions attributable to the recourse debt can also have economic effect.

[74] Treas. Reg. § 1.704-1(b)(3).

[75] 461 U.S. 300 (1983).

taxpayer will have to recognize. While A and B may not be required to restore the deficits in their capital accounts, we may still be able to bring their capital accounts back to at least zero. This is done by allocating minimum gain to each partner in an amount at least sufficient to bring the capital account to zero. In Example 1, if the AB partnership defaults on the loan after the first year, the partnership and its two partners will have $20,000 of gain on the foreclosure ($200,000 debt minus $180,000 basis). Allocating that gain equally to A and B will bring their capital accounts back to zero. Thus, if allocations of nonrecourse deductions are made and the basis of the property is reduced below the amount of the debt, we can commonly be assured that at some point there will be compensating minimum gain. Generally, the Regulations allow allocations of nonrecourse deductions to a partner as long as an equal amount of minimum gain is allocated to that partner (this minimum gain is unrecognized but inherent in the property), though as we will see, the Regulations focus on book value rather than tax basis.[76] Further, partners may generally have negative capital accounts, even if they do not have deficit restoration obligations, to the extent of their shares of minimum gain. There can be a genuine economic impact to this minimum gain. If the only gain that is recognized is the amount of the minimum gain, no cash will be going to the taxpayer and he will have to reach into his pocket to pay the taxes on the minimum gain (another example of "phantom income").

B.   The Regulatory Safe Harbor

Because the allocation of deductions attributable to nonrecourse debt cannot have economic effect, the Regulations provide that they must be allocated in accordance with the partners' interests in the partnership.[77] The Regulations provide a complex safe harbor that contain a number of specialized terms. "Partnership minimum gain" is determined by computing for each partnership nonrecourse liability any *book* gain the partnership would realize if it disposed of the property subject to that liability for no consideration other than the full satisfaction of the liability; in other words, the amount by which the nonrecourse liabilities exceed the property's book value.[78] If A contributes property to a partnership with a tax basis of $10,000, a fair market value of $20,000 and subject to a nonrecourse debt of $20,000, initially there is no minimum gain as the nonrecourse debt does not exceed the $20,000 book value of the property. Indeed, it should be borne in mind that book value rules here. When we, for example, discuss depreciation in this context, book depreciation is meant. Of course, if property is acquired with cash, there will be no book/tax disparities (barring a revaluation).[79] I.R.C. § 704(c) governs book/tax disparities.

---

[76] Technically, the Regulations provide that if the allocation of nonrecourse deductions is in accordance with the regulatory rules, it will also be in accordance with the partner's interest in the partnership. Treas. Reg. § 1.704-2(b)(1).

[77] Treas. Reg. § 1.704-2(b)(1).

[78] Treas. Reg. § 1.704-2(d)(1), (3).

[79] Revaluations, however, generally cannot reduce minimum gain. *See* Treas. Reg. § 1.704-2(d)(4)(ii).

The amount of nonrecourse deductions for a partnership taxable year equals the net increase in partnership minimum gain during that year.[80] In Example 1, if the property generates $20,000 of depreciation deductions in the first year, the property's book value is reduced by $20,000, meaning that the increase in partnership minimum is also $20,000. It went from zero to $20,000. Note that the partnership can have nonrecourse debt without generating nonrecourse deductions. Until there is minimum gain, any deductions are considered to come from the equity in the property. Nonrecourse deductions are created when the partnership generates minimum gain. Nonrecourse deductions and minimum gain are two sides of one coin. Nonrecourse deductions consist first of depreciation deductions with respect to property that is subject to nonrecourse debt and then, generally, pro rata portions of the partnership's other deductions and I.R.C. § 705(a)(2)(B) expenditures.[81]

The formal regulatory rules that have to be met in order for an allocation of nonrecourse deductions to be allowed under the safe harbor are:[82]

1. The partnership must comply with the economic effect test described earlier in this chapter. Recall that part 3 of that test either requires a partner to have an unlimited deficit restoration obligation or meet the qualified income offset rules. Also, recall that under the qualified income offset rules a partner may have a deficit capital account to the extent of any "limited" deficit restoration obligation. Partnerships using nonrecourse debt commonly do not have deficit restoration obligations. At one point in time, the qualified income offset rules and the nonrecourse deduction rules were in mortal conflict. The nonrecourse deduction rules allow for deficit capital accounts notwithstanding the lack of a deficit restoration obligation to the extent of a partner's share of minimum gain, but the qualified income offset rules did not permit a deficit capital account absent a deficit restoration obligation. The regulatory error was corrected, and the qualified income offset rules now provide that partners may have negative capital accounts to the extent of their shares of minimum gain. A partner's share of minimum gain is considered to be a "limited" deficit restoration obligation for purposes of the qualified income offset rules.[83]

2. Beginning in the first taxable year of the partnership in which there are nonrecourse deductions and thereafter throughout the full term of the partnership, the partnership agreement provides for allocations of nonrecourse deductions in a manner that is "reasonably consistent" with allocations of some other significant partnership item attributable to the property securing the nonrecourse liabilities that has substantial economic effect. For example, assume depreciation deductions are exactly equal to

---

[80] Treas. Reg. § 1.704-2(c)(1). This is reduced by any distributions of nonrecourse liabilities that are allocable to an increase in minimum gain, a subject we will discuss below. Increases in partnership minimum gain resulting from conversions, refinancing, and other changes to the debt instrument do not generate nonrecourse deductions.

[81] Treas. Reg. § 1.704-2(j)(1).

[82] Treas. Reg. § 1.704-2(e).

[83] Treas. Reg. § 1.704-2(g)(1).

the nonrecourse deductions. Allocation of any other deductions (e.g., interest on the debt) fall within the substantial economic effect rules. In an example in the Regulations, allocations that have substantial economic effect are allocated initially 90% to the limited partner and 10% to the general partner until the items of income equal the items of loss, then shift to 50%-50%. The Regulations state that the nonrecourse deductions may be allocated anywhere from 50%-50% to 90%-10%, but may not be allocated 99%-1%.[84] Of course, if nonrecourse deductions are allocated in the exact same manner as all other deductions (in this case starting at 90%-10% and shifting with the other items to 50%-50%), they are as "reasonably consistent" as is possible.

3. The partnership has a "minimum gain chargeback" provision, discussed below.

4. The partnership otherwise complies with the regulatory rules for allocations.

Eventually, minimum gain inherent in partnership property will be reduced. The partnership might sell the underlying property (meaning the associated minimum gain drops to zero), or it might pay down some or all of the nonrecourse debt. Of course, the key item that has been driving this whole allocation system is that there is minimum gain available to offset the nonrecourse deductions. What does the partnership do when the minimum gain decreases? The Regulations provide that at that time there is a "minimum gain chargeback," meaning that the partners must be allocated items of income and gain equal to their shares of the net decrease in minimum gain.[85] Of course, if the partnership sells the underlying property (or has it taken in foreclosure), finding the gain will not be a problem. The gain from the sale or foreclosure will be available for this purpose. Indeed, the Regulations provide that any minimum gain chargeback must consist first of gains recognized from the disposition of partnership property subject to partnership nonrecourse liabilities. But if there is no such disposition gain because, for example, the reduction in minimum gain resulted from paying down the debt, then the partnership must allocate a pro rata portion of the partnership's other items of income and gain to the partners to offset the drop in minimum gain. If insufficient income and gain is available in the year in which the drop in minimum gain occurs, the allocations continue in future years until the full offset has been made. This minimum gain chargeback allocation is made before any other I.R.C. § 704 allocations.[86]

Example 2[87]

A and B form the AB limited partnership. Neither partner makes a capital contribution. Under the partnership agreement, the partners do not have a deficit restoration obligation, but the agreement contains a qualified income offset provision and otherwise complies with the substantial economic effect rules as well

---

[84] Treas. Reg. § 1.704-2(m), example 1(ii).

[85] Treas. Reg. § 1.704-2(f)(1).

[86] Treas. Reg. § 1.704-2(j).

[87] This example is based on Treas. Reg. § 1.704-2(f)(7), example 1.

as the rules for allocating nonrecourse deductions. As a consequence, the partnership agreement meets the first test for allocating nonrecourse deductions. All losses are allocated 90% to A and 10% to B. All income is allocated first to restore previous losses and thereafter 50% to A and 50% to B. The partnership borrows $200,000 on a nonrecourse basis from a commercial lender and purchases an apartment building. Interest only is due on the note for the first five years. For its first three years, the partnership breaks even on its operations except for depreciation. Depreciation is $10,000 per year, so the partnership operates at a loss of $10,000 for each of its first three years. The book value of the apartment building is thus reduced by $10,000 per year.

After three years, the partnership's book value in the building is reduced to $170,000. The debt remains at $200,000. Thus, there is $30,000 of minimum gain inherent in the property. Nonrecourse deductions exist to the extent of the increase in minimum gain, or $30,000 over the three years. The nonrecourse deductions must be allocated in a manner that is reasonably consistent with the allocations of items that have substantial economic effect. Note that the partnership is incurring other expenses, for example, interest on the debt. The interest expense does not contribute to the nonrecourse deductions as they come first out of cost recovery deductions attributable to the property securing the debt, and the nonrecourse deductions are exactly equal to the depreciation deductions. Thus, the allocation of all other items of income and expense fall within the regular allocation rules. The allocation of the nonrecourse deductions must be reasonably consistent with these other allocations. Here they are exactly the same, as everything is allocated the same way, thus the second part of the nonrecourse allocation rules is met.

After three years, A and B's capital accounts are as follows:

A	B
($27,000)	($3,000)

Recall that the partners may have negative capital accounts notwithstanding the fact that they do not have actual deficit restoration obligations. A partner is deemed to have a deficit restoration obligation to the extent of that partner's share of minimum gain. The partners' shares of minimum gain are the same as the nonrecourse allocations made to them; that is, $27,000 for A and $3,000 for B.[88] Thus, A is allowed to have a $27,000 negative capital account and B is allowed to have a $3,000 negative capital account.

At the beginning of year four, the partnership sells the apartment building for $300,000. The total gain of the partnership on the sale is $300,000 - $170,000 = $130,000. Minimum gain drops to zero as the partnership no longer holds the property. Under the minimum gain chargeback rules, gain first must be allocated to the partners in the same manner as nonrecourse deductions were allocated to

---

[88] Treas. Reg. § 1.704-2(g)(1). Recall from out prior discussion that under the qualified income offset rules a partner may have a negative capital account to the extent of any limited deficit restoration obligation as long as the partnership otherwise complies with the qualified income offset rules, as is the case here.

the partners. Here there is gain available from the sale to do this, so the first $30,000 of gain from the sale is allocated $27,000 to A and $3,000 to B. Note this will eliminate the deficit capital accounts of each partner, a primary goal of the system. The one thing the IRS would not want to happen is for someone to be able to walk away from a negative capital account. Even if the partner has an unlimited deficit restoration obligation, as mentioned above, it may not be meaningful in this context as there is no one to enforce it. The minimum gain chargeback solves the problem by requiring an income allocation that offsets the negative capital account.

Having satisfied the minimum gain chargeback rule, we turn to the partnership agreement to determine the balance of the gain allocation. Under that agreement, income is first allocated in the same manner as losses were allocated. As it happened, this occurred when we allocated the first $30,000 of gain to A and B as discussed. Under the partnership agreement, the balance of the $100,000 of gain is allocated equally between the partners. Thus the partners" capital accounts are as follows:

	A	B
Years 1-3	($27.000)	($3,000)
Min. Gain Chargeback	$27,000	$3,000
Other Gain	$50,000	$50,000
Balance	$50,000	$50,000

If the partnership were to now liquidate, it would be required to distribute $50,000 to each partner.[89]

If there is a reduction in partnership minimum gain that does not result from the sale of the underlying asset, the minimum gain chargeback rules require that other items of income and gain must be allocated pro rata to the partners to offset their reductions in minimum gain. In a traditional general partnership, this may have no net effect because the partners will be allocated offsetting expenses. But in a limited partnership where the limited partners do not have a deficit restoration obligation, there could well be an adverse tax consequence. Likely, the limited partners would be allocated income sufficient to offset the minimum gain reduction, but would not be allocated offsetting expenses and would perhaps not receive cash to pay the tax on that income. Any remaining income and expenses would be allocated to the general partner assuming the general partner has an unlimited deficit restoration obligation. This process will undoubtedly wreak havoc on the partnership's allocation system, and partnership agreements often provide that as soon as possible allocations should be made to get everyone back to where they would have been had no minimum gain chargeback occurred.

---

[89] We kept this problem simple for pedagogical purposes, but when nonrecourse debt is used, the way the flip happens must be fine-tuned. In our Example 2, a distortion could have resulted if the flip occurred before the sale and minimum gain chargeback. The minimum gain chargeback would have had to flow mostly to A as he received most of the nonrecourse deductions, which would have been inconsistent with the overall economic structure had the flip already taken place. Generally, nonrecourse deductions should only be able to be offset by the minimum gain chargeback and should be "pulled out" of the general flip arrangement. See Willis, Pennell, and Postlewaite, *Partnership Taxation* ¶ 10.05 [7][d].

C. Subsequent Nonrecourse Borrowing

Of course, a partnership might take out a nonrecourse loan other than for the purchase of a property. If, for example, a real estate venture goes well and the property goes up in value, the partnership might choose to borrow additional funds on a nonrecourse basis. If the funds are invested in the property, creating additional basis and book value, the rules we discussed above would govern the tax consequences. But what if the funds create additional minimum gain because they are invested in an unrelated project or distributed to the partners? The Regulations provide the additional guidance that is needed in this regard.

Previously, we stated that nonrecourse deductions generally equal the net increase in partnership minimum gain. While that can be true, the total picture is, alas, more complex. (Hey, we never said partnership tax was easy.) The amount of partnership minimum gain is computed by taking all partnership nonrecourse debt into account, including debt arising from additional borrowings.[90] A partner's share of that minimum gain is based not only on the nonrecourse deductions allocated to that partner, but also distributions of proceeds of nonrecourse debt made to that partner.[91] Distributions, of course, reduce a partner's capital account, potentially causing or increasing a deficit capital account. But because a partner's share of partnership minimum gain is increased for proceeds of nonrecourse debt distributed to that partner, that is normally not a problem. Recall that a partner's share of minimum gain is considered to be a deficit restoration obligation.[92] The partnership may use any reasonable method to determine whether the source of a distribution is, in fact, nonrecourse borrowing.[93]

§ 6.07 FAMILY MEMBERS AS PARTNERS

A. Introduction

As you know from your basic tax course, under the assignment of income doctrine (it really should be called the nonassignment of income doctrine), one person generally may not gift income to another. Could a partnership be used to end-run the assignment of income doctrine? Is it possible, for example, for a parent to give a partnership interest to a child and for the partnership to then allocate income to the interest and thereby to the child? Under a substance over form argument you might think the answer is no, but often it is in fact yes. Congress preempted much of the area with I.R.C. § 704(e), though case law that predates the statute remains relevant in many cases.

---

[90] Treas. Reg. § 1.704-2(d)(1).

[91] Treas. Reg. § 1.704-2(g)(1). To avoid double counting, nonrecourse deductions equal the increase in partnership minimum gain reduced by the amount of nonrecourse debt proceeds that are distributed to the partners. Treas. Reg. § 1.704-2(c).

[92] Treas. Reg. § 1.704-2(g)(1).

[93] *See* Treas. Reg. §§ 1.704-2(h)(2), 1.704-2(h)(4) and 1.704-2(m), example (1)(vi), for rules that apply if the distribution in a given year is less than the minimum gain increase caused by the nonrecourse borrowing and how that interplays with nonrecourse deductions in this regard.

B. Pre-I.R.C. § 704(e) Case Law

Prior to the enactment of I.R.C. § 704(e), cases addressed whether a donee of a partnership interest should be respected as a bona fide partner. In *Commissioner v. Tower*,[94] the Supreme Court concluded that the parties must have bona fide intent to create a partnership. If a party provided either "original capital" or "vital services" to the partnership, that would be indicative of an intent to become a member of the partnership. The Tax Court then held that in order for a person to be respected as a partner, she must contribute either original capital or vital services.[95] The Supreme Court responded in *Commissioner v. Culbertson*[96] that no, that is not what it said, neither original capital nor vital services are required. The fact that participants are family members is not fatal, though it may justify further inquiry. The real question is "whether, considering all the facts — the agreement, the conduct of the parties in execution of its provisions, their statements, the testimony of disinterested persons, the relationship of the parties, their respective abilities and capital contributions, the actual control of income and the purposes for which it is used, and any other facts throwing light on their true intent — the parties in good faith and acting with a business purpose intended to join together in the present conduct of the enterprise."[97]

C. I.R.C. § 704(e)

Congress ultimately stepped in and enacted I.R.C. § 704(e). I.R.C. § 704(e)(1) provides that a person shall be recognized as a partner if she owns a capital interest in a partnership in which capital is a material income-producing factor, whether or not that interest was derived by purchase or gift from any other person.[98] Accordingly, I.R.C. § 704(e) trumps the assignment of income doctrine, at least as it was interpreted in the partnership context in early case law. Income may be allocated to a donee partner in a partnership in which capital is a material income-producing factor even if the partner contributed nothing to the partnership.

When is capital a material income-producing factor? While this can sometimes be difficult to ascertain, usually it is not, and generally means what you would expect. For example, a partnership that derives its income mainly from an apartment building will meet the test. A partnership that derives its income from the performance of services (e.g., a partnership of accountants or lawyers) will not. Note that when capital is not a material income-producing factor, I.R.C. § 704(e) does not apply, and we must rely on the *Tower/Culbertson* line of cases in determining whether a person's partnership status is to be respected.

---

[94] 327 U.S. 280 (1946).

[95] Culbertson v. Commissioner, 1947 T.C.M. (P-H) ¶ 47,168, *rev'd* 168 F.2d 979 (5th Cir. 1948), *rev'd* 337 U.S. 733 (1949); also see *Monroe v. Commissioner*, 7 T.C. 278 (1946).

[96] Commissioner v. Culbertson, 337 U.S. 733 (1949).

[97] *Id* at 742.

[98] I.R.C. § 704(e)(1).

There are other potential ways to game the system. One would be to underpay the donor partner for services he renders to the partnership, leaving more income for the donee partners. In response, I.R.C. § 704(e)(2) requires that the partnership pay the donor partner reasonable compensation for his services. It also effectively requires that the rate of return on the donee's capital not exceed the rate of return on the donor' capital.

§ 6.08   CHANGES IN PARTNERSHIP INTERESTS DURING THE TAX YEAR

A.   General Rules

I.R.C. § 706(a) provides that a partner is required to include the partner's distributive share of the income, gain, loss, deduction, or credit of the partnership for the taxable year of the partnership ending within or with the taxable year of the partner. The partnership's tax year of a given partner will close early if the partner's entire interest in the partnership is sold, exchanged or liquidated.

Further, a partner's interest in the partnership can change during the tax year. A partner's percentage interest in the partnership can vary during a tax year if, for example, part of his or another partner's interest is sold or redeemed, if he or another partner contributes new capital to the partnership, or if new partners enter the partnership.

I.R.C. § 706 and its Regulations address how partnership items of income, gain, loss, deduction or credit are to be allocated when partnership interests change.

B.   Closing of Partnership Taxable Year

I.R.C. § 706(c)(1) sets forth the general rule that the taxable year of the partnership is not closed as the result of the death of a partner, the entry of a new partner, the liquidation of a partner's interest in the partnership or the sale or exchange of a partner's interest in the partnership. This is true, whether or not any of such transactions result in the partnership being dissolved or liquidated for state law purposes.[99] I.R.C. § 706(c)(2) provides, however, significant exceptions to the general rule, at times saying just the opposite.

I.R.C. § 706(c)(2)(A) provides that the taxable year of the partnership indeed closes *with respect to a partner* whose entire interest in the partnership terminates. The closing of the partnership's taxable year is only with respect to the partner disposing of her interest, not the other partners. It does not matter whether the partner's interest terminates because of sale or exchange, death, liquidation, or any other event. The partnership tax year should also close on the death of a partner (even if the partnership interest does not terminate, but, for example, is placed in the decedent's estate), though the statute does not expressly address this issue.[100] I.R.C. § 706(c)(2)(B), however, provides that the partnership's

---

[99] Treas. Reg. § 1.706-1(c)(1).

[100] HR Conf. Rep. No. 220, 105th Cong., 1st Sess. 688–689 (1997); see McKee, Nelson, Whitmire,

taxable year does not close with respect to a partner who sells or exchanges less than her entire interest in the partnership.

C. Requirement to Account for Varying Interests

I.R.C. § 706(d)(1) sets forth the general rule that if there is any change in a partner's partnership interest during the year, each partner's distributive share of the items of income, gain, loss, deduction or credit of the partnership for that taxable year is determined by taking into account the varying interests of the partners during the year. Treas. Reg. § 1.706-1(c)(2)(ii) provides that in the case of a sale or exchange of a partner's entire partnership interest, or liquidation of the entire partnership interest, the partner includes in her taxable income for her taxable year within or with which her membership interest in the partnership ends, her distributive share of the items of income, gain, loss, deduction or credit, and any guaranteed payments under I.R.C. § 707(c). Recall that her partnership taxable year ends with the date of such sale or exchange or liquidation.[101]

If, on the other hand, the partner's partnership tax year does not close, then the partner needs to take into account her varying share of partnership items as discussed below.

D. Methods of Allocation

The partnership has two options for allocating partnership items when the partners' interests change during the year if a partner terminates her entire interest in the partnership: It can do an "interim closing of the books" or it can prorate the partnership items to the partners based on their varying interests in the partnership during the year.[102] Specifically, Treas. Reg. § 1.706-1(c)(2)(ii) provides that in order to avoid an interim closing of the partnership's books, the terminating partner's distributive share of such items may, if agreed to by the partners,[103] be estimated by taking into account her pro rata share of the amount of such items that would have been included in her taxable income had she remained a partner until the end of the partnership's taxable year. If such alternative method is used, the transferee also includes in her taxable income a pro rata share of the amount of the items that would have been included in her income had she been a partner from the beginning of the taxable year. The pro rata portions that are included in the transferor and transferee partners' income must be determined in the same fashion.

For example, assume in the equal ABC partnership, B sells his interest (one-third interest in the partnership) to D on October 1, so that after that date A has a

---

Federal Taxation of Partnerships and Partners ¶ 12.02[4][c].

[101] It should be noted that, although Treas. Reg. § 1.706-1(c)(3) provides that when a partner dies the taxable year of the partnership does not close, I.R.C. § 706(c)(1) now provides the taxable year of a partnership does close on the death of a partner.

[102] *See* Treas. Reg. § 1.706-1(c)(2)(ii).

[103] The Regulation does not indicate whether this agreement must be unanimous or whether the general voting rules applicable to the partners is sufficient.

one-third interest, and C and D each has a one-third interest.[104] If the interim closing of the books method is used, the partnership calculates what its income and expenses are for the first three-quarters of the year and allocates one-third of those amounts each to A, B and C. It makes the same calculation for the final quarter and allocates one-third to A, C and D.

Closing the books in this fashion and determining exactly what was incurred when can be challenging and expensive. Partnerships thus often prefer the pro rata method.[105] The pro rata method is based on the period a partner held a particular percentage interest in the partnership, without regard to when a partnership item was actually incurred. Continuing with the above example, under the pro rata method, A and C are allocated one-third of all partnership items for the year. B is allocated $1/3 \times 9/12$[106] of partnership items with respect to the portion of the year he was a partner. Finally, D is allocated $1/3 \times 3/12$ of partnership items with respect to the portion of the year he was a partner.

The Regulations do not provide specific guidance on how to allocate partnership items where the tax year of a partner does not close, but the same principles should apply.[107] For example, assume in the equal AB partnership, B sells half of his interest (one-quarter interest in the partnership) to C on October 1, so that after that date A has a one-half interest, and B and C each have a one-quarter interest. If the interim closing of the books method is used, the partnership would calculate what its income and expenses were for the first three-quarters of the year and allocate half of those amounts each to A and B. It would make the same calculation for the final quarter and allocate one-half to A and one-quarter each to B and C. Under the pro rata method, A would be allocated half of all partnership items for the year. B would be allocated $1/2 \times 9/12$ of partnership items with respect to the portion of the year he was a one-half partner and $1/4 \times 3/12$ of partnership items with respect to the portion of the year he was a one-quarter partner. Finally, C would be allocated $1/4 \times 3/12$ of partnership items with respect to the portion of the year he was a partner.

Cash method partnerships could take advantage of the rules as discussed to this point. Assume in the above example where B sold his entire interest that when D became a partner, the partnership is cash basis and has a $60,000 expense that it has incurred, but not paid. Under the pro rata method, D's share of that loss is $1/3 \times 1/4 \times \$60,000$, or $5,000. If, however, the cash-method partnership used the interim closing of the books method, then paid the expense after D became a partner, D is entitled to a full one-third share or $20,000.[108]

---

[104] *See* Willis, Pennell, and Postlewaite, *Partnership Taxation* ¶ 9.06[7]; this assumes the partnership is on a calendar year, as would typically be the case.

[105] Treas. Reg. § 1.706-1(c)(2)(ii).

[106] *I.e.*, 9 months divided by 12 months.

[107] S. Rep. No. 938, 94th Cong., 2d Sess. 98 (1976); accord HR Rep. No. 658, 94th Cong., 1st Sess. 124 (1975).

[108] The partnership successfully used this technique in *Richardson v. Commissioner*, 76 T.C. 512 (1981), *aff'd on other issues* 693 F.2d 1189 (5th Cir. 1982).

I.R.C. § 706(d)(2)(a) for the most part has stopped this ploy, and applies whenever a partner's interest in the partnership changes, not only when it terminates as in the example. Cash-method partnerships must now allocate listed "cash basis items" to the time during the taxable year to which these items are attributable, regardless of whether the partnership uses the interim closing of the books method or the pro rata method. The listed items are therefore treated as if the partnership were on the accrual method of accounting. The allocable cash basis items are interest, taxes, payments for services or for the use of property, and any other item specified in the Regulations (though to date the Regulations have not specified any). Thus, in the above example where B sold his entire interest, if the $60,000 loss were for services and was attributable to a time before D became a partner, D could be allocated none of it. It would have to be allocated entirely to A, B and C. If, on the other hand, the $60,000 loss was not an allocable cash basis item (a judgment against the partnership, for example), it should still be possible to close the books and allocate a portion to D. Note that the rules for allocating cash basis items cover most of the waterfront and thus will typically be the rule that applies whether a partner's interest in the partnership terminates or is merely changed. Of course, as you now know, I.R.C. § 704(b) permits the partnership to make allocations other than based on strict partnership ownership percentages. But what I.R.C. § 706(d) does not permit, and in this regard it trumps I.R.C. § 704(b), is for the partnership to make a retroactive allocation to a partner of deductions and losses that the partnership incurred prior to that person becoming a partner.[109]

---

[109] *See* Staff of the Joint Committee on Taxation, *General Explanation of Tax Reform Act of 1976*, 94th Cong., 2d Sess. 91-94 (1976).

Chapter 7

DISPOSITIONS OF PARTNERSHIP INTERESTS

BASIC OVERVIEW

In this chapter we discuss the tax consequences of the sale by a partner of his partnership interest.

I.R.C. § 741 provides that in the case of a sale or exchange of a partnership interest, gain is recognized by the transferring partner. As in the case of all sales or exchanges, in order to be able to compute the gain or loss recognized by the transferring partner, it is necessary to know the amount realized and the partner's basis for the partnership interest transferred.[1] I.R.C. § 751(d) provides, in effect, that when a partner sells a partnership interest, any associated liabilities are included in her amount realized.

Under I.R.C. § 741, the gain or loss from the sale or exchange of a partnership interest is treated as gain or loss from the sale or exchange of a capital asset, i.e., as capital gain or loss, except as otherwise provided in I.R.C. § 751.

Without I.R.C. § 751, it would be easy for a partner to convert ordinary income into capital gains, something that is usually utterly unacceptable to Congress. Without I.R.C. § 751, if the partnership holds ordinary income assets, a partner could avoid the ordinary income by dint of selling his partnership interest before the partnership sells the ordinary income assets. The value of those ordinary income assets would increase the value of his partnership interest, but that might mean more long-term capital gain taxed at more favorable rates on a sale of the partnership interest rather than, if the partner stayed in the partnership, more ordinary income from the sale of the partnership ordinary income assets taxed at less favorable rates.

I.R.C. § 751(a) provides that the amount received by a partner upon a disposition of all or portion of a partnership interest that is attributable to (i) unrealized receivables of the partnership, or (ii) inventory items of the partnership, is treated as an amount realized from the sale or exchange of property other than a capital asset. Thus, amounts so treated will result in ordinary income or ordinary loss (and almost always ordinary income).

Typically, an unrealized receivable is an accounts receivable from the performance of services or sale of inventory.[2] We will hold off on the brutal details until the Detailed Analysis.

---

[1] I.R.C. § 1001(a).

[2] I.R.C. § 751(c).

I.R.C. § 751(d) defines the term "inventory items" to mean (i) for the most part, what is commonly understood to be inventory, i.e., goods the taxpayer is in the business of selling, (ii) any other property the sale or exchange of which would be considered property other than a capital asset or property described in I.R.C. § 1231, and (iii) any other property that, if held by the selling partner would be considered property of the type described in (i) or (ii) above. This definition is so broad that it can also include unrealized receivables. This is likely unintentional, but the Service enforces this view. It is relevant primarily for I.R.C. § 751(b) purposes, discussed in Chapter 8.

Clause (iii) above significantly broadens the scope of the term inventory item. It is likely mostly applicable to situations in which the partnership is not a dealer with respect to its property, but a partner might be a dealer with respect to such property. But we are not really sure how this works. A person can hold the same kind of asset both for investment or resale, so the question becomes quite metaphysical. How would the partner have held it?

The Regulations generally require a partner selling her partnership interest to recognize any ordinary income she would have recognized if the partnership had sold all its assets before the sale of the partnership interest. Assume, for example, that a partner sells her partnership interest held for more than one year. Before the application of I.R.C. § 751(a), the partner has $50,000 of I.R.C. § 741 gain. (There is no special term for this in the Regulations, but one of the authors calls this "initial I.R.C. § 741 gain"). Assume the partner's share of partnership ordinary income from unrealized receivables is $10,000 and from inventory is $20,000. The partner is required to recognize this ordinary income and the initial I.R.C. § 741 gain is reduced to $20,000 ($50,000 - $10,000 - $20,000). The Regulations call this $20,000 "pre-look through" capital gain. Next the regulations require the partner to determine if the partnership holds assets with more highly taxed long-term capital gains. To simplify a bit, these are gains from collectibles, typically taxed at a rate of 28%, or gains from real estate equal to the depreciation taken, i.e., unrecaptured I.R.C. § 1250 gain, typically taxed at a rate of 25%. Assume in our example that the partnership has no unrecaptured I.R.C. § 1250 gain, but that the selling partner's share of collectible gain is $5,000. The Regulations require that on the sale of the partnership interest she recognize this $5,000 of collectible gain, reducing the "pre-look through" capital gain by that amount, i.e. $20,000 - $5,000 = $15,000. The Regulations call this $15,000 "residual" capital gain (typically taxed at a 15% rate if it is long term).[3]

Under the general rule of I.R.C. § 743(a), if a partner purchases a partnership interest from another partner, the purchase of that partnership interest has no effect on the partnership's basis in its assets.[4] This can produce an inequitable result for the purchasing partner. To illustrate, if a partnership's sole assets are marketable securities with a basis of $200,000 and a fair market value of $1 million, and A purchases a 50% interest in that partnership for $500,000, the partnership's basis for the marketable securities remains $200,000. If the partnership then sells

---

[3] *See* I.R.C. § 1(h) for long term capital gain rates.

[4] I.R.C. § 743(a).

one-half of its assets for $500,000, the partnership recognizes a $400,000 gain, $200,000 of which is allocated to A. As to A, however, there has been no appreciation since A acquired her interest in the partnership. Nevertheless, she will be subject to tax on her $200,000 share of the partnership's gain. Note further that if the partnership holds I.R.C. § 751 assets instead of marketable securities, A recognizes ordinary income. The gain A recognizes will increase A's basis in her partnership interest, creating an inherent loss, but that loss may not be recognized for some time, creating a timing distortion. If the partnership holds I.R.C. § 751 assets, there is also a character distortion, because normally under I.R.C. § 741, any loss on the sale or exchange of the partnership interest is a capital loss. To correct these distortions, I.R.C. § 743(b) was enacted. Note that it can prevent a partner from recognizing gain that arose before she became a partner (a good thing), but also can prevent a partner from recognizing a loss that arose before she became a partner (not as good a thing, at least from the buying partner's perspective). We explain and give an example of the operation of I.R.C. § 743(b) below, but first a few other details.

The optional adjustment to the basis of partnership property provided by I.R.C. § 743(b) is only available in the case of a sale or exchange of a partnership interest or upon the death of a partner. Thus, the provisions of I.R.C. § 743(b) do not apply to partnership interests acquired directly from a partnership or acquired by gift.[5] In order for I.R.C. § 743(b) to be applicable, the partnership must have in effect an "I.R.C. § 754 election." In fact, if an election was made before our partner bought the partnership interest, an I.R.C. § 743(b) adjustment is mandatory. Therefore, an I.R.C. § 743(b) adjustment is only optional if the partnership has not yet made an I.R.C. § 754 election. I.R.C. § 754 elections are difficult to revoke, as we discuss in the Detailed Analysis.

So how does all of this work? I.R.C. § 743(b) provides that the partnership shall (i) increase the adjusted basis of its assets by the excess of the basis of the transferee partner for his partnership interest over his proportionate share of the adjusted basis of the partnership's assets, or (ii) decrease the adjusted basis of its assets by the excess of the transferee partner's proportionate share of the adjusted basis of the partnership's assets over the basis of the transferee for his partnership interest. Notwithstanding the language of I.R.C. § 743(b), it would now be more accurate to state that the transferee partner is given an I.R.C. § 743(b) adjustment with respect to the partnership assets, rather than a special basis in those assets. In our example, because A is a 50% partner, half of the gain in the marketable securities would be allocable to her, or $400,000. That is A's total I.R.C. § 743(b) adjustment with respect to the marketable securities. The partnership sold half the securities, so A offsets the $200,000 of gain allocable to her with half of the $400,000 I.R.C. § 743(b) adjustment, or $200,000, generating no net gain to A. If, rather than selling half the securities for $500,000, the partnership sells half for $600,000, A offsets the $300,000 of gain allocable to her with the $200,000 I.R.C. § 743(b)

---

[5] In many instances, this same inequity resulting from a purchase of a partnership interest will not result in the case of a contribution to a partnership, either because the existing partners will be subject to tax on the appreciation by virtue of a revaluation of the partnership assets and the making of reverse section 704(c) allocations or because of a special allocation of the pre-contribution gain to the existing partners. *See* Chapter 6.

adjustment, for net gain of $100,000. Conversely, if the partnership sells half of the securities for $400,000, A offsets the $150,000 of gain allocable to her with the $200,000 I.R.C. § 743(b) adjustment, for a net loss of $50,000. If the marketable securities are capital assets, as typically would be the case, the gains and losses are capital in nature.

The I.R.C. § 743(b) adjustment is made solely with respect to the transferee partner, and not the other partners. Further, this is purely a tax adjustment, and does not affect capital accounts.

If the assets held by the partnership are depreciable property, the I.R.C. § 743(b) adjustment of $400,000 generates extra depreciation deductions for A (for now we will spare you the complex details).[6] Further, if the partnership sells depreciable personal property held when A purchased the partnership interest, the unused portion of the I.R.C. § 743(b) adjustment offsets depreciation recapture allocable to A.

And it can all work in reverse. If there is a net loss inherent in the partnership assets and a I.R.C. § 754 election has been made, then any loss allocable to A is offset by the I.R.C. § 743(b) adjustment. A might not prefer this outcome, but usually would be stuck with it if the partnership previously made an I.R.C. § 754 election. If no such election has been made, A might still be stuck. Even if the partnership has not made a § 754 election, if the partnership has a substantial built-in loss in its assets immediately after the purchase of the partnership interest (or death of a partner), the partnership is usually required to give an I.R.C. § 743(b) adjustment to the purchasing or inheriting partner (meaning that the purchasing or inheriting partner does not get the benefit of the preexisting loss).[7] I.R.C. § 743(d)(1) provides that a partnership has a substantial built-in loss if the partnership's adjusted basis for its property exceeds by more than $250,000 the fair market value of the partnership's property.

If property with an I.R.C. § 743(b) adjustment is distributed to A, A's basis in the distributed property is the partnership's basis plus (for gain assets) or minus (for loss assets) the I.R.C. § 743(b) adjustment.

Having to keep track of I.R.C. § 743(b) and (as we will discuss in the next chapter) I.R.C. § 734(b) adjustments can pose a substantial administrative burden on the partnership, particularly if they arise with some frequency. Historically, that has caused partnerships often to resist making I.R.C. § 754 elections. However, because of the mandatory step downs, these elections are becoming more common.

Changing gears, I.R.C. § 708(a) provides that a partnership is considered to continue until it is terminated. Okay, sometimes the Code states the obvious. Under I.R.C. § 708(b)(1)(A), a partnership is terminated if no part of any business, financial operation or venture of the partnership continues to be carried on by any of its partners (still obvious). Under I.R.C. § 708(b)(1)(B), a partnership is also terminated if within a 12-month period there is a sale or exchange of 50% or more

---

[6] Treas. Reg. § 1.743-1(j)(4).

[7] I.R.C. § 743(a),(d).

of the total interest in partnership capital and profits (not so obvious).[8] For purposes of this chapter, we will focus on I.R.C. § 708(b)(1)(B).

Not all transfers of partnership interests are necessarily taken into account in determining whether the required 50% change has occurred. A sale from one partner to an existing partner is taken into account.[9] A transfer of a partnership interest by gift, bequest, or inheritance and a liquidation of a partnership interest are not treated as a sale or exchange for purposes of I.R.C. § 708(b)(1)(B).[10] Likewise, a contribution of property to a partnership is not treated as a sale or exchange.[11]

Treas. Reg. § 1.708-1(b)(4) provides that if a partnership is terminated pursuant to I.R.C. § 708(b)(1)(B) as a result of a sale or exchange, the partnership is deemed to have contributed all of its assets and liabilities to a new partnership in exchange for the interests in the new partnership (tax free under I.R.C. § 721(a)) and to immediately thereafter distribute those interests in the new partnership to the purchasing partner and the other continuing partners, in proportion to their respective interests in the terminated partnership, in liquidation of the terminated partnership (tax free under I.R.C. § 731(a)). As a result of these deemed transactions, the new partnership's basis for its assets is unchanged, as are the capital accounts of the new and continuing partners.[12]

DETAILED DISCUSSION

§ 7.01   INTRODUCTION

In this chapter we will discuss the tax consequences of the sale by a partner of his partnership interest. Our discussion will include consideration of the amount realized upon the sale, the partner's basis for the partner's partnership interest, the partner's holding period for the partnership interest sold, the character of the gain or loss recognized, dispositions that do not qualify as sales or exchanges, and the special election that may be made by a partnership in the case of a purchase of a partnership interest. We will also discuss when a transfer of partnership interests can cause a tax termination of the partnership.

§ 7.02   RECOGNITION OF GAIN OR LOSS

I.R.C. § 741 provides that in the case of a sale or exchange of a partnership interest, gain or loss is recognized by the transferring partner. As in the case of all sales or exchanges, in order to be able to compute the gain or loss recognized by the transferring partner, it is necessary to know the amount realized and the partner's

---

[8] For special rules with respect to the termination of a partnership in the case of mergers or divisions, *see* § 9.02.

[9] Treas. Reg. § 1.708-1(b)(2).

[10] *Id.*

[11] *Id.*

[12] Treas. Reg. § 1.708-1(b)(4), example (ii); Treas. Reg. § 1.704-1(b)(2)(iv)(*l*).

basis for the partnership interest transferred.[13]

A. Amount Realized

I.R.C. § 1001(b) provides the general rule that the amount realized from the sale or other disposition of property is equal to the sum of any money received plus the fair market value of any property other than money received. This general rule is applicable in the case of a sale of a partnership interest. If a partnership has no liabilities, then there are no unique issues with respect to the amount realized. Where, however, the partnership has liabilities, the provisions of I.R.C. § 752(d) must be taken into account.

I.R.C. § 752, a partner is permitted to increase the basis of his partnership interest by his share of the liabilities of the partnership. If the liabilities of the partnership were not taken into account upon the sale by a partner of a partnership interest, the increase in the partner's basis for her partnership interest resulting from including her share of partnership liabilities in basis would artificially reduce the amount of gain, or increase the amount of loss, recognized by the partner upon the sale of the partnership interest. As a consequence, I.R.C. § 752(d) provides that the partner's share of the partnership's liabilities of which the partner is deemed relieved is treated as part of the amount realized from the sale or exchange of her partnership interest.

Where a partner disposes of the partner's entire partnership interest, the amount of the partnership's liabilities of which the transferor is deemed relieved is simply the partner's share of the partnership's liabilities immediately prior to the disposition. Where, however, only a portion of a partner's partnership interest is disposed of, it is necessary to determine the extent to which there has been a decrease in the partner's share of the partnership's liabilities. That decrease is then included in the amount realized.

B. Basis

Where a partner disposes of his entire interest in the partnership, the partner's entire basis is used to determine whether the taxpayer has recognized a gain or loss. Where a partner disposes of only a portion of her partnership interest, however, more difficult rules come into play. The IRS has held that a partner has a single basis for a partnership interest, even if the partner is both a general partner and a limited partner.[14] Presumably, this rule would also apply if a partner had different classes of partnership interests (e.g., Class A Units and Class B Units, or Common Interests and Preferred Interests).

Treas. Reg. § 1.61-6(a) provides that when a taxpayer sells a part of a larger property, the basis of the entire property is apportioned among the several parts. Rev. Rul. 84-53 provides that when a partner disposes of a portion of a partnership interest, the basis of the transferred portion is generally equal to the amount that bears the same relationship to the partner's basis in the partnership as the fair

---

[13] I.R.C. § 1001(a).

[14] Rev. Rul. 84-53, 1984-1 C.B. 159.

market value of the transferred portion bears to the entire fair market value of the interest. Where a partner's basis includes his share of partnership liabilities, however, additional rules come into play that can become surprisingly complex. We do not think it likely you will cover this in a typical law school course, so we will skip over these rules here. If we are wrong, you will need to slug your way through Rev. Rul. 84-53.

§ 7.03 CHARACTER OF GAIN OR LOSS

A. General Rule

I.R.C. § 741 provides that upon a sale or exchange of a partnership interest, the gain or loss is treated as gain or loss from the sale or exchange of a capital asset, i.e., as capital gain or loss, except as otherwise provided in I.R.C. § 751. Unrealized Receivables and Inventory Items.

1. Ordinary Income Recognition

I.R.C. § 751(a) provides that the amount received by a partner upon a disposition of all or a portion of a partnership interest that is attributable to (i) unrealized receivable of the partnership, or (ii) inventory items of the partnership, is treated as an amount realized from the sale or exchange of property other than a capital asset. Thus, amounts so treated will result in ordinary income or ordinary loss (usually ordinary income).

2. Unrealized Receivables

I.R.C. § 751(c) provides three categories of "unrealized receivables." The first two categories include "to the extent not previously includible in income under the method of accounting used by the partnership, any rights (contractual or otherwise) to payment for — (1) goods delivered, or to be delivered, to the extent the proceeds therefrom would be treated as amounts received from the sale or exchange of property other than a capital asset, or (2) services rendered, or to be rendered." The third category of unrealized receivables include (i) mining property (as defined in I.R.C. § 617(f)(2)), (ii) stock in a DISC, (iii) section 1245 property, (iv) stock in certain foreign corporations, (v) section 1250 property (mostly now a dead letter), (vi) farmland described in I.R.C. § 1252(a), (vii) franchises, trademarks or trade names and (viii) oil, gas or geothermal property, but only to the extent of the amount that would be treated as ordinary income under I.R.C. §§ 617(d)(1), 995(c), 1245(a), 1248(a), 1250(a), 1252(a), 1253(a) or 1254(a) if the property had been sold for its fair market value.

The first category of unrealized receivables, receivables from goods delivered or to be delivered, generally applies to the sale of inventory or property held for sale in the ordinary course of business where the cash method of accounting[15] is used.

---

[15] To oversimplify, under cash method accounting, a taxpayer has income when he gets cash constituting income and has an expense when he pays it. Under accrual method accounting, a taxpayer has income when he earns it and has an expense when he owes it.

But taxpayers who hold inventory are generally required to use the accrual method of accounting, meaning that the relevant receivables will not usually constitute unrealized receivables under I.R.C. § 751(c).

The second category of unrealized receivables for "services rendered, or to be rendered" principally arises in cash method service businesses. The cases have given this provision wide applicability. Thus, contracts to manage a business,[16] and exclusive distribution agreements[17] have been held to be unrealized receivables in situations in which the contracts were not cancelable by the party for whom the services were be rendered. Where the contracts are terminable by the party for whom the services are to be rendered, the issue is less clear.

The third category of unrealized receivables includes gains from properties that, if sold, would be ordinary income under specific "recapture" provisions of the Code. The purpose of this category is to put the selling partner in the same place he would have been in if the he had directly sold the asset of the partnership. Perhaps the most important of these is "section 1245 property." I.R.C. § 1245 provides that gain from the sale of depreciable personal property is ordinary income (sometimes called recapture gain or just recapture) to the extent of depreciation taken. This recapture is treated as an unrealized receivable. The balance of the gain (which does not count as an unrealized receivable), if any, is covered by I.R.C. § 1231.

3. Inventory Items

I.R.C. § 751(d) defines the term "inventory items" to mean (i) property described in I.R.C. § 1221(a)(1), i.e. stock in trade, (ii) any other property the sale or exchange of which would be considered the sale or exchange of property other than a capital asset or property described in I.R.C. § 1231, and (iii) any other property which if held by the selling partner would be considered property of the type described in (i) or (ii) above. Though probably unintended, the definition of inventory items is so broad that it includes items that are also unrealized receivables. For example, most of the recapture-type items that are part of the definition of unrealized receivables would also fall within the class of property described in clause (ii) above. As we will see in a later chapter, this overlap between unrealized receivables and inventory plays an important role in I.R.C. § 751(b).

Clause (iii) above significantly broadens the scope of the term inventory item. It is likely mostly applicable to situations in which the partnership is not a dealer with respect to a given type of property, but a partner might be a dealer with respect to such property. Its scope is unclear, however, as a dealer can hold the same type of property he holds for resale for investment. The question thus becomes how would a partner hold it if he did, which can get more than a little metaphysical.

---

[16] United States v. Woosey, 326 F.2d. 287 (5th Cir. 1963); Ledux v. Commissioner, 77 T.C. 293 (1981), aff'd per curiam, 695 F.2d. 1320 (11th Cir. 1983).

[17] Roth v. Commissioner, 321 F.2d 607 (9th Cir. 1963).

§ 7.04   HOLDING PERIOD

Assuming that some portion of the gain or loss recognized upon the sale or exchange of a partnership interest is treated as a gain or loss from a sale of a capital asset, it is then necessary to determine whether the gain or loss is a long-term gain or loss or a short-term gain or loss. I.R.C. § 1222, in effect, provides that a gain or loss from the sale or exchange of a capital asset is a short-term capital gain or loss if the asset has not been held for more than one year, whereas it is a long-term capital gain or loss if the asset has been held for more than one year. This general rule is applicable to sales or exchanges of partnership interests.

Treas. Reg. § 1.1223-3(a) provides that a partner will have a multiple holding periods in his partnership interest if (i) the partner acquired portions of the partnership interest at different times or (ii) the partner contributed property at the same time, but the nature of the property contributed results in different holding periods. Thus, it is possible that a sale of a partnership interest will result in both long-term capital gain or loss and short-term capital gain or loss.

§ 7.05   DISPOSITIONS OTHER THAN SALES OR EXCHANGES

A.   Death of a Partner

If an individual dies owning real property encumbered by a mortgage, no deemed sale of the property is deemed to have occurred in which gain or loss is recognized. The same should be true upon the death of a partner owning a partnership interest, even if the partnership has liabilities and the deceased partner has a negative capital account. In this context, I.R.C. § 752(b) should not be available to treat the transaction as a sale or exchange.

The basis of a partnership interest acquired from a decedent is equal to the fair market value of the partnership interest on the date of death (or alternative valuation date if elected), increased by the successor's share of partnership liabilities as of the date of death, reduced to the extent that any of such value is attributable to items constituting income in respect of a decedent under I.R.C. § 691.[18] Thus, the death of a partner has the potential to eliminate permanently gain or loss, which otherwise would be recognized by the partner upon a disposition of the partnership interest.

B.   Exchanges of Partnership Interest

The exchange of property held for investment or use in a trade or business for like-kind property is generally a tax-free transaction under I.R.C. § 1031(a)(1). However, an exchange of one partnership interest for another partnership interest does not qualify for tax-free treatment, even if the assets of the partnerships would meet the like-kind requirement.[19] Where, however, the partnership has in effect a

---

[18]   Treas. Reg. § 1.742-1.

[19]   I.R.C. § 1031(a)(2)(D).

valid election under I.R.C. § 761(a) to be excluded from the application of Subchapter K of the Code, a partnership interest is treated as an interest in each of the assets of the partnership, and not as an interest in the partnership.[20] In these circumstances, a partnership interest may be exchanged for another partnership interest tax free, if both partnerships have made elections under I.R.C. § 761(a), provided the partnerships hold assets that are like kind with each other (typically real property).

C. Abandonment and Worthlessness

Generally, when a taxpayer abandons property, the taxpayer is entitled to an ordinary loss in an amount equal to the tax basis for the property abandoned.[21] This is true even if the property abandoned is a capital asset. The reason this is the case is that there is no sale or exchange in the case of an abandonment, and in order to have a capital gain or capital loss, there must be a sale or exchange.[22] It is then necessary to determine whether this general rule is equally applicable to partnerships.

If the partner abandoning the partnership interest does not have a share of the partnership's liabilities, either because the partnership has no liabilities, or because the partner does not have a share of the partnership's liabilities, then the general rule for abandonment applies.[23] Where, however, the partner has a share of partnership liabilities, a sale or exchange is created.

If a partner abandons a partnership interest, and the partner has a share of partnership liabilities, the act of abandonment will result in the rules of I.R.C. § 752 coming into play. Under I.R.C. § 752(d), the transaction can be viewed as a sale or exchange to the extent of the partner's share of liabilities. If so, I.R.C. § 741 characterizes the loss as a capital loss. Alternatively, to the extent of any liability relief, the transaction can be viewed as a distribution by the partnership to the abandoning partner pursuant to the provisions of I.R.C. § 752(b), with the same capital loss consequences.[24]

What happens if a taxpayer abandons his partnership interest, but the taxpayer nevertheless remains liable for a partnership liability (e.g., because of a guaranty given by the abandoning partner or because the partner was a general partner and the partnership had recourse liabilities)? At least one court has held that in these circumstances the abandoning partner does not realize his share of partnership liabilities (conceivably permitting an ordinary loss, though the court in question remanded the case).[25]

---

[20] I.R.C. § 1031(a).

[21] Rev. Rul. 57-503, 1957- 2 C.B. 139.

[22] I.R.C. § 1222.

[23] Rev. Rul. 93-80, 1993-2 C.B. 239; if there is debt, the revenue ruling would apply I.R.C. § 751(b). *See also*, Gannon v. Commissioner, 16 T.C. 1134 (1951).

[24] *See* O'Brien v. Commissioner, 77 T.C. 113 (1981); Stillwell v. Commissioner, 46 T.C. 247 (1966).

[25] Weiss v. Commissioner, 956 F.2d 242 (11th Cir. 1992).

Precisely what is required in order for a partner to abandon her partnership interest is unclear. The Tax Court has stated, "for an abandonment to be effective for purposes of I.R.C. § 165(a), the abandoning party must manifest an intent to abandon by some overt act or statement reasonably calculated to give a third party notice of the abandonment."[26] In that case, a partner announced at a partners meeting that he would no longer make contributions to the partnership and that he would convey his partnership interest to anyone who would assume his portion of the debt payments. The Tax Court found that this was not sufficient to constitute an abandonment, while the Fifth Circuit held that it was. In another case,[27] the limited partner told the general partner that the limited partner would not contribute additional funds to the partnership and wanted nothing further to do with the partnership. This was held to constitute a sufficient manifestation of his intention to abandon his partnership interest by an overt act.

D. Conversion to Corporation

If taxpayers transfer property to a corporation and the transferors in the aggregate own at least 80% of the stock of the transferee corporation, under I.R.C. § 351(a), no gain or loss is recognized by the taxpayers upon the receipt of the stock of the corporation. Under I.R.C. § 357(a), if a transfer is otherwise tax-free under I.R.C. § 351(a), but as part of the consideration for the property transferred, the corporation assumes the liability of the transferor, or acquires the property subject to a liability, the assumption of the liability or taking of the property subject to the liability is not treated as money or other property for purposes of I.R.C. § 351(a). Under I.R.C. § 357(c), however, if in a transaction to which I.R.C. § 351 applies the amount of liabilities assumed and to which the transferred property is subject exceeds the basis of the property transferred, then the excess is treated as a gain from the sale or exchange of property.

How do these rules apply in the partnership context? If the partnership has no liabilities, I.R.C. § 351(a) applies in a straightforward manner. If the partnership has liabilities, I.R.C. § 752 once more enters the fray. If a taxpayer transfers his partnership interest to a corporation in a transaction to which I.R.C. § 351 applies, then the liabilities of which the taxpayer is deemed relieved are subject to the rules of I.R.C. § 357. Thus, if the liabilities of which the taxpayer is deemed relieved are less than the taxpayer's basis for his partnership interest, then no gain or loss will be recognized by virtue of the liabilities. If the liabilities of which the taxpayer is deemed relieved exceed the taxpayer's basis for his partnership interest, then gain or loss will be recognized.[28]

---

[26] Echols v. Commissioner, 93 T.C. 553, 557 (1989), rev'd 935 F.2d 703 (5th Cir. 1991).

[27] Citron v. Commissioner, 97 T.C. 200 (1991).

[28] Rev. Rul. 84-111, 1984-2 C.B. 88; Rev. Rul. 81-38, 1981-1 C.B. 386; Rev. Rul. 80-323, 1980-2 C.B. 124. If, however, the principal purpose of a taxpayer with respect to the assumption of the liability or the taking of the property subject to the liability, was to avoid federal income tax or not for a bona fide purpose, then all of the liabilities involved are treated as boot. I.R.C. § 357(b).

Rev. Rul. 84-111[29] describes three methods pursuant to which a partnership may be converted to a corporation:

1. The assets of the partnership may be contributed to a newly formed corporation in exchange for stock of the corporation, and then the partnership is terminated by distributing all of the stock of the corporation ("the Assets-Over form");

2. The assets of the partnership may be distributed out to the partners in liquidation of the partnership, and the partners then contribute the assets to a newly formed corporation in exchange for stock in the corporation; and

3. The partners of the partnership contribute all of their partnership interests to a newly formed corporation in exchange for stock in the corporation. The partnership, which now only has one owner, is deemed to liquidate.

The Ruling assumes that the steps chosen for the particular structure actually occur. As the Ruling discusses, the alternatives must be analyzed based upon the general rules for contributions of assets under I.R.C. § 351 and partnership distributions.

Further, the check-the-box Regulations themselves contemplate that a partnership may file Form 8832 and elect to be treated as a corporation even though the entity continues as a partnership or LLC for state law purposes. If a partnership makes this election, the partnership is deemed to use the Assets-Over Form described above.[30]

Many states have cross-entity merger or formless conversion statutes, permitting, for state law purposes, one entity to convert to another entity without having to go through a liquidation and formation process. For example, a statute might permit an LLC to convert to a corporation by dent of a simple filing. No formal election under the check-the-box Regulations might be filed. Rev. Rul. 2004-59[31] provides that if a partnership converts to a corporation for state law purposes using a method that does not require an actual transfer of assets or interests, the partnership will be deemed to use the Assets-Over Form.

E.   Transfers to Other Partnerships

Under I.R.C. § 721(a), no gain or loss is recognized if a person transfers property to a partnership in exchange for a partnership interest. This rule applies if a partnership interest is contributed to another partnership. Again, however, it is necessary to consider the effect of the liabilities of the partnership whose interest is transferred, as well as the liabilities of the partnership to which the partnership interest is transferred.

---

[29] 1984-2 C.B. 88.

[30] Treas. Reg. § 301.7701-3(g)(1)(i).

[31] 2004-1 C.B. 1050.

Treas. Reg. § 1.752-1(f) provides that if, as a result of a single transaction, a partner incurs both an increase in the partner's share of partnership liabilities and a decrease in the partner's share of partnership liabilities, only the net decrease is treated as a distribution from the partnership and only a net increase is treated as a contribution to the partnership. Thus, if a partner transfers a partnership interest to another partnership, it is necessary to determine the partner's share of the transferee partnership's liabilities (which includes the share of the liabilities of the partnership whose interest was transferred) to determine whether there is a deemed net distribution to or net contribution from the contributing partner.

For example, assume that A is a 25% partner of partnership ABCD, that A's basis for his partnership interest is $10,000, and that A's share of the $60,000 of nonrecourse liabilities of ABCD is $15,000. If A transfers A's partnership interest in ABCD to a newly formed partnership AZ, which has no other liabilities and of which A is a 50% partner, A's share of the liabilities of ABCD drops to $7,500, and there is a decrease in A's share of ABCD's liabilities of $7,500. Because this is less than A's basis for his partnership interest in ABCD, no gain or loss is recognized by A on the transfer.[32] A's basis in AZ is $2,500 ($10,000 - $7,500).

If AZ has liabilities, those liabilities need to be taken into consideration in determining the net result to A. If we assume that AZ has $5,000 of nonrecourse liabilities in addition to those attributable to A's contribution of A's interest in ABCD, then A's 50% of the additional liabilities is included in the calculation. A's share of AZ's liabilities attributable to ABCD is $7,500, and A's share of the additional liabilities of AZ is $2,500. So the net distribution to A on the contribution of A's interest in ABCD to AZ is $5,000 (($7,500) + $2,500). A's basis in AZ is also $5,000 under these facts ($10,000 - $5,000).

§ 7.06   OPTIONAL ADJUSTMENT TO BASIS OF PARTNERSHIP PROPERTY

As we never tire of observing, Subchapter K sometimes treats the partnership as an aggregate of its partners and sometimes treats the partnership as an entity apart from its partners. In many instances, treating a partnership as an aggregate is beneficial to the partners and provides flexibility that is not available for corporations. One example of this is the ability to adjust the basis of partnership property when there is a sale or exchange of a partnership interest.

Under the general rule of I.R.C. § 743(a), if a buyer purchases a partnership interest from a partner, the purchase has no effect on the partnership's basis in its assets.[33] This can produce an inequitable result for the transferee partner. To illustrate, if a partnership's sole assets are marketable securities with a basis of $200,000 and a fair market value of $1 million, and A purchases a 50% interest in that partnership for $500,000, the partnership's basis for the marketable securities remains $200,000. If the partnership then sells one-half of its assets for $500,000,

---

[32] *See* Rev. Rul. 79-205, 1979-2 C.B. 255; Rev. Rul. 77-309, 1977-2 C.B. 216; and Rev. Rul. 87-120, 1987-2 C.B. 161.

[33] I.R.C. § 743(a).

the partnership recognizes a $400,000 gain, $200,000 of which is allocated to A. As to A, however, there has been no appreciation in the marketable securities since A acquired her interest in the partnership. Nevertheless, she will be subject to tax on her $200,000 share of the partnership's gain. To correct these distortions, I.R.C. § 743(b) was enacted. It should be noted that there is no comparable provision in the case of an S corporation, even though the same inequity exists.

A.   I.R.C. § 743(b)

Three code sections interplay to address this problem. I.R.C. § 754 provides the election, I.R.C. § 743(b) provides the adjustment, and I.R.C. § 755 provides rules for how the adjustment is applied. The adjustment provided by I.R.C. § 743(b) is only available in the case of a sale or exchange of a partnership interest or upon the death of a partner. Thus, the provisions of I.R.C. § 743(b) do not apply to partnership interests acquired directly from a partnership or acquired by gift.[34] In order for I.R.C. § 743(b) to be applicable, the partnership must make an I.R.C. § 754 election. In fact, if an I.R.C. § 754 election has already been made, an adjustment is mandatory under I.R.C. § 743(b), and no longer optional. This is true even if there is a negative I.R.C. § 743(b) adjustment, because the partnership holds primarily loss assets, rather than a positive adjustment, as in our example. Of course, the transferee partner would not mind being allocated losses that occurred before his watch, but if an I.R.C. § 754 election has been made, he will not be able to do so. Indeed, even if the partnership has not made a § 754 election, if the partnership has a substantial built-in loss in its assets immediately after the transfer, the partnership is required to make an I.R.C. § 743(b) adjustment, notwithstanding the lack of an I.R.C. § 754 election. I.R.C. § 743(d)(1) provides that a partnership has a substantial built-in loss if the partnership's adjusted basis for its property exceeds by more than $250,000 the fair market value of the partnership's property.[35]

B.   Making the I.R.C. § 754 Election

As noted, I.R.C. § 754 provides that once an election is made, it applies to all transfers of partnership interests during the taxable year in which the election is made, as well as for all subsequent taxable years.[36]

Treas. Reg. § 1.754-1(b) provides that an election under I.R.C. § 754 is to be made in a written statement filed with the partnership return for the taxable year in which the transfer (or as we will see, distribution) occurs. For the election to be

---

[34] In many instances, this same inequity resulting from a purchase of a partnership interest will not result in the case of a contribution to a partnership, either because the existing partners will be subject to tax on the appreciation by virtue of a revaluation of the partnership assets and the making of reverse section 704(c) allocations or because of a special allocation of the pre-contribution gain to the existing partners.

[35] Exceptions to this rule are provided in I.R.C. § 743(e) and 743(f) in the case of investment partnerships and securitization partnerships. I.R.C. § 743(d)(2) authorizes the IRS to issue Regulations to carry out the purposes of I.R.C. § 743(d)(1), which may include aggregating related partnerships or disregarding property acquired by a partnership in an attempt to avoid this rule.

[36] And all distributions of property by the partnership for I.R.C. § 734 purposes.

valid, the return must be timely filed (including extensions).

If a partnership wishes to revoke an election under I.R.C. § 754, it must file with the IRS an application setting forth the grounds on which the revocation is desired. The application has to be filed not later than 30 days after the close of the partnership taxable year with respect to which the revocation is intended to apply.[37] The Regulations give as examples of situations that might result in a favorable response to an application for revocation (i) a change in the nature of the partnership's business, (ii) a substantial increase in the assets of the partnership, (iii) a change in the character of partnership assets, or (iv) an increased frequency of retirements or shifts of partnership interests that would result in an administrative burden to the partnership. The Regulations make clear, however, that an application for revocation will not be approved where the revocation is intended (in our current context) to permit a transferee partner from taking advantage of preexisting losses.[38]

C.   Effect of I.R.C. § 743(b)

I.R.C. § 743(b) provides that the partnership shall (i) increase the adjusted basis of its assets by the excess of the basis of the transferee partner for his partnership interest over his proportionate share of the adjusted basis of the partnership's assets, or (ii) decrease the adjusted basis of its assets by the excess of the transferee partner's proportionate share of the adjusted basis of the partnership's assets over the basis of the transferee for his partnership interest. The Regulations have evolved over time. Notwithstanding the language of I.R.C. § 743(b), it would now be more accurate to state that the transferee partner is given an I.R.C. § 743(b) adjustment with respect to the partnership assets, rather than a special basis in those assets, as we discuss below. The I.R.C. § 743(b) adjustment is made solely with respect to the transferee partner, and not the other partners. Further, this is purely a tax adjustment, and does not affect capital accounts.

We will steep you in the details of an I.R.C. § 743(b) adjustment shortly, but first let's zoom out.

Returning to the prior example, if no I.R.C. § 754 election is in effect, A has $200,000 of gain at the time of the sale of one-half of the securities. The $200,000 of gain increases A's basis for his partnership interest by $200,000. When A sells his partnership interest, or when the partnership interest is liquidated, this $200,000 increase in basis will ultimately result in less income or more loss in an equal amount. If, on the other hand, an I.R.C. § 754 election is in effect, A has a $400,000 total I.R.C. § 743(b) adjustment, $200,000 of which offsets his share of the gain, and thus no income is recognized by A in the example upon the sale of one-half of the marketable securities; nor does A have a $200,000 basis increase. Thus, in the example, there has been solely a timing difference (though that is no small thing). Note that the character of all of the gains and losses is capital.

---

[37] Treas. Reg. § 1.754-1(c)(1).

[38] *Id.*

Instead of the partnership having marketable securities as its assets, assume that the partnership holds inventory. If an I.R.C. § 754 election is in effect, then A avoids being taxed on the ordinary income inherent in the partnership assets at the time of purchase. Thus, an I.R.C. § 754 election affects both timing and character.

Assume now that the partnership holds depreciable personal or real property. Upon the purchase of the partnership interest, if an I.R.C. § 754 election is in effect, A has a $400,000 I.R.C. § 743(b) adjustment. That adjustment gives A additional depreciation deductions.[39]

And all of this can work in reverse. As indicated above, if the partnership primarily has losses inherent in its assets, then an I.R.C. § 754 election gives A, in effect, a negative I.R.C. § 743(b) adjustment. This offsets losses or "extra depreciation" that would otherwise be allocable to A.

Having to keep track of I.R.C. § 743(b) adjustments (and as we will discuss in the next chapter, their cousins I.R.C. § 734(b) adjustments) can pose a substantial administrative burden on the partnership, particularly if they arise with some frequency. Historically, that has caused partnerships often to resist making I.R.C. § 754 elections. However, because of the mandatory negative I.R.C. § 743(b) adjustments, these elections are becoming more common.

D. Computation of Transferee's Proportionate Share of I.R.C. § 743(b) Adjustment

Fasten your seat belts. It is time to slog through the details. In order to determine the adjustment that will result from a transfer of a partnership interest when an I.R.C. § 754 election is in effect, it is necessary to determine the transferee partner's proportionate share of the adjusted basis of the partnership's assets. Treas. Reg. § 1.743-1(d)(1) provides that a transferee partner's share of the adjusted basis of partnership property is equal to the transferee's interest in the partnership's "previously taxed capital" plus the transferee's share of partnership liabilities. A transferee partner's share of the previously taxed capital is equal to (i) the amount of cash that the transferee would receive in liquidation if the partnership sold all of its assets for their fair market value (a hypothetical sale), increased by (ii) the amount of tax loss that would be allocated to the transferee from the hypothetical sale, and decreased by (iii) the amount of tax gain that would be allocated to the transferee from the hypothetical sale.

Treas. Reg. § 1.743-1(d)(3), Example 1 provides an illustration. In that example, the partnership owns assets having a fair market value of $76,000, which have a basis of $55,000 and the partnership has liabilities of $10,000. A partner sells his one-third interest in the partnership to a transferee for $22,000. The transferee's basis for his partnership interest is $25,333 ($22,000 + ($10,000/3)). The transferee's share of the previously taxed capital is $15,000 (the $22,000 of cash which he would have received in liquidation following the hypothetical sale — ($76,000-$10,000)/3 — minus the $7,000 of gain that would have been allocated to him in the hypothetical sale). The transferee's share of the adjusted basis of the

---

[39] Treas. Reg. § 1.743-1(j)(4).

partnership property is thus $18,333 (the $15,000 of previously taxed capital plus his $3,333 share of the partnership's liabilities). This results in an I.R.C. § 743(b) adjustment of $7,000 (the difference between the $25,333 "outside basis" and the $18,333 share of partnership "inside basis").

The formula provided for in the Regulations is complex, and its provisions only have to be followed in situations in which the partnership either has non pro rata allocations, adjustments under I.R.C. § 704(c), or reverse section 704(c) allocations (resulting from prior revaluations). In simpler situations, the basis adjustment would simply be the excess of the purchase price (including liabilities, here $25,333) over the transferee partner's one-third interest in the adjusted basis of the partnership's assets ($55,000/3 = $18,333).

E. Allocation of Basis Adjustment among Partnership Assets under I.R.C. § 755

If a partnership has a single asset, it is obvious that any adjustment available under I.R.C. § 743(b) will be allocated to that asset. In most cases, however, a partnership does not have a single asset. Therefore, it becomes necessary to determine how the adjustment under I.R.C. § 743(b) is to be allocated among the various assets of the partnership.

I.R.C. § 755(a) generally provides that the adjustment to be made under I.R.C. § 743(b) shall be made in a fashion that will result in a reduction of the difference between the fair market value and the adjusted basis of partnership properties. I.R.C. § 755(b) provides that, in applying the allocation rules provided for in I.R.C. § 755(a), increases or decreases allocable to (i) capital assets and property described in I.R.C. § 1231(b), and (ii) other property, shall be allocated to partnership property of a like character, except that the basis of any partnership assets shall not be reduced below zero. As you likely already have recognized, the rules of I.R.C. § 755 are not at all clear as to how the allocation is to be made. The Regulations, however, go into great detail as to the manner in which the allocation is to be made.

Let's first zoom out. For the most part, I.R.C. § 755 will allocate a I.R.C. § 743(b) adjustment per asset equal to the transferee partner's share of the gain or loss in that asset, irrespective of whether they are capital or ordinary income assets. Note that even if an overall I.R.C. § 743(b) adjustment is positive, if the partnership holds both appreciated and depreciated assets, the I.R.C. § 743(b) adjustment for the appreciated assets will be positive and for the depreciated assets will be negative. For example assume A buys a 25% interest in a partnership with many assets. Assume Asset 1 has $10,000 of appreciation (i.e., fair market value in excess of basis) and Asset 2 has $8,000 of depreciation (i.e. basis in excess of fair market value). As a 25% partner, A's I.R.C. § 743(b) adjustment for Asset 1 is positive $2,500 and for Asset 2 is a negative $2,000. If Asset 1 is sold, and values have not changed, A will be allocated $2,500 of gain, offset it with the $2,500 I.R.C. § 743(b) adjustment, for no net gain. If Asset 1 continues to increase in value, so that A is allocated $3,000 of gain, after the $2,500 I.R.C. § 743(b) adjustment, the net gain to A will be $500. Conversely, if Asset 1 drops in value before the sale so that A's share of the gain is only $2,000, after the $2,500 I.R.C. § 743(b) adjustment,

A will net to a $500 loss (the character of which will be a function of the character of the asset to the partnership). These are strictly tax adjustments and do not affect capital accounts.

Now let's zoom back in.[40] The amount of I.R.C. § 743(b) adjustment that is allocated to the ordinary income class of property is equal to the total amount of gain or loss that would be allocated to the transferee from the sale of all of the ordinary income property in this hypothetical sale. The amount of the I.R.C. § 743(b) adjustment that is allocable to the capital gain property is equal to the total amount of the I.R.C. § 743(b) adjustment less the amount of the I.R.C. § 743(b) adjustment allocated to the ordinary income class of property.[41] There is also a special rule that provides that in no event may the amount of any negative I.R.C. § 743(b) adjustment allocable to capital gain property exceed the partnership's basis for the capital gain property. In such circumstances, the negative I.R.C. § 743(b) adjustment is allocated to the capital gain property to the extent of the partnership's basis for the capital gain property, and any excess is applied to ordinary income property.[42] Allocations to particular property within a class are generally made on a similar basis.[43] Recall again that within a given class, there may be upward and downward adjustments if the class contains assets with fair market values in excess of their bases and others with fair market values less than their bases. The point of the adjustment is, as of the date of the purchase, to eliminate any net gain or loss from partnership assets to the purchasing partner. In determining the amount of gain or loss that would be allocated to the purchasing partner, allocations under I.R.C. § 704(c) must be taken into account, as must reverse section 704(c) allocations.[44]

---

[40] An issue that must be determined is whether I.R.C. § 743(b) applies in a situation in which the amount paid by the transferee partner is equal to the transferee partner's share of the partnership's basis. Despite the language of I.R.C. § 743(b), the Regulations take the position that an allocation may nevertheless be required. This rare fact pattern would occur in a situation in which some partnership assets have fair market values in excess of their bases, and others have fair market values less than their bases, netting to zero. Treas. Reg. § 1.755-1(b)(1)(i).

[41] Treas. Reg. § 1.755-1(b)(2)(i).

[42] Id.

[43] Treas. Reg. § 1.755-1(b)(3).

[44] Treas. Reg. § 1.755-1(b)(1)(ii); Treas. Reg. § 1.755-1(b)(2)(ii), example 1. The Regulations provide for coordination between I.R.C. § 755 and 1060. If there is a basis adjustment under I.R.C. § 743(b) and the assets of the partnership constitute a trade or business (within the meaning of Treas. Reg. § 1.1060-1(d)(2)), then the partnership is required to use the residual method to assign values to the partnership's section 197 intangibles. Under this method, it is first necessary to determine the value of the assets other than section 197 intangibles and the amount in excess of the value of such non-section 197 intangibles is allocated to section 197 intangibles. Treas. Reg. § 1.755-1(a)(2). The Regulations provide that in determining the value of partnership property other than section 197 intangibles, the provisions of I.R.C. § 7701(g) must be taken into account. Under I.R.C. § 7701(g), in determining the amount of gain or loss with respect to any property, the property is treated as having a fair market value which is not less than the amount of any nonrecourse indebtedness to which the property is subject. Id. If, as a result of applying the residual method, any portion of the I.R.C. § 743(b) adjustment is to be allocated to section 197 intangibles, the value allocated to section 197 intangibles must be divided into two classes: (i) section 197 intangibles other than goodwill and going concern value, and (ii) goodwill and going concern value. Treas. Reg. § 1.755-1(a)(5). After an appropriate amount of value is allocated to the section 197 intangibles other than goodwill and going concern value, any remaining value is then

F. Additional Aspects of Adjustment

1. Transfer of Partnership Interest

Any positive or negative I.R.C. § 743(b) adjustment is an adjustment only with respect to the transferee. If a transferee who has a I.R.C. § 743(b) adjustment subsequently transfers all or a portion of the partnership interest, the new transferee's I.R.C. § 743(b) adjustment is determined without regard to the prior transferee's adjustment.[45] If the transfer is by gift, however, then the donee stands in the shoes of the donor with respect to the adjustment.[46]

2. Distribution of Partnership Property

If there is distributed to a partner of a partnership an asset with respect to which he has a I.R.C. § 743(b) adjustment, then the adjustment is taken into account for purposes of calculating the basis the partner takes in the distributed property under I.R.C. § 732.[47] For example, a positive adjustment would increase the partner's basis in the distributed property. If a partner receives a partnership asset with respect to which there is a I.R.C. § 743(b) adjustment as to another partner, that adjustment is not taken into account by the distributee partner for purposes of I.R.C. §732.[48] In such circumstances, the partner having the I.R.C. § 743(b) adjustment with respect to the property distributed reallocates the adjustment among the remaining items of partnership property in accordance with the rules of Treas. Reg. § 1.755-1(c).[49]

3. Contribution of Property to Lower-Tier Partnership

If a partnership contributes property to another partnership in a transaction to which I.R.C. § 721(a) applies and a partner of the transferring partnership has a I.R.C. § 743(b) adjustment, then the adjustment is treated as contributed to the lower-tier partnership regardless of whether the lower-tier partnership has an election under I.R.C. § 754 in effect.[50] Nevertheless, the upper-tier partnership's I.R.C. § 743(b) adjustment with respect to the partnership interest in the lower-tier partnership must be allocated solely to the transferee partner having that adjustment.

4. Contribution of Property to Corporation

If a partnership contributes an asset to a corporation in a transaction to which I.R.C. § 351 applies with respect to which a partner of the transferring partnership has an I.R.C. § 743(b) adjustment, the corporation's basis for such property

---

allocated to the goodwill and going concern value. Treas. Reg. § 1.755-1(a)(5)(iii).

[45] Treas. Reg. § 1.743-1(f).

[46] *Id.*

[47] Treas. Reg. § 1.743-1(g)(1).

[48] Treas. Reg. § 1.743-1(g)(2).

[49] *Id.*

[50] Treas. Reg. § 1.743-1(h)(1).

generally includes the adjustment.[51] If any gain is recognized by the contributing partnership in such transaction, the contributing partnership determines the amount of gain *without* regard to the basis adjustment, but when allocating the gain to the transferee partner having the I.R.C. § 743(b) adjustment, the adjustment is taken into account.[52] The partnership's basis in the stock of the corporation is determined *without* regard to the I.R.C. § 743(b) adjustment, but the transferee partner has a I.R.C. § 743(b) adjustment with respect to the stock.[53]

5. Special Basis Adjustment and Depreciable Property

If a property with respect to which a I.R.C. § 743(b) adjustment is in effect is depreciable property, and the adjustment is positive, as noted above, the adjustment gives the transferee partner additional depreciation deductions. The adjustment is treated as if it were newly purchased property placed in service when the transfer occurs.[54] The I.R.C. § 743(b) adjustment may be depreciated using any applicable recovery period and method. No change, however, is made with respect to the portion of the basis of the asset for which there is no increase.[55]

To illustrate, assume that partnership AB has a single asset that is depreciable personal property having a recovery period of five years. The asset was originally purchased for $5,000 with the result that there is $1,000 of depreciation available each year, one-half of which is allocated to each of A and B. At the end of year four, when the partnership's basis in the property is $1,000, A sells her partnership interest to C for $1,500 (meaning that the asset owned by partnership AB is worth $3,000). C has a I.R.C. § 743(b) adjustment with respect to the asset of $1,000 ($1,500 - $500). During year five, C's share of the depreciation deduction with respect to the partnership's basis for the asset is $500. In addition, C is entitled to depreciate the $1,000 I.R.C. § 743(b) adjustment over five years. If the straight line method is used, C has an additional depreciation deduction in each of years five through nine of $200. (To keep things simple, or at least simpler, we have ignored depreciation conventions.)

If an I.R.C. § 743(b) adjustment with respect to depreciable property is negative, the adjustment first decreases the transferee partner's distributive share of the depreciation for that item of property for a given tax year. If the amount of the adjustment exceeds the transferee's distributive share of the depreciation, then the transferee's distributive share of depreciation of other items of partnership property is decreased. If the amount recovered in any year exceeds the transferee partner's distributive share of all of the partnership's depreciation for that year, then the transferee is required to recognize income to the extent of such excess.[56] The portion of the decrease that is recovered in any year is based upon the

---

[51] Treas. Reg. § 1.743-1(h)(2)(i).

[52] Treas. Reg. § 1.743-1(h)(2)(ii).

[53] Treas. Reg. § 1.743-1(h)(2)(iii).

[54] Treas. Reg. § 1.743-1(j)(4)(i)(B)(1).

[55] *Id.*

[56] Treas. Reg. § 1.743-1(j)(4)(ii)(A).

remaining useful life of the property to which the I.R.C. § 743(b) adjustment is allocated.[57]

So far, neither of the authors have had the courage to put an I.R.C. § 743(b)/ depreciation combo question on an exam.

§ 7.07   TERMINATION OF PARTNERSHIPS

I.R.C. § 708(a) provides that a partnership is considered to continue until it is terminated (it is rare, but sometimes the Code states the obvious). Under I.R.C. § 708(b)(1), a partnership is terminated if (i) no part of any business, financial operation or venture of the partnership continues to be carried on by any of its partners, (still pretty obvious) or (ii) within a 12-month period there is a sale or exchange of 50% or more of the total interest in partnership capital and profits (not obvious).[58] It is the latter provision that is, of course, relevant in the case of transfers of partnership interests.

A.   What Transactions Are Taken Into Account

Not all transfers of partnership interests are necessarily taken into account in determining whether the required 50% change has occurred. A sale from one partner to an existing partner is taken into account.[59] A transfer of a partnership interest by gift, bequest, or inheritance and a liquidation of a partnership interest are not treated as a sale or exchange for purposes of I.R.C. § 708(b)(1)(B).[60] Likewise, a contribution of property to a partnership is not treated as a sale or exchange.[61]

If a sale or exchange of an interest in an upper-tier partnership results in a termination of the upper-tier partnership, the upper-tier partnership is treated as exchanging its interest in the capital and profits of the lower-tier partnership. If, however, the sale or exchange of an interest in the upper-tier partnership does not result in a termination of the upper-tier partnership, then the sale or exchange is *not* treated as a sale or exchange of a proportionate part of the upper-tier partnership's interest in the capital and profits of the lower-tier partnership.[62]

Is there a sale or exchange for purposes of I.R.C. § 708(b)(1)(B) where a partnership interest is transferred in a nontaxable transaction? The IRS has generally taken the position that as long as there is an exchange, the fact that the exchange qualifies for tax-free treatment does not prevent the transaction from being treated as an exchange for purposes of I.R.C. § 708(d)(1)(B). It has been held that a transfer of a 50% interest in capital and profits by a partner to a corporation

---

[57] Treas. Reg. § 1.743-1(j)(4)(ii)(B).

[58] For special rules with respect to the termination of a partnership in the case of mergers or divisions, *see* § 9.02.

[59] Treas. Reg. § 1.708-1(b)(2).

[60] *Id.*

[61] *Id.*

[62] *Id.*

in a transaction that was tax-free pursuant to I.R.C. § 351 qualified as an exchange for purposes of I.R.C. § 708(b)(1)(B).[63] In Private Rulings, the IRS has held that the transfer of a partnership interest to another partnership is an exchange for purposes of I.R.C. § 708(b)(1)(B).[64]

I.R.C. § 761(e) provides that for purposes of I.R.C. § 708, any distribution of an interest in a partnership is treated as an exchange. That a distribution by a partnership to its partners is treated as an exchange for purposes of I.R.C. § 708(b)(1)(B) is not intuitive. If the partnership distributed an interest in a lower-tier partnership pro rata to its partners, the partners are now merely holding directly that which they previously owned indirectly, and the transaction would not appear to be an appropriate transaction to be taken into account for purposes of I.R.C. § 708(b)(1)(B). Nonetheless, it would appear to be covered by I.R.C. § 761(e) given the IRS rulings.

If a partnership, however, has terminated under I.R.C. § 708(b)(1)(B) (the consequences of which are discussed in more detail below), the deemed distribution by the old partnership of the partnership interests in the new partnership pursuant to Treas. Reg. § 1.708-1(d)(1)(iv) is not treated as a sale or exchange of an interest in the new partnership.[65]

B. Computing Capital and Profits

As indicated above, in order for there to be a termination of a partnership under I.R.C. § 708(b)(1)(B), there must be a sale or exchange of 50% or more of both the capital interests and the profits interests. The Regulations made clear that a sale of a 30% interest in partnership capital and a 60% interest in partnership profits does not result in a termination of the partnership.[66] The Regulations also make clear that a sale by partner A of a 30% interest in a partnership to D, followed by the sale by D of the same 30% interest in the partnership to E, is not treated as a sale of more than a 50% interest in partnership capital and profits because the same 30% interest was transferred.[67]

The Regulations do not indicate how to determine a partner's capital interest. For example, assume partnership AB is comprised of A, a service partner, who has made no capital contribution to the partnership, and B, who has contributed all of the capital to the partnership, and B transfers 60% of his interest in the partnership to C. Is this necessarily a transfer of a 50% interest in partnership capital? Suppose further that the partnership agreement provided that gain from the sale of AB's assets is to be allocated 70% to A and 30% to B. If B transfers 60% of his interest to A, has he triggered I.R.C. § 708(b)(1)(B)? What if, at the time of the transfer by B, the assets of AB have significantly increased in value so that on

---

[63] Evans v. Commissioner, 54 T.C. 40 (1970), aff'd 447 F.2d 547 (7th Cir. 1971); See also Rev. Rul. 81-38, 1981-1 C.B. 386.

[64] PLR 8116041(Jan. 21, 1981) and 8229034 (Apr. 20, 1982).

[65] Treas. Reg. § 1.761-1(e).

[66] Treas. Reg. § 1.708-1(b)(2).

[67] Id.

a sale of the assets of AB at fair market value and a subsequent liquidation, A would receive more money than B?

There appear to be two methods for determining a partner's capital interest for purposes of I.R.C. § 708(b)(1)(B). The first is to assume that all assets are worth their book value and simply look to the capital accounts of the partners. This would be consistent with the rules set forth in Treas. Reg. § 1.704-1(b)(3)(iii)(D) for purposes of determining a partner's interest in the partnership. Alternatively, a partner's percentage interest in capital may be the percentage of the funds of the partnership that a partner would receive if the partnership sold all of its assets for their fair market value. This is consistent with the rule for determining a partner's interest in capital for purposes of I.R.C. § 704(e).[68]

Determining a partner's interest in partnership profits is straightforward if under the partnership agreement a partner has a fixed interest in partnership profits. Where, as is often the case, a partner's profit interest varies over time, or varies depending upon whether it is an ordinary transaction or a capital transaction, how to determine profit interests is not clear. Is the determination based upon the income or loss of the partnership through the date of the sale? If so, what happens if there has been a loss through the date of sale? What happens if under I.R.C. § 706 the pro rata method is to be used in determining the income allocated to the selling partner, making it impossible to determine the allocation of profits for the year until the year ends?

C. The 12-Month Rule

Because there must be a sale or exchange of a 50% interest in both capital and profits during a 12-month period, can a transaction be structured so that less than 50% is sold within the 12-month period, and the balance is sold following the expiration of the 12-month period? In Private Rulings, the IRS has approved transactions of this type.[69]

The issue becomes more complicated if the transaction involves the sale of a 49% interest in the partnership and the purchaser has either an option or an obligation to purchase an additional 1% after the expiration of 12 months from the date of the initial purchase. Under these circumstances, a question is raised as to whether the option is a true option, or whether the future sale is really consummated at the time of the first sale.

D. Effect of Partnership Termination

1. Transactions Deemed to Occur

Treas. Reg. § 1.708-1(b)(4) provides that if a partnership is terminated pursuant to I.R.C. § 708(b)(1)(B) as a result of a sale or exchange, the partnership is deemed to have contributed all of its assets and liabilities to a new partnership in exchange for the interests in the new partnership. Thereafter, the terminated partnership is

---

[68] Treas. Reg. § 1.704-1(e)(1)(v).

[69] *See* PLR 8517022 (Jan. 25, 1985); PLR 7952057 (Sept. 25, 1979).

deemed to liquidate, distributing the interests in the new partnership to the purchasing and continuing partners, in proportion to their respective interests in the terminated partnership. As a result of these deemed transactions, the new partnership's basis for its assets is unchanged, as are the capital accounts of the partners.[70] Even though the assets of the old partnership may have been appreciated, no new section 704(c) gain is created as a result of the deemed transfer by the old partnership of its assets to the new partnership.[71] In order for a purchasing partner to obtain the benefit of a I.R.C. § 743(b) adjustment, the old partnership must have an I.R.C. § 754 election in effect (which can be made on the final return of the old partnership).[72] The new partnership retains the taxpayer identification number of the old partnership.[73]

2. Elections

Because the Regulations treat the old partnership as having transferred its assets to a new partnership, the new partnership should be able to make all new tax elections, although this is not specifically stated. If the new partnership wishes to have a I.R.C. § 754 election in effect, prudence dictates that the new partnership make a new election.

3. IRC §§ 704(c)(1)(B) and 737

A termination of a partnership under I.R.C. § 708(b)(1)(B), will not trigger gain recognition under either I.R.C. §§ 704(c)(1)(B) or 737.[74]

4. Depreciation and Amortization

The principal issue that occurs with respect to a termination of a partnership under I.R.C. § 708(b)(1)(B) relates to depreciation. Under I.R.C. § 168(i)(7)(A), if depreciable property is transferred to a partnership in a transaction to which I.R.C. § 721 applies, the transferee partnership steps in the shoes of the transferor with respect to depreciation. The provisions of I.R.C. § 168(i)(7)(A), however, do not apply in the case of a termination of a partnership under I.R.C. § 708(b)(1)(B). Thus, the new partnership is treated as having newly acquired the assets of the old partnership and must restart depreciation using the appropriate life under the modified accelerated cost recovery system of I.R.C. § 168.

To illustrate, assume that the old partnership held commercial real property with a remaining basis of $390,000 and that it had 10 years remaining in its depreciable life. Thus, the partnership would claim $39,000 of depreciation deductions in each of the next 10 years. Upon a termination of that partnership under I.R.C. § 708(b)(1)(B), the new partnership has a basis for the real property of $390,000, but is required to depreciate that basis over 39 years, resulting in a depreciation

---

[70] Treas. Reg. § 1.708-1(b)(4), example (ii); Treas. Reg. § 1.704-1(b)(2)(iv)(l).

[71] Treas. Reg. § 1.708-1(b)(4), example (iii); Treas. Reg. § 1.704-3(a)(3)(i).

[72] Treas. Reg. § 1.708-1(b)(5).

[73] Treas. Reg. § 1.708-1(b)(4), example (ii); Treas. Reg. § 301.6109-1(d)(2)(iii).

[74] Treas. Reg. §§ 1.704-4(c)(3); 1.737-2(a).

deduction of only $10,000 per year. Thus, the termination of the partnership under I.R.C. § 708(b)(1)(B) resulted in reducing the depreciation deduction of the partnership by $29,000 per year for 10 years. (We have again simplified the depreciation rules.)

I.R.C. § 197 allows the amortization of certain intangible costs incurred by a taxpayer. I.R.C. § 197(f)(2) provides for a step-in-the-shoes rule in the case of transactions described in I.R.C. §§ 721 and 731, which covers an I.R.C. § 708(b)(1)(B) termination. Thus, unlike the situation with depreciation generally, the step-in-the-shoes rule applies in the case of intangibles where there is a termination of a partnership under I.R.C. § 708(b)(1)(B). Thus, the new partnership continues the old partnership's I.R.C. § 197 amortization schedule.

I.R.C. § 709(b)(1) provides for the amortization of organization expenses if the partnership has properly elected to do so. I.R.C. § 709(b)(2)(B) provides that if a partnership is liquidated before the organization expenses have been fully amortized, the unamortized expenses may be deducted to the extent provided under I.R.C § 165 (the general provision for loss deductions). The question presented, therefore, is whether a deemed liquidation under I.R.C. § 708(b)(1)(B) constitutes a liquidation that would permit the claim of a deduction for the unamortized organization expenses. Although there does not appear to be any authority directly in point, it would appear that the deduction should be available.

Chapter 8

PARTNERSHIP DISTRIBUTIONS

BASIC OVERVIEW

Subchapter K prefers not to tax distributions from a partnership to a partner, just as it prefers not to tax contributions by a partner to a partnership. It will make a transaction taxable when necessary to prevent a negative basis, the conversion of ordinary income into capital gain, and abuse. Sometimes the rule of nontaxation seems to be overwhelmed by the exceptions, and the exceptions are often quite complex. If, however, you keep track of the general rule as we proceed with this Chapter, it will help you understand the material that follows.

Under I.R.C. § 731(a), a partner generally recognizes no gain or loss on the receipt of money from a partnership. Under I.R.C. § 733, the partner's basis in the partnership interest is reduced by the amount of money distributed, but not below zero. Recall that a partner's basis is increased by the amount of money and basis of property he contributes to the partnership as well as by his share of partnership income.[1] To the extent that any distribution represents a return of capital or a return of income that was previously allocated to him, not taxing the distribution makes sense. If the money distributed to a partner exceeds that partner's basis in the partnership interest, the distribution exceeds his tax investment in the partnership. Because the partner cannot have a negative basis, the only answer is to tax the partner on the amount by which the distribution exceeds the outside basis, and I.R.C. § 731(a)(1) so provides.

Under I.R.C. § 731(a), that gain is characterized as gain from the sale of the partnership interest, typically capital gain (long or short term, depending on the holding period in the partnership interest). Generally, I.R.C. § 731(a)(1) looks at the basis of the partner at the time the distribution is made. The Regulations, however, provide that distributions that are draws against a partner's share of income are considered to be made on the last day of the partnership tax year, when the partner's outside basis is first increased by his share of any partnership income.[2] The draw "exception" largely swallows the rule in real life as most partnerships consider current distributions to be draws against income.

The amount of the reduction in a partner's share of partnership liabilities is treated as a distribution of money to the partner.[3] That distribution is treated as if

---

[1] I.R.C. §§ 722, 705(a)(1).

[2] Treas. Reg. § 1.731-1(a)(1)(ii); I.R.C. § 706(a).

[3] I.R.C. § 752(b).

it were a draw against income and is thus considered to be made on the last day of the partnership tax year.[4]

The distribution rules only apply to bona fide distributions. A loan to a partner, for example, is not a distribution and is governed by I.R.C. § 707(a).[5] If a loan is canceled, however, the partner is considered to have received a distribution of the money at the time of the cancellation.[6]

In line with the general bias against gain recognition, I.R.C. §§ 731(a) and (b), respectively, provide that neither the distributee partner nor the partnership recognizes a gain or loss on the distribution of property to a partner.[7] The distributee partner takes a carryover basis in the property under I.R.C. § 732. The gain or loss inherent in the distributed property is thus preserved and the gain or loss awaits recognition at a later date when the partner disposes of the property in a taxable transaction. I.R.C. § 733 requires the partner to reduce her basis in her partnership interest by the carryover basis taken in the distributed property. This makes sense. To the extent the partner received property with a carryover basis tax-free, she should give up a concomitant part of her basis in the partnership interest. If cash is distributed in the same transaction, the partner's outside basis is first reduced for the cash, then for the carryover basis in the distributed property.

If a partnership distributes to a partner property encumbered by a liability, the partner's share of partnership liabilities goes down, but his personal liabilities go up. Assume for example that the AB partnership with two equal partners holds a property with a basis of $1,000, subject to a $500 liability. The property is distributed to B in a nonliquidating distribution. Both A's and B's share of partnership liabilities go down, and A and B each have a deemed distribution of $250 under I.R.C. § 752(b). Because B is taking on the full liability, however, he will be deemed to make a contribution to the partnership under I.R.C. § 752(a) of $500. The liability decrease and increase simultaneously offset one another, for a deemed net contribution under I.R.C. § 752(a) by B of $250 with a concomitant increase in the basis of B's partnership interest.[8]

Sometimes, however, the partner does not have enough outside basis in his partnership interest to go around. If the outside basis is less than the basis of the distributed property, reducing the outside basis by the full amount of the partnership's inside basis in the distributed asset would give the partner a negative outside basis. The one consistent rule in tax is that one cannot have a negative basis. To resolve this problem, I.R.C. § 732(a)(2) provides that if the outside basis (after first reducing it for any cash distributed in the same transaction) is less than the inside basis of the distributed asset, then the partner's basis in the distributed

---

[4] Rev. Rul. 94-4, 1994-1 C.B. 196.

[5] Treas. Reg. § 1.731-1(c)(2).

[6] Id.

[7] There are a number of exceptions, including those for marketable securities and I.R.C. § 751 assets discussed below and those contained in I.R.C. §§ 704(c)(1)(B) and 737 discussed in Chapter 11.

[8] Rev. Rul. 79-205, 1979-2 C.B. 255.

asset is limited to the available outside basis. Under I.R.C. § 733, the outside basis is then reduced to zero.

For example, assume the partnership distributes property to a partner with a fair market value of $100 and a basis of $50. The partner has an outside basis of $40. Under these rules, the partner's basis in the distributed property is limited to $40 and her basis in the partnership interest is reduced to zero. Note that on the sale of the property the partner will necessarily recognize more gain than the partnership would have recognized.

Recall that capital accounts are designed to measure the economic value of a partner's partnership interest. At the time property is distributed to a partner, there may be inherent in it both book and tax gain or loss. As we have seen, the tax gain or loss is generally not recognized on the distribution. The capital accounts would be distorted if they were reduced for the fair market value of distributed property (as the Regulations require), but not adjusted for the book gain or loss inherent in distributed property. Consequently, the Regulations also require that book gain or loss be recognized on the distribution of property (which is allocated under the allocation formula in the partnership agreement).[9] For example, assume A and B are equal partners in the AB partnership and the partnership distributes $10,000 to A and land (which is a capital asset to the partnership) to B. The land has a fair market value of $10,000 and a book value and tax basis of $6,000. None of the tax gain is recognized. The $4,000 of book gain, however, is recognized for book purposes, and the capital accounts of A and B are increased for half of the book gain, or $2,000 each. B's capital account is reduced by the fair market value of the distributed land or $10,000.

As you now know, partnership income is normally characterized at the partnership level. As you hopefully also recall, I.R.C. § 724 provides an exception under which unrealized receivables, inventory, and capital loss property that were contributed to the partnership by a partner can be characterized by reference to their status in the hands of the contributing partner. I.R.C. § 735 is the analogue of I.R.C. § 724 for distributions. Under I.R.C. §§ 735(a)(1) and (2), when a distributee partner sells distributed unrealized receivables or inventory, he generally recognizes ordinary gain or loss. Unrealized receivables stay tainted forever; inventory loses its taint after five years and is then characterized based on how the distributee holds it. There is no capital loss property rule.

Under I.R.C. § 734(a), the distribution of property to a partner does not affect the inside basis of partnership property. This can lead to distortions. Consider the equal ABC partnership with the following balance sheet:

P/S Assets	Adj. Basis	F.M.V.	Partners	Adj. Basis	F.M.V.
Cash	$12,000	$12,000	A	$6,000	$12,000
Land	$6,000	$24,000	B	$6,000	$12,000
			C	$6,000	$12,000
Total	$18,000	$36,000		$18,000	$36,000

---

[9] Treas. Reg. § 1.704-1(b)(2)(iv)(e)(1).

Assume the land is a capital asset and that the partnership distributes $12,000 of cash to C in liquidation of C's interest. Under I.R.C. § 731(a)(1), C recognizes $6,000 of gain on the distribution. This is appropriate enough because that is the gain inherent in her interest. But look at the problem that creates for A and B. Before the liquidation of C's interest, their shares of the $18,000 of gain inherent in the land were $6,000 each. After the distribution, their shares of that gain become $9,000 each. If later recognized, that gain will increase their bases in the partnership interest to $15,000, notwithstanding the fact that the fair market value of the interest remains at $12,000. Assuming no change in the figures, on a subsequent sale or liquidation of their partnership interests, A and B will recognize a $3,000 loss that, when offset against the $9,000 of gain, will give them the same $6,000 of gain C recognized. But the sale or liquidation could be years away, and if A or B dies in the interim, he will take the losses with him.

In a manner that is reminiscent of the I.R.C. § 743(b) adjustment, if an I.R.C. § 754 election is in effect, I.R.C. § 734(b) provides an adjustment that can solve the problem. In our example, the basis of the land is increased by the gain C recognized on the distribution or $6,000. That gives the partnership a basis in the land of $12,000, and A's and B's shares of the remaining gain return to being $6,000 each.

The devil is in the details, which are discussed in the Detailed Discussion.

Congress would not have been wise to stop with the rules we have discussed so far, for if it did, it would be easy for a distributee partner to avoid ordinary income recognition, at least if her other partners were cooperative. For example, assume that a partner in a partnership has a $10,000 basis in her partnership interest. Assume further that the partner receives $15,000 of cash in complete liquidation of the partnership interest. Based on the rules we have discussed so far, the partner recognizes *capital* gain of $5,000 on the distribution under I.R.C. § 731(a)(1). It is capital gain because I.R.C. § 731(a) provides that any gain or loss recognized is considered to be gain or loss from the sale or exchange of the distributee's partnership interest, and under I.R.C. § 741 the partnership interest is (essentially) a capital asset to the distributee.

But what if the partnership holds ordinary income assets such as receivables and inventory? Without other Code provisions, the distributee partner could avoid recognizing her share of any ordinary income she would have recognized had she stayed a partner and the partnership had collected the receivables or sold the inventory. Or saying the same thing in other words, she would have converted ordinary income into capital gain. Congress hates that and enacted I.R.C. § 751(b) in response. In Chapter 7 we discussed I.R.C. § 751(a) which performs a similar function in the case of a sale of a partnership interest. Effectively, I.R.C. § 751(b) trumps the other rules of I.R.C. §§ 731 and 732 and requires ordinary income (and possibly other gain or loss) recognition on the part of the partner and/or the partnership if a distribution shifts the partners' interests in certain ordinary income property. Again, the devil is in the details, which are discussed in the Detailed Discussion.

We will conclude our basic overview with a discussion of liquidation either of the partnership as a whole, or of the interest of a single partner. State law on partnership termination is not controlling for federal tax purposes. [10] I.R.C. § 708(b)(1)(A) provides that a partnership terminates "if no part of any business, financial operation, or venture of the partnership continues to be carried on by any of its partners in a partnership." Note that this definition is met if one partner buys the interests of the other partners and continues the partnership business as the partnership form is no longer used.[11] On the other hand, the death of one partner in a two-person partnership will not terminate the partnership if the estate or other successor of the deceased partner continues to share in profits or losses of the partnership business.[12] If the surviving partner purchases the interest of the deceased partner, the partnership would, of course, terminate.

If a partnership terminates, its tax year closes for all of the partners.[13] Any successor partnership would thus be a new partnership permitting (or requiring) fresh elections. Similarly, if the interest of a particular partner terminates, the tax year closes with regard to that partner; the relevant share of income and expense arising from the beginning of the partnership tax year up to when it closes is allocated to that partner.[14]

If a partnership terminates or if the interest of an individual partner is liquidated, the rules we discussed above generally govern with a few additions. As we noted, if a partner's outside basis is less than the partnership's inside basis in distributed property, under I.R.C. § 732(a)(2), the partner's basis in that property is limited to the outside basis. But what if the converse is the case and the partner's outside basis exceeds the partnership's basis in the distributed property?

I.R.C. § 732 provides that a distributee partner cannot take a greater basis in distributed inventory and unrealized receivables than that which the partnership had. To permit the partner to take a greater basis in these assets would enable the distributee partner to avoid ordinary income. Under I.R.C. § 731(a)(2), if the only assets that are distributed in liquidation to a partner are cash, unrealized receivables, and inventory, and the partner's outside basis exceeds the amount of distributed cash and the carryover basis in the unrealized receivables and inventory, the partner recognizes a loss to the extent of any unused basis. The loss is considered to arise from the sale or exchange of the partnership interest and is, therefore, a capital loss.

For example, assume that A is a one-third partner in the ABC partnership with a $20,000 basis in his partnership interest. The partnership uses the calendar year for reporting and makes a liquidating distribution to A on January 1 (making it unnecessary to allocate any income or expense from the current year to A). The

[10] *See* the Revised Uniform Partnership Act ("RUPA") § 801 for events causing dissolution and winding up of a state law partnership. RUPA § 802 provides that a partnership is terminated after it has been wound up. This may or may not coincide with the tax definition. Also *see* Fuchs v. Commissioner, 80 T.C. 506 (1983).

[11] Treas. Reg. § 1.708-1(b)(1); *see also* Harbor Cove Marina Partners Partnership v. Commissioner, 123 T.C. 64 (2004).

[12] Treas. Reg. § 1.708-1(b)(1)(i).

[13] I.R.C. § 706(c)(1).

[14] I.R.C. § 706(c)(2)(A); *see* § 5.09.

partnership distributes to A in complete liquidation of his interest $10,000 of cash and inventory with a basis of $4,000 and a fair market value of $15,000. After reducing A's basis for the cash and a carryover basis in the inventory, A has $6,000 of basis left over. A recognizes a $6,000 capital loss from the sale or exchange of the partnership interest as a consequence. Note that the fair market value of the assets and cash A receives is $25,000, which exceeds his basis of $20,000. Economically, therefore, A has a gain on the transaction. Nonetheless, A recognizes a loss to preserve the ordinary income in the inventory. When A sells the inventory for $15,000, he will recognize $11,000 of ordinary income. Offset that against the $6,000 loss, and it nets to the $5,000 economic gain A had on the liquidation, and all is right with the world. Also note that if A does not receive his proportional share of I.R.C § 751 property, I.R.C. § 751(b) will apply.

Recall that fundamental to all of Subchapter K is the preference for avoiding gain or loss on contributions of property to a partnership and distributions of property to a partner. In the above example, Congress could not avoid loss recognition. There was $6,000 of unused basis, and Congress could not give A a greater basis in I.R.C § 751 property than that which the partnership had and still maintain one of the holier principles in the world of tax, preserving ordinary income. However, if A receives any other assets, we can simply shift any unused basis to those assets, even if it means that A takes a greater basis in those assets than that which the partnership had. Assume in the above example that A's partnership interest is more valuable and that in addition to the cash and inventory, the partnership also distributes land to A and that the land is a capital asset to the partnership. The land has basis to the partnership of $2,000 and a fair market value of $10,000. After reducing his basis for the cash and the inventory, A has $6,000 of basis in the partnership interest left. That $6,000 is allocated to the land, giving A greater basis in the land than that which the partnership had.

I.R.C. § 736 applies when a partner retires from the partnership and the partnership continues.[15] It is in some ways a curious provision. Subchapter K could probably live without I.R.C. § 736 and instead merge its key provisions into I.R.C. § 751(b). But to date Congress has not seen fit to do that, and as a consequence, you will have to learn to juggle the two Code sections. I.R.C. § 736 does serve a useful function. If payments made to a retiring partner are either guaranteed payments (discussed in Chapter 9) or a distributive share of partnership income, they reduce the income of the other partners. If payments are for the partner's share of partnership property, they generally fall within the regular rules for distributions (and thus do not reduce partnership income). Which category a particular payment fits into obviously has a great deal of tax significance. I.R.C. § 736 gives a substantial measure of certainty to this area, though questions remain.

A primary focus of I.R.C. § 736 is the tax treatment of payments of money to a retiring partner over time, but it can also apply when a retiring partner's interest is fully liquidated with a single payment. Further, while the clear implication of the statute is that payments will be made with money, there is nothing in the statute to

---

[15] It can also apply to payments made to the successor-in-interest of a deceased partner. I.R.C. § 736(a).

prevent payments being made with property other than money.[16] Making payments with property can create a number of theoretical problems.[17] Further, as I.R.C. § 736 applies to "payments," it suggests that the partner is being "paid" (typically with money) for his interest in something else (typically partnership property or a right to partnership income). Therefore, if a partner only receives a pro rata distribution of the assets of the partnership, it does not seem that I.R.C. § 736 should apply.

I.R.C. § 736 divides the world into I.R.C. § 736(a) payments and I.R.C. § 736(b) payments. I.R.C. § 736(b) applies to payments for the retiring partner's interest in partnership property. I.R.C. § 736(a) applies to all other payments. I.R.C. § 736(a) and (b) merely classify payments. Other Code provisions that we have covered in this and other Chapters govern the tax treatment of those payments. Generally, I.R.C. § 736(a) payments are for unrealized receivables in services partnerships and are generally ordinary income to the retiring partner and in some fashion deductible to the partnership. I.R.C. § 736(b) payments are for most other items and, subject to I.R.C. § 751(b), are given regular distribution treatment, meaning often that the retiring partner will have a capital loss if the total I.R.C. § 736(b) payments are less than the partner's outside basis, and a capital gain if they exceed that basis.

We leave the details for the Detailed Discussion.

DETAILED DISCUSSION

§ 8.01   INTRODUCTION

Subchapter K prefers not to tax distributions from a partnership to a partner, just as it prefers not to tax contributions by a partner to a partnership. It will only make a transaction taxable when necessary to prevent a negative basis, the conversion of ordinary income into capital gain, and abuse. Sometimes the rule of nontaxation seems to be overwhelmed by the exceptions, and the exceptions are often quite complex. If, however, you keep track of the general rule as we proceed with this Chapter, it will help you understand the material that follows.

In Chapter 7 we discussed the distortions in inside and outside bases that can arise when a partner sells her partnership interest.[18] I.R.C. § 743(b) usually provides an optional adjustment that can address this issue. Distributions can cause similar distortions between inside and outside basis. I.R.C. § 734(b) again usually provides optional adjustments to reduce or eliminate the distortion. We will discuss these as well.

Finally, we will look at I.R.C. § 736, which in principle is designed to address how to treat the retirement of a partner from the partnership where payments are made over time. As we shall see, the reach of I.R.C. § 736 is far broader, however.

---

[16] *See* Willis, Pennell, Postlewaite, *Partnership Taxation* ¶ 15.06[1], [2].

[17] *Id* at ¶ 15.06.

[18] Recall that a partner's basis in her partnership interest is called the "outside basis," and the partnership's basis in its assets is called the "inside basis."

§ 8.02 NONLIQUIDATING DISTRIBUTIONS OF MONEY

Under I.R.C. § 731(a), a partner generally recognizes no gain or loss on the receipt of money from a partnership. Under I.R.C. § 733, the partner's basis in the partnership interest is reduced by the amount of money distributed, but not below zero. Recall that a partner's basis is increased by the amount of money and basis of property he contributes to the partnership as well as by his share of partnership income.[19] To the extent that any distribution represents a return of capital or a return of income that was previously allocated to him, not taxing the distribution makes sense. If the money distributed to a partner exceeds that partner's basis in the partnership interest, the distribution exceeds his tax investment in the partnership. Because the partner cannot have a negative basis, the only answer is to tax the partner on the amount by which the distribution exceeds the outside basis, and I.R.C. § 731(a)(1) so provides. Under I.R.C. § 731(a), that gain is characterized as gain from the sale of the partnership interest, typically capital gain.

Generally, I.R.C. § 731(a)(1) looks at the basis of the partner at the time the distribution is made. The Regulations, however, provide that distributions that are draws against a partner's share of income are considered to be made on the last day of the partnership tax year, when the partner's outside basis is first increased by his share of any partnership income.[20] To ensure draw status, it may be advisable for the partnership agreement to contain a provision requiring repayment of any amount distributed that ultimately exceeds the partner's share of partnership income.[21] The draw "exception" largely swallows the rule in real life as most partnerships consider current distributions to be draws against income.

The amount of the reduction in a partner's share of partnership liabilities is treated as a distribution of money to the partner.[22] The distribution is treated as if it were a draw against income and is thus considered to be made on the last day of the partnership tax year.[23]

The distribution rules only apply to bona fide distributions. A loan to a partner, for example, is not a distribution and is governed by I.R.C. § 707(a).[24] If a loan is canceled, however, the partner is considered to have received a distribution of the money at the time of the cancellation.[25]

---

[19] I.R.C. §§ 722, 705(a)(1).

[20] Treas. Reg. § 1.731-1(a)(1)(ii); I.R.C. § 706(a).

[21] *See* McKee, Nelson, Whitmire, *Federal Taxation of Partnerships and Partners* ¶ 19.03[2]; contra Willis, Pennell, Postlewaite, *Partnership Taxation* ¶ 13.02[1][b].

[22] I.R.C. § 752(b).

[23] Rev. Rul. 94-4, 1994-1 C.B. 196.

[24] Treas. Reg. § 1.731-1(c)(2).

[25] *Id.*

§ 8.03 NONLIQUIDATING DISTRIBUTIONS OF PROPERTY

A. General Rules

In line with the general bias against gain recognition, I.R.C. §§ 731(a) and (b), respectively, provide that neither the distributee partner nor the partnership recognizes a gain or loss on the distribution of property to a partner.[26] The distributee partner takes a carryover basis in the property under I.R.C. § 732. The gain or loss inherent in the distributed property is thus preserved and the gain or loss awaits recognition at a later date when the partner disposes of the property in a taxable transaction. I.R.C. § 733 requires the partner to reduce his basis in his partnership interest by the carryover basis taken in the distributed property. This makes sense. To the extent the partner received property with a basis tax-free, he should give up a concomitant part of his basis in the partnership interest. If cash is distributed in the same transaction, the partner's outside basis is first reduced for the cash, then for the carryover basis in the distributed property.

If a partnership distributes property encumbered by a liability to a partner, the partner's share of partnership liabilities decreases, but his personal liabilities increase. Assume, for example, that the AB partnership with two equal partners holds a property with a basis of $1,000, subject to a $500 liability. The property is distributed to B in a nonliquidating distribution. Both A's and B's share of partnership liabilities decrease, and A and B each have a deemed distribution of $250 under I.R.C. § 752(b). Because B is taking on the full liability, however, he will be deemed to make a contribution to the partnership under I.R.C. § 752(a) of $500. The liability decrease and increase simultaneously offset one another, for a deemed net contribution under I.R.C. § 752(a) by B of $250 with a concomitant increase in the basis of B's partnership interest.[27]

In Rev. Rul. 2007-40[28], a partnership was obligated to make a I.R.C. § 707(c) guaranteed payment to a partner. In lieu of distributing cash in satisfaction of the guaranteed payment, the partnership distributed real property having a fair market value equal to the guaranteed payment. Generally, as we noted above, if a partnership makes a distribution of property to a partner, it recognizes no gain or loss under I.R.C. § 731(b). On the other hand, if a taxpayer conveys property to another in satisfaction of an obligation, or in exchange for the performance of services, the taxpayer must recognize gain or loss measured by the difference between the basis of the property conveyed and the fair market value of the property. Rev. Rul. 2007-40 holds that the conveyance of the real property to the partner was not a distribution, bringing it within the general taxable exchange rules.

In Chief Counsel Advice 20065014 (Dec 15, 2006), the taxpayer's interest in a partnership was to be liquidated. To accomplish the liquidation, the partnership formed a single member LLC (treated as a disregarded entity) that purchased a

---

[26] There are a number of exceptions, including those for marketable securities and I.R.C. § 751 assets discussed below and those contained in I.R.C. §§ 704(c)(1)(B) and 737.

[27] Rev. Rul. 79-205, 1979-2 C.B. 255.

[28] 2007-1 C.B. 1426.

house that it then transferred to the partner in exchange for his partnership interest. The taxpayer treated the transaction as a liquidating distribution in which neither he nor the partnership had any gain or loss pursuant to I.R.C. § 731. The IRS concluded, however, that I.R.C. § 731 did not apply because the house was acquired solely for the purpose of the distribution, and was not related to the partnership's business. It also stated that the partnership was never the owner of the house for tax purposes. Lastly, the IRS stated that there was no economic substance to the transaction.

B. Outside Basis Less Than Inside Basis

Sometimes, however, the partner does not have enough outside basis in his partnership interest to go around. If the outside basis is less than the basis of the distributed property, reducing the outside basis by the full amount of the partnership's inside basis in the distributed asset would give the partner a negative outside basis. The one consistent rule in tax is that one cannot have a negative basis. To resolve this problem, I.R.C. § 732(a)(2) provides that if the outside basis (after first reducing it for any cash distributed in the same transaction) is less than the inside basis of the distributed asset, then the partner's basis in the distributed asset is limited to the available outside basis. Under I.R.C. § 733, the outside basis is then reduced to zero.

For example, assume the partnership distributes property to a partner with a fair market value of $100 and a basis of $50. The partner has an outside basis of $40. Under these rules, the partner's basis in the distributed property is limited to $40 and her basis in the partnership interest is reduced to zero. Note that on the sale of the property the partner will necessarily recognize more gain than the partnership would have recognized.

What happens if the partnership distributes several properties to a partner and the partner's outside basis is insufficient to give her a full carryover basis in the distributed properties? The maximum basis the partner is allowed in all of the properties is limited to the outside basis. How is it allocated among the distributed properties? I.R.C. § 732(c) provides the applicable rules. These rules are somewhat complex. The outside basis is first allocated to unrealized receivables and inventory to the extent possible. Note that this is taxpayer friendly, as it limits the extent to which the distributee partner may have more ordinary income to recognize than the partnership would have had.[29] If the outside basis of the partner is insufficient to give the partner a full carryover basis in those assets, then the basis of the assets must be reduced to equal the available outside basis. Any decrease in the basis of the distributed assets is first allocated to assets with built-in loss (i.e., a basis in excess of fair market value) in proportion to the respective built-in losses, but not in an amount in excess of any property's built-in loss. (Unrealized receivables and inventory are unlikely to have built-in losses.) If an additional decrease in basis in the distributed unrealized receivables and inventory is

---

[29] I.R.C. § 735, discussed below, generally provides that the character of the assets to the partner will be the same as they were to the partnership.

necessary, it is allocated among the distributed assets in proportion to their respective bases.[30]

If there is sufficient outside basis to give the distributee partner a full carryover basis in the inventory and unrealized receivables, then the balance of the basis is again allocated to any other distributed assets. Again, the basis decrease to those assets is first allocated to assets with built-in loss in proportion to the built-in losses (but not in excess of any built-in loss in a given asset) and any remaining decrease is allocated in proportion to the respective bases of the other distributed assets.[31]

For example, assume partner A has an outside basis of $9,000 and the partnership distributes to A inventory with a basis to the partnership of $5,000 and a fair market value of $9,000, and two parcels of land (both capital assets) each with a basis to the partnership of $3,000 and a fair market value of $500. A's outside basis of $9,000 is first allocated to the inventory, giving A a full carryover basis in the inventory of $5,000 and reducing his outside basis to $4,000 ($9,000 - $5,000). A's remaining outside basis of $4,000 is insufficient to give him a full carryover basis in the two parcels of land which together have a basis of $6,000. The bases of the two parcels thus must be reduced by $2,000. The relative depreciation in each parcel is the same, $2,500, so the basis of each parcel is reduced by 50% of the total $2,000 reduction, or $1,000 each. Thus A's basis in each parcel is $3,000 - $1,000 = $2,000.

C. Marketable Securities

As we have seen, a distribution of money is only tax-free to the extent of a partner's outside basis. Any distribution of money in excess of the basis causes the partner to recognize gain. A distribution of property, on the other hand, can be tax-free irrespective of the partner's outside basis. If marketable securities were treated like any other non-cash property, a partnership might be inclined to distribute them instead of money in situations where a money distribution would cause the partner to recognize gain. For that reason, I.R.C. § 731(c) generally treats a distribution of marketable securities as a distribution of money to the extent of their fair market value at the time of the distribution. Marketable securities are primarily financial instruments and foreign currencies that are actively traded, including interests in common trust funds, and mutual funds.[32] The partner's basis in the marketable security will be a carryover basis under I.R.C. § 732 increased by any gain recognized to the partner on the distribution,[33] though for purposes of reducing the distributee's basis under I.R.C. § 733, the gain is ignored.[34] If different marketable securities are distributed in the same transaction and gain is recognized, the basis increase in the securities is allocated in proportion

---

[30] I.R.C. § 732(c)(3).

[31] Id.

[32] This is a partial list, see I.R.C. § 732(c)(2) for the full definition.

[33] I.R.C. § 732(c)(4). The gain will normally be capital gain, as it would be with a distribution of money, unless the marketable securities constitute unrealized receivables or inventory items, in which case the gain will be ordinary income. I.R.C. § 731(c)(6).

[34] I.R.C. § 731(c)(5).

to the built-in gain in the securities (i.e., the amount by which the fair market value exceeds basis).[35]

Assume, for example, that A and B form the AB partnership as equal partners. A contributes an asset with a fair market value of $1,000 and an adjusted basis of $300, and B contributes $1,000 of cash. AB subsequently purchases Marketable Security Y for $200 that appreciates in value to $500 and then distributes it to A in a current distribution. AB holds no other marketable securities. Under I.R.C. § 722, A's basis in his partnership interest is $300. The distribution of the security is treated as a distribution of money in the amount of $500. Ignoring (for the sake of simplicity) I.R.C. § 731(c)(3)(B), A recognizes a gain of $200 under I.R.C. § 731(a)(1). A's basis in the security is initially a carryover basis of $200 under I.R.C. § 732(a)(1), but is then increased for the $200 of gain recognized under I.R.C. § 731(c)(4)(A), giving A a basis in the security of $400. A's basis in the partnership interest, after factoring in I.R.C. § 731(c)(5), is $300 - $200, or $100.[36]

I.R.C. § 731(c)(3)(A), in conjunction with the Regulations contains a number of exceptions. A distribution of a marketable security to a partner who contributed it will not ordinarily be treated as a distribution of money. The same is generally true if the marketable securities distributed were acquired by the partnership in a nonrecognition transaction if two conditions are met: (1) The marketable securities constituted less than 20% of the value of all the assets exchanged by the partnership in the nonrecognition transaction; and (2) the marketable securities are distributed within five years of either the date the partnership acquired them or the date the security became marketable.[37] Another exception is provided under certain circumstances if the security was not marketable when acquired by the partnership.[38] Finally, there is also an exception for a distribution by an investment partnership if the distributee partner did not contribute any property to the partnership other than money or securities.[39]

Under I.R.C. § 731(c)(3)(B), the fair market value of marketable securities distributed generally is reduced by the excess of

1. the distributee partner's share of the net gain that would have been recognized if all of the marketable securities held by the partnership were sold over

2. the distributee partner's share of that gain for the marketable securities held by the partnership immediately after the distribution.[40]

Assume, for example, that A and B form partnership AB as equal partners. AB subsequently distributes security X to A in a current distribution. Immediately before the distribution, AB held the following securities:

---

[35] I.R.C. § 731(c)(4)(B).

[36] This example is based on Treas. Reg. § 1.731-2(j), example 1.

[37] Treas. Reg. § 1.731-2(d)(1)(ii).

[38] Treas. Reg. § 1.731-2(d)(1)(iii).

[39] I.R.C. §§ 731(c)(3)(A)(iii), (c)(3)(C).

[40] See Treas. Reg. § 1.731-2(b).

	FMV	Basis	Gain (Loss)
Security X	100	70	30
Security Y	100	80	20
Security Z	100	110	(10)

If AB had sold the securities for their fair market values immediately before the distribution, AB would have recognized $40 of net gain. A's distributive share would have been $20. If AB had sold Securities Y and Z immediately after the distribution of Security X to A, the partnership would have recognized $10 of net gain. A's distributive share of that would have been $5. Thus, the distribution resulted in a $15 reduction in A's distributive share of the net gain in AB's securities ($20 before - $5 after). Under I.R.C. § 731(c)(3)(B), the amount of the distribution of Security X that is treated as a distribution of money is reduced to $85 ($100 - $15).[41]

§ 8.04   CAPITAL ACCOUNTS

Recall that capital accounts are designed to measure the economic value of a partner's partnership interest. At the time property is distributed to a partner, there may be inherent in it both book and tax gain or loss. As we have seen, the tax gain or loss is generally not recognized on the distribution. The capital accounts would be distorted if they were reduced for the fair market value of distributed property (as the Regulations require), but not adjusted for the book gain or loss inherent in distributed property. Consequently, the Regulations also require that book gain or loss be recognized on the distribution of property (which is allocated under the allocation formula in the partnership agreement).[42] For example, assume A and B are equal partners in the AB partnership and the partnership distributes $10,000 to A and land (which is a capital asset to the partnership) to B. The land has a fair market value of $10,000 and a book value and tax basis of $6,000. None of the tax gain is recognized. The $4,000 of book gain, however, is recognized for book purposes, and the capital accounts of A and B are increased for half of the book gain or $2,000 each. B's capital account is reduced by the fair market value of the distributed land or $10,000.

§ 8.05   I.R.C. § 732(D)

I.R.C. § 732(d) applies to partners who receive distributions of property from the partnership, but acquired their partnership interests by sale, exchange or inheritance[43] from another partner when an I.R.C. § 754 election was *not* in effect. The distribution must occur within two years of the transfer of the partnership interest

---

[41] This example is based on Treas. Reg. § 1.731-2(j), example 2.

[42] Treas. Reg. § 1.704-1(b)(2)(iv)(e)(1).

[43] I.R.C. § 732(d) provides that the partner is given an often modified version of the I.R.C. § 743(b) adjustment. The I.R.C. § 743(b) adjustment in turn applies when the partner acquired the partnership interest by sale, exchange or purchase. *See* Willis, Pennell, Postlewaite *Partnership Taxation* ¶ 13.03[6][a].

to the distributee partner. In determining the basis of the distributed assets, the distributee partner receives the basis adjustment provided in I.R.C. § 743(b) notwithstanding the lack of an I.R.C. § 754 election. This adjustment applies only for the purpose of determining the basis of distributed property and not (as would be the case with an actual I.R.C. § 754 election) for purposes of partnership depreciation, depletion, or gain or loss on disposition of partnership property.[44] The transferee partner, not the partnership as is the case with I.R.C. § 754, must make an election to use I.R.C. § 732(d).[45]

The I.R.C. § 732(d) option may be particularly valuable when the partnership is about to sell ordinary income property that would be eligible for an I.R.C. § 743(b) adjustment had an I.R.C. § 754 election been made. If the partnership distributes to the transferee partner his share of that ordinary income property within two years of when the partnership interest was acquired, then when that partner sells the property he can avoid, or at least reduce, the ordinary income realized due to the I.R.C. § 743(b) adjustment.[46] Of course, this assumes the transferee partner has sufficient outside basis to be able to take meaningful advantage of the I.R.C. § 743(b) adjustment.[47]

The Regulations require the distributee partner to apply the special basis rule contained in I.R.C. § 732(d) to any distribution of property made by the partnership to him at any time (not just within two years of acquiring the interest) if at the time of the acquisition of the transferred interest:

1. The fair market value of all partnership property (other than money) exceeded 110 % of its adjusted basis to the partnership.

2. An allocation of basis under I.R.C. § 732(c) upon a liquidation of his interest immediately after the transfer of the interest would have resulted in a shift of basis from property not subject to an allowance for depreciation, depletion, or amortization, to property subject to such an allowance; and

3. An I.R.C. § 743(b) basis adjustment would change the basis to the transferee partner of the property actually distributed.[48]

The point here is to prevent the distributee from obtaining tax benefits that might arise as the result of shifting basis from, for example, nondepreciable property to depreciable property via a distribution. The likelihood of this Regulation applying is somewhat reduced by I.R.C. § 197, which allows the amortization of intangible assets that were often not amortizable before its enactment.

---

[44] Treas. Reg. § 1.732-1(d)(1)(vi).

[45] Treas. Reg. § 1.732-1(d)(1)(iii).

[46] See Willis, Pennell, Postlewaite, *Partnership Taxation* ¶ 13.03[6][a].

[47] See I.R.C. § 732(a)(2).

[48] Treas. Reg. § 1.732-1(d)(4).

§ 8.06   THE SALE OF DISTRIBUTED PROPERTY

Recall that partnership income is normally characterized at the partnership level. I.R.C. § 724 provides an exception under which unrealized receivables, inventory, and capital loss property that were contributed to the partnership by a partner are characterized by reference to their status in the hands of the contributing partner. I.R.C. § 735 is the analogue of I.R.C. § 724 for distributions. Under I.R.C. §§ 735(a)(1) and (2), when a distributee partner sells distributed unrealized receivables or inventory, he generally recognizes ordinary gain or loss. Unrealized receivables stay tainted forever; inventory loses its taint after five years and is then characterized based on how the distributee holds it. Neither the partner nor the partnership can end-run I.R.C. § 735 by swapping the distributed unrealized receivables or inventory for other property in a nonrecognition transaction. I.R.C. § 735(c)(2) provides that the provisions of I.R.C. § 735 will apply to the property received in such an exchange. The Code, however, excepts from this rule C corporation stock received in an exchange under I.R.C. § 351, apparently figuring that the burden of corporate double taxation outweighs the need to continue the ordinary income taint.

I.R.C. § 735 defines unrealized receivables by reference to I.R.C. § 751(c). While the definition of unrealized receivables in I.R.C. § 751(c) can include I.R.C. § 1245 recapture property,[49] it does not do so for I.R.C. § 735 purposes. The "recomputed basis" rules of I.R.C. § 1245, however, will keep the recapture taint attached to the property. Thus, when the partner sells a distributed depreciable, personal property, I.R.C. § 1245, will apply to the sale.[50]

I.R.C. § 735(b) generally gives the distributee partner a tacked holding period in the distributed property, though there is of course no tacking for purposes of the five-year taint that applies to inventory. There is no capital loss property rule.

§ 8.07   I.R.C. § 734(B) ADJUSTMENTS

A.   Introduction

Under I.R.C. § 734(a), the distribution of property to a partner does not affect the inside basis of partnership property. This can lead to distortions. Consider the equal ABC partnership with the following balance sheet:

---

[49] Generally, I.R.C. § 1245 provides that if a taxpayer sells depreciable personal property at a gain, he recognizes ordinary income on the sale to the extent of any depreciation taken on the property. Any additional gain is normally governed by I.R.C. § 1231 which would generally characterize the additional gain as long-term capital gain if total I.R.C. § 1231 gains exceed total I.R.C. § 1231 losses.

[50] I.R.C. §§ 1245(b)(3), (6).

P/S Assets	Adj. Basis	F.M.V.	Partners	Adj. Basis	F.M.V.
Cash	$12,000	$12,000	A	$6,000	$12,000
Land	$6,000	$24,000	B	$6,000	$12,000
			C	$6,000	$12,000
Total	$18,000	$36,000		$18,000	$36,000

Assume the land is a capital asset and that the partnership distributes $12,000 of cash to C in liquidation of C's interest. Under I.R.C. § 731(a)(1), C recognizes $6,000 of gain on the distribution. This is appropriate enough because that is the gain inherent in her interest. But look at the problem that creates for A and B. Before the liquidation of C's interest, their shares of the $18,000 of gain inherent in the land were $6,000 each. After the distribution, their shares of that gain become $9,000 each. Assuming the values don't change, if and when recognized, that gain will increase their bases in the partnership interest to $15,000, notwithstanding the fact that the fair market value of the interests remains at $12,000. On a subsequent sale or liquidation of their partnership interests, A and B will recognize a $3,000 loss that, when offset against the $9,000 of gain, will give them the same $6,000 of gain C recognized. But the sale or liquidation could be years away, and if A or B dies in the interim, she will take the losses with her. Note there is a timing distortion, but no character distortion. Character distortion would be unusual due to the application of I.R.C. § 751(b), discussed below.

In a manner that is reminiscent of the I.R.C. § 743(b) adjustment, if an I.R.C. § 754 election is in effect, I.R.C. § 734(b) provides an adjustment that can solve the problem. In our example, the basis of the land would be increased by the gain C recognized on the distribution, or $6,000. That would give the partnership a basis in the land of $12,000, and A's and B's shares of the remaining gain would return to being $6,000 each.

B.   The Devil is in the Details

I.R.C. § 754 and its Regulations provide for the election, I.R.C. § 734(b) and its Regulations provide the amount of the adjustment, and I.R.C. § 755 and its Regulations provide for how the adjustment is allocated to the partnership assets. While I.R.C. § 743(b) adjustments only benefit the buying partner, I.R.C. § 734(b) adjustments benefit all of the continuing partners as the basis adjustments apply to partnership property and do not belong to a particular partner.

There are four ways for an I.R.C. § 734(b) adjustment to arise:[51]

1. When a distributee partner recognizes a gain on a distribution under I.R.C. § 731(a)(1).[52] The amount of the adjustment is the amount of the gain.

2. When a distributee partner recognizes a loss on a distribution under

---

[51] Treas. Reg. § 1.735-1(b).

[52] Note that in each of the four cases the partnership must have made a bona fide distribution and not, for example, a disguised sale under I.R.C. § 707(a)(2)(A).

I.R.C. § 731(a)(2). This can only happen in liquidation of a partner's interest, discussed below. The amount of the adjustment is the amount of the loss.

3. When a distributee partner takes a lesser basis under I.R.C. § 732(a)(2) in distributed property than that which the partnership had. As discussed above, this will occur when the distributee partner has insufficient outside basis to give her a full carryover basis in the distributed property. The amount of the adjustment is the difference between the basis the partnership has in the property and the basis the distributee partner takes in the property. For example, assume the partnership's basis in distributed property is $10,000 and the distributee's outside basis in the partnership interest is $8,000. The adjustment is $2,000.

4. When a distributee partner takes a greater basis under I.R.C. § 732(b) in distributed property than that which the partnership had. This again can only happen in liquidation of a partner's interest, discussed below. For example, if the partnership's basis in distributed property is $6,000 but the distributee's basis in the partnership interest is $9,000 and as a consequence of the rules discussed below the distributee takes a $9,000 basis in the distributed property, the adjustment is $3,000.

How the adjustments are allocated to partnership property is provided in I.R.C. § 755 and its Regulations. As was the case for I.R.C. § 743(b) adjustments, the partnership's assets are divided into two categories: (1) the capital asset and I.R.C. § 1231 property class and (2) the ordinary income class. If the adjustment results from the distributee partner recognizing a gain or loss, the capital asset and I.R.C. § 1231 property class of assets is adjusted.[53] Under I.R.C. §§ 734(b)(1)(A) and (B), gain gives an upward adjustment, loss yields a downward adjustment. Note that any gain or loss recognized by a partner will normally be a capital gain or loss. If the relevant I.R.C. § 734(b) adjustment could be allocated to the ordinary income class, the parties would be able to arbitrage tax rates. Capital gains to the distributee would reduce ordinary income to the remaining partners.[54] To prevent that, the Regulations require that the adjustment resulting from a gain or loss to be allocated to the capital asset and I.R.C. § 1231 property class.

If the adjustment results from the distributee partner taking a different basis in distributed property than that which the partnership had, the class of assets adjusted is the same as the class to which the distributed property belongs.[55] Thus, if a capital asset is distributed and the distributee partner takes a different basis in that asset than that which the partnership had, the capital and I.R.C. § 1231 property class is adjusted. If an ordinary income class asset is distributed, that class of assets would be adjusted. Under I.R.C. §§ 734(b)(1)(B) and (b)(2)(B), if the distributee takes a lesser basis, it is an upward adjustment; if the distributee takes a greater basis, it is a downward adjustment.

---

[53] Treas. Reg. § 1.755-1(c)(1)(ii).

[54] *See* Willis, Pennell, Postlewaite, *Partnership Taxation* ¶ 13.05[8].

[55] Treas. Reg. § 1.755-1(c)(1)(i).

An upward adjustment is allocated in up to two steps. Step 1: The adjustment is allocated to appreciated assets within a class in proportion to the appreciation inherent in each asset, but under this step the amount allocated to a property cannot exceed the appreciation inherent in that property. Step 2: If the first step does not fully use the available I.R.C. § 734(b) adjustment, any remaining upward adjustment is allocated to *all* of the assets in the class in proportion to their fair market values.[56]

A downward adjustment is allocated in up to three steps. Step 1: The adjustment is allocated to depreciated assets within a class in proportion to the depreciation inherent in each asset, but under this step the amount allocated to a property cannot exceed the depreciation inherent in that property. Step 2: If the first step does not fully use the available I.R.C. § 734(b) adjustment, any remaining downward adjustment is allocated to *all* of the assets in the class in proportion to their adjusted bases.[57] The basis of property cannot, of course, be reduced below zero, which leads to Step 3: Any unused adjustment remaining after Step 2 is held in abeyance until assets with basis are added to that class. Thus, if the downward adjustment held in abeyance is to the ordinary income class, assets will have to be acquired in *that* class that have basis that can then be adjusted downward.[58]

First return to the example presented at the start of this section and make sure you understand how the I.R.C. § 734(b) adjustment works with those facts. Then take a look at an expanded version of that example:

P/S Assets	Adj. Basis	F.M.V.	Partners	Adj. Basis	F.M.V.
Cash	$18,000	$18,000	A	$10,000	$18,000
Land #1	$6,000	$24,000	B	$10,000	$18,000
Land #2	$6,000	$12,000	C	$10,000	$18,000
Total	$30,000	$54,000		$30,000	$54,000

Again, both parcels of land are capital assets. $18,000 is distributed to C in liquidation of her interest.[59] C has gain under I.R.C. § 731(a)(1) of $8,000. An I.R.C. § 754 election is in effect. Because there is a gain, there is an $8,000 upward adjustment to the capital asset and I.R.C. § 1231 property class, the only class of assets that exists in this example. There is a total of $24,000 of gain inherent in the two parcels of land, $18,000 in land #1 and $6,000 in land #2. Land #1 thus has 75% of the total gain (18,000/24,000) and land #2 has 25% (6,000/24,000). Thus 75% of the $8,000 upward adjustment, or $6,000, is allocated to land #1 and 25% of $8,000, or $2,000, is allocated to land #2. The partnership's ending balance sheet thus would be:

---

[56] Treas. Reg. § 1.755–1(c)(2)(i).

[57] Treas. Reg. § 1.755–1(c)(2)(ii).

[58] Treas. Reg. §§ 1.755-1(c)(3), (4).

[59] Note that while in our example we are liquidating C's interest, in part to simplify the math, I.R.C. § 734(b) also applies when a partner's interest in the partnership is merely reduced.

P/S Assets	Adj. Basis	F.M.V.	Partners	Adj. Basis	F.M.V.
			A	$10,000	$18,000
Land #1	$12,000	$24,000	B	$10,000	$18,000
Land #2	$8,000	$12,000			
Total	$20,000	$36,000		$20,000	$36,000

I.R.C. § 734(b) can interact with both I.R.C. § 732(d) (discussed above) and I.R.C. § 743(b). Assume that E buys A's interest in the ABC partnership and no I.R.C. § 754 election is in effect. Within two years of the purchase, the partnership makes an I.R.C. § 754 election and distributes property to E that reduces E's interest in the partnership from one-third to one-quarter. Assume E's outside basis in the partnership interest is $10,000. The partnership's "regular" basis in the distributed property is $8,000, but the basis in that property for I.R.C. § 732(d) purposes is $12,000. It is that latter basis that is used for determining whether I.R.C. § 734(b) applies.[60] Because for these purposes the partnership's inside basis of $12,000 exceeds E's outside basis of $10,000, there is an upward I.R.C. § 734(b) adjustment of $2,000 that applies to the same class of property as the class to which the distributed property belonged.

Assume the same facts set forth above except that an I.R.C. § 754 election was in effect before E's purchase and at the time of the distribution.[61] Assume after making the I.R.C. § 743(b) adjustment, with regard to E, the property's basis is $12,000. The answer would be the same as when I.R.C. § 732(d) applied.[62]

C. Mandatory "As If" I.R.C. § 754 Elections

As we noted above, I.R.C. § 754 elections can result in downward adjustments as well as upward adjustments. Downward adjustments are much less fun. Assume, for example, that A, B and C form a partnership. In year 1, A and B each contribute $300,000 and C contributes $600,000. The partnership purchases two parcels of land. Both are capital assets. The partnership pays $400,000 for Parcel #1 and $800,000 for Parcel #2. In year 2 Parcel #2 drops in value to $400,000. In year 2 the partnership distributes Parcel #1 to C in liquidation of his interest. Under the liquidation rules, discussed in detail below, C's basis in Parcel #1 is $600,000, her entire outside basis.[63] If the values do not change, C will recognize a $200,000 capital loss when he sells this parcel. As we discussed above, if an I.R.C. § 754 election is in effect, the partnership must reduce its basis in Parcel #2 by $200,000, the excess of C's basis in Parcel #1 over the basis it had to the

---

[60] *See* I.R.C. § 734(b)(1)(B), (2)(B).

[61] To create the higher I.R.C. § 743(b) adjustment in the distributed property, E's outside basis must exceed E's share of the inside basis. So why is E's outside basis now less than the basis of the partnership property after accounting for I.R.C. § 743(b)? Perhaps E's outside basis was reduced in the interim by cash distributions or partnership losses.

[62] For an article discussing some of the problems with I.R.C. § 734(b), *see* Howard Abrams, *The Section 734(b) Basis Adjustment Needs Repair*, 57 Tax Law. 343 (2004).

[63] I.R.C. § 732(b).

partnership. That would give the partnership a basis of $600,000 in Parcel #2. Assuming no value changes, the partnership would then recognize a $200,000 capital loss on the sale of Parcel #2 ($400,000 - $600,000). But if an I.R.C. § 754 election is not in effect, there is no basis adjustment, and the partnership will recognize a $400,000 loss on the sale of Parcel #2 ($400,000 - $800,000), effectively duplicating C's loss on the sale of Parcel #1.

Congress was unenthusiastic about this duplication (though gains can also be duplicated if no I.R.C. § 754 election is in effect — though it is more likely to be in effect if the partnership is sane, or at least well-advised). As a consequence, the American Jobs Creation Act of 2004 amended I.R.C. § 734(b) to mandate a downward basis adjustment, even if no I.R.C. § 754 election is in effect, if there is a "substantial basis reduction." New I.R.C. § 734(d) provides that a substantial basis reduction exists if the downward adjustments provided in I.R.C. § 734(b)(2) exceed $250,000.[64] As we discussed above, I.R.C. § 734(b)(2) provides for a downward basis adjustment if a distributee partner recognizes a loss on distribution or takes a greater basis in distributed partnership property than that which the partnership had, both of which can only happen in liquidation. Normally, an I.R.C. § 754 election must be in effect for the I.R.C. § 734(b)(2) adjustments to be applicable, but the amendments to the code trigger the adjustments when an I.R.C. § 754 election is not in effect if the adjustment would exceed $250,000. In the above example, this new rule would not apply as the basis adjustment would have only been $200,000, but had it exceeded $250,000, the partnership would have had to reduce the basis of Parcel #2 even if an I.R.C. § 754 election were not in effect.[65]

§ 8.08 SHIFTS IN ORDINARY INCOME PROPERTY

A. Introduction

Congress would not have been wise to stop with the rules we have discussed so far, for if it did, it would be easy for a distributee partner to avoid ordinary income recognition, at least if her other partners were cooperative. For example, assume that a partner in that partnership with a $10,000 basis in her partnership interest receives $15,000 of cash in complete liquidation of the partnership interest. Based on the rules we have discussed so far, the partner recognizes *capital* gain of $5,000 on the distribution under I.R.C. § 731(a)(1). It would be capital gain because I.R.C. § 731(a) provides that any gain or loss recognized is considered to be gain or loss from the sale or exchange of the distributee's partnership interest, and under I.R.C. § 741 the partnership interest is (essentially) a capital asset to the distributee.

But what if the partnership holds ordinary income assets such as receivables and inventory? Without other Code provisions, the distributee partner could avoid recognizing her share of any ordinary income she would have recognized had she

---

[64] There is an exception for "securitization partnerships." *See* I.R.C. § 734(e).

[65] There is a corresponding rule in I.R.C. § 743, discussed in Chapter 6. *See* Jeffery Rosenberg, *AJCA Imposes New Burdens for Partnership Basis Adjustments Under Sections 734 and 743*, 101 J. Tax'n 334 (2004).

stayed a partner and the partnership had collected the receivables or sold the inventory. Or saying the same thing in other words, she would have converted ordinary income into capital gain. Congress hates that and enacted I.R.C. § 751(b) in response. In Chapter 7 we discussed I.R.C. § 751(a), which performs a similar function in the case of a sale of a partnership interest. Effectively, I.R.C. § 751(b) trumps the other rules of I.R.C. §§ 731 and 732 and requires ordinary income (and possibly other gain or loss) recognition on the part of the partner and/or the partnership if a distribution shifts the partners' interests in certain ordinary income property.

B. Unrealized Receivables and Substantially Appreciated Inventory

I.R.C. § 751(b) will apply if the partnership holds unrealized receivables or substantially appreciated inventory.[66] To simplify our lives, we will sometimes call unrealized receivables and inventory "I.R.C. § 751 property." You should know that tax professionals also sometimes refer to these assets as "hot assets." We will sometimes call any other property "I.R.C. § 741 property." We covered I.R.C. § 751 property in detail in Chapter 7, but some additional rules apply to inventory.

Inventory is an I.R.C. § 751(b) asset only if it is "substantially appreciated," meaning that it has a fair market value in excess of 120 percent of its adjusted basis.[67] It would conceivably be possible to manipulate this test by buying inventory for quick resale. The basis and fair market value would be about the same. When added to the "genuine" inventory, it would increase the basis of the inventory proportionately more than the fair market value, and it might help the partnership avoid the substantial appreciation test. To help thwart such efforts, I.R.C. § 751(b)(3)(B) contains an anti-stuffing rule, which provides that any property acquired for the principal purpose of avoiding the application of I.R.C. § 751(b) will not be counted as inventory.

Under I.R.C. § 751(d)(2), inventory includes any property that would not constitute a capital or I.R.C. § 1231 asset. As a consequence, unrealized receivables usually also meet the definition for inventory (though this outcome was probably unintended). This is important because it makes it far easier for inventory to meet the substantial appreciation test for partnerships on the cash method of accounting.[68] The typical unrealized receivable will have a basis of zero. It would thus add nothing to basis, but increase the overall fair market value of inventory items, making it more likely that the fair market value of the inventory will exceed 120% of their adjusted basis. Of course, for I.R.C. § 751(b) purposes, you cannot count an asset more than once. Thus, while unrealized receivables can count as inventory for purposes of the substantial appreciation test, they go back to their

---

[66] Note that for I.R.C. § 751(a) purposes, the inventory does not need to be substantially appreciated.

[67] I.R.C. § 751(b)(3)(A); special basis adjustments of a partner are ignored for these purposes. Treas. Reg. § 1.751-1(d)(1).

[68] Though, typically, businesses with inventory are required to use accrual accounting; see I.R.C. §§ 446, 471 and Rev. Proc. 2002-28, 2002-18 I.R.B. 815.

regular status for purposes of implementing I.R.C. § 751(b).[69]

Assume a partnership has the following balance sheet:

P/S Assets	Adj. Basis	F.M.V.	Partners	Adj. Basis	F.M.V.
Cash	$30,000	$30,000	A	$16,000	$26,600
Inventory	$18,000	$19,800	B	$16,000	$26,600
Acct. Rec.	0	$30,000	C	$16,000	$26,800
Total	$48,000	$79,000		$48,000	$79,000

Note that the "true" inventory by itself is not substantially appreciated. The fair market value of $19,800 is only 110% of the $18,000 basis. But when the accounts receivable are added in, the inventory becomes substantially appreciated. The combined fair market value of $49,800 is more than double the combined basis of $18,000.

If a partnership is on the accrual method of accounting, on the other hand, counting the accounts receivable as inventory might actually prevent the inventory from being substantially appreciated. For example:

P/S Assets	Adj. Basis	F.M.V.	Partners	Adj. Basis	F.M.V.
Cash	$21,000	$21,000	A	$21,000	$22,000
Inventory	$2,000	$5,000	B	$21,000	$22,000
Acct. Rec.	$40,000	$40,000	C	$21,000	$22,000
Total	$63,000	$66,000		$63,000	$66,000

In this example, the fair market value of the inventory is more than double its basis, but when the accounts receivable are added in, the fair market value of $45,000 is less than 120% of the basis of $42,000.

C. The Nuts and Bolts

Now let's take a more detailed look. Assume that A, B, and C are equal partners in the ABC partnership. The partnership has the following balance sheet:

P/S Assets	Adj. Basis	F.M.V.	Partners	Adj. Basis	F.M.V.
Cash	$30,000	$30,000	A	$18,000	$30,000
Inventory	$18,000	$30,000	B	$18,000	$30,000
Cap. Asset	$6,000	$30,000	C	$18,000	$30,000
Total	$54,000	$90,000		$54,000	$90,000

Assume that partner C receives the inventory in liquidation of his interest. It is of no particular significance that it is a liquidating as opposed to an nonliquidating distribution; we have made it a liquidating distribution in order to make the

---

[69] *See* Treas. Reg. § 1.751-1(g), example 2.

numbers easier to follow. Note that the inventory is substantially appreciated. The fair market value of $30,000 exceeds 120% of the basis of $18,000 (120% of $18,000 is $21,600). Also, assume that the capital asset has been held for over one year. If I.R.C. § 751(b) did not exist, C would receive the inventory with a basis of $18,000 and a fair market value of $30,000 and his basis in his partnership interest would be reduced to zero.[70] There is $12,000 of gain inherent in the inventory in C's hands. There is $24,000 of gain inherent in the capital asset that the partnership continues to hold, or $12,000 each for A and B. Thus, all the partners have the same *amount* of gain that they had before C's interest was liquidated. But, the *character* of the gain has changed. If the partnership had sold all of its assets before C's interest was liquidated, each partner would have had $4,000 of ordinary income and $8,000 of long-term capital gain. If the partnership sells all of its assets and C sells the inventory after C's interest is liquidated, A and B each have $12,000 of long-term capital gain and C has $12,000 of ordinary income.[71] A and B have shifted their shares of the ordinary income that was inherent in the inventory to C; that is, A and B have converted ordinary income into capital gains. I.R.C. § 751(b) stops this, though as we will see, it does not always do so perfectly. While it prevents partners from converting ordinary income into capital gains, it does not always prevent partners from shifting ordinary income amongst themselves.[72]

The mechanics of I.R.C. § 751(b) are complex. The starting point of I.R.C. § 751(b) is that each partner has, in effect, an undivided interest in the assets that constitute I.R.C. § 751 property and I.R.C. § 741 property. If an interest in one class is swapped for an interest in the other class, a taxable event has occurred. Note that partners (or LLC members) are generally not considered to have an ownership interest in partnership (or LLC) property for state law purposes.[73] I.R.C. § 751(b) creates a fiction to avoid ordinary income shifting. From the perspective of I.R.C. § 751(b), C holds a one-third interest in the partnership assets consisting of:

Assets	Adjusted Basis	F.M.V.
Cash	$10,000	$10,000
Inventory	$6,000	$10,000
Capital Asset	$2,000	$10,000
Total	$18,000	$30,000

C effectively exchanged his interest in the cash and the capital asset (the I.R.C. § 741 assets) for the "extra" two-thirds of the inventory (the I.R.C. § 751(b) asset). I.R.C. § 751(b) requires C and the partnership (now A and B) to treat what is an exchange in substance as an exchange for tax purposes.[74]

---

[70] I.R.C. §§ 731(a), 732(b), (c)(1)(A).

[71] I.R.C. § 735(a)(2).

[72] *See* Monte Jackel and Avery Stok, *Blissful Ignorance: Section 751(b) Uncharted Territory*, 98 Tax Notes 1557 (2003).

[73] *See* Revised Uniform Partnership Act ("RUPA") § 203.

[74] Treas. Reg. § 1.751-1(b)(2)(i).

The partnership is deemed to make a phantom distribution of the I.R.C. § 741 assets to C. The partners may actually choose which I.R.C. § 741 assets are deemed to be distributed to C. The partners could, for example, choose just the cash or just the capital asset. If there is no specific agreement, as we will assume here, C is deemed to receive a pro rata share of each I.R.C. § 741 asset.[75] Thus, the partnership is thus deemed to make a phantom distribution to C of one-third of the cash and the capital asset. The "regular" distribution rules apply to this phantom distribution. C thus first reduces his $18,000 basis for the $10,000 of cash deemed received, leaving him with a basis of $8,000 in the partnership interest. C then reduces his basis by the partnership's $2,000 basis in the capital asset and takes a full carryover basis in that asset, leaving C with a $6,000 basis in his partnership interest. Under I.R.C. § 731, C recognizes no gain or loss.

C now enters into a phantom, taxable exchange with the partnership, as follows:

C		Partnership
Cash $10,000 and		Inventory
Capital Asset	For	F.M.V. $20,000
F.M.V. $10,000		Basis $12,000
Basis $2,000		

C recognizes $8,000 of capital gain on the capital asset and the partnership recognizes $8,000 of ordinary income on the inventory.[76] Logically enough, the Regulations require that the partnership's ordinary income be allocated to A and B.[77] Note that at this point A and B have recognized their pro rata shares of the ordinary income inherent in the inventory and each will increase his basis in his partnership interest by the $4,000 of income recognized.[78] C will take a fair market basis of $20,000 in two-thirds of the inventory, and the partnership will take a fair market value basis of $10,000 in one-third of the capital asset.[79]

After the phantom exchange (but prior to the distribution of the remaining one-third of the inventory to C), the balance sheet of the partnership is as follows:

Assets	Adj. Basis	F.M.V.	Partners	Adj. Basis	F.M.V.
Cash	$30,000	$30,000	A	$22,000	$30,000
Inventory	$6,000	$10,000	B	$22,000	$30,000
Cap. Asset	$14,000	$30,000	C	$6,000	$10,000
Total	$50,000	$70,000		$50,000	$70,000

The regular operating rules are now back in effect, and the final one-third of the inventory is deemed distributed to C. C takes a basis of $6,000 in the one-third of

---

[75] Treas. Reg. § 1.751-1(g), example 4(c).

[76] I.R.C. §§ 1001(a), (c).

[77] Treas. Reg. §§ 1.751-1(b)(2)(ii), (b)(3)(ii).

[78] I.R.C. § 705(a)(1)(A).

[79] I.R.C. § 1012.

the inventory, his partnership interest basis is reduced to zero, and he recognizes no gain on the distribution.[80] C thus now holds the inventory with a total basis of $26,000 (fair market value basis of $20,000 in two-thirds of the inventory under I.R.C. § 1012 plus a $6,000 carryover basis under I.R.C. § 732(b) for the final one-third of the inventory considered distributed). Assuming its value does not change, when C sells the inventory for $30,000, he recognizes $4,000 of ordinary income. This is what his share of ordinary income inherent in the inventory was to begin with when the partnership held it, and all is right with the world.

The balance sheet of the partnership after completion of the transaction is as follows:

Assets	Adj. Basis	F.M.V.	Partners	Adj. Basis	F.M.V.
Cash	$30,000	$30,000	A	$22,000	$30,000
Cap. Asset	$14,000	$30,000	B	$22,000	$30,000
Total	$44,000	$60,000		$44,000	$60,000

Note that in order for I.R.C. § 751(b) to apply, an interest in the I.R.C § 751 property must be swapped for an interest in the I.R.C. § 741 property. If C had simply received a distribution with a value of $30,000 consisting of his proportionate one-third share of I.R.C. § 751(b) property plus cash and/or a portion of the capital asset to make up the difference, no deemed swap would have occurred, and I.R.C. § 751(b) would not have applied. Further, I.R.C. § 751(b) will not apply to a distribution of property that the distributee contributed to the partnership.[81] I.R.C. § 751(b) also will not apply to I.R.C. § 736(a) payments[82] (discussed below), draws or advances that a partner receives against his distributive share of partnership income, or to gifts, payments for services, or use of capital.[83]

Now let's look at an example involving a nonliquidating distribution.[84] Assume the ABC Partnership has the following balance sheet:

Assets	Adj. Basis	F.M.V.	Partners	Adj. Basis	F.M.V.
Cash	$24,000	$24,000	A	$12,000	$24,000

---

[80] I.R.C. §§ 731(a)(1), 732(b) and 733(2). Technically, because it is a liquidating distribution, C does not take a carryover basis in the one-third of the inventory, as would be the case if it had been an operating distribution. Instead, his basis in his partnership interest of $6,000 becomes the basis in this part of the inventory. Note that if it had been an operating distribution, C's carryover basis would have been the same $6,000. Further, a partner is never permitted to take a greater basis than that which the partnership had in inventory and unrealized receivables, regardless of the type of distribution involved. I.R.C. § 732(c)(1).

[81] I.R.C. § 751(b)(2)(A).

[82] I.R.C. § 751(b)(2)(B).

[83] Treas. Reg. § 1.751-1(b)(i)(ii).

[84] See Treas. Reg. § 1.751-1(g), Ex. 6. For a discussion of some special problems that can arise with nonliquidating distributions, see Federal Taxation of Partnerships and Partners at ¶ 21.03[8].

Equipment	0	$24,000	B	$12,000	$24,000
Cap. Asset	$12,000	$24,000	C	$12,000	$24,000
Total	$36,000	$72,000		$36,000	$72,000

Assume all of the gain inherent in the equipment is I.R.C. § 1245 recapture and thus is treated as an unrealized receivable. Assume the partnership distributes $12,000 of cash to C and C is reduced to a one-fifth partner.

To ascertain whether C has "exchanged" his interest in I.R.C. § 751 property for additional I.R.C. § 741 property, we can either compare his interest in I.R.C § 751 property before and after the distribution, or his interest in I.R.C. § 741 property before and after the distribution. Either approach will yield the same result.

C's indirect interest in I.R.C § 751 property:

Before the Distribution	1/3 of recapture of $24,000 =	$8,000
After the Distribution	1/5 of recapture of $24,000 =	$4,800
C's share dropped by		($3,200)

Similarly, C's indirect interest in I.R.C. § 741 property:

Before the Distribution	1/3 of combined value of cash and capital asset or 1/3 of $48,000 =	$16,000
After the Distribution	1/5 of combined value cash and capital asset, or 1/5 of $36,000 = $7,200 plus distributed cash of $12,000 =	$19,200
C's share increased by		$3,200

Accordingly, C must receive a phantom distribution of $3,200 of the "recapture unrealized receivable" that he will be deemed to exchange with the partnership for $3,200 of cash that was actually received. C's carryover basis in the recapture unrealized receivable is zero, C will have $3,200 of ordinary income on the transaction and the partnership will have a basis step-up in the equipment of the same amount. Then, under the regular distribution rules, C receives the balance of the cash of $8,800, reducing his basis in the partnership interest to $3.200. Thus, the partnership's balance sheet is as follows:

Assets	Adj. Basis	F.M.V.	Partners	Adj. Basis	F.M.V.
Cash	$12,000	$12,000	A	$12,000	$24,000
Equipment	$3,200	$24,000	B	$12,000	$24,000
Cap. Asset	$12,000	$24,000	C	$3,200	$12,000
Total	$27,200	$60,000		$27,200	$60,000

D. Associated Issues

In the example just above, assume that C purchased his interest in the partnership from X for $24,000 and that since the time of the purchase both the value of the partnership assets and their bases are as stated above. Assume further that no I.R.C. § 754 election is in effect and more than two years has elapsed since C's purchase. C would in effect have paid $8,000 of the purchase price for an indirect one-third interest in the equipment. Nonetheless, C will have to recognize the same amount of ordinary income as in the example above because no I.R.C. § 754 election was made. If, on the other hand, C's share of the equipment is distributed to C within two years of C's purchase of the interest, then I.R.C. § 732(d), discussed above, would provide relief and for purposes of the distribution give C the equivalent of an I.R.C. § 754 election.[85]

In Rev. Rul. 77-412,[86] the IRS ruled that I.R.C. § 751(b) applies to the liquidation of a two-person partnership, even though the partnership ceased to exist with the liquidating distributions. Under the Ruling "the distribution is treated as a sale or exchange of such properties between the distributee partner and the partnership (as constituted after the distribution), even though after the distribution the partnership consists of a single individual." The Ruling notes that it does not make any difference which partner is considered to be the distributee partner and which partner is considered to be "the partnership" for purposes of making the I.R.C. § 751(b) exchange. While this was true under the facts of the Ruling, it will not necessarily be true with partnerships with more than two members that make disproportionate distributions of I.R.C § 751 property.

Liability shifts can also create I.R.C. § 751(b) issues. Assume a partnership with liabilities and I.R.C § 751 property distributes cash to a partner in liquidation of that partner's partnership interest. The total amount of cash considered to be distributed for purposes of doing the I.R.C. § 751(b) calculation would include both the money actually distributed and the money deemed distributed under I.R.C. § 752(b) as a result of the distributee partner's reduction in his share of partnership liabilities.

I.R.C. §§ 751(b)/752(b) issues can also arise when a partner enters the partnership. In Revenue Ruling 84-102,[87] a partnership had liabilities and unrealized receivables. When the new partner entered the partnership, he was allocated a share of the existing partnership liabilities under I.R.C. § 752(a) and concomitantly, the other partners' shares of partnership liabilities were reduced, resulting in a deemed distribution of money under I.R.C. § 752(b). Because the new partner also was considered to share in the existing unrealized receivables, all the elements necessary to trigger I.R.C. § 751(b) were in place. The existing partners' shares of the unrealized receivables changed, and they were deemed to receive a distribution of money. Consequently, the IRS ruled that I.R.C. § 751(b) applied to the existing partners. The IRS also ruled that I.R.C. § 751(b) did not apply to the entering partner as there was no actual or constructive distribution of property to

---

[85] *See* Treas. Reg. § 1.751-1(b)(2)(iii) and (b)(3)(iii).

[86] 1977-2 C.B. 223.

[87] 1984-2 C.B. 119.

him. The consequences of the Revenue Ruling can be avoided if the partnership does not allocate existing liabilities or a share of the unrealized receivables to the incoming partner. The latter could be achieved by a revaluation or an appropriate allocation provision.

Note that unlike I.R.C. § 751(a), which focuses on giving a selling partner his share of the gain or loss inherent in each hot asset of the partnership, I.R.C. § 751(b) focuses on whether the partner received his proportionate share of I.R.C § 751 property based on the overall fair market values. This can permit some ordinary income shifting. Assume, for example, that the one-third interest of partner A in the ABC partnership is liquidated. The partnership has $30,000 of I.R.C § 751 property, including $15,000 of unrealized receivables with a zero basis and $15,000 of substantially appreciated inventory with a significant basis. Assume there is more gain inherent in the unrealized receivables than in the inventory and that the partnership wishes to distribute to A his one-third share of I.R.C § 751 property. In doing so, the partnership can choose $10,000 of higher gain unrealized receivables or $10,000 of lower gain inventory or a combination of both.[88]

§ 8.09 LIQUIDATIONS OF PARTNERSHIPS AND PARTNERSHIP INTERESTS

A. Introduction

We will cover two topics, the complete liquidation of a partnership and the liquidation of a partner's interest where the partnership, as such, continues. There are a number of variations on this theme. Many of the rules we have discussed so far will apply and, in some cases, fully resolve the tax issues. But some additional rules are necessary to address differences between the partner's outside basis and the basis of distributed property.

B. Liquidations of the Partnership or of a Partnership Interest

State law on partnership termination is not controlling for federal tax purposes. [89] I.R.C. § 708(b)(1)(A) provides that a partnership terminates "if no part of any business, financial operation, or venture of the partnership continues to be carried on by any of its partners in a partnership." Note that this definition is met if one partner buys the interests of the other partners and continues the partnership

---

[88] The IRS has indicated that it is considering extensive changes to the I.R.C. § 751(b) rules. One possible change would make the I.R.C. § 751(b) rules similar to the I.R.C. § 751(a) rules and prevent this type of income shifting. Notice 2006-14, 2006-1 C.B. 498 (Feb 2, 2006). Similar changes were proposed in2014 by the House Ways in Means Committee in its Tax Reform Act.

[89] *See* the Revised Uniform Partnership Act ("RUPA") § 801 for events causing dissolution and winding up of a state law partnership. RUPA § 802 provides that a partnership is terminated after it has been wound up. This may or may not coincide with the tax definition. Also see *Fuchs v. Commissioner*, 80 T.C. 506 (1983).

business, but no longer in partnership form.[90] On the other hand, the death of one partner in a two-person partnership will not terminate the partnership if the estate or other successor of the deceased partner continues to share in profits or losses of the partnership business.[91] If the surviving partner purchases the interest of the deceased partner, the partnership would, of course, terminate.

If a partnership terminates, its tax year closes for all of the partners.[92] Any successor partnership would thus be a new partnership permitting (or requiring) fresh elections. Similarly, if the interest of a particular partner terminates, the tax year closes with regard to that partner; the relevant share of income and expense arising from the beginning of the partnership tax year up to when it closes is allocated to that partner.[93]

If a partnership terminates or if the interest of an individual partner is liquidated, the rules we have discussed generally govern with a few additions. As we discussed above, if a partner's outside basis is less than the partnership's inside basis in distributed property, under I.R.C. § 732(a)(2), the partner's basis in that property is limited to the outside basis. But what if the converse is the case and the partner's outside basis exceeds the partnership's basis in the distributed property?

I.R.C. § 732 provides that a distributee partner cannot take a greater basis in distributed inventory and unrealized receivables than that which the partnership had. To permit the partner to take a greater basis in these assets would enable the distributee partner to avoid ordinary income. Under I.R.C. § 731(a)(2), if the only assets that are distributed to a partner are cash, unrealized receivables, and inventory, and the partner's outside basis exceeds the amount of distributed cash and the carryover basis in the unrealized receivables and inventory, the partner recognizes a loss to the extent of any unused basis. The loss is considered to arise from the sale or exchange of the partnership interest and is, therefore, a capital loss.

For example, assume that A is a one-third partner in the ABC partnership. The partnership uses the calendar year for reporting and makes a liquidating distribution to A on January 1 (making it unnecessary to allocate any income or expense from the current year to A). The partnership distributes to A in complete liquidation of his interest $10,000 of cash and inventory with a basis of $4,000 and a fair market value of $15,000. A's outside basis in his partnership interest is $20,000. After reducing A's basis for the cash and a carryover basis in the inventory, A has $6,000 of basis left over. A recognizes a $6,000 capital loss from the sale or exchange of the partnership interest as a consequence. Note that the fair market value of the assets and cash A receives is $25,000, which exceeds her basis of $20,000. Economically, therefore, A has a gain on the transaction. Nonetheless, A recognizes a loss to preserve the ordinary income in the inventory. When A sells the inventory for $15,000, she will recognize $11,000 of ordinary income. Offset that

---

[90] Treas. Reg. § 1.708-1(b)(1); *see also* Harbor Cove Marina Partners Partnership v. Commissioner, 123 T.C. 64 (2004).

[91] Treas. Reg. § 1.708-1(b)(1)(i).

[92] I.R.C. § 706(c)(1).

[93] I.R.C. § 706(c)(2)(A); *see* § 5.09.

against the $6,000 loss, and it nets to the $5,000 economic gain A had on the liquidation and all is right with the world. Also note that if A does not receive his proportional share of I.R.C § 751 property, I.R.C. § 751(b) will apply.

Recall that fundamental to all of Subchapter K is the preference for avoiding gain or loss on contributions of property to a partnership and distributions of property to a partner. In the above example, Congress could not avoid loss recognition. There was $6,000 of unused basis, and Congress could not give A a greater basis in I.R.C § 751 property than that which the partnership had and still maintain one of the holier principles in the world of tax, preserving ordinary income. However, if A receives any other assets, we can simply shift any unused basis to those assets, even if it means that A takes a greater basis in those assets than that which the partnership had. Assume in the above example that A's partnership interest is more valuable and that in addition to the cash and inventory, the partnership also distributes land to A and that the land is a capital asset to the partnership. The land has basis to the partnership of $2,000 and a fair market value of $10,000. After reducing her basis for the cash and the inventory, A has $6,000 of basis in the partnership interest left. That $6,000 is allocated to the land, giving A greater basis in the land than that which the partnership had.

If a partnership distributes several assets to a partner (excluding I.R.C § 751 property) and the partner's outside basis exceeds the partnership's aggregate bases in the distributed properties, the Code provides rules for allocating the "extra" basis among the distributed properties. It is first allocated in proportion to the relative appreciation inherent in the distributed properties. If the extra basis exceeds the inherent appreciation, any remaining amount is allocated based on the relative fair market values of the distributed assets. In the above example, assume that instead of one parcel of land, A receives two parcels each with a basis of $1,000 and a fair market value of $6,000. A has $6,000 of available basis. A carryover basis in each asset would use $2,000 of that $6,000. The extra $4,000 must be allocated based on the relative appreciation in the assets. In this example, each asset has the same amount of appreciation, or $5,000. Accordingly, half of the extra $4,000 of basis is allocated to each asset, or $2,000 each. Thus, A's basis in each parcel of land is $3,000.

Recall that a partner is ordinarily paid the balance of his capital account on the liquidation of his partnership interest. As we discussed above, for the capital accounts to perform their function properly, the Regulations provide that they must be adjusted for any book gain or loss inherent in distributed property, notwithstanding the fact that tax gain or loss might not be recognized.[94]

---

[94] Treas. Reg. § 1.704-1(b)(2)(iv)(e)(1).

C. I.R.C. § 736 Payments

1. Introduction

I.R.C. § 736 applies when a partner retires from the partnership and the partnership continues.[95] It is in some ways a curious provision. Subchapter K could probably live without I.R.C. § 736 and instead merge its key provisions into I.R.C. § 751(b). But to date Congress has not seen fit to do that, and as a consequence, you will have to learn to juggle the two Code sections. I.R.C. § 736 does serve a useful function. If payments made to a retiring partner are either guaranteed payments (discussed in Chapter 9) or a distributive share of partnership income, they reduce the income of the other partners. If payments are for the partner's share of partnership property, they generally fall within the regular rules for distributions (and thus do not reduce partnership income). Which category a particular payment fits into obviously has a great deal of tax significance. I.R.C. § 736 gives a substantial measure of certainty to this area, though questions remain.

A primary focus of I.R.C. § 736 is the tax treatment of payments of money to a retiring partner over time, but it can also apply when a retiring partner's interest is fully liquidated with a single payment. Further, while the clear implication of the statute is that payments will be made with money, there is nothing in the statute to prevent payments being made with property other than money.[96] Making payments with property can create a number of theoretical problems.[97] Further, as I.R.C. § 736 applies to "payments," it suggests that the partner is being "paid" (typically with money) for his interest in something else (typically partnership property). Therefore, if a partner only receives a pro rata distribution of the assets of the partnership, it does not seem that I.R.C. § 736 should apply.

I.R.C. § 736 divides the world into I.R.C. § 736(a) payments and I.R.C. § 736(b) payments. I.R.C. § 736(b) applies to payments for the retiring partner's interest in partnership property. I.R.C. § 736(a) applies to all other payments. I.R.C. § 736(a) and (b) merely classify payments. Other Code provisions that we have covered in this and other chapters govern the tax treatment of those payments.

2. I.R.C. § 736(a) Payments

I.R.C. § 736(a) covers all payments not within I.R.C. § 736(b). I.R.C. § 736(a) does not apply to all partnerships in the same way. I.R.C. § 736 has different rules for partnerships in which "capital is an income producing factor" and for limited partners in all partnerships on the one hand, and for *general* partners in partnerships in which capital *is not* a material income-producing factor on the other hand.[98] According to the legislative history, capital is not an income producing factor where substantially all of the gross income of the business consists of fees,

---

[95] It can also apply to payments made to the successor-in-interest of a deceased partner. I.R.C. § 736(a).

[96] *See* Willis, Pennell, Postlewaite, *Partnership Taxation* ¶ 15.06[1], [2].

[97] *Id* at ¶ 15.06.

[98] *See* I.R.C. § 736(b)(2), (3).

commissions, or other compensation for personal services. Note that under this definition the practice of her profession by a lawyer, accountant, doctor, or architect will not be treated as a trade or business in which capital is a material income-producing factor even though the professional may have a substantial capital investment in professional plant or equipment if that investment is merely incidental to the performance of the services.[99] We will call these "services partnerships."

In a services partnership, I.R.C. § 736(a) applies to payments to withdrawing general partners for:

1. Partnership unrealized receivables to the extent their fair market value exceeds any basis the partnership has in them (unrealized receivables do not include recapture for these purposes),[100] and

2. "Unstated goodwill" to the extent the fair market value exceeds the partnership's basis. Unstated goodwill exists where part of the value of the partnership indeed includes goodwill, but the partnership agreement does not provide for payments for goodwill. Thus the goodwill is unstated.[101]

In any kind of partnership (services or nonservices), I.R.C. § 736(a) applies to the portion of the payment that exceeds the partner's share of the fair market value of all partnership property (including goodwill), sometimes known as "premium payments."[102] Note that premium payments are the only item included in I.R.C. § 736(a) if capital is a material income-producing factor. Premium payments are also the only item included in I.R.C. § 736(a) for services partnerships making payments to *non*general partners (i.e., limited partners).

3.   I.R.C. § 736(b) Payments

I.R.C. § 736(b) applies to all payments for a partner's interest in partnership property. Thus, in a *non*services partnership, I.R.C. § 736(b) will apply to all payments to a retiring partner except premium payments. In a services partnership, I.R.C. § 736(b) will apply to payments attributable to any basis the partnership has in unrealized receivables and goodwill as well, in the case of payments to a general partner, to payments for goodwill in excess of that basis if goodwill is stated.[103] Thus, services partnerships making payments to general partners have the option of having I.R.C. § 736(b) cover the appreciation in goodwill or not by their choice to include a relevant provision in the partnership agreement (i.e., to state goodwill), or not. As the tax consequences of I.R.C. §§ 736(a) and (b) are different, this provides for a planning opportunity depending on the tax circumstances of the partners.

A question that is unanswered by the Code and Regulations is what constitutes goodwill. Items that might be included are customer lists, insurance agency listings,

---

[99] H.R. No. 103-11, 103rd Cong., 1st Sess. 345 (1993).

[100] I.R.C. § 751(c) flush language.

[101] *See* I.R.C. § 736(b)(2)(B).

[102] Treas. Reg. § 1.736-1(a)(3).

[103] Treas. Reg. § 1.736-1(b)(2), (3).

formulas, know-how, going concern value (i.e., the fact that a business is up and running), the value of the company's name, to name but a few).[104]

The distribution rules discussed earlier in this chapter apply to I.R.C. § 736(b) payments. Thus, the relevant Code sections are I.R.C. §§ 731, 741, and 751(b). We address these rules in detail below.

4.   Allocating and Taxing I.R.C. § 736 Payments

I.R.C. § 736 applies whether a retiring partner receives a single payment for his partnership interest or is paid for it over time. If a partner receives a single payment in liquidation of his partnership interest, the payment is allocated between the I.R.C. §§ 736(a) and (b) payments pursuant to the rules discussed above. If a partner receives payments over a period of years, the parties may agree on how a payment in a given year is allocated provided that the aggregate amount allocated to property under I.R.C. § 736(b) does not exceed the fair market value of such property at the date of the retirement.[105] Barring that, the Regulations provide a formula for allocating the payment; this varies depending on whether the payments are fixed in amount or not. If the partnership pays the retiring partner a fixed amount over a fixed number of years, the following formula is used to allocate a portion of each annual payment to I.R.C. § 736(b):[106]

$$\text{I.R.C. § 736(b) amount} = \text{Total Payment Fixed for Year} \times \frac{\text{Total Fixed Agreed 736(b) Payments}}{\text{Total I.R.C. §§ 736(a) and (b) Fixed Agreed Payments}}$$

The balance, if any, of the amount received in the same taxable year falls within I.R.C. § 736(a). If the payments are not fixed because, for example, the retiring partner is paid a percentage of partnership profits each year, the partnership's payments are first considered to be I.R.C. § 736(b) payments. Once the I.R.C. § 736(b) amount has been fully paid, payments are then considered to be I.R.C. § 736(a) payments.[107]

If the payments are fixed, I.R.C. § 736(a) payments are treated as guaranteed payment under I.R.C. § 707(c),[108] with the proviso that they are deductible to the partnership and considered ordinary income to the retiring partner.[109] Following the general rules for guaranteed payments (discussed in Chapter 9), it is income to a recipient for his tax year with or within which ends the partnership tax year in which the guaranteed payment may be deducted. When the payments are not fixed, the portion falling within I.R.C. § 736(a) is treated as a distributive share of partnership under I.R.C. § 702. For example, if a partner is allocated a 10% share of partnership income and the partnership incurs ordinary income and capital gains,

---

[104]   *See* Willis, Pennell, Postlewaite, *Partnership Taxation* at ¶ 15.03[2].

[105]   Treas. Reg. § 1.736-1(b)(5)(iii).

[106]   Treas. Reg. § 1.736-1(b)(5)(i).

[107]   Treas. Reg. § 1.736-1(b)(5)(ii).

[108]   I.R.C. § 736(a)(2).

[109]   Treas. Reg. § 1.736-1(a)(4).

then the portion of the payments falling within I.R.C. § 736(a) is partly ordinary income and partly capital gains.[110] These I.R.C. § 736(a) payments are again income to the retiring partner for his tax year with or within which ends the partnership tax year to which the allocable share is attributable.

Note that if the partnership can fit a payment within I.R.C. § 736(a), it gets a deduction or its equivalent and the withdrawing partner has income. If the payment falls within I.R.C. § 736(b), the partnership gets no deduction or its equivalent and the withdrawing partner normally recovers basis or has capital gain or loss (subject to the application of I.R.C. § 751(b)). Thus, from both the partner's and the partnership's perspectives, how a payment is classified can be highly important.

I.R.C. § 736(a) used to apply to all partnerships in the way it currently applies to general partners in services partnerships. Congress changed it because of a perceived abuse.[111] Assume A operates a nonservices business as a sole proprietor and the business has significant goodwill. B wants to buy the business. To optimize the tax consequences from B's perspective, the parties often would engage in the following planning transaction. A and B would form a partnership. A would contribute the business and B would contribute cash. A would then withdraw from the partnership with the partnership paying A for her interest with the cash. There would be no provision made for goodwill. B (as the partnership) now has a current deduction for payments made for goodwill (in excess of any basis).[112] If B had bought the business directly, the payments for goodwill would have had to have been capitalized and amortized over 15 years under I.R.C. § 197.

As noted above, I.R.C. § 736(b) payments fall within the distribution rules and are taken into account when actually paid.[113] Under the general rule, whether or not the payments are fixed, the partner first recovers her basis in the partnership interest. Any payment in excess of that basis is treated as gain from the sale or exchange of a partnership interest, typically capital gain.[114] Under this method, any loss recognition is postponed until the final payment is received (and the retiring partner has partnership interest basis left over).[115] There is an alternative when the total I.R.C. § 736(b) payments are fixed. The retiring partner may elect to prorate the partnership interest basis over the payments being made, and recognize gain or loss as each payment is made.[116] Of course, this election is more likely to be made when it accelerates the recognition of losses rather than gain.

As we discussed above, I.R.C. § 751(b) can apply to restructure a distribution if there is a shift in partners' interests in unrealized receivables and substantially

---

[110] Treas. Reg. §§ 1.736-1(a)(3), (4).

[111] H.R. Rep. No. 103-11, 103rd Cong, 1st Sess. 344 (1993).

[112] Even though the partnership will cease to be a partnership as a matter of law once A's interest is purchased, it should be viewed as a partnership for I.R.C. § 736 purposes until payment is complete. *See e.g.* Rev. Rul. 77-137, 1977-1 C.B. 178, Rev. Rul. 77-332, 1977-2 C.B. 484, and Willis, Pennell, Postlewaite, *Partnership Taxation* at ¶ 15.01[3].

[113] I.R.C. § 736(b)(1).

[114] I.R.C. § 731(a)(1); Treas. Reg. §§ 1.736-1(b)(6), (7), example 1.

[115] Treas. Reg. § 1.731-1(a)(2).

[116] Treas. Reg. § 1.736-1(b)(6).

appreciated inventory. To the extent unrealized receivables are covered by I.R.C. § 736(a), they are not subject to I.R.C. § 751(b). I.R.C. § 751(b) continues to apply to substantially appreciated inventory and to unrealized receivables not covered by I.R.C. § 736(a) (and thus instead covered by I.R.C. § 736(b)). I.R.C. § 736(a) does not cover unrealized receivables at all for partnerships in which capital *is* a material income-producing factor or for services partnerships making payments to *non-general* partners. Just to keep life interesting, I.R.C. § 736(a) also does not apply to certain types of "special" unrealized receivables, such as recapture, in the case of services partnerships making payments to general partners.

If there is a single I.R.C. § 736 payment, particularly if it is in cash, there is no great (additional) challenge; one simply applies I.R.C. § 751(b) to the payments falling within I.R.C. § 736(b). But in situations where payments are made over time, how does I.R.C. § 751(b) apply? The answer is not clear, but likely the parties would calculate the I.R.C. § 751(b) impact assuming a single payment and then allocate the ordinary income (or, unusually, loss) over all of the payments that are made. This assumes that the payments are fixed. If they are not, things get even murkier. Because I.R.C. § 736(a) payments (along with their typically ordinary income consequence) are considered to be made after the I.R.C. § 736(b) payments have been completed, there is an argument that the I.R.C. § 751(b) ordinary income treatment also should only come after the I.R.C. § 736(b) payments have been completed.[117]

The following flow chart, prepared by Professor James Maule at Villanova Law School, summarizes I.R.C. § 736:

Liquidating Distributions § 736

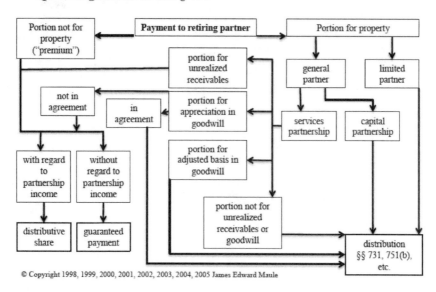

© Copyright 1998, 1999, 2000, 2001, 2002, 2003, 2004, 2005 James Edward Maule

---

[117] *See* Willis, Pennell, Postlewaite, *Partnership Taxation* at ¶ 15.05[2].

Chapter 9

TRANSACTIONS BETWEEN PARTNER AND PARTNERSHIP; ISSUANCE OF A PARTNERSHIP INTEREST FOR SERVICES

BASIC OVERVIEW

This chapter focuses on I.R.C. § 707(a) partner-partnership transactions, guaranteed payments under I.R.C. § 707(c), the special rules relating to controlled partnerships under I.R.C. §§ 267 and 707(b), and the tax consequences of the issuance of partnership interests for services.

In general, transactions between partners and partnerships fall into one of three categories for federal income tax purposes. The three categories are: (i) all payments to a partner in the partner's capacity as a partner other than guaranteed payments to a partner for the use of capital or for services. (ii) guaranteed payments to a partner for the use of capital or for services rendered in the partner's capacity as a partner, where the amount the partner is to receive is guaranteed, at least to the extent the partnership has the capacity to make it, and (iii) transactions with a partner other than in the partner's capacity as a partner. I.R.C. §§ 702, 703, 704 and 731 are applicable to the first category of transactions. I.R.C. § 707(c) is applicable to the second category. I.R.C. § 707(a) is applicable to the third category. Which category a particular transaction, relationship or arrangement falls into may affect the timing, character and, potentially, amount of income on which a partner is subject to tax. It is also important to note that which category a payment falls into is not optional. If a particular payment falls in a given category, it must be taxed in accordance with the rules of that category. Thus, distributions to a partner in his capacity as a partner that were not guaranteed mandatorily fall within the first category.

Guaranteed payments are made to a partner in a partner's capacity as a partner. An example would be the manager of a real estate partnership who is guaranteed a payment of $100,000 per year. Another example would be a partner who is guaranteed a 10% return on capital contributed. Guaranteed payments are always ordinary income to the recipient. Generally, the partnership treats the payment as if it were made to a nonpartner third party, deducting or capitalizing it as appropriate. It may seem self-evident that guaranteed payments have to be fixed in amount, and cannot be made with reference to partnership income, and indeed that is usually true. In the Detailed Discussion we will see that this may not be perfectly true, however.

A partner may also have a pure third-party relationship with a partnership. For example, in the above real estate partnership example, if a partner who is an attorney gives legal advice to the partnership, he is acting in a third-party capacity, and payments by the partnership to him would have to be treated as if he were not a partner, expensed or capitalized as fits the facts.

Partnerships can be tempted to convert capital expenditures into ordinary deductions using partnership allocations. Assume again, that an attorney is a partner in a real estate partnership. He advises the partnership on the acquisition of a new apartment building. His normal fee for this service is $10,000. If the partnership pays him the $10,000 and treats it as an I.R.C. § 707(a) payment, the amount is capitalized into the cost of the property, an unappealing result. More appealing would be for the partnership to allocate an extra $10,000 of the partnership's income to the attorney/partner. The tax consequence to the attorney is the same, assuming ordinary income is allocated. But the partnership, by having less income to allocate thereafter, is given the equivalent of a deduction. Thus, if allowed, by using partnership allocations, the partnership can turn a capital item into an ordinary deduction.

Needless to say, Congress was unenthusiastic about this result. To deal with this and similar abuses, it enacted I.R.C. § 707(a)(2)(A), which generally disallows this type of allocation. We review this code section more thoroughly in the Detailed Discussion.

As we have learned in prior chapters, both contributions to and distributions from partnerships can be tax free. A partner who wants to sell property to the partnership could be tempted to take advantage of these rules to avoid gain recognition. Instead of selling property to the partnership, she could contribute it to the partnership and have the partnership make a distribution to her. Congress has enacted a number of rules to stop this and other "mixing bowl" transactions. One of them is contained in I.R.C. § 707(a)(2)(B) which, along with its regulations, generally assumes that a contribution and nonprorata distribution that occur within two years of each other constitute a disguised sale. See Detailed Discussion.

Although I.R.C. § 707(a) provides that a transaction between a partner and a partnership may be treated as a transaction between the partnership and a person who is not a partner, I.R.C. § 707(b)(1) provides that no deduction shall be allowed for losses from sales or exchanges of property (other than an interest in the partnership) between a partnership and a person owning, directly or indirectly, more than 50 percent of the capital interest or the profits interest in the partnership or between two partnerships in which the same persons own, directly or indirectly, more than 50 percent of the capital interests or profits interests. For example, if the ABC partnership sold its property at a loss to the BCD partnership, and each partnership was owned by the same partners, the loss recognized by the ABC partnership would not be deductible by ABC. Instead, the disallowed loss is treated as a reduction of gain on subsequent sale by BCD.[1]

For the purposes of I.R.C. § 707(b), the constructive ownership rules of I.R.C. § 267(c) apply except that there is no attribution among partners solely because they are partners.[2] Under these attribution rules, (i) stock owned, directly or

---

[1] I.R.C. § 267(d).

[2] I.R.C. § 707(b)(3).

indirectly, by or for a corporation, partnership, estate or trust is considered owned proportionately by or for its shareholders, partners or beneficiaries and (ii) an individual is considered to own the stock owned, directly or indirectly, by or for the individual's family. The family of an individual for these purposes includes the individual's siblings, spouse, ancestors and lineal descendants. Stock owned constructively by reason of attribution from a corporation, partnership, estate or trust is considered owned by the person to whom the ownership is attributed for further application of the constructive ownership rules as well. Example: If a husband and wife are each 50% partners, for purposes of the attribution rules each owns 100% of the partnership.

Assume an accrual basis partnership and a cash basis partner who performs services for the partnership in a nonpartner capacity. Assume they are both on calendar years. The temptation would be for the partnership to accrue the expense in year one, but not pay the partner until January of year two. That gives the partnership an immediate deduction, but defers when the partner needs to take the income into account. Generally, I.R.C. § 267(e) and I.R.C. § 267(a)(2) stop this, deferring the partnership's deduction until year two.

When gain is recognized in certain transactions between a person related to a partnership and the partnership, the gain is recharacterized as ordinary income. I.R.C. § 707(b)(2)(B) provides that in the case of a sale or exchange, directly or indirectly, of property that in the hands of the transferee is property other than a capital asset (as defined in I.R.C. § 1221), any recognized gain shall be considered as gain from the sale or exchange of property other than a capital asset, if the sale or exchange is between partnerships in which the same persons own, directly or indirectly, more than 50 percent of the capital or profits interests in each partnership or between a partnership and a person owning, directly or indirectly, more than 50 percent of the capital interests, or profits interests in such partnership. As with the rules on loss disallowance, in determining ownership for the purposes of I.R.C. § 707(b)(2)(B), the rules for the constructive ownership of stock provided in I.R.C. § 267(c) (1), (2), (4) and (5) are applied.

In general, a service recipient recognizes gain and (if allowed by I.R.C. § 165) loss on the transfer of property to a service provider in payment for the performance of services.[3] The service recipient is treated as having sold the transferred property.[4] The service provider has income equal to the fair market value of the property received (and takes a fair market value basis in the property).[5] When the service recipient issues equity in itself to the service provider, this general approach creates an issue because the service recipient will generally have a zero basis in its own equity. I.R.C. § 721 provides that neither a partner nor the partnership recognizes gain or loss when property is contributed to the partnership in exchange for a partnership interest, but it does not apply to services.

---

[3] Treas. Reg. § 1.83-6(b).

[4] U.S. v. General Shoe Corp., 282 F.2d 9 (6th Cir. 1960).

[5] *See, e.g.,* International Freighting Corporation, Inc. v. Commissioner, 135 F.2d 310 (2d Cir. 1943).

In the case of partnerships, it is necessary to distinguish between two types of interests, profits interests and capital interests. Profits interests, as used here, mean a right to share in future profits only. Thus, if a partnership is liquidated immediately after a service provider is given a profits interest, the service provider would receive nothing in the liquidation. A capital interest, on the other hand, gives the service provider a right to the existing capital of the partnership. If capital accounts are kept in accordance with the Regulations, a partner receiving a capital interest starts with a positive capital account. If the partnership is liquidated immediately after a service provider is given a capital interest, the service provider would receive a distribution in the liquidation.

I.R.C. § 83 requires that, in general, if property is issued in connection with the performance of services, the excess of the value of the property over the amount paid for the property is included in the gross income of the service provider in the first year the rights of the recipient of the property are transferable or not subject to a substantial risk of forfeiture.[6] Thus, if property is subject to a substantial risk of forfeiture, it is taken into income at its value when the substantial risk for forfeiture lapses. If the partner makes an I.R.C. § 83(b) election, he can take the property into income in the year of receipt (valued as if there were no substantial risk of forfeiture).[7] For example, assume an employee receives stock in the corporation for which he works, but has to give it back if he does not work there for five years. He would have income after the five years, equal to the value of the stock at that time, unless he made an I.R.C. § 83(b) election to take the value of the stock into income in the year of receipt (which he might do if the stock had a low value at that time).

Notwithstanding the general rule of I.R.C. § 83 that property received for services is income, for historical reasons discussed in the Detailed Discussion, in Rev. Proc. 93-27[8] the Service ruled that in most cases if a person receives a profits interest for the provision of services, the IRS will not treat the receipt of such an interest as a taxable event for the partner or the partnership. The services must be provided to or for the benefit of the partnership by the partner in his capacity as a partner or in anticipation of becoming a partner. Thus it is possible for a partner to receive a profits interest for services tax free (and with a zero basis), and no gain or loss is recognized by the partnership.

Note that this gives partnerships a major advantage over corporations. Subject to the rules of I.R.C. § 83, the fair market value of stock received in exchange for services is income to the service provider.

---

[6] I.R.C. § 83(a). The rights of a person in property are subject to a substantial risk of forfeiture if such person's rights to full enjoyment of such property are conditioned upon the future performance of substantial services by any individual. I.R.C. § 83(c)(1).

[7] I.R.C. § 83(b).

[8] 1993-2 C.B. 343. *See* Paravano, "IRS Adopts 'Capacity' Approach for Treatment of Receipt of a Partnership Profits Interest," 94 TNT 4-57 (Jan. 3, 1994).

DETAILED DISCUSSION

§ 9.01 INTRODUCTION

This chapter focuses on I.R.C. § 707(a) partner-partnership transactions, guaranteed payments under I.R.C. § 707(c), the special rules relating to controlled partnerships under I.R.C. §§ 267 and 707(b), and the tax consequences of the issuance of partnership interests for services.

§ 9.02 THE DIFFERENT ROLES OF PARTNERS IN TRANSACTIONS WITH A PARTNERSHIP

In general, transactions between partners and partnerships fall into one of three categories for federal income tax purposes. The three categories are: (i) all payments to a partner in the partner's capacity as a partner other than guaranteed payments to a partner for the use of capital or for services, (ii) guaranteed payments to a partner for the use of capital or for services rendered in the partner's capacity as a partner, and (iii) transactions with a partner other than in the partner's capacity as a partner. I.R.C. §§ 702, 703, 704 and 731 are applicable to the first category of transactions. I.R.C. § 707(c) is applicable to the second category. I.R.C. § 707(a) is applicable to the third category. Which category a particular transaction, relationship or arrangement falls into may affect the timing, character and, potentially, amount of income in respect of which a partner is subject to tax. It is also important to note that which category a payment falls into is not optional. If a particular payment falls in a given category, it must be taxed in accordance with the rules of that category. Thus, for example, distributions to a partner in his capacity as a partner that are not guaranteed mandatorily fall within the first category. Payments to a partner for services not performed in his capacity as a partner always fall into the third category.

§ 9.03 PAYMENTS TO A PARTNER AS A PARTNER OTHER THAN GUARANTEED PAYMENTS

Payments (other than guaranteed payments) to a partner in the partner's capacity as a partner are generally distributions of partnership income or returns of capital. Under I.R.C. § 731, generally, distributions of money to a partner are not taxable unless they exceed the partner's basis in the partnership interest. Where they do not exceed the basis, they are generally returns of capital or distributions of income taxable to the partner, making the norm of nontaxation appropriate. Thus, the term *payments* here is not really a good fit. In this context, instead, tax professionals typically speak simply of distributions.

§ 9.04 GUARANTEED PAYMENTS

I.R.C. § 707(c) guaranteed payments are made to a partner in a partner's capacity as a partner, but the amount to be paid is made without regard to partnership income and is fixed in amount. If a payment to a partner is a guaranteed payment, the payment is treated as ordinary income to the recipient partner irrespective of the character of the income earned by the partnership.[9] In addition, the payment is taken into income by the partner based upon the accounting method of the partnership rather than the accounting method of the partner.[10] In general, so long as the payment meets the requirements of an ordinary and necessary business expense requirement of under I.R.C. § 162, a guaranteed payment is deductible to the partnership in the year the services are performed for an accrual basis partnership or the year in which payment is made for a cash basis partnership. In other words, if a payment is for services and the services are performed in 2014 for an accrual basis partnership, the partner will take the payment into income in 2014 even if the payment is made in 2015 — without regard to whether the partner is a cash basis or an accrual basis taxpayer. Conversely, if the partnership is on the cash method of accounting, the payment is income to the partner in 2015, if that is when it is made. Guaranteed payments for services that do not meet the ordinary and necessary test of I.R.C. § 162 are typically capitalized. Guaranteed payments that are returns on capital are normally deductible by the partnership.

The leading case interpreting guaranteed payments is *Pratt v. Commissioner*.[11] In *Pratt*, the general partners of a real estate limited partnership received a fee of 5% of the gross rentals received by the partnership for management services provided to the partnership by the general partners. The taxpayers in *Pratt* contended that the management fees should either be treated as guaranteed payments or payments to a partner other than in the partner's capacity as a partner (which would have made them deductible to the partnership in either case). The Tax Court and the Fifth Circuit held that the management fees were not deductible. Both courts held that the fees were not payments to a partner other than in the partner's capacity as a partner because the general partners were acting in their capacities as partners performing basic duties of the partnership business pursuant to the partnership agreement.

Once the determination is made that a distribution is made to a partner in the partner's capacity as a partner, the question of the characterization of payments to a partner becomes limited to whether the distributions are guaranteed payments or allocations and distributions of partnership income under I.R.C. §§ 702, 703, 704 and 731. Guaranteed payments only include amounts that are paid without regard to the income of the partnership. In *Pratt*, the Tax Court held that the management fees were not guaranteed payments because they were computed as a percentage of gross rental income received by the partnership. The court reasoned that the gross rental income was "income" of the partnership and, thus, the requirement that a guaranteed payment be determined without regard to the income of the partnership was not satisfied. (For technical reasons, the Fifth Circuit did not address this issue on appeal.) However, in Rev. Rul. 81-300,[12] the IRS ruled that the fees based upon gross income of a partnership should not be treated as being

---

[9] Treas. Reg. § 1.707-1(c).

[10] *Id.*

[11] 64 T.C. 203 (1975), *aff'd in part, rev'd in part*, 550 F.2d 1023 (5th Cir. 1977).

[12] 1981-2 C.B. 143.

determined with regard to partnership income, and so, under Rev. Rul. 81-300, the payment in *Pratt* would have been treated as a guaranteed payment.

§ 9.05   PAYMENTS TO A PARTNER OTHER THAN IN THEIR CAPACITY AS A PARTNER

A partner may have more than one relationship with a partnership. In other words, some of the actions of the partner may be in the partner's capacity as a partner and some of the actions may be in some other capacity, not as a partner.

For example, in Rev. Rul. 81-301,[13] a general partner was also an investment adviser to the partnership, which ran a mutual fund. The adviser performed substantially the same services for other persons as an independent contractor or agent. The adviser was responsible for the adviser's own expenses and could be removed as the investment adviser for the partnership on 60 days' notice. The IRS concluded that because of the factors just listed, the adviser was acting as an investment adviser for the partnership not in its capacity as a partner, but rather in the capacity of a person who is not a partner.

I.R.C. § 707(a) provides that if a partner engages in a transaction with a partnership other than in the capacity of a member of the partnership, the transaction will, except as otherwise provided, be considered as occurring between the partnership and one who is not a partner. In other words, the payments normally are classified as deductible or capital in the same manner that they would be if made to a nonpartner third party.

Partnerships can be tempted to convert capital expenditures into ordinary deductions using partnership allocations. Assume, for example, that an attorney is a partner in a real estate partnership. He advises the partnership on the acquisition of a new apartment building. His normal fee for this service is $10,000. If the partnership pays him the $10,000 and treats it as an I.R.C. § 707(a) payment, the amount is capitalized into the cost of the property, an unappealing result. (I.R.C. § 162 does not allow for the deduction of acquisition expenditures.) More appealing would be for the partnership to allocate an extra $10,000 of the partnership's income to the attorney/partner. The tax consequence to the attorney is the same, assuming ordinary income is allocated. But the partnership, by having $10,000 less income to allocate to the partners thereafter, is given the equivalent of a deduction. Thus, if allowed, by using partnership allocations, the partnership can turn a capital item into an ordinary deduction.

Needless to say, Congress was unenthusiastic about this result. To deal with this and similar abuses, it enacted I.R.C. § 707(a)(2)(A). I.R.C. § 707(a)(2)(A) provides that if a partner performs services for a partner or transfers property to a partnership and there is a related direct or indirect allocation and distribution to the partner, and the performance of services and the allocation and distribution, when viewed together, are properly characterized as occurring between the partnership and a person acting other than in his capacity as a partner, that is how it will be treated. Thus, in the above example, the purported allocation/distribution

---

[13] 1981-2 C.B. 144.

to the attorney/partner will not be respected and instead will be treated as a payment to a nonpartner and required to be capitalized.[14] Transfers of property in this context usually involve disguised leases as opposed to disguised sales, which we discuss, in part, below.

The legislative history behind I.R.C. § 707 provides some guidance in determining whether a partner is receiving a distribution in the partner's capacity as a partner.[15] According to the Senate Finance Committee Report, the first and generally the most important factor is whether the payment is subject to an appreciable risk.[16] Equity owners of all sorts generally make profits based upon the success of the business venture, while third parties generally receive payments that are not subject to this risk (except to the extent that a failed business may not be able to pay its creditors). An allocation and related distribution to a partner that subjects the partner to significant entrepreneurial risk as to both the amount and the fact of payment generally should be recognized as an allocation of a partner's distributive share and a partnership distribution. In contrast, a distribution provided for a service partner that involves limited risk as to amount and payment should generally be treated as a fee under I.R.C. § 707(a), if the services are not performed in the partner's capacity as a partner.

The second factor mentioned by the Senate Finance Committee Report is whether the partner status of the recipient is transitory. If a so-called partner has claimed partnership status for only a short period, it suggests that a payment to the transitory partner is a fee under I.R.C. § 707(a).[17]

The third factor in the Senate Finance Committee Report is whether a distribution to a partner is close in time to the partner's performance of services for, or transfers of property to, the partnership.[18] A distribution close in time to the performance of services or the transfer of property is more likely to be related to the services or property.

The fourth factor from the Senate Finance Committee Report is whether the recipient of a distribution became a partner primarily to obtain tax benefits for himself or the partnership, such as the avoidance of capitalization requirements, which would not have been available if the recipient had rendered services to the partnership in a third-party capacity.[19]

The fifth factor from the Senate Finance Committee Report is whether the value of the recipient's interest in partnership profits is generally small in relation to the allocation in question.[20] In other words, if a partner has a very small continuing interest, but for a period of time (probably contemporaneous with the period during

---

[14] It is unlikely that I.R.C. § 707(a)(2)(A) would apply to a disguised sale of property to the partnership. *See* § 13.04.E.

[15] S. Rep. No. 169, vol. 1., 98th Cong., 2d Sess., 227, April 2, 1984.

[16] *Id.*

[17] *Id.*

[18] *Id.*

[19] *Id.* at 228.

[20] S. Rep. No. 169, vol. 1., 98th Cong., 2d Sess., 228, April 2, 1984.

which services or property is being provided) the partner has a disproportionately large interest, this factor suggests that a distribution based on the disproportionately large interest is being paid to the partner in a third-party capacity.

The sixth factor from the Senate Finance Committee Report is whether the partnership maintains capital accounts under the rules of Treas. Reg. § 1.704-1(b)(2)(iv) and otherwise economically respects the capital accounts so that allocations which are disguised payments for capital may be economically unfeasible and therefore less likely to occur.[21] From the Regulations promulgated under I.R.C. § 707(a)(2), discussed below, one could conclude, however, that the Treasury is less optimistic than the Senate Finance Committee appears to have been about the effectiveness of the capital account maintenance rules in preventing disguised sales.

The Senate Finance Committee Report also provided the following example: An office building to be constructed by a partnership is projected to generate at least $100,000 per year indefinitely from high credit tenants. The architect for the partnership, who usually charges $40,000 for her services, contributes cash for a 25 percent interest in the partnership and receives both a 25 percent distributive share of net income for the life of the partnership, and a disproportionate allocation of $20,000 of partnership gross income for the first two years of partnership operations after lease-up. The projections indicate that there will be sufficient cash-flow to pay $20,000 to the architect in each of the first two years, and the agreement requires such a distribution. The report concludes that the $20,000 disproportionate gross income allocation and partnership distribution should be treated as a fee under I.R.C. § 707(a), rather than as a distributive share. The report indicated that the factors which contribute to this conclusion are: (i) the allocation is fixed in amount and there is a substantial probability that there will be sufficient income and cash to make the allocation/distribution; (ii) the allocation is disproportionate to the architect's general interest in the partnership; (iii) the distribution is fairly close in time to the services provided; and (iv) it is not unreasonable to conclude from all the facts and circumstances that the architect became a partner primarily for tax-motivated reasons. If, on the other hand, the project were a "spec building," and the architect assumed significant entrepreneurial risk that the partnership would be unable to lease the building, the disproportionate allocation might, depending on all the facts and circumstances, properly be treated as an allocation of the architect's distributive share and a partnership distribution.[22] Note that the partnership is in the business of operating an office building. Arguably, therefore, the architect did not perform his services in her capacity as a partner. Nonetheless, income allocated to her will be treated as her distributive share if it does not meet either the definition of a guaranteed payment or a third-party payment.

---

[21] S. Rep. No. 169, vol. 1., 98th Cong., 2d Sess., 228, April 2, 1984.

[22] *Id.* at 228-29.

§ 9.06   DISGUISED SALES

A.   The Disguised Sale of Assets

In addition to a service partner potentially entering into a relationship with the partnership other than in the service partner's capacity as a partner, a partner contributing property to a partnership may more properly be treated as selling the property to the partnership if a distribution to the contributing partner is associated with the contribution.

Because the general rule is that property may be contributed to a partnership without gain recognition under I.R.C. § 721 and also distributed from a partnership without gain recognition under I.R.C. § 731, partnerships have provided a tempting arena for taxpayers to attempt to structure otherwise taxable sales as nonrecognition transactions. One of the most successful of these attempts was described in the case of *Otey v. Commissioner*.[23] In *Otey*, the taxpayer contributed property to a partnership, after which the partnership borrowed against the property contributed, distributing a portion of the proceeds of the loan to the taxpayer. The Tax Court respected the form of the transaction as a contribution to capital followed by a current distribution with the result that the taxpayer had no current gain. Although there were cases before and after *Otey* that came to similar results, the provisions in the Code designed to stop disguised sales through the use of partnership structures, I.R.C. §§ 704(c)(1)(B), 707(a)(2)(B), and 737, are often called the anti-*Otey* provisions. We discuss I.R.C. § 707(a)(2)(B) below, and I.R.C. §§ 704(c)(1)(B) and 737 in Chapter 11.

I.R.C. § 707(a)(2)(B) provides that if (i) there is a direct or indirect transfer of money or other property by a partner to a partnership, (ii) there is a related direct or indirect transfer of money or other property by the partnership to such partner (or another partner), and (iii) the transfers described in clauses (i) and (ii), when viewed together, are properly characterized as a sale or exchange of property, such transfers shall be treated either as occurring between the partnership and one who is not a partner, or as a transaction between two or more partners acting other than in their capacity as members of the partnership.

In general, a transfer of property by a partner to a partnership and a transfer of money or other consideration by the partnership to the partner constitute a sale of the property only if based on all the facts and circumstances (i) the transfer of money or other consideration would not have been made but for the transfer of property and, (ii) in cases in which the transfers are not made simultaneously, the subsequent transfer is not dependent on the entrepreneurial risks of the partnership operations.[24] The facts and circumstances that are taken into consideration in making the determination include:

    i. whether the timing and amount of a subsequent transfer are determinable with reasonable certainty at the time of an earlier transfer;

---

[23] 70 T.C. 312 (1978).

[24] Treas. Reg. § 1.707-2(b)(1).

ii. whether the transferor has a legally enforceable right to the subsequent transfer;

iii. whether the partner's right to receive the transfer of money or other consideration is secured;

iv. whether any person has made or is legally obligated to make contributions to the partnership in order to enable the partnership to make the transfer;

v. whether any person has loaned the partnership the money or other consideration to enable the partnership to make the transfer;

vi. whether the partnership holds liquid assets, beyond those required by the reasonable needs of the business, that are expected to be available to make the transfer;

vii. whether partnership distributions, allocations or control of partnership operations are designed to effect an exchange of the burdens and benefits of ownership of property;

viii. whether the transfer by the partnership to the partner is disproportionately large in relationship to the partner's general and continuing interest in partnership profits; and

ix. whether the recipient partner has an obligation to return or repay the distribution.[25]

To address the difficult factual determination of whether a transfer from the partnership is related to a transfer to the partnership, Treas. Reg. § 1.707-3(c) provides that if within a two-year period a partner transfers property to a partnership and the partnership transfers money or other consideration to the partner (without regard to the order of the transfers), the transfers are presumed to be a sale of the property to the partnership unless the facts and circumstances clearly establish that the transfers do not constitute a sale.

If a taxpayer takes the position that a pair of transfers that would otherwise be presumed to be a sale is, under all the facts and circumstances, not a sale, the taxpayer is required to disclose the transfers to the IRS, unless the transfer from the partnership is a guaranteed payment, a reasonable preferred return or an operating cash flow distribution.[26] Operating cash flow distribution means, generally, distributions of partnership income made proportionately to all of the partners. Thus, a typical operating distribution made proportionately to all of the partners does not trigger I.R.C. § 707(a)(2)(B).[27]

If a transfer of money or other consideration is made to a partner by a partnership and the recipient partner made a transfer to the partnership more than two years before or after the transfer to the partnership, the transfers are presumed not to be a sale of the property to the partnership unless the facts and

---

[25] Treas. Reg. § 1.707-2(b)(2).

[26] Treas. Reg. § 1.707-3(c). Proposed Regulations would extend the period during which disclosure is required to seven years. Prop. Treas. Reg. § 1.707-5(a)(8).

[27] Treas. Reg. § 1.704-4(b)(2).

circumstances clearly establish that the transfers constitute a sale.[28]

The Regulations illustrate these rules with the following example:

> A transfers property X to partnership AB on April 9, 1992, in exchange for
> an interest in the partnership. At the time of the transfer, property X has
> a fair market value of $4,000,000 and an adjusted tax basis of $1,200,000.
> Immediately after the transfer, the partnership transfers $3,000,000 in
> cash to A. Assume that, under this section, the partnership's transfer of
> cash to A is treated as part of a sale of property X to the partnership.
> Because the amount of cash A receives on April 9, 1992, does not equal the
> fair market value of the property, A is considered to have sold a portion of
> property X with a value of $3,000,000 to the partnership in exchange for the
> cash. Accordingly, A must recognize $2,100,000 of gain ($3,000,000 amount
> realized less $900,000 adjusted tax basis ($1,200,000 multiplied by
> $3,000,000/$4,000,000)). Assuming A receives no other transfers that are
> treated as consideration for the sale of the property under this section, A
> is considered to have contributed to the partnership, in A's capacity as a
> partner, $1,000,000 of the fair market value of the property with an
> adjusted tax basis of $300,000.[29]

In other words, when the consideration given in the deemed sale is less than the
fair market value of the property contributed, the transaction is divided into two
transactions: a sale of the portion of the property contributed represented by the
relationship of the consideration given by the partnership to the fair market value
of the entire property and, second, a contribution of the remaining portion of the
fair market value of the property contributed, with the carryover basis also based
upon the same proportion of the basis of the property contributed.

Special safe harbors are provided for reasonable guaranteed payments for
capital and reasonable preferred returns. In this context, a guaranteed payment
means any payment to a partner by a partnership for the use of capital and that is
determined without regard to partnership income.[30] A guaranteed payment for
these purposes does not include payments designed to liquidate all or part of the
partner's interest in partnership property.[31] A preferred return in this context
means a preferential distribution of partnership cash flow to a partner with respect
to capital contributed to the partnership by the partner that will be matched, to the
extent available, by an allocation of income or gain.[32] A preferred return or a
guaranteed payment is viewed as reasonable for the purposes of the deemed sale
rules only if (i) the payment is reasonable in amount, (ii) the payment is pursuant
to a written provision in the partnership agreement, and (iii) the payment is made
after the provision providing for the payment is added to the partnership
agreement.[33] A preferred return or guaranteed payment is reasonable in amount if

---

[28] Treas. Reg. § 1.707-3(d).

[29] Treas. Reg. § 1.707-3(f), example 1.

[30] Treas. Reg. § 1.707-4(a)(1)(i).

[31] *Id.*

[32] Treas. Reg. § 1.707-4(a)(2).

[33] Treas. Reg. § 1.707-4(a)(3)(i).

the sum of any preferred return and any guaranteed payment does not exceed the product of the partner's unreturned capital at the beginning of the year (or the partner's weighted average capital balance for the year) multiplied by a rate that does not exceed 150 percent of the highest applicable Federal rate,[34] at the appropriate compounding period or periods, in effect at any time from the time that the right to the payment is established through the end of the taxable year.[35]

An exception is also provided for reimbursement of preformation expenditures.[36] Preformation expenditures are limited to the amounts incurred during the two years prior to the transfer by the partner to the partnership and are incurred by the partner for organization and syndication costs or property contributed to the partnership by the partner (subject to a limitation of 20 percent of the fair market value of the property contributed).[37]

Partners or partnerships might try to end-run I.R.C. § 707(a)(2)(B) using debt. For example, instead of having the partnership distribute money to the partner, the partner might borrow money against the contributed property, giving him his wanted consideration (or at least much of it), and then contribute the property to the partnership with the partnership taking over the debt. The problem becomes how to distinguish "legitimate debt" from debt incurred in an effort to avoid the application of I.R.C. § 707(a)(2)(B). In the lingo of the Regulations, if the partnership takes property subject to "qualified liabilities," that (mostly) will not trigger I.R.C. § 707(a)(2)(B). As a rule of thumb, a qualified liability is one over two years old, incurred to buy or improve property, or incurred in the ordinary course of business if all genuine assets of the business are transferred to the partnership. To the extent nonqualified liabilities are assumed, I.R.C. § 707(a)(2)(B) is in play, generally to the extent the partner is deemed relieved of the liability under I.R.C. § 752(b).

Specifically, a "qualified liability" means a liability assumed or taken subject to by a partnership in connection with a transfer of property to the partnership by a partner that (i) was incurred by the partner more than two years prior to the transfer and that has continually encumbered the transferred property, (ii) was not incurred in anticipation of the transfer, but was incurred within the two-year period prior to the transfer, and that has continually encumbered the transferred property (a tough test to meet, see below), (iii) is allocable under the rules of Treas. Reg. § 1.163-8T to capital expenditures with respect to the property, or (iv) is incurred in the ordinary course of the trade or business in which the property transferred to the partnership was used or held, but only if all the assets related to that trade or business are transferred other than assets that are not material to a continuation of the trade or business.[38] If within a two-year period a partner incurs a liability and transfers property to a partnership, and in connection with the transfer the

---

[34] The applicable federal rate is a rate that is published monthly by the Treasury pursuant to I.R.C. § 1274(d) based upon the term of the obligation and the compounding period.

[35] Treas. Reg. § 1.707-4(a)(3)(ii).

[36] Treas. Reg. § 1.707-4(b) and (d).

[37] Treas. Reg. § 1.707-4(d).

[38] Treas. Reg. § 1.707-5(a)(6).

partnership assumes or takes the property subject to the liability, the liability is presumed to be incurred in anticipation of the transfer unless the facts and circumstances clearly establish that the liability was not incurred in anticipation of the transfer.[39]

If a partnership assumes or takes property subject to a qualified liability of a partner, the partnership is treated as transferring consideration to the partner only to the extent provided in Treas. Reg. § 1.707-5(a)(5).[40] What this Regulation addresses is what to do if, for example, the partner transfers property subject to a qualified liability but for other reasons still triggers I.R.C. § 707(a)(2)(B). Treas. Reg. § 1.707-5(a)(5) provides that if a transfer of property by a partner to a partnership is not otherwise treated as part of a sale, the partnership's assumption of or taking subject to a qualified liability in connection with a transfer of property is not treated as part of a sale. On the other hand, if a transfer subject to a qualified liability is treated as part of a sale without regard to the partnership's assumption of or taking subject to a qualified liability, the assumption of or taking subject to the qualified liability is treated as consideration in a sale to the extent of the lesser of:

i. the amount of consideration that the partnership would be treated as transferring if the liability were not a qualified liability, or

ii. the amount obtained by multiplying the amount of the qualified liability by the partner's net equity percentage[41] with respect to the property contributed by the partner.

By contrast, if the partnership assumes or takes property subject to a liability of the partner other than a qualified liability, the partnership is treated as transferring consideration to the partner to the extent that the amount of the liability exceeds the partner's share of that liability immediately after the partnership assumes or takes subject to the liability.[42] In general, a partner's share of a liability after the partnership assumes or takes subject to the liability for the purposes of the disguised sale rules is the partner's share of the liability determined under Treas. Reg. § 1.752, with the exception that a partner's share of partnership liabilities is reduced by any amount of liabilities to the extent that it is anticipated that the transferring partner's share of liabilities will be subsequently reduced and the subsequent reduction is part of a plan to minimize the impact of the disguised sale rules.[43]

---

[39] Treas. Reg. § 1.707-5(a)(7)(i). If a partner treats a liability incurred within two years of the transfer as not being in anticipation of the transfer, the partner must disclose the treatment. Treas. Reg. § 1.707-5(a)(7)(ii).

[40] Treas. Reg. § 1.707-5(a)(1).

[41] A partner's net equity percentage with respect to a property equals the percentage determined by dividing (i) the aggregate consideration provided by the partnership to the partner that is treated as proceeds realized on the sale of the transferred property by (ii) the excess of the fair market value of the property over any qualified liability encumbering or properly allocable to the property. Treas. Reg. § 1.707-5(a)(5)(ii).

[42] Treas. Reg. § 1.707-5(a)(1).

[43] Treas. Reg. § 1.707-5(a)(2) and (3).

§ 9.07   LIMITATIONS ON RECOGNITION OF LOSSES AND RECHARACTERIZATION OF GAINS IN RELATED PARTY TRANSACTIONS

A.   Limitations on Recognition of Losses

In many contexts, the Code disallows losses between related parties on the assumption that since the property is staying with related parties, the parties are trying to recognize a tax loss while maintaining control over the property. In other words, no genuine sale has taken place. One example of such a provision is I.R.C. § 707(b)(1), which provides that no deduction shall be allowed for losses from sales or exchanges of property (other than an interest in the partnership) between a partnership and a person owning, directly or indirectly, more than 50 percent of the capital interest or the profits interest in the partnership or between two partnerships in which the same persons own, directly or indirectly, more than 50 percent of the capital interests or profits interests.

For example, if the ABC partnership sold its property at a loss to the BCD partnership, and each partnership was owned by the same partners, the loss recognized by the ABC partnership would not be deductible by ABC. Instead, the disallowed loss is treated as a reduction of gain on subsequent sale by BCD.[44]

For the purposes of I.R.C. § 707(b), the constructive ownership rules of I.R.C. § 267(c) apply except that there is no attribution among partners solely because they are partners.[45] Under these attribution rules, (i) stock owned, directly or indirectly, by or for a corporation, partnership, estate or trust is considered owned proportionately by or for its shareholders, partners or beneficiaries and (ii) an individual is considered to own the stock owned, directly or indirectly, by or for the individual's family. The family of an individual for these purposes includes the individual's siblings, spouse, ancestors and lineal descendants. Stock owned constructively by reason of attribution from a corporation, partnership, estate or trust is considered owned by the person to whom the ownership is attributed for further application of the constructive ownership rules as well. For example, assume A sells property to the ABC partnership. A, his wife B, and son C each are one-third partners. A is deemed to own the partnership interests owned by B and C and thus would be considered to own 100% of the partnership. Thus, any loss on the sale would be disallowed.

B.   Recharacterization of Gains

I.R.C. § 707(b)(2)(B) can recharacterize capital gain as ordinary income on certain sales between related parties. Specifically, it provides that in the case of a sale or exchange, directly or indirectly, of property which in the hands of the transferee is property other than a capital asset (as defined in I.R.C. § 1221), any recognized gain is considered to be gain from the sale or exchange of property other than a capital asset. The sale or exchange must be between partnerships in

---

[44] I.R.C. § 267(d).
[45] I.R.C. § 707(b)(3).

which the same persons own, directly or indirectly, more than 50 percent of the capital or profits interests in each partnership or between a partnership and a person owning, directly or indirectly, more than 50 percent of the capital interests, or profits interests, in the partnership. I.R.C. § 707(b)(2)(B) overlaps with I.R.C. § 1239, which in these and other circumstances characterize gain as ordinary income if it is depreciable in the hands of the transferee.

As with the rules on loss disallowance, in determining ownership for the purposes of I.R.C. § 707(b)(2)(B), the rules for the constructive ownership of stock provided in I.R.C. § 267(c) (1), (2), (4) and (5) are applied.

§ 9.08 ISSUANCE OF A PARTNERSHIP INTEREST IN EXCHANGE FOR SERVICES

A. Potential Income to Partner and Gain to Partnership

In general, a service recipient recognizes gain and (if allowed by I.R.C. § 165) loss on the transfer of property to a service provider in payment for the performance of services.[46] The service recipient is treated as having sold the transferred property.[47] The service provider has income equal to the fair market value of the property received (and takes a fair market value basis in the property).[48]

When the service recipient is issuing equity in itself to the service provider, this general approach creates an issue because the service recipient will generally have a zero basis in its own equity.

Under I.R.C. § 721, neither the partnership nor a partner recognizes gain or loss when contributing property or money to the partnership in exchange for a partnership interest. I.R.C. § 721, however, does not apply to the contribution of services in exchange for a partnership interest.

In the case of partnerships, it is necessary to distinguish between two types of interests, profits interests and capital interests. Profits interests, as used here, mean a right to share in future profits only. Thus, if a partnership were liquidated immediately after a service provider was given a profits interest, the service provider would receive nothing in the liquidation. A capital interest, on the other hand, gives the service provider a right to the existing capital of the partnership. If capital accounts are kept in accordance with the Regulations, a partner receiving a capital interest starts with a positive capital account. If the partnership were liquidated immediately after a service provider was given a capital interest, the service provider would receive a distribution in the liquidation.

The Regulations under I.R.C. § 721 provide:

---

[46] Treas. Reg. § 1.83-6(b).

[47] U.S. v. General Shoe Corp., 282 F.2d 9 (6th Cir. 1960).

[48] See, e.g., International Freighting Corporation, Inc. v. Commissioner, 135 F.2d 310 (2d Cir. 1943).

> To the extent that any of the partners gives up any part of his right to be repaid his contributions (as distinguished from a share in partnership profits) in favor of another partner as compensation for services (or in satisfaction of an obligation), section 721 does not apply.[49]

This language states that if a partner receives a capital interest (i.e., via another partner giving up his "right to be repaid his contributions"), I.R.C. § 721 does not apply. The Regulation suggests that I.R.C. § 721 continues to apply if only a profits interest is received via the following language in the parenthetical: ". . . as distinguished from a share in partnership profits." We will return to profits interests. Staying with capital interests for now, as I.R.C. § 721 does not apply, a partner who receives a capital interest in the partnership in exchange for services should fall under the regular income tax rules and have income equal to the fair market value of the interest received. Her basis in the partnership interest is that same fair market value. Further, partnerships arguably are subject to income recognition on the issuance of their own interests in exchange for services under the current Regulations because the partnership is paying compensation with a partnership interest in which the partnership has a zero basis. That said, no case has concluded this, and the Service has never issued a ruling arguing for this position.

I.R.C. § 83 requires that, in general, if property is issued in connection with the performance of services, the excess of the value of the property over the amount paid for the property is included in the gross income of the service provider in the first year the rights of the recipient of the property are transferable or not subject to a substantial risk of forfeiture.[50] Long before I.R.C. § 83 was enacted, it was clear that the value of property received in exchange for services was income. What I.R.C. § 83 added was the ability to defer the income if the property was subject to a substantial risk of forfeiture (or not transferable — which is typically tacked on to the substantial risk of forfeiture). For example, if someone is given stock in a start-up corporation, but has to give it back (and cannot transfer it in the interim) if he does not stay employed by the start-up for five years, the stock is subject to a substantial risk of forfeiture. The employee only has income when the substantial risk of forfeiture lapses, at the value the stock has at that time. Alternatively, the employee can make "an I.R.C. § 83(b) election," and take the stock into income at its value on receipt (ignoring the substantial risk of forfeiture for valuation purposes). Taxpayers only have 30 days from receipt to make an I.R.C. § 83(b) election. Hoping that their company is the next Apple, employees often make an I.R.C. § 83(b) election, provided only a relatively small amount needs to be taken into income currently. If they are right in their hopes, they avoid having to take a much larger amount into income upon vesting.

The service provider is not allowed a loss deduction, should an I.R.C. § 83(b) election be made, but the property forfeited. Except as otherwise provided in Treas.

---

[49] Treas. Reg. § 1.721-1(b).

[50] I.R.C. § 83(a). The rights of a person in property are subject to a substantial risk of forfeiture if such person's rights to full enjoyment of such property are conditioned upon the future performance of substantial services by any individual. I.R.C. § 83(c)(1).

Reg. § 1.83-6(a)(3),[51] I.R.C. § 83(h) provides that any deduction allowable to the person for whom the services are provided will be in an amount equal to the amount included in the service provider's income. Further, any deduction is taken into account in the taxable year of the person for whom the services are provided in which or with which ends the taxable year in which the amount is included in the gross income of the service provider. Thus, an I.R.C. § 83(b) election will also affect the amount and timing of the service recipient's deduction.

Generally, if property is transferred in connection with the performance of services but is not vested, the transferee is not treated as the owner of the property (and the holding period does not begin) until such property becomes substantially vested, unless the recipient files an I.R.C. § 83(b) election.[52]

If a capital interest is subject to a substantial risk of forfeiture at the time of grant, the partner does not recognize income on the grant,[53] but the partner is also not recognized as a partner unless a I.R.C. § 83(b) election is made.[54] This means that no amounts may be allocated to the partner until the interest vests. However, this rule does not apply to a profits interest granted to a service provider for services to the issuing partnership if all parties have consistently treated the recipient as a partner. The IRS has ruled that a profits interest that is excluded from income under Rev. Proc. 93-27 (discussed below), is excluded both at the time of the grant and, if subject to a substantial risk of forfeiture, at the time of vesting.[55]

We discuss I.R.C. § 83 in additional detail below in our discussion of the Compensatory Interest Proposed Regulations.

B. Receipt of Profits Interests by Service Partners

How to tax profits interests has been the subject of a meaningful amount of litigation.

In *Hale v. Commissioner*,[56] a pre-I.R.C. § 83 case, the court concluded that the income recognized on the assignment of a profits interest should be given ordinary income treatment, although the partnership interest itself was a capital asset. The court also observed in a footnote that the mere receipt of a profits interest in a partnership does not create a current tax liability.[57] For many years, that footnote was the sole authority for the position that the value of a profits interest was not income to the service provider.

---

[51] Treas. Reg. § 1.83-6(a)(3) provides two exceptions. First, when property is substantially vested upon transfer, an otherwise allowable deduction is allowed to the service recipient in accordance with its method of accounting (in conformity with I.R.C. §§ 446 and 461). Also, in the case of a transfer to an employee benefit plan described in Treas. Reg. § 1.162-10(a) or a transfer to an employees' trust or annuity plan described in I.R.C. § 404(a)(5), section 83(h) does not apply.

[52] I.R.C. § 83(f); Treas. Reg. § 1.83-1; Treas. Reg. § 1.1361-1(b)(3).

[53] I.R.C. § 83(a).

[54] Crescent Holdings, LLC v. Commissioner, 141 T.C. No. 15 (2013).

[55] Rev. Proc. 2001-43, 2001-2 C.B. 191.

[56] T.C. Memo. 1965-274.

[57] *Id.* at 65-1646 fn.3.

In *Diamond v. Commissioner*,[58] also a pre-I.R.C. § 83 case, the court found that the taxpayer had taxable ordinary income treated as compensation for services on the receipt of a profits interest where the profits interest had clearly determinable fair market value because of a sale of the interest within a month of receipt.

In other cases, the court has concluded, or the IRS has conceded, that receipt of a profits interest by a service partner creates no tax liability, primarily because it could not be reliably valued.[59] Similarly, in *Campbell v. Commissioner*,[60] the Eighth Circuit found that a profits interest had only speculative, if any, value and, therefore, was not taxable.

Much of the uncertainty and litigation over the treatment of profits interests was resolved by the IRS through the promulgation of Rev. Proc. 93-27, essentially trumping the possible application of I.R.C. § 83.[61] Under Rev. Proc. 93-27, if a taxpayer receives a partnership profits interest for the provision of services to or for the benefit of a partnership, the IRS will not treat the receipt of such an interest as a taxable event for the partner or the partnership. The taxpayer must be acting in a partner capacity or in anticipation of becoming a partner.

Under Rev. Proc. 93-27, a profits interest is defined as an interest that would not give the holder a share of the proceeds if the partnership's assets were sold at fair market value and then the proceeds were distributed in a complete liquidation of the partnership at the time of the receipt of the partnership interest. Rev. Proc. 93-27 does not apply, however, if (i) the profits interest relates to a substantially certain and predicable stream of income from partnership assets; (ii) the partner disposes of the profits interest within two years of receipt; or (iii) the profits interest is a limited partnership interest in a "publicly traded partnership" within the meaning of I.R.C. § 7704(b). In these latter cases, both the taxpayer and the IRS fall under existing case law, which is to say it is not clear what the tax consequence is.

Rev. Proc. 93-27 was further clarified in Rev. Proc. 2001-43.[62] Rev. Proc. 2001-43 provides that if a partnership grants a nonvested interest to a service provider, the time for testing whether the interest qualifies as a profits interest is, under certain circumstances, is at the time the interest is granted (rather than at the time of vesting, when profits could have been earned — those profits increase the partner's capital account and entitle him to a distribution if the partnership interest is liquidated). To qualify under the revenue procedure, (i) the service provider must be treated as a partner from the time of grant; (ii) neither the partnership nor the other partners may deduct any amount in respect of the vesting of the interest; and

---

[58] 492 F.2d 286 (7th Cir. 1974).

[59] *See* National Oil Co. v. Commissioner, 52 T.C.M. (CCH) 1223, 1228 (1986) (Commissioner conceded that if taxpayer received only profits interest, no taxable event had occurred); Kenroy, Inc. v. Commissioner, 47 T.C.M. (CCH) 1749, 1756-59 (1984) (profits interest had no fair market value, thus no tax liability upon receipt).

[60] 943 F.2d 815 (8th Cir. 1991).

[61] 1993-2 C.B. 343. *See* Paravano, "IRS Adopts 'Capacity' Approach for Treatment of Receipt of a Partnership Profits Interest," 94 TNT 4-57 (Jan. 3, 1994).

[62] 2001-2 C.B. 191. *See* Mincey, Sloan and Banoff, "Rev. Proc. 2001-43, Section 83(b), and Unvested Profits Interests — the Final Facet of Diamond?" 95 JTAX 205 (Oct. 2001).

(iii) the interest otherwise must qualify as a profits interest under Rev. Proc. 93-27.

Thus, as to a profits interest under Rev. Proc. 93-27, neither the recipient partner nor the partnership will recognize income on the issuance of the interest in exchange for services if the requirements of Rev. Proc. 93-27 and Rev. Proc. 2001-43 are satisfied.

§ 9.09   COMPENSATORY INTEREST PROPOSED REGULATIONS

On May 24, 2005, the Treasury and I.R.S. released proposed regulations (the "*Compensatory Interest Proposed Regulations*") addressing the issuance of equity and equity related interests in partnerships in exchange for services.[63] The Compensatory Interest Proposed Regulations effectively trump Rev. Proc. 93-27 and provide that the transfer of a partnership capital *or* profits interest in connection with the performance of services *is* subject to I.R.C. § 83. The Compensatory Interest Proposed Regulations also provide that no gain or loss is recognized by a partnership on the transfer or vesting of an interest in the transferring partnership in connection with the performance of services for the transferring partnership. The Compensatory Interest Proposed Regulations provide a default rule that the gross income of the recipient of the interest will include an amount based upon the fair market value of the interest at the time of the transfer or vesting. However, the Treasury also issued Notice 2005-43[64] together with the Compensatory Interest Proposed Regulations, which describes a proposed revenue procedure that would, subject to some limitations, permit the amount included in the gross income of the recipient of the interest to be based upon the liquidation value of the interest when issued, for profits interests normally zero. Thus, while the applicable law for profits interests would be changed, the tax outcome typically would be the same.

The Compensatory Interest Proposed Regulations provide that a partnership interest is property within the meaning of I.R.C. § 83 and that the transfer of a partnership interest in connection with the performance of services is subject to I.R.C. § 83.[65] Thus, as noted, the Compensatory Interest Proposed Regulations apply I.R.C. § 83 equally to partnership capital interests and partnership profits interests. However, a right to receive allocations and distributions from a partnership that is treated under I.R.C. § 707(a)(2)(A) as being more properly treated as a disguised payment of compensation to the service provider is not a partnership interest under the proposed Regulations.[66]

As discussed above, I.R.C. § 83(b) allows a person who receives property subject to a substantial risk of forfeiture in connection with the performance of services to

[63] REG-105346-03, 70 Fed. Reg. 29675 (May 24, 2005) (the "*Compensatory Interest Proposed Regulations*").

[64] 2005-1 C.B. 1221.

[65] Prop. Treas. Reg. § 1.83-3(e) is amended by the Proposed Regulations to explicitly provide that "property" includes a partnership interest.

[66] *See* S. Rep. No. 98-169 v.1, 98 Cong. 2d Sess., 226 (Apr. 2, 1984).

elect to include in gross income the difference between: (i) the fair market value of the property at the time of transfer (determined without regard to the risk of forfeiture); and (ii) the amount paid for the property. Under I.R.C. § 83(b)(2), the election under I.R.C. § 83(b) must be made within 30 days of the date of the transfer of the property to the service provider. If the partnership interest has appreciated in value between the time of grant and the time of vesting, the service provider may include a greater amount in income than the service provider might otherwise have included in income had an I.R.C. § 83(b) election been timely made — depending upon the value of the interest when it vests compared to the service provider's allocable share of income over the period of vesting and the fair market value at the time of grant. Indeed, hoping their company is a Microsoft of the future, taxpayers commonly make the I.R.C. § 83(b) election provided only a relatively small amount of income need be taken into account currently rather than (they hope) a much larger amount when the property interest vests.

Except as otherwise provided in Treas. Reg. § 1.83-6(a)(3),[67] I.R.C. § 83(h) provides that any deduction allowable to the person for whom the services are provided will be in an amount equal to the amount included in the service provider's income. Further, any deduction is taken into account in the taxable year of the person for whom the services are provided in which or with which ends the taxable year in which the amount is included in the gross income of the service provider. Thus, an I.R.C. § 83(b) election will also affect the amount and timing of the service recipient's deduction.

The Compensatory Interest Proposed Regulations provide that the I.R.C. § 83 timing rules override the timing rules in Subchapter K to the extent that they are inconsistent.[68] Accordingly, under the Compensatory Interest Proposed Regulations, if a partnership transfers a partnership interest to a partner in connection with the performance of services, the timing and the amount of the related income inclusion and deduction are determined by I.R.C. § 83 and the regulations thereunder.[69]

Consistent with the current treatment of S corporation shareholders, the Compensatory Interest Proposed Regulations provide that if a partnership interest that was transferred in connection with the performance of services is subject to a substantial risk of forfeiture, and if an election under I.R.C. § 83(b) is not made, then the holder of the partnership interest is not treated as a partner for federal tax purposes until the interest becomes substantially vested.

If an election under I.R.C. § 83(b) has been made with respect to a substantially nonvested interest, the holder of the nonvested interest may be allocated partnership items that may later be forfeited. Under the proposed Regulations, for this

---

[67] Treas. Reg. § 1.83-6(a)(3) provides two exceptions. First, when property is substantially vested upon transfer, an otherwise allowable deduction is allowed to the service recipient in accordance with its method of accounting (in conformity with I.R.C. §§ 446 and 461). Also, in the case of a transfer to an employee benefit plan described in Treas. Reg. § 1.162-10(a) or a transfer to an employees' trust or annuity plan described in I.R.C. § 404(a)(5), section 83(h) does not apply.

[68] Prop. Treas. Reg. § 1.707-1(c).

[69] The Treasury Department and the Service have requested comments on alternative approaches to resolving the timing inconsistency between I.R.C. § 83 and I.R.C. § 707(c).

reason, allocations of partnership items while the interest is substantially nonvested cannot have economic effect.[70] Under the proposed Regulations, these allocations will be deemed to be in accordance with the partners' interests in the partnership if: (i) the partnership agreement requires that the partnership make forfeiture allocations[71] if the interest for which the I.R.C. § 83(b) election is made is later forfeited and (ii) all material allocations and capital account adjustments under the partnership agreement not pertaining to substantially nonvested partnership interests for which an I.R.C. § 83(b) election has been made are recognized under I.R.C. § 704(b).[72] This safe harbor does not apply if, at the time of the I.R.C. § 83(b) election, there is a plan that a substantially nonvested interest will be forfeited.[73] All of the facts and circumstances (including the tax status of the holder of the substantially nonvested interest) will be considered in determining whether there is a plan that the interest will be forfeited. In such a case, the partners' distributive shares of partnership items shall be determined in accordance with the partners' interests in the partnership under Treas. Reg. § 1.704-1(b)(3).[74]

Forfeiture allocations are allocations of gross income and gain or gross deduction and loss (to the extent such items are available) to the service partner that offset prior distributions and allocations of partnership items with respect to the forfeited partnership interest. Forfeiture allocations may be made out of the partnership's items for the entire taxable year, whether or not the forfeiting partner was a partner for the entire taxable year.[75] The formula for forfeiture allocations is (i) the excess (which cannot be less than zero) of (a) the amount of distributions (including deemed distributions and the adjusted tax basis of any property distributed) to the partner with respect to the forfeited interest (to the extent such distributions were not taxable under I.R.C. § 731) over (b) the amount paid for the interest (including any deemed contributions) and the adjusted basis of property contributed, minus (ii) the cumulative net income or loss allocated to the partner with respect to the forfeited partnership interest.[76]

§ 9.10   CURRENT LEGISLATIVE PROPOSALS

Several recent legislative proposals would change the way in which the issuance of a partnership interest in exchange for services would be taxed.[77] One such bill, H.R. 1935, would amend I.R.C. § 83 to treat the fair market value of a partnership

---

[70] Prop. Treas. Reg. § 1.704-1(b)(4)(xii).

[71] Most of the discussion of the proposed regulations is beyond where you will go in a typical law school class, so we do not address the forfeiture allocations. If your professor is a complete sadist, you will need to review these in the proposed regulations.

[72] Prop. Treas. Reg. § 1.704-1(b)(4)(xii)(b).

[73] Prop. Treas. Reg. § 1.704-1(b)(4)(xii)(e).

[74] *Id.*

[75] Prop. Reg. § 1.706-3(b).

[76] Prop. Reg. § 1.704-1(b)(4)(xii)(c). For these purposes, items of income and gain are reflected as positive amounts, and items of deduction and loss are reflected as negative amounts. Prop. Reg. § 1.704-1(b)(4)(xii)(d).

[77] *See, e.g.*, H.R. 1935, 11th Cong. 1st Sess. (April 2, 2009). Howard E. Abrams has predicted that the

interest issued in connection with the performance of services as the liquidation value of the partnership interest unless the recipient partner elected not to have the provision apply. Such a provision would expand the treatment now provided by Rev. Proc. 93-27[78] to types of partnership interests excluded by Rev. Proc. 93-27.

H.R. 1935 would also add a new I.R.C. § 710 that would provide that, in the case of an investment services partnership interest, net income with respect to such interest will be treated as ordinary income for the performance of services, and net loss with respect to such interest (to the extent not disallowed) will be treated as ordinary loss.[79] In addition, any gain realized on the disposition of an investment services partnership interest would be treated as ordinary income for the performance of services.[80] This provision is designed to cover so-called "carried interests" and have been discussed at length in the popular press. In brief, investment advisors for investment partnerships often take partnership profits interests in those funds. Due to the nature of the funds, the income earned by the funds, and allocable to an investment advisor's profits interest, is often capital gain. Some argue that because the investment advisor received the profits interest for services, all allocable income should be ordinary income.

An "investment services partnership interest" means any interest in a partnership that is held by any person if such person provides (directly or indirectly) a substantial quantity of any of the following services to the partnership: (i) advising the partnership as to the value of any specified asset; (ii) advising the partnership as to the advisability of investing in, purchasing or selling any specified asset; (iii) arranging financing with respect to acquiring specified assets; or (iv) any activity in support of the forgoing services.[81] "Specified asset" means, in this context, securities, real estate, interests in partnerships, commodities, or options or derivative contracts with respect to securities, real estate or commodities.

The bill provides an exception to the general recharacterization treatment for a portion of the investment services partnership interest that is acquired for invested capital.

As of the time of this writing, the adoption of the proposals remains unclear. However, the president has incorporated a similar proposal in his budget.

---

current form of the proposal will ultimately be abandoned by Congress because of the technical flaws in the proposal. Howard E. Abrams, "Carried Interests: The Past is Prologue" at 9 (Jan. 19, 2008), available at SSRN: http://ssrn.com/abstract=1085582.

[78] 1993-2 C.B. 343.

[79] Prop. I.R.C. § 710(a)(1). The designation "Prop." has been used to indicate a portion of the bill that would change or add a current Code provision.

[80] Prop. I.R.C. § 710(b)(1).

[81] Prop. I.R.C. § 710(c)(1).

Chapter 10

BUSINESS COMBINATIONS: PARTNERSHIP MERGERS AND DIVISIONS

BASIC OVERVIEW

I.R.C. § 708(b)(2)(A) provides that in the case of a merger or consolidation of two or more partnerships, the resulting partnership is, for purposes of I.R.C. § 708, considered the continuation of any merging or consolidating partnership whose members own an interest of more than 50 percent in the capital and profits of the resulting partnership. Treas. Reg. § 1.708-1(c)(2) provides that if the resulting partnership could otherwise be considered a continuation of more than one of the merging partnerships, the resulting partnership is solely the continuation of the partnership that is credited with the contribution of assets having the greatest fair market value (net of liabilities) to the resulting partnership. Any other merging or consolidating partnerships are considered to be terminated.[1] If the members of none of the merging partnerships own more than a 50 percent interest in the capital and profits of the resulting partnership, all of the merged partnerships are considered terminated, and a new partnership results.[2] The taxable years of the merging partnerships that are considered terminated are closed under I.R.C. § 706(c) ending upon the date of the merger or consolidation.[3]

Generally, there are two ways in which the form of a partnership merger may be characterized for tax purposes, as the Assets-Over Form or as the Assets-Up Form. In the Assets-Over Form, any merged or consolidated partnership that is treated as terminated is first treated as contributing its assets and liabilities to the resulting partnership in exchange for interests in the resulting partnership.[4] Immediately after the contribution, the terminated partnership is treated as distributing interests in the resulting partnership to its partners in liquidation of the terminating partnership. In the Assets-Up Form, the terminating partnership distributes its assets and liabilities to its partners who then contribute the assets and liabilities to the resulting partnership.[5]

If two or more partnerships merge or consolidate into one partnership under the applicable local jurisdictional law without undertaking a form for the merger or consolidation, or undertake a form for the merger or consolidation that is not the Assets-Up Form, then the Assets-Over Form is deemed to apply. This means, for

---

[1] Treas. Reg. § 1.708-1(c)(1).

[2] *Id.*

[3] Treas. Reg. § 1.708-1(c)(2).

[4] Treas. Reg. § 1.708-1(c)(3)(i).

[5] Treas. Reg. § 1.708-1(c)(3)(ii).

example, that a merger of two partnerships under a state law pursuant to which the merger is accomplished merely by filing articles or a certificate of merger is deemed to be undertaken in the Assets-Over Form.

If a merger or consolidation is treated as using the Assets-Over Form, the normal rules under I.R.C. § 721, relating to the contribution of assets to a partnership in exchange for a partnership interest, would apply to the deemed contribution by any terminating partnerships. In the Assets-Up Form, I.R.C. § 721 would apply to the contribution by the partners of any assets of the terminating partnership to the continuing partnership. I.R.C. §§ 731 and 736 would similarly apply to the deemed or actual distribution of the partnership interests or assets of the terminating partnership to its partners (depending upon whether the transaction is characterized under the Assets-Over Form or Assets-Up Form).

I.R.C. § 708(b)(2)(B) provides that, in the case of a division of a partnership into two or more partnerships, all the resulting partnerships the members of which had an interest of more than 50 percent in the capital and profits of the preexisting partnership are considered a continuation of the preexisting partnership. Treas. Reg. § 1.708-1(b)(2)(ii) provides that any other resulting partnership is not considered a continuation of the preexisting partnership but is considered a new partnership. If the members of none of the resulting partnerships owned an interest of more than 50 percent in the capital and profits of the preexisting partnership, the preexisting partnership is terminated.[6] If members of a preexisting partnership do not become members of a resulting partnership that is considered a continuation of the preexisting partnership, such members' interests are considered liquidated as of the date of the division.[7]

As with partnership mergers, the divided partnership in a partnership division is treated as transferring all or a portion of its assets and liabilities to one or more resulting partnerships either in the Assets-Over Form or the Assets-Up Form.[8] A "divided partnership," for the purposes of this discussion, means the continuing partnership that is treated as transferring assets and liabilities to the recipient partnership or partnerships.[9] If a partnership divides into two or more partnerships and only one of the resulting partnerships is a continuation of the prior partnership, then the partnership that is a continuation of the prior partnership is the divided partnership. If more than one resulting partnership is a continuation of the prior partnership, the resulting partnership that, in form, transferred the assets and liabilities of the prior partnership will be treated as the divided partnership (if it is also treated as a continuation of the prior partnership). If a preexisting partnership divides and more than one resulting partnership is a continuing partnership (but the rule in the preceding sentence does not apply), then the continuing resulting partnership with assets having the greatest fair market value (net of liabilities) will be treated as the divided partnership.[10]

---

[6] Treas. Reg. § 1.708-1(d)(1).

[7] Id.

[8] Treas. Reg. § 1.708-1(d)(3).

[9] Treas. Reg. § 1.708-1(d)(4)(i).

[10] Id.

All resulting partnerships that are continuing partnerships are subject to preexisting elections that were made by the preexisting partnership.[11] However, a post-division election that is made by a resulting partnership will not bind any of the other resulting partnerships.

In partnership divisions, a preexisting partnership generally transfers certain assets and liabilities to a resulting partnership in exchange for interests in the resulting partnership, and immediately thereafter, the preexisting partnership distributes the resulting partnership interests to partners who are designated to receive interests in the resulting partnership (the "Assets-Over Form").[12] Alternatively, the preexisting partnership may distribute certain assets and liabilities to some or all of its partners who then contribute the assets and liabilities to a resulting partnership in exchange for interests in the resulting partnership (the "Assets-Up Form").[13] As with partnership mergers, the default rule for partnership divisions is the Assets-Over Form, so that if a transaction does not follow the formal steps of the Assets-Up Form, the transaction will be characterized under the Assets-Over Form regardless of whether that form is followed.[14] Also, as with mergers, the Assets-Up Form will be respected for divisions where the assets are conveyed to the partners under the laws of the applicable jurisdiction and then reconveyed to the resulting partnership.[15]

Whether a merger or division of a partnership is structured as an Assets-Up Transaction or an Assets-Over Transaction, two steps occur: there is a transfer of property to a partnership and a distribution of property from the partnership to the partners. Although the sequence and nature of the property distributed varies between the two structures, the partners receive their property as a distribution from the partnership and will have their bases determined in the property received under I.R.C. § 732, which generally provides that the bases to the partners in the property received will be the same as the bases were to the partnership immediately before the distribution. The partners reduce their bases in the partnership interests by the basis of the property received.[16]

In each case, a contribution is made to a resulting partnership, and the basis of the partnership interest received in exchange for the contribution will generally be determined under I.R.C. § 722, which generally provides that the basis in the partnership interest will equal the basis of the property contributed to the resulting partnership in the transaction. Similarly, the partnership would generally have a basis in the property contributed equal to the basis in the contributed property in the hands of the party that contributed that property.[17] The holding period of the resulting partnerships will include the holding periods of the

---

[11] Treas. Reg. § 1.708-1(d)(2)(ii).

[12] Treas. Reg. § 1.708-1(d)(i)(A).

[13] Treas. Reg. § 1.708-1(d)(ii)(A).

[14] Treas. Reg. § 1.708-1(d)(3)(i).

[15] Treas. Reg. § 1.708-1(d)(ii)(A).

[16] I.R.C. § 733.

[17] I.R.C. § 723.

contributors of the property, assuming no gain is recognized on the transaction.[18]

The result of these rules in the context of a merger is that the partners of the terminating partnerships will generally have bases in their partnership interests in the continuing partnership equal to their bases in their partnership interests in the terminating partnership (assuming no gain is recognized in the transaction).

DETAILED DISCUSSION

§ 10.01 PARTNERSHIP MERGERS

A. General Rules

I.R.C. § 708(b)(2)(A) provides that in the case of a merger or consolidation of two or more partnerships, the resulting partnership is, for purposes of I.R.C. § 708, considered the continuation of any merging or consolidating partnership whose members own an interest of more than 50 percent in the capital and profits of the resulting partnership. Treas. Reg. § 1.708-1(c)(2) provides that if the resulting partnership could otherwise be considered a continuation of more than one of the merging partnerships, the resulting partnership is solely the continuation of the partnership that is credited with the contribution of assets having the greatest fair market value (net of liabilities) to the resulting partnership. Any other merging or consolidating partnerships are considered to be terminated.[19] If the members of none of the merging partnerships own more than a 50 percent interest in the capital and profits of the resulting partnership, all of the merged partnerships are considered terminated, and a new partnership results.[20] The taxable years of the merging partnerships that are considered terminated are closed under I.R.C. § 706(c), ending upon the date of the merger or consolidation.[21]

The resulting partnership's taxable year does not close, and the partnership files a return for the taxable year of the merging or consolidating partnership that it is considered to be continuing.[22] The resulting partnership retains the taxpayer identification number of the partnership that is continuing.[23]

> *Example 1.* Partnership AB, in whose capital and profits A and B each own a 50-percent interest, and partnership CD, in whose capital and profits C and D each own a 50-percent interest, merge on September 30, and form partnership ABCD. Partners A, B, C, and D are on a calendar year, and partnership AB and partnership CD also are on a calendar year. After the merger, the partners have capital and profits interests as follows: A, 30 percent; B, 30 percent; C, 20 percent; and D, 20 percent. Since A and B together own an interest of more than 50 percent in the capital and profits

---

[18] I.R.C. § 1223(2); Treas. Reg. § 1.723-1.

[19] Treas. Reg. § 1.708-1(c)(1).

[20] *Id.*

[21] Treas. Reg. § 1.708-1(c)(2).

[22] *Id.*

[23] *Id.*

of partnership ABCD, partnership ABCD is considered a continuation of partnership AB and continues to file returns on a calendar year basis. Since C and D own an interest of less than 50 percent in the capital and profits of partnership ABCD, the taxable year of partnership CD closes as of September 30, the date of the merger, and partnership CD is terminated as of that date. Partnership ABCD is required to file a return for the taxable year January 1 to December 31, indicating that, until September 30, it was partnership AB. Partnership CD is required to file a return for its final taxable year, January 1 through September 30.[24]

The determination of which of the partnerships continues for tax purposes is made without regard to which partnership is treated as continuing for state law purposes.

Example 2. (i) Partnership X, in whose capital and profits A owns a 40-percent interest and B owns a 60-percent interest, and partnership Y, in whose capital and profits B owns a 60-percent interest and C owns a 40-percent interest, merge on September 30. The fair market value of the partnership X assets (net of liabilities) is $100X, and the fair market value of the partnership Y assets (net of liabilities) is $200X. The merger is accomplished under state law by partnership Y contributing its assets and liabilities to partnership X in exchange for interests in partnership X, with partnership Y then liquidating, distributing interests in partnership X to B and C.

(ii) B, a more than 50-percent partner in both partnerships prior to the merger, owns a greater than 50-percent interest in the resulting partnership following the merger. Thus, the "fair market value of assets" rule applies. Because the fair market value of partnership Y's assets (net of liabilities) was greater than that of partnership X's, under Treas. Reg. § 1.708-1(c)(1), partnership X will be considered to terminate in the merger. As a result, even though, for state law purposes, the transaction was undertaken with partnership Y contributing its assets and liabilities to partnership X and distributing interests in partnership X to its partners, pursuant to Treas. Reg. § 1.708-1(c)(3)(i), for Federal income tax purposes, the transaction will be treated as if partnership X contributed its assets to partnership Y in exchange for interests in partnership Y and then liquidated, distributing interests in partnership Y to A and B.[25]

B. Form of a Merger

Generally, there are two ways in which the form of a partnership merger may be characterized for tax purposes, as the Assets-Over Form or as the Assets-Up Form. In the Assets-Over Form, any merged or consolidated partnership that is treated as terminated is first treated as contributing its assets and liabilities to the

---

[24] Treas. Reg. § 1.708-1(c)(5), example 1.

[25] Treas. Reg. § 1.708-1(c)(5), example 2.

resulting partnership in exchange for interests in the resulting partnership.[26] Immediately after the contribution, the terminated partnership is treated as distributing interests in the resulting partnership to its partners in liquidation of the terminating partnership. In the Assets-Up Form, the terminating partnership distributes its assets and liabilities to its partners who then contribute the assets and liabilities to the resulting partnership.[27]

If two or more partnerships merge or consolidate into one partnership under the applicable local jurisdictional law without undertaking a form for the merger or consolidation, or undertake a form for the merger or consolidation that is not the Assets-Up Form (described below), then the Assets-Over Form is deemed to apply. This means, for example, that a merger of two partnerships under a state law pursuant to which the merger is accomplished merely by filing articles or a certificate of merger is deemed to be undertaken in the Assets-Over Form.

> *Example 3.* The facts are the same as in Example 2, except that partnership X is engaged in a trade or business and has, as one of its assets, goodwill. In addition, the merger is accomplished under state law by having partnership X convey an undivided 40-percent interest in each of its assets to A and an undivided 60-percent interest in each of its assets to B, with A and B then contributing their interests in such assets to partnership Y. Partnership Y also assumes all of the liabilities of partnership X.[28]

In this example, because partnership X followed the Assets-Up Form for state law purposes, the choice of the form of the partnership merger will be respected so that partnership X will be treated as following the Assets-Up Form for federal income tax purposes. However, if partnership X had chosen a form other than the Assets-Up Form or Assets-Over Form, the choice of the form would not be respected.

> *Example 4.* Partnership X and partnership Y merge when the partners of partnership X transfer their partnership X interests to partnership Y in exchange for partnership Y interests. Immediately thereafter, partnership X liquidates into partnership Y. The resulting partnership is considered a continuation of partnership Y, and partnership X is considered terminated.[29]

The partnerships in this example attempted to use what is sometimes called an "interests over" form[30] — the partners contribute their partnership interest to the partnership that continues for state law purposes. However, the partnerships are treated as undertaking the Assets-Over Form for tax purposes because the "interests over" form is not one of the permitted forms for partnership mergers

---

[26] Treas. Reg. § 1.708-1(c)(3)(i).

[27] Treas. Reg. § 1.708-1(c)(3)(ii).

[28] Treas. Reg. § 1.708-1(c)(5), example 3.

[29] Treas. Reg. § 1.708-1(c)(5), example 4.

[30] The "interests over" form is one of the three permitted structures for converting a partnership to a corporation. *See* Rev. Rul. 84-111, 1984-2 C.B. 88. *See* Eric. B. Sloan, Richard M. Lipton, Deborah Harrington and Marc Frediani, *New Prop. Regs. Provide Expanded Guidance on Partnership Mergers and Divisions — Part 1*, 93 J. Tax'n 198 (2000).

under the Regulations. Accordingly, for federal income tax purposes, partnership X is deemed to contribute its assets and liabilities to partnership Y in exchange for interests in partnership Y. Immediately thereafter, partnership X is deemed to have distributed the interests in partnership Y to its partners in liquidation of their interests in partnership X.

While a partnership merger may be accomplished by using any number of transactional structures, the result is a single transaction that combines two partnerships. In the two alternatives permitted by the Regulations, each partner must participate (or will be deemed to participate) in the partnership merger in the same manner (with the exception of those partners who are subject to the buy-out rule). Therefore, if the partners wish for a partnership merger to be characterized under the Assets-Up Form, the terminated partnership must undertake the steps of the Assets-Up Form for all of its assets when it distributes the assets to its partners. Otherwise, the transaction will be characterized under the Assets-Over Form. However, where more than two partnerships are combined, each combination will be viewed as a separate merger so that the characterization of a merger of one partnership into the resulting partnership under the Assets-Over Form will not prevent a simultaneous merger of another partnership into the same resulting partnership from being characterized under the Assets-Up Form.

Most partnership mergers are characterized under the Assets-Over Form, because of the greater simplicity in undertaking the form. But sometimes the Assets-Up Form is viewed as advantageous because of the way in which the basis of the property is calculated in a liquidating distribution. I.R.C. § 732(b) requires that the basis of property (other than money) distributed by a partnership in liquidation of the partner's interest will be equal to the partner's basis in the partnership interest reduced by the amount of any money distributed in the same transaction. This means that if a partner's basis in her partnership interest were greater than her proportionate share of the partnership's bases in its assets, the partner could obtain a step-up in the bases of the assets distributed to her and re-contributed if the partnership merged using an Assets-Up Form.

Consider the ABC partnership, which holds three properties of equal value: Whiteacre, Blackacre and Redacre. C's total proportionate share of the inside bases of the three properties is $300, but her basis in her partnership interest is $500. If ABC were to merge with DEF in a transaction in which ABC was the terminated partnership and the Asset-Over Form were used, the bases of the three properties would carry over without change. However, if the Asset-Up Form were used, C's proportionate share of the bases of the three properties would be increased to $500.

If a partnership merger is part of a larger series of transactions, the Regulations give the IRS authority to disregard the form if the substance of the larger series of transactions is inconsistent with following the form.[31]

---

[31] Treas. Reg. § 1.708-1(c)(6)(i).

C. Built-In Gain Resulting from the Merger

If a merger or consolidation is treated as using the Assets-Over Form, the normal rules under I.R.C. § 721, relating to the contribution of assets to a partnership in exchange for a partnership interest, would apply to the deemed contribution by any terminating partnerships. In the Assets-Up Form, I.R.C. § 721 would apply to the contribution by the partners of any assets of the terminating partnership to the continuing partnership. I.R.C. §§ 731 and 736 would similarly apply to the deemed or actual distribution of the partnership interests or assets of the terminating partnership to its partners (depending upon whether the transaction is characterized under the Assets-Over Form or Assets-Up Form).

In general, I.R.C. § 704(c)(1)(B) provides that if any property contributed to a partnership is distributed to a partner, other than the contributing partner, within seven years of the contribution, the contributing partner will recognize gain or loss in an amount equal to the remaining gain allocable to the contributing partner from the built-in gain in the property at the time of contribution. Similarly, I.R.C. § 737 provides that a partner who contributed property with built-in gain and who receives a distribution (other than the property originally contributed) from a partnership within seven years of the contribution may recognize gain on the distribution. However, Treas. Reg. § 1.704-4(c)(4) provides that I.R.C. § 704(c)(1)(B) does not apply to a transfer by a partnership of all of its assets and liabilities to a second partnership in an exchange described in I.R.C. § 721, followed by a distribution of the interest in the transferee partnership in a liquidation of the contributing partnership. Instead, a subsequent distribution of I.R.C. § 704(c) property by the continuing partnership is subject to I.R.C. § 704(c)(1)(B) to the same extent that a distribution by the transferor partnership would have been subject to I.R.C. § 704(c)(1)(B).[32] Similarly, Treas. Reg. § 1.737-2(b)(1) provides that I.R.C. § 737 does not apply under the same conditions as described in Treas. Reg. § 1.704-4(c)(4).

Neither section provides relief from the application of the seven-year holding period if the Assets-Up Form is used.

In spite of the apparent exception from the seven-year holding period provided in Treas. Reg. § 1.704-4(c)(4) and Treas. Reg. § 1.737-2(b)(1) for the Assets-Over Form, the Treasury took the position in Rev. Rul. 2004-43[33] that both I.R.C. § 704(c)(1)(B) and I.R.C. § 737 would still apply to the built-in gain or loss that existed in the assets of a continuing partnership that were deemed to be contributed by the terminating partnership to the continuing partnership. Under this interpretation, although gain recognition under I.R.C. § 704(c)(1)(B) and I.R.C. § 737 are not triggered by the deemed contribution and distribution resulting from the merger or consolidation, the merger or consolidation itself begins a new seven-year holding period during which the built-in gain in existence at the time of the merger or consolidation could be recognized by the partners of a

---

[32] Treas. Reg. § 1.704-4(c)(4).

[33] 2004-1 C.B. 842, revoked by Rev. Rul. 2005-10, 2005-1 C.B. 492. Although Rev. Rul. 2005-10 revoked Rev. Rul. 2004-43, the Treasury has proposed Regulations implementing the principles of Rev. Rul. 2004-43. *See* Prop. Treas. Reg. §§ 1.704-4(c)(4) and 1.737-2(b).

partnership that is treated as terminating in a merger or consolidation.

Rev. Rul. 2004-43[34] illustrated its conclusions with the following example:

> Example 5. On January 1, 2004, A contributed Asset 1, with a basis of $200x and a fair market value of $300x to partnership AB in exchange for a 50 percent interest. On the same date, B contributed $300x of cash to AB in exchange for a 50 percent interest. Also on January 1, 2004, C contributed Asset 2, with a basis of $100x and a fair market value of $200x to partnership CD in exchange for a 50 percent interest. D contributed $200x of cash to CD in exchange for a 50 percent interest.
>
> On January 1, 2006, AB and CD undertake an assets-over partnership merger in which AB is the continuing partnership and CD is the terminating partnership. At the time of the merger, AB's only assets are Asset 1, with a fair market value of $900x, and $300x in cash, and CD's only assets are Asset 2, with a fair market value of $600x and $200x in cash. After the merger, the partners have capital and profits interests in AB as follows: A, 30 percent; B, 30 percent; C, 20 percent; and D, 20 percent.
>
> On January 1, 2012, which is eight years after the initial contributions and six years after the merger, AB has the same assets that it had immediately after the merger. Each asset has the same value that it had at the time of the merger. On this date, AB distributes Asset 2 to A in liquidation of A's interest in AB.

In this example, on the date of the partnership merger, CD contributes cash and Asset 2 to AB in exchange for an interest in AB. Immediately thereafter, CD distributes, in liquidation, interests in AB to C and D. Under Treas. Reg. § 1.704-4(c)(4) and Treas. Reg. § 1.737-2(b)(1), the transaction considered in the example would appear to meet the exception from the application of I.R.C. § 704(c)(1)(B) and I.R.C. § 737. However, Rev. Rul. 2004-43 applies an I.R.C. § 704(c)(1)(B) analysis as if the exceptions in Treas. Reg. § 1.704-4(c)(4) and Treas. Reg. § 1.737-2(b)(1) did not apply.

As Rev. Rul. 2004-43 continues its analysis, Asset 2 has a basis of $100x and a fair market value of $600x upon contribution. Of the $500x of built in gain in Asset 2, $100x is pre-existing I.R.C. § 704(c) gain attributable to C's contribution of Asset 2 to CD, and $400x is additional I.R.C. § 704(c) gain created as a result of the merger. Rev. Rul. 2004-43 concludes, applying Treas. Reg. § 1.704-3(a)(7), that as the transferees of CD's partnership interest in AB, C and D each succeed to one-half of CD's $400x of I.R.C. § 704(c) gain in Asset 2 (each $200x). Thus, C's share of I.R.C. § 704(c) gain is $300x, and D's share of I.R.C. § 704(c) gain is $200x.

The distribution of Asset 2 to A occurs more than seven years after the contribution of Asset 2 to CD. Therefore, I.R.C. § 704(c)(1)(B) does not apply to the $100x of pre-existing 704(c) gain attributable to that contribution. However, the distribution of Asset 2 to A occurs within seven years of the contribution of Asset 2 by CD to AB. According to Rev. Rul. 2004-43, the contribution of Asset 2 by CD to

---

[34] 2004-1 C.B. 842, revoked by Rev. Rul. 2005-10, 2005-1 C.B. 492. We include Rev. Rul. 2004-43 in the text, as its principles were followed by the Proposed Regulations discussed below.

AB creates I.R.C. § 704(c) gain of $400x subject to the seven-year holding period. As the transferees of CD's partnership interest in AB, C and D each succeed to one-half of the $400x of 704(c) gain created by the merger. Under the analysis of Rev. Rul. 2004-43, I.R.C. § 704(c)(1)(B) applies to that I.R.C. § 704(c) gain because of the distribution of Asset 2 to A within seven years of the merger, causing C and D each to recognize $200x of gain.

It should be particularly noted that in this example, D, who originally contributed only cash, and who received nothing in the distribution from AB, has been required to recognize $200x of gain on the distribution of Asset 2 to A. This gain is solely attributable to the start of another I.R.C. § 704(c)(1)(B) seven-year period at the time of the merger of the two partnerships.

Proposed Regulations that implement the principles articulated in Rev. Rul. 2004-43 have now been issued. Prop. Treas. Reg. §§ 1.704-4(c)(4) and 1.737-2(b) provide that in an assets-over merger, I.R.C. §§ 704(c)(1)(B) and 737 do not apply to the transfer by a partnership (the transferor partnership) of all of its assets and liabilities to another partnership (the transferee partnership), followed by a distribution of the interests in the transferee partnership in liquidation of the transferor partnership as part of the same plan or arrangement. The Proposed Regulations, however, provide that I.R.C. § 704(c)(1)(B) applies to a subsequent distribution by the transferee partnership of I.R.C. § 704(c) property contributed in the assets-over merger by the transferor partnership to the transferee partnership. The Proposed Regulations also provide that I.R.C. § 737 applies when a partner of the transferor partnership receives a subsequent distribution of property (other than money) from the transferee partnership.

D. Buy-Out Rule

The Regulations contain a special buy-out rule that allows a resulting partnership in a merger to fund the purchase of one or more partners' interests in a terminating partnership without triggering the disguised sale rules, which otherwise could cause all of the partners in the terminating partnership to recognize gain or loss as a result of the purchase. Specifically, the Regulations provide that if the merger agreement (or similar document) specifies that the resulting partnership is purchasing the exiting partner's interest in the terminating partnership and also specifies the amount paid for the interest, the transaction will be treated as a sale of the exiting partner's interest to the resulting partnership.[35] The partner who is being bought out must also consent to the treatment.

Example 5 in Treas. Reg. § 1.708-1(c)(4) indicates that the partner who is being bought out is treated as if his interest was purchased immediately prior to the merger. Thus, the resulting partnership, and the partners (determined prior to the merger) of the partnership that is treated as continuing, would succeed to the withdrawing partner's capital account and built-in gain.[36] Although not discussed in the Regulations, it follows from treating the buyout as a sale to the resulting

---

[35] Treas. Reg. § 1.708-1(c)(4).

[36] Treas. Reg. § 1.708(c)(5), example 5(iii).

partnership occurring immediately prior to the merger that, if exiting partners sell 50 percent or more of the total interest in the terminating partnership's capital and profits as part of a merger, then a partnership termination under I.R.C. § 708(b)(1)(B) will occur immediately before the merger.

§ 10.02 PARTNERSHIP DIVISIONS

A. General Rules

I.R.C. § 708(b)(2)(B) provides that, in the case of a division of a partnership into two or more partnerships, all the resulting partnerships the members of which had an interest of more than 50 percent in the capital and profits of the preexisting partnership are considered a continuation of the preexisting partnership. Treas. Reg. § 1.708-1(b)(2)(ii) provides that any other resulting partnership is not considered a continuation of the preexisting partnership but is considered a new partnership. If the members of none of the resulting partnerships owned an interest of more than 50 percent in the capital and profits of the preexisting partnership, the preexisting partnership is terminated.[37] If members of a preexisting partnership do not become members of a resulting partnership that is considered a continuation of the preexisting partnership, such members' interests are considered liquidated as of the date of the division.[38]

As with partnership mergers, the divided partnership in a partnership division is treated as transferring all or a portion of its assets and liabilities to one or more resulting partnerships either in the Assets-Over Form or the Assets-Up Form.[39] A "divided partnership," for the purposes of this discussion, means the continuing partnership that is treated as transferring assets and liabilities to the recipient partnership or partnerships.[40] If a partnership divides into two or more partnerships and only one of the resulting partnerships is a continuation of the prior partnership, then the partnership that is a continuation of the prior partnership is the divided partnership. If more than one resulting partnership is a continuation of the prior partnership, the resulting partnership that, in form, transferred the assets and liabilities of the prior partnership will be treated as the divided partnership (if it is also treated as a continuation of the prior partnership). If a preexisting partnership divides and more than one resulting partnership is a continuing partnership (but the rule in the preceding sentence does not apply), then the continuing resulting partnership with assets having the greatest fair market value (net of liabilities) will be treated as the divided partnership.[41]

The divided partnership that is regarded as continuing is required to file a return for the taxable year of the partnership that has been divided.[42] The divided

---

[37] Treas. Reg. § 1.708-1(d)(1).

[38] *Id.*

[39] Treas. Reg. § 1.708-1(d)(3).

[40] Treas. Reg. § 1.708-1(d)(4)(i).

[41] *Id.*

[42] Treas. Reg. § 1.708-1(d)(2)(i).

partnership will also retain the employer identification number of the preexisting partnership. All other resulting partnerships that are regarded as continuing and all new partnerships (i.e., resulting partnerships that are not considered continuing) will file separate returns for the taxable year beginning on the day after the date of the division with new employer identification numbers for each partnership.[43]

All resulting partnerships that are continuing partnerships are subject to preexisting elections that were made by the preexisting partnership.[44] However, a post-division election that is made by a resulting partnership will not bind any of the other resulting partnerships.

> *Example 6.* Partnership ABCD owns three parcels of property: property X, with a value of $500; property Y, with a value of $300; and property Z, with a value of $200. A and B each own a 40-percent interest in the capital and profits of partnership ABCD, and C and D each own a 10 percent interest in the capital and profits of partnership ABCD. On November 1, partnership ABCD divides into three partnerships (AB1, AB2, and CD) by contributing property X to a newly formed partnership (AB1) and distributing all interests in such partnership to A and B as equal partners, and by contributing property Z to a newly formed partnership (CD) and distributing all interests in such partnership to C and D as equal partners in exchange for all of their interests in partnership ABCD. While partnership ABCD does not transfer property Y, C and D cease to be partners in the partnership. Accordingly, after the division, the partnership holding property Y is referred to as partnership AB2.[45]

In this example, partnerships AB1 and AB2 are both continuations of partnership ABCD (because A and B own more than 50 percent of the capital and profits of the preexisting partnership), while partnership CD is considered a new partnership formed at the beginning of the day on November 2. For each of the divisions, partnership ABCD will be treated as following the Assets-Over Form, with partnership ABCD contributing property X to partnership AB1 and property Z to partnership CD, and distributing the interests in such partnerships to the designated partners. ABCD will also be treated as contributing property Y to partnership AB2 for tax purposes even though no transfer occurs for state law purposes. Because property X has a greater fair market value than property Y, partnership AB1 will be viewed as the divided partnership.

The Regulations do not define what constitutes a partnership division. However, the Regulations do clarify that, in order to have a division, at least two members of the preexisting partnership must be members of each resulting partnership that exists after the transaction.[46]

---

[43] *Id.*

[44] Treas. Reg. § 1.708-1(d)(2)(ii).

[45] Treas. Reg. § 1.708-1(d)(5), example 4.

[46] Treas. Reg. § 1.708-1(d)(4)(iv).

B. Form of a Division

In partnership divisions, a preexisting partnership generally transfers certain assets and liabilities to a resulting partnership in exchange for interests in the resulting partnership, and immediately thereafter, the preexisting partnership distributes the resulting partnership interests to partners who are designated to receive interests in the resulting partnership (the *"Assets-Over Form"*).[47] Alternatively, the preexisting partnership may distribute certain assets and liabilities to some or all of its partners who then contribute the assets and liabilities to a resulting partnership in exchange for interests in the resulting partnership (the *"Assets-Up Form"*).[48] As with partnership mergers, the default rule for partnership divisions is the Assets-Over Form, so that if a transaction does not follow the formal steps of the Assets-Up Form, the transaction will be characterized under the Assets-Over Form regardless of whether that form is followed.[49] Also, as with mergers, the Assets-Up Form will be respected for divisions where the assets are conveyed to the partners under the laws of the applicable jurisdiction and then reconveyed to the resulting partnership.[50]

The rules for divisions also parallel the rules for mergers in that a division resulting in a single new partnership cannot be treated both in the Assets-Over Form and the Assets-Up Form. If a partnership attempted to combine the two forms so that the choice of form was not clear, the Assets-Over Form would be applied. However, where a single partnership is divided in a transaction that involves a transfer of assets (either actual or deemed) to multiple partnerships, the transfer to each resulting partnership should be viewed separately. If a partnership division is part of a larger series of transactions, the Regulations give the IRS authority to disregard the form if the substance of the larger series of transactions is inconsistent with following the form.[51]

C. Built-In Gain in Divisions

The preamble to the Regulations under I.R.C. § 708 dealing with partnership divisions indicates that the IRS and Treasury agree that, in general, a partnership division should not create new I.R.C. § 704(c) property or I.R.C. § 737 net precontribution gain.[52] However, the preamble also indicates that the Treasury was not certain that this result is necessarily appropriate where a division is non-pro rata as to the partners, where some property is extracted from or added to the partnerships in connection with the division, or where new partners are added to the ownership group in connection with the division.

---

[47] Treas. Reg. § 1.708-1(d)(i)(A).

[48] Treas. Reg. § 1.708-1(d)(ii)(A).

[49] Treas. Reg. § 1.708-1(d)(3)(i).

[50] Treas. Reg. § 1.708-1(d)(ii)(A).

[51] Treas. Reg. § 1.708-1(d)(6).

[52] T.D. 8925, 66 Fed. Reg. 715 (Jan. 4, 2001).

§ 10.03   THE EFFECT ON THE PARTNERS AND THE PARTNERSHIP

Whether a merger or division of a partnership is structured as an Assets-Up Transaction or an Assets-Over Transaction, two steps occur: There is a transfer of property to a partnership and a distribution of property from the partnership to the partners. Although the sequence and nature of the property distributed varies between the two structures, the partners receive their property as a distribution from the partnership and will have their bases determined in the property received under I.R.C. § 732, which generally provides that the bases to the partners in the property received will be the same as the bases were to the partnership immediately before the distribution. If the distribution was made other than in liquidation of the partner's partnership interest, the partner would reduce her basis in the partnership interest by the basis of the property received.[53]

In each case, a contribution is made to a resulting partnership, and the basis of the partnership interest received in exchange for the contribution will generally be determined under I.R.C. § 722, which generally provides that the basis in the partnership interest will equal the basis of the property contributed to the resulting partnership in the transaction. Similarly, the partnership would generally have a basis in the property contributed equal to the basis in the contributed property in the hands of the party that contributed that property.[54] The holding period of the resulting partnerships will include the holding periods of the contributors of the property, assuming no gain is recognized on the transaction.[55]

The result of these rules in the context of a merger is that the partners of the terminating partnerships will generally have bases in their partnership interests in the continuing partnership equal to their bases in their partnership interests in the terminating partnership (assuming no gain is recognized in the transaction).

However, the form, and thus the sequence, of the transaction chosen may create a difference in the bases of the assets held by the resulting partnerships when there is a difference between the bases of the assets held by a terminating partnership and the aggregate bases of the partners' partnership interests in the terminating partnership. I.R.C. § 732(b) provides that the basis of property other than money distributed to a partner in liquidation of the partner's interest will be equal to the adjusted basis of such partner's interest in the partnership reduced by any money distributed in the same transaction. This means that if partnership ABC merges into partnership DEF using an Assets-Up Form, because the property of ABC is first distributed to partners A, B and C in liquidation of their partnership interests prior to contribution to DEF, DEF will have a basis in the former property of ABC equal to the aggregate bases of A, B and C in their partnership interests (rather than the basis that such property had in the hands of ABC). In contrast, if the Assets-Over Form is used, the continuing partnership has the same basis in the assets as the terminating partnership had in the assets. The same type of difference between inside and outside bases can result in similar differences between the

---

[53] I.R.C. § 733.

[54] I.R.C. § 723.

[55] I.R.C. § 1223(2); Treas. Reg. § 1.723-1.

Assets-Over Form and Assets-Up Form in partnership divisions.

Chapter 11

ANTI-ABUSE PROVISIONS

BASIC OVERVIEW

As you have seen from the prior chapters, Subchapter K gives partnerships and their partners a great deal of flexibility in structuring their transactions for tax purposes. In many transactions, a partnership can avoid taxation where a corporation could not. Both the Congress and the IRS have thought the flexibility afforded partnerships can sometimes be too much of a good thing. Congress has enacted a number of statutes and the IRS has promulgated Regulations designed to rein in taxpayers' more aggressive tendencies. Further, a number of judicial doctrines are relevant to the application of Subchapter K. These provisions, beginning with the latter, are the focus of this chapter.

There is a limit on the extent to which the courts will allow taxpayers to run with the ball. When a literal application of the law overly strains the courts' sense of tax justice, they will often step in and apply one or more of a variety of judicial doctrines to set things right. These doctrines have different names, but the purpose is always the same: Not to let overly clever taxpayers (or, more likely, their overly clever tax advisers) allow a literal application of the tax law or the external form of the transaction trump reason. Indeed, commonly the various doctrines can be applied interchangeably and yield the same result.[1]

From the earliest days of the tax law, the courts have held that there is a limit on the extent to which form can control substance. Particularly when the taxpayer controls the relevant aspects of the form of the transaction, or when the transaction only involves related parties, the courts will commonly feel free to ignore the form and look at the substance of the transactions. The substance over form doctrine is also sometimes called the "sham transaction" doctrine or, due to a statute discussed below, the "economic substance" doctrine.

That does not mean form never counts. Often form absolutely controls. If a taxpayer has two identical assets, one with an inherent loss and one with an inherent gain, he has complete control over which one to sell and whether or not to recognize a gain or a loss. If, however, the loss sale is to a relative or friend, who sells the property back shortly after buying it, the courts may step in even where the legislature has not.[2] If, on the other hand, the form reflects the substance, the fact that there was also a desire to obtain tax benefits will not usually cause a problem.

---

[1] See *ASA Investering Partnership v. United States*, 201 F.3d 505 (D.C. Cir. 2000), *cert. denied* 531 U.S. 871 (2000), at 512 note 4: "Because of the ultimate unity of the tests . . . ."

[2] Often in this context, the legislature has stepped in. *See* I.R.C. § 267.

Usually, the substance over form doctrine may only be used by the government. A taxpayer normally is bound by the form he uses (and the associated tax consequences).[3]

In 2010, Congress codified the economic substance doctrine in I.R.C. § 7701(o). Under the codified version, any transaction to which the economic substance doctrine is relevant will be treated as having economic substance only if (i) the transaction changes in a meaningful way (apart from federal income tax effects) the taxpayer's economic position, *and* (ii) the taxpayer has a substantial purpose (apart from federal income tax effects) for entering into the transaction. For the purposes of the first requirement, a profit potential for the transaction is taken into account only if the present value of pre-tax profit from the transaction is substantial in relation to the present value of the expected net tax benefits from the transaction if the transaction were respected. More on this in the Detailed Discussion.

The business purpose doctrine originated in the Second Circuit in the case of *Helvering v. Gregory*.[4] There, taxpayers attempted to use the tax-free corporate reorganization provisions to avoid a taxable dividend. The court held that the transaction did not qualify as a reorganization as it was not part of the conduct of the business of the relevant organizations, the sole motivation being tax savings. Again, there is no bright line and the application of the business purpose doctrine will depend upon the facts of each case.

In *Lynch v. United States*,[5] a corporation declared a dividend in kind of boxes of apples. Instead of actually distributing the apples, however, the shareholders agreed that the corporation should sell the apples and distribute the proceeds to them. The corporation then sold the apples in the ordinary course of its business. The court, citing the business purpose doctrine, held that the dividend should be ignored and the gain on the sale of the apples be taxed directly to the corporation.

Under the step transaction doctrine, interrelated steps are collapsed and treated as part of a single transaction. *McDonald's Restaurant v. Commissioner*[6] applied the step transaction doctrine. The hamburger giant was the taxpayer. It issued stock to acquire the interests of franchise holders. The question was whether that issuance should be stepped together with a subsequent registration of the stock and sale of the stock by the erstwhile franchise holders. If not stepped

---

[3] See *Commissioner v. Danielson*, 378 F.2d 771, 775 (1967), holding that a taxpayer may only "challenge the tax consequences of his agreement as construed by the Commissioner only by adducing proof which in an action between the parties to the agreement would be admissible to alter that construction or to show its unenforceablility because of mistake, undue influence, fraud, duress, etc." Some circuit courts and the Tax Court somewhat more liberally permit a taxpayer to disavow the form of an agreement if the taxpayer provides "strong proof" that the parties intended a different arrangement. *See* Coleman v. Commissioner, 87 T.C. 178 (1986); Kreider v. Commissioner, 762 F.2d 580 (7th Cir. 1985). The burden in the former courts will usually be impossible to overcome, in the latter courts it will merely by highly difficult. The moral? For planning purposes assume the taxpayer will be stuck with the form he chooses.

[4] 69 F.2d 809 (2d Cir. 1934), *aff'd sub nom* Gregory v. Helvering, 293 U.S. 465 (1935)

[5] 192 F.2d 718 (9th Cir. 1951).

[6] 688 F.2d 520 (7th Cir. 1982).

together, the first step could be seen as a tax-free reorganization under I.R.C. § 368. That treatment would not have been beneficial for McDonald's as it meant a lower basis in the acquired assets and thus lower depreciation deductions. The court held, however, that the transactions should be stepped together and the first step was thus not a tax-free reorganization.[7] In the court's view, the franchise holders would not have entered into the transaction without the assurance that the stock they received would be registered so that they could sell it (which they promptly did).[8]

Several recent cases have concluded that a taxpayer's tax avoidance motives prevented the taxpayer from forming a valid partnership for tax purposes. These cases are sometimes referred to as the *"ACM"* decisions after the first such decision.[9] The facts of these cases are highly complex. See Detailed Discussion.

The IRS often has had to play catch-up to crafty tax planners and in 1994 it decided it needed a more powerful weapon and promulgated the anti-abuse Regulations of Treas. Reg. § 1.701-2. These Regulations essentially permit the IRS to ignore the structure of a transaction that might technically comply with partnership tax law if the transaction is deemed to be abusive under these Regulations.

Specifically, the Regulations provide that three requirements are implicit in the intent of Subchapter K:

1. The partnership must be bona fide and each partnership transaction or series of related transactions must be entered into for a substantial business purpose.

2. The form of each partnership transaction must be respected under substance over form principles.

3. The application of a given Code provision and the ultimate tax results, taking into account all the relevant facts and circumstances, must be clearly contemplated by that provision.[10]

If this all sounds a little squishy, it is because it is. More details are provided in the Detailed Discussion.

A number of Code sections address what have become known as "mixing bowl" transactions. Recall that contributions to and distributions from partnerships can be tax free under I.R.C. §§ 721 and 731. Partners may attempt to disguise what

---

[7] When stepped together, the reorganization lacked "continuity of interest," a necessary component to a tax-free reorganization. *McDonald's Restaurant v. Commissioner, supra.*

[8] Indeed, the court held that any of the three forms of the step transaction doctrine could have been applied.

[9] *See generally* ACM Partnership v. Commissioner, TCM 1997-115, aff'd 157 F.3d 231 (3d Cir. 1998), and Lipton, *The Tax Court Upsets New Corporate Tax Shelter — Lessons From the Colgate Case*, 86 JTAX 331 (1997), and Lipton, *Brush Up Your Planning — More Lessons From the Colgate Case.* 90 JTAX 89 (1999); Boca Investering Partnership v. United States, 167 F. Supp. 2d 298 (D.C. 2001), *rev'd* 314 F.3d 625 (D.C. Cir. 2003), *cert. denied* 540 U.S. 826 (2003); *see also* Saba Partnership v. Commissioner, 273 F.3d 1135 (D.C. Cir. 2001). We discuss some of these cases in Chapter 1.

[10] Treas. Reg. § 1.702-2(a).

really is a sale as a contribution and distribution. It is true that the economic substance doctrine could be used to attack these, but Congress wanted a more precise weapon.

I.R.C. § 707(a)(2)(B) was the first of these rules to be enacted, discussed in Chapter 9. Congress thought it was not sufficient by itself and enacted two other code sections.

I.R.C. § 704(c)(1)(B) applies if property contributed by one partner is distributed to another partner within seven years of the original contribution. In that event, the contributing partner recognizes the gain or loss he would have recognized under I.R.C. § 704(c)(1)(A) had the contributed property been sold for its fair market value to the distributee. The character of the gain or loss is the same as the character that would have resulted had the property actually been sold to the distributee.[11] For example, assume A contributes land to a partnership with a fair market value of $10,000 and a basis of $6,000 and B contributes cash of $10,000. Further assume that, three years later, when the land has appreciated in value to $15,000, it is distributed to B when B's basis in his partnership interest is $10,000. Under I.R.C. § 704(c)(1)(B), A will recognize $4,000 of gain, the gain he would have recognized under I.R.C. § 704(c)(1)(A) had the property been sold at its fair market value.[12] Note that while there is $9,000 of gain inherent in the distributed property, not all of that gain is recognized, only the portion to which I.R.C. § 704(c)(1)(A) would have applied.

I.R.C. § 704(c)(1)(B)(iii) provides that "appropriate adjustments" are made to the basis of the contributed property and the contributing partner's basis in the partnership interest. The Regulations provide that the contributing partner's partnership interest basis is increased for gain and reduced for any loss resulting from the distribution. The partnership's basis in the contributed property is also increased for any gain and reduced for any loss, and this is deemed to occur immediately before the distribution of the property.[13] Thus, continuing with the above example, because A recognized $4,000 of gain, A's basis in the partnership interest and, immediately before the distribution, the partnership's basis in the land, is increased by $4,000 to $10,000. When the land is distributed to B, he takes it with a $10,000 carryover basis, and his basis in the partnership interest is reduced to zero.[14]

The I.R.C. § 704(c)(1)(B) "taint" attaches to the partnership interest. Thus, if all or a portion of A's partnership interest is transferred, a proportionate share of the I.R.C. § 704(c)(1)(B) gain or loss goes with it.[15]

---

[11] The fact that it is deemed sold to the distributee can have unexpected consequences. For example, if the distributee owns over 50 percent of the partnership, and the asset is not a capital asset to him, the gain will be ordinary income under I.R.C. § 707(b)(2) even if the asset was a capital asset to the contributing partner and the partnership. I.R.C. § 707(b)(1) could deny a loss.

[12] Note that the I.R.C. § 704(c)(1)(A) method used, whether it be the traditional, traditional with curative allocations, or remedial method, will determine the amount of gain or loss that is allocated.

[13] Treas. Reg. § 1.704-4(e)(1) and (2).

[14] See I.R.C. §§ 732(a)(1) and 733.

[15] Treas. Reg. § 1.704-4(d)(2). See Willis, Pennell, Postlewaite, *Partnership Taxation* ¶ 10.08[5][b][v]

I.R.C. § 737 requires the contributing partner to recognize gain (but not loss) if he contributes *appreciated* property to the partnership and within seven years receives a current or liquidating distribution of property other than money from the partnership.[16] The amount of gain that is recognized is the lesser of:

1. The fair market value of the distributed property less the partner's outside basis just before the distribution (the basis is first reduced by any money received as part of the same distribution), or

2. The "net precontribution gain."

The net precontribution gain is the net gain that would have been recognized by the distributee partner under I.R.C. § 704(c)(1)(B) if all property held by the partnership that had been contributed to the partnership by that partner within seven years of the distribution had been distributed to another partner. This latter amount is the same as the net I.R.C. § 704(c)(1)(A) gain allocable to the partner.

The character of the gain the distributee partner recognizes is determined by reference to the character of the net precontribution gain inherent in the contributed property *to the partnership*.[17] The gain increases the partner's outside basis immediately before the property distribution.[18] The gain also generally increases the inside basis of the property the partner contributed to the partnership.[19] The distributee takes the normal I.R.C. § 732 basis in the distributed property.[20]

I.R.C. § 737 is perhaps most easily understood by way of an example. Assume A contributes land #1 to a partnership with a fair market value of $10,000 and an adjusted basis of $6,000. B contributes cash of $3,000 and land #2 with an adjusted basis and fair market value of $7,000. Within seven years, Land #2 is distributed to A in an operating distribution and the facts and the values otherwise remain unchanged. Under I.R.C. § 737, A's gain is the lesser of:

1. $1,000, the fair market value of the distributed land of $7,000 less A's outside basis of $6,000, or

2. $4,000, A's net precontribution gain.

Thus, in this case A recognizes $1,000 of gain. A increases his outside basis to $7,000 for the gain and this is done immediately before the distribution. A then takes a $7,000 adjusted basis in the distributed property under I.R.C. § 732(a)(1), and his adjusted basis in the partnership is reduced to zero under I.R.C. § 733.[21] Finally, the partnership increases its adjusted basis in land #1 that A contributed by $1,000 to $7,000.

---

for some interesting planning opportunities in this regard.

[16] Marketable securities can be treated as money. I.R.C. §§ 737(e) and 731(c).

[17] *See* Treas. Reg. § 1.737-1(d).

[18] I.R.C. § 737(c)(1); Treas. Reg. § 1.737-3(a).

[19] *See* Treas. Reg. § 1.737-3(c) for a fairly involved set of rules in this regard.

[20] Treas. Reg. § 1.737-3(b).

[21] Note that the basis increase to A's interest only occurs for purposes of determining his basis in the distributed property and not for purposes of determining his gain or loss on the I.R.C. § 737 transaction.

I.R.C. §§ 737 and 704(c)(1)(B) can apply simultaneously. See Detailed Discussion.

DETAILED DISCUSSION

§ 11.01 INTRODUCTION

As you have seen from the prior chapters, Subchapter K gives partnerships and its partners a great deal of flexibility in structuring their transactions for tax purposes. In many transactions, a partnership can avoid taxation where a corporation could not. Both the Congress and the IRS have thought that the flexibility afforded partnerships can sometimes be too much of a good thing. Congress has enacted a number of statutes and the IRS has promulgated Regulations designed to rein in taxpayers' more aggressive tendencies. Further, a number of judicial doctrines are relevant to the application of Subchapter K. These provisions, beginning with the latter, are the focus of this chapter.

§ 11.02 JUDICIAL DOCTRINES

A. Introduction

To begin at the beginning, no taxpayer is required to pay more taxes than he owes and can arrange his tax affairs so as to minimize taxes. In the famous words of Judge Learned Hand:

> [A] transaction, otherwise within an exception of the tax law, does not lose its immunity, because it is actuated by a desire to avoid, or, if one choose, to evade taxation. Any one may so arrange his affairs that his taxes shall be as low as possible; he is not bound to choose that pattern which will best pay the Treasury; there is not even a patriotic duty to increase one's taxes.[22]

Still, there is a limit on the extent to which the courts will allow taxpayers to run with the ball. When a literal application of the law overly strains the courts' sense of tax justice, they will often step in and apply one or more of a variety of judicial doctrines to set things right. These doctrines have different names, but the purpose is always the same: Not to let overly clever taxpayers (or, more likely, their overly clever tax advisers) allow a literal application of the tax law or the external form of the transaction trump reason. Indeed, commonly the various doctrines can be applied interchangeably and yield the same result.[23] Of course, no one can exactly pinpoint the line that cannot be crossed, and what might seem to be properly arranging one's affairs to lower taxes to one judge might seem grossly over the line to another judge or appellate court. Further, even if a particular taxpayer's hands

---

[22] Helvering v. Gregory, 69 F.2d 809, 810 (2d Cir. 1934), aff'd sub nom Gregory v. Helvering, 293 U.S. 465 (1935); as the lingo of tax law has developed since this case, the term "tax evasion" has come to be associated with criminal conduct, so the reader may want to substitute "avoidance" for "evasion" in Judge Hand's opinion. It is also noteworthy that the taxpayer actually lost in this case.

[23] See ASA Investering Partnership v. United States, 201 F.3d 505 (D.C. Cir. 2000), cert. denied 531 U.S. 871 (2000), at 512 note 4: "Because of the ultimate unity of the tests . . . ."

are reasonably clean, courts may still rule against him if they fear that other taxpayers might take inappropriate advantage of the structure he used.[24] Consequently, it is very difficult to provide ready touchstones for when the judicial doctrines will apply. Finally, courts often combine the doctrines discussed below. Thus, a court might conclude that a transaction lacks substance *and* a business purpose.

B. Substance Over Form

From the earliest days of the tax law, the courts have held that there is a limit on the extent to which form can control substance. Particularly when the taxpayer controls the relevant aspects of the form of the transaction, or when the transaction only involves related parties, the courts will commonly feel free to ignore the form and look at the substance of the transactions. This doctrine is also sometimes called the "sham transaction" doctrine or, as a consequence of a fairly new statute discussed below, the "economic substance" doctrine.

The substance over form doctrine does not mean form never counts. Often form absolutely controls. If a taxpayer has two identical assets, one with an inherent loss and one with an inherent gain, he has complete control over which one to sell and whether or not to recognize a gain or a loss. If, however, the loss sale is to a relative or friend, who sells the property back shortly after buying it, the courts may step in even where the legislature has not.[25]

The court applied the substance over form doctrine in *Norton v. Commissioner*.[26] There the taxpayer placed business and personal assets in three domestic trusts and moved income and expenses amongst them and a foreign trust in an effort to avoid taxable income.[27] The taxpayer effectively had complete control over what went on in the domestic trusts and it was apparent that the foreign trust was operated in a cooperative manner. The court ignored the trusts under the substance over form doctrine and treated their income as directly earned by the taxpayer.

Courts commonly intervene where the economic profit from a transaction is primarily based on the tax savings. For example, in *Winn-Dixie Stores, Inc. v. Commissioner*,[28] Winn-Dixie embarked on a broad based, company-owned life-insurance program whose sole purpose, as shown by contemporary memoranda, was to give Winn-Dixie interest deductions. Under the program, Winn-Dixie purchased whole life insurance policies on almost all of its full-time employees, who numbered in the tens of thousands. Winn-Dixie was the sole beneficiary of the policies. Winn-Dixie would borrow against those policies' account values at an interest rate of more than 11%. The high interest rate and the administrative fees that came with the program outweighed the net cash surrender value and benefits

---

[24] Boris Bittker and Martin McMahon, Jr., *Federal Income Taxation of Individuals* ¶ 1.3[2] ("Federal Income Taxation").

[25] Often in this context, the legislature has stepped in. *See* I.R.C. § 267.

[26] 2002 T.C.M. (RIA) ¶ 2002-137.

[27] It is not uncommon to see similar structures used by "tax protestors."

[28] 254 F.3d 1313 (11th Cir. 2001).

paid on the policies, with the result that in pre-tax terms Winn-Dixie lost money on the program. The deductibility of the interest and fees, however, yielded a post-tax benefit projected to reach into the billions of dollars over 60 years. Winn-Dixie participated until 1997, when a change in tax law jeopardized this tax arbitrage, and it eased its way out.[29] The court affirmed the Tax Court's application of the sham transaction doctrine as the structure was not expected to generate a pre-tax profit and thus was purely a tax savings maneuver.

If, on the other hand, the form reflects the substance, the fact that there was also a desire to obtain tax benefits will not usually cause a problem. Thus, for example, in *Winn Dixie*, if the company had only insured key employees, and the insurance had served the needs of the business to protect against financial disruption that might occur on a key employee's death, the structure probably would have passed muster. The fact that there also would have been tax benefits from borrowing against the policies, which in part motivated the transaction, should not have changed the result.

Transactions that are at arm's length are more likely to survive scrutiny than transactions between related parties, though it should be noted that the Code often has something to say about related party transactions. For example, I.R.C. § 267 often denies losses on sales between related parties.

Usually, the substance over form doctrine may only be used by the government. A taxpayer normally is bound by the form he uses (and the associated tax consequences).[30]

In 2010, Congress codified the economic substance doctrine in I.R.C. § 7701(o). Under the codified version, any transaction to which the economic substance doctrine is relevant will be treated as having economic substance only if (i) the transaction changes in a meaningful way (apart from federal income tax effects) the taxpayer's economic position, *and* (ii) the taxpayer has a substantial purpose (apart from federal income tax effects) for entering into the transaction. For the purposes of the first requirement, a profit potential for the transaction is taken into account only if the present value of pre-tax profit from the transaction is substantial in relation to the present value of the expected net tax benefits from the transaction if the transaction were respected.

The new provisions are only intended to apply to transactions entered into in connection with a trade or business or for the production of income. The new

---

[29] *Id.* at 1314. *See* I.R.C. § 264(e)(2) which lowered the interest rate that could be used beginning on January 1, 1996.

[30] See *Commissioner v. Danielson*, 378 F.2d 771, 775 (1967), holding that a taxpayer may only "challenge the tax consequences of his agreement as construed by the Commissioner only by adducing proof which in an action between the parties to the agreement would be admissible to alter that construction or to show its unenforceablility because of mistake, undue influence, fraud, duress, etc." Some circuit courts and the Tax Court somewhat more liberally permit a taxpayer to disavow the form of an agreement if the taxpayer provides "strong proof" that the parties intended a different arrangement. *See* Coleman v. Commissioner, 87 T.C. 178 (1986); Kreider v. Commissioner, 762 F.2d 580 (7th Cir. 1985). The burden in the former courts will usually be impossible to overcome, in the latter courts it will merely by highly difficult. The moral? For planning purposes assume the taxpayer will be stuck with the form he chooses.

provision expresses an intent not to change the determination of whether the economic substance doctrine is relevant to a transaction, thus maintaining the importance of prior case law.

The report of the Staff of the Joint Committee indicates that if the realization of the tax benefits of a transaction is consistent with the congressional purpose or plan that the tax benefits were designed by Congress to effectuate, it is not intended that such tax benefits be disallowed under the new provision. Thus, for example, the report of the Staff of the Joint Committee indicates that it is not intended that a tax credit (e.g., I.R.C. § 42 (low-income housing credit), I.R.C. § 45 (production tax credit), I.R.C. § 45D (new markets tax credit), I.R.C. § 47 (rehabilitation credit), I.R.C. § 48 (energy credit), etc.) be disallowed in a transaction pursuant to which, in form and substance, a taxpayer makes the type of investment or undertakes the type of activity that the credit was intended to encourage.

According to the legislative history, the provision is not intended to alter the tax treatment of certain basic business transactions that, under long-standing judicial and administrative practice, are respected, merely because the choice between meaningful economic alternatives is largely or entirely based on comparative tax advantages. Among these basic transactions are (1) the choice between capitalizing a business enterprise with debt or equity; (2) a U.S. person's choice between utilizing a foreign corporation or a domestic corporation to make a foreign investment; (3) the choice to enter into a transaction or series of transactions that constitute a corporate organization or reorganization under subchapter C of the Code; and (4) the choice to utilize a related party entity in a transaction, provided that the arm's length standard of I.R.C. § 482 and other applicable concepts are satisfied. Leasing transactions, like all other types of transactions, will continue to be analyzed in light of all the facts and circumstances. As under present law, whether a particular transaction meets the requirements for specific treatment under any of these provisions is a question of facts and circumstances.

The amendment, which is immediately effective, also increases penalties for transactions without economic substance in some circumstances. A new 20% strict liability penalty is added for understatements due to the failure of a transaction to satisfy the economic substance doctrine, which is increased to 40% if the transaction is not disclosed. There is no reasonable cause defense to the penalty.

C. Business Purpose

The business purpose doctrine originated in the Second Circuit in the case of *Helvering v. Gregory*.[31] There, taxpayers attempted to use the tax-free corporate reorganization provisions to avoid a taxable dividend. The court held that the transaction did not qualify as a reorganization as it was not part of the conduct of the business of the relevant organizations, the sole motivation being tax savings. Judge Learned Hand, who authored the Second Circuit's opinion in *Helvering v. Gregory*, later summarized the business purpose doctrine as follows:

---

[31] 69 F.2d 809 (2d Cir. 1934), *aff'd sub nom* Gregory v. Helvering, 293 U.S. 465 (1935)

> The doctrine of *Gregory v. Helvering* . . . means that in construing words of a tax statute which describe commercial or industrial transactions we are to understand them to refer to transactions entered upon for commercial or industrial purposes and not to include transactions entered upon for no other motive but to escape taxation.[32]

Again, there is no bright line and the application of the business purpose doctrine will depend upon the facts of each case. As one court noted:

> "[T]he "business purpose" doctrine is hazardous. It is uniformly recognized that taxpayers are entitled to structure their transactions in such a way as to minimize tax. When the business purpose doctrine is violated, such structuring is deemed to have gotten out of hand, to have been carried to such extreme lengths that the business purpose is no more than a facade. But there is no absolutely clear line between the two. Yet the doctrine seems essential. A tax system of rather high rates gives a multitude of clever individuals in the private sector powerful incentives to game the system. Even the smartest drafters of legislation and Regulations cannot be expected to anticipate every device."[33]

D. Step Transaction Doctrine

Under the step transaction doctrine, interrelated steps are collapsed and treated as part of a single transaction. The doctrine has three variations, the "binding commitment" test, the "interdependence" test, and the "end result" test.[34] The binding commitment test will apply if the parties are legally required to take each of the steps. In *Gordon v. Commissioner*,[35] it was actually the taxpayer that was endeavoring to have the doctrine applied. The case involved a "spin-off" of a subsidiary corporation that would have been tax-free if the requirements of I.R.C. § 355 had been met. That section requires an amount of stock equal to control (generally 80% of the stock) of the subsidiary be distributed. Initially, the amount distributed did not constitute control. The court noted that there may have been an intention at the time of the earlier distribution to distribute an additional amount in the future that combined would have constituted control (and indeed it was distributed). But because at the time of the initial distribution the distributing corporation was under no binding obligation to make the subsequent distribution, the step transaction doctrine was not applied.

The interdependence test looks to whether the various steps taken were so interrelated that it would have been pointless to have taken any single step without taking the others. In *McDonald's Restaurant v. Commissioner*,[36] the hamburger giant was the taxpayer. It issued stock to acquire the interests of franchise holders. The question was whether that issuance should be stepped together with a

---

[32] Commissioner v. Transport Trading & Terminal Corp., 176 F.2d 570, 572 (2d Cir. 1949).

[33] ASA Investering Partnership v. Commissioner, 201 F.3d 505, 513 (D.C. Cir. 2000).

[34] *See* McDonald's Restaurant v. Commissioner, 688 F.2d 520 (7th Cir. 1982).

[35] 391 U.S. 83 (1968).

[36] 688 F.2d 520 (7th Cir. 1982).

subsequent registration of the stock and sale of the stock by the erstwhile franchise holders. If not stepped together, the first step could be seen as a tax-free reorganization under I.R.C. § 368. That treatment would not have been beneficial for McDonald's as it meant a lower basis in the acquired assets and thus lower depreciation deductions. The court held, however, that the transactions should be stepped together and the first step was thus not a tax-free reorganization.[37] In the court's view, the franchise holders would not have entered into the transaction without the assurance that the stock they received would be registered so that they could sell it (which they promptly did).[38]

Finally, the end result test combines the various steps together if the intention is to reach a particular "end result." In *Kornfield v. United States*,[39] the taxpayer created a revocable trust that held bonds. He engaged in a series of transactions in an attempt to separate a life estate from the remainder interest, with the hope of creating the equivalent of amortization deductions on bonds. Bonds are normally not amortizable. The court applied the end result test to disallow the scheme.[40]

E. Failure to Form a Valid Partnership for Tax Purposes

Several recent cases have concluded that a taxpayer's tax avoidance motives prevented the taxpayer from forming a valid partnership for tax purposes. These cases are sometimes referred to as the *"ACM"* decisions after the first such decision.[41] The facts of these cases are highly complex. We will very briefly summarize the facts in *ASA Investing Partnership v. Commissioner*,[42] which is representative of the other cases. In this case, the taxpayer was trying to shelter substantial gains the taxpayer had from an unrelated transaction. In a strategy proposed by Merrill Lynch & Co.,[43] the taxpayer formed a partnership with a foreign entity, initially with the foreign entity holding the substantial majority of the interests in the partnership. The foreign entity was ultimately controlled by a large foreign lending institution. The partnership bought debt instruments and sold them on the installment basis. The partnership took advantage of the installment sale rules of I.R.C. § 453 that apply when the sales price is contingent. It sold the debt instrument partly for a fixed amount and partly for a contingent amount. Under the rules of I.R.C. § 453, this initially created a substantial gain.

---

[37] When stepped together, the reorganization lacked "continuity of interest," a necessary component to a tax-free reorganization. *McDonald's Restaurant v. Commissioner, supra.*

[38] Indeed, the court held that any of the three forms of the step transaction doctrine could have been applied.

[39] 137 F.3d 1231 (10th Cir. 1998).

[40] The court also noted that the interdependence test could have been applied as well.

[41] *See generally* ACM Partnership v. Commissioner, TCM 1997-115, aff'd 157 F.3d 231 (3d Cir. 1998), and Lipton, *The Tax Court Upsets New Corporate Tax Shelter — Lessons From the Colgate Case*, 86 JTAX 331 (1997), and Lipton, *Brush Up Your Planning — More Lessons From the Colgate Case*, 90 JTAX 89 (1999); Boca Investering Partnership v. United States, 167 F. Supp. 2d 298 (D.C. 2001), *rev'd* 314 F.3d 625 (D.C. Cir. 2003), *cert. denied* 540 U.S. 826 (2003); *see also* Saba Partnership v. Commissioner, 273 F.3d 1135 (D.C. Cir. 2001).

[42] 201 F.3d 505 (D.C. Cir. 2000), *cert. denied* 531 U.S. 871 (2000).

[43] Merrill Lynch's fee for proposing and fostering the transaction in one case was $7,000,000; ASA Investering Partnership v. Commissioner, 201 F.3d 505 (D.C. Cir. 2000).

That gain was allocated to the foreign partner, who as a nonresident alien was not subject to U.S. tax on the gain. Subsequently, the ownership of the partnership was adjusted so that the taxpayer owned the substantial majority of the partnership interests. When the transaction was brought to closure, the rules of I.R.C. § 453 generated a large loss that was mostly allocated to the taxpayer, sheltering the large gain on the unrelated transaction. Overall the transactions were approximately a wash, but because of the timing of the gain and loss and the partnership ownership interest changes, the transactions generated a large paper loss for the taxpayer. The D.C. Circuit noted that the transaction could have been attacked as a sham transaction.[44] Instead, though, the court affirmed the Tax Court's conclusion that the parties had failed to form a valid partnership for tax purposes under the principles of *Commissioner v. Culbertson*[45] that we discuss in Chapter 2. The appellate court concluded that the partnership could not be respected as it was formed for no significant reason other than tax avoidance.[46]

§ 11.03 ANTI-ABUSE REGULATIONS

The IRS often has had to play catch up to crafty tax planners and in 1994 it decided it needed a more powerful weapon and promulgated the anti-abuse Regulations of Treas. Reg. § 1.701-2. These Regulations essentially permit the IRS to ignore the structure of a transaction that might technically comply with partnership tax law if the transaction is deemed to be abusive under these Regulations.

Specifically, the Regulations provide that three requirements are implicit in the intent of Subchapter K:

1. The partnership must be bona fide and each partnership transaction or series of related transactions must be entered into for a substantial business purpose.

2. The form of each partnership transaction must be respected under substance over form principles.

3. The application of a given Code provision and the ultimate tax results, taking into account all the relevant facts and circumstances, must be clearly contemplated by that provision.[47]

The Regulations go on to provide that if a partnership is used in a transaction the principal purpose of which is to reduce the present value of the partners' aggregate federal tax liability in a manner that is inconsistent with the intent of Subchapter K, the IRS is authorized to recast the transaction for federal tax purposes as

---

[44] *Id.*

[45] 337 U.S. 733 (1949).

[46] An important, related line of cases is commonly known as the *Castle Harbour* Decisions. They provide a valuable review of many partnership tax rules. The trial court and the Second Circuit saw things rather differently, and the case bounced back and forth between the trial court and the Second Circuit. *See* TIFD III-E Inc. v. United States, 342 F.Supp.2d 94 (D. Conn. 2004), *rev'd* 459 F.3d 220 (2d Cir. 2006), *on remand* 660 F. Supp. 2d 367 (DC Conn 2009), *rev'd* 666 F.3d 836 (2d Cir 2012),

[47] Treas. Reg. § 1.702-2(a).

appropriate to achieve tax results that are consistent with the intent of Subchapter K. The Regulations specifically note that literal compliance with the rules of Subchapter K will not save the day. The transaction must be consistent with the intent of Subchapter K. The Regulations give the IRS very broad authority to restructure the transaction, including disregarding the partnership, not treating a purported partner as a partner, adjusting the partnership's method of accounting, and reallocating income and loss.

The anti-abuse Regulations have met with substantial criticism from tax professionals, partly because of their ambiguous nature and partly because transactions in compliance with the tax law can run afoul of the Regulations, injecting much uncertainty into the planning process. It is also true, however, that Subchapter K was often used abusively to inappropriately reduce taxes. Of course, as we discussed above, there are judicial doctrines available to the IRS with which to attack such transactions, including substance over form, step transaction, and business purpose. Some view the Regulations as an attempt to codify these doctrines, though the IRS appears to believe the Regulations give it an additional weapon.[48]

The Regulations contain a nonexclusive list of facts and circumstances that could be relevant in determining whether or not a partnership was formed or availed of with a principal purpose to reduce substantially the present value of the partners' aggregate tax liabilities in a manner inconsistent with the intent of Subchapter K. The weight given a factor can vary, depending on the totality of the circumstances, and the presence or absence of a factor is neither fatal nor a guarantee of safety. Ultimately, it comes down to whether the transaction meets the "smell test," but because you may be new to tax and not yet have had the chance to fully develop your olfactory senses, the list of the facts and circumstances can be helpful in getting a feel for the area. These include:

1. The present value of the partners' aggregate federal tax liability is substantially less than if the partners had owned the partnership's assets and conducted the partnership's activities directly.

2. The present value of the partners' aggregate federal tax liability is substantially less than would be the case if purportedly separate transactions designed to achieve a particular end result are integrated and treated as steps in a single transaction. For example, this analysis may indicate that it was contemplated that a partner would be a partner only temporarily in order to provide the claimed tax benefits to the remaining partners.

3. One or more partners who are necessary to achieve the claimed tax results either have a nominal interest in the partnership, are substantially protected from any risk of loss from the partnership's activities (through distribution preferences, indemnity or loss guaranty agreements, or other arrangements), or have little or no participation in the profits from the partnership's activities other than a preferred return that is in the nature of a payment for the use of capital.

---

[48] *See* Willis, Pennell, Postlewaite, *Partnership Taxation* ¶ 1.03[6].

4. Substantially all of the partners (measured by number or interests in the partnership) are related (directly or indirectly) to one another.

5. Partnership items are allocated in compliance with the literal language of Treas. Reg. §§ 1.704-1 and 1.704-2, but with results that are inconsistent with the purpose of I.R.C. § 704(b) and those Regulations. In this regard, particular scrutiny will be paid to partnerships in which income or gain is specially allocated to one or more partners that may be legally or effectively exempt from federal taxation (for example, a foreign person, an exempt organization, an insolvent taxpayer, or a taxpayer with unused federal tax attributes such as net operating losses, capital losses, or foreign tax credits).

6. The benefits and burdens of ownership of property nominally contributed to the partnership are in substantial part retained (directly or indirectly) by the contributing partner (or a related party).

7. The benefits and burdens of ownership of partnership property are in substantial part shifted (directly or indirectly) to the distributee partner before or after the property is actually distributed to the distributee partner (or a related party).[49]

The examples in the Regulations endeavor to provide taxpayers with a greater sense of what does and does not cross the line. The Regulations contain 11 examples. Eight pass muster and often involve transactions that have been commonly used by tax professionals. One such example gives its blessing to a partnership between an S corporation and a nonresident alien.[50] A nonresident alien cannot be a shareholder of an S corporation.[51] There might have been an argument that a nonresident alien was essentially end-running this prohibition by forming a partnership with an S corporation. For that reason, there might have been an argument that the structure violated the anti-abuse Regulations. But the example finds this commonly used approach unobjectionable.

Like to see an example? We would like to give you one, but the examples in the Regulations that are still relevant are very complex. So we decided to spare you an example. We encourage you to review the examples in the Regulations if you ever decide to be a partnership tax specialist.

§ 11.04   MIXING BOWL TRANSACTIONS

A.   Introduction

A number of Code sections address what have become known as "mixing bowl" transactions. Recall that contributions to and distributions from partnerships can be tax free under I.R.C. §§ 721 and 731. Partners may attempt to disguise what really is a sale as a contribution and distribution. It is true that the economic

---

[49] Treas. Reg. § 1.701-2(c).

[50] Treas. Reg. § 1.701-2(d), example 2.

[51] I.R.C. § 1361(b)(1)(c).

substance doctrine could be used to attack these, but Congress wanted a more precise weapon.

I.R.C. § 707(a)(2)(B) was enacted in 1984 and applies to a "disguised sale" of property between the partnership and a partner. For a full discussion, see Chapter 9. I.R.C. § 707(a)(2)(B) has a somewhat limited application given its (typically) two-year window. Congress wanted some additional tools, and so enacted two other code sections.

B.   I.R.C. § 704(c)(1)(B)

I.R.C. § 704(c)(1)(A) requires gain or loss inherent in contributed property to be allocated to the contributing partner, subject to the adjustments it provides. Prior to the enactment of I.R.C. § 704(c)(1)(B), however, there was no tax impact to the contributing partner if the property he contributed was distributed to another partner. The partnership took a carryover basis in the property under I.R.C. § 723 and that basis in the property then generally carried over to the distributee under I.R.C. § 732. Thus, the gain or loss inherent in the property could be shifted to another partner, possibly one in a lower tax bracket. Moreover, if the distribution was in liquidation and the distributee had a high basis in her partnership interest, the gain or loss in the distributed property could disappear as the outside basis of the partner is shifted to the distributed asset under I.R.C. § 732(b). The partnership would not be required to adjust the inside bases of its assets to account for this unless an I.R.C. § 754 election were in effect.

I.R.C. § 704(c)(1)(B) applies if property contributed by one partner is distributed to another partner within seven years of the original contribution. In that event, the contributing partner recognizes the gain or loss he would have recognized under I.R.C. § 704(c)(1)(A) had the contributed property been sold for its fair market value to the distributee. The character of the gain or loss is the same as the character that would have resulted had the property actually been sold to the distributee.[52] For example, assume A contributes land to a partnership with a fair market value of $10,000 and a basis of $6,000, and B contributes cash of $10,000. Further assume that, three years later, when the land has appreciated in value to $15,000, it is distributed to B when B's basis in his partnership interest is $10,000. Under I.R.C. § 704(c)(1)(B), A will recognize $4,000 of gain, the gain he would have recognized under I.R.C. § 704(c)(1)(A) had the property been sold at its fair market value.[53] Note that while there is $9,000 of gain inherent in the distributed property, not all of that gain has to be recognized, only the portion to which I.R.C. § 704(c)(1)(A) would have applied.

I.R.C. § 704(c)(1)(B)(iii) provides that "appropriate adjustments" are made to the basis of the contributed property and the contributing partner's basis in the

---

[52] The fact that it is deemed sold to the distributee can have unexpected consequences. For example, if the distributee owns over 50 percent of the partnership, and the asset is not a capital asset to him, the gain will be ordinary income under I.R.C. § 707(b)(2) even if the asset was a capital asset to the contributing partner and the partnership. I.R.C. § 707(b)(1) could deny a loss.

[53] Note that the I.R.C. § 704(c)(1)(A) method used, whether it be the traditional, traditional with curative allocations, or remedial method, will determine the amount of gain or loss that is allocated.

partnership interest. The Regulations provide that the contributing partner's partnership interest basis is increased for gain and reduced for any loss resulting from the distribution. The partnership's basis in the contributed property is also increased for any gain and reduced for any loss, and this is deemed to occur immediately before the distribution of the property.[54] Thus, continuing with the above example, because A recognized $4,000 of gain, A's basis in the partnership interest is increased by that $4,000 to $10,000. Further, immediately before the distribution, the partnership's basis in the land is increased by $4,000 to $10,000. When the land is distributed to B, he takes it with a $10,000 carryover basis, and his basis in the partnership interest is reduced to zero.[55]

The I.R.C. § 704(c)(1)(B) "taint" attaches to the partnership interest. Thus, if all or a portion of A's partnership interest is transferred, a proportionate share of the I.R.C. § 704(c)(1)(B) gain or loss goes with it.[56]

Note that there has to be both a contribution of property and its subsequent distribution. If property is, for example, purchased or sold by the partnership, including a disguised sale under I.R.C. § 707(a)(2)(B), I.R.C. § 704(c)(1)(B) does not apply. I.R.C. § 704(c)(1)(B) also provides that it does not apply if property is distributed to the partner who contributed it.

The Regulations provide a number of exceptions to the application of I.R.C. § 704(c)(1)(B). It does not apply in the case of an I.R.C. § 708 termination, though the relevant property would be subject to I.R.C. § 704(c)(1)(B) in the hands of the new partnership to the same extent it would have been in the old partnership. Thus, if the old partnership held the property for four years, the new partnership would have to hold the property for three years before I.R.C. § 704(c)(1)(B) would cease to apply. I.R.C. § 704(c)(1)(B) also does not apply in the case of partnership mergers, but as with I.R.C. § 708, continues to apply to the property in the hands of the transferee partnership.[57] It also does not apply in the case of the incorporation of a partnership, unless the property of the partnership is distributed to the partners and they transfer it to the corporation.[58] There is a complex exception for undivided interests.[59] There is another complex exception

---

[54] Treas. Reg. § 1.704-4(e)(1) and (2).

[55] See I.R.C. §§ 732(a)(1) and 733.

[56] Treas. Reg. § 1.704-4(d)(2). See Willis, Pennell, Postlewaite, *Partnership Taxation* ¶ 10.08[5][b][v] for some interesting planning opportunities in this regard.

[57] Treas. Reg. § 1.704-4(c)(3). See Prop. Treas. Reg. §§ 1.704-4(c)(4) and 1.737-2(b), providing that in a merger I.R.C. § 704(c)(1)(B) applies to the appreciation that accrued in the assets of the nonsurviving partnership while the partnership held those assets.

[58] This assumes the erstwhile partnership is liquidated, see Treas. Reg. § 1.704-4(c)(5).

[59] I.R.C. § 704(c)(1)(B) does not apply to a distribution of an undivided interest in property to the extent that the undivided interest does not exceed the undivided interest, if any, contributed by the distributee partner in the same property. The portion of the undivided interest in property retained by the partnership after the distribution, if any, that is treated as contributed by the distributee partner, is reduced to the extent of the undivided interest distributed to the distributee partner. Treas. Reg. § 1.704-4(c)(2). For example, it two partners contribute undivided interests in property to the partnership, the distribution of an undivided interest to one partner does not trigger gain recognition to the other partner, provided what the distributee partner received does not exceed what he contributed to the partnership. See Willis, Pennell, Postlewaite, *Partnership Taxation* at ¶ 10.08[5][b][v].

that can apply in liquidations.[60] It also does not apply to a distribution that is treated as a sale or exchange of unrealized receivables or substantially appreciated inventory under I.R.C. § 751(b) or a distribution that is treated as a guaranteed payment under I.R.C. § 736(a).[61]

Generally, if the partnership disposes of the I.R.C. § 704(c)(1)(B) property in a nonrecognition transaction, such as a like-kind exchange under I.R.C. § 1031, I.R.C. § 704(c)(1)(B) is not triggered, but applies to the replacement property to the same extent.[62] If the I.R.C. § 704(c)(1)(B) property is distributed to a noncontributing partner, to the extent I.R.C. § 1031 like-kind property is distributed to the contributing partner within the I.R.C. § 1031 times frame, I.R.C. § 704(c)(1)(B) is again not triggered.[63] Finally, the Regulations contain an anti-abuse rule that permits the IRS to recast the transaction if the rules of I.R.C. § 704(c)(1)(B) are literally met, if the principal purpose of the transaction is to achieve a tax result inconsistent with the purpose of I.R.C. § 704(c)(1)(B).[64]

C. I.R.C. § 737

I.R.C. § 737 requires the contributing partner to recognize gain (but not loss) if he contributes *appreciated* property to the partnership and within seven years receives a current or liquidating distribution of property other than money from the partnership.[65] The amount of gain that is recognized is the lesser of:

1. The fair market value of the distributed property less the partner's outside basis just before the distribution (the basis is first reduced by any money received as part of the same distribution), or

2. The "net precontribution gain."

The net precontribution gain is the net gain that would have been recognized by the distributee partner under I.R.C. § 704(c)(1)(B) if all property held by the partnership that had been contributed to the partnership by that partner within seven years of the distribution had been distributed to another partner. This latter amount is the same as the net I.R.C. § 704(c)(1)(A) gain allocable to the partner.

The character of the gain the distributee partner recognizes is determined by reference to the character of the net precontribution gain inherent in the

---

[60] I.R.C. § 704(c)(1)(B) does not apply to a distribution of an interest in I.R.C. § 704(c) property to a partner other than the contributing partner in a liquidation of the partnership if (i) the contributing partner receives an interest in the I.R.C. § 704(c) property contributed by that partner (and no other property); and (ii) the built-in gain or loss in the interest distributed to the contributing partner, determined immediately after the distribution, is equal to or greater than the built-in gain or loss on the property that would have been allocated to the contributing partner under § 704(c)(1)(A). Treas. Reg. § 1.704-4(c)(2).

[61] Treas. Reg. § 1.704-4(a)(2).

[62] *See* Treas. Reg. § 1.704-4(d)(1) and (2).

[63] *See* Treas. Reg. § 1.704-4(d)(3).

[64] *See* Treas. Reg. § 1.704-4(f).

[65] Marketable securities can be treated as money. I.R.C. §§ 737(e) and 731(c).

contributed property *to the partnership*.[66] The gain increases the partner's outside basis immediately before the property distribution.[67] The gain also generally increases the inside basis of the property the partner contributed to the partnership.[68] The distributee takes the normal I.R.C. § 732 basis in the distributed property.[69]

I.R.C. § 737 is perhaps most easily understood by way of an example. Assume A contributes land #1 to a partnership with a fair market value of $10,000 and an adjusted basis of $6,000. B contributes cash of $3,000 and land #2 with an adjusted basis and fair market value of $7,000. Within seven years, Land #2 is distributed to A in an operating distribution and the facts and the values otherwise remain unchanged. Under I.R.C. § 737, A's gain is the lesser of

1. $1,000, the fair market value of the distributed land of $7,000 less A's outside basis of $6,000, or

2. $4,000, A's net precontribution gain.

Thus, in this case A recognizes $1,000 of gain. A increases his outside basis to $7,000 for the gain and this is done immediately before the distribution. A then takes a $7,000 adjusted basis in the distributed property under I.R.C. § 732(a)(1), and his adjusted basis in the partnership is reduced to zero under I.R.C. § 733. Finally, the partnership increases its adjusted basis in land #1 that A contributed by $1,000 to $7,000. If A contributes multiple properties at different times to the partnership, allocating the basis increase among partnership properties can become quite complex.[70] If the increase in basis is made to depreciable property, the increase is depreciated using any applicable recovery method that applies to newly purchased property.[71]

I.R.C. §§ 737 and 704(c)(1)(B) can apply simultaneously. This will occur, for example, if one partner contributes appreciated property to the partnership, bringing I.R.C. § 737 into play, and a second partner contributes appreciated or depreciated property to the partnership, bringing I.R.C. § 704(c)(1)(B) into play. If the property contributed by the second partner is distributed to the first partner, both Code sections will apply, assuming the contributions and distribution occur within the seven-year time frame. I.R.C. § 704(c)(1)(B) is applied (with the concomitant partnership interest basis adjustment) before I.R.C. § 737 is applied.[72]

There are exceptions to the application of I.R.C. § 737. They are similar to the exceptions applicable to I.R.C. § 704(c)(1)(B). Under I.R.C. § 737(d), if any portion of the property distributed consists of property that had been contributed by a distributee partner to the partnership, that property is not taken into account in

---

[66] *See* Treas. Reg. § 1.737-1(d).

[67] I.R.C. § 737(c)(1); Treas. Reg. § 1.737-3(a).

[68] *See* Treas. Reg. § 1.737-3(c) for a fairly involved set of rules in this regard.

[69] Treas. Reg. § 1.737-3(b).

[70] *See* Treas. Reg. § 1.737-3(c). If an I.R.C. § 754 election is in effect, any I.R.C. § 734(b) adjustments are made after the I.R.C. § 737 adjustments.

[71] Treas. Reg. § 1.737-3(d).

[72] Treas. Reg. § 1.737-3(e), example 2.

determining whether the fair market value of the distributed property exceeds the outside basis or in determining the amount of the net precontribution gain.[73] There must be both a contribution of property and a subsequent distribution to the contributing partner. If property is, for example, purchased or sold by the partnership, including a disguised sale under I.R.C. § 707(a)(2)(B), I.R.C. § 737 would not apply. I.R.C. § 737 does not apply to the extent I.R.C. § 751(b) applies to the distribution. It also does not apply to a distribution that is treated as a guaranteed payment under I.R.C. § 736(a).[74]

I.R.C. § 737 will not apply in the case of an I.R.C. § 708 termination, but I.R.C. § 737 will apply to a subsequent distribution of property by the new partnership to a partner who was also a partner in the terminated partnership to the same extent it would have applied to the old partnership.[75] Thus, if the old partnership held the property for four years, the new partnership would have to hold the property for three years before I.R.C. § 737 would cease to apply. I.R.C. § 737 also does not apply in the case of partnership mergers but, as with I.R.C. § 704(c)(1)(B), continues to apply to the property in the hands of the transferee partnership.[76] It also does not apply in the case of the incorporation of a partnership, unless the property of the partnership is distributed to the partners and they transfer it to the corporation.[77] There is a complex exception for undivided interests.[78]

Generally, if the partnership disposes of the contributed appreciated property in a nonrecognition transaction, such as a like-kind exchange under I.R.C. § 1031, I.R.C. § 737 is not triggered, but applies to the replacement property to the same extent.[79] Finally, the I.R.C. § 737 Regulations also contain an anti-abuse rule that permits the IRS to recast a transaction if the principal purpose of the transaction

---

[73] Under Treas. Reg. § 1.737-2(b)(2), if both previously contributed and other property are distributed in the same distribution, the previously contributed property is considered to be distributed first in a separate distribution. Any resulting basis reduction increases the possibility of I.R.C. § 737 gain. If the property distributed consists of an interest in an entity, the exception does not apply to the extent that the value of such interest is attributable to property contributed to such entity after such interest had been contributed to the partnership. For example, assume A contributes corporate stock to the partnership and the partnership than contributed property to the corporation, increasing the corporation's value. I.R.C. § 737 still applies to the increased value of the stock. See I.R.C. § 737(d). Query: What happens if the property contributed to the partnership is improved and that improved property is then distributed back to the contributing partner. See Willis, Pennell, Postlewaite, *Partnership Taxation* at ¶ 10.08[5][c][iv].

[74] Treas. Reg. § 1.737-1(a)(2).

[75] Treas. Reg. § 1.737-2(a), *see* Prop. Treas. Reg. §§ 1.704-4(c)(4) and 1.737-2(b), providing that in merger I.R.C. § 737 applies to the appreciation that accrued in the assets of the nonsurviving partnership while the partnership held them.

[76] Treas. Reg. § 1.737-2(b)(1); I.R.C. § 737 will also not apply in the case of certain divisive transactions. *See* Treas. Reg. § 1.737-2(b)(2).

[77] Treas. Reg. § 1.737-2(c). This assumes the erstwhile partnership is liquidated.

[78] I.R.C. § 737 does not apply to the distribution of an undivided interest in property to the extent that the undivided interest does not exceed the undivided interest, if any, contributed by the distributee partner in the same property. The portion of the undivided interest in property retained by the partnership after the distribution, if any, that is treated as contributed by the distributee partner, is reduced to the extent of the undivided interest distributed to the distributee partner. Treas. Reg. § 1.737-2(d)(4).

[79] *See* Treas. Reg. § 1.737-2(d)(3).

is to achieve a tax result inconsistent with the purpose of I.R.C. § 737.[80]

D.   I.R.C. § 707(a)(2)(A)

We discussed this Code section in detail in Chapter 9. While it is not likely to apply to a mixing bowl transaction, it is possible. Recall that I.R.C. § 707(a)(2)(A) can apply when there is a transfer of property to the partnership and a related *allocation* and distribution to the partner, and the transaction is properly characterized as one occurring between the partnership and a partner acting other than in his capacity as a partner. But for I.R.C. § 707(a)(2)(A), a partnership might be tempted to use allocations to convert a capital expense into an immediately deductible item. It is unlikely, however, that in the I.R.C. § 707(a)(2)(A) context there would be disguised sale. If capital accounts are kept normally, they are increased for the fair market value of contributed property. I.R.C. § 707(a)(2)(A) also requires that there be an allocation to the contributing partner. If income equal to the fair market value of the contributed property were also allocated to the contributing partner, while there would be an income tax effect to the partner, his capital account would in effect be increased twice for the same property. It would be increased by the fair market value once on contribution, and by that same amount again on the allocation. If the partnership keeps capital accounts in accordance with the I.R.C. § 704(b) Regulations, a partner is entitled to receive the balance of his capital account on liquidation. The other partners would normally object to the partner receiving two such bites of the apple.

For example, A contributes equipment with a fair market value of $10,000 and an adjusted basis of $4,000 to the equal ABC partnership. B and C each contribute $10,000. Following the capital account rules in the Regulations,[81] the capital account of each partner is increased by $10,000. If the partnership now also allocates the first $10,000 of income to A for the contributed equipment (and the rest of the income and deductions are allocated equally), A's capital account will be increased by $20,000 for a $10,000 property. Assuming B and C are independent third parties, they will not agree to that. However, if capital accounts are not kept in accordance with the Regulations, I.R.C. § 707(a)(2)(A) becomes more relevant. Thus, if A's capital account is only increased by $100 for the contributed property, it would not cause the partners any great pain to allocate $10,000 of income disproportionately to A. I.R.C. § 707(a)(2)(A) would prevent this attempt to convert a capital acquisition expenditure into an immediate deduction.

---

[80] *See* Treas. Reg. § 1.737-4.

[81] Treas. Reg. § 1.704-1(b)(2)(iv)(b).

Chapter 12

DEATH OF A PARTNER

BASIC OVERVIEW

The death of a partner raises some unique issues, but for the most part, the death of a partner raises issues already discussed in prior chapters. Even in the Detailed Discussion, we keep our review of those prior chapters fairly brief, while alerting you where to read up on the details.

I.R.C. § 708 provides that a partnership is considered terminated only if (i) no part of any business, financial operation, or venture of the partnership continues to be carried on by any of its partners in a partnership, or (ii) within a 12-month period there is a sale or exchange of 50% or more of the total interests in partnership capital and profits. Death of the partner does not ordinarily result in the termination of the partnership under I.R.C. § 708(b)(1)(B), because a disposition by gift, bequest or inheritance is not considered a sale or exchange.[1] The death of a partner may result in the termination of a partnership under I.R.C. § 708(b)(1)(A) when the partnership is a two-person partnership because it is not possible to have a one-person partnership. In that case, the death of the partner will cause the partnership to terminate unless the estate or other successor-in-interest continues to share in the profits or losses of the partnership business.[2]

Often partnership agreements will contain "buy-sell" provisions that allow or require the partnership interest to be sold upon the death of a partner. The manner of the sale may be in the form of a redemption by the partnership or a purchase of the interest by the remaining partners. Ordinarily, the sale of a partnership interest by a partner owning 50% or more of the capital and profits interest of the partnership within a 12-month period will cause the partnership to terminate.[3] However, for the purposes of calculating whether the requisite 50% or more has been sold, liquidations of a partnership interest are excluded.[4] Thus, assume that A, B and C are 20%, 20% and 60% partners respectively in the ABC partnership. If C were to die, and if the partnership liquidated C's interest in the partnership, the partnership would not terminate under I.R.C. § 708(b). However, if a buy-sell agreement provides for A and B to each purchase half of C's interest, the partnership would have a sale or exchange of more than 50% of the interests in profits and capital, terminating the partnership under I.R.C. § 708(b).

---

[1] Treas. Reg. § 1.708-1(b)(2).

[2] Treas. Reg. § 1.708-1(b)(1)(i).

[3] I.R.C. § 708(b).

[4] Treas. Reg. § 708-1(b)(2).

Someone can die with a right to income not yet received, including, of course, a partner who has a right to share in the income that a partnership earns. This right to income gets special treatment. I.R.C. § 691(a)(1)(A) provides, generally, that these item of "income in respect of a decedent" are included in the gross income of the successor-in-interest of the decedent.[5] This means, typically, that the successor-in-interest will be taxed on the income at ordinary income rates. (Note that an estate of a decedent is a taxable entity.)

I.R.C. § 753 provides that the amount includible in the gross income of the successor-in-interest of a deceased partner under I.R.C. § 736(a) is considered income in respect of a decedent under I.R.C. § 691. Recall that I.R.C. § 736 covers payments by the partnership to a retiring partner. It can also cover payments to redeem the interest of a successor-in-interest to a deceased partner. The legislative history to I.R.C. § 753 indicates that Congress intended to cause the I.R.C. § 736(a) payment to be income in respect of a decedent to the successor to the extent such amounts are attributable to the decedent's interest in the partnership's unrealized receivables and fees.[6]

Of course, if the successor-in-interest continues as a partner in the partnership rather than withdrawing from the partnership upon the death of the partner, I.R.C. § 736 does not apply to the distributions that this partner receives.[7] Instead, the successor-in-interest is taxed on its share of income under I.R.C. § 702 and distributions during the period in which the successor continues as a partner would be treated under the normal rules under I.R.C. § 731.

Under I.R.C. § 706(c)(2)(A), the partnership taxable year will close for a deceased partner on the date of death, and the decedent and the successor-in-interest must each report his share of partnership income, loss, deductions and credits for the part of the year he was a partner.[8]

I.R.C. § 1014(a) generally provides that the basis of property in the hands of a person acquiring the property from a decedent is its fair market value of the property at the date of the decedent's death, or the alternate valuation date (generally six months later), if applicable. I.R.C. § 1014(c) provides that I.R.C. § 1014 does not apply to property that constitutes a right to receive an item of income in respect of a decedent under I.R.C. § 691.

If a partnership files an election under I.R.C. § 754, a death of a partner can give rise to a I.R.C. § 743(b) adjustment.

---

[5] Or other successor-in-interest. Throughout the chapter we will assume the estate is the successor-in-interest.

[6] H.R. Rep. 1337, 83d Cong., 2d Sess. 237 (1954).

[7] Treas. Reg. § 1.736-1(a)(1)(i).

[8] *See* Treas. Reg. § 1.706-1(c)(3)(iv) & (vi) Example (2).

DETAILED DISCUSSION

§ 12.01 INTRODUCTION

The death of a partner raises some unique issues, but for the most part, the death of a partner raises issues already discussed in prior chapters. Even in the Detailed Discussion, we keep our review of those prior chapters fairly brief, while alerting you where to read up on the details.

§ 12.02 TERMINATION OF A PARTNERSHIP

I.R.C. § 708 provides that a partnership is considered as terminated only if (i) no part of any business, financial operation, or venture of the partnership continues to be carried on by any of its partners in a partnership, or (ii) within a 12-month period there is a sale or exchange of 50% or more of the total interests in partnership capital and profits. Death of the partner does not ordinarily result in the termination of the partnership under I.R.C. § 708(b)(1)(B), because a disposition by gift, bequest or inheritance is not considered a sale or exchange.[9] The death of a partner may result in the termination of a partnership under I.R.C. § 708(b)(1)(A) when the partnership is a two-person partnership, as there cannot be a one-person partnership. Whether it does or does not typically depends upon whether there is a buy-sell agreement in effect triggered by the death, or whether the decedent partner's estate or other successor-in-interest continues to share in the profits or losses of the partnership business.[10]

For example, suppose D and E are equal partners in a two-person partnership engaged in the wholesale produce business. Upon D's death, E purchases with cash, pursuant to a buy-and-sell agreement, and through the use of E's own funds, the decedent's interest in the partnership from his estate. Thereafter, the business is continued by E as a sole proprietorship. The sale of D's partnership interest to E results in the termination of the partnership under I.R.C. § 708(b)(1)(A) because the business is no longer carried on by any of its partners in a partnership.[11]

On the other hand, an example from a revenue ruling: A and B were equal partners in AB, a calendar year partnership. B died on January 1, 1983. Upon B's death, B's estate succeeded to B's interest in AB. The value of B's partnership interest as determined for federal estate tax purposes greatly exceeded the adjusted basis of B's share of partnership assets. During 1983, B's estate was taxable on its distributable share of partnership income. Although AB was a two-person partnership, the partnership did not terminate because the estate succeeded to the interest of the decedent.[12]

[9] Treas. Reg. § 1.708-1(b)(2).
[10] Treas. Reg. § 1.708-1(b)(1)(i).
[11] Rev. Rul. 67-65, 1967-1 C.B. 168.
[12] Rev. Rul. 86-139, 1986-2 C.B. 95.

A partner in a two-person partnership who retires and receives payments under I.R.C. § 736, may die before all payments have been made. The deceased partner's successor-in-interest who receives the remaining payments is regarded as a partner until the entire interest of the deceased partner is liquidated. Therefore, the partnership is not considered to have terminated upon the death of the partner, but terminates as to both partners only when the entire interest of the decedent is liquidated.[13]

Often partnership agreements will contain "buy-sell" provisions which allow or require the partnership interest to be sold upon the death of a partner. The manner of the sale may be in the form of a redemption by the partnership or a purchase of the interest by the remaining partners. As noted above, the sale of a partnership interest by a partner owning 50% or more of the capital and profits interest of the partnership within a 12-month period will cause the partnership to terminate.[14] However, for the purposes of calculating whether the requisite 50% or more has been sold, only purchases by other partners (or third parties) count, not payments (i.e., redemptions) by the partnership.[15] Thus, assume that A, B and C are 20%, 20% and 60% partners respectively in ABC. If C were to die, and if the partnership liquidated C's interest in the partnership, the partnership would not terminate under I.R.C. § 708(b). However, if a buy-sell agreement provides for A and B to each purchase half of C's interest, the partnership would have a sale or exchange of more than 50% of the interests in profits and capital, terminating the partnership under I.R.C. § 708(b).

§ 12.03   INCOME IN RESPECT OF A DECEDENT

Someone can die with a right to income not yet received, including, of course, a partner who has a right to share in the income that a partnership earns. This right to income gets special treatment. I.R.C. § 691(a)(1)(A) provides, generally, that these items of "income in respect of a decedent" are included in the gross income of the successor-in-interest. This means, typically, that the successor-in-interest will be taxed on the income at ordinary income rates. (Note that a decedent's estate is a taxable entity.)

I.R.C. § 691 does not actually contain a definition of income in respect of a decedent. A definition is provided, however, by Treas. Reg. § 1.691(a)-1(b) which states:

> In general, the term "income in respect of a decedent" refers to those amounts to which a decedent was entitled as gross income but which were not properly includible in computing his taxable income for the taxable year ending with the date of his death or for a previous taxable year under the method of accounting employed by the decedent. . . . Thus, the term includes —
>
> (1)   all accrued income of a decedent who reported his income by use

---

[13]   Treas. Reg. § 1.736-1(a)(6).

[14]   I.R.C. § 708(b).

[15]   Treas. Reg. § 708-1(b)(2).

of the cash receipts and disbursements method;

(2)   income accrued solely by reason of the decedent's death in case of a decedent who reports his income by use of an accrual method of accounting; and

(3)   income to which the decedent had a contingent claim at the time of his death.

I.R.C. § 753 provides that the amount includible in the gross income of a successor-in-interest of a deceased partner under I.R.C. § 736(a) is considered income in respect of a decedent under I.R.C. § 691. Recall that I.R.C. § 736 covers payments by the partnership to a retiring partner. It can also cover payments to redeem the interest of a successor-in-interest to a deceased partner.

The legislative history to I.R.C. § 753 indicates that Congress intended to cause the I.R.C. § 736(a) payment to be income in respect of a decedent to the successor to the extent such amounts are attributable to the decedent's interest in partnership's unrealized receivables and fees.[16] In contrast with the somewhat narrower scope of the legislative history, the Regulations under I.R.C. § 753 provide that all payments coming within the provisions of I.R.C. § 736(a) made by a partnership to the successor-in-interest of a deceased partner are considered income in respect of a decedent under I.R.C. § 691.[17]

Of course, if the successor-in-interest continues as a partner in the partnership rather than withdrawing from the partnership upon the death of the partner, I.R.C. § 736 does not apply to the distributions that this partner receives.[18] Instead, the successor-in-interest is taxed on its share of income under I.R.C. § 702 and distributions during the period in which the successor continues as a partner would be treated under the normal rules under I.R.C. § 731.[19]

An example of partner income in respect of a decedent:

A and the decedent B are equal partners in a cash basis business having assets worth $40,000 with an adjusted basis of $10,000. B dies. Certain partnership business is well advanced toward completion before B's death and after B's death, but before the end of the partnership year, payment of $2,000 is made to the partnership for this work. The partnership agreement provides that, upon the death of one of the partners, all partnership property, including unfinished work, passes to the surviving partner. It further provides that the surviving partner pays the decedent's estate what the decedent partner's share of undistributed partnership earnings in the year of death would have been if the decedent had not died plus $10,000 in each of the three years after death. B's estate's share of earnings for the year of his death is $1,000. Assume that the value of B's interest in partnership

---

[16]   H.R. Rep. 1337, 83d Cong., 2d Sess. 237 (1954).

[17]   Treas. Reg. § 1.753-1(a).

[18]   Treas. Reg. § 1.736-1(a)(1)(i).

[19]   Payments to the estate of a deceased law partner that represent a share of profits attributable to work completed after his death on matters in process at the date of his death, and post death partnership income were held to be income in respect of a decedent in *Estate of Riegelman v. Commissioner*, 253 F.2d 315 (2d Cir. 1958).

property at the date of his death is $20,000. Under the partnership agreement, A is to pay B's estate a total of $31,000. The difference of $11,000 between the amount to be paid by A ($31,000) and the value of B's interest in partnership property ($20,000) comes within I.R.C. § 736(a) and, thus, constitutes income in respect of a decedent.[20] The payments by the partnership in this example had three components. First, the $1,000 share of date-of-death earnings is an I.R.C. § 736(a)(1) payment. The $10,000 in excess of B's share of partnership property and not based upon the income of the partnership is an I.R.C. § 736(a)(2) payment. The $20,000 paid in respect of B's interest in partnership property is an I.R.C. § 736(b) payment.

If the partnership is on the cash basis method of accounting, items not received before the date of death will properly be in the successor-in-interest's taxable year, rather than the decedent's final taxable year. However, if the partnership is on the accrual method of accounting, it is possible that items may appear in the final taxable year of the decedent if all events have occurred to make them fixed and determinable. Thus, an item that might otherwise be income in respect of a decedent in the successor-in-interest's return may more properly be treated as included in the final year of the decedent, depending upon the facts and circumstances.

It should be noted that this particular issue is reconciled within I.R.C. § 736(b). Although unrealized receivables are excluded from partnership property for the purposes of I.R.C. § 736(b) for partnerships in which capital is not a material income-producing factor, "unrealized receivables" are defined in this context by cross reference to I.R.C. § 751. I.R.C. § 751 only includes in unrealized receivables items that have not previously been taken into income by the partnership. Thus, an accrual basis partnership that takes an unrealized receivable into income prior to the death of a decedent should then include that unrealized receivable as property for the purposes of I.R.C. § 736(b).

§ 12.04　CLOSING OF THE PARTNERSHIP YEAR

I.R.C. § 706(a) provides that, in computing the taxable income of a partner for a taxable year, the inclusions required by I.R.C. §§ 702 and 707(c) with respect to a partnership is based on the income, gain, loss, deduction, or credit of the partnership for any taxable year of the partnership ending within or with the taxable year of the partner.

Under I.R.C. § 706(c)(2)(A), the partnership taxable year will close for a deceased partner on the date of death, and the decedent and the successor-in-interest must each report his proportionate share of partnership income, loss, deductions and credits for the part of the year he was a partner.[21]

For example, B has a taxable year ending December 31 and is a member of partnership ABC, the taxable year of which ends on June 30. B dies on October 31,

[20] This example is based upon the example in Treas. Reg. § 1.753-1(c) modified to reflect that I.R.C. § 706 now requires the taxable year of the partnership to close with respect to the decedent on the death of a partner.

[21] See Treas. Reg. § 1.706-1(c)(3)(iv) & (vi) Example (2).

2014. When B dies on October 31, 2014, the partnership's taxable year beginning July 1, 2014 closes with respect to him. Therefore, the return for B's last taxable year (January 1 to October 31, 2014) will include B's distributive share of taxable income of the partnership for its taxable year ending June 30, 2014, plus B's distributive share of partnership taxable income for the period July 1 to October 31, 2014. B's successor will include the distributive share for the portion of the partnership year after October 31, 2014. [22]

To avoid the expense of an actual closing of the books, which would presumably require all of the same types of calculations for the segment created by the death of a partner that one would normally expect to be made at the end of the full taxable year, many smaller partnerships and partnerships that have frequent changes of interests have adopted the proration method.

§ 12.05 ADJUSTMENT TO BASIS

I.R.C. § 1014(a) generally provides that the basis of property in the hands of a person acquiring the property from a decedent is its fair market value of the property at the date of the decedent's death, or the alternate valuation date (generally six months later), if applicable.

I.R.C. § 1014(c) provides that I.R.C. § 1014 does not apply to property that constitutes a right to receive an item of income in respect of a decedent under I.R.C. § 691. Consistent with I.R.C. § 1014(c), Treas. Reg. § 1.742-1 provides that the basis of a partnership interest acquired from a decedent is the fair market value of the interest at the date of the partner's death or at the alternate valuation date, increased by the successor-in-interest's share of partnership liabilities on that date, and reduced to the extent that such value is attributable to items constituting income in respect of a decedent.

If a partnership files an election under I.R.C. § 754, a death of a partner can give rise to a I.R.C. § 743(b) adjustment.[23]

---

[22] This is based upon Treas. Reg. § 1.706-1(c)(3)(vi), Example (2). The example assumes a closing of the books method.

[23] A coordination issue also exists between I.R.C. § 1014, § 736 and § 753 if the deceased partner was a general partner and the business of the partnership is providing services. I.R.C. § 1014 would theoretically take into consideration in determining the value of the partnership all assets of the partnership, including goodwill, resulting in a basis adjustment under I.R.C. § 1014 and § 742. On the other hand, I.R.C. § 736(b)(3) may cause the payment for the deceased partner's share of goodwill to be an I.R.C. § 736(a) payment if goodwill is "unstated." Because payments for partnership property are generally not based upon the income of the partnership, the payment for unstated goodwill may well be an I.R.C. § 736(a)(2) guaranteed payment. I.R.C. § 736(a)(2) payments do not reduce the partnership interest basis, so the successor-in-interest may end up with a capital loss from the I.R.C. § 736(b) payments. In addition, I.R.C. § 753 may require the estate to treat the payment as income in respect of a decedent because the payment is an I.R.C. § 736(a) payment. The issue becomes even more complex if an I.R.C. § 754 election is in place. See Gary R. McBride, "Alice's Estate in the Wonderland of Subchapter K,"122 Tax Notes 971 (Feb. 23, 2009).

PART II:
C CORPORATIONS

Chapter 13

TAXING C CORPORATIONS IN GENERAL

BASIC OVERVIEW

Under the Code, a C corporation is a taxable entity.[1] Thus, like an individual or other non-corporate taxpayer, a C corporation determines its regular federal income tax liability by applying prescribed tax rates to its taxable income. C corporations are also subject to the alternative minimum tax. This chapter provides a review of the general rules for the taxation of C corporations. Later chapters address specific tax consequences to C corporations on transactions such as distributions to shareholders (liquidating and nonliquidating), reorganizations, corporate divisions and certain acquisitions of a corporation's stock.

A. Determination of Taxable Income

Under section 63(a), a C corporation's taxable income is defined as gross income minus allowable deductions. In general, the determination of the taxable income of a C corporation is quite similar to that of an individual, but there are some differences that are described in the Detailed Analysis. Transactions between related parties, whether corporate or non-corporate, are typically subject to special tax rules. An important related party rule for C corporations is section 482, and under this section's regulations, transactions between members of a controlled group of corporations will be tested to see whether a transaction's results are consistent with the results that would have occurred if uncontrolled corporations had engaged in the same transaction under the same circumstances.[2]

While most of tax law is statutory in nature, there is a body of tax common law that applies to both corporate and non-corporate taxpayers. The common law of taxation contains the doctrine of substance over form, where courts and the Service endeavor to ascertain the substance of a transaction and tax it accordingly, rather than simply respecting a transaction's form. A tool used in the search for the substance of a transaction is the step-transaction doctrine. Rather than respecting and taxing (or not) the separate transactional steps engaged in by a taxpayer, the courts and the Service will collapse the separate steps and consider only the net result, provided the transactional steps can be viewed as interrelated. The business purpose doctrine is another strand of tax common law, under which tax benefits are sometimes denied where the only motivation is tax avoidance. And under the common law economic substance doctrine, tax benefits have generally been denied where a transaction does not have economic substance apart from the economic

---

[1] In contrast, an S corporation is generally not subject to federal income tax. *See* Chapter 24.

[2] See Treas. Reg. § 1.482-1(b)(1).

benefit resulting from the tax benefits.[3] Because of a lack of uniformity in applying the economic substance doctrine, in 2010 Congress codified the meaning of economic substance,[4] which is examined in the Detailed Analysis.

B.   Tax Rates

Under section 11, a C corporation is generally subject to tax rates on its taxable income that range from 15 to 35 percent. Qualified personal service corporations (defined in the Detailed Analysis) are subject to a flat 35 percent tax rate on all of their taxable income, regardless of the amount.[5] Unlike non-corporate taxpayers,[6] C corporations are currently not entitled to a rate preference on their net capital gains.

C.   Taxable Year

A C corporation can generally adopt as its taxable year either the calendar year or a fiscal year,[7] the latter being any 12-month period that ends on the last day of a month other than December.[8] As an exception, a personal service corporation (defined in the Detailed Analysis) generally must use the calendar year as its taxable year.[9]

D.   Accounting Methods

A C corporation is generally required under section 448 to use the accrual method of accounting.[10] Exceptions are carved out for farming businesses,[11] qualified personal service corporations,[12] as well as corporations that satisfy a $5,000,000 gross receipts test.[13]

E.   Special Rules for Certain Affiliated Corporations

Under section 1561(a), the members of a "controlled group of corporations" (defined in the Detailed Analysis) are limited to receiving one helping, so to speak, of certain tax benefits. For example, the rate brackets in section 11 are applied to the combined taxable income of the members of the controlled group of corporations, as opposed to applying the rate brackets to each member's separate

---

[3] *See* ACM Partnership v. Commissioner, 73 T.C.M. 2189 (1997).

[4] *See* Section 7701(o).

[5] I.R.C. §§ 11(b)(2).

[6] *See* I.R.C. § 1(h).

[7] *See* I.R.C. § 441(a), (b), (c).

[8] *See* I.R.C. § 441(e).

[9] *See* I.R.C. § 441(i)(1).

[10] *See* I.R.C. § 448(a).

[11] I.R.C. § 448(b)(1).

[12] I.R.C. § 448(b)(2).

[13] I.R.C. § 448(b)(3).

taxable income.[14] In addition, an "affiliated group" (defined in the Detailed Analysis) of corporations may elect to file a consolidated return rather than separate returns.[15] In very general terms, an affiliated group that has made the election is treated as if it were a single corporation for tax purposes.

F. Alternative Minimum Tax

Like an individual, a C corporation is also potentially subject to the alternative minimum tax. The purpose of the alternative minimum tax is to ensure that taxpayers with substantial economic income do not avoid significant tax liability through the use of exclusions, deductions and credits.[16] The alternative minimum tax ("AMT") for a taxable year is equal to the excess (if any) of (i) the "tentative minimum tax" for the year over (ii) the regular tax for the year.[17] For corporations, the "tentative minimum tax" is generally equal to 20 percent of the excess of (i) alternative minimum taxable income ("AMTI") over (ii) an exemption amount;[18] the exemption amount is generally $40,000, but begins to be phased out once alternative minimum taxable income exceeds $150,000.[19] AMTI is a corporation's taxable income increased by certain tax preference items along with other adjustments to more closely reflect a corporation's economic income.[20] The AMT is imposed in addition to a taxpayer's regular tax.[21]

DETAILED ANALYSIS

§ 13.01 DETERMINATION OF TAXABLE INCOME

A. In General

The taxable income of a C corporation is determined in a manner similar to that of an individual. Under section 63(a), taxable income is defined as gross income minus allowable deductions. Because a C corporation does not receive a standard deduction, there is no need to distinguish between "above-the-line" and "below-the-line" deductions, as in the case of individuals.[22] There are also other differences in computing the taxable income of C corporations as compared to individuals; these differences are due to one of the following reasons: the fact that corporations do not have personal expenses, a presumption that all activities relate to a trade or business, or certain legislative decisions to treat C corporations differently than

---

[14] *See* I.R.C. § 1561(a)(1)

[15] *See* I.R.C. § 1501.

[16] *See* Senate Finance Comm. Rep. No. 313, 99th Cong., 2d Sess. 518-519.

[17] *See* I.R.C. § 55(a).

[18] *See* I.R.C. § 55(b)(1)(B).

[19] *See* I.R.C. § 55(d)(2), (d)(3)(A).

[20] *See* I.R.C. § 55(b)(2).

[21] I.R.C. § 55(a).

[22] *See* I.R.C. §§ 62(a), 63(b).

individuals.[23] Included among these differences are:

- No personal deductions (e.g., medical expenses,[24] alimony[25])

- Lower charitable deduction limit[26]

- Different capital loss limitations[27]

- Non-application of certain limits on deductions (e.g., for nonbusiness losses,[28] for nonbusiness bad debts[29])

- General non-application of at risk[30] and passive loss rules[31]

- Allowance of deductions for organizational expenses[32]

- Allowance of dividends-received deductions[33]

B.   Special Rules for Transactions between Related Parties

Transactions between related parties, whether corporate or non-corporate, are typically subject to special tax rules. For example, section 267(a)(1) disallows a loss deduction where a corporation sells property to a more than 50 percent shareholder (by value), or vice versa.[34] Also, where a corporation using the accrual method of accounting incurs an expense owed to a more than 50 percent shareholder (by value) who uses the cash method of accounting, section 267(a)(2) postpones the corporation's deduction until the shareholder includes the amount in gross income (which would typically be when payment is made).[35]

Another related party rule is section 482, which provides the Service with the authority to allocate income, deductions, credits, or allowances between taxpayers that are controlled by the same interests.[36] Section 482 is primarily used in the

---

[23] *See* Stephen Schwarz and Daniel J. Lathrope, Fundamentals of Corporate Taxation 15-16 (2012).

[24] *See* I.R.C. § 213.

[25] *See* I.R.C. § 215.

[26] *See* I.R.C. § 170(b)(2) (limit being 10 percent of taxable income).

[27] *See* I.R.C. § 1211(a) (capital losses deductible to extent of capital gains), 1212(a) (excess capital losses generally carried back three years and carried forward five years).

[28] *See* I.R.C. § 165(c).

[29] *See* I.R.C. § 166(d).

[30] *See* I.R.C. § 465(a) (only certain closely-held C corporations subject to at risk rules).

[31] *See* I.R.C. § 469(a)(2) (only certain closely-held C corporations and personal service corporations subject to passive loss rules).

[32] *See* I.R.C. § 248. Upon making an election, a corporation can generally deduct up to $5,000 of organizational expenditures in the year it begins business; any remaining organizational expenditures are amortized over a 180 month period beginning in the month the corporation begins business. I.R.C. § 248(a). Organizational expenditures are expenditures (i) incident to the creation of a corporation, (ii) chargeable to capital account, and (iii) of a character which, if expended to create a corporation having a limited life, would be amortizable over that life. I.R.C. § 248(b).

[33] *See* I.R.C. § 243. The dividends-received deduction is examined in Chapter 16.

[34] *See* I.R.C. § 267(a)(1), (b)(2). Section 267(a)(1) also applies to other types of related parties as specified in section 267(b).

[35] *See* I.R.C. § 267(a)(2), (b)(2).

[36] *See* also Treas. Reg. § 1.482-1(a).

context of a controlled group of corporations, and in particular, where one of the corporations is domestic and the other foreign. Under section 482 (and its lengthy regulations), transactions between members of a controlled group of corporations will be tested under the arm's length standard, which is whether a transaction's results are consistent with the results that would have occurred if uncontrolled corporations had engaged in the same transaction under the same circumstances.[37]

C. Common Law of Taxation

Most of tax law is statutory in nature. There is, however, a body of tax common law that applies to both corporate and non-corporate taxpayers.

1. Substance over Form

The common law of taxation contains the doctrine of substance over form, where courts and the Service endeavor to ascertain the substance of a transaction and tax it accordingly, rather than simply respecting a transaction's form. Examples of this include reclassifying a purported debt instrument issued by a corporation as stock, and treating purported compensation paid by a corporation to an employee/shareholder as a constructive dividend, both of which are examined later in this book.[38]

2. Step-Transaction Doctrine

A tool used in the search for the substance of a transaction is the step-transaction doctrine. Rather than respecting and taxing (or not) the separate transactional steps engaged in by a taxpayer, the courts and the Service will collapse the separate steps and consider only the net result, provided the transactional steps can be viewed as interrelated. Regarding the relationship necessary to apply the doctrine, the courts and the Service have used different tests, sometimes requiring a binding commitment at the outset to complete all of the steps, and other times invoking the doctrine where subsequent steps were intended or where the steps are mutually interdependent.[39]

3. Business Purpose Doctrine

The business purpose doctrine is another strand of tax common law, under which tax benefits are sometimes denied where the only motivation is tax avoidance. Under current law, this doctrine has been subsumed within the economic substance doctrine (discussed below). In addition, having a business purpose is an independent requirement for corporate reorganizations[40] and corporate divisions,[41] discussed later is this book.

---

[37] *See* Treas. Reg. § 1.482-1(b)(1).

[38] *See* Chapter 15 (debt-equity classification), Chapter 16 (constructive dividends).

[39] The step-transaction doctrine is discussed in connection with corporate formations (*see* Chapter 14) and corporate reorganizations (*see* Chapter 21).

[40] *See* Chapter 21.

[41] *See* Chapter 22.

4.   Economic Substance Doctrine

Under the common law economic substance doctrine, tax benefits have generally been denied where a transaction does not have economic substance apart from the economic benefit resulting from the tax benefits.[42] The business purpose doctrine has often been considered together with the economic substance doctrine.[43] Both doctrines allow the courts to disallow tax benefits that would otherwise be permitted under a literal application of the Code.

Because of a lack of uniformity in applying the economic substance doctrine, in 2010 Congress codified the meaning of economic substance.[44] Section 7701(o) provides that any transaction to which the economic substance doctrine is relevant shall be treated as having economic substance only if:

- the transaction changes the taxpayer's economic position in a meaningful way (apart from the effect of federal income taxes) and

- the taxpayer has a substantial purpose (apart from federal income taxes) for entering into the transaction.[45]

Thus, for a transaction to have economic substance, it must meet both an objective requirement regarding its effect on the taxpayer's economic position, and a subjective requirement regarding the taxpayer's purpose for the transaction. For both requirements, the statute provides that a transaction's potential for profit will be taken into account only if the present value of the reasonably expected pre-tax profit is substantial when compared to the present value of the net tax benefits expected if the transaction were respected.[46] Penalties are provided for transactions lacking economic substance.[47]

§ 13.02   TAX RATES

Under section 11, a C corporation is generally subject to the following tax rates on its taxable income:

Taxable income of $0 to $50,000:	15%
Taxable income of $50,001 to $75,000:	25%
Taxable income of $75,001 to $100,000:	34%
Taxable income of $100,001 to $335,000:	39%
Taxable income of $335,001 to $10,000,000:	34%
Taxable income of $10,000,001 to $15,000,000:	35%
Taxable income of $15,000,001 to $18,333,333:	38%

---

[42] *See* ACM Partnership v. Commissioner, 73 T.C.M. 2189 (1997).

[43] *See* Staff of the Joint Committee on Taxation, General Explanation of Tax Legislation Enacted in the 111th Congress (JCS-2-11) 369-372 (March 2011).

[44] *See id.*

[45] I.R.C. § 7701(o)(1).

[46] I.R.C. § 7701(o)(2)(A).

[47] I.R.C. § 6662(b)(6), (i), 6664(c)(2).

Taxable income in excess of $18,333,333: 35%[48]

Notice that the tax rates contain two "bubbles": higher rates for a limited amount of taxable income, and then lower rates after that amount of taxable income is exceeded. The rate bubble of 39 percent is to eliminate the tax savings resulting from applying the 15 and 25 percent rates on the first $75,000 of taxable income. The effect is that C corporations with total taxable income in excess of $335,000 but not greater than $10,000,000 are taxed at a flat 34 percent rate on their total taxable income. Similarly, the rate bubble of 38 percent wipes out the benefit from applying the 34 percent rate to the first $10,000,000 of taxable income, and its effect is to apply a flat 35 percent rate on the total taxable income of C corporations with taxable income of at least $18,333,333.

Qualified personal service corporations are subject to a flat 35 percent tax rate on all of their taxable income, regardless of the amount.[49] In general, under section 448(d)(2) a "qualified personal service corporation" is a corporation that meets the following requirements:

- substantially all of its activities involve performing services in the fields of health, law, engineering, architecture, accounting, actuarial sciences, performing arts, or consulting, and

- substantially all of its stock (by value) is held (directly or indirectly) by employees performing services, retired employees who had performed services, or their estates.

This special corporate tax rate prevents certain service professionals from benefiting from the lower marginal rates applicable to a C corporation's first $75,000 of income, which the professionals could otherwise do by performing services through a C corporation and having the corporation be taxable on some of the income generated by the professionals' services by paying them compensation that is less than the income generated.

Unlike non-corporate taxpayers,[50] C corporations are currently not entitled to a rate preference on their net capital gains. Section 1201(a) provides that if the highest tax rate exceeds 35 percent, ignoring the rate bubbles (described above), the maximum rate on a C corporation's net capital gain will be 35 percent. Because this is currently not the case, section 1201(a) has no current effect.

§ 13.03 TAXABLE YEAR

A C corporation can generally adopt as its taxable year either the calendar year or a fiscal year,[51] the latter being any 12-month period that ends on the last day of a month other than December.[52]

---

[48] I.R.C. § 11(b)(1).

[49] I.R.C. § 11(b)(2).

[50] See I.R.C. § 1(h).

[51] See I.R.C. § 441(a), (b), (c).

[52] See I.R.C. § 441(e).

As an exception, a personal service corporation generally must use the calendar year as its taxable year.[53] For this purpose, a "personal service corporation" is a corporation whose principal activity is the performance of personal services that are substantially performed by employee-owners — employees who also own (actually or constructively) stock in the corporation, provided that employee-owners own in the aggregate more than 10 percent of the stock (by value) in the corporation.[54] A personal service corporation can use a fiscal year as its taxable year if it can establish a business purpose for its use; in this regard, a desire to defer income to shareholders is not a business purpose.[55] Such a corporation can also select a taxable year that ends on either September 30, October 31, or November 30 without establishing a business purpose by making an election under section 444.[56] If this election is made, the personal service corporation must make certain minimum payments (excluding dividends and sale proceeds) to employee-owners during the period between the end of its fiscal year and December 31, or else have its deduction for payments to employee-owners limited.[57]

§ 13.04   ACCOUNTING METHODS

A C corporation is generally required under section 448 to use the accrual method of accounting.[58] Exceptions are carved out for a farming business,[59] a qualified personal service corporation[60] (defined above[61]), as well as a corporation that for all of its prior taxable years (beginning after 1985) satisfies a $5,000,000 gross receipts test. In general, a corporation meets this $5,000,000 gross receipts test for any prior taxable year if the corporation's average annual gross receipts for the three-year period ending with the prior year do not exceed $5,000,000.[62]

§ 13.05   SPECIAL RULES FOR CERTAIN AFFILIATED CORPORATIONS

A.   Limitation on Multiple Tax Benefits

Under section 1561(a), the members of a "controlled group of corporations" are limited to receiving one helping, so to speak, of certain tax benefits. For example, in applying the rate brackets in section 11, a controlled group of corporations as a whole will have its first $50,000 of combined taxable income taxed at 15 percent, its

---

[53] *See* I.R.C. § 441(i)(1).

[54] *See* I.R.C. § 441(i)(2), 269A(b). Note that a personal service corporation has a different meaning than a qualified personal service corporation (discussed above).

[55] *See* I.R.C. § 441(i)(1).

[56] *See* I.R.C. § 444(a), (b), (e).

[57] *See* I.R.C. § 280H.

[58] *See* I.R.C. § 448(a).

[59] I.R.C. § 448(b)(1).

[60] I.R.C. § 448(b)(2).

[61] *See* § 13.02

[62] I.R.C. § 448(c).

next $25,000 of combined taxable income taxed at 25 percent, and so on.[63] This is opposed to allowing each member to apply the section 11 tax rates to that member's separate taxable income, which if allowed, would permit a corporate enterprise to divide itself into several separate corporations and thus receive several times the $75,000 of taxable income that is taxed at rates below 34 percent.[64] Section 1561 also applies to other tax benefits, including the minimum accumulated earnings credit of $250,000 ($150,000, in some cases)[65] and the $40,000 exemption for purposes of the alternative minimum tax[66] (which are discussed later[67]).

Under section 1563(a), a "controlled group of corporations" includes a parent-subsidiary controlled group or a brother-sister controlled group.[68] In general, a parent-subsidiary controlled group is one or more chains of corporations with a common parent, which are connected through stock ownership that consists of at least 80 percent of the vote or value of a corporation's stock.[69] In general, a brother-sister controlled group is two or more corporations if five or fewer persons who are individuals, estates or trusts own more than 50 percent of the vote or value of each corporation's stock; for this purpose, each person's stock ownership is taken into account only to the extent it is identical with respect to each corporation.[70] Stock ownership for purposes of section 1563 is determined by taking into account both actual and constructive ownership.[71]

B.   Privilege to File a Consolidated Return

An "affiliated group" of corporations may elect to file a consolidated return rather than separate returns.[72] In very general terms, an affiliated group that has made the election is treated as if it were a single corporation for tax purposes. Thus, intercompany transactions are generally disregarded, and the affiliated group's consolidated taxable income mainly represents its transactions with persons outside of the group.[73] In general terms, an "affiliated group" of corporations is defined as one or more chains of corporations with a common

---

[63] *See* I.R.C. § 1561(a)(1)

[64] For example, absent section 1561, a corporate enterprise could subdivide into 10 separate but related corporations and have up to $750,000 of its aggregate taxable income taxed at the 15 percent and 25 percent rates.

[65] *See* I.R.C. § 1561(a)(2)

[66] *See* I.R.C. § 1561(a)(3)

[67] *See* Chapter 20 (accumulated earnings credit); Chapter 13.06 (exemption for alternative minimum tax).

[68] *See* I.R.C. § 1563(a)(1), (a)(2). Also included are certain combinations of parent-subsidiary and brother-sister groups, and certain groups of insurance companies. *See* I.R.C. § 1563(a)(3), (a)(4).

[69] *See* I.R.C. § 1563(a)(1).

[70] *See* I.R.C. § 1563(a)(2).

[71] *See* I.R.C. § 1563(d). In this regard, constructive ownership rules are prescribed under section 1563(e).

[72] *See* I.R.C. § 1501.

[73] *See* Boris I. Bittker & James S. Eustice, Federal Income Taxation of Corporations and Shareholders 13-95 – 13-96 (2000)

parent, which are connected through stock ownership that consists of at least 80 percent of the vote and value of a corporation's stock.[74]

§ 13.06 ALTERNATIVE MINIMUM TAX

Like an individual, a C corporation is also potentially subject to the alternative minimum tax. The purpose of the alternative minimum tax is to ensure that taxpayers with substantial economic income do not avoid significant tax liability through the use of exclusions, deductions and credits.[75] This is accomplished by effectively requiring that taxpayers have a minimum tax that is equal to a flat rate tax imposed on an income base that more closely reflects economic income than does taxable income.[76]

Under section 55(a), the alternative minimum tax is imposed in addition to a taxpayer's regular tax. The alternative minimum tax ("AMT") for a taxable year is equal to the excess (if any) of (i) the "tentative minimum tax" for the year, over (ii) the regular tax for the year.[77] For corporations, the "tentative minimum tax" ("TMT") is generally equal to 20 percent of the excess of (i) alternative minimum taxable income ("AMTI") (described below) over (ii) the exemption amount;[78] the exemption amount is generally $40,000, but begins to be phased out once alternative minimum taxable income exceeds $150,000.[79]

The above rules for determining a corporation's AMT can be expressed as follows:

- AMT = TMT – regular tax
- TMT = .20 (AMTI – exemption amount)
- Therefore, AMT = .20 (AMTI – exemption amount) – regular tax

Because a corporation pays the AMT in addition to the regular tax, for a year when a corporation has an AMT liability, its *total tax* (AMT plus regular tax) is generally equal to:

.20 (AMTI – exemption amount) – regular tax + regular tax = **. 20 (AMTI – exemption amount)**,[80]

i.e., a flat tax on a broader income base than taxable income (which is described immediately below).

AMTI is a corporation's taxable income increased by certain tax preference items along with other adjustments to more closely reflect a corporation's economic

---

[74] *See* I.R.C. § 1504.

[75] *See* Senate Finance Comm. Rep. No. 313, 99th Cong., 2d Sess. 518-519.

[76] *See* Schwarz & Lathrope, *supra* note 23 at 19.

[77] *See* I.R.C. § 55(a).

[78] *See* I.R.C. § 55(b)(1)(B). In determining the tentative minimum tax, there is also a reduction for the alternative minimum foreign tax credit for the year. *See* I.R.C. § 55(b)(1)(B)(ii).

[79] *See* I.R.C. § 55(d)(2), (d)(3)(A).

[80] This ignores the reduction in the TMT and AMT by the amount of the alternative minimum foreign tax credit.

income.[81] For example, a corporation is required to add back the interest received on certain private activity bonds, the interest on which is tax exempt for regular tax purposes.[82] As far as adjustments, a corporation is generally required to depreciate tangible personal property more slowly for AMTI purposes as compared to depreciation for taxable income purposes,[83] based on the recognition that depreciation for regular tax purposes is more accelerated than the actual decline in the assets' values.

Another important adjustment is the adjusted current earnings ("ACE") adjustment. Under the ACE adjustment, AMTI is increased by 75 percent of the excess (if any) of ACE over AMTI determined without regard to the ACE adjustment or the alternative minimum net operating loss deduction ("interim AMTI"[84]).[85] The ACE adjustment can also be negative — AMTI is generally decreased by 75 percent of the excess (if any) of interim AMTI over ACE.[86] In general terms, ACE is interim AMTI with certain additional adjustments that are similar to the adjustments made to taxable income in determining "earnings and profits,"[87] a concept that aims to reflect a corporation's economic profits and that is examined later in this book.[88] The purpose of the ACE adjustment is to move AMTI even closer to a corporation's economic income.

Certain corporations are exempt from the AMT. In general, the AMT does not apply to a corporation for a taxable year if the corporation's average annual gross receipts for all three-year periods (beginning after 1993) ending before the year do not exceed $7,500,000.[89] In addition, a corporation is exempt from the AMT for its first year of existence.[90]

A corporation is generally permitted to credit a portion of the AMT imposed for a taxable year against the corporation's regular tax liability for later years.[91] The allowance of this credit is in recognition of the fact that a corporation's AMT liability may be largely due to timing differences for certain deductions (e.g., depreciation) in determining AMTI versus taxable income, and that without a credit the corporation would be forever losing the accelerated portions of these deductions.[92]

---

[81] *See* I.R.C. § 55(b)(2).

[82] *See* I.R.C. § 57(a)(5).

[83] *See* I.R.C. § 56(a)(1).

[84] *See* Bittker & Eustice, *supra* note 74 at 5-85 – 5-86 of 2011 Cumulative Supplement (providing this handy label).

[85] I.R.C. § 56(g)(1).

[86] *See* I.R.C. § 56(g)(2). This decrease is subject to a certain limitation. *See* I.R.C. § 56(g)(2)(B).

[87] *See* I.R.C. § 56(g)(3), (4).

[88] *See* Chapter 16.

[89] *See* I.R.C. § 55(e)(1). For the first three-year period that is taken into account in applying this rule, the gross receipts limit is $5,000,000. I.R.C. § 55(e)(1)(B).

[90] I.R.C. § 55(e)(1)(C).

[91] *See* I.R.C. § 53(a), (b), (c), (d). The amount of the credit for a taxable year cannot exceed the excess (if any) of the regular tax for such year over the TMT for the year. *See* I.R.C. § 53(c).

[92] *See* Senate Finance Comm. Rep. No. 313, 99th Cong., 2d Sess. 521.

Chapter 14

CORPORATE FORMATION

BASIC OVERVIEW

This chapter examines the tax consequences to shareholders and the corporation upon the formation of a corporation and related transactions.

A. General Shareholder Consequences

On the formation of a corporation, shareholders will typically capitalize the corporation by transferring property and money to it. Absent special rules, the formation of a corporation would be a taxable event to the shareholders transferring property to the corporation, and possibly to the corporation as well. As far as the shareholders are concerned, a transfer of property in exchange for corporate stock is a realization event, thus requiring that the shareholders pay tax on any realized gain in the absence of a nonrecognition rule.

Section 351(a) provides a nonrecognition rule that can apply to corporate formations as well as to transfers to existing corporations. Section 351(a) provides that no gain or loss is recognized if:

- One or more persons transfer property to a corporation,
- Solely in exchange for stock, and
- The person or persons transferring property to the corporation ("transferor(s)") are in control of the corporation immediately after the exchange.

If the requirements are met, section 351(a) would also provide for nonrecognition treatment where two or more persons each transfer property to the corporation as part of a single exchange. In this regard, transfers need not be simultaneous to be a part of one exchange.[1]

For purposes of section 351, property is generally broadly construed to include a wide range of assets, including money[2] and accounts receivable.[3] Section 351(d) specifically excludes certain items from the term property — e.g., services.

For purposes of section 351, section 368(c) defines control as:

- Ownership of at least 80% of the total combined voting power of all classes of stock entitled to vote, and

---

[1] *See* Treas. Reg. § 1.351-1(a)(1).

[2] *See* Rev. Rul. 69-357, 1969-1 C.B. 101.

[3] *See* Hempt Brothers v. United States, 490 F.2d 1172 (3rd Cir. 1974), *cert. denied* 419 U.S. 826 (1974).

- Ownership of at least 80% of the total number of shares of all other classes of stock.

Under section 358(a)(1), a shareholder's basis in stock received in a section 351 exchange is the same as the shareholder's basis in the property exchanged for the stock, with some adjustments that will be discussed later. This special basis rule applies instead of the regular rule under which a taxpayer would take a cost basis in the property received.[4]

Under section 1223(1), a taxpayer's holding period in the property received in a section 351 exchange includes the taxpayer's holding period in the property exchanged, referred to as a tacked holding period, provided:

- the taxpayer's basis in the property received in an exchange is the same in whole or part as the basis of the property exchanged ("exchanged basis"), and

- the property exchanged is either a capital asset or a section 1231 asset.

Because a shareholder takes an exchanged basis under Section 358(a)(1) in the stock received in a section 351 transaction, the shareholder would take a tacked holding period in the stock if the property exchanged is either a capital asset or a section 1231 asset.

B.   General Corporation Consequences

Under section 1032(a), no gain or loss is recognized by a corporation on the receipt of money or other property in exchange for its stock. Under section 362(a), a corporation's basis in the property received in a section 351 exchange is generally the same as the shareholder's basis in property exchanged for the stock, with some adjustments that will be discussed later. Section 362(e)(2) contains an exception that provides that if a corporation's aggregate section 362(a) basis in the properties transferred in a section 351 transaction exceeds the aggregate fair market value of the properties at the time of the transfer, then the corporation's aggregate basis in the properties is generally limited to their aggregate fair market value.

Under section 1223(2), a corporation receives a tacked holding period in the property received in a section 351 transaction; that is, the corporation includes in its holding period the shareholder's holding period in that property. Section 1223(2) provides for a tacked holding period whenever a taxpayer takes a transferred basis in property, which is the type of basis the corporation takes under section 362(a) in a section 351 transaction.

C.   Shareholders' Receipt of Boot

Pursuant to section 351(b)(1), if an exchange otherwise would have qualified under 351(a) but for the fact that the transferor received money or other property, commonly referred to as "boot," then any realized gain is recognized by the transferor to the extent of money plus fair market value of the other property. Under section 351(b)(2), if the exchange otherwise would have qualified under

---

[4] *See* I.R.C. § 1012.

351(a) but for the fact that transferor received boot, the transferor cannot recognize any realized loss.

The receipt of boot in a section 351 transaction necessitates the consideration of adjustments in the section 358(a) basis rule mentioned above. Stating this basis rule fully, a shareholder's basis in stock received in a 351 exchange is:

- Same as the shareholder's basis in the property exchanged for the stock,
- Plus the gain recognized by the shareholder on the exchange,
- Minus the money received by the shareholder on the exchange,
- Minus the fair market value of other property received by the shareholder on the exchange.[5]

The shareholder's basis in other property received in the exchange is its fair market value at the time of receipt.[6]

The receipt of boot in a section 351 transaction also necessitates an adjustment to the rule for determining the corporation's basis in property received. Stating this rule fully, generally[7] the corporation's basis in property acquired in a section 351 exchange is:

- Same as the shareholder's basis in the property exchanged for the stock,
- Plus gain recognized by the shareholder on the exchange.[8]

D. Corporation's Assumption of Shareholder Liabilities

Section 357(a) provides that the assumption of liabilities generally will not constitute the receipt of boot for purposes of section 351.[9] Consequently, in general the corporation's assumption of shareholder liabilities upon the formation of a corporation will not cause the shareholder to recognize gain. There are, however, shareholder stock basis consequences, as well as few exceptions to this general rule.

Section 358(d) treats the assumption of liabilities as money received by the shareholder for purposes of determining the shareholder's basis in the stock received in a section 351 transaction. As an exception to section 357(a), section 357(b) treats the assumption of liabilities as the receipt of money if the shareholder's principal purpose with respect to the assumption either was a purpose to avoid federal income tax or was not a bona fide business purpose. If the bad purpose exists, the *total* amount of the transferor's liabilities assumed is treated as money received. In addition, section 357(c) provides that a shareholder in a section 351 transaction will recognize gain to the extent that the total liabilities

---

[5] I.R.C. § 358(a)(1).

[6] I.R.C. § 358(a)(2).

[7] This is subject to the rule in section 362(e)(2) described above and another rule that is discussed in the Detailed Analysis.

[8] I.R.C. § 362(a).

[9] Section 357(a) also applies to section 361 transactions in the context of corporate reorganizations.

assumed by the corporation exceed the shareholder's aggregate adjusted basis in the properties transferred.[10]

DETAILED ANALYSIS

§ 14.01   GENERAL SHAREHOLDER CONSEQUENCES

A.   Nonrecognition of Gain or Loss

On the formation of a corporation, shareholders will typically capitalize the corporation by transferring property and money to it. As described below, section 351(a) generally provides that shareholders will not recognize any gain or loss in these situations. An example suggests the apparent need for the nonrecognition treatment for shareholders upon the formation of a corporation.

> *Example 14.1.* A forms X Corp. A transfers real estate used in business with a fair market value of $1,000,000 and an adjusted basis of $200,000 to X Corp., in exchange for all 100 shares of X Corp. stock.

Under 1001(a), A has realized gain on the exchange equal to $800,000:

- The fair market value of the property received (100 shares of X Corp. stock), which is $1,000,000, minus

- A's $200,000 adjusted basis in the real estate transferred.

Under section 1001(c), except as otherwise provided in the Code, a realized gain or loss is recognized — i.e., included in gross income (absent an exclusion provision) or potentially allowed as a deduction.

There are arguably a few policy reasons for not recognizing A's $800,000 of realized gain. There may be a concern that because the transaction mainly changes the form rather than the substance of A's holdings and therefore appears to lack significance, taxing contributions of property to newly formed corporations may impede such transactions. There may also be valuation and liquidity concerns in taxing such transactions, although these concerns are always present where a taxpayer disposes of property for other property rather than cash, yet nonrecognition is not afforded for all in-kind transactions.

To alleviate these concerns, section 351(a) provides a nonrecognition rule that can apply to corporate formations as well as to transfers to existing corporations.[11] Section 351(a) provides that no gain or loss is recognized if:

- One or more persons transfer property to a corporation,

---

[10] Where a section 351 transaction involves more than one transferor, section 357(c) is applied separately to each transferor. Rev. Rul. 66-142, 1966-2 C.B. 66.

[11] Two types of transactions are outside of section 351's coverage. First, section 351 does not apply to a transfer of property to an investment company, as defined in section 351(e)(1) and Treas. Reg. § 1.351-1(c). I.R.C. § 351(e)(1). In addition, section 351 does not apply to a transfer of property of a debtor pursuant to a plan while the debtor is under the jurisdiction of a court in a title 11 or similar case, to the extent that stock received in the exchange is used to satisfy the debtor's indebtedness. I.R.C. § 351(e)(2).

- Solely in exchange for stock, and
- The person or persons transferring property to the corporation ("transferor(s)") are in control of the corporation immediately after the exchange.

If the requirements are met, section 351(a) would also provide for nonrecognition treatment where two or more persons each transfer property to the corporation as part of a single exchange. In this regard, transfers need not be simultaneous to be a part of one exchange.[12] For example, if A, B and C each transferred property to a newly formed corporation in exchange for one-third of the stock of the corporation, the transferors would not recognize any of their realized gain or loss on the exchange. It may be difficult to justify nonrecognition here on the basis of a change in form rather than substance, given that each transferor has exchanged a 100 percent direct interest in a single property for a 33⅓ percent indirect interest in multiple properties. Nonetheless, section 351 was crafted to accommodate a wide variety of corporate formations.[13]

1. Property

For purposes of section 351, property is generally broadly construed to include a wide range of assets, including money[14] and accounts receivable.[15] Section 351(d) specifically excludes certain items from the term property — e.g., services. The specific consequences of having a shareholder contribute services for her stock are discussed below.

2. Control

For purposes of section 351, section 368(c) defines control as:

- Ownership of at least 80% of the total combined voting power of all classes of stock entitled to vote, and
- Ownership of at least 80% of the total number of shares of all other classes of stock.

Applying section 351(a) to Example 14.1:

- A transfers property to X Corp.
- A receives solely stock, and
- A is in control of X Corp. immediately after the exchange.

Therefore, A does not recognize her $800,000 of realized gain on the exchange.

Section 351 can also apply to transfers to pre-existing corporations. For example, in Example 14.1 if, prior to the transaction, X Corp. had been in existence and A had

---

[12] *See* Treas. Reg. § 1.351-1(a)(1).

[13] *See* Stephen Schwarz and Daniel J. Lathrope, Fundamentals of Corporate Taxation 57 (2012).

[14] *See* Rev. Rul. 69-357, 1969-1 C.B. 101.

[15] *See* Hempt Brothers v. United States, 490 F.2d 1172 (3rd Cir. 1974), *cert. denied* 419 U.S. 826 (1974). The transfer of accounts receivable to corporation in a section 351 transaction does raise the issue of the assignment of income doctrine. *See* § 14.08[A].

owned 100 shares of X Corp. stock, A's transfer of the real estate would still qualify for nonrecognition under section 351(a). There is no requirement that the transferor obtain control of the corporation in the exchange, only that the transferor has control immediately after the exchange.

B. Basis in Stock Received

Under section 358(a)(1), a shareholder's basis in stock received in a Section 351 exchange is the same as shareholder's basis in the property exchanged for the stock, with some adjustments that will be discussed later. This type of basis is generally referred to as an exchanged basis.[16] This special basis rule applies instead of the regular rule under which a taxpayer would take a cost basis in the property received.[17]

Applying section 358(a)(1) to Example 14.1:

A's basis in the stock is the same as her basis in the real estate, or $200,000. The special basis rule preserves in the stock received in the section 351 transaction the gain or loss realized on the exchange that went unrecognized. This is viewed as appropriate so that such preserved gain or loss can be recognized on a subsequent disposition of the stock — on such a disposition the change-in-form policy that drives nonrecognition is no longer implicated. The preservation principle underlying the special basis rule contained in section 358(a)(1) can be expressed as follows:

gain or loss *realized* on property transferred to corporation = any gain *recognized* on property transferred to corporation + gain or loss preserved in stock.

Applying the preservation principle to Example 14.1:

gain or loss realized on property transferred to corporation ($800,000) = any gain recognized on property transferred to corporation ($0) + gain or loss preserved in stock ($800,000, which is equal to stock's fair market value of $1,000,000 minus the stock's basis of $200,000).

If a shareholder receives stock of different classes in a section 351 exchange, pursuant to Treas. Reg. § 1.358-2(b), the basis amount determined under section 358(a)(1) is allocated between the different classes of stock based on the relative fair market values of the different classes of stock. To illustrate, assume that in Example 14.1 A had received X Corp. common stock with a value of $250,000 and X Corp. preferred stock with a value of $750,000. The basis amount of $200,000 determined under section 358(a)(1) would be allocated as follows: $50,000 to the common stock (which constitutes 25 percent of the total value of the stock received) and $150,000 to the preferred stock (which constitutes 75 percent of the total value of the stock received).

---

[16] I.R.C. § 7701(a)(44).

[17] *See* I.R.C. § 1012.

C. Holding Period in Stock Received

Under section 1223(1), a taxpayer's holding period in the property received in an exchange includes the taxpayer's holding period in the property exchanged, referred to as a tacked holding period, provided:

- the taxpayer's basis in the property received in an exchange is the same in whole or part as the basis of the property exchanged ("exchanged basis"), and

- the property exchanged is either a capital asset or a section 1231 asset.

Because a shareholder takes an exchanged basis in the stock received in a section 351 transaction, the shareholder would take a tacked holding period in the stock if the property exchanged is either a capital asset or a section 1231 asset.

Applying section 1223(1) to Example 14.1:

A should receive a tacked holding period in the stock, because:

- the stock takes an exchanged basis under section 358(a)(1), and

- the real estate should be a section 1231 asset.

§ 14.02   GENERAL CORPORATION CONSEQUENCES

A. Nonrecognition of Gain or Loss

Under section 1032(a), no gain or loss is recognized by a corporation on the receipt of money or other property in exchange for its stock.

Applying section 1032(a) to Example 14.1:

X Corp. recognizes no gain or loss on the receipt of the real estate for its stock.

B. Basis in Property Received

1. In General

Under section 362(a), a corporation's basis in the property received in a section 351 exchange is the same as the shareholder's basis in the property exchanged for the stock with some adjustments that will be discussed later. This type of basis is generally referred to as a transferred basis.[18] Section 362 generally preserves in the hands of the corporation the gain or loss that was realized by the shareholder but not recognized on the transaction. Thus, sections 358 and 362 work to generally preserve the realized yet unrecognized gain or loss at both the shareholder and corporate levels.

Applying section 362(a) to Example 14.1:

X Corp.'s basis in the real estate is the same as A's basis in the real estate, or $200,000.

---

[18] I.R.C. § 7701(a)(43).

2. Basis Limitation on Transfers of Property with Built-In Losses

Under section 362(e)(2), if a corporation's aggregate section 362(a) basis in the properties transferred in a section 351 transaction exceeds the aggregate fair market value of the properties at the time of the transfer, then the corporation's aggregate basis in the properties is limited to their aggregate fair market value. This limitation is applied separately to each transferor in a section 351 transaction.[19] Alternatively, a shareholder and corporation can jointly elect under section 362(e)(2)(C) to limit the shareholder's basis in the stock received to its fair market value.

> *Example 14.2.* A forms X Corp. A transfers to X Corp., in exchange for all 100 shares of X Corp. stock, real property J held for investment with a fair market value of $1,000,000 and an adjusted basis of $1,400,000.

Applying section 362(e)(2) to Example 14.2:

Because X Corp.'s basis in real property J of $1,400,000 under 362(a) exceeds the property's fair market value of $1,000,000, X Corp.'s basis in real property J is limited to its fair market value of $1,000,000. Alternatively, if A and X Corp. had jointly elected to limit A's basis in the 100 shares of stock to their fair market value of $1,000,000, then X Corp.'s basis in real property J would be $1,400,000.

Where a person transfers multiple properties, section 362(e)(2)(B) provides that a reduction in aggregate basis is allocated among the properties in proportion to their respective built-in losses.

> *Example 14.3.* A forms X Corp. A transfers to X Corp., in exchange for all 100 shares of X Corp. stock, (i) real property J held for investment with a fair market value of $1,000,000 and an adjusted basis of $1,400,000 and (ii) real property K used in business with a fair market value of $1,000,000 and an adjusted basis of $800,000.

Applying section 362(e)(2) to Example 14.3:

Because X Corp.'s aggregate basis in the properties of $2,200,000 under 362(a) exceeds the properties' aggregate fair market value of $2,000,000, X Corp.'s aggregate basis in the properties is limited to their aggregate fair market value of $2,000,000. The basis of real property J is $1,200,000 — a section 362(a) basis of $1,400,000 reduced by the entire $200,000 built-in loss. The basis of real property K is $800,000 — a section 362(a) basis of $800,000 unreduced by the built-in loss.

Alternatively, if A and X Corp. had jointly elected to limit A's basis in the 100 shares of stock to their fair market value of $2,000,000, then X Corp.'s basis in real property J would be $1,400,000 (and its basis in real property K would remain at $800,000).

---

[19] *See* Treas. Reg. § 1.362-4(b).

C. Holding Period in Property Received

Under section 1223(2), a corporation receives a tacked holding period in the property received in a section 351 transaction; that is, the corporation includes in its holding period the shareholder's holding period in that property. Section 1223(2) provides for a tacked holding period whenever a taxpayer takes a transferred basis in property, which is the type of basis the corporation takes under section 362(a) in a section 351 transaction.

Applying section 1223(2) to Example 14.1:

X, Inc. will receive a tacked holding period in the real estate, because the real estate takes a transferred basis under section 362(a).

§ 14.03   EFFECT OF SUBSEQUENT STOCK TRANSFERS ON SECTION 351 QUALIFICATION

Example 14.4. A forms X Corp. A transfers real estate used in business with a fair market value of $1,000,000 and an adjusted basis of $200,000 to X Corp., in exchange for all 100 shares of X Corp. stock. One month after the formation of X Corp., A sells 25 shares of X Corp. stock to B for $250,000.

Control for purposes of section 351 is determined by taking into account a subsequent disposition of stock that is pursuant to a binding commitment that existed when the stock was received by the shareholder.[20] This is an application of the step transaction doctrine, discussed in Chapter 13. Note that in applying the control requirement, the Service has ignored a subsequent *nontaxable* disposition of stock, even though pursuant to a binding commitment.[21]

Applying this rule to Example 14.4:

If the subsequent transfer of stock was pursuant to a preexisting binding commitment, A only "owns" 75 shares, or 75 percent of the stock, immediately after the exchange. Consequently, the control requirement and section 351 are not satisfied. If the subsequent transfer of stock was not pursuant to a preexisting binding commitment, the subsequent transfer is not taken into account, and the control requirement and section 351 are satisfied.

---

[20] *See, e.g.,* Intermountain Lumber v. Commissioner, 65 T.C. 1025 (1976).

[21] *See* Rev. Rul. 2003-51, 2003-1 C.B. 938.

§ 14.04   TRANSFERORS OF PROPERTY FOR PURPOSES OF SECTION 351

A.   Exclusion of Services

As stated above, "property" for purposes of section 351 excludes services,[22] along with a few other items.[23] The exclusion for services can present complications for qualifying under section 351 where stock is issued for services rendered or to be rendered for the corporation.

> *Example 14.5.* A and B form X Corp. A transfers real estate used in business with a fair market value of $1,000,000 and an adjusted basis of $200,000 to X Corp., in exchange for 70 shares of X Corp. stock. B agrees to perform services for X Corp. in exchange for 30 shares of X Corp. stock.

Applying section 351(a), (d) to Example 14.5:

Because the services to be rendered by B to X Corp. are not property for purposes of section 351(a), B is not a transferor of property. The transferor of property, A, only has 70 shares after the exchange, or 70 percent of the stock, and thus the control requirement and section 351 are not satisfied.

> *Example 14.6.* A and B form X Corp. A transfers real estate used in business with a fair market value of $1,000,000 and an adjusted basis of $200,000 to X Corp., in exchange for 70 shares of X Corp. stock. B agrees to perform services for X Corp. in exchange for 29 shares of X Corp. stock and transfers $10,000 in cash for 1 share of X Corp. stock.

In general, if a person receives stock in exchange for both property and services, all of the stock counts for purposes of the control requirement.[24] However, this is subject to an anti-abuse rule contained in Treas. Reg. § 1.351-1(a)(1)(ii): stock will not be treated as having been issued for property:

- if the primary purpose of the transfer is to qualify the exchanges of other transferors of property for nonrecognition, and

- if the stock issued for property is "of relatively small value" in comparison to the value of the stock to be received for services by the person transferring property.

According to the Service's policy for issuing favorable rulings, property transferred will *not* be considered to be of relatively small value if:

$$\frac{\text{fair market value of property transferred}}{\text{fair market value of stock received for services}} \qquad \text{equals or exceeds } 0.10.^{[25]}$$

---

[22]   I.R.C. § 351(d)(1).

[23]   Also excluded from "property" are (i) the transferee corporation's indebtedness that is not a security and (ii) interest on the transferee corporation's indebtedness that accrued on or after the start of the transferor's holding period for the debt. I.R.C. § 351(d)(2), (3).

[24]   *See* Treas. Reg. § 1.351-1(a)(2), ex. 3.

[25]   Rev. Proc. 77-37, 1977-2 C.B. 568.

Applying Treas. Reg. § 1.351-1(a)(1)(ii) to Example 14.6:

Because the fair market value of the property transferred by B ($10,000 of cash) is less than 10% of the fair market value of the stock received by B for services ($290,000), it would appear that B will not be treated as a transferor of property. If that is the case, the transferor of property, A, only owns 70 shares after the exchange, or 70 percent of the stock, and thus the control requirement and section 351 are not satisfied.

> *Example 14.7.* A and B form X Corp. A transfers real estate used in business with a fair market value of $1,000,000 and an adjusted basis of $200,000 to X Corp., in exchange for 70 shares of X Corp stock. B agrees to perform services to X Corp. in exchange for 25 shares of X Corp. stock and transfers $50,000 in cash for five shares of X Corp. stock.

Applying Treas. Reg. § 1.351-1(a)(1)(ii) to Example 14.7:

Because the fair market value of the property transferred by B ($50,000) exceeds 10% of the fair market value of the stock received by B for services ($250,000), B will be treated as a transferor of property. The transferors of property, A and B, own all 100 shares after the exchange, and thus the control requirement and section 351 are satisfied.

B. Accommodation Transfers In Connection with Pre-Existing Corporations

As discussed previously, section 351 can also apply to transfers to pre-existing corporations if the provision's requirements are satisfied. Where a new shareholder transfers property to a pre-existing corporation, a current shareholder may also transfer property to the corporation as a part of the same transaction in order to qualify the new shareholder for section 351(a) nonrecognition.

> *Example 14.8.* A owns 50 shares of the stock of X Corp., all of the outstanding stock, which has a fair market value of $500,000. Pursuant to a plan, (i) B transfers equipment with a fair market value of $500,000 and an adjusted basis of $80,000 to X Corp. in exchange for 50 shares of X Corp. stock, and (ii) A transfers $10,000 of cash to X Corp. in exchange for one share of X Corp. stock.

Absent a special rule, the transaction would qualify for nonrecognition treatment under section 351, as A and B have each transferred property to the corporation, solely in exchange for stock, and immediately after the exchange the transferors, A and B, are in control of the corporation — they own 100 percent of the stock. However, the anti-abuse rule, along with the Service's ruling policy, mentioned above, can also apply in this situation.

Specifically, under Treas. Reg. § 1.351-1(a)(1)(ii), stock will not be treated as having been issued for property:

- if the primary purpose of the transfer is to qualify the exchanges of other transferors of property for nonrecognition, and

- if the stock issued for property is "of relatively small value" in comparison to the value of the stock already owned by the person transferring property.

According to the Service's policy for issuing favorable rulings, the property transferred will not be considered to be of relatively small value if:

$$\frac{\text{fair market value of property transferred}}{\text{fair market value of stock already owned}} \quad \text{equals or exceeds } 0.10.\text{[26]}$$

Applying Treas. Reg. 1.351-1(a)(1)(ii) to Example 14.8:

Because the fair market value of the property transferred by A ($10,000 of cash) is less than 10% of the fair market value of the stock already owned by A ($500,000), it would appear that A will not be treated as a transferor of property. If that is the case, the transferor of property, B, only owns 50 shares after the exchange, or 49.5% of the stock, and thus the control requirement and section 351 are not satisfied.

§ 14.05   SHAREHOLDERS' RECEIPT OF BOOT

A.   Recognition of Gain

1.   In General

Example 14.9. A and B form X Corp. A transfers real estate used in business with a fair market value of $500,000 and an adjusted basis of $100,000 to X Corp., in exchange for 40 shares of X Corp. stock and $100,000 of cash. B transfers equipment with a fair market value of $500,000 and an adjusted basis of $80,000 along with $100,000 in cash to X Corp., in exchange for 60 shares of X Corp. stock.

As discussed previously, section 351(a) provides that no gain or loss is recognized if:

- One or more persons transfer property to a corporation,
- Solely in exchange for stock, and
- The person or persons transferring property to the corporation ("transferor(s)") are in control of the corporation immediately after the exchange.

B's exchange qualifies under section 351(a), but A's exchange does not because she does not receive solely stock in the exchange, as she also receives $100,000 in cash. Does this mean that A has to recognize all of her realized gain of $400,000?

The answer in this situation is no. Pursuant to section 351(b)(1), if an exchange otherwise would have qualified under section 351(a) but for the fact that the transferor received money or other property, commonly referred to as "boot," then

---

[26] Rev. Proc. 77-37, 1977-2 C.B. 568.

any realized gain is recognized by transferor to the extent of the money plus the fair market of the other property. In another words, a transferor's recognized gain equals the lesser of:

- Realized gain, or
- Money and fair market value of other property.

Applying section 351(b)(1) to Example 14.9:

A qualifies under 351(a) except for the solely stock requirement. A recognizes the lesser of $400,000 (realized gain) or $100,000 (money received), or $100,000 of gain.

2. Timing of Gain

Shareholders receiving a debt instrument in a section 351 exchange are generally permitted to use the installment sale method to recognize section 351(b) gain as payments of boot are received.[27] The amount of gain recognized per payment of boot is essentially equal to:

$$\frac{\text{Total Recognized Gain on Exchange}}{\text{Total Payments of Boot}} \quad \text{x} \quad \text{Payment of Boot}$$

To illustrate, if in Example 14.9 A had received, instead of cash, X Corp.'s note calling for $100,000 to be paid in two equal installments over the next two years (along with adequate interest), A would generally recognize the gain on the transaction as the payments are received. Thus, on each of the two payments, A would recognize $50,000 of gain, which is equal to:

$$\frac{\text{Total Recognized Gain on Exchange (\$100,000)}}{\text{Total Payments of Boot (\$100,000)}} \quad \text{x} \quad \text{Payment of Boot (\$50,000)}$$

B. Nonrecognition of Loss

Example 14.10. A and B form X Corp. A transfers real estate used in business with a fair market value of $500,000 and an adjusted basis of $600,000 to X Corp., in exchange for 50 shares of X Corp. stock and $100,000 of cash. B transfers equipment with a fair market value of $400,000 and an adjusted basis of $80,000 along with $100,000 in cash to X Corp., in exchange for 50 shares of X Corp. stock.

Now A has a realized loss of $100,000. Is A permitted to recognize her realized loss to the extent of the boot received?

The answer is no. Under section 351(b)(2), if the exchange otherwise would have qualified under section 351(a) but for fact that the transferor received money or other property, the transferor cannot recognize any realized loss.

---

[27] *See* Prop. Reg. § 1.453-1(f)(1), (3).

C. Nonqualified Preferred Stock

For purposes of recognizing gain under section 351(b), "nonqualified preferred stock" is treated as boot.[28] In general, "nonqualified preferred stock" is "preferred stock" that meets one of the following conditions:

- The shareholder has the right to require the corporation or a related person[29] to redeem or purchase the stock,

- The corporation or related person is required to redeem or purchase the stock,

- The corporation or related person has the right to redeem or purchase the stock, and as of the stock's issue date, it is more likely than not that this right will be exercised, or

- The stock's dividend rate varies in whole or in part (directly or indirectly) with reference to interest rates, commodity rates, or similar indices.[30]

Any of the first three conditions exists only if (i) the right or obligation may be exercised within 20 years of the stock's issue date and (ii) the right or obligation is not subject to a contingency that, as of the issue date, makes the likelihood of redemption or purchase remote.[31] "Preferred stock" for purposes of this rule is stock that is limited and preferred as to dividends and does not participate in corporate growth to any significant extent.[32]

Nonqualified preferred stock is treated as boot because of its debt-like features. Accordingly, if a shareholder in a section 351 transaction receives nonqualified preferred stock along with other stock, then under section 351(b) the shareholder will recognize any realized gain to the extent of the fair market value of the nonqualified preferred stock, but is not permitted to recognize any realized loss.[33] However, if the shareholder only receives nonqualified preferred stock in the transaction, then under section 351(g)(1) the shareholder would recognize the total amount of any realized gain or loss.[34] While nonqualified preferred stock is treated as boot for section 351(b) purposes, it is still treated as stock for purposes determining whether a transaction satisfies the control requirement under section 351(a) until and unless regulations say otherwise.[35]

---

[28] I.R.C. § 351(g)(1).

[29] Related person is a person related to the corporation under either section 267(b) or section 707(b). I.R.C. § 351(g)(3)(B).

[30] I.R.C. § 351(g)(2)(A).

[31] I.R.C. § 351(g)(2)(B).

[32] I.R.C. § 351(g)(3)(A).

[33] I.R.C. § 351(g)(1)(B), 351(b).

[34] *See* I.R.C. § 351(g)(1)(B).

[35] *See* Boris I. Bittker & James S. Eustice, Federal Income Taxation of Corporations and Shareholders 3-24 and n.91 (2000) (referring to the provision's legislative history).

D. Basis in Stock Received

Previously it was stated that under section 358(a)(1), a shareholder's basis in stock received in a section 351 exchange is the same as shareholder's basis in property exchanged for the stock, with some adjustments to be discussed later. The receipt of boot in a section 351 transaction necessitates these adjustments. Stating the basis rule fully, a shareholder's basis in stock received in a section 351 exchange is:

- Same as the shareholder's basis in property exchanged for the stock,
- Plus the gain recognized by the shareholder on the exchange,
- Minus the money received by the shareholder on the exchange,
- Minus the fair market value of other property received by the shareholder on the exchange.[36]

The shareholder's basis in other property received in the exchange is its fair market value at the time of receipt.[37]

Applying section 358(a)(1) to A in Example 14.9:

A's basis in the 40 shares of X Corp. stock received is:

- A's adjusted basis in the real estate ($100,000),
- Plus gain recognized by A on the exchange, ($100,000)
- Minus money received by A on the exchange ($100,000),
- Minus fair market value of other property received by A on the exchange ($0),

which equals $100,000.

As previously discussed, the preservation principle underlying the special basis rule contained in section 358(a)(1) can be expressed as follows:

gain or loss realized on property transferred to corporation = any gain recognized on property transferred to corporation + gain or loss preserved in stock.

Applying the preservation principle to A's consequences in Example 14.9:

gain or loss realized on property transferred to corporation ($400,000) = any gain recognized on property transferred to corporation ($100,000) + gain or loss preserved in stock ($300,000, which is equal to stock's fair market value of $400,000 minus the stock's basis of $100,000).

E. Corporation's Basis in Property Received

Previously it was stated that under section 362(a), a corporation's basis in property received in a section 351 exchange is the same as the shareholder's basis in property exchanged for the stock with some adjustments to be discussed. The

---

[36] I.R.C. § 358(a)(1).

[37] I.R.C. § 358(a)(2).

receipt of boot in a section 351 transaction also necessitates an adjustment to the corporation's basis in property received.

Generally,[38] the corporation's basis in property acquired in a section 351 exchange is the:

- Same as the shareholder's basis in property exchanged for the stock,
- Plus gain recognized by shareholder on the exchange.[39]

As previously mentioned, the general aim of section 362 is to preserve in the hands of the corporation the gain or loss that was realized by the shareholder but not recognized on the transaction. Thus, sections 358 and 362 work to preserve (generally) the realized yet unrecognized gain or loss at both the shareholder and corporate levels.

Applying section 362(a) to the real estate transferred by A in Example 14.9:

X Corp.'s basis in the real estate is the:

- Same as A's basis in the real estate ($100,000),
- Plus gain recognized by A on the exchange ($100,000),

which equals $200,000.

§ 14.06   TRANSFER OF MULTIPLE ASSETS

A.   Separate Application of Section 351(b) and Allocation of Boot

When a person transfers multiple assets to a corporation in a section 351 exchange and receives stock and boot, this raises questions of (i) whether section 351(b) should be applied to the transferred properties separately or in the aggregate, and if separately, (ii) how the boot should be allocated to the transferred properties for purposes of applying section 351(b). Revenue Ruling 68-55[40] and, more recently, Prop. Reg. § 1.351-2(b), answer these questions by providing that section 351(b) applies separately to the transferred properties, and that for this purpose, boot is allocated to the transferred assets based on their relative fair market values.

> *Example 14.11.* A and B form X Corp. A transfers the following assets to X Corp., in exchange for 40 shares of X Corp. stock and $100,000 of cash: (i) improved real estate used in business with a fair market value of $250,000 and an adjusted basis of $100,000, (ii) inventory with a fair market value of $100,000 and an adjusted basis of $90,000, and (iii) land held for investment with a fair market value of $150,000 and an adjusted basis of $200,000. B

---

[38] This is subject to the rule in section 362(e)(2) described above and another rule to be discussed below.

[39] I.R.C. § 362(a).

[40] 1968-1 C.B. 140.

transfers equipment with a fair market value of $500,000 and an adjusted basis of $80,000 along with $100,000 in cash to X Corp., in exchange for 60 shares of X Corp. stock.

Applying Rev. Rul. 68-55 and Prop. Reg. § 1.351-2(b) to A in Example 14.11:

The $100,000 of cash received by A is allocated to the properties transferred by A as follows:

- $50,000 is allocated to the improved real estate (which constitutes 50 percent of the total value of the properties transferred).

- $20,000 is allocated to the inventory (which constitutes 20 percent of the total value of the properties transferred).

- $30,000 is allocated to the land (which constitutes 30 percent of the total value of the properties transferred).

Under section 351(b), A has the following consequences:

- $50,000 of recognized gain on the improved real estate (the lesser of the realized gain of $150,000 and the allocated boot of $50,000).

- $10,000 of recognized gain on the inventory (the lesser of the realized gain of $10,000 and the allocated boot of $20,000).

- $0 of recognized loss on the land (none of the $50,000 of realized loss is recognized even with the receipt of boot).

B. Split Holding Period in Stock

As previously discussed, under section 1223(1), the shareholder would take a tacked holding period in the stock received in a section 351 transaction if the property exchanged is either a capital asset or a section 1231 asset. When a person transfers multiple properties in a section 351 exchange, it could well be the case that some but not all of the properties qualify the stock for a tacked holding period; moreover, the transferor's holding period in the particular assets will almost certainly be different.

Pursuant to Revenue Ruling 85-164,[41] a person transferring multiple properties to a corporation in a section 351 exchange takes a split holding period in each share of stock received. This is opposed to determining holding periods of stock by assigning particular shares of stock to particular assets. The split holding period that each share of stock takes is determined by reference to the relative fair market values of the properties transferred. To illustrate, in Example 14.11 A should take a tacked holding period in 80 percent of each share of stock received, because 80 percent of the assets transferred are either section 1231 assets (the business real estate) or capital assets (the investment land), and a non-tacked holding period in 20 percent of each share received, because 20 percent of the assets transferred are inventory (which is neither a section 1231 asset nor a capital asset).

---

[41] Rev. Rul. 85-164, 1985-2 C.B. 117.

§ 14.07   CORPORATION'S ASSUMPTION OF SHAREHOLDER LIABILITIES

A.   General Rule

Absent a special rule, the assumption of shareholder liabilities by the corporation in a section 351 transaction would be considered the receipt of boot by the shareholder, thereby requiring the transferor to recognize any realized gain to the extent of the assumed liabilities.[42] This treatment would cause many incorporations of going businesses to become taxable events, and thus frustrate the policy of section 351.

Section 357(a), enacted to prevent this result,[43] provides that the assumption of liabilities generally will not constitute the receipt of boot for purposes of section 351.[44] Consequently, in general, the corporation's assumption of shareholder liabilities upon the formation of a corporation will not cause the shareholder to recognize gain. There are, however, shareholder stock basis consequences, as well as few exceptions that are discussed below.

B.   Assumption of Liabilities

Under section 357(d), a recourse liability is treated as having been assumed if, on the basis of all the facts and circumstances, the transferee corporation has agreed to, and is expected to, satisfy the liability, regardless of whether the transferor shareholder has been relieved of the liability. A nonrecourse liability is generally treated as having been assumed where the transferee corporation takes an asset subject to the liability.[45]

C.   Effect on Shareholder's Basis in Stock

In order to preserve the appropriate amount of gain or loss in the shareholder's stock, section 358(d) treats the assumption of liabilities as money received by the shareholder for purposes of determining the shareholder's basis in the stock received in the section 351 transaction. The following example illustrates the application of sections 357(a) and 358(d).

> *Example 14.12.* A transfers an asset with a fair market value of $100,000 and an adjusted basis of $20,000 to X Corp. in a transaction qualifying under section 351. In exchange, X Corp. transfers to A $90,000 of stock and assumes (for purposes of section 357) $10,000 of section 357(a) liabilities of the individual (e.g., longstanding business liabilities).

Applying sections 357(a) and 358 to A in Example 14.12:

---

[42] *See* United States v. Hendler, 303 U.S. 564 (1938) (holding that for purposes of the reorganization provisions, the assumption of liabilities is considered the equivalent of cash received by the party whose liabilities are assumed, therefore triggering the recognition of boot gain).

[43] *See* H.R. REP. 76-875 (1939), *reprinted in* 1939-2 C.B. 504, 518-520.

[44] Section 357(a) also applies to section 361 transactions in the context of corporate reorganizations.

[45] I.R.C. § 357(d)(1), (2).

Pursuant to section 357(a), the assumption of liabilities will not be treated as boot, and therefore, under section 351(a), A will recognize none of her realized gain of $80,000 (amount realized of $100,000 less adjusted basis of $20,000) on the transaction. Under section 358, A will take a $10,000 basis in the X Corp. stock received, which is equal to:

- A's basis in the property transferred ($20,000),

- plus the gain recognized by A ($0),

- minus the money or other boot received by A ($10,000, due to the assumption of liabilities, which is treated as money received for basis purposes).

Applying the preservation principle to A's consequences in Example 14.12:

gain or loss realized on property transferred to corporation ($80,000) = any gain recognized on property transferred to corporation ($0) + gain or loss preserved in stock ($80,000, which is equal to stock's fair market value of $90,000 minus the stock's basis of $10,000).

D. Tax Avoidance Exception

As an exception to section 357(a), section 357(b) treats the assumption of liabilities as the receipt of money if the shareholder's principal purpose with respect to the assumption either was a purpose to avoid federal income tax or was not a bona fide business purpose. If the bad purpose exists, the *total* amount of the transferor's liabilities assumed is treated as money received.[46]

Section 357(b) is aimed at the situation where a shareholder borrows on the eve of incorporation and then transfers the liability to the corporation, which effectively results in the receipt of cash by the shareholder.[47] Also covered are transfers of personal liabilities to the transferee corporation.[48]

E. Gain Recognition Where Assumed Liabilities Exceed Shareholder's Basis in Transferred Property

1. Basic Rule

If in Example 14.12 the asset had a basis of $5,000 in A's hands, a straightforward application of sections 357(a) and 358 would result in no gain recognized and a basis of *negative* $5,000 in the stock ($5,000 basis in the asset, plus $0 gain recognized, minus $10,000 money received for basis purposes). However, the tax law does not permit a negative basis.[49] And providing a stock basis of zero without the recognition of gain on these facts would violate the gain/loss preservation principle:

---

[46] *See* I.R.C. § 357(b).

[47] *See* Bittker & Eustice, *supra* note 35, at 3-29 – 3-30.

[48] *See id.*

[49] *See, e.g., Easson v. Commissioner*, 33 T.C. 963 (1960) (acq. and nonacq.), rev'd on other grounds, 294 F.2d 653 (9th Cir. 1961).

the $95,000 of realized gain (amount realized of $100,000 less the asset's adjusted basis of $5,000) would *not* equal the $0 of recognized gain plus the $90,000 of gain inherent in the stock following the transaction (the difference between the stock's fair market value of $90,000 and its basis of $0).

To avoid having a negative basis while adhering to the gain/loss preservation principle, Congress enacted section 357(c),[50] which provides that a shareholder in a section 351 transaction will recognize gain to the extent that the total liabilities assumed by the corporation exceed the shareholder's aggregate adjusted basis in the properties transferred.[51]

Applying section 357(c) to determine A's consequences in modified Example 14.12:

A would have $5,000 of recognized gain ($10,000 of assumed liabilities less $5,000 of adjusted basis) and per section 358(a), a basis in X Corp. stock of $0 ($5,000 basis in the asset, plus $5,000 gain recognized, minus $10,000 money received for basis purposes). With these results, the gain/loss preservation principle is satisfied — $95,000 of realized gain equals $5,000 of recognized gain plus $90,000 of gain inherent in the stock following the transaction.

2. Effect on Corporation's Basis in Property Received

As with section 351(b) gain, section 357(c) gain will generally result in an increase in the corporation's basis in the property received pursuant to section 362(a).[52] However, section 362(d)(1) provides a limitation, under which a corporation's basis in the property received cannot be increased above the fair market value of the property as a result of the recognition of gain under section 357(c). Congress's apparent reason for enacting section 362(d)(1) was to create a general anti-abuse measure aimed at perceived corporate tax shelter abuses.[53]

3. Avoiding Section 357(c) Gain

Prior to 1999, section 357(c) gain was recognized to the extent that "the sum of the liabilities assumed, plus the amount of liabilities to which the property is subject" exceeded the transferor's aggregate basis in the transferred assets.[54] Under this rule, recourse liabilities secured by the transferred assets were taken into account in determining section 357(c) gain, regardless of whether the transferor remained personally liable on the obligations.[55] Taxpayers attempted to avoid section 357(c) gain by contributing their own promissory notes in an attempt to

---

[50] *See* George Cooper, *Negative Basis*, 75 Harv. L. Rev. 1352, 1358-60 (1962).

[51] Where a section 351 transaction involves more than one transferor, section 357(c) is applied separately to each transferor. Rev. Rul. 66-142, 1966-2 C.B. 66.

[52] As discussed earlier, under section 362(a) the corporation's basis in the property received in a section 351 transaction is equal to the transferor's basis in the property, increased by the amount of gain recognized by the transferor on the transaction.

[53] *See* Staff of Joint Comm. on Taxation, 107th Cong., General Explanation of Tax Legislation Enacted in the 106th Congress 10 (Comm. Print 2001).

[54] *See* I.R.C. § 357(c)(1) (prior to amendments made by P.L. 106-36, § 3001(d)(4)).

[55] *See* Treas. Reg. § 1.357-2(a).

increase the basis of the property transferred to the corporation. This led to the rejection by the Service[56] and the U.S. Tax Court[57] of this technique for eliminating section 357(c) gain, its acceptance by two federal circuit courts[58] and a great deal of scholarship on the issue.[59]

Under the current rule, section 357(c) only takes into account liabilities assumed which, in the case of recourse liabilities, are treated as having been assumed if, on the basis of all the facts and circumstances, the transferee corporation has agreed to, and is expected to, satisfy the liability, regardless of whether the transferor has been relieved of the liability.[60] With the current rule, transferor shareholders may be able to avoid section 357(c) gain with respect to secured recourse liabilities by agreeing with the transferee corporations that the transferors, rather than the corporations, will satisfy the recourse liability.[61] With respect to recourse liabilities, this may moot the promissory note issue. Nevertheless, there is some possibility that given the "on the basis of all the facts and circumstances" language contained in the statute, the Service could establish that the parties agreed and expected that the corporation, rather than the transferor, would satisfy the liability, despite an express agreement to the contrary.[62]

4. Excluded Liabilities

In determining the amount of liabilities assumed for purposes of section 357(c), 357(c)(3) generally excludes obligations that would give rise to a deduction (or that would be described in section 736(a)) if paid by the shareholder.[64] Also excluded under Rev. Rul. 95-74[65] are liabilities that have neither given rise to a deduction to the transferor nor resulted in the creation of, or increase in, basis in the transferor's property.[66] Under section 358(d)(2), excluded liabilities are not treated as money received by the shareholder for stock basis purposes.

---

[56] *See* Rev. Rul. 68-629, 1968-2 C.B. 154.

[57] *See, e.g.*, Alderman v. Commissioner, 55 T.C. 662 (1971).

[58] *See* Lessinger v. Commissioner, 872 F.2d 519 (2d Cir. 1989); Peracchi v. Commissioner, 143 F.3d 487 (9th Cir. 1998).

[59] *See, e.g.*, John Bogdanski, *Shareholder Debt, Corporate Debt; Lessons from Leavitt and Lessinger*, 16 J. Corp. Tax'n 348 (1990); Susan Kalinka, *Peracchi: What is the Right Result?*, 80 Tax Notes 1615 (Sept. 28, 1998); Lipton and Bender, *Peracchi and Making Something Out of Nothing, or Does Debt Have a Zero Basis to its Maker and Further Ruminations on the Substance and Form of Transaction*, 77 Taxes 13 (Mar. 1999).

[60] *See* I.R.C. § 357(d)(1)(A).

[61] *See* John A. Bogdanski, *Section 357(d) – Old Can, New Worms*, 27 J. Corp. Tax'n 17, 26 (2000).

[62] *See* Bogodanski, *supra* note, at 22-24, 27.

[64] I.R.C. § 357(c)(3)(A). Excepted from these excluded liabilities are the liabilities that resulted in the creation of, or increase in, the basis of any property. I.R.C. § 357(c)(3)(B). An example of such liabilities is where a cash basis taxpayer purchases small tools on credit. The payment of the liabilities would give rise to a deduction, but the taxpayer has a basis in the tools equal to their purchase price. *See* Bittker & Eustice, *supra* note 35 at 3-38.

[65] 1995-2 C.B. 36.

[66] The revenue ruling involved contingent environmental liabilities that had neither been deducted by the transferor nor increased the basis in any of the transferor's property. *See id.*

5. Character of Section 357(c) Gain

With regard to the character of section 357(c) gain, the statute provides that such gain is treated as from the sale or exchange of property that is a capital asset or is not a capital asset, as the case may be. By way of examples, the regulations provide that the character of section 357(c) gain is determined based on the relative fair market value of the assets transferred to the corporation.[67] According to the regulations, if half of the transferred assets, based on their fair market values, are capital assets and half are not, then half of the section 357(c) gain will be treated as capital gain and half will be other than capital gain. Despite the relative fair market value approach called for by the regulations, a few U.S. Tax Court decisions have allocated section 357(c) gain solely to assets with realized gain.[68]

§ 14.08 EFFECT OF OTHER DOCTRINES ON SECTION 351 NONRECOGNITION

A. Assignment of Income Doctrine

Under the assignment of income doctrine, where a right to receive income is gifted to another person, the transferor is taxed on the income when collected by the transferee.[69] Generally, the assignment of income doctrine does not override nonrecognition treatment under section 351.[70] Consequently, if, for example, a cash method individual were to transfer accounts receivable to a corporation in a section 351 transaction as part of the incorporation of a going concern, the transferor would not recognize income with respect to the accounts receivable either when the stock is received or the receivables are collected. However, the assignment of income doctrine will override section 351 if there was a tax avoidance purpose for the transaction — for example, where the accounts receivable were the only assets transferred in the section 351 transaction.[71]

B. Tax Benefit Rule

The tax benefit rule applies where an amount had been deducted and a subsequent event occurs that is "fundamentally inconsistent" with the provision allowing for the previous deduction. Where this occurs, the amount of the previous deduction must be added back into income in the year that the fundamentally inconsistent event occurs, in effect eliminating the earlier deduction.[72] The possible application of the tax benefit rule in a section 351 transaction can arise where a taxpayer transfers to the corporation assets that were deducted upon acquisition

---

[67] *See* Treas. Reg. § 1.357-2(b), Examples 1, 2.

[68] *See* Raich v. Commissioner, 46 T.C. 604 (1966); Rosen v. Commissioner, 62 T.C. 11 (1974), *aff'd without opinion*, 515 F.2d 507 (3d Cir. 1975).

[69] *See* Lucas v. Earl, 280 U.S. 538 (1929); *see also* Commissioner v. P.G. Lake, Inc., 356 U.S. 260 (1958).

[70] *See* Hempt Brothers v. United States, 490 F.2d 1172, *cert. denied*, 419 U.S. 826 (1974).

[71] *See* Rev. Rul. 80-198, 1980-2 C.B. 113.

[72] *See* Hillsboro National Bank v. Commissioner, 460 U.S. 370 (1983).

(e.g., supplies) in an exchange otherwise qualifying under section 351. It appears to be unsettled whether the tax benefit rule overrides section 351. To date, no case has ever applied the tax benefit rule to require the recognition of income in a section 351 transaction,[73] and one case has rejected its application.[74]

§ 14.09　CONTRIBUTIONS TO CAPITAL

A contribution to capital occurs when a shareholder or other person transfers property to a corporation and receives no stock or other consideration.[75]

A.　Consequences to the Contributor

The tax treatment to shareholders on contributions to capital is basically the same as in a section 351 transaction.[76] A shareholder recognizes no gain or loss upon the transfer of the contributed property to the corporation.[77] The contribution is treated as an additional price paid for the stock,[78] and thus the shareholder will increase her basis in stock by the amount of money and the adjusted basis of property contributed.

Where a non-shareholder contributes to the capital of a corporation, the contribution may constitute a deductible expense to the contributor.[79] Otherwise, there are probably no other tax consequences to non-shareholders on contributions to capital.[80]

B.　Consequences to the Corporation

Under section 118(a), a contribution to capital by a shareholder is excluded from the gross income of the corporation.[81] Some capital contributions by non-shareholders are also excluded from the corporation's gross income, such as property contributed to a corporation by a governmental unit to induce a

---

[73] *See generally* Nash v. United States, 398 U.S. 1 (1970).

[74] *See* Mars v. Commissioner, 88 T.C. 428 (1987); *Cf.* section 1245(b)(3).

[75] However, where a sole shareholder contributes money or property and receives no stock, the transaction is treated as a section 351 exchange because the issuance of additional stock to the shareholder would be a meaningless gesture. *See* Lessinger v. Commissioner, 872 F.2d 519 (2d Cir. 1989). As a consequence, section 357(c), which applies to section 351 transactions but not to contributions to capital, can apply to such a transaction.

[76] As noted above, a difference is that section 357(c) does not apply to contributions to capital.

[77] *See* Commissioner v. Fink, 483 U.S. 89 (1987) (applying this rule to a shareholder's non-pro rata contribution of a portion of her stock in the corporation).

[78] Treas. Reg. § 1.118-1.

[79] *See* Treas. Reg. § 1.162-15(b) (providing as an example a contribution of money by a transit company to a corporation in order to induce the corporation to hold a convention in the city in which the transit company operates, where the transit company reasonably expects that holding of such convention will increase its income).

[80] *See* Bittker & Eustice, supra note 35 at 3-82.

[81] *See* Treas. Reg. § 1.118-1.

corporation to locate or expand its business in a particular community.[82] However, the section 118 exclusion does not apply to money or property transferred to a corporation as consideration for goods or services rendered, or as a subsidy to induce the corporation to limit production.[83] In addition, the term "contribution to capital" generally does not include any contribution in aid of construction or any other contribution as a customer or potential customer.[84]

Under section 362(a)(2), the corporation's basis in the property contributed by a shareholder is the same as shareholder's adjusted basis in the property. With regard to non-shareholder contributions to capital, section 362(c) provides that the corporation takes a zero basis in property (other than money) contributed,[85] and that the corporation must reduce the basis of its property by the amount of money received as a contribution to capital.[86]

---

[82] *See id.*

[83] *See id.*

[84] I.R.C. § 118(b). There is an exception for certain contributions made to a regulated public utility company providing water or sewerage disposal services. *See* 118(c).

[85] I.R.C. § 362(c)(1).

[86] I.R.C. § 362(c)(2). More specifically, the corporation first reduces the basis of property that is acquired with such money within the 12-month period beginning on the day of the contribution, and to the extent that the amount of money contributed exceeds this reduction, the excess amount is applied to reduce the basis of any other property held by the corporation on the last day of the 12-month period. *See id.*

Chapter 15

DEBT/EQUITY CLASSIFICATION

BASIC OVERVIEW

Corporations raise capital by issuing debt instruments and stock to investors for money or property. This chapter examines the tax treatment of corporate debt and stock, and the standards used for classifying an instrument as either debt or stock.

A. General Tax Advantages of Debt Over Equity

From a tax perspective, debt generally has several advantages over stock. First, interest paid on debt is deductible to the corporation,[1] but dividends paid on stock are not. Both interest and dividends are included in the gross income of the recipients. Consequently, to the extent that the earnings of a C corporation are paid as interest on debt rather than dividends on stock, these earnings are not subject to tax at the corporate level. In other words, C corporate earnings paid out as interest are subject to one level of tax (at the debt holder level), whereas C corporate earnings paid out as dividends on stock are subject to two levels of tax (at the shareholder and corporate levels). In addition, when a corporation repays its debt, this is generally a tax-free return of capital to the holder. On the other hand, when a corporation redeems its stock (repurchases it from the shareholder), the shareholder may be allowed to offset her stock basis against the amount received, but this is not always the case. A stock redemption can be treated as either an exchange, allowing for basis offset, or as a dividend (to the extent of corporate earnings and profits), not allowing for basis offset.[2] Other advantages of debt versus stock, and the treatment of the worthlessness of debt and stock instruments are examined in the Detailed Analysis.

B. Reclassifying Debt as Equity

Because of the general tax advantages of debt over equity, C corporations and their shareholders have a tax bias for issuing corporate debt rather than stock. Especially in the context of closely held C corporations, this can lead to situations where purported debt issued to persons who are also shareholders may in substance resemble stock. Consequently, the courts and Service have developed standards to reclassify purported debt as stock where appropriate; these standards are addressed below.

---

[1] *See* I.R.C. § 163(a).

[2] *See* I.R.C. §§ 302, 301, 316. Redemptions are discussed in Chapter 17; dividends and earnings and profits are discussed in Chapter 16.

A major effect of reclassifying debt as stock is that purported interest is treated as dividends, and thus the corporate deduction for the interest is denied. Consequently, reclassification of debt as equity results in a corporate level tax on the earnings paid on the reclassified instrument. Another effect of reclassification is that the repayment of purported debt will be treated as a redemption of stock, which could result in dividend treatment for the amount received by the holder (and thus no basis offset).[3]

C.   Factors for Classifying Shareholder-Held Debt

Unlike most other areas of tax law, the approach for classifying shareholder-held debt does not contain definite rules. Instead, classification involves an application of certain factors in deciding whether purported debt should be treated as equity. While the courts and Services may sometimes use other factors,[4] what appear to be the principal factors are examined below.

1.   Form

In the case of shareholder-held debt, it appears that the form of the instrument must conform to classic debt, lest the risk of reclassification will be high.[5] Thus, it seems that having good form is almost a must factor to avoid reclassification, and that an instrument should contain the following:

- Unconditional promise to pay
- Specific term or repayment upon demand, and
- Stated reasonable rate of interest payable unconditionally.[6]

2.   Corporation's Debt/Equity Ratio

In determining the economic reality of purported debt, the courts and Service will often determine the corporation's debt-equity ratio, which is:

$$\frac{\text{Liabilities}}{\text{Assets} - \text{Liabilities}}$$

A high ratio is a factor that favors equity, based on the view that an independent creditor would not lend money to a corporation that is thinly capitalized.[7] A low ratio is a factor that favors debt.[8] There is, however, uncertainty as to what is a good debt-equity ratio. In general, a ratio of three to one or less is usually assumed

---

[3] *See* Chapter 17.

[4] *See, e.g.,* Fin Hay Realty Co. v. United States, 398 F.2d 694 (3rd Cir. 1968) (court announced a 16-factor test, but only applied some of the factors in concluding that the shareholder advances were equity).

[5] *See* Stephen Schwarz and Daniel J. Lathrope, Fundamentals of Corporate Taxation 122 (2012).

[6] *See id.*

[7] *See id;* Boris I. Bittker & James S. Eustice, Federal Income Taxation of Corporations and Shareholders 4-44 – 4-45 (2000).

[8] *See* Bittker & Eustice, *supra* note 7 at 4-45.

to provide immunity from reclassification.[9] A ratio of five to one or greater generally appears to pose a greater risk of reclassification. However, the cases lack consistency, with very high ratios not leading to reclassification,[10] and debt reclassified as equity in situations involving very low ratios.[11]

3. Proportionality

Proportionality is a factor in favor of equity treatment and thus raises the risk that debt will be reclassified as stock.[12] Proportionality exists where the debt held by shareholders is held in the same proportions as their stock holdings.[13] An example of proportionate shareholder-held debt is where two 50 percent shareholders each hold 50 percent of the shareholder-held debt. In such circumstances, it appears that the shareholders do not have the intention or incentive to act like real creditors — to the extent that they advance their interests as creditors that would equally harm their interests as shareholders.[14]

4. Subordination

Subordination exists where shareholder-held debt is subordinated to the claims of non-shareholder creditors. Its presence can be a factor in favor of reclassifying debt as stock, although it may be treated as a practical necessity of operating a closely held corporation.[15]

5. Hindsight

By the time a court is asked to decide whether an instrument is debt or equity, there is often a history concerning the instrument — that is, whether or not principal and interest were paid in a timely manner. Courts will often use this hindsight as a factor in classifying an instrument.[16] If principal and interest were paid in a timely manner, this is a factor against reclassifying the instrument as equity.[17] If the opposite, this is a factor in favor of treating the instrument as equity.[18]

---

[9] *See* Bittker & Eustice, *supra* note 7 at 4-44 – 4-45.

[10] *See* Bradshaw v. United States, 683 F.2d 365 (Ct. Cl. 1982).

[11] *See* Schnitzer v. Commissioner, 13 T.C. 43 (1949). The fact that the debt was issued to the shareholders for core assets of the corporation's business could have been an important factor in this decision. *See* Bittker & Eustice, *supra* note 7 at 4-46.

[12] *See* Schwarz and Lathrope, *supra* note 5 at 124; Bittker & Eustice, *supra* note 7 at 4-42 — 4-43.

[13] *See* Bittker & Eustice, *supra* note 7 at 4-42 — 4-43.

[14] *See* Schwarz and Lathrope, *supra* note 5 at 124.

[15] *See id.* at 124.

[16] *See* Bittker & Eustice, *supra* note 7 at 4-49.

[17] *See id.*

[18] *See* Schwarz and Lathrope, *supra* note 5 at 124; Bittker & Eustice, *supra* note 7 at 4-49.

6. Applying the Factors

Courts generally apply the debt-equity factors by evaluating whether a given factor as applied to the facts signifies debt or equity, and then determining whether overall the factors indicate debt or equity. A good example of this is Indmar Products Co., Inc. v. Commissioner.[19] Here, the Court of Appeals for the Sixth Circuit reversed the U.S. Tax Court and found that the shareholder advances were debt rather than equity. The Court determined that demand notes without a fixed maturity date did not strongly favor equity given the fixed interest rate and regular interest payments, and that except for a lack of security for the advances, the other factors examined pointed to debt:

- the corporation was adequately capitalized (going towards debt-equity ratio)
- proportionality was not present
- subordination did not exist as to all creditors
- regular monthly interest payments were made, and shareholders demanded and received numerous partial payments of principal (hindsight)

DETAILED ANALYSIS

§ 15.01 TAX TREATMENT OF DEBT VERSUS EQUITY

A. General Tax Advantages of Debt over Equity

1. Interest versus Dividends

Interest paid on debt is deductible to the corporation,[20] but dividends paid on stock are not. Both interest and dividends are included in the gross income of the recipients. Consequently, to the extent that the earnings of a C corporation are paid as interest on debt rather than dividends on stock, these earnings are not subject to tax at the corporate level. In other words, C corporate earnings paid out as interest are subject to one level of tax (at the debt holder level), whereas C corporate earnings paid out as dividends on stock are subject to two levels of tax (at the shareholder and corporate levels).

Mitigating to an extent this advantage of interest over dividends are some rules that can reduce the shareholder-level tax on dividends. First, most dividends paid by domestic corporations to non-corporate shareholders constitute qualified dividend income that are subject to preferential capital gains rates[21] — generally a

---

[19] Indmar Products Co., Inc. v. Commissioner, 444 F.3d 771 (6th Cir. 2006). I thank the authors of Schwarz & Lathrope, supra note 5, for bringing this case to my attention by including it in their book.

[20] See I.R.C. § 163(a).

[21] See I.R.C. § 1(h)(11). Dividends paid by certain foreign corporations also constitute qualified dividend income. Qualified dividend income is discussed in Chapter 16.

maximum rate of 15 percent.[22] Second, corporate shareholders generally receive a dividends-received deduction, which allows corporations to generally deduct 70 percent of the amount of the dividend.[23] Interest, on the other hand, is fully included in taxable income and taxed at ordinary income rates. In addition, corporations and their shareholders can control the timing of the tax on dividends by accumulating earnings and not paying dividends on a current basis, whereas interest is often taxable on an annual basis, whether or not it is paid.[24]

2. Repayment of Debt versus Redemption of Stock

When a corporation repays its debt, this is generally a tax-free return of capital to the holder. That is, upon the repayment of debt, the holder offsets her basis in the debt against the amount received,[25] with the holder's basis in the debt typically equal to the amount repaid. On the other hand, when a corporation redeems its stock (repurchases it from the shareholder), the shareholder may be allowed to offset her stock basis against the amount received, but this is not always the case. A stock redemption is either treated either as an exchange, allowing for basis offset, or as a dividend (to the extent of corporate earnings and profits), not allowing for basis offset.[26] Exchange versus dividend treatment generally depends on the extent to which the redemption reduced the shareholder's stock interest in the corporation.[27]

3. Other Advantages of Debt as Compared to Stock

The accumulation of earnings by a C corporation to retire a debt instrument may well constitute a reasonable accumulation for purposes of the accumulated earnings tax.[28] On the other hand, it is unusual for accumulations to redeem stock to be considered as accumulations for the reasonable needs of the corporation's business.[29]

In some cases, a corporation may issue debt rather than stock to allow a person transferring property to the corporation to intentionally fail section 351.[30] This may be done to permit a transferor to recognize a loss on a transfer of depreciated property, or to allow a transferor to recognize capital gain on a transfer of real

---

[22] For lower income taxpayers, the maximum rate is 0 percent, and for higher income taxpayers, it is 20 percent. *See* I.R.C. § 1(h).

[23] The dividends-received deduction is discussed in Chapter 16.

[24] This is a result of the rules applying to debt instruments with original issue discount. *See* I.R.C. §§ 1272-1275.

[25] *See* I.R.C. §§ 1001, 1271(a).

[26] *See* I.R.C. § 302, 301, 316. Redemptions are discussed in Chapter 17; dividends and earnings and profits are discussed in Chapter 16.

[27] *See* Chapter 17.

[28] *See* Schwarz and Lathrope, *supra* note 5 at 115. See Chapter 20 for a discussion of the accumulated earnings tax.

[29] *See* Schwarz and Lathrope, *supra* note 5 at 115-116.

[30] *See id* at 116.

estate prior to development and thereby reduce the amount of ordinary income to be recognized by the corporation.[31]

B. Worthlessness of Debt and Stock

In examining the tax treatment of debt versus stock, the character of the loss upon the worthlessness of an instrument should be considered. In particular, it is important to determine whether the loss would be an ordinary loss, which can be deducted without restriction against the holder's taxable income,[32] or instead a capital loss, which in general can only be deducted to the extent of the holder's capital gains for the particular year.[33]

1. Debt

The character of the loss upon the worthlessness of a corporate indebtedness depends on whether the indebtedness is a security as defined under the Code.

a.   Securities

If corporate indebtedness is a security, then assuming it is a capital asset in the hands of the holder, which would typically be the case, it is treated as sold or exchanged on the last day of the taxable year in which it became worthless.[34] Thus, the worthlessness of a corporate debt instrument that is a security would typically result in a capital loss. A security is defined as evidence of indebtedness issued by a corporation that is either in registered form or with interest coupons.[35]

b.   Non-Securities

For a corporate holder, the worthlessness of corporate indebtedness that is not a security gives rise to an ordinary loss.[36] For a non-corporate holder, the worthlessness of corporate indebtedness that is not a security is either a (i) business bad debt giving rise to an ordinary loss or (ii) nonbusiness bad debt giving rise to a short-term capital loss.[37] A nonbusiness bad debt results from a debt *other* than (i) a debt created or acquired in connection with a business of the holder or (ii) a debt whose loss upon worthlessness is incurred in the holder's business.[38] Any other bad debt is a business bad debt.

An issue that often arises is whether the worthlessness of corporate indebtedness that is not a security and is held by a shareholder should be treated

---

[31] *See id* at 110-111.

[32] *See* I.R.C. § 165(a).

[33] *See* I.R.C. § 1211. Capital losses in excess of capital gains can be carried over to other taxable years. *See* I.R.C. § 1212.

[34] *See* I.R.C. § 165(g)(1).

[35] *See* I.R.C. § 165(g)(2).

[36] *See* I.R.C. § 166(a).

[37] *See* I.R.C. § 166(d)(1).

[38] *See* I.R.C. § 166(d)(2).

as a business or nonbusiness bad debt. In *Generes v. Commissioner*,[39] the U.S. Supreme Court held that for such indebtedness to be a business bad debt, the shareholder/creditor's dominant motivation must be business. A motivation to protect an interest as an employee of the corporation is a business motivation,[40] whereas a motivation to protect an interest as a shareholder is an investment motivation. In *Generes*, the Court found that the shareholder's dominant motivation was not to protect his salary as an employee of the corporation, but instead to protect his investment as a shareholder, and thus nonbusiness bad debt treatment was accorded.

2. Stock

a.   In General

Stock and rights to acquire stock are securities.[41] Therefore, assuming that stock is a capital asset in the hands of the shareholder, which would typically be the case, the stock is treated as sold or exchanged on the last day of the taxable year in which it became worthless.[42] Thus, absent the application of a special rule, the worthlessness of stock would typically result in a capital loss.

b.   Section 1244 Stock

An exception to capital loss treatment applies to the worthlessness (or sale or exchange) of section 1244 stock held by an individual to whom the stock was issued (or an individual who was a partner at the time that a partnership acquired the stock).[43] Upon the worthlessness (or sale or exchange) of section 1244 stock held by these taxpayers, the loss is an ordinary loss to the extent of $50,000 per year (or $100,000 per year for a married taxpayer filing jointly).[44]

Section 1244 stock is stock that meets all of the following requirements:

- Issued for money or property (other than stock and securities);[45]
- At the time issued, the corporation was a "small business corporation,"[46] i.e., aggregate amount of money and other property received by the corporation for stock or as a contribution to capital does not exceed $1,000,000;[47] and
- For the five years prior to the year of loss, the corporation derived more than 50 percent of its aggregate gross receipts from sources *other* than

---

[39] 405 U.S. 93 (1972).

[40] Performing services as an employee is considered a business activity for tax purposes.

[41] *See* I.R.C. § 165(g)(2).

[42] *See* I.R.C. § 165(g)(1).

[43] *See* I.R.C. § 1244(a).

[44] *See* I.R.C. § 1244(a), (b).

[45] I.R.C. § 1244(c)(1)(B).

[46] I.R.C. § 1244(c)(1)(A).

[47] I.R.C. § 1244(c)(3)(A).

passive investment income items.[48]

§ 15.02 RECLASSIFYING DEBT AS EQUITY

A. In General

Because of the general tax advantages of debt over equity, C corporations and their shareholders have a tax bias for issuing corporate debt rather than stock. Especially in the context of closely held C corporations, this can lead to situations in which purported debt issued to persons who are also shareholders may in substance resemble stock. Where shareholders occupy both sides of a transaction involving purported debt — on one side as the debt holders and on the other side representing the corporation — it could be that the parties are simply labeling the instrument as debt for tax purposes, and that there is a lack of intention and/or economic reality for the instrument to function as debt. Consequently, the courts and Service have developed standards to reclassify purported debt as stock where appropriate. These standards are addressed below.

Besides situations involving shareholder-held debt, classification controversies can also arise where there are so-called hybrid instruments that have both debt-like and stock-like features. Classification standards for hybrid instruments are briefly mentioned below.

B. Effect of Reclassification

A major effect of reclassifying debt as stock is that purported interest is treated as dividends, and thus the corporate deduction for the interest is denied. Consequently, reclassification of debt as equity results in a corporate level tax on the earnings paid on the reclassified instrument. Another effect of reclassification is that the repayment of purported debt will be treated as a redemption of stock, which could result in dividend treatment for the amount received by the holder (and thus no basis offset).[49]

§ 15.03 FACTORS FOR CLASSIFYING SHAREHOLDER-HELD DEBT

A. Overview

Unlike most other areas of tax law, the approach for classifying shareholder-held debt does not contain definite rules. Instead, classification involves an application of certain factors in deciding whether purported debt should be treated as equity. The inquiry is highly fact specific, and because the area is governed by tax common law, a uniform approach is lacking. Nevertheless, certain factors do predominate, and they will be analyzed below.

---

[48] *See* I.R.C. § 1244(c)(1)(C).

[49] *See* Chapter 17.

Before discussing the key common law factors for debt-equity classification, section 385 should be mentioned. Section 385 was enacted to address debt-equity classification, but the provision is not self-executing and only provides Treasury with authority to promulgate regulations.[50] And while proposed regulations were once issued, it has been more than 30 years since they were withdrawn.[51] Thus, at least for the foreseeable future, and maybe forever, debt-equity classification is governed by common law standards without the aid of statutes or regulations.[52]

While the courts and Services may sometimes use other factors,[53] it appears that the principal classification factors are as follows:

- Form
- Debt/Equity Ratio
- Proportionality
- Subordination
- Hindsight[54]

Each of these factors will be explored below.

B.   Form

In the case of shareholder-held debt, it appears that the form of the instrument must conform to classic debt, lest the risk of reclassification be high.[55] In other words, hybrid instruments (e.g., with interest contingent on earnings) held by shareholders are particularly subject to being reclassified as stock.[56] Thus, it seems that having good form is almost a must factor to avoid reclassification, and an instrument should contain the following:

- Unconditional promise to pay

---

[50]   See I.R.C. 385(a).

[51]   *See* Bittker & Eustice, *supra* note 7 at 4-18.

[52]   The now-defunct regulations did contain a *safe harbor* for classifying instruments as debt. Debt bearing a reasonable interest rate would not be reclassified as equity provided that the corporation had a:
- total debt-equity ratio of 10 to 1 or less, and
- shareholder-held debt-equity ratio of 3 to 1 or less. Prop. Reg. § 1.385-6(g)(3).

In determining these ratios, assets were valued using adjusted basis. Prop. Reg. § 1.385-6(g)(3). While the section 385 regulations were never in effect, it is understood that some practitioners may have used the safe harbor as an indication of when the Service would challenge the classification of purported debt instruments.

[53]   *See, e.g.*, Fin Hay Realty Co. v. United States, 398 F.2d 694 (3d Cir. 1968) (court announced a 16-factor test, but only applied some of the factors in concluding that the shareholder advances were equity).

[54]   *See* Schwarz and Lathrope, *supra* note 5 at 122-124; Bittker & Eustice, *supra* note 7 at 4-42 – 4-49. Except for the hindsight factor, these factors are the ones listed in section 385(b) (along with convertibility into stock) as factors (among other factors) that Treasury may include in regulations that reclassify debt as stock.

[55]   *See* Schwarz and Lathrope, *supra* note 5 at 122.

[56]   *See id.*

- Specific term or repayment upon demand
- Stated reasonable rate of interest payable unconditionally.[57]

C. Corporation's Debt/Equity Ratio

In determining the economic reality of purported debt, the courts and Service will often determine the corporation's debt-equity ratio, which is:

$$\frac{\text{Liabilities}}{\text{Assets} - \text{Liabilities}}$$

A high ratio is a factor that favors equity, based on the view that an independent creditor would not lend money to a corporation that is thinly capitalized.[58] A low ratio is a factor that favors debt.[59]

Several issues arise in connection with using the debt-equity ratio as a classification factor. First, in computing the ratio, how are assets to be valued? While the use of fair market value appears to be the norm,[60] some cases have used adjusted bases to value assets.[61] There are also issues in determining liabilities — that is, whether to include all corporate liabilities or just shareholder-held debt, with the former apparently being the general approach.[62] Another question is whether trade payables are included in liabilities.[63]

Perhaps more fundamentally, there is uncertainty as to what is a good debt-equity ratio. In general, a ratio of three to one or less is usually assumed to provide immunity from reclassification.[64] A ratio of five to one or greater generally appears to pose a greater risk of reclassification. However, the cases lack consistency, with very high ratios not leading to reclassification,[65] and debt reclassified as equity in situations involving very low ratios.[66]

---

[57] *See id.*

[58] *See id;* Bittker & Eustice, *supra* note 7 at 4-44 – 4-45.

[59] *See* Bittker & Eustice, *supra* note at 4-45.

[60] *See id.*

[61] *See* Schwarz and Lathrope, *supra* note 5 at 123.

[62] *See* Bittker & Eustice, *supra* note 7 at 4-44 – 4-45.

[63] *See* Schwarz and Lathrope, *supra* note 5 at 123.

[64] *See* Bittker & Eustice, *supra* note 7 at 4-44 – 4-45.

[65] *See* Bradshaw v. United States, 683 F.2d 365 (Ct. Cl. 1982).

[66] *See* Schnitzer v. Commissioner, 13 T.C. 43 (1949). The fact that the debt was issued to the shareholders for core assets of the corporation's business could have been an important factor in this decision. *See* Bittker & Eustice, *supra* note 7 at 4-46.

D. Proportionality

Proportionality is a factor in favor of equity treatment and thus raises the risk that debt will be reclassified as stock.[67] Proportionality exists where the debt held by shareholders is held in the same proportions as their stock holdings.[68] An example of proportionate shareholder-held debt is where two 50 percent shareholders each hold 50 percent of the shareholder-held debt. In such circumstances, it appears that the shareholders do not have the intention or incentive to act like real creditors — to the extent that they advance their interests as creditors that would equally harm their interests as shareholders.[69]

E. Subordination

Subordination exists where shareholder-held debt is subordinated to the claims of non-shareholder creditors. Its presence can be a factor in favor of reclassifying debt as stock, although it may be treated as a practical necessity of operating a closely held corporation.[70]

F. Hindsight

By the time a court is asked to decide whether an instrument is debt or equity, there is often a history concerning the instrument — that is, whether or not principal and interest were paid in a timely manner. Courts will often use this hindsight as a factor in classifying an instrument.[71] If principal and interest were paid in a timely manner, this is a factor against reclassifying the instrument as equity.[72] If the opposite, this is a factor in favor of treating the instrument as equity.[73] The hindsight factor seems to go to both the intention and reality of having the instrument function as debt.

G. Applying the Factors

Courts generally apply the debt-equity factors by evaluating whether a given factor as applied to the facts signifies debt or equity, and then determining whether overall the factors indicate debt or equity. A good example of this is *Indmar Products Co., Inc. v. Commissioner*.[74] Here, the Court of Appeals for the Sixth Circuit reversed the U.S. Tax Court and found that the shareholder advances were debt rather than equity. The Court determined that demand notes without a fixed maturity did not strongly favor equity given the fixed interest rate and regular

---

[67] *See* Schwarz and Lathrope, *supra* note 5 at 124; Bittker & Eustice, *supra* note 7 at 4-42 — 4-43.

[68] *See* Bittker & Eustice, *supra* note 7 at 4-42 — 4-43.

[69] *See* Schwarz and Lathrope, *supra* note 5 at 124.

[70] *See* Schwarz and Lathrope, *supra* note 5 at 124.

[71] *See* Bittker & Eustice, *supra* note 7 at 4-49.

[72] *See id.*

[73] *See* Schwarz and Lathrope, *supra* note 5 at 124; Bittker & Eustice, *supra* note 7 at 4-49.

[74] Indmar Products Co., Inc. v. Commissioner, 444 F.3d 771 (6th Cir. 2006). I thank the authors of Schwarz & Lathrope, supra note 5, for bringing this case to my attention by including it in their book.

interest payments, and that except for a lack of security for the advances, the other factors examined pointed to debt:

- the corporation was adequately capitalized (going toward debt-equity ratio)

- proportionality was not present

- subordination did not exist as to all creditors

- regular monthly interest payments were made, and shareholders demanded and received numerous partial payments of principal (hindsight).

Example 15.1. A and B form X Corp. by each transferring $100,000 in cash to X Corp. in exchange for 50 shares of X Corp. stock. In addition, A and B each loan X Corp. $600,000 and take back X Corp.'s note to repay $600,000 plus interest payable at a commercially reasonable rate, in equal annual installments over the next 10 years. X Corp.'s obligation to A and B on the notes is subordinated to any claims of non-shareholder creditors.

Applying the debt-equity factors to A and B's loan to X Corp. in Example 15.1:

- Proper form signifies debt.

- Total debt-equity ratio of

$$\frac{\$1,200,000 \text{ (total liabilities)}}{\$200,000 \text{ (assets minus liabilities)}}$$

or 6 to 1 appears high, signifying equity.

- Proportionality is present as shareholders hold debt in the same proportion to stock — each 50 percent shareholder holds 50 percent of the shareholder-held debt — signifying equity.

- Subordination is present, signifying equity.

- At this point, the instrument has no history to consider hindsight.

Conclusion: it seems likely that the shareholder advances would be reclassified as stock, given the equity determinations under the debt-equity ratio, proportionality and subordination factors.

Example 15.2. A and B form X Corp. by each transferring $100,000 in cash to X Corp. in exchange for 50 shares of X Corp. stock. In addition, A loans X Corp. $1,200,000 and takes back X Corp.'s note to repay $1,200,000 plus interest payable at a commercially reasonable rate, in equal annual installments over the next 10 years. X Corp.'s obligation to A on the note is subordinated to any claims of non-shareholder creditors.

Applying the debt-equity factors to A's loan to X Corp. in Example 15.2:

- Proper form signifies debt.

- Total debt-equity ratio of

$1,200,000 (total liabilities)

$200,000 (assets minus
liabilities)

- Proportionality is *not* present as shareholders do not hold debt in the same proportion to stock – one 50 percent shareholder holds 100 percent of the shareholder-held debt — signifying debt.
- Subordination is present, signifying equity.
- At this point, the instrument has no history to consider hindsight.

    Conclusion: less likely (compared to Example 15.1) that shareholder advances would be reclassified as stock, given the debt determination under proportionality, even though there are equity determinations under the debt-equity ratio and subordination factors.

Example 15.3. A and B form X Corp. by each transferring $100,000 in cash X Corp. in exchange for 50 shares of X Corp. stock. In addition, A loans X Corp. $1,200,000 and takes back X Corp.'s note to repay $1,200,000 plus interest payable at a commercially reasonable rate, in equal annual installments over the next 10 years. X Corp.'s obligation to A on the note is subordinated to any claims of non-shareholder creditors. Four years after the loan is made, X Corp. is unable to make the annual principal and interest payments called for under the note, and A permits X Corp. to suspend making payments indefinitely.

Applying the debt-equity factors to A's loan to X Corp. in Example 15.3:

- Proper form signifies debt.
- Total debt-equity ratio of

$1,200,000 (total liabilities)
$200,000 (assets minus
liabilities)

    or 6 to 1 is high, signifying equity.

- Proportionality is *not* present as shareholders do not hold debt in the same proportion to stock — one 50 percent shareholder holds 100 percent of the shareholder-held debt — signifying debt.
- Subordination is present, signifying equity.
- The suspension of payments on the note signifies equity under the hindsight factor.

    Conclusion: more likely (compared to Example 15.2) that the shareholder advances would be reclassified as stock, given the equity determination under the hindsight factor.

H.   Effect of Shareholder Guarantees of Third Party Loans

In certain situations, a shareholder guarantee of a third-party loan to the corporation could result in the following recharacterization for tax purposes: the third-party loan would be treated as a loan to the shareholder guaranteeing the loan, followed by a capital contribution to the corporation. The effect would be that the corporation would be denied interest deductions on the payments to the third party. This is what occurred in *Plantation Patterns, Inc. v. Commissioner*.[75]

Such a recharacterization would probably only occur where there is a very high debt-equity ratio — in *Plantation Patterns, Inc.*, the corporation had a debt-equity ratio of apparently 150 to 1.[76] The basis for recharacterizing shareholder-guaranteed third-party debt in these situations is that in light of the very high debt-equity ratio, the third-party lender is really looking to the shareholder for repayment rather than the corporation.

§ 15.04   HYBRID INSTRUMENTS

Hybrid instruments are instruments with both debt and equity features, such as: long maturity dates, subordination, interest contingent on earnings, ability to defer interest payments, convertibility to stock, and management rights. As mentioned previously, where hybrid instruments are issued to shareholders, they would appear to be particularly subject to reclassification as stock. Where such instruments are issued to persons who are not otherwise shareholders, the Service and the courts usually approach their classification as debt or equity by determining whether the debt or equity features dominate, as well as considering the corporation's financial strength.[77] The Code supplements the common law rules for hybrid instruments by providing that interest deductions are denied for certain instruments payable in stock.[78]

---

[75] 462 F.2d 712 (5th Cir. 1972)

[76] *See id.*

[77] *See* Notice 94-47, 1994-1 C.B. 357; Rev. Rul. 85-119, 1985-2 C.B. 60; Rev. Rul. 83-98, 1983-2 C.B. 40; CCA 200932049.

[78] *See* I.R.C. § 163(l).

Chapter 16

NONLIQUIDATING DISTRIBUTIONS OF PROPERTY

BASIC OVERVIEW

This chapter addresses the tax treatment of distributions of cash and property by a corporation to its shareholders in the nonliquidating context. Later chapters will address other types of distributions by a corporation to its shareholders in the nonliquidating context and distributions by a corporation to its shareholders in the liquidating context. This chapter examines the consequences of nonliquidating distributions to both shareholders and the corporation, as well as some special rules applying to the taxation of dividends.

A. General Shareholder Treatment on Distributions of Cash and Other Property

The shareholder treatment of nonliquidating distributions of property by a corporation to shareholders is governed by section 301(c).[1] For this purpose, property is defined as money, securities, and any other property, except stock of the corporation making the distribution.[2] The amount of a distribution is the amount of money plus the fair market value of other property received by the shareholder (reduced by any corporate liabilities assumed or taken subject to by the shareholder in connection with the distribution).[3]

Section 301(c) contains a three-part rule for treating distributions:

- The portion of the distribution that is a dividend (as defined in section 316) is included in the shareholder's gross income.[4]

- The portion that is not a dividend reduces the shareholder's basis in the stock on which the distribution is made (but not below zero).[5]

- The excess of the portion that is not a dividend over the shareholder's basis in the stock is considered gain from the sale of stock (with a very limited exception for distributions out of an increase in value occurring prior to March 1, 1913).[6]

---

[1] *See* I.R.C. § 301(a).

[2] *See* I.R.C. § 317(a).

[3] *See* I.R.C. § 301(b).

[4] *See* I.R.C. § 301(c)(1).

[5] *See* I.R.C. § 301(c)(2).

[6] *See* I.R.C. § 301(c)(3).

Under section 301(d), a shareholder's basis in the distributed property is equal to the property's fair market value at the time of the distribution.

B.   Dividends and Earnings & Profits

Under section 316(a), a dividend is a distribution of property out of either:

- Earnings and profits accumulated for periods after February 28, 1913 ("Accumulated E&P"), or

- Earnings and profits of the corporation's taxable year in which the distribution occurs ("Current E&P").

Per section 316(a), every distribution is out of earnings and profits ("E&P") to the extent thereof, and from the most recently accumulated E&P. This prevents the claim that distributions should first be traced to capital invested by the shareholders.

The purpose of E&P is to measure a corporation's capacity to make distributions out of corporate profits as opposed to capital invested by the shareholders. Thus, E&P aims to reflect a corporation's economic profits, and consequently differs from taxable income, which is influenced by other policies.

E&P is determined by starting with a corporation's taxable income for a particular year and then making certain adjustments generally aimed at moving taxable income closer to economic income. While the Code and Regulations do not comprehensively define E&P, they do provide for some of these adjustments, while others are provided under common law.

Adjustments to Taxable Income in Determining E&P:

- Add back certain items that are excluded from taxable income but represent an accession to corporate wealth.[7]

- Add back certain items that are deductible in determining taxable income but do not represent actual expenditures for the particular taxable year.

- Subtract certain items that are nondeductible in determining taxable income yet represent actual expenditures for the particular taxable year.

- Make certain timing adjustments.

In determining whether there is enough E&P for a distribution to be a dividend, the Regulations provide that Current E&P is considered first.[8] To the extent that distributions during a taxable year exceed Current E&P, Accumulated E&P is considered.[9] Where the total amount of distributions made during a taxable year is greater than the total amount of E&P, it is necessary to allocate E&P to the distributions. The Regulations provide for different methods for allocating Current E&P and Accumulated E&P that are explored in the Detailed Analysis.

---

[7] Treas. Reg. § 1.312-6(b).

[8] Treas. Reg. § 1.316-2(a).

[9] *Id.*

Accumulated E&P is generally reduced by the amount of a distribution. However, the reduction or charge to Accumulated E&P cannot exceed the amount of Accumulated E&P prior to the E&P charge.[10] Consequently, a deficit in Accumulated E&P cannot be created or increased as a result of a distribution, but E&P can be negative as a result of operations. The rules generally result in an E&P charge that is equal to the amount of dividend received by the shareholder.

C. Corporate Consequences on Distributions of Property

When a corporation distributes appreciated property to its shareholders, i.e., property with a fair market value in excess of the corporation's adjusted basis in the property, pursuant to section 311(b)(1), the corporation recognizes gain as if it had sold the property to the shareholder for its fair market value.[11] At one time under the so-called *General Utilities* doctrine,[12] distributions of property, whether in the nonliquidating or liquidating context, did not give rise to corporate-level gain or loss. The current rule represents a repeal of the *General Utilities* doctrine for nonliqudating distributions of appreciated property. The gain recognition rule does not apply to a distribution of a corporation's own obligations.[13]

When a corporation distributes depreciated property to its shareholders, i.e., property with a fair market value that is less than the corporation's adjusted basis in the property, pursuant to section 311(a)(1), the corporation recognizes no loss. Thus, Congress retained the *General Utilities* doctrine for nonliquidating distributions of depreciated property, presumably because of a concern that corporations could abuse loss recognition with regard to timing or the bona fide nature of such transactions.[14]

Current E&P is increased by the amount of gain recognized on a distribution of appreciated property.[15] The increase in Current E&P on the distribution of appreciated property can in turn cause some or all of the distribution to be a dividend. Because E&P tracks taxable income with respect to recognized gains and losses,[16] the nonrecognition of loss on the distribution of depreciated property has no effect on Current E&P.

D. Constructive Distributions

Traditionally, C corporations and their shareholders have sought to reduce the double taxation of distributed corporate earnings by employing certain techniques. Most of the techniques aim to pay corporate earnings to shareholders in a manner

---

[10] I.R.C. § 312(a).

[11] I.R.C. § 311(b)(1).

[12] The doctrine is based on General Utilities & Operating Co. v. Helvering, 296 U.S. 200 (1935).

[13] *Id.*

[14] *See* BORIS I. BITTKER & JAMES S. EUSTICE, FEDERAL INCOME TAXATION OF CORPORATIONS AND SHAREHOLD-ERS 8-77 (2000).

[15] I.R.C. § 312(b)(1). The property's adjusted basis for E&P purposes is used to determine the amount of gain that is added to Current E&P. I.R.C. § 312(b).

[16] I.R.C. § 312(f)(1).

that, unlike a dividend, is deductible to the corporation. Other maneuvers try to avoid an inclusion in gross income at either the shareholder or corporate level.

To combat these attempts at reducing the sting of the double tax, the courts, Service, Treasury, and occasionally Congress have developed certain responses. Prominent among them are rules that can recharacterize payments as constructive distributions in order to reflect the substance of the transaction. These are explored in the Detailed Analysis.

E. Taxation of Dividends Received by Non-Corporate Shareholders

Dividends received by individuals and other non-corporate taxpayers are generally subject to the preferential tax rates that apply to long-term capital gains. More specifically, qualified dividend income received by non-corporate taxpayers is treated as adjusted net capital gain for purposes of the preferential rates provided in section 1(h).[17] Adjusted net capital gain is generally taxed at a maximum rate of 15 percent, with maximum rates of 0 percent for lower income taxpayers[18] and 20 percent for higher income taxpayers.[19] Accordingly, a non-corporate taxpayer's qualified dividend income is generally taxed at 15 percent. Qualified dividend income generally includes dividends paid by taxable domestic (U.S.) corporations, as well as dividends paid by qualified foreign corporations.[20]

F. Dividends-Received Deduction for Corporate Shareholders

Corporations are generally entitled to a deduction equal to a certain percentage of a dividend received from another corporation. More specifically, the dividends-received deduction percentages are as follows:

- 70% of the amount of the dividend in general.[21]

- 80% of the amount of the dividend if the corporation receiving the dividend owns at least 20% of the stock (by vote and value) of the corporation paying the dividend.[22]

- 100% of the amount of "qualifying dividends," which are generally dividends (i) from a corporation that is a member of the receiving corporation's affiliated group and (ii) which were distributed out of the E&P of a year in which the distributing and receiving corporations were members of the same affiliated group;[23] generally, two corporations are members of an affiliated group where one corporation owns at least 80% of

---

[17] I.R.C. § 1(h)(11), (4), (5), (6), (7).

[18] These are taxpayers in the 10 or 15 percent tax brackets.

[19] These are taxpayers in the 39.6 percent tax bracket.

[20] I.R.C. § 1(h)(11)(B)(i).

[21] I.R.C. § 243(a)(1).

[22] I.R.C. § 243(c).

[23] I.R.C. § 243(a)(3), (b)(1).

the stock (by vote and value) of the other corporation.[24]

The purpose of the dividends-received deduction is to prevent three or more full levels of taxation as dividends wend their way through multiple corporations.

The ability of a corporate shareholder to deduct at least 70 percent of the amount of a dividend opens the door to certain abuses. The Code contains three provisions to combat these abuses: holding period requirements, a rule that reduces stock basis in connection with extraordinary dividends, and a rule that reduces the dividends-received deduction in connection with certain debt-financed stock. These provisions are examined in the Detailed Analysis.

DETAILED ANALYSIS

§ 16.01   DISTRIBUTIONS OF CASH AND OTHER PROPERTY

The shareholder treatment on nonliquidating distributions of property by a corporation to shareholders is governed by section 301(c).[25] For this purpose, property is defined as money, securities, and any other property, except stock of the corporation making the distribution.[26] The amount of a distribution is the amount of money plus the fair market value of other property received by the shareholder (reduced by any corporate liabilities assumed or taken subject to by the shareholder in connection with the distribution).[27]

Section 301(c) contains a three-part rule for treating distributions:

- The portion of the distribution that is a dividend (as defined in section 316) is included in the shareholder's gross income.[28]

- The portion that is not a dividend reduces the shareholder's basis in the stock on which the distribution is made (but not below zero).[29]

- The excess of the portion that is not a dividend over the shareholder's basis in the stock is considered gain from the sale of stock (with a very limited exception for distributions out of an increase in value occurring prior to March 1, 1913).[30]

In general terms, a dividend is a distribution of a corporation's profits as opposed to the capital invested by shareholders. Dividends will be addressed in more detail below.

---

[24] I.R.C. § 1504(a).

[25] *See* I.R.C. § 301(a).

[26] *See* I.R.C. § 317(a).

[27] *See* I.R.C. § 301(b).

[28] *See* I.R.C. § 301(c)(1).

[29] *See* I.R.C. § 301(c)(2).

[30] *See* I.R.C. § 301(c)(3).

Example 16.1. A owns all 100 shares of X Corp. A's basis in the X Corp. stock is $4,000. During 2014, X Corp. distributes $10,000 to A. $3,000 of the distribution is a dividend.

Applying section 301(c) to Example 16.1:

- The portion of the distribution that is a dividend is included in gross income — $3,000.

- The portion that is not a dividend ($7,000) reduces shareholder's basis in stock — from $4,000 to $0.

- The excess of the portion that is not a dividend ($7,000) over the shareholder's basis in stock ($4,000) is considered gain from the sale of stock — $3,000 gain.

Under section 301(d), a shareholder's basis in the distributed property is equal to the property's fair market value at the time of the distribution.

§ 16.02 DIVIDENDS AND EARNINGS & PROFITS

A. Dividends in General

Under section 316(a), a dividend is a distribution of property out of either:

- Earnings and profits accumulated for periods after February 28, 1913 ("Accumulated E&P"), or

- Earnings and profits of the corporation's taxable year in which the distribution occurs ("Current E&P").

Per section 316(a), every distribution is out of earnings and profits ("E&P") to the extent thereof, and from the most recently accumulated E&P. This prevents the claim that distributions should first be traced to capital invested by the shareholders.

Example 16.2. A owns all 100 shares of X Corp. A's basis in the X Corp. stock is $4,000. During 2014, X Corp. distributes $10,000 to A. For 2014, X Corp. had $3,000 of Current E&P and no Accumulated E&P for prior years.

Applying section 316 to Example 16.2:

$3,000 of the distribution is out of Current E&P and is a dividend. The results to A are the same as in Example 16.1.

Example 16.3. A owns all 100 shares of X Corp. A's basis in the X Corp. stock is $4,000. During 2014, X Corp. distributes $10,000 to A. For 2014, X Corp. had $3,000 of Current E&P and Accumulated E&P for prior years of *negative* $20,000.

Applying section 316 to Example 16.3:

$3,000 of the distribution is out of Current E&P and is a dividend. The results to A are the same as in Example 16.1. The fact that X Corp. has an overall deficit in E&P of $17,000 since its formation (Current E&P of $3,000 less Accumulated E&P

of negative $20,000) has no effect. A distribution is a dividend if it is out of *either* pool of E&P, and thus a distribution out of Current E&P is a dividend regardless of a deficit in Accumulated E&P. This is known as the nimble dividend rule.

B. Determining E&P

The purpose of E&P is to measure a corporation's capacity to make distributions out of corporate profits as opposed to capital invested by the shareholders. Thus, E&P aims to reflect a corporation's economic profits, and consequently differs from taxable income, which is influenced by other policies.

E&P is determined by starting with a corporation's taxable income for a particular year and then making certain adjustments generally aimed at moving taxable income closer to economic income. While the Code and Regulations do not comprehensively define E&P, they do provide for some of these adjustments, while others are provided under common law.

Adjustments to Taxable Income in Determining E&P:

- Add back certain items that are excluded from taxable income but represent an accession to corporate wealth.[31] Examples include tax-exempt interest[32] and life insurance proceeds.[33] Realized yet unrecognized gains on the disposition of property are not added back.[34]

- Add back certain items that are deductible in determining taxable income but do not represent actual expenditures for the particular taxable year. Examples include the dividends-received deduction[35] and deductions for net operating loss and capital loss carryovers.[36]

- Subtract certain items that are nondeductible in determining taxable income yet represent actual expenditures for the particular taxable year. Examples include federal income taxes, expenses disallowed under section 265,[37] losses disallowed under section 267,[38] net operating losses,[39] and capital losses in excess of capital gains.[40]

- Make certain timing adjustments. These include using the alternative depreciation system instead of ACRS,[41] amortizing the section 179 deduction over five years,[42] generally not using the installment method for

---

[31] Treas. Reg. § 1.312-6(b).

[32] *See* I.R.C. § 103.

[33] *See* I.R.C. § 101.

[34] I.R.C. § 312(f)(1).

[35] *See* I.R.C. § 243.

[36] *See* I.R.C. § 172, 1212(a).

[37] These are expenses related to tax-exempt income.

[38] These are losses on sales of property between related persons.

[39] *See* I.R.C. § 172.

[40] *See* I.R.C. § 1222(10).

[41] I.R.C. § 312(k)(3)(A).

[42] I.R.C. § 312(k)(3)(B).

reporting gains on installment sales,[43] and using FIFO instead of LIFO for inventory income.[44]

Example 16.4. X Corp. is a cash method, calendar year taxpayer. During 2014, X Corp. has the following items of economic income and expenses:

Item	Amount
Gross profits from sales	$475,000
Salaries paid to employees	$300,000
Tax-exempt interest received	$90,000
Dividends received on publicly-traded stock	$40,000
Long-term capital gain	$100,000
Long-term capital loss	$110,000
Estimated federal income taxes paid	$20,000
Depreciation on equipment using ACRS	$50,000

(depreciation would have been $25,000 under the alternative depreciation system (ADS)).

Determining E&P in Example 16.4:

Taxable Income Determination —

Gross Income

Gross profits from sales	$475,000
Dividends received on publicly traded stock	40,000
Long-term capital gain	100,000
Total	615,000

Deductions

Salaries paid to employees	300,000	
Dividends received deduction	28,000	(70% of dividend)
Long-term capital loss	100,000	(to extent of capital gains)
Depreciation	50,000	
Total	478,000	

Taxable Income   137,000

E&P Determination —

Taxable Income	$137,000
Add tax-exempt interest	90,000
Add dividends-received deduction	28,000

---

[43] I.R.C. § 312(n)(5).

[44] I.R.C. § 312(n)(4).

Subtract excess capital loss	(10,000)
Subtract federal income taxes	(20,000)
Make timing adjustment to depreciation (add difference between ACRS and ADS)	25,000
E&P	250,000

C.　Allocating E&P to Distributions

In determining whether there is enough E&P for a distribution to be a dividend, the regulations provide that Current E&P is considered first.[45] To the extent that distributions during a taxable year exceed Current E&P, Accumulated E&P is considered.[46]

Where the total amount of distributions made during a taxable year is greater than the total amount of E&P, it is necessary to allocate E&P to the distributions. The regulations provide for different methods for allocating Current E&P and Accumulated E&P.

1.　Allocating Current E&P

Current E&P is allocated to a particular distribution according to the following method:[47]

$$\text{amount of Current E\&P allocated to distribution} =$$
$$\text{amount of distribution} \times \frac{\text{total Current E\&P}}{\text{total distributions during the year}}$$

2.　Allocating Accumulated E&P

A distribution is out of Accumulated E&P to the extent of the amount of Accumulated E&P that is available on the date of the distribution.[48] As discussed below, a distribution reduces the amount of Accumulated E&P that is available for subsequent distributions. Thus, the effect is that Accumulated E&P is allocated to distributions chronologically.

Where Current E&P is negative, the current year's deficit in E&P will reduce the amount of Accumulated E&P that is available on the date of a distribution.[49] The Regulations provide that where the actual amount of the current deficit to the date of distribution cannot be shown, the current deficit will be prorated throughout the year.[50] Accordingly, if a distribution is made at a time that is one-third into the year,

---

[45] Treas. Reg. § 1.316-2(a).

[46] *Id.*

[47] Treas. Reg. § 1.316-2(b).

[48] *Id.*

[49] *See* Treas. Reg. § 1.316-2(b); Rev. Rul. 74-164. 1974-1 C.B. 74.

[50] Treas. Reg. § 1.316-2(b); *see* Rev. Rul. 74-164, 1974-1 C.B. 74. (prorating the current deficit without mentioning whether or not the actual deficit to the date of distribution could be shown).

one-third of the current deficit will be deemed to have occurred at the time of the distribution for purposes of determining available Accumulated E&P on the date of the distribution (assuming that the actual deficit to date cannot be shown).

D. Examples

The following examples illustrate the E&P allocation rules, along with the complete results under section 301(c).

> *Example 16.5.* As of January 1, 2014, A owns all 100 shares of X Corp. A's basis in the X Corp. stock is $4,000. On May 1, 2014, X Corp. distributes $10,000 to A. On July 1, 2014, A sells all 100 shares of X Corp. stock to B. B's basis in the X Corp. stock is $12,000. On September 1, 2014, X Corp. distributes $20,000 to B. For 2014, X Corp. has $15,000 of Current E&P and no Accumulated E&P for prior years.

Determining the tax consequences to A and B in Example 16.5:

A's Consequences —

The amount of Current E&P allocated to A's 5/1/14 distribution of $10,000 is equal to:

$$\text{amount of distribution (\$10,000)} \times \frac{\text{total Current E\&P (\$15,000)}}{\text{total distributions during the year (\$30,000)}}$$

This equals $5,000. Because there is no Accumulated E&P, $5,000 of A's $10,000 distribution is a dividend. The complete treatment of A's distribution under section 301(c) is as follows:

- The portion of distribution that is a dividend is included in gross income — $5,000

- The portion that is not a dividend ($5,000) reduces the shareholder's basis in the stock — from $4,000 to $0.

- The excess of portion that is not a dividend ($5,000) over the shareholder's basis in stock ($4,000) is considered gain from the sale of stock — $1,000 gain.

B's Consequences —

The amount of Current E&P allocated to B's 9/1/14 distribution of $20,000 is equal to:

$$\text{amount of distribution (\$20,000)} \times \frac{\text{total Current E\&P (\$15,000)}}{\text{total distributions during the year (\$30,000)}}$$

This equals $10,000. Because there is no Accumulated E&P, $10,000 of B's $20,000 distribution is a dividend. The complete treatment of B's distribution under section 301(c) is as follows:

- The portion of the distribution that is a dividend is included in gross income — $10,000

- The portion that is not a dividend ($10,000) reduces the shareholder's basis in stock — from $12,000 to $2,000.

- The excess of portion that is not a dividend ($10,000) over the shareholder's basis in the stock ($12,000) is considered gain from sale of stock – $0 gain.

Example 16.6. As of January 1, 2014, A owns all 100 shares of X Corp. A's basis in the X Corp. stock is $4,000. On July 1, 2014, A sells all 100 shares of X Corp. stock to B. B's basis in the X Corp. stock is $12,000. On May 1, 2014, X Corp. distributes $10,000 to A. On September 1, 2014, X Corp. distributes $20,000 to B. For 2014, X Corp. has $15,000 of Current E&P and $10,000 of Accumulated E&P for prior years.

Determining the tax consequences to A and B in Example 16.6:

A's Consequences —

As in example 16.5, the amount of Current E&P allocated to A's 5/1/14 distribution of $10,000 is equal to $5,000. In addition, with $10,000 of Accumulated E&P available on 5/1/14, $5,000 of Accumulated E&P is allocated to A's distribution. Consequently, A's entire $10,000 distribution is a dividend, and A has no other consequences under section 301(c).

B's Consequences —

As in Example 16.5, the amount of Current E&P allocated to B's 9/1/14 distribution of $20,000 is equal to $10,000. After allocating $5,000 of Accumulated E&P to A's 5/1/14 distribution, there is $5,000 of Accumulated E&P available for B's 9/1/14 distribution — $10,000 of Accumulated E&P at the start of the year less the $5,000 allocated to A's distribution. The $5,000 of available Accumulated E&P is allocated to B's distribution. Consequently, $15,000 of B's $20,000 distribution is a dividend. The complete treatment of B's distribution under section 301(c) is as follows:

- The portion of the distribution that is a dividend is included in gross income — $15,000

- The portion that is not a dividend ($5,000) reduces the shareholder's basis in the stock — from $12,000 to $7,000.

- The excess of portion that is not a dividend ($5,000) over the shareholder's basis in the stock ($12,000) is considered gain from the sale of the stock — $0 gain.

Example 16.7. As of January 1, 2014, A owns all 100 shares of X Corp. A's basis in the X Corp. stock is $4,000. On July 1, 2014, A sells all 100 shares of X Corp. stock to B. B's basis in the X Corp. stock is $12,000. On May 1, 2014, X Corp. distributes $10,000 to A. On September 1, 2014, X Corp. distributes $20,000 to B. For 2014, X Corp. has *negative* $15,000 of Current E&P and $30,000 of Accumulated E&P for prior years.

Determining the tax consequences to A and B in Example 16.7:

A's Consequences —

With negative Current E&P, there is only Accumulated E&P to allocate to the distributions. Assuming that the actual deficit in Current E&P to the date of distributions cannot be shown, the current deficit will be prorated throughout the year. Since A's 5/1/14 distribution occurs at a time that is one third into the year, one third of the current deficit of $15,000, or $5,000, will be deemed to have occurred at the time of the distribution. Consequently, the Accumulated E&P available on the date of A's distribution is $25,000 — $30,000 of Accumulated E&P at the start of the year less the $5,000 of prorated current deficit. $10,000 of the available Accumulated E&P is allocated to A's $10,000 distribution. Thus, A's entire $10,000 distribution is a dividend, and A has no other consequences under section 301(c).

B's Consequences —

After allocating $10,000 of Accumulated E&P to A's 5/1/14 distribution, there is $15,000 of Accumulated E&P available following A's distribution — $25,000 of Accumulated E&P available on 5/1/14 less the $10,000 allocated to A's distribution. Between 5/1/14 and 9/1/14, the date of B's distribution, another one third of the current deficit, or $5,000, will be deemed to have occurred. Consequently, the Accumulated E&P available on the date of B's distribution is $10,000 — $15,000 of Accumulated E&P following A's 5/1/14 distribution less the $5,000 of prorated current deficit. The $10,000 of available Accumulated E&P is allocated to B's $20,000 distribution. Consequently, $10,000 of B's $20,000 distribution is a dividend. The complete treatment of B's distribution under section 301(c) is as follows:

- The portion of distribution that is a dividend is included in gross income — $10,000.

- The portion that is not a dividend ($10,000) reduces the shareholder's basis in the stock — from $12,000 to $2,000.

- The excess of portion that is not a dividend ($10,000) over the shareholder's basis in the stock ($12,000) is considered gain from the sale of the stock — $0 gain.

E.   Reduction of E&P Due to Distributions

Accumulated E&P is generally reduced by the amount of a distribution. However, the reduction or charge to Accumulated E&P cannot exceed the amount of Accumulated E&P prior to the E&P charge.[51] Consequently, a deficit in Accumulated E&P cannot be created or increased as a result of a distribution, but E&P can be negative as a result of operations. The rules generally result in an E&P charge that is equal to the amount of dividend received by the shareholder.

Subject to the limit referred to above, there are specific E&P charging rules for different types of distributions.

- On a distribution of cash, Accumulated E&P is reduced by the amount of cash distributed.[52]

---

[51] I.R.C. § 312(a).

[52] I.R.C. § 312(a)(1).

- On a distribution of property other than cash (and other than a corporation's own obligations):

  ○ If the property is appreciated, i.e., its fair market value exceeds its adjusted basis in the hands of the corporation, Accumulated E&P is reduced by the fair market value of the property.[53]

  ○ If the property is depreciated, i.e., its fair market value is less than the corporation's adjusted basis, the charge to Accumulated E&P is the corporation's adjusted basis in the property.[54]

- On a distribution of a corporation's own obligations, Accumulated E&P is generally reduced by the principal amount of the obligation. An exception applies if the obligation has original issue discount, in which case the charge to the Accumulated E&P is the issue price of the obligation.[55]

Where a shareholder assumes a liability of the corporation in connection with a distribution or takes property subject to a corporate liability, the charge to Accumulated E&P is reduced by the amount of the liability.[56] This is consistent with a reduction in the amount of the distribution due to the corporate liability assumed or taken subject to.

§ 16.03   CORPORATE CONSEQUENCES ON DISTRIBUTIONS OF PROPERTY

A.   Taxable Income Consequences

1.   Distributions of Appreciated Property

When a corporation distributes appreciated property to its shareholder, i.e., property with a fair market value in excess of the corporation's adjusted basis in the property, pursuant to section 311(b)(1), the corporation recognizes gain as if it had sold the property to the shareholder for its fair market value.[57] At one time under the so-called *General Utilities*[58] doctrine, distributions of property, whether in the nonliquidating or liquidating context, did not give rise to corporate-level gain or loss. The current rule represents a repeal of the *General Utilities* doctrine for nonliqudating distributions of appreciated property. The gain recognition rule does not apply to a distribution of a corporation's own obligations.[59]

> *Example 16.8.* A owns all 100 shares of X Corp. During 2014, X Corp. distributes to A real estate with a fair market value of $100,000 and an adjusted basis in X Corp.'s hands of $60,000.

---

[53] I.R.C. § 312(a)(3), (b)(2).

[54] I.R.C. § 312(a)(3).

[55] I.R.C. § 312(a)(2).

[56] I.R.C. § 312(c); Treas. Reg. § 1.312-3.

[57] I.R.C. § 311(b)(1).

[58] The doctrine is based on General Utilities & Operating Co. v. Helvering, 296 U.S. 200 (1935).

[59] I.R.C. § 311(b)(1).

Applying section 311(b)(1) to X Corp. in Example 16.8:

Because the real estate is appreciated property, on the distribution X Corp. recognizes gain as if it had sold the real estate to A for its fair market value of $100,000. Thus, X Corp. recognizes gain of $40,000 — the difference between the deemed amount realized of $100,000 and X Corp.'s adjusted basis in the real estate of $60,000.

2. Distributions of Depreciated Property

When a corporation distributes depreciated property to its shareholder, i.e., property with a fair market value that is less than the corporation's adjusted basis in the property, pursuant to section 311(a)(1), the corporation recognizes no loss. Thus, Congress retained the *General Utilities* doctrine for nonliquidating distributions of depreciated property, presumably because of a concern that corporations could abuse loss recognition with regard to the timing or the bona fide nature of such transactions.[60]

> *Example 16.9.* A owns all 100 shares of X Corp. During 2014, X Corp. distributes to A real estate with a fair market value of $50,000 and an adjusted basis in X Corp.'s hands of $60,000.

Applying section 311(a)(1) to X Corp. in Example 16.9:

Because the real estate is depreciated property, X Corp. recognizes no loss on the distribution. Note that pursuant to section 301(d), A's basis in the real estate is the property's fair market value at the time of the distribution, or $50,000. Consequently, the real estate's inherent loss of $10,000, which is not recognized by X Corp., is also *not* preserved in the hands of the shareholder.

B. E&P Consequences

Current E&P is increased by the amount of gain recognized on a distribution of appreciated property.[61] The increase in Current E&P on the distribution of appreciated property can in turn cause some or all of the distribution to be a dividend. Because E&P tracks taxable income with respect to recognized gains and losses,[62] the nonrecognition of loss on the distribution of depreciated property has no effect on Current E&P.

---

[60] *See* Bittker & Eustice, *supra* note 14 at 8-77.

[61] I.R.C. § 312(b)(1). The property's adjusted basis for E&P purposes is used to determine the amount of gain that is added to Current E&P. I.R.C. § 312(b).

[62] I.R.C. § 312(f)(1).

§ 16.04   EXAMPLES DEMONSTRATING CORPORATE AND SHAREHOLDER CONSEQUENCES ON DISTRIBUTIONS OF PROPERTY

A.   Distribution of Appreciated Property

Example 16.10. A owns all 100 shares of X Corp. A's basis in the X Corp. stock is $40,000. During 2014, X Corp. distributes to A real estate with a fair market value of $100,000 and an adjusted basis in X Corp.'s hands of $60,000. Aside from any consequences on the distribution, X Corp. had no Current E&P for 2014 and no Accumulated E&P for prior years.

Determining the taxable income and E&P consequences to X Corp. and the distribution consequences to A in Example 16.10:

As in Example 16.8, on the distribution of the real estate, X Corp. recognizes gain of $40,000 for taxable income purposes. Current E&P is increased by the $40,000 of gain to a total of $40,000 (this ignores any reduction in E&P due to any increase in federal and state taxes as a result of the gain). The amount of A's distribution is $100,000 (the fair market value of the real estate). $40,000 of the distribution is out of Current E&P and is a dividend. The complete treatment of A's distribution under section 301(c) is as follows:

- The portion of the distribution that is a dividend is included in gross income — $40,000

- The portion that is not a dividend ($60,000) reduces the shareholder's basis in the stock — from $40,000 to $0.

- The excess of portion that is not a dividend ($60,000) over the shareholder's basis in the stock ($40,000) is considered gain from the sale of the stock — $20,000 gain.

Per 301(d), A's basis in the real estate is the property's fair market value, or $100,000.

X Corp.'s Accumulated E&P at the start of 2015 is equal to Accumulated E&P at the start of 2014 ($0), plus Current E&P for 2014 ($40,000), minus the E&P charge for the 2014 distribution. Because the distribution consisted of appreciated property, per section 312(b)(2) the E&P charge is the fair market value of the property, or $100,000, but not greater than the pre-charge amount of Accumulated E&P, which is $40,000. Therefore, the E&P charge is $40,000, and X Corp. has $0 Accumulated E&P at the start of 2015.

B.   Distribution of Depreciated Property

Example 16.11. A owns all 100 shares of X Corp. A's basis in the X Corp. stock is $40,000. During 2014, X Corp. distributes to A real estate with a fair market value of $50,000 and an adjusted basis in X Corp.'s hands of $60,000. Aside from any consequences on the distribution, X Corp. has $20,000 of Current E&P for 2014 and no Accumulated E&P for prior years.

Determining the taxable income and E&P consequences to X Corp. and the distribution consequences to A in Example 16.11:

As in Example 16.9, on the distribution of the real estate, X Corp. recognizes no loss for taxable income purposes. Current E&P is not affected by the distribution and thus remains at $20,000. The amount of A's distribution is $50,000 (the fair market value of the real estate). $20,000 of the distribution is out of Current E&P and is a dividend. The complete treatment of A's distribution under section 301(c) is as follows:

- The portion of the distribution that is a dividend is included in gross income — $20,000

- The portion that is not a dividend ($30,000) reduces the shareholder's basis in the stock — from $40,000 to $10,000.

- The excess of the portion that is not a dividend ($30,000) over the shareholder's basis in the stock ($40,000) is considered gain from the sale of the stock — $0 gain.

Per 301(d), A's basis in the real estate is the property's fair market value, or $50,000.

X Corp.'s Accumulated E&P at the start of 2015 is equal to Accumulated E&P at the start of 2014 ($0), plus Current E&P for 2014 ($20,000), minus the E&P charge for the 2014 distribution. Because the distribution consisted of depreciated property, per section 312(a)(3) the E&P charge is the adjusted basis of the property, or $60,000, but not greater than the pre-charge amount of Accumulated E&P, which is $20,000. Therefore, the E&P charge is $20,000, and X Corp. has $0 Accumulated E&P at the start of 2015.

C. Distribution of Property Subject to a Liability

Example 16.12. A owns all 100 shares of X Corp. A's basis in the X Corp. stock is $40,000. During 2014, X Corp. distributes to A real estate with a fair market value of $100,000, an adjusted basis in X Corp.'s hands of $60,000, and subject to a liability of $70,000. The real estate remains subject to the $70,000 liability following the distribution to A. Aside from any consequences on the distribution, X Corp. has no Current E&P for 2014 and no Accumulated E&P for prior years.

Determining the taxable income and E&P consequences to X Corp. and the distribution consequences to A in Example 16.12:

Per section 311(b)(1), X Corp. recognizes gain of $40,000 for taxable income purposes — the difference between the property's fair market value of $100,000 and its adjusted basis of $60,000. The fact that the real estate is subject to a liability of $70,000 has no effect on the amount of gain recognized by X Corp. Current E&P is increased by the $40,000 of gain to a total of $40,000 (this ignores any reduction in E&P due to any increase in federal and state taxes as a result of the gain). The amount of A's distribution is $100,000 (the fair market value of the real estate), reduced, per section 301(b)(2), by the $70,000 liability, resulting in a distribution of $30,000. The entire $30,000 distribution is out of Current E&P and is a dividend, and A has no other consequences under section 301(c). Per section 301(d), A's basis in the real estate is the property's fair market value, or $100,000.

X Corp.'s Accumulated E&P at the start of 2015 is equal to Accumulated E&P at the start of 2014 ($0), plus Current E&P for 2014 ($40,000), minus the E&P charge for the 2014 distribution. The E&P charge is the fair market value of the appreciated property, $100,000, reduced, per Treas. Reg. § 1.312-3, by the $70,000 liability to which the property is subject. Therefore, the E&P charge is $30,000, and X Corp. has $10,000 of Accumulated E&P at the start of 2015.

D. Distribution of Corporation's Own Obligation

Example 16.13. A owns all 100 shares of X Corp. A's basis in the X Corp. stock is $40,000. During 2014, X Corp. distributes to A an X Corp. obligation to pay a principal amount of $50,000 in five years, with annual payments of interest that qualify as adequate stated interest under section 1274 (and thus no original issue discount). The X Corp. obligation has a fair market value of $50,000. Aside from any consequences on the distribution, X Corp. has $20,000 of Current E&P for 2014 and no Accumulated E&P for prior years.

Determining the taxable income and E&P consequences to X Corp. and the distribution consequences to A in Example 16.13:

On the distribution of its own obligation, X Corp. recognizes no gain or loss for taxable income purposes.[63] Current E&P is not affected by the distribution and thus remains at $20,000. The amount of A's distribution is $50,000 (the fair market value of the obligation). $20,000 of the distribution is out of Current E&P and is a dividend. The complete treatment of A's distribution under section 301(c) is as follows:

- The portion of the distribution that is a dividend is included in gross income — $20,000

- The portion that is not a dividend ($30,000) reduces the shareholder's basis in the stock — from $40,000 to $10,000.

- The excess of portion that is not a dividend ($30,000) over the shareholder's basis in the stock ($40,000) is considered gain from the sale of the stock — $0 gain.

Per section 301(d), A's basis in the X Corp. obligation is its fair market value, or $50,000.

X Corp.'s Accumulated E&P at the start of 2015 is equal to Accumulated E&P at the start of 2014 ($0), plus Current E&P for 2014 ($20,000), minus the E&P charge for the 2014 distribution. Because the distribution consisted of X Corp.'s own obligation, per section 312(a)(2), the E&P charge is the principal amount of the obligation,[64] or $50,000, but not greater than the pre-charge amount of Accumulated

---

[63] I.R.C. § 311(a)(2), (b)(1).

[64] The exception for obligations with original issue discount does not apply here. Under this exception, the charge to E&P would be the obligation's issue price. I.R.C. § 312(a)(2).

E&P, which is $20,000. Therefore, the E&P charge is $20,000, and X Corp. has $0 Accumulated E&P at the start of 2015.

§ 16.05   CONSTRUCTIVE DISTRIBUTIONS

Traditionally, C corporations and their shareholders have sought to reduce the double taxation of distributed corporate earnings by employing certain techniques. Most of the techniques aim to pay corporate earnings to shareholders in a manner that, unlike a dividend, is deductible to the corporation.[65] Other maneuvers try to avoid an inclusion in gross income at either the shareholder or corporate level.

To combat these attempts at reducing the sting of the double tax, the courts, Service, Treasury, and occasionally Congress have developed certain responses. Prominent among them are rules that can recharacterize payments as constructive distributions in order to reflect the substance of the transaction.[66]

A.   Excessive Compensation Paid to Shareholder-Employees

A common way of paying out corporate earnings in a manner that can be deductible to the corporation is to pay compensation to shareholders who are also employees of the corporation. If the courts or Service find the compensation to be unreasonable, the amounts are treated as a constructive distribution and a corporate deduction is denied.[67] In this regard, the authorities have used different tests in determining whether compensation is unreasonable, including looking at the compensation levels of comparable employees in comparable companies,[68] and calculating whether the net investment return of the corporation after taking into account the purported compensation is comparable to that received by independent investors in comparable companies.[69]

B.   Interest Paid on Shareholder-held Corporate Debt

Another common technique is to have shareholders double as lenders to the corporation, with the goal of paying out corporate earnings to the shareholder-lenders as interest that is deductible to the corporation. As discussed in Chapter 15, the courts and the Service will sometimes recharacterize purported shareholder loans as stock and thus treat the interest on such loans as nondeductible constructive distributions.

---

[65] With preferential capital gains rates applying to most dividends received by individuals, there may be situations where the payment of a nondeductible dividend would result in lower combined corporate and shareholder taxes as compared to paying earnings in a deductible form such as compensation or interest. For example, earnings paid out as dividends would be subject to a full corporate tax and a preferential dividend tax, whereas earnings paid out as compensation would be subject to a full individual tax along with employment taxes.

[66] While the recharacterized payments are often termed constructive dividends, they are actually constructive section 301 distributions, which would be treated as dividends to the extent of a corporation's E&P.

[67] I.R.C. § 162(a)(1).

[68] Charles McCandless Tile Service v. United States, 422 F.2d 1336 (Ct. Cl. 1970).

[69] Exacto Spring Corp. v. Commissioner, 196 F.3d 833 (7th Cir. 1999).

C.   Excessive Rent Paid to Shareholder-Lessors

Similar to compensation paid to shareholder-employees, corporations may attempt to provide shareholders with corporate earnings in a deductible fashion by paying rent to shareholders who lease property to the corporation. As with compensation, if the rent is found to be excessive when compared to market rents,[70] it is treated as a nondeductible constructive distribution.

D.   Bargain Sales of Property to Shareholders

Another way in which corporations and shareholders attempt to reduce the double tax is for the corporation to sell property to a shareholder at a price below the property's fair market value. The aim is to provide the shareholder with value attributable to the property's fair market value over the amount paid without the imposition of a dividend tax. The Regulations prevent this tactic by generally treating the difference between the property's fair market value and the amount paid for the property as a distribution subject to section 301.[71]

E.   Interest-free Loans to Shareholders

Interest-free loans by corporations to shareholders have also been used to reduce the double tax. The goal with this device is to avoid a corporate-level tax on the income earned on the loaned amounts. Section § 7872 combats this technique by generally imputing interest payments from the shareholder-borrower to the corporation-lender, along with section 301 distributions from the corporation to the shareholder in the same amounts as the imputed interest.[72] While the shareholder-borrower may be entitled to a deduction on the imputed interest payment that could offset any dividend income, the corporation-lender will be taxed on the imputed interest income, thereby ensuring a corporate-level tax on an investment return on the loaned amounts.

§ 16.06   TAXATION OF DIVIDENDS RECEIVED BY NON-CORPORATE SHAREHOLDERS

Dividends received by individuals and other non-corporate taxpayers are generally subject to the preferential tax rates that apply to long-term capital gains. More specifically, qualified dividend income received by non-corporate taxpayers is treated as adjusted net capital gain for purposes of the preferential rates provided in section 1(h).[73] Adjusted net capital gain is generally taxed at a maximum rate of 15 percent, with maximum rates of 0 percent for lower income taxpayers[74] and 20

---

[70]   I.R.C. § 162(a)(3).

[71]   Treas. Reg. § 1.301-1(j).

[72]   *See* I.R.C. § 7872(a), (b), (c)(1)(C), (e).

[73]   I.R.C. § 1(h)(11), (4), (5), (6), (7). It should be noted that qualified dividend income is not otherwise treated as capital gain, and thus cannot be used to increase the limit on deducting capital losses under section 1211(b).

[74]   These are taxpayers in the 10 or 15 percent tax brackets.

percent for higher income taxpayers.[75] Accordingly, a non-corporate taxpayer's qualified dividend income is generally taxed at 15 percent.

Qualified dividend income generally includes dividends paid by taxable domestic (U.S.) corporations,[76] as well as dividends paid by qualified foreign corporations.[77] Excluded from qualified dividend income is a dividend on stock that the shareholder has not held for at least 61 days during the 121-day period that begins 60 days before the "ex-dividend date" for the dividend (the earliest date on which a buyer of stock does not acquire the right to the dividend).[78] Absent this exclusion from qualified dividend income, a taxpayer could effectively convert a short-term capital gain taxable at non-preferential rates into a dividend taxable at preferential rates by doing the following: purchase stock just before the ex-dividend date, collect the dividend and then soon thereafter sell the stock at a loss that would reflect the difference in the price of the stock before the imminent dividend and the stock's value after the dividend is paid.

§ 16.07 DIVIDENDS-RECEIVED DEDUCTION FOR CORPORATION SHAREHOLDERS

A. Dividends-Received Deduction: General Rules

Corporations are generally entitled to a deduction equal to a certain percentage of a dividend received from another corporation. More specifically, the dividends-received deduction percentages are as follows:

- 70% of the amount of the dividend in general.[79]

- 80% of the amount of the dividend if the corporation receiving the dividend owns at least 20% of the stock (by vote and value) of the corporation paying the dividend.[80]

- 100% of the amount of "qualifying dividends," which are generally dividends (i) from a corporation that is a member of the receiving corporation's affiliated group and (ii) which were distributed out of the E&P of a year in which the distributing and receiving corporations were members of the same affiliated group;[81] generally, two corporations are

---

[75] These are taxpayers in the 39.6 percent tax bracket.

[76] I.R.C. § 1(h)(11)(B)(i)(I).

[77] I.R.C. § 1(h)(11)(B)(i)(II). A qualified foreign corporation is generally a foreign corporation (i) that is incorporated in a U.S. possession, (ii) that is eligible for benefits under an income tax treaty with the United States which includes an exchange of information provision and is deemed satisfactory by Treasury, or (iii) whose stock is readily tradable on an established securities market in the United States.

[78] Also excluded are dividends to the extent that a taxpayer is under an obligation to make related payments with respect to substantially similar or related property, as well as dividends that a taxpayer elects to treat as investment income under section 163(d)'s investment interest limitation. I.R.C. § 1(h)(11)(B)(iii)(II), (D)(i).

[79] I.R.C. § 243(a)(1).

[80] I.R.C. § 243(c).

[81] I.R.C. § 243(a)(3), (b)(1).

members of an affiliated group where one corporation owns at least 80% of the stock (by vote and value) of the other corporation.[82]

The purpose of the dividends-received deduction is to prevent three or more full levels of taxation as dividends wend their way through multiple corporations. If not for the dividends-received deduction, the earnings of a first-tier subsidiary corporation that are ultimately distributed to the individual shareholders of its parent corporation would be subject to three full levels of tax: once when earned by the subsidiary corporation, a second time when received by the parent corporation, and a third time when received by the parent corporation's shareholders. For a second-tier subsidiary, there would be four full levels of taxation on earnings that are ultimately distributed to the parent's individual shareholders; for a third-tier subsidiary, there would be five levels of tax, and so on. While the dividends-received deduction does not (except for qualifying dividends) completely remove inter-company dividends from the receiving corporation's taxable income, the deduction substantially prevents more than two levels of taxation of corporate earnings.

> *Example 16.14.* For all of 2014, Y Corp. owns 10 percent of the common stock (the only stock outstanding) of X Corp. On July 1, 2014, X Corp. pays a $1,000 dividend to Y Corp.

Determining Y Corp.'s dividend-sreceived deduction in Example 16.14:

Under the general rule, Y Corp. is entitled to a dividends-received deduction equal to 70 percent of the amount of the dividend, or $700. Consequently, Y Corp. has $300 of taxable income in connection with the dividend ($1,000 of gross income less the dividends-received deduction of $700).

> *Example 16.15.* For all of 2014, Y Corp. owns 30 percent of the common stock (the only stock outstanding) of X Corp. On July 1, 2014, X Corp. pays a $1,000 dividend to Y Corp.

Determining Y Corp.'s dividends-received deduction in Example 16.15:

Because Y Corp. owns at least 20 percent of the stock (by vote and value) of X Corp., Y Corp. is entitled to a dividends-received deduction equal to 80 percent of the amount of the dividend, or $800. Consequently, Y Corp. has $200 of taxable income in connection with the dividend ($1,000 of gross income less the dividends-received deduction of $800).

B. Dividends-Received Deduction: Limitations and Special Rules

The ability of a corporate shareholder to deduct at least 70 percent of the amount of a dividend opens the door to certain abuses, discussed below. The Code contains three provisions to combat these abuses: holding period requirements, a rule that reduces stock basis in connection with extraordinary dividends, and a rule that reduces the dividends-received deduction in connection with certain debt-financed stock.

---

[82] I.R.C. § 1504(a).

1. Holding Period Requirements

In general, the dividends-received deduction is denied if the stock on which the dividend is paid is held for 45 days or less during 91-day period that begins 45 days before the "ex-dividend date" for the dividend (the earliest date on which a buyer of stock does not acquire the right to the dividend).[83] For certain preferred stock, the dividends-received deduction is denied if the stock on which the dividend is paid is held for 90 days or less during 181-day period surrounding the ex-dividend date.[84] The shareholder's holding period with respect to the stock is reduced for periods when the shareholder enters into certain transactions that diminish the shareholder's risk of loss with respect to the stock.[85]

Without this limitation on the dividends-received deduction, a corporation could effectively convert a capital gain (for which a corporation receives no rate preference) into income that is at least 70 percent sheltered by the dividends-received deduction, as demonstrated by the following example.

> *Example 16.16.* On June 24, 2014, X Corp., a publicly traded corporation (with 1,000,000 shares of common stock outstanding), declares a dividend of $1 per share on its common stock (with an ex-dividend date of July 3, 2014). On July 1, 2014, Y Corp. purchases 10,000 shares of the common stock of X Corp. for $21 per share or a total cost of $210,000. On July 10, 2014, Y Corp. collects a total dividend of $10,000 on its shares of X Corp stock. On July 11, 2014, Y Corp. sells the X Corp. shares for their current price of $20 per share or a total price of $200,000. For 2014, Y Corp. also has $10,000 of capital gain from a sale of investment property.

Determining Y Corp.'s consequences for 2014 *in the absence* of the holding period requirement for the dividends-received deduction:

Receipt of dividend	$10,000 gross income
Capital gain from investment property	$10,000 capital gain
Sale of X Corp. stock	($10,000) capital loss[86]
Dividend-received deduction	($7,000)[87]
Taxable Income	**$3,000**

Had Y Corp. not engaged in the transactions with respect to X Corp. stock, Y Corp. would have had taxable income of $10,000 due to the capital gain on the sale of the investment property. Consequently, the transactions with respect to X Corp. stock allowed Y Corp. to reduce its taxable income from $10,000 to $3,000.

---

[83] I.R.C. § 246(c)(1)(A). The dividends-received deduction is also denied to the extent that a taxpayer is under an obligation to make related payments with respect to substantially similar or related property. I.R.C. § 246(c)(1)(B).

[84] I.R.C. § 246(c)(2).

[85] I.R.C. § 246(c)(4).

[86] This is equal to the $200,000 amount realized on the sale minus $210,000 cost basis in the X Corp. stock.

[87] This is equal to 70 percent of the $10,000 dividend on the X Corp. stock.

Determining Y Corp.'s consequences for 2014 with the holding period requirement for the dividends-received deduction:

Because Y Corp. had held the X Corp. stock for only 10 days, the holding period requirement is not satisfied, and Y Corp. is denied the dividends-received deduction. Consequently, the transactions with respect to X Corp. stock do not reduce Y Corp.'s taxable income.

Receipt of dividend	$10,000 gross income
Capital gain from investment property	$10,000 capital gain
Sale of X Corp. stock	($10,000) capital loss
Dividends-received deduction	$0
Taxable Income	**$10,000**

If Y Corp. in Example 16.16 had held the X Corp. stock until August 16, 2014, then Y Corp. would have been entitled to the dividends-received deduction as it would have held the stock for more than 45 days in the 91-day period surrounding the ex-dividend date. Of course, Y Corp. may not be willing to incur a market risk with respect to the X Corp. stock for that length of time in order to receive the desired tax benefits.

2. Extraordinary Dividends

If in Example 16.16 the dividend paid by X Corp. were $4 per share or a total dividend of $40,000, then the allowance of the dividends-received deduction would permit Y Corp. to effectively convert $40,000 of capital gain into $12,000 of taxable income — i.e., shelter $28,000 income via the dividends-received deduction.[88] Now with the tax benefits being a larger percentage of Y Corp.'s investment in the X Corp. stock, Y Corp. may be willing to incur a market risk with respect to the stock for 46 days (or even 91 days if the stock were preferred stock), thus satisfying the holding period requirement.

To combat abuse where there are relatively large dividends, Congress enacted section 1059, which provides:

- If a corporate shareholder receives an "extraordinary dividend," and

- the shareholder did not hold the stock on which the dividend is paid for more than two years before the "dividend announcement date,"[89]

- then the shareholder's basis in the stock is reduced (but not below zero) by the amount of the dividends-received deduction; if the amount of the dividends-received deduction exceeds the shareholder's basis in the stock, the excess is treated as gain from the sale of the stock in the year in which the dividend is received.[90]

---

[88] With a $40,000 dividend, the dividends-received deduction would be $28,000 — 70 percent of the $40,000 dividend.

[89] The "dividend announcement date" is the earliest date on which the corporation declares, announces or agrees to the amount or payment of the dividend. I.R.C. § 1059(d)(5).

[90] I.R.C. § 1059(a).

An "extraordinary dividend" occurs when the amount of a dividend equals or exceeds a certain percentage of the adjusted basis of the stock on which the dividend is paid:

- for preferred stock, the dividend equals or exceeds 5% of the stock's adjusted basis

- for other stock, the dividend equals or exceeds 10% of stock's adjusted basis.[91]

Example 16.17. On June 24, 2014, X Corp., a publicly traded corporation (with 1,000,000 shares of common stock outstanding), declares a dividend of $4 per share on its common stock (with an ex-dividend date of July 3, 2014). On July 1, 2014, Y Corp. purchases 10,000 shares of the common stock of X Corp. for $24 per share or a total cost of $240,000. On July 10, 2014, Y Corp. collects a total dividend of $40,000 on its shares of X Corp stock. On August 16, 2014, Y Corp. sells the X Corp. shares for their current price of $20 per share or a total price of $200,000. For 2014, Y Corp. also has $40,000 of capital gain from a sale of investment property.

Determining Y Corp.'s consequences for 2014:

Y Corp. is entitled to the dividends-received deduction of $28,000[92] because it has held the stock for more than 45 days in the 91-day period surrounding the ex-dividend date. However, pursuant to section 1059, Y Corp.'s adjusted basis in its X Corp. stock would be reduced by the amount of the dividends-received deduction because:

- Y Corp. has received an extraordinary dividend — the $40,000 dividend on the X Corp. common stock equals or exceeds 10% of the stock's $240,000 adjusted basis, and

- Y Corp. had not held the X Corp. stock for more than two years before the June 24, 2014 declaration date for the dividend[93] — Y Corp. acquired the stock on July 1, 2014.

Therefore, Y Corp.'s adjusted basis in its X Corp. stock is reduced by the amount of the dividends-received deduction, or $28,000, from $240,000 to $212,000. The complete consequences for Y Corp. for 2014 are as follows:

Receipt of dividend $40,000 gross income

---

[91] I.R.C. § 1059(c)(1), (2). A taxpayer can elect to use the fair market value of the stock in lieu of the stock's adjusted basis in determining whether a dividend is an extraordinary dividend. I.R.C. § 1059(c)(4). There are also rules that aggregate dividends in certain circumstances for purposes of the extraordinary dividend determination; for example, all dividends that have ex-dividend dates within 85 days are treated as one dividend. I.R.C. § 1059(c)(3)(A). In addition, the provision contains special rules that automatically include or exclude dividends in certain circumstances as extraordinary dividends; for example, qualifying dividends entitled to the 100 percent dividends-received deduction are generally not extraordinary dividends. I.R.C. § 1059(d), (e).

[92] This is equal to 70 percent of the $40,000 dividend on the X Corp. stock.

[93] The latest dividend announcement date on these facts is June 24, 2014. The dividend announcement date would be earlier than June 24, 2014 if X Corp. had agreed to the payment of the dividend on a date prior to the date it formally declared the dividend.

Capital gain from investment property	$40,000 capital gain
Sale of X Corp. stock	($12,000) capital loss[94]
Dividends-received deduction	($28,000)
Taxable Income	**$40,000**

Consequently, the transactions with respect to X Corp. stock do not reduce Y Corp.'s taxable income.

3. Debt-Financed Portfolio Stock

Absent a special provision, a corporate taxpayer would be able to shelter income through a combination of a dividends-received deduction and interest deduction where it financed the purchase of stock by borrowing funds.

Example 16.18. On January 1, 2014, Y Corp. purchases 10,000 shares of the common stock of X Corp. for $200,000. X Corp. is a publicly traded corporation (with 1,000,000 shares of common stock outstanding). Y Corp. finances the purchase of X Corp. stock by borrowing $200,000. During 2014, Y Corp. pays $10,000 of interest on the loan to purchase the shares of X Corp. stock. During 2014, Y Corp. collects a total dividend of $10,000 on its shares of X Corp. stock. For 2014, Y Corp. also has $10,000 of ordinary income from business operations.

In the absence of a special provision, Y Corp.'s consequences for 2014 would be as follows:

Receipt of dividend	$10,000 gross income
Ordinary income from business operations	$10,000 gross income
Interest expense on loan	($10,000)[95]
Dividends-received deduction	($7,000)[96]
Taxable Income	**$3,000**

Had Y Corp. not engaged in the transactions with respect to X Corp. stock, Y Corp. would have had taxable income of $10,000 due to business operations. Consequently, the transactions with respect to X Corp. stock allowed Y Corp. to reduce its taxable income from $10,000 to $3,000.

To combat abuse where there are borrowings in connection with the purchase of stock, Congress enacted section 246A, which generally reduces the dividends-received deduction percentage with respect to dividends on "debt-financed portfolio stock."[97]

---

[94] This is equal to the $200,000 amount realized on the sale minus the $212,000 adjusted basis in the X Corp. stock.

[95] This is deductible under section 163(a).

[96] This is equal to 70 percent of the $10,000 dividend on the X Corp. stock.

[97] Section 246A does not apply to qualifying dividends entitled to the 100 percent dividends-received deduction under section 243(b). I.R.C. § 246A(b)(1).

"Debt-financed portfolio stock" is "portfolio stock" if there is "portfolio indebtedness" with respect to it during the "base period."[98] "Portfolio stock" is generally stock held in corporations in which the taxpayer owns less than 50 percent of the vote or value of the stock.[99] "Portfolio indebtedness" is indebtedness directly attributable to investment in portfolio stock.[100]

With respect to dividends on debt-financed portfolio stock, the dividends-received deduction percentage is equal to:

- Regular dividends-received deduction percentage, *multiplied by*
- 100% minus the "average indebtedness percentage."[101]

The "average indebtedness percentage" is equal to:

- The average amount of portfolio indebtedness during the base period, *divided by*
- The average amount of adjusted basis of the stock during the base period.

Applying section 246A to determine Y Corp.'s consequences in Example 16.18:

The X Corp. stock purchased by Y Corp. is debt-financed portfolio stock because (i) it is portfolio stock (Y Corp. owns less than 50 percent of X Corp.) and (ii) there is portfolio indebtedness with respect to the stock — the fact that Y Corp. incurred the indebtedness to acquire the stock should result in the indebtedness being considered as directly attributable to Y Corp.'s investment in the stock. Assuming that the amount of the indebtedness and Y Corp.'s basis in the X Corp. stock remain at $200,000 throughout the base period, the average indebtedness percentage is 100 percent ($200,000 divided by $200,000). As a result, the dividends-received deduction percentage is the regular dividends-received deduction of 70 percent multiplied by (100 percent minus 100 percent), which is 0. In short, because the acquisition of the stock is 100 percent debt financed, the dividends-received deduction is reduced to $0. The complete results for Y Corp. for 2014 are as follows:

Receipt of dividend	$10,000 gross income
Ordinary income from business operations	$10,000 gross income
Interest expense on loan	($10,000)
Dividend-received deduction	$0
Taxable Income	**$10,000**

Consequently, the debt-financed acquisition of the X Corp. stock does not reduce Y Corp.'s taxable income.

---

[98] I.R.C. § 246A(c)(1).

[99] I.R.C. § 246A(c)(2).

[100] I.R.C. § 246A(d)(3). The "base period" with respect to a dividend is the shorter of (i) the period between the most recent previous and current ex-dividend dates or (ii) the one year period before the current ex-dividend date. I.R.C. § 246A(d)(4).

[101] I.R.C. § 246A(a).

C. Use of Dividends in Bootstrap Acquisitions

Where a corporation sells stock in another corporation, a pre-sale dividend, if respected as such, can reduce the selling corporation's taxable income on the sale given the general availability of the dividends-received deduction.

> *Example 16.19.* As of January 1, 2014, Y Corp. owns all 100 shares of the stock of X Corp., which have a fair market value of $10,000,000. Y Corp.'s adjusted basis in the stock of X Corp. is $2,000,000. X Corp. has $1,000,000 of cash, which it uses for working capital, and $1,000,000 of E&P (all of which was accumulated while Y Corp. owned all 100 shares of X Corp.). On January 1, 2014, Y Corp. causes X Corp. to pay Y Corp. a dividend of $1,000,000. On January 2, 2014, Y Corp. sells all of its X Corp. stock to Z Corp. for $9,000,000 (the fair market value of the X Corp. stock following the payment of the $1,000,000 dividend). On January 5, 2014, Z Corp. contributes $1,000,000 of cash to X Corp., to be used for working capital.

If the form of the transactions is respected, Y Corp.'s consequences for 2014 would be as follows:

Receipt of dividend	$1,000,000 gross income
Dividends-received deduction	($1,000,000)[102]
Gain on sale of stock	$7,000,000 gain[103]
Taxable Income	**$7,000,000**

In connection with the dividend and sale, Y Corp. receives a total of $10,000,000 and disposes of stock with an adjusted basis of $2,000,000; yet, Y Corp. only has $7,000,000 of taxable income if the form is respected. Compare this to the situation where there is no pre-sale dividend and the X Corp. stock is sold for its pre-dividend value of $10,000,000, in which case Y Corp. would have had $8,000,000 of gain on the sale.[104] Consequently, unless the form of the transaction is disregarded, the pre-sale dividend allows Y Corp. to reduce its taxable income on the sale by $1,000,000.

In certain situations, courts have prevented the reduction of taxable income where dividends are paid in connection with stock sales. For example, in *Waterman Steamship Corp. v. Commissioner*,[105] a pre-sale distribution by the acquired corporation to the seller was treated as part of the sales proceeds where the distribution was a promissory note that was repaid with funds loaned to the

---

[102] Because Y Corp. and X Corp. are members of an affiliated group (connected by at least 80 percent ownership) and the dividend was paid out of E&P accumulated while Y Corp. and X Corp. are affiliated, the dividend is a qualifying dividend giving rise to a 100 percent dividends-received deduction. I.R.C. § 243(b)(1).

[103] This is equal to the amount realized of $9,000,000 on the sale less Y Corp.'s adjusted basis in the X Corp. stock of $2,000,000. Section 1059 will not result in a reduction in Y Corp.'s adjusted basis in the X Corp. stock because of the exception for qualifying dividends. I.R.C. § 1059(e)(2).

[104] This is equal to the amount realized of $10,000,000 on the sale less Y Corp.'s adjusted basis in the X Corp. stock of $2,000,000.

[105] 430 F.2d. 1185 (5th Cir. 1970).

acquired corporation by the buyer, and the pre-sale distribution and sale occurred almost simultaneously. The seller was required to include the amount of the pre-sale distribution in determining the gain on the sale.

On the other hand, in *TSN Liquidating Corp., Inc. v. United States*,[106] the court refused to treat a pre-sale distribution as part of the sales proceeds for the stock where the assets distributed to the seller were markedly different from the assets subsequently infused by the buyer. In *Litton Industries, Inc. v. Commissioner*,[107] the court also did not treat a pre-sale distribution as part of the sales proceeds where the distribution was several months prior to any negotiations with the buyer, although the seller had an intention to sell the corporation at the time of the distribution.

Based on the above case law, it appears that a pre-sale distribution will be treated as part of the seller's proceeds on the stock sale where (i) the distribution and sale are considered to be a part of the same transaction and (ii) taking into account subsequent events, the pre-sale distribution does *not result in real removal of assets* from the acquired corporation.

The application of this doctrine to Example 16.19 should result in the $1,000,000 pre-sale distribution being treated as part of Y Corp.'s amount realized on the sale of the X Corp. stock. This is because the distribution appears to be part of the stock sale given the timing of the distribution and sale, and taking into account the buyer's subsequent infusion of cash, no assets are actually removed from X Corp. Consequently, Y Corp. should be treated as having an amount realized of $10,000,000 on the sale of the X Corp. stock and thus $8,000,000 of gain on the sale.[108]

---

[106] 624 F.2d. 1328 (5th Cir. 1980).

[107] 89 T.C. 1086 (1987).

[108] This is equal to the amount realized of $10,000,000 on the sale less Y Corp.'s adjusted basis in the X Corp. stock of $2,000,000.

Chapter 17

STOCK REDEMPTIONS

BASIC OVERVIEW

This chapter addresses the tax consequences where a corporation distributes money or property to a shareholder in a redemption of stock, as well as situations involving purchases of stock by related corporations.

A. General Framework for Treating Redemptions as Either Exchanges or Section 301 Distributions

A stock redemption occurs when a corporation acquires its stock from a shareholder in exchange for money or other property.[1] The economic effect of a stock redemption may resemble that of a sale to a third party or a section 301 distribution, depending on the circumstances. Section 302 was enacted to distinguish between these two economic effects and provide appropriate treatment. Under section 302:

- If a redemption meets one of five tests (set forth in section 302(b)), it is treated as a distribution in exchange for stock.[2] The shareholder would offset her basis in the stock against the amounts distributed, and the resulting gain or loss would likely be capital gain or loss.[3]

- If redemption fails all five tests, it is generally[4] treated as a section 301 distribution of property.[5] The amount of the distribution would be a dividend to the extent of the distributing corporation's E&P, with a recovery of the shareholder's stock basis and possible gain to the extent that the distribution is not a dividend.[6]

The five tests contained in section 302(b) are as follows:

- Redemption not essentially equivalent to a dividend.[7]
- Substantially disproportionate redemptions.[8]

---

[1] I.R.C. § 317(b).

[2] I.R.C. § 302(a).

[3] The stock is likely to be a capital asset in the shareholder's hands. I.R.C. § 1221.

[4] Even if the redemption fails all five tests, all or part of the distribution may receive exchange treatment under section 303, which deals with redemptions to pay death taxes.

[5] I.R.C. § 302(d).

[6] *See* Chapter 16.

[7] I.R.C. § 302(b)(1).

[8] I.R.C. § 302(b)(2).

- Complete termination redemptions.[9]
- Partial liquidations.[10]
- Redemptions by certain regulated investment companies.[11]

These tests are analyzed below,[12] but before doing so, constructive stock ownership rules for applying the tests are addressed.

B. Constructive Ownership of Stock

1. In General

To address the concern that actual ownership alone may not accurately measure a shareholder's real stock interest in a corporation, section 302(c)(1) generally provides that in applying the section 302(b) tests, stock ownership is determined by using constructive ownership rules contained in section 318.[13] Section 318 contains four categories of rules that attribute stock owned by one person to another person for purposes of the section 302(b) tests:

- Family Attribution
- Entity to Owner or Beneficiary Attribution
- Owner or Beneficiary to Entity Attribution
- Option Attribution

Under family attribution, an individual constructively owns stock owned by the individual's spouse, children, grandchildren, and parents.[14] For purposes of this rule, a legally adopted child is considered to be a child by blood.[15]

Under attribution from an entity to owner or beneficiary:

- A partner constructively owns the stock owned by her partnership in proportion to the partner's interest in the partnership.[16]
- A beneficiary of an estate constructively owns stock owned by the estate in proportion to the beneficiary's interest in the estate.[17]
- A beneficiary of a trust constructively owns stock owned by the trust in proportion to the beneficiary's actuarial interest in the trust.[18]

---

[9] I.R.C. § 302(b)(3).

[10] I.R.C. § 302(b)(4).

[11] I.R.C. § 302(b)(5).

[12] The last test is only discussed in the Detailed Analysis.

[13] There is an exception for applying the family attribution rules for constructive stock ownership in connection with certain complete termination redemptions. See § 17.03[B][1].

[14] I.R.C. § 318(a)(1)(A).

[15] I.R.C. § 318(a)(1)(B).

[16] I.R.C. § 318(a)(2)(A).

[17] I.R.C. § 318(a)(2)(A).

[18] I.R.C. § 318(a)(2)(B). The attribution rule does not apply to beneficiaries of a qualified employees' trust described in section 401(a).

- A shareholder of a corporation constructively owns stock owned by the corporation in proportion to the shareholder's interest in the stock of the corporation by value, *provided* that the shareholder owns at least 50 percent of the stock of the corporation by value.[19]

Under attribution from an owner or beneficiary to entity:

- A partnership constructively owns in full the stock owned by its partners.[20]
- An estate constructively owns in full the stock owned by its beneficiaries.[21]
- A trust constructively owns in full the stock owned by its beneficiaries.[22]
- A corporation constructively owns in full the stock owned by its shareholders, *provided* that the shareholder owns at least 50 percent of the stock of the corporation by value.[23]

Under option attribution, a person constructively owns the stock that the person has an option to acquire.[24]

In general, in applying the constructive ownership rules, "chain" attribution is permitted: stock constructively owned by a person under the attribution rules is considered as actually owned by that person for purposes of applying the attribution rules to make another person the constructive owner of the stock.[25] There are two exceptions to chain attribution that are discussed in the Detailed Analysis.

C. Tests for Treating Redemptions as Exchanges

1. Substantially Disproportionate Redemptions

Under section 302(b)(2), if three requirements are satisfied, a redemption is considered substantially disproportionate and the amounts received by the shareholder are treated as a distribution in exchange for stock. The three requirements are:

- Immediately after the redemption, the shareholder owns less than 50% of the total combined voting power of the corporation's stock.
- The shareholder's percentage of the corporation's voting stock owned immediately after the redemption is less than 80% of the shareholder's

---

[19] I.R.C. § 318(a)(2)(C).

[20] I.R.C. § 318(a)(3)(A).

[21] I.R.C. § 318(a)(3)(A).

[22] I.R.C. § 318(a)(3)(B). The attribution rule does not apply to a qualified employees' trust described in section 401(a). The attribution rule also does not apply to the stock owned by a beneficiary that has a remote contingent interest in the trust; an interest is remote where under the maximum exercise of discretion by the trustee, the beneficiary's interest computed actuarially is not more than five percent of the value of the trust property. I.R.C. § 318(a)(3)(B)(i).

[23] I.R.C. § 318(a)(3)(C).

[24] I.R.C. § 318(a)(4).

[25] I.R.C. § 318(a)(5)(A).

percentage of the voting stock owned immediately before the redemption, and

- The shareholder's percentage of the corporation's common stock owned immediately after the redemption is less than 80% of the shareholder's percentage of the common stock owned immediately before the redemption.

2. Complete Termination Redemptions

Under section 302(b)(3), where there is a redemption of all of a shareholder's stock in a corporation, the amounts received by the shareholder are treated as a distribution in exchange for stock. To allow redemptions in family owned corporations to achieve exchange treatment, a waiver of family attribution is permitted if the following requirements are satisfied:

- Immediately after redemption, the redeemed shareholder has no interest in the corporation, *other than as a creditor* — prohibited interests specifically include interests as an officer, director, or employee.

- The redeemed shareholder does not acquire any prohibited interest within 10 years of the redemption, except for stock acquired by bequest or devise.

- The redeemed shareholder files an agreement promising to notify the Service of an acquisition of a prohibited interest within the 10-year period and to retain necessary records.[26]

Even if the above requirements are satisfied, a waiver of family attribution is not permitted if within the 10-year period ending on the date of the redemption:

- A person whose stock is attributed to the redeemed shareholder under the constructive stock ownership rules had acquired stock from the redeemed shareholder (unless such stock is redeemed as well in the same transaction), or

- The redeemed shareholder had acquired the redeemed stock from a person whose stock is attributed to the redeemed shareholder under the constructive stock ownership rules,

unless the disposition or acquisition by the redeemed shareholder did not have the avoidance of federal income taxes as one of its principal purposes.[27] It should be emphasized that only family attribution can be waived for purposes of the complete termination redemption test. Other types of attribution can never be waived.

3. Redemptions Not Essentially Equivalent to Dividends

Under section 302(b)(1), if a redemption is not essentially equivalent to a dividend, the amounts received by the shareholder are treated as a distribution in exchange for stock. According to the Supreme Court in *U.S. v. Davis*,[28] the standard is whether the redemption results in a meaningful reduction in the shareholder's

---

[26] I.R.C. § 302(c)(2)(A).

[27] I.R.C. § 302(c)(2)(B).

[28] 397 U.S. 301 (1970).

proportionate interest in the corporation. Unlike the fairly mechanical approaches contained in the other section 302(b) tests, section 302(b)(1) uses a facts and circumstances approach. Nevertheless, there are established guidelines in applying the meaningful reduction standard:

- Where the redeemed shareholder has a controlling stock interest in the corporation before the redemption, a loss of control is required to satisfy the test.[29]

- Where before the redemption, the redeemed shareholder does not have a controlling stock interest but does have the potential for exercising group control, a loss of that same potential for exercising group control is required to satisfy the test.[30] A potential for exercising group control is where the shareholder can control the corporation by teaming up with one or more other shareholders.

- Where before the redemption, the redeemed shareholder does not have a controlling stock interest or the potential for exercising group control but does own voting stock, insignificant reductions in voting stock can satisfy the test.[31]

- Where the redeemed shareholder holds only nonvoting preferred stock before the redemption, a redemption of any stock will apparently satisfy the test.[32]

4. Partial Liquidation Redemptions

Under section 302(b)(4), amounts received by a shareholder on a redemption are treated as a distribution in exchange for stock if:

- The shareholder is not a corporation, and

- The distribution is in "partial liquidation" of the distributing corporation.

A "partial liquidation" is defined as a distribution that is:

- Not essentially equivalent to a dividend (determined at the *corporate* level rather than shareholder level),[33] and

- Pursuant to a plan and occurs within the taxable year that the plan is adopted or within the succeeding year.[34]

---

[29] Rev. Rul. 75-502, 1975-2 C.B. 111 (test satisfied where percentage of stock went from 57% to 50%, with one other shareholder holding the other 50%).

[30] Rev. Rul. 85-106, 1985-2 C.B. 116 (test not satisfied where same potential for group control after redemption).

[31] Rev. Rul. 75-512, 1975-2 C.B. 112 (test satisfied where percentage of stock went from 30% to 24.3%, with no potential for group control before or after redemption); Rev. Rul. 76-385, 1976-2 C.B. 92. (test satisfied where percentage of stock went from .0001118% to .0001081%).

[32] *See* Treas. Reg. § 1.302-2(a) (test satisfied where half of shareholder's nonvoting preferred stock is redeemed); Rev. Rul. 77-426, 1977-2 C.B. 87 (test satisfied where 5% of shareholder's nonvoting preferred stock is redeemed).

[33] I.R.C. § 302(e)(1)(A).

[34] I.R.C. § 302(e)(1)(B).

For the "not essentially equivalent to a dividend" standard to be satisfied, there must be a genuine contraction of corporate business. As an example, the provision's legislative history refers to a situation where, after a fire destroyed a portion of a corporation's factory, the corporation distributed the insurance proceeds to its shareholders and continued its operations on a smaller scale.[35] Voluntary contractions of corporate business can also qualify for partial liquidation treatment. The provision contains a *safe harbor* for meeting the standard, which provides that a distribution is not essentially equivalent to a dividend at the corporate level if:

- It is attributable to corporation's ceasing to conduct, or consists of the assets of, a "qualified trade or business," and

- Immediately after the distribution, the corporation is actively engaged in the conduct of a "qualified trade or business."[36]

A "qualified trade or business" is a trade or business that was:

- Actively conducted throughout the five-year period ending on the date of the redemption, and

- Not acquired by the corporation within the five-year period in a transaction in which gain or loss was recognized.[37]

Under either the general corporate contraction standard or the safe harbor, the fact that a redemption is pro rata with respect to all of the shareholders (and thus does not alter their proportionate stock interests) is irrelevant.[38]

D. Stock Purchases by Related Corporations Treated as Redemptions

In the absence of a special rule, a shareholder who owns a controlling interest in two corporations would be able to receive exchange treatment in a transaction that may well have the economic effect of a dividend by selling stock in one of the corporations to the other corporation. Section 304 addresses this situation by subjecting transactions of this type to the section 302(b) tests to determine whether exchange treatment or section 301 distribution treatment will be accorded. Section 304 applies to two categories of transactions: so-called "brother-sister acquisitions" and "parent-subsidiary acquisitions."

1. Brother-Sister Acquisitions

One situation in which section 304 applies is when:

- One or more persons "control" each of two corporations, and

- One corporation (referred to as the "acquiring corporation") acquires stock in the other corporation (referred to as the "issuing corporation") from the

---

[35] S. Rep. No. 1622, 83 Cong., 2d Sess. 49 (1954). The example in the legislative history is based on Imler v. Commissioner, 11 T.C. 836 (1948).

[36] I.R.C. § 302(e)(2).

[37] I.R.C. § 302(e)(3).

[38] *See* I.R.C. § 302(e)(4) (stating this in connection with the safe harbor).

controlling person (or persons) for property.[39]

"Control" is defined as having at least 50 percent of the voting power of the stock of a corporation or at least 50 percent of the value of the stock of a corporation.[40] For purposes of determining control, stock ownership is determined by using the constructive ownership rules contained in section 318, with some modifications.[41] When the above requirements are met, the transaction is treated as a *redemption* of stock in the acquiring corporation.[42] Nevertheless, the section 302(b) tests are applied with reference to the controlling person's stock in the issuing corporation.[43]

If a section 302(b) test is satisfied with respect to the controlling person's stock interest in the issuing corporation, the disposition of the issuing corporation stock is treated as an exchange,[44] and thus the controlling person has a gain or loss equal to the difference between the controlling person's amount realized on the transaction and that person's basis in the transferred stock. In this case, the acquiring corporation takes a cost basis in the issuing corporation stock that it acquires, and the controlling person's basis in the stock of the acquiring corporation is unchanged. In short, if a section 302(b) test is satisfied, the tax consequences follow the form of the transaction, i.e., a sale of issuing corporation stock by the controlling person to the acquiring corporation.

If all of the section 302(b) tests are failed with respect to the controlling person's stock interest in the issuing corporation, the amount received by the controlling person is treated as a section 301 distribution of property.[45] In determining the amount of the dividend on the distribution, the E&P of *both* the acquiring corporation and the issuing corporation is used.[46] For basis purposes, the transaction is treated as if the controlling person had transferred the issuing corporation stock to the acquiring corporation in a transaction qualifying under section 351.[47] Accordingly, the acquiring corporation's basis in the issuing corporation stock acquired is the same as the basis that the controlling person had in such stock.[48] In addition, the controlling person increases her basis in the stock of the acquiring corporation by the amount of basis she had in the issuing corporation stock that was transferred.[49]

2. Parent-Subsidiary Acquisitions

Another situation in which section 304 applies is when:

---

[39] I.R.C. § 304(a)(1).

[40] I.R.C. § 304(c)(1).

[41] I.R.C. § 304(c)(3).

[42] I.R.C. § 304(a)(1).

[43] I.R.C. § 304(b)(1).

[44] I.R.C. § 302(a).

[45] I.R.C. § 302(d).

[46] I.R.C. § 304(b)(2).

[47] I.R.C. § 304(a)(1).

[48] I.R.C. § 362(a).

[49] I.R.C. § 358(a)(1).

- One corporation (referred to as the "acquiring corporation") acquires from a shareholder of another corporation (referred to as the "issuing corporation") stock in the issuing corporation for property, and

- The issuing corporation controls the acquiring corporation.[50]

Thus, this other section 304 situation occurs when a subsidiary corporation acquires stock in its parent corporation from a shareholder of the parent. When this occurs, the transaction is treated as a redemption of stock in the parent corporation,[51] and the section 302(b) tests are applied with reference to stock in the parent corporation.[52] Following the application of the section 302(b) tests, the possible results are substantially the same as in the brother-sister acquisition context: exchange treatment if a section 302(b) test is satisfied, and section 301 distribution treatment if all of the section 302(b) tests are failed.

DETAILED ANALYSIS

§ 17.01 GENERAL FRAMEWORK FOR TREATING REDEMPTIONS AS EITHER EXCHANGES OR SECTION 301 DISTRIBUTIONS

A stock redemption occurs when a corporation acquires its stock from a shareholder in exchange for money or other property.[53] While the form of a stock redemption is a sale or exchange of stock, the economic effect may sometimes be similar to a section 301 distribution of money or property to a shareholder. The following examples illustrate this.

Example 17.1. Individual A owns 100 shares of X Corp. stock as an investment. There are 100,000 shares of X Corp. stock outstanding. A's basis in the stock is $400. A sells 50 shares of X Corp. stock (with a basis of $200) to B for $500.

On the sale, A would have a capital gain equal to A's amount realized of $500 minus A's adjusted basis in the stock of $200, or $300.[54]

Example 17.2. Individual A owns 100 shares of X Corp. stock as an investment. There are 100,000 shares of X Corp. stock outstanding. A's basis in the stock is $400. X Corp. redeems 50 shares of A's X Corp. stock (with a basis of $200) for $500.

The economic effect of this transaction is similar to a sale of the stock to a third party, and accordingly the Code will treat it that way; the details will be explored below. As in the previous example, A would have $300 of capital gain on the disposition of the stock.

---

[50] I.R.C. § 304(a)(2).

[51] *Id.*

[52] I.R.C. § 304(b)(1).

[53] I.R.C. § 317(b).

[54] I.R.C. §§ 1001, 1222, 1221.

Example 17.3. Individual A owns all 100 shares of X Corp. stock as an investment. A's basis in the stock is $400. X Corp. redeems 50 shares of A's X Corp. stock (with a basis of $200) for $500.

The economic effect of this transaction is similar to a nonliquidating distribution of cash subject to section 301,[55] and the Code will generally treat it that way (details later). Thus, A would generally have a section 301 distribution of $500. If X Corp. has enough E&P, the $500 distribution would be dividend.[56]

As the foregoing illustrates, the economic effect of a stock redemption may resemble that of a sale to a third party or a section 301 distribution, depending on the circumstances. Section 302 was enacted to distinguish between these two economic effects and provide appropriate treatment. Under section 302:

- If a redemption meets one of five tests (set forth in section 302(b)), it is treated as a distribution in exchange for stock.[57] The shareholder would offset her basis in the stock against the amounts distributed, and the resulting gain or loss would likely be capital gain or loss.[58]

- If redemption fails all five tests, it is generally[59] treated as a section 301 distribution of property.[60] The amount of the distribution would be a dividend to the extent of the distributing corporation's E&P, with a recovery of the shareholder's stock basis and possible gain to the extent that the distribution is not a dividend.[61]

The five tests contained in section 302(b) are as follows:

- The redemption is not essentially equivalent to a dividend.[62]

- Substantially disproportionate redemptions.[63]

- Complete termination redemptions.[64]

- Partial liquidations.[65]

- Redemptions by certain regulated investment companies.[66]

The first three tests examine whether there has been a sufficient reduction in the shareholder's ownership interest in the corporation to justify exchange treatment.

---

[55] *See* Chapter 16.

[56] *See id.*

[57] I.R.C. § 302(a).

[58] The stock is likely to be a capital asset in the shareholder's hands. I.R.C. § 1221.

[59] Even if the redemption fails all five tests, all or part of the distribution may receive exchange treatment under section 303, which deals with redemptions to pay death taxes. § 17.07 addresses section 303.

[60] I.R.C. § 302(d).

[61] *See* Chapter 16.

[62] I.R.C. § 302(b)(1).

[63] I.R.C. § 302(b)(2).

[64] I.R.C. § 302(b)(3).

[65] I.R.C. § 302(b)(4).

[66] I.R.C. § 302(b)(5).

The fourth test examines whether there has been a sufficient contraction of the corporation's business. Each of these tests is analyzed below, but before doing so, constructive stock ownership rules for applying the tests are addressed.

§ 17.02 CONSTRUCTIVE OWNERSHIP OF STOCK

A. In General

A redemption could result in a significant reduction in a shareholder's actual stock interest in a corporation, but because other stock in the corporation is held by related persons who the shareholder may be able to control and/or financially benefit from, the redemption's effect on the shareholder's interest in the corporation may not be meaningful.

> *Example 17.4.* Individual A owns 50 shares of X Corp as an investment. There are 100 shares of X Corp. outstanding. A's basis in the stock is $200. The other 50 shares of X Corp. stock are owned by A's son B. X Corp. redeems 40 shares of A's X Corp. stock (with a basis of $160) for $400.

A's percentage of the X Corp. stock has gone from 50 percent (50 out of 100 shares) to 16.67 percent (10 out of 60 shares), but this reduction in stock interest may not be meaningful because A's son owns the remaining stock in X Corp. Through her son, A may able to exercise control over the corporation's affairs, and through such control, A may be able to reap financial benefits from the corporation to the same extent as if no stock had been redeemed.

To address the concern that actual ownership alone may not accurately measure a shareholder's real stock interest in a corporation, section 302(c)(1) generally provides that in applying the section 302(b) tests, stock ownership is determined by using constructive ownership rules contained in section 318.[67] Section 318 contains four categories of rules that attribute stock owned by one person to another person for purposes of the section 302(b) tests:

- Family Attribution
- Entity to Owner or Beneficiary Attribution
- Owner or Beneficiary to Entity Attribution
- Option Attribution

B. Family Attribution

Under family attribution, an individual constructively owns stock owned by the individual's spouse, children, grandchildren, and parents.[68] For purposes of this rule, a legally adopted child is considered to be a child by blood.[69]

---

[67] There is an exception for applying the family attribution rules for constructive stock ownership in connection with certain complete termination redemptions. *See* § 17.03[B][1].

[68] I.R.C. § 318(a)(1)(A).

[69] I.R.C. § 318(a)(1)(B).

Applying family attribution in Example 17.4:

A constructively owns the shares of X Corp. stock that are owned by her son. Consequently, before the redemption, A owns 50 shares actually and 50 shares constructively, or 100 shares, which is 100 percent of the X Corp. stock; after the redemption, A owns 10 shares actually and 50 shares constructively, or 60 shares, which is 100 percent of the X Corp. stock. Therefore, the redemption has not changed A's proportionate interest in the X Corp. stock.

C. Entity to Owner or Beneficiary Attribution

Under attribution from an entity to owner or beneficiary:

- A partner constructively owns the stock owned by her partnership in proportion to the partner's interest in the partnership.[70]
- A beneficiary of an estate constructively owns stock owned by the estate in proportion to the beneficiary's interest in the estate.[71]
- A beneficiary of a trust constructively owns stock owned by the trust in proportion to the beneficiary's actuarial interest in the trust.[72]
- A shareholder of a corporation constructively owns stock owned by the corporation in proportion to the shareholder's interest in the stock of the corporation by value, *provided* that the shareholder owns at least 50 percent of the stock of the corporation by value.[73]

> *Example 17.5.* Individual A owns 50 shares of X Corp. There are 100 shares of X Corp. outstanding. The other 50 shares of X Corp. stock are owned by A/B Partnership, in which A is a 50 percent partner.

Applying partnership to partner attribution in Example 17.5:

A constructively owns a portion of the shares of X Corp. stock that are owned by the A/B Partnership, in proportion to her interest in the partnership; thus, because A is a 50 percent partner, A constructively owns 50 percent of the shares owned by the partnership. Consequently, A owns 50 shares actually and 25 shares constructively, which is 50 percent of the 50 shares owned by A/B Partnership, for a total of 75 shares of X Corp. stock.

> *Example 17.6.* Individual A owns 50 shares of X Corp. There are 100 shares of X Corp. outstanding. The other 50 shares of X Corp. stock are owned by a trust in which A is a beneficiary with a 30 percent actuarial interest.

Applying trust to beneficiary attribution in Example 17.6:

A constructively owns a portion of the shares of X Corp. stock that are owned by the trust, in proportion to her actuarial interest in the trust; thus, because A has a

---

[70] I.R.C. § 318(a)(2)(A).

[71] *Id.*

[72] I.R.C. § 318(a)(2)(B). The attribution rule does not apply to beneficiaries of a qualified employees' trust described in section 401(a).

[73] I.R.C. § 318(a)(2)(C).

30 percent actuarial interest in the trust, A constructively owns 30 percent of the shares owned by the trust. Consequently, A owns 50 shares actually and 15 shares constructively, which is 30 percent of the 50 shares owned by the trust, for a total of 65 shares of X Corp. stock.

> *Example 17.7.* Individual A owns 50 shares of X Corp. There are 100 shares of X Corp. outstanding. The other 50 shares of X Corp. stock are owned by Y Corp.; A is a shareholder of Y Corp. and owns 60 percent of the Y Corp. stock by value.

Applying corporation to shareholder attribution in Example 17.7:

Because A owns at least 50 percent of the stock of Y Corp. by value, A constructively owns a portion of the shares of X Corp. stock that are owned by Y Corp., in proportion to her stock interest in Y Corp. by value; thus, because A has a 60 percent stock interest in the corporation by value, A constructively owns 60 percent of the shares owned by the corporation. Consequently, A owns 50 shares actually and 30 shares constructively, which is 60 percent of the 50 shares owned by Y Corp., for a total of 80 shares of X Corp. stock.

> *Example 17.8.* Individual A owns 50 shares of X Corp. There are 100 shares of X Corp. outstanding. The other 50 shares of X Corp. stock are owned by Y Corp.; A is a shareholder of Y Corp. and owns 40 percent of the Y Corp. stock by value.

Applying corporation to shareholder attribution in Example 17.8:

Because A does not own at least 50 percent of the stock of Y Corp. by value, A does not constructively own any of the X Corp. stock that is owned by Y Corp.

D. Owner or Beneficiary to Entity Attribution

Under attribution from an owner or beneficiary to entity:

- A partnership constructively owns in full the stock owned by its partners.[74]

- An estate constructively owns in full the stock owned by its beneficiaries.[75]

- A trust constructively owns in full the stock owned by its beneficiaries.[76]

- A corporation constructively owns in full the stock owned by its shareholders, *provided* that the shareholder owns at least 50 percent of the stock of the corporation by value.[77]

---

[74] I.R.C. § 318(a)(3)(A).

[75] *Id.*

[76] I.R.C. § 318(a)(3)(B). The attribution rule does not apply to a qualified employees' trust described in section 401(a). The attribution rule also does not apply to the stock owned by a beneficiary that has a remote contingent interest in the trust; an interest is remote where under the maximum exercise of discretion by the trustee, the beneficiary's interest computed actuarially is not more than five percent of the value of the trust property.

[77] I.R.C. § 318(a)(3)(C).

Example 17.9. A/B Partnership owns 50 shares of X Corp. There are 100 shares of X Corp. outstanding. The other 50 shares of X Corp. stock are owned by A, a 50 percent partner in A/B Partnership.

Applying partner to partnership attribution in Example 17.9:

A/B Partnership constructively owns the shares of X Corp. stock that are owned by A. Consequently, A/B Partnership owns 50 shares actually and 50 shares constructively, for a total of all 100 shares of X Corp. stock.

Example 17.10. A trust owns 50 shares of X Corp. There are 100 shares of X Corp. outstanding. The other 50 shares of X Corp. stock are owned by A, a beneficiary of the trust with a 30 percent actuarial interest in the trust.

Applying beneficiary to trust attribution in Example 17.10:

The trust constructively owns the shares of X Corp. stock that are owned by A. Consequently, the trust owns 50 shares actually and 50 shares constructively, for a total of all 100 shares of X Corp. stock.

Example 17.11. Y Corp. owns 50 shares of X Corp. There are 100 shares of X Corp. outstanding. The other 50 shares of X Corp. stock are owned by A; A is a shareholder of Y Corp. and owns 60 percent of the Y Corp. stock by value.

Applying shareholder to corporation attribution in Example 17.11:

Because A owns at least 50 percent of the stock of Y Corp. by value, Y Corp. constructively owns the shares of X Corp. stock that are owned by A. Consequently, Y Corp. owns 50 shares actually and 50 shares constructively, for a total of all 100 shares of X Corp. stock.

Example 17.12. Y Corp. owns 50 shares of X Corp. There are 100 shares of X Corp. outstanding. The other 50 shares of X Corp. stock are owned by A; A is a shareholder of Y Corp. and owns 40 percent of the Y Corp. stock by value.

Applying shareholder to corporation attribution in Example 17.12:

Because A does not own at least 50 percent of the stock of Y Corp. by value, Y Corp. does not constructively own any of the X Corp. stock that is owned by A.

E. Option Attribution

Under option attribution, a person constructively owns stock that the person has an option to acquire.[78]

F. Chain Attribution

In general, "chain" attribution is permitted stock constructively owned by a person under the attribution rules is considered as actually owned by that person for purposes of applying the attribution rules to make another person the

---

[78] I.R.C. § 318(a)(4).

constructive owner of the stock.[79]

> *Example 17.13.* Y Corp. owns 100 shares of X Corp. A/B Partnership owns 60 percent of the Y Corp. stock by value. A is 50 percent partner in A/B Partnership.

Applying chain attribution to Example 17.13:

Under corporation to shareholder attribution, A/B Partnership constructively owns 60 shares of X Corp. stock.[80] Under partnership to partner attribution, A owns 50 percent of the 60 shares of X Corp. stock that are constructively owned by A/B Partnership, or 30 shares of X Corp. stock.[81]

There are two exceptions to chain attribution. First, there is no double family attribution: stock that is constructively owned by a person under family attribution is *not* considered as owned by that person for purposes of applying family attribution to make another person the owner of the stock.

> *Example 17.14.* B owns 50 shares of X Corp. B's mother is M, and B has a sibling, who is S.

Applying the no double family attribution rule to Example 17.14:

Under child to parent attribution, M constructively owns the 50 shares of X Corp. stock owned by B. However, the 50 shares of X Corp. stock constructively owned by M are not reattributed to S under parent to child attribution because of the bar against double family attribution. Therefore, S does not constructively own the 50 shares of X Corp. stock actually owned by B.[82]

In addition, there is no "sidewise"[83] attribution: stock that is constructively owned by a person under "owner or beneficiary to entity attribution" is *not* considered as owned by that person for purposes of applying "entity to owner or beneficiary attribution" to make another person the owner of the stock.

> *Example 17.15.* A owns 50 shares of X Corp. A and B are 50 percent partners in A/B Partnership.

Applying the no sidewise attribution rule to Example 17.15.

Under partner to partnership attribution, A/B Partnership constructively owns the 50 shares of X Corp. stock owned by A. However, a portion of the 50 shares of

---

[79] I.R.C. § 318(a)(5)(A).

[80] Because A/B Partnership owns at least 50 percent of the stock of Y Corp. by value, A/B Partnership constructively owns a portion of the shares of X Corp. stock that are owned by Y Corp., in proportion to A/B Partnership's stock interest in Y Corp. by value; thus, because A/B Partnership has a 60 percent stock interest in Y Corp. by value, A/B Partnership constructively owns 60 percent of the 100 shares owned by the corporation, or 60 shares of X Corp. stock.

[81] A constructively owns a portion of the shares of X Corp. stock that are owned by the A/B Partnership, in proportion to her interest in the partnership; thus, because A is a 50 percent partner, A constructively owns 50 percent of the shares owned by the partnership.

[82] There is no direct attribution of the stock from B to S because section 318 does not provide for sibling attribution.

[83] *See* Stephen Schwarz and Daniel J. Lathrope, Fundamentals of Corporate Taxation 200 (2012).

X Corp. stock constructively owned by A/B partnership is *not* reattributed to B under partnership to partner attribution because of the bar against sidewise attribution. Therefore, B does not constructively own any of the 50 shares of X Corp. stock actually owned by A.

§ 17.03   TESTS FOR TREATING REDEMPTIONS AS EXCHANGES

A.   Substantially Disproportionate Redemptions

1.   In General

Under section 302(b)(2), if three requirements are satisfied, a redemption is considered as substantially disproportionate and the amounts received by the shareholder are treated as a distribution in exchange for stock. The shareholder would then offset her basis in the stock against the amounts distributed, and the resulting gain or loss would likely be capital gain or loss. The three requirements are:

- Immediately after the redemption, the shareholder owns less than 50% of the total combined voting power of the corporation's stock.

- The shareholder's percentage of the corporation's voting stock owned immediately after the redemption is less than 80% of the shareholder's percentage of the voting stock owned immediately before the redemption, *and*

- The shareholder's percentage of the corporation's common stock owned immediately after the redemption is less than 80% of the shareholder's percentage of the common stock owned immediately before the redemption.[84]

Example 17.16. X Corp. has 100 shares of voting common stock outstanding (its only class of stock). A owns 60 shares of the X Corp. stock, and B owns 40 shares of the X Corp. stock. A and B are unrelated for purposes of the constructive stock ownership rules. A has a total basis of $6,000 in her 60 shares of X Corp. stock. On January 1, 2014, X Corp. distributes $12,000 to A in redemption of 30 shares of A's X Corp. stock.

Applying section 302(b)(2) to A in Example 17.16:

Before the redemption, A owns 60 out of 100 shares of voting common stock of X Corp., or 60%. After the redemption, A owns 30 out of 70 shares of voting common stock, or 42.9%. The redemption of A's 30 shares of X Corp. stock satisfies the three requirements of section 302(b)(2):

- Immediately after the redemption, A owns less than 50% of the total combined voting power of the corporation's stock — after the redemption, A owns 42.9% of the voting power.

---

[84] I.R.C. § 302(b)(2); Boris I. Bittker & James S. Eustice, Federal Income Taxation of Corporations and Shareholders 9-22 (2000).

- A's percentage of the corporation's voting stock owned immediately after the redemption is less than 80% of A's percentage of the voting stock owned immediately before the redemption — 42.9% (percentage of voting stock after) < 48% (80% of 60% (percentage of voting stock before))

- A's percentage of the corporation's common stock owned immediately after the redemption is less than 80% of A's percentage of the common stock owned immediately before the redemption — 42.9% (percentage of common stock after) < 48% (80% of 60% (percentage of common stock before)).

Consequently, the $12,000 received by A is treated as in exchange for A's stock, and thus A has a gain of $9,000 on the redemption ($12,000 amount received minus A's basis of $3,000 in the 30 shares redeemed), which would likely be a capital gain.[85]

2. Simultaneous Redemption of Nonvoting Preferred Stock

If a redemption satisfies section 302(b)(2), a simultaneous redemption of nonvoting preferred stock (other than section 306 stock[86]) also gets exchange treatment under a "piggy back" rule.[87] For example, if in Example 17.16 A also owned 100 shares of X Corp. nonvoting preferred stock, and this stock was redeemed along with 30 shares of X Corp. voting common stock on January 1, 2014, A would also receive exchange treatment on the redemption of the nonvoting preferred stock (provided it was not section 306 stock).

3. Series of Redemptions

Under section 302(b)(2)(D), a series of redemptions pursuant to a plan are tested in the aggregate.[88] Thus, if the overall result with respect to a shareholder of two or more planned redemptions does not satisfy the section 302(b)(2) requirements, the shareholder does not receive exchange treatment even if the shareholder's redemption in isolation would have satisfied the requirements.

> *Example 17.17.* X Corp. has 100 shares of voting common stock outstanding (its only class of stock). A owns 60 shares of the X Corp. stock, and B owns 40 shares of the X Corp. stock. A and B are unrelated for purposes of the constructive stock ownership rules. Pursuant to a plan, on January 1, 2014, X Corp. distributes $12,000 to A in redemption of 30 shares of A's X Corp. stock, and on February 1, 2014, X Corp. distributes $8,000 to B in redemption of 20 shares of B's X Corp. stock.

Applying section 302(b)(2) to A in Example 17.17:

---

[85] The stock is likely to be a capital asset in the shareholder's hands. I.R.C. § 1221.

[86] Section 306 stock is addressed in Chapter 18.

[87] Treas. Reg. § 1.302-3(a).

[88] This represents a codification of the step transaction doctrine for a series of redemptions in connection with the section 302(b)(2) test. Whether a plan exists is based on the facts and circumstances. Treas. Reg. § 1.302-3(a). The Service has ruled that a design by a single shareholder can constitute a plan for purposes of this rule — thus, an agreement between two or more shareholders is not necessary. Rev. Rul. 85-14, 1985-1 C.B. 83.

Because A's redemption is part of a planned series of redemptions that includes B's redemption, section 302(b)(2) is applied to A's redemption by taking into account the effect of B's redemption. Before the two redemptions, A owns 60 out of 100 shares of voting common stock of X Corp., or 60%. After the two redemptions, A owns 30 out of 50 shares of voting common stock, or 60%. Thus, A's redemption fails the section 302(b)(2) test.

B. Complete Termination Redemptions

Under section 302(b)(3), where there is a redemption of all of a shareholder's stock in a corporation, the amounts received by the shareholder are treated as a distribution in exchange for stock.

> *Example 17.18.* X Corp. has 100 shares of voting common stock outstanding (its only class of stock). A owns 60 shares of the X Corp. stock, and B owns 40 shares of the X Corp. stock. A and B are unrelated for purposes of the constructive stock ownership rules. A has a total basis of $6,000 in her 60 shares of X Corp. stock. On January 1, 2014, X Corp. distributes $24,000 to A in redemption of all 60 shares of A's X Corp. stock.

Applying section 302(b)(3) to A in Example 17.18:

Because all of A's stock is redeemed, the $24,000 received by A is treated as in exchange for A's stock, and thus A has a gain of $18,000 on the redemption ($24,000 amount received minus A's basis of $6,000 in the 60 shares redeemed), which would likely be a capital gain.

If in Example 17.18 A and B were family members for purposes of the constructive ownership rules, absent a special rule, the redemption would not completely terminate A's stock interest in X Corp. because A would continue to constructively own the 40 shares owned by B. In such circumstances, the redemption would also not satisfy the substantially disproportionate redemption test, as A's percentage interest in the stock of the corporation would be 100% both before and after the redemption and thus fail the section 302(b)(2) requirements.

1. Waiver of Family Attribution by Individuals

To allow redemptions in family-owned corporations to achieve exchange treatment, a waiver of family attribution is generally permitted in applying the complete termination redemption test provided the redeemed shareholder severs her financial connection to the corporation for a sufficient period of time. Specifically, to waive family attribution, the following requirements must be satisfied:

- Immediately after the redemption, the redeemed shareholder has no interest in the corporation, *other than as a creditor* — prohibited interests specifically include interests as an officer, director, or employee.

- The redeemed shareholder does not acquire any prohibited interest within 10 years of the redemption, except for stock acquired by bequest or devise.

- The redeemed shareholder files an agreement promising to notify the Service of an acquisition of a prohibited interest within the 10-year period and to retain necessary records.[89]

Even if the above requirements are satisfied, a waiver of family attribution is not permitted if within the 10-year period ending on the date of the redemption:

- A person whose stock is attributed to the redeemed shareholder under the constructive stock ownership rules had acquired stock from the redeemed shareholder (unless such stock is redeemed as well in the same transaction), or

- The redeemed shareholder had acquired the redeemed stock from a person whose stock is attributed to the redeemed shareholder under the constructive stock ownership rules,

unless the disposition or acquisition by the redeemed shareholder did not have the avoidance of federal income taxes as one of its principal purposes.[90]

It should be emphasized that only family attribution can be waived for purposes of the complete termination redemption test. Other types of attribution can never be waived.

> *Example 17.19.* X Corp. has 100 shares of voting common stock outstanding (its only class of stock). A owns 60 shares of the X Corp. stock, and B owns 40 shares of the X Corp. stock. Both A and B have held their shares of X Corp. stock for the past 10 years. A and B are mother and son, respectively. A has a total basis of $6,000 in her 60 shares of X Corp. stock. On January 1, 2014, X Corp. distributes $24,000 to A in redemption of all 60 shares of A's X Corp. stock. A refrains from any interest in X Corp. for the next 10 years, including an interest as an employee, director or officer.

Applying section 302(b)(3) to A in Example 17.19:

Absent a waiver of family attribution, A would constructively own her son B's shares after the redemption and thus would not completely terminate her stock interest in X Corp. Provided that A files the required agreement with the Service, A would be able to waive family attribution and satisfy the complete termination redemption test because she has no interest in X Corp. immediately after the redemption and refrains from acquiring a prohibited interest for the 10-year period following the redemption. Also, the "ten year look back" rule does not disqualify the waiver because both A and B have held their stock for the past 10 years. Consequently, the $24,000 received by A is treated as in exchange for A's stock, and thus A has a gain of $18,000 on the redemption ($24,000 amount received minus A's basis of $6,000 in the 60 shares redeemed), which would likely be a capital gain.

If in Example 17.19 X Corp. transfers its note calling for future payments to A in redemption of A's 60 shares of X Corp. stock, A would still be able to waive family attribution and satisfy the complete termination redemption test, because a post-redemption interest as a creditor is permitted. The Service has ruled that an interest as a lessor of property to the corporation is generally permitted, apparently

---

[89] I.R.C. § 302(c)(2)(A).

[90] I.R.C. § 302(c)(2)(B).

analogizing a lessor's interest to a creditor's interest.[91]

If in Example 17.19 A performs services for X Corp. as an independent contractor within the 10-year period following the redemption, this may constitute a prohibited interest that would prevent the waiver of family attribution. The Ninth Circuit in *Lynch v. Commissioner*[92] held that a redeemed shareholder's performance of any services within the 10-year post-redemption period, whether as an independent contractor or an employee, would disqualify the waiver of family attribution. On the other hand, the U.S. Tax Court appears to use a balancing test in the case of services performed as an independent contractor, holding that such services would constitute a prohibited interest only where the redeemed shareholder has a financial stake in, or exercises managerial control over, the corporation.[93]

If in Example 17.19 B had acquired his 40 shares of X Corp. stock from A during the 10-year period prior to the redemption, this would disqualify the waiver of family attribution unless A's transfer of stock to B did not have as one of its principal purposes the avoidance of federal income taxes. According to the Service, a lack of tax avoidance can be demonstrated by showing that the person acquiring stock from the redeemed shareholder is active and knowledgeable in the corporation's business and intends to manage and control the corporation.[94]

2. Waiver of Family Attribution by Entities

Where the redeemed shareholder is a partnership, estate, trust or corporation, a waiver of family attribution is permitted provided that the entity having its shares redeemed and each "related person:"

- Refrain from holding a prohibited interest in the corporation for the 10-year period following the redemption,

- File an agreement promising to notify the Service of an acquisition of a prohibited interest within the 10-year period and to retain necessary records, and

- Agree to be jointly and severally liable for any deficiency resulting from an acquisition of a prohibited interest within the 10-year period.[95]

A "related person" is a person to whom ownership of stock in the corporation is attributed under family attribution, if the stock is further attributed to the entity under owner or beneficiary to entity attribution.[96]

> *Example 17.20.* X Corp. has 100 shares of voting common stock outstanding (its only class of stock). Trust owns 60 shares of the X Corp. stock, and B owns 40 shares of the X Corp. stock. A is the sole beneficiary of Trust. Both

---

[91] Rev. Rul. 77-467, 1977-2 C.B. 92.

[92] 801 F.2d 1176 (9th Cir. 1986).

[93] *See* Seda v. Commissioner, 82 T.C. 484 (1984).

[94] Rev. Rul. 77-293, 1977-2 C.B. 91.

[95] I.R.C. § 302(c)(2)(C)(i), (ii)(I).

[96] I.R.C. § 302(c)(2)(C)(ii)(II).

Trust and B have held their shares of X Corp. stock for the past 10 years. A and B are mother and son, respectively. Trust has a total basis of $6,000 in its 60 shares of X Corp. stock. On January 1, 2014, X Corp. distributes $24,000 to Trust in redemption of all 60 shares of its X Corp. stock. Trust and A refrain from any interest in X Corp. for the next 10 years, including an interest as an employee, director or officer.

Applying section 302(b)(3) to Trust in Example 17.20:

Absent a waiver of family attribution, the redemption would not completely terminate Trust's stock interest in X Corp as Trust would constructively own B's shares after the redemption: A would own B's shares under family attribution (child to parent) and the shares would be reattributed to Trust under beneficiary to entity attribution. A is a related person for purposes of the rule allowing entities to waive family attribution — A constructively owns B's stock under family attribution, and the stock is further attributed to the Trust under beneficiary to entity attribution. Consequently, provided both Trust and A file the required agreement with the Service and agree to be jointly and severally liable, Trust would be able to waive family attribution because both Trust and A have no interest in X Corp. immediately after the redemption and they refrain from acquiring a prohibited interest for the 10-year period following the redemption.[97] With the waiver of family attribution, Trust satisfies the complete termination test because A no longer constructively owns B's shares, and thus no shares are reattributed to Trust under beneficiary to entity attribution.

As with individual shareholders, entities can only waive family attribution; other types of attribution can *never* be waived. Accordingly, if, in Example 17.20, A rather than B had owned 40 shares of X Corp. stock, the complete termination test would not have been satisfied because Trust is not permitted to waive the attribution of stock from A, its beneficiary.

C. Redemptions Not Essentially Equivalent to Dividends

Under section 302(b)(1), if a redemption is not essentially equivalent to a dividend, the amounts received by the shareholder are treated as a distribution in exchange for stock. According to the Supreme Court in *U.S. v. Davis*,[98] the standard is whether the redemption results in a meaningful reduction in the shareholder's proportionate interest in the corporation. *Davis* also made clear that the section 318 attribution rules apply in making this determination.[99]

Unlike the fairly mechanical approaches contained in the other section 302(b) tests, section 302(b)(1) uses a facts and circumstances approach. Nevertheless, there are established guidelines in applying the meaningful reduction standard:

- Where the redeemed shareholder has a controlling stock interest in the corporation before the redemption, a loss of control is required to satisfy

---

[97] Also, the "ten year look back" rule does not disqualify the waiver because both Trust and B have held their stock for the past 10 years.

[98] 397 U.S. 301 (1970).

[99] *Id.*

the test.[100]

- Where before the redemption, the redeemed shareholder does not have a controlling stock interest but does have the potential for exercising group control, a loss of that same potential for exercising group control is required to satisfy the test.[101] A potential for exercising group control is where the shareholder can control the corporation by teaming up with one or more other shareholders.

- Where before the redemption, the redeemed shareholder does not have a controlling stock interest or the potential for exercising group control but does own voting stock, insignificant reductions in voting stock can satisfy the test.[102]

- Where the redeemed shareholder holds only nonvoting preferred stock before the redemption, a redemption of any stock will apparently satisfy the test.[103]

These guidelines reflect the view that while a redemption of any stock will reduce a shareholder's proportionate interest in the earnings and net assets of the corporation, a reduction in a shareholder's stock interest is not meaningful where the shareholder continues to have either control or the same voting interest.

Example 17.21. X Corp. has 100 shares of voting common stock outstanding (its only class of stock). A owns 60 shares of the X Corp. stock, and B owns 40 shares of the X Corp. stock. A and B are unrelated for purposes of the constructive stock ownership rules. On January 1, 2014, X Corp. distributes $8,000 to A in redemption of 20 shares of A's X Corp. stock.

Applying section 302(b)(1) to A in Example 17.21:

The redemption should satisfy the meaningful reduction standard because A has lost her controlling interest in X Corp. Before the redemption, A had a controlling interest in X Corp. (60 out of 100 shares of voting common stock, or 60 percent), and after the redemption, A no longer has a controlling interest in X Corp. (40 out of 80 shares of voting common stock, or 50 percent).[104]

Example 17.22.[105] X Corp. has 100 shares of voting common stock outstanding (its only class of stock). The X Corp. stock is owned as follows:

---

[100] Rev. Rul. 75-502, 1975-2 C.B. 111 (test satisfied where percentage of stock went from 57% to 50%, with one other shareholder holding the other 50%).

[101] Rev. Rul. 85-106, 1985-2 C.B. 116 (test not satisfied where same potential for group control after redemption).

[102] Rev. Rul. 75-512, 1975-2 C.B. 112 (test satisfied where percentage of stock went from 30% to 24.3%, with no potential for group control before or after redemption); Rev. Rul. 76-385, 1976-2 C.B. 92 (test satisfied where percentage of stock went from .0001118% to .0001081%).

[103] *See* Treas. Reg. § 1.302-2(a) (test satisfied where half of shareholder's nonvoting preferred stock is redeemed); Rev. Rul. 77-426, 1977-2 C.B. 87 (test satisfied where 5% of shareholder's nonvoting preferred stock is redeemed).

[104] *See* Rev. Rul. 75-502 ,1975-2 C.B. 111 (test satisfied where percentage of stock went from 57% to 50%, with one other shareholder holding the other 50%).

[105] *See* Schwarz & Lathrope, supra note 82 at 235, for a problem with similar facts.

A owns 27 shares, B owns 25 shares, C owns 24 shares, and D owns 24 shares. None of the shareholders are related for purposes of the constructive stock ownership rules. On January 1, 2014, X Corp. distributes $2,000 to A in redemption of 5 shares of A's X Corp. stock.

Applying section 302(b)(1) to A in Example 17.22:

The redemption appears to satisfy the meaningful reduction standard because A has lost the same potential to exercise group control.[106] Before the redemption, A could team up with any other shareholder to muster more than 50 percent of the X Corp. stock:

- A's shares (27) plus B's shares (25) equals 52 out of 100 shares, or 52 percent.

- A's shares (27) plus C's shares (24) equals 51 out of 100 shares, or 51 percent.

- A's shares (27) plus D's shares (24) equals 51 out of 100 shares, or 51 percent.

After the redemption, A cannot team up with any shareholder to muster more than 50 percent of the X Corp. stock:

- A's shares (22) plus B's shares (25) equals 47 out of 95 shares, or 49 percent.

- A's shares (22) plus C's shares (24) equals 46 out of 95 shares, or 48 percent.

- A's shares (22) plus D's shares (24) equals 46 out of 95 shares, or 48 percent.

Example 17.23. X Corp. has 100 shares of voting common stock outstanding (its only class of stock). The X Corp. stock is owned as follows: A owns 27 shares, B owns 22 shares, and C owns 51 shares. None of the shareholders are related for purposes of the constructive stock ownership rules. On January 1, 2014, X Corp. distributes $2,000 to A in redemption of 5 shares of A's X Corp. stock.

Applying section 302(b)(1) to A in Example 17.23:

The redemption should satisfy the meaningful reduction standard. Before the redemption, A does not have a controlling stock interest or the potential for exercising group control, because C owns more than 50 percent of the X Corp. stock. Consequently, any reduction in A's percentage of the voting stock should satisfy the meaningful reduction standard.[107]

Example 17.24. X Corp. has outstanding 100 shares of voting common stock and 100 shares of nonvoting, nonconvertible preferred. A owns all 100 shares of the X Corp. preferred stock, and B owns all 100 shares of the X Corp. common stock. A and B are unrelated for purposes of the constructive stock ownership rules. On January 1, 2014, X Corp. distributes $5,000 to A in redemption of 5 shares of A's X Corp. preferred stock.

---

[106] *See* 76-364, 1976-2 C.B. 91; *cf.* Rev. Rul. 85-106, 1985-2 C.B. 116.

[107] *See* Rev. Rul. 75-512, 1975-2 C.B. 112 (test satisfied where percentage of stock went from 30% to 24.3%, with no potential for group control before or after redemption)

Applying section 302(b)(1) to A in Example 17.24:

The redemption should satisfy the meaningful reduction standard. Because A holds only nonvoting preferred stock before the redemption, a redemption of any stock will apparently satisfy the test.[108]

D. Partial Liquidation Redemptions

Under section 302(b)(4), amounts received by a shareholder on a redemption are treated as a distribution in exchange for stock if:

- The shareholder is not a corporation,[109] and
- The distribution is in "partial liquidation" of the distributing corporation.

A "partial liquidation" is defined as a distribution that is:

- Not essentially equivalent to a dividend (determined at the *corporate* level rather than shareholder level),[110] and
- Pursuant to a plan and occurs within the taxable year that the plan is adopted or within the succeeding year.[111]

While the "not essentially equivalent to a dividend" language contained in the partial liquidation definition is also used in the section 302(b)(1) test, the parenthetical directs that the determination be made at the corporate level rather than the shareholder level. For this standard to be satisfied, there must be a genuine contraction of corporate business. As an example, the provision's legislative history refers to a situation where after a fire destroyed a portion of a corporation's factory, the corporation distributed the insurance proceeds to its shareholders and continued its operations on a smaller scale.[112] Voluntary contractions of corporate business can also qualify for partial liquidation treatment.[113]

Because the application of the corporate contraction standard can be uncertain, the provision contains a *safe harbor* for meeting the standard. Specifically, a distribution is not essentially equivalent to a dividend at the corporate level if:

- It is attributable to the corporation's ceasing to conduct, or consists of the

---

[108] *See* Rev. Rul. 77-426, 1977-2 C.B. 87 (test satisfied where 5% of shareholder's nonvoting preferred stock is redeemed).

[109] The purpose for denying partial liquidation treatment to corporate shareholders was to prevent acquiring corporations from receiving a stepped-up basis on selective, in-kind distributions from target corporations without the recognition of gain to the target corporation, by taking advantage of a partial liquidation exception to limitations on the *General Utilities* doctrine that applied to most nonliquidating distributions after 1969. *See* Bittker & Eustice, *supra* note 83 at 9-55 – 9-56.

[110] I.R.C. § 302(e)(1)(A).

[111] I.R.C. § 302(e)(1)(B).

[112] S. Rep. No. 1622, 83 Cong., 2d Sess. 49 (1954). The example in the legislative history is based on *Imler v. Commissioner*, 11 T.C. 836 (1948).

[113] *Id.* The Service will not issue a favorable ruling on whether there is a sufficient contraction of corporate business unless there is at least a 20 percent reduction in the corporation's gross income, net fair market value of assets, and employees. Rev. Proc. 2015-3, 2014-1 I.R.B.

assets of, a "qualified trade or business," and

- Immediately after the distribution, the corporation is actively engaged in the conduct of a "qualified trade or business."[114]

A "qualified trade or business" is a trade or business that was:

- Actively conducted throughout the five-year period ending on the date of the redemption, and

- Not acquired by the corporation within the five-year period in a transaction in which gain or loss was recognized.[115]

Under either the general corporate contraction standard or the safe harbor, the fact that a redemption is pro rata with respect to all of the shareholders (and thus does not alter their proportionate stock interests) is irrelevant.[116]

> *Example 17.25.* X Corp. has 100 shares of voting common stock outstanding (its only class of stock). A owns 50 shares of the X Corp. stock, and Y Corp. owns 50 shares of the X Corp. stock. X Corp. operates a business that manufactures and sells widgets. X Corp. decides to scale back on its operations, and on January 1, 2014, it sells for $1,000,000 one of its two widget manufacturing facilities that are of equal size. On February 1, 2014, X Corp. distributes $500,000 to A and $500,000 to Y Corp. in redemption of 25 shares of each shareholder's X Corp. stock.

Applying section 302(b)(4) to A and Y Corp. in Example 17.25:

As a corporation, Y Corp. cannot qualify for exchange treatment under section 302(b)(4). Because the redemption is pro rata and Y Corp.'s proportionate stock interest in X Corp. is therefore unchanged (50 out of 100 shares, or 50 percent before — 25 out of 50 shares, or 50 percent after), Y Corp. cannot satisfy any of the other section 302(b) tests.[117] Consequently, Y Corp.'s redemption is treated as a section 301 distribution of property.

As a non-corporate shareholder, assuming that the plan requirement is satisfied, A would qualify for exchange treatment under section 302(b)(4) if the distribution is not essentially equivalent to a dividend at the corporate level. Because X Corp. has reduced its manufacturing operations by one half, the corporate contraction standard should be satisfied, and thus A's redemption should be treated as an exchange under the provision.

> *Example 17.26.* X Corp. has 100 shares of voting common stock outstanding (its only class of stock). A owns 50 shares of the X Corp. stock, and Y Corp. owns 50 shares of the X Corp. stock. X Corp. operates a business that

---

[114] I.R.C. § 302(e)(2).

[115] I.R.C. § 302(e)(3). The dual five year requirements for having a qualified trade or business are aimed at preventing partial liquidation treatment where a corporation invests E&P in a business that the shareholders would have otherwise acquired with taxable dividends, with the intention of promptly distributing the acquired business assets to the shareholders. *See* Bittker and Eustice, *supra* note 83 at 9-64–9-65.

[116] *See* I.R.C. § 302(e)(4) (stating this in connection with the safe harbor).

[117] This assumes that the section 302(b)(5) test is not applicable. *See* § 17.03[E].

manufactures and sells widgets, and another business that manufactures and sells gadgets. X Corp. has operated both businesses for five years. On January 1, 2014, X Corp. sells its gadget manufacturing business for $1,000,000. On February 1, 2014, X Corp. distributes $500,000 to A and $500,000 to Y Corp. in redemption of 25 shares of each shareholder's X Corp. stock. Following the redemption, X Corp. continues to operate its widget manufacturing business.

Applying section 302(b)(4) to A and Y Corp. in Example 17.26:

As in Example 17.25, Y Corp.'s redemption is treated as a section 301 distribution of property: Y Corp. cannot qualify for exchange treatment under section 302(b)(4) because it is a corporation, and it cannot satisfy any of the other section 302(b) tests because its proportionate stock interest in X Corp. is unchanged.

As in Example 17.25, assuming that the plan requirement is satisfied, A can qualify for exchange treatment under section 302(b)(4) if the distribution is not essentially equivalent to a dividend at the corporate level. In this regard, A's redemption should satisfy the safe harbor: X Corp. had conducted two businesses for at least five years, it terminated one business and distributed the proceeds, and it continued to conduct the other business. Thus, A's redemption should be treated as an exchange under the provision.

If in Example 17.26 X Corp. had acquired either the widgets business or the gadgets business within the five-year period ending on the date of the redemption in a transaction in which the transferor recognized gain or loss, then the safe harbor would not have been met. Nevertheless, partial liquidation treatment may still be available in this situation by satisfying the corporate contraction doctrine. Alternatively, if in Example 17.26 X Corp. had acquired either business within the five-year period in a tax-free reorganization, the safe harbor would have been satisfied.

E. Redemptions by Certain Regulated Investment Companies

Under section 302(b)(5), amounts received by a shareholder on a redemption of stock in a "publicly offered regulated investment company" are treated as a distribution in exchange for stock if:

- The redemption is upon the demand of the shareholder, and
- The company issues only stock that is redeemable upon the demand of the shareholder.

A "publicly offered regulated investment company" is defined as a regulated investment company the shares of which are:

- Continuously offered pursuant to a public offering,
- Regularly traded on an established securities market, or
- Held by (or for) 500 or more persons at all times during the taxable year.[118]

---

[118] I.R.C. § 67(c)(2)(B).

Congress added section 302(b)(5) in 2010.

§ 17.04 SHAREHOLDER BASIS CONSEQUENCES WHERE REDEMPTION TREATED AS 301 DISTRIBUTION

A. Current Law

Where a redemption fails to satisfy any of the section 302(b) tests and thus is treated as a section 301 distribution of property, the shareholder is unable to use the adjusted basis of the redeemed stock to offset the amount distributed in the redemption. To prevent a shareholder from permanently losing the ability to use this amount of basis, the current regulations provide that this amount is added to the shareholder's adjusted basis in the stock of the corporation that the shareholder retains.[119]

> *Example 17.27.* X Corp. has 100 shares of voting common stock outstanding (its only class of stock), all of which is owned by A. A has a total basis of $10,000 in her 100 shares of X Corp. stock. On January 1, 2014, X Corp. distributes $25,000 to A in redemption of 50 shares of A's X Corp. stock. X Corp. did not contract its business operations in connection with the redemption. X Corp. has $100,000 of Current E&P for 2014 and no Accumulated E&P for prior years.

Applying the basis rule to A in Example 17.27:

The redemption is treated as a section 301 distribution because all of the section 302(b) tests are failed: A's proportionate stock interest is not altered (100 percent both before and after the redemption) and there is no contraction of corporate business to satisfy the partial liquidation test. Because X Corp. has enough E&P, the $25,000 distribution is a dividend. Under the regulations, A increases her basis in the 50 shares of X Corp. stock that she retains by the amount of her basis in the 50 shares redeemed. Therefore, A's new basis in the 50 shares retained is $10,000 ($5,000 original basis plus $5,000 basis in the shares redeemed).

Where a redemption is treated as a section 301 distribution but the redeemed shareholder retains no stock in the corporation, the amount of basis in the redeemed shares is added to the basis of the stock held by a person whose stock is attributed to the shareholder under section 318.[120]

> *Example 17.28.* X Corp. has 100 shares of voting common stock outstanding (its only class of stock). A owns 60 shares of the X Corp. stock, and B owns 40 shares of the X Corp. stock. A and B are mother and son, respectively. A has a total basis of $6,000 in her 60 shares of X Corp. stock, and B has a total basis of $4,000 in his 40 shares. On January 1, 2014, X Corp. distributes $24,000 to A in redemption of all 60 shares of A's X Corp. stock. Following the redemption, A works for X Corp. as an employee. X Corp. did

---

[119] Treas. Reg. § 1.302-2(c), Example 1.

[120] Treas. Reg. § 1.302-2(c), Example 2.

not contract its business operations in connection with the redemption. X Corp. has $100,000 of Current E&P for 2014 and no Accumulated E&P for prior years.

Applying the basis rule to A in Example 17.28:

The redemption is treated as a section 301 distribution because all of the section 302(b) tests are failed. A's proportionate stock interest is not altered: before the redemption, A owns 60 shares actually and 40 shares constructively via family attribution, or 100 percent; after the redemption, A owns no shares actually and 40 shares constructively via family attribution, or 100 percent. Because A is an employee of X Corp. after the redemption, the waiver of family attribution is not available. Also, there is no contraction of corporate business to satisfy the partial liquidation test. Because X Corp. has enough E&P, the $24,000 distribution is a dividend. Under the regulations, B, the person whose stock is attributed to A via family attribution, increases his basis in his 40 shares of X Corp. stock by the amount of A's basis in the 60 shares redeemed. Therefore, B's new basis in his 40 shares is $10,000 ($4,000 original basis plus $6,000 basis in A's shares that are redeemed).

B.   Proposed Regulations § 1.302-5

Proposed regulations would change the basis rule in the situation where the redeemed shareholder retains no shares of the redeemed class of stock. If a redemption is treated as a dividend and all of the shares of the redeemed class held by the redeemed shareholder are redeemed, the amount of basis in the redeemed stock is treated as a loss from a disposition of the redeemed stock.[121] However, the recognition of this loss must be deferred until the "inclusion date,"[122] which is the earlier of:

- The first date when either section 302(b)(1), (2) or (3) is met with regard to redemption, if the facts and circumstances that exist on that date had existed immediately after redemption, or

- The first date when all of the stock of the corporation becomes worthless.[123]

Example 17.29. X Corp. has 100 shares of voting common stock outstanding (its only class of stock). A owns 60 shares of the X Corp. stock, and B owns 40 shares of the X Corp. stock. A and B are mother and son, respectively. A has a total basis of $6,000 in her 60 shares of X Corp. stock. On January 1, 2013, X Corp. distributes $24,000 to A in redemption of all 60 shares of A's X Corp. stock. Following the redemption, A works for X Corp. as an employee. X Corp. did not contract its business operations in connection with the redemption. X Corp. has $100,000 of Current E&P for 2013 and no Accumulated E&P for prior years. On January 1, 2014, B sells his 40 shares

---

[121] Prop. Reg. § 1.302-5(a)(3).

[122] *Id.*

[123] Prop. Reg. 1.302-5(b)(4).

of X Corp. stock for $16,000 to C, an unrelated individual for purposes of the section 318 constructive stock ownership rules.

Applying the proposed regulations' basis rule to A in Example 17.29:

As in Example 17.28, the redemption is treated as a section 301 distribution because all of the section 302(b) tests are failed. Because X Corp. has enough E&P, the $24,000 distribution is a dividend. The amount of A's basis in the 60 shares of X Corp. stock that are redeemed is treated as a loss from the disposition of this stock — resulting in a $6,000 loss. This loss is deferred until the inclusion date, which occurs on January 1, 2014 when B sells his shares in X Corp. to C: if on the date of the redemption B had not owned any shares of X Corp. stock, then A's redemption would have satisfied the complete termination test under section 302(b)(3). Therefore, A can recognize the $6,000 loss in 2014.

§ 17.05   REDUCTION OF E&P DUE TO REDEMPTIONS

The rules for charging Accumulated E&P due to a redemption depend on whether the redemption is treated as a section 301 distribution or an exchange. If a redemption is treated as a section 301 distribution, then the rules discussed in Chapter 16 apply to determine the reduction to Accumulated E&P. Under these rules, Accumulated E&P is generally reduced by the amount of a distribution.

If a redemption is treated as an exchange, the charge to Accumulated E&P is generally equal to the lesser of:

- The redeemed stock's ratable share of Accumulated E&P at the time of the redemption, or

- The amount distributed to the shareholder on the redemption.[124]

Example 17.30. X Corp. has 100 shares of voting common stock outstanding (its only class of stock). A owns 50 shares of the X Corp. stock, and B owns 50 shares of the X Corp. stock. A and B are unrelated individuals for purposes of the section 318 constructive stock ownership rules. On January 1, 2014, X Corp. distributes $75,000 to A in redemption of all 50 shares of A's X Corp. stock. X Corp. has no Current E&P for 2014 and $100,000 of Accumulated E&P for prior years.

Determining the charge to X Corp.'s E&P in Example 17.30:

Because A has completely terminated her stock interest in X Corp., her redemption qualifies as an exchange under section 302(b)(3). Consequently, the charge to E&P is the lesser of the amount of the distribution, $75,000, or A's 50 shares' ratable portion of the $100,000 of Accumulated E&P. Because A's shares constitute 50 percent of the outstanding stock, their ratable share of the Accumulated E&P is $50,000. Therefore, the charge to Accumulated E&P is $50,000 (the lesser of $75,000 or $50,000).

---

[124] I.R.C. § 312(a), (n)(7). The legislative history to section 312(n)(7) provides that special rules should apply to redemptions of preferred stock and redemptions of common stock where different classes of common stock have different distribution rights. *See* Staff of Joint Committee on Taxation, General Explanation of the Tax Reform Act of 1984, 98th Cong., 2d Sess. 181 (1984).

§ 17.06   REDEMPTIONS AND INTEGRATED TRANSACTIONS

Where redemptions and other transactions involving the stock of the corporation are parts of an integrated plan, the overall result of the integrated transactions will be evaluated for purposes of the section 302(b) tests. This is an application of the step-transaction doctrine. For example, where pursuant to an integrated plan, a shareholder sells a portion of her stock and the corporation redeems the remaining portion of the shareholder's stock, the redemption will qualify for exchange treatment as a complete termination redemption under section 302(b)(3).[125] This should be the case regardless of the order of the steps.[126] Similarly, where pursuant to an integrated plan, a shareholder has a portion of her stock redeemed and other shareholders are issued additional stock, whether the redemption is substantially disproportionate under the section 302(b)(2) test will be determined by taking into account the effect of the stock issuances on the redeemed shareholder's proportionate stock interest in the corporation.[127]

> *Example 17.31.* X Corp. has 100 shares of voting common stock outstanding (its only class of stock). A owns 60 shares of the X Corp. stock, and B owns 40 shares of the X Corp. stock. A and B are unrelated individuals for purposes of the section 318 constructive stock ownership rules. Pursuant to an integrated plan, (i) on January 1, 2014, X Corp. distributes $20,000 to A in redemption of 20 shares of A's X Corp. stock and (ii) on January 15, 2014, X Corp. issues 20 shares of voting common stock to B. X Corp. has no Current E&P for 2014 and $100,000 of Accumulated E&P for prior years.

Determining A's tax consequences on the redemption in Example 17.31:

Because A's redemption and the issuance of stock to B are parts of an integrated plan, the section 302(b) tests are applied by considering the overall effect of these transactions. Prior to the first step in the plan, A owns 60 out of 100 shares of voting common stock of X Corp., or 60%. After the last step in the plan, A owns 40 out of 100 shares of voting common stock, or 40%. Thus, A's redemption satisfies the substantially disproportionate test under section 302(b)(2): after the last step in the plan, A has less than 50 percent of the voting power of the X Corp. stock, and A's percentage of the X Corp. voting and common stock after the last step (40%) is less than 80% of A's percentage of the X Corp. voting and common stock before the first step (80% of 60% = 48%)

---

[125] *See* Zenz v. Quinlivan, 213 F.2d 914 (6th Cir. 1954); Rev. Rul. 55-745, 1955-2 C.B. 223; *cf.* 75-447, 1975-2 C.B. 113 (situation 2) (qualifying for exchange treatment under section 302(b)(2)'s substantially disproportionate redemption test). Qualification under section 302(b)(3) assumes that after the redemption the shareholder does not constructively own stock in the corporation.

[126] *See* Rev. Rul. 75-447, 1975-2 C.B. 113.

[127] Rev. Rul. 75-447 (situation 1), 1975-2 C.B. 113.

§ 17.07 REDEMPTIONS TO PAY DEATH TAXES AND EXPENSES

Besides satisfying a section 302(b) test, a redemption is treated as an exchange under section 303 to the extent that the amount distributed to the shareholder does not exceed the sum of (i) federal and state death taxes and (ii) funeral and administrative expenses that are deductible for federal estate tax purposes,[128] provided the following requirements are met:

- The redeemed stock is included in a decedent's gross estate for federal estate tax purposes;[129]

- The value of all of the stock of the redeeming corporation included in the decedent's gross estate exceeds 35% of the value of the decedent's gross estate (less certain deductible expenses);[130]

- The redemption generally occurs within the statute of limitations for assessing federal estate taxes or within 90 days after the expiration of this period;[131] and

- The redeemed shareholder's interest is reduced directly (or through a binding obligation to contribute) by any payment of federal and state death taxes and deductible funeral and administrative expenses; for the most part, it is the estate that is an eligible shareholder under this requirement.[132]

As a result of the date-of-death basis under section 1014, exchange treatment under section 303 may well result in no gain or loss on the redemption.

> *Example 17.32.* X Corp. has 100 shares of voting common stock outstanding (its only class of stock). A owns 50 shares of X Corp. stock, and B owns 50 shares of X Corp. stock. A and B are mother and daughter, respectively. On January 1, 2014, A dies, and A's 50 shares of X Corp. stock passes to her estate, whose sole beneficiary is B. The 50 shares of X Corp. stock are the only assets of the estate. On February 1, 2014, X Corp. distributes $25,000 to A's estate in redemption of 25 shares of A's X Corp. stock. The federal and estate death taxes resulting from A's death exceed $25,000. The 50 shares of X Corp. stock are included in A's gross estate for federal estate tax purposes, and the shares take a date-of-death adjusted basis of $50,000 under section 1014.

Applying sections 302 and 303 to Example 17.32:

---

[128] I.R.C. § 303(a).

[129] I.R.C. § 303(a).

[130] I.R.C. § 303(b)(2)(A). Under a special aggregation rule, the stock of two or more corporations shall be treated as the stock of a single corporation for purposes of the greater than 35% requirement, provided the decedent's gross estate includes 20% or more of the value of the stock of such corporations. I.R.C. § 303(b)(2)(B).

[131] I.R.C. § 303(b)(1)(A). The time period is extended in situations where a U.S. Tax Court petition is filed with respect to estate taxes and where an election is made under section 6166 to pay estate taxes in installments. I.R.C. § 303(b)(1)(B), (C).

[132] I.R.C. § 303(b)(3).

Because of beneficiary to estate attribution,[133] A's estate owns 100% of the X Corp. stock both before and after the redemption. Consequently, none of the section 302(b) tests are satisfied.[134]

However, the redemption of the estate's 25 shares qualifies for exchange treatment under section 303: (i) the amount distributed is not in excess of federal and state death taxes plus deductible funeral and administrative expenses resulting from A's death — the death taxes exceed the amount distributed in the redemption, (ii) the redeemed stock is included in A's gross estate for federal estate tax purposes; (iii) the value of the X Corp. stock included in A's estate exceeds 35% of the value of A's gross estate — the stock constitutes 100% of A's gross estate; (iv) the redemption occurs within the statute of limitations for assessing federal estate taxes — the redemption occurs one month after A's death, and the statute of limitations does not expire until three years after the estate tax return is filed; and (v) the estate's interest is reduced by any payment of death taxes and deductible funeral and administrative expenses. Consequently, the estate has $0 gain or loss on the redemption of the 25 shares of X Corp. stock ($25,000 amount realized minus the estate's $25,000 stepped-up basis in the shares redeemed[135]).

§ 17.08   STOCK PURCHASES BY RELATED CORPORATIONS TREATED AS REDEMPTIONS

A.   Introduction

In the absence of a special rule, a shareholder who owns a controlling interest in two corporations would be able to receive exchange treatment in a transaction that may well have the economic effect of a dividend by selling stock in one of the corporations to the other corporation.

> *Example 17.33.* A owns all 100 shares of the voting common stock of both X Corp. and Y Corp. (the only class outstanding of each corporation). A has a total basis of $100,000 in both her 100 shares of X Corp. stock and her 100 shares of Y Corp. stock. On January 1, 2014, A sells 50 shares of her X Corp. stock (with a basis of $50,000) to Y Corp. for $200,000. X Corp. and Y Corp. each have no Current E&P for 2014 and $300,000 of Accumulated E&P for prior years.

Without a special rule, in Example 17.33 A would have a gain of $150,000 on the sale of the 50 shares of X Corp. stock to Y Corp. ($200,000 amount realized minus A's basis of $50,000 in the 50 shares sold), which would likely be a capital gain.[136] However, the economic effect of this transaction resembles a dividend in that A is able to extract $200,000 from Y Corp., which has ample E&P, while effectively maintaining the same proportionate stock interest in both Y Corp. and X Corp.

---

[133] I.R.C. § 318(a)(3)(A).

[134] This assumes that neither the partial liquidation test (section 302(b)(4)) nor the regulated investment company test (section 302(b)(5)) is satisfied.

[135] This is ½ of the $50,000 basis in the 50 shares of X Corp. stock that passed from A to the estate.

[136] The stock is likely to be a capital asset in the shareholder's hands. *See* I.R.C. § 1221.

Although A transferred 50 shares of X Corp. to Y Corp., she still controls those shares through her 100% control of Y Corp. And note that because A's sale of X Corp. stock is not a redemption,[137] absent a special rule the transaction receives sale treatment without regard to whether it satisfies a section 302(b) test.

Section 304 addresses this situation by subjecting transactions of this type to the section 302(b) tests to determine whether exchange treatment or section 301 distribution treatment will be accorded. Section 304 applies to two categories of transactions: so-called "brother-sister acquisitions" and "parent-subsidiary acquisitions."

B. Brother-Sister Acquisitions

One situation in which section 304 applies is when:

- One or more persons "control" each of two corporations, and
- One corporation (referred to as the "acquiring corporation") acquires stock in the other corporation (referred to as the "issuing corporation") from the controlling person (or persons) for "property."[138]

"Control" is defined as having at least 50 percent of the voting power of the stock of a corporation or at least 50 percent of the value of the stock of a corporation.[139] For purposes of determining control, stock ownership is determined by using the constructive ownership rules contained in section 318, with some modifications.[140] "Property" includes money, securities and any other property, except stock of the corporation making the distribution,[141] i.e., stock of the acquiring corporation.

When the above requirements are met, the transaction is treated as a *redemption* of stock in the acquiring corporation.[142] Nevertheless, the section 302(b) tests are applied with reference to the controlling person's stock in the issuing corporation.[143]

1. Consequences Where a Section 302(b) Test Is Satisfied

If a section 302(b) test is satisfied with respect to the controlling person's stock interest in the issuing corporation, the disposition of the issuing corporation stock is treated as an exchange,[144] and thus the controlling person has a gain or loss equal to the difference between the controlling person's amount realized on the transaction and that person's basis in the transferred stock. In this case, the acquiring

---

[137] A redemption is where a corporation acquires its stock from a shareholder in exchange for money or other property. I.R.C. § 317(b).

[138] I.R.C. § 304(a)(1).

[139] I.R.C. § 304(c)(1).

[140] I.R.C. § 304(c)(3).

[141] I.R.C. § 317(a).

[142] I.R.C. § 304(a)(1).

[143] I.R.C. § 304(b)(1).

[144] I.R.C. § 302(a).

corporation takes a cost basis in the issuing corporation stock that it acquires, and the controlling person's basis in the stock of the acquiring corporation is unchanged. In short, if a section 302(b) test is satisfied, the tax consequences follow the form of the transaction, i.e., a sale of the issuing corporation stock by the controlling person to the acquiring corporation.

2. Consequences Where All of the Section 302(b) Tests Are Failed

If all of the section 302(b) tests are failed with respect to the controlling person's stock interest in the issuing corporation, the amount received by the controlling person is treated as a section 301 distribution of property.[145] In determining the amount of the dividend on the distribution, the E&P of *both* the acquiring corporation and the issuing corporation is used.[146]

For basis purposes, the transaction is treated as if the controlling person had transferred the issuing corporation stock to the acquiring corporation in a transaction qualifying under section 351.[147] Accordingly, the acquiring corporation's basis in the issuing corporation stock acquired is the same as the basis that the controlling person had in such stock.[148] In addition, the controlling person increases her basis in the stock of the acquiring corporation by the amount of basis she had in the issuing corporation stock that was transferred.[149]

> *Example 17.34.* A owns all 100 shares of the voting common stock of both X Corp. and Y Corp. (the only class outstanding of each corporation). A has a total basis of $100,000 in both her 100 shares of X Corp. stock and her 100 shares of Y Corp. stock. On January 1, 2014, A sells 50 shares of her X Corp. stock (with a basis of $50,000) to Y Corp. for $200,000. X Corp. and Y Corp. each have no Current E&P for 2014 and $100,000 of Accumulated E&P for prior years.

Applying section 304 to Example 17.34:

Section 304 applies because (i) A is in control of X Corp. and Y Corp. (she owns 100% of each) and (ii) Y Corp. (the acquiring corporation) acquires stock in X Corp. (the issuing corporation) from A (the controlling person) for cash (which is property). Thus the transaction is treated as a redemption of Y Corp. stock, and section 302(b) is applied to A's stock interest in X Corp.

Before the transfer of the X Corp. stock, A owns 100% of the stock of X Corp.; after the transfer, A still owns 100% of the stock of X Corp. — 50% of the stock actually and 50% of the stock constructively because the 50 shares of X Corp. stock owned by Y Corp. are attributed to A under corporation to shareholder attribu-

---

[145] I.R.C. § 302(d).

[146] I.R.C. § 304(b)(2).

[147] I.R.C. § 304(a)(1).

[148] I.R.C. § 362(a).

[149] I.R.C. § 358(a)(1).

tion.[150] Therefore, all of the section 302(b) tests are failed,[151] and the transaction is treated as a section 301 distribution of $200,000. The E&P of both Y Corp. and X Corp. is used to determine the amount of the dividend, and because there is a total of $200,000 of E&P, the entire $200,000 distribution is a dividend.

Y Corp.'s basis in the 50 shares of X Corp. stock acquired is $50,000, the same basis that A had in these shares. A's basis in her stock in Y Corp. is increased by $50,000 — the amount of basis that she had in the 50 shares of X Corp. stock transferred to Y Corp.; therefore, A's new basis in her 100 shares of Y Corp. stock is $150,000.

C. Parent-Subsidiary Acquisitions

Another situation in which section 304 applies is when:

- One corporation ("acquiring corporation") acquires from a shareholder of another corporation ("issuing corporation") stock in the issuing corporation for property, and

- The issuing corporation controls the acquiring corporation.[152]

Thus, this other section 304 situation is where a subsidiary corporation acquires stock in its parent corporation from a shareholder of the parent. When this occurs, the transaction is treated as a redemption of stock in the parent corporation,[153] and the section 302(b) tests are applied with reference to the stock in the parent corporation.[154] Following the application of the section 302(b) tests, the possible results are substantially the same as in the brother-sister acquisition context:[155] exchange treatment if a section 302(b) test is satisfied, and section 301 distribution treatment if all of the section 302(b) tests are failed.

---

[150] I.R.C. § 318(a)(2)(C).

[151] This assumes that neither the partial liquidation test (section 302(b)(4)) nor the regulated investment company test (section 302(b)(5)) is satisfied. As pointed out by Professors Bittker and Eustice, it is awkward to apply the partial liquidation test in the context of section 304, because the test would be applied with reference to the issuing corporation stock, while the acquiring corporation is the corporation making the distribution. See Bittker and Eustice, *supra* note 83 at 9-83.

[152] I.R.C. § 304(a)(2). The terms "property" and "control" have the same meaning as stated above.

[153] *Id.*

[154] I.R.C. § 304(b)(1).

[155] The basis results are different in the parent-subsidiary context. The subsidiary takes a cost basis in the parent's stock that it acquires regardless of whether the transaction is treated as an exchange or section 301 distribution. See Rev. Rul. 80-189, 1980-2 C.B. 106. And if the transaction is treated as a section 301 distribution, the shareholder's basis in the transferred stock in the parent is added to the shareholder's basis in other parent stock that the shareholder owns. Treas. Reg. § 1.304-3(a).

Where a situation is both a brother-sister situation and a parent-subsidiary situation, the parent-subsidiary rules take precedence. I.R.C. § 304(a)(1). Such overlap can occur through the application of the section 318 constructive ownership rules. Despite the tie-breaking rule contained in the statute, the regulations under section 304 implicitly assume that brother-sister rules apply in a situation that involves an *actual* brother-sister relationship and *constructive* parent-subsidiary relationship. See Treas. Reg. § 1.304-2(c), Ex. 1; Bittker & Eustice, *supra* note 83 at 9-83.

D.   Section 304 versus Section 351

It is possible for a transaction to meet the requirements of both section 304 and section 351, as illustrated by the following example.

> *Example 17.35.* A owns all 400 shares of the voting common stock of both X Corp. and Y Corp. (the only class outstanding of each corporation). A has a total basis of $300,000 in both her 400 shares of X Corp. stock and her 400 shares of Y Corp. stock. On January 1, 2014, A transfers 200 shares of her X Corp. stock (with fair market value of $200,000 and a basis of $150,000) to Y Corp. for $150,000 in cash and 57 shares of Y Corp. stock with a fair market value of $50,000. X Corp. and Y Corp. each have no Current E&P for 2014 and $100,000 of Accumulated E&P for prior years.

To the extent of A's transfer of the 150 shares of X Corp. stock for $150,000 in cash, section 304 applies because (i) A is in control of X Corp. and Y Corp. (she owns 100% of each) and (ii) Y Corp. (the acquiring corporation) acquires stock in X Corp. (the issuing corporation) from A (the controlling person) for cash (which is property). As in Example 17.34, the amount of cash received by A would be treated as a dividend, resulting in a $150,000 dividend.

In addition, the entire transaction qualifies under section 351. In this regard, A transfers property (stock in X Corp.) to Y Corp., in exchange for stock of Y Corp., and A controls Y Corp. immediately after the exchange (A owns all of the Y Corp. stock). Because A does not receive solely Y Corp. stock in the exchange, under section 351(b) A would have to recognize her realized gain of $50,000 to the extent of the boot received of $150,000, or $50,000 of recognized gain. Because the results under section 351 are different (and in this case better) than the results under section 304, a rule coordinating the applications of the two sections is needed.

Generally, if a transaction meets the requirements of both section 304 and section 351, section 304 will supersede section 351 to the extent that the shareholder receives property in the transaction.[156] Property excludes the stock of the acquiring corporation.[157] Consequently, where both provisions are applicable, section 304 will govern the part of the transaction that consists of the receipt of property for a portion of the issuing corporation stock transferred, while section 351 will govern the part of the transaction that consists of the receipt of stock in the acquiring corporation for a portion of the issuing corporation stock transferred.

Applying this rule to Example 17.35:

Section 304 applies to the extent that A transfers 150 shares of X Corp. stock for $150,000 in cash. As discussed above, this results in a dividend of $150,000. Section 351 applies to the extent that A transfers 50 shares of X Corp. stock in exchange for 57 shares of Y Corp. stock, and A does not recognize any of her realized gain of $12,500[158] on this exchange.

---

[156]   I.R.C. § 304(b)(3)(A).

[157]   I.R.C. § 317(a).

[158]   This is equal to the fair market value of the 57 shares of Y Corp. stock, $50,000, less A's basis of

As an exception to the rule above, section 304 generally will not apply to a liability assumed by the acquiring corporation, or to which stock in the issuing corporation is subject, where the liability was incurred by the transferor to acquire stock in the issuing corporation.[159] Consequently, in this situation, even though the assumption of liabilities by the acquiring corporation is the receipt of property by the shareholder transferring stock in the issuing corporation, section 351, rather than section 304, will generally apply. Because the assumption of liabilities in a section 351 transaction is generally not treated as the receipt of boot,[160] the application of section 351 in this situation would likely result in the nonrecognition of any realized gain on the transaction.

$37,500 in the 50 shares of X Corp. stock transferred (1/4 of the $150,000 basis in A's 200 shares of X Corp. stock transferred).

[159] I.R.C. § 304(b)(3)(B)(i). An exception to the exception is where the stock was acquired from a person whose stock is attributable to the transferor under section 318 (other than option attribution), unless the person satisfies requirements similar to those for waiving family attribution with respect to both the acquiring and issuing corporations. I.R.C. § 304(b)(3)(B)(iii).

[160] *See* I.R.C. § 357(a).

Chapter 18

STOCK DIVIDENDS AND SECTION 306 STOCK

BASIC OVERVIEW

This chapter examines the tax consequences when a corporation distributes its own stock to its shareholders. The chapter also discusses the related topic of "section 306 stock," which is stock subject to special treatment in light of its potential for bailing out earnings via its disposition.

A. General Framework for Treating Stock Distributions as Either Taxable or Nontaxable

Where a corporation distributes its own stock to its shareholders, the distribution may in some situations have no effect on the shareholders' proportionate ownership interest in the corporation, resulting in a mere change in the form of the shareholders' ownership interests. On the other hand, sometimes a stock distribution does affect the shareholders' proportionate interests in the corporation. Section 305 governs the tax consequences of stock distributions, and basically provides that a stock distribution is taxable where it affects the shareholders' proportionate interests, and it is generally not taxable where shareholder's proportionate interests are unaffected.

Specifically, section 305(a) states that except as provided in section 305(b), a corporation's distribution of its own stock is not included in the gross income of a shareholder. As exceptions to section 305(a), section 305(b) provides for five situations where a distribution of a corporation's own stock is treated as a section 301 distribution of property:

- Distributions in lieu of money,[1]
- Disproportionate distributions,[2]
- Distributions of common and preferred stock,[3]
- Distributions on preferred stock,[4]
- Certain distributions of convertible preferred stock.[5]

---

[1] I.R.C. § 305(b)(1).

[2] I.R.C. § 305(b)(2).

[3] I.R.C. § 305(b)(3).

[4] I.R.C. § 305(b)(4).

[5] I.R.C. § 305(b)(5).

B. Taxable Stock Distributions Under Section 305(b)

1. Stock Distributions in Lieu of Money

Under section 305(b)(1), a stock distribution is treated as a section 301 distribution of property if the distribution is payable at the election of any shareholder in either stock or property (which includes money[6]).[7] The theory underlying this provision is that if a shareholder has a choice between receiving stock or money (or other property) and chooses to receive stock, the shareholder is treated as if she first received the cash and then purchased the stock from the corporation.

2. Disproportionate Stock Distributions

Under section 305(b)(2), a stock distribution is treated as a section 301 distribution of property if a distribution or series of distributions has the result of:

- The receipt of property by some shareholders, and
- An increase in the proportionate interests of other shareholders in the assets or E&P of the corporation.

Section 305(b)(2) represents the purest expression of the increase in proportionate interest principle that generally underlies section 305.

Under the regulations, two distributions are treated as part of *a series of distributions* if the distributions are within 36 months of each other, even though they are not made pursuant to a plan calling for the distributions.[8] Distributions separated by more than 36 months are treated as part of a series of distributions only if pursuant to a plan.[9]

3. Distributions of Common and Preferred Stock

Under section 305(b)(3), a stock distribution is treated as a section 301 distribution of property if a distribution or series of distributions has the result of:

- Receipt of preferred stock by some common shareholders, and
- Receipt of common stock by other common shareholders.

The theory underlying this provision is that where its requirements are satisfied, all of the common shareholders receiving stock distributions increase their proportionate interests in the assets or E&P of the corporation: the common shareholders receiving common stock increase their residual interest in corporate assets and earnings, while the common shareholders receiving preferred stock obtain a more senior interest in assets and earnings.[10]

---

[6] I.R.C. § 317(a).

[7] I.R.C. § 305(b)(1).

[8] Treas. Reg. § 1.305-3(b)(4).

[9] *Id.*

[10] Section 305(b)(3) applies whether or not the preferred stock distributed is convertible. Treas. Reg. § 1.305-4(a).

4. Stock Distributions on Preferred Stock

Under section 305(b)(4), any stock distribution with respect to preferred stock is generally treated as a section 301 distribution of property. The underlying theory is that preferred shareholders only have a limited (albeit prior) interest in corporate assets or earnings and that any stock distribution thus increases a preferred shareholder's proportionate interest in the corporation.

5. Distributions of Convertible Preferred Stock

Under section 305(b)(5), a distribution of convertible preferred stock is treated as a section 301 distribution of property, unless it is established that the distribution will *not* have the result of a disproportionate distribution under section 305(b)(2). As discussed earlier, a disproportionate distribution is where a distribution or series of distributions has the result of (i) the receipt of property by some shareholders, and (ii) an increase in the proportionate interests of other shareholders in the assets or E&P of the corporation.

6. Constructive Stock Distribution

Pursuant to section 305(c), the regulations provide that certain transactions are treated as stock distributions for purposes of section 305 with respect to shareholders whose proportionate interests in the assets or E&P of the corporation are increased by the transaction. Such transactions include:

- A change in conversion ratio,
- A change in redemption price,
- A difference between redemption price and issue price,
- A redemption treated as a section 301 distribution, or
- Any similar transaction.[11]

Under the regulations, a transaction deemed to be a stock distribution is treated as a section 301 distributions of property if the transaction has the result described in one of the section 305(b) categories (except for the distributions in lieu of money under section 305(b)(1)).[12] The rules for constructive stock distributions prevent the avoidance of taxable treatment on transactions that in substance increase the proportionate interests of shareholders.

---

[11] Treas. Reg. § 1.305-7(a).

[12] *Id.*

C. Treatment of Taxable and Nontaxable Stock Distributions

1. Taxable Stock Distributions

On a stock distribution that is treated as a section 301 distribution of property, the amount of the distribution is the fair market value of the stock on the date of the distribution.[13] As with other distributions of property, this amount will be treated as a dividend to the extent of the corporation's E&P, and a reduction in stock basis and possible gain to the extent that there is not enough E&P to cover the distribution as a dividend.[14] The shareholder's basis in the stock distributed is its fair market value on the date of the distribution,[15] and the shareholder's holding period in the distributed stock begins on the day following the distribution date.[16]

A corporation recognizes no gain or loss on the distribution of its own stock, whether or not the distribution is taxable to the shareholder.[17] On a taxable stock distribution, the corporation reduces its Accumulated E&P by the fair market value of the stock on the date of the distribution.[18]

2. Nontaxable Stock Distributions

On a stock distribution that is not included in the shareholder's gross income under section 305(a), the amount of the distribution is, of course, irrelevant. Under section 307(a) and its regulations, the shareholder's basis in the stock received ("new stock") in a nontaxable distribution and the basis of the stock with respect to which the distribution was made ("old stock") is generally determined by allocating the original basis in the old stock to the old stock and new stock based on their relative fair market values. The shareholder's holding period in the stock received in a nontaxable stock distribution is determined by tacking the shareholder's holding period in the old stock.[19]

As mentioned above, a corporation recognizes no gain or loss on the distribution of its own stock, whether or not the distribution is taxable to the shareholder.[20] On a nontaxable stock distribution, a corporation does not reduce its Accumulated E&P,[21] which is consistent with the treatment at the shareholder level.

---

[13] Treas. Reg. § 1.305-1(b)(1).

[14] *See* Chapter 16.

[15] I.R.C. § 301(d).

[16] This follows from an application of the normal rule for measuring holding periods. *See* Rev. Rul. 66-7, 1966-1 C.B. 188.

[17] I.R.C. § 311(a)(1).

[18] Treas. Reg. § 1.312-1(d).

[19] I.R.C. § 1223(4).

[20] I.R.C. § 311(a)(1).

[21] I.R.C. § 312(d)(1)(B).

D. Section 306 Stock

1. Preferred Stock Bailout

In the absence of a special rule, a corporation could effectively distribute earnings to its shareholders in a manner that allows for basis offset and capital gain treatment by distributing preferred stock to its shareholders, which is then sold to a third party for cash. To combat the preferred stock bailout, Congress enacted section 306. In general, the provision (i) brands certain stock that is ripe for bailout as "section 306 stock," and (ii) imposes special treatment on the disposition of section 306 stock, which can result in all or a portion of sale (or redemption) proceeds being treated as ordinary income.

2. Definition of Section 306 Stock

The principal category of section 306 stock is stock that meets the following requirements:

- The stock is distributed to the shareholder disposing of such stock,
- The distribution is nontaxable under section 305(a), and
- The stock is *other* than common stock that is distributed with respect to common stock.[22]

Stock distributions meeting the third requirement are (i) common stock distributed on preferred stock, (ii) preferred stock distributed on preferred stock, or (iii) preferred stock distributed on common stock. Of these three distributions, only the third type of distribution also meets the second requirement, as any stock distributed on preferred stock is taxable under section 305(b)(4). Therefore, section 306 stock is ordinarily preferred stock distributed on common stock. Other categories of section 306 stock are examined in the Detailed Analysis.

However, stock falling within any of the categories of section 306 stock is not section 306 stock if the distributing corporation had no Current E&P for the year of the distribution and no Accumulated E&P at the time of the distribution. [23] The rationale for this exception is that distributed stock does not have bailout potential if there are no earnings to bail out.

3. Dispositions of Section 306 Stock

On a disposition of section 306 stock, special rules apply that can result in all or a portion of sale (or redemption) proceeds being treated as ordinary income. There are separate rules for redemptions and dispositions other than redemptions. There are also exceptions to the application of these rules that are discussed in the Detailed Analysis.

In general, on a disposition of section 306 stock that is not a redemption, e.g., a sale to a third party, section 306(a)(1) provides for the following treatment:

---

[22] I.R.C. § 306(c)(1)(A).
[23] I.R.C. § 306(c)(2).

- The amount realized on the disposition is treated as ordinary income to the extent of the stock's ratable share of the amount that would have been a dividend if the corporation had distributed cash equal to the fair market value of the stock at time of distribution.[24] Any ordinary income is treated as a dividend for purposes of applying the preferential capital gain rates that apply to most dividends received by individuals.[25]

- Any remaining portion of the amount realized in excess of the adjusted basis of the stock is treated as gain from the sale of stock.[26]

- If the adjusted basis of the stock exceeds the remaining portion of the amount realized, then no loss is recognized.[27] The unrecovered basis is allocated to the basis of the stock with respect to which the section 306 stock was distributed.[28]

In general, under section 306(a)(2) the amount realized on a redemption of section 306 stock is treated as a section 301 distribution of property.[29] Here, section 301 distribution treatment is "automatic," i.e., without regard to whether the section 302(b) tests are failed.

DETAILED ANALYSIS

§ 18.01 GENERAL FRAMEWORK FOR TREATING STOCK DISTRIBUTIONS AS EITHER TAXABLE OR NONTAXABLE

Where a corporation distributes its own stock to its shareholders, the distribution may in some situations have no effect on the shareholders' proportionate ownership interest in the corporation, resulting in a mere change in the form of the shareholders' ownership interests. This is illustrated by the following example.

Example 18.1. X Corp. has 100 shares of voting common stock outstanding (its only class of stock). A owns 50 shares of X Corp. stock, and B owns 50 shares of X Corp. stock. On January 1, 2014, X Corp. distributes 25 shares of X Corp. voting common stock to each shareholder.

The stock distribution does not affect A and B's proportionate interests in the corporation — before the distribution, each shareholder holds 50 shares out of 100 shares, or 50% of the stock, and after the redemption, each shareholder holds 75 shares out of 150 shares, or 50% of the stock. Thus, the distribution merely affects the form of A and B's stock holdings as they now have more pieces of paper to represent the same ownership interest. Appropriately, the Code treats this

---

[24] I.R.C. § 306(a)(1)(A).

[25] I.R.C. § 306(a)(1)(D). The amount of ordinary income is not treated as a dividend for other purposes under the Code in the absence of regulations providing for such. *Id.*

[26] I.R.C. § 306(a)(1)(B).

[27] I.R.C. § 306(a)(1)(C).

[28] Treas. Reg. § 1.306-1(b)(2), Example 2.

[29] I.R.C. § 306(a)(2).

distribution as nontaxable to the shareholders, the details of which are discussed below.

On the other hand, sometimes a stock distribution does affect the shareholders' proportionate interests in the corporation, as illustrated in the next example.

> *Example 18.2.* X Corp. has 100 shares of voting common stock outstanding (its only class of stock). A owns 50 shares of X Corp. stock, and B owns 50 shares of X Corp. stock. On January 1, 2014, X Corp. distributes 25 shares of X Corp. voting common stock to A and $25,000 of cash to B.

The stock distribution in Example 18.2 does affect the shareholders' proportionate interests in the corporation. As a result of the distribution, A's proportionate interest in the X Corp. stock increases from 50% (50 shares out of 100 shares) to 60% (75 shares out of 125 shares). And correspondingly, B's proportionate interest in the X Corp. stock decreases from 50% (50 shares out of 100 shares) to 40% (50 shares out of 125 shares). Because the stock distribution to A affects the substance of her stock holdings, the Code treats this distribution as taxable to A — more precisely, as a section 301 distribution of property; again, the details will be examined below. Of course, the $25,000 cash distribution to B is also treated as a section 301 distribution of property.

Section 305 governs the tax consequences of stock distributions, and basically follows the principles discussed above: a stock distribution is taxable where it affects the shareholders' proportionate interests, and it is generally not taxable where shareholder's proportionate interests are unaffected. Specifically, section 305(a) states that except as provided in section 305(b), a corporation's distribution of its own stock is not included in the gross income of a shareholder. In addition, section 317(a) provides that a distribution of a corporation's own stock is not treated as a distribution of property for purposes of section 301.

As exceptions to sections 305(a) and 317(a), section 305(b) provides for five situations where a distribution of a corporation's own stock is treated as a section 301 distribution of property:

- Distributions in lieu of money,[30]
- Disproportionate distributions,[31]
- Distributions of common and preferred stock,[32]
- Distributions on preferred stock,[33]
- Certain distributions of convertible preferred stock.[34]

These section 305(b) exceptions are analyzed in the next part.

Treating a stock distribution as a section 301 distribution of property does not always mean that the shareholder receiving the distribution will be taxable on the

---

[30] I.R.C. § 305(b)(1).

[31] I.R.C. § 305(b)(2).

[32] I.R.C. § 305(b)(3).

[33] I.R.C. § 305(b)(4).

[34] I.R.C. § 305(b)(5).

distribution. As with other distributions of property, the amount distributed, which is the fair market value of the stock,[35] will be treated as a dividend to the extent of the corporation's E&P.[36] And where there is not enough E&P to cover the distribution as a dividend, the stock distribution will reduce the shareholder's basis in the stock on which the distribution is made, and result in the recognition of gain to the extent that the non-dividend stock distribution exceeds the shareholder's basis in the underlying stock.[37] The complete consequences of taxable and nontaxable stock distributions are examined below.

§ 18.02   TAXABLE STOCK DISTRIBUTIONS UNDER SECTION 305(b)

A.   Stock Distributions in Lieu of Money

Under section 305(b)(1), a stock distribution is treated as a section 301 distribution of property if the distribution is payable at the election of any shareholder in either stock or property (which includes money[38]).[39] The theory underlying this provision is that if a shareholder has a choice between receiving stock or money (or other property) and chooses to receive stock, the shareholder is treated as if she first received the cash and then purchased the stock from the corporation. Had this actually occurred, the shareholder would have had a section 301 distribution on the receipt of the cash.

> *Example 18.3.* X Corp. has 100 shares of voting common stock outstanding (its only class of stock). A owns 50 shares of X Corp. stock, and B owns 50 shares of X Corp. stock. On January 1, 2014, X Corp. provides A and B with the option of receiving via a distribution either 25 shares of X Corp. voting common stock or $25,000 of cash. Both A and B opt for the stock distribution, and on February 1, 2014, X Corp. distributes to each shareholder 25 shares of X Corp. voting common stock.

Applying section 305(b)(1) to A and B in Example 18.3:

For A and B, the distribution of the 25 shares of X Corp. voting common stock is a section 301 distribution of property because the shareholders were given an option to receive stock or cash. Notice that distributions are taxable even though A and B's proportionate interest in the X Corp. stock is unaffected by the distribution (each shareholder has a 50% stock interest before and after the distribution).

If in Example 18.3 A had been given the option to receive stock or cash but B could only receive stock, the result would still be the same. Section 305(b)(1) only requires that *any* shareholder have the option of receiving stock or property.[40]

----

[35] Treas. Reg. § 1.305-1(b)(1).

[36] *See* Chapter 16.

[37] *See id.*

[38] I.R.C. § 317(a).

[39] I.R.C. § 305(b)(1).

[40] Treas. Reg. § 1.305-2(a)(5).

Therefore, even though only A is given the election, both A and B have taxable stock distributions.

B. Disproportionate Stock Distributions

Under section 305(b)(2), a stock distribution is treated as a section 301 distribution of property if a distribution or series of distributions has the result of:

- The receipt of property by some shareholders, and
- An increase in the proportionate interests of other shareholders in the assets or E&P of the corporation.

Section 305(b)(2) represents the purest expression of the increase in proportionate interest principle that generally underlies section 305.

Under the regulations, two distributions are treated as part of *a series of distributions* if the distributions are within 36 months of each other, even though they are not made pursuant to a plan calling for the distributions.[41] Distributions separated by more than 36 months are treated as part of a series of distributions only if pursuant to a plan.[42]

> *Example 18.4.* X Corp. has 100 shares of voting common stock outstanding (its only class of stock). A owns 50 shares of X Corp. stock, and B owns 50 shares of X Corp. stock. On January 1, 2014, X Corp. distributes 25 shares of X Corp. voting common stock to A and $25,000 of cash to B.

Applying section 305(b)(2) to A in Example 18.4:

The distribution of 25 shares of X Corp. voting common stock to A is a section 301 distribution of property because the result of the distribution is (i) a receipt of property by some shareholders — B receives cash; and (ii) an increase in the proportionate interest of other shareholders in the assets or E&P of the corporation — A's stock interest in the corporation increases from 50% (50 shares out of 100 shares) to 60% (75 shares out of 125 shares).

For purposes of section 305, stock includes rights to acquire stock,[43] and shareholders include holders of stock rights or securities convertible into stock.[44] The following example illustrates these aspects of section 305.

> *Example 18.5.* X Corp. has 100 shares of voting common stock outstanding (its only class of stock), all of which are owned by A. X Corp. also has issued 100 of its bonds, each with a face amount of $1,000 and paying interest at an annual rate of 5%, with each bond convertible into one share of X Corp. voting common stock. B holds all of the X Corp. bonds. On January 1, 2014, X Corp. distributes 100 shares of X Corp. voting common stock to A. During 2014, X Corp. makes the annual interest payments on its bonds.

---

[41] Treas. Reg. § 1.305-3(b)(4).

[42] *Id.*

[43] I.R.C. § 305(d)(1).

[44] I.R.C. § 305(d)(2).

Applying section 305(b)(2) to A in Example 18.5:

The distribution of 100 shares of X Corp. voting common stock to A is a section 301 distribution of property because the result of the distribution is (i) a receipt of property by some shareholders and (ii) an increase in the proportionate interest of other shareholders in the assets or E&P of the corporation.[45] Regarding the first requirement, B, the holder of the X Corp. convertible bonds, is treated as a shareholder,[46] and pursuant to the regulations, her receipt of interest is treated as a distribution of property.[47] Regarding the second requirement, A, the holder of the X Corp. voting common stock, has increased her proportionate interest in the X Corp. stock, given that B's rights to acquire stock by converting the bonds are considered stock;[48] taking into account B's 100 shares of *potential* stock, A's stock interest in the corporation increases from 50% (100 shares out of 200 shares) to 66.67% (200 shares out of 300 shares).

C. Distributions of Common and Preferred Stock

Under section 305(b)(3), a stock distribution is treated as a section 301 distribution of property if a distribution or series of distributions has result of:

- Receipt of preferred stock by some common shareholders, and

- Receipt of common stock by other common shareholders.

The theory underlying this provision is that where its requirements are satisfied, all of the common shareholders receiving stock distributions increase their proportionate interests in the assets or E&P of the corporation: the common shareholders receiving common stock increase their residual interest in corporate assets and earnings, while the common shareholders receiving preferred stock obtain a more senior interest in assets and earnings.[49]

> *Example 18.6.* X Corp. has 100 shares of voting common stock outstanding. A owns 50 shares of X Corp. stock, and B owns 50 shares of X Corp. stock. On January 1, 2014, X Corp. distributes 50 shares of X Corp. voting common stock to A and 100 shares of a new class of nonvoting preferred stock to B.

Applying section 305(b)(3) to A and B in Example 18.6:

The distribution of 50 shares of X Corp. voting common stock to A and 100 shares of nonvoting preferred stock to B are both section 301 distributions of property because the result of the distribution is (i) the receipt of preferred stock by some common shareholders — B; and (ii) the receipt of common stock by other common shareholders — A.

---

[45] *See* I.R.C. § 1.305-3(e), Example 4.

[46] I.R.C. § 305(d)(2).

[47] Treas. Reg. § 1.305-3(b)(3).

[48] I.R.C. § 305(d)(1).

[49] Section 305(b)(3) applies whether or not preferred stock distributed is convertible. Treas. Reg. § 1.305-4(a).

D. Stock Distributions on Preferred Stock

Under section 305(b)(4), any stock distribution with respect to preferred stock is generally treated as a section 301 distribution of property. The underlying theory is that preferred shareholders only have a limited (albeit prior) interest in corporate assets or earnings and that any stock distribution thus increases a preferred shareholder's proportionate interest in the corporation. In this regard, the regulations provide that the distinguishing feature of preferred stock is that it enjoys limited rights to dividends and liquidating distributions and does not participate in corporate growth to a significant extent.[50]

> *Example 18.7.* X Corp. has 100 shares of voting common stock outstanding, all of which are owned by A. X Corp. also has outstanding 100 shares of nonvoting, nonconvertible preferred stock, all of which are owned by B. On January 1, 2014, X Corp. distributes another 100 shares of X Corp. nonvoting, nonconvertible preferred stock to B.

Applying section 305(b)(4) to B in Example 18.7:

The distribution of 100 shares of X Corp. nonvoting, nonconvertible preferred stock to B is a section 301 distribution of property because it is a stock distribution with respect to preferred stock.

As discussed below, certain transactions, including an increase in the conversion ratio of convertible preferred stock, can be treated as constructive stock distributions for purposes of section 305. Thus, an increase in the conversion ratio of convertible preferred stock, as a constructive stock distribution with respect to preferred stock, would generally be treated as a section 301 distribution of property under section 305(b)(4). However, an exception applies where an increase in the conversion ratio of convertible preferred stock is made solely to take account of stock distributions with respect to stock into which convertible stock is convertible.[51] In this case, the increase in the conversion ratio does not add to the preferred shareholders' proportionate interest in the corporation.

> *Example 18.8.* X Corp. has 100 shares of voting common stock outstanding, all of which are owned by A. X Corp. also has outstanding 100 shares of nonvoting, *convertible* preferred stock, which can be converted into X Corp. voting common stock on a one-to-one basis; B owns all of the X Corp. preferred stock. On January 1, 2014, X Corp. distributes another 100 shares of X Corp. voting common stock to A and increases the conversion ratio on the X Corp. preferred stock so that one share of preferred stock can be converted into two shares of common stock.

Applying section 305(b)(4) to B in Example 18.8:

The increase in the conversion ratio of the X Corp. preferred stock is not a section 301 distribution of property because it is done to take account of the X Corp. common stock distributions with respect to the X Corp. common stock. The doubling of the conversion ratio does not add to the preferred shareholder's

---

[50] Treas. Reg. § 1.305-5(a).

[51] I.R.C. § 305(b)(4).

proportionate interest in corporate assets or earnings because the amount of outstanding common stock is also doubled.

The distribution of the X Corp. common stock to A is also not a section 301 distribution of property under section 305(b)(2): there is no increase in A's proportionate interest in corporate assets or earnings because the conversion ratio of the preferred stock is fully adjusted to reflect the distribution.[52]

E. Distributions of Convertible Preferred Stock

Under section 305(b)(5), a distribution of convertible preferred stock is treated as a section 301 distribution of property, unless it is established that the distribution will *not* have the result of a disproportionate distribution under section 305(b)(2). As discussed earlier, a disproportionate distribution is where a distribution or series of distributions has the result of (i) the receipt of property by some shareholders, and (ii) an increase in the proportionate interests of other shareholders in the assets or E&P of the corporation.

According to the regulations, a distribution is likely to result in a disproportionate distribution if:

- The conversion right must be exercised within a relatively short time period, and

- Taking into account the terms and marketability of the convertible preferred stock, it may be anticipated that some shareholders will convert and others will not.[53]

The regulations go on to state that there is no basis for predicting the time and extent to which stock will be converted and it is unlikely that a disproportionate distribution will result if:

- The conversion right may be exercised over many years, and

- The dividend rate is consistent with market conditions at the time of distribution.

Example 18.9.[54] X Corp. has outstanding a class of common stock. On January 1, 2014, X Corp. distributes shares of a new class of preferred stock to its common shareholders. The X Corp. preferred stock is convertible into X Corp. common stock for a period of 20 years from the date of issuance. The preferred stock provides for a dividend rate that is consistent with existing market conditions.

Applying section 305(b)(5) to Example 18.9:

The distribution of the X Corp. convertible preferred stock is not a section 301 distribution of property as it is not likely that a disproportionate distribution will result. This is because it is impossible to predict the extent to which the preferred stock will be converted into common stock given the preferred stock's lengthy

---

[52] *See* Treas. Reg. § 1.305-3(e), Example 4.

[53] Treas. Reg. § 1.305-6(a)(2).

[54] This example is based on Treas. Reg. § 1.305-6(b), Example 1.

conversion period and the normal dividend rate.[55]

> *Example 18.10.*[56] X Corp. has outstanding a class of common stock. On
> January 1, 2014, X Corp. distributes shares of a new class of preferred
> stock to its common shareholders. The X Corp. preferred stock is convert-
> ible into X Corp. common stock for a period of four months from the date
> of issuance at a price slightly above the market price of the X Corp.
> common stock on the date of issuance. Y Corp. has agreed to purchase the
> X Corp. preferred stock from any shareholder who does not want to convert
> her shares. It is anticipated that some shareholders will sell their preferred
> shares to Y Corp. for cash and some will convert, and this is what occurs.

Applying section 305(b)(5) to Example 18.10:

The distribution of the X Corp. convertible preferred stock is a section 301
distribution of property because it results in a disproportionate distribution: the
receipt of cash by shareholders who sell their preferred shares, and an increase in
the proportionate interests of shareholders who convert their preferred shares into
common shares.[57]

F. Constructive Stock Distribution

Pursuant to section 305(c), the regulations provide that certain transactions are
treated as stock distributions for purposes of section 305 with respect to
shareholders whose proportionate interests in the assets or E&P of the
corporation are increased by the transaction. Such transactions include:

- A change in conversion ratio,
- A change in redemption price,
- A difference between redemption price and issue price,
- A redemption treated as a section 301 distribution, or
- Any similar transaction (including a recapitalization[58]).[59]

Under the regulations, a transaction deemed to be a stock distribution is treated as
a section 301 distributions of property if the transaction has the result described in
one of the section 305(b) categories (except for distributions in lieu of money under
section 305(b)(1)).[60] The rules for constructive stock distributions prevent the
avoidance of taxable treatment on transactions that in substance increase the
proportionate interests of shareholders.

> *Example 18.11.* X Corp. has 100 shares of voting common stock outstand-
> ing, all of which are owned by A. X Corp. also has outstanding 100 shares
> of nonvoting, convertible preferred stock, which can be converted into X

---

[55] *See* Treas. Reg. § 1.305-6(b), Example 1.

[56] This example is based on Treas. Reg. § 1.305-6(b), Example 2.

[57] *See* Treas. Reg. § 1.305-6(b), Example 2.

[58] *See* Chapter 21.

[59] I.R.C. § 305(c); Treas. Reg. § 1.305-7(a).

[60] *Id.*

Corp. voting common stock on a one-to-one basis; B owns all of the X Corp. preferred stock. On January 1, 2014, X Corp. increases the conversion ratio on the X Corp. preferred stock so that one share of preferred stock can be converted into two shares of common stock. During 2014, X Corp. pays an annual cash dividend on the voting common stock held by A.

Applying the section 305(c) regulations and section 305(b) to B in Example 18.11:

The increase in the conversion ratio of the X Corp. preferred stock is treated as a stock distribution because it is a transaction listed in the section 305(c) regulations and it increases B's proportionate interest in the assets or E&P of X Corp. — B's *potential* voting common stock interest in the corporation increases from 50% (100 shares out of 200 shares) to 66.67% (200 shares out of 300 shares). The constructive stock distribution is a section 301 distribution of property because it, along with the annual cash dividend on the X Corp. common stock,[61] results in a disproportionate distribution under section 305(b)(2): (i) a receipt of property by some shareholders — A receives cash; and (ii) an increase in the proportionate interest of other shareholders in the assets or E&P of the corporation — B's potential stock interest in the corporation increases.[62]

As mentioned above, a type of transaction that can result in a constructive stock distribution is a redemption treated as a section 301 distribution. Thus, it is possible for a redemption of stock of one shareholder to cause a taxable stock distribution to another shareholder. The following example illustrates this.

Example 18.12. X Corp. has 100 shares of voting common stock outstanding (its only class of stock). A owns 70 shares of X Corp. stock, and B owns 30 shares of X Corp. stock. Pursuant to a plan for periodic redemptions, X Corp. redeems up to 10 percent of each shareholder's stock each year. In 2014, A has five shares of her stock redeemed for cash.

Applying the section 305(c) regulations and section 305(b) to B in Example 18.12:

The redemption of five shares of A's stock is treated as a stock distribution *to B* because it is a transaction listed in the section 305(c) regulations — a redemption treated as a section 301 distribution — and it increases B's proportionate interest in the assets or E&P of X Corp. Regarding the first requirement, the redemption would be treated as a section 301 distribution because none of the section 302(b) tests are satisfied as A's stock interest goes from 70% (70 shares out of 100 shares) to 68.4% (65 shares out of 95 shares).[63] Regarding the second requirement, B's proportionate interest increases as B's stock interest goes from 30% (30 shares out of 100 shares) to 31.6% (30 shares out of 95 shares). This constructive stock distribution is a section 301 distribution of property to B because it results in a disproportionate distribution under section 305(b)(2): (i) a receipt of property by some shareholders — A receives cash on the redemption; and (ii) an increase in the

---

[61] The constructive stock distribution and the annual cash dividend are part of a series of distributions because they are made within 36 months of each other. *See* § 18.02[B].

[62] *See* Treas. Reg. § 1.305-3(e), Example 6.

[63] This assumes that neither the partial liquidation test (section 302(b)(4)) nor the regulated investment company test (section 302(b)(5)) is satisfied.

proportionate interest of other shareholders in the assets or E&P of the corporation — B's stock interest in the corporation increases.[64]

The rule for treating redemptions as stock distributions does not apply to isolated redemptions.[65] Accordingly, if in Example 18.12 the redemption had not been pursuant to a periodic redemption plan but instead had been an isolated redemption, then the redemption would not result in a constructive stock distribution under section 305(c) to which section 305(b)(2) and section 301 apply.[66]

§ 18.03   TREATMENT OF TAXABLE STOCK DISTRIBUTIONS

A.   Shareholder Consequences

On a stock distribution that is treated as a section 301 distribution of property, the amount of the distribution is the fair market value of the stock on the date of the distribution.[67] As with other distributions of property, this amount will be treated as a dividend to the extent of the corporation's E&P, and a reduction in stock basis and possible gain to the extent that there is not enough E&P to cover the distribution as a dividend.[68] The shareholder's basis in the stock distributed is its fair market value on the date of the distribution,[69] and the shareholder's holding period in the distributed stock begins on the day following the distribution date.[70]

B.   Corporation Consequences

A corporation recognizes no gain or loss on the distribution of its own stock, whether or not the distribution is taxable to the shareholder.[71] On a taxable stock distribution, the corporation reduces its Accumulated E&P by the fair market value of the stock on the date of the distribution.[72] This is consistent with the treatment of the stock distribution at the shareholder level.

---

[64] *See* Treas. Reg. § 1.305-3(e), Example 8; Rev. Rul. 78-60, 1978-1 C.B. 81.

[65] Treas. Reg. § 1.305-3(b)(3).

[66] *See* Treas. Reg. § 1.305-3(e), Example 10.

[67] Treas. Reg. § 1.305-1(b)(1).

[68] *See* Chapter 16.

[69] I.R.C. § 301(d).

[70] This follows from an application of the normal rule for measuring holding periods. *See* Rev. Rul. 66-7, 1966-1 C.B. 188.

[71] I.R.C. § 311(a)(1).

[72] Treas. Reg. § 1.312-1(d).

§ 18.04   TREATMENT OF NONTAXABLE STOCK DISTRIBUTIONS

A.   Shareholder Consequences

On a stock distribution that is not included in the shareholder's gross income under section 305(a), the amount of the distribution is, of course, irrelevant. Under section 307(a) and its regulations, the shareholder's basis in the stock received ("new stock") in a nontaxable distribution and the basis of the stock with respect to which the distribution was made ("old stock") is generally determined by applying the following rule:

basis of new stock =

$$\text{original basis of old stock} \quad \times \quad \frac{\text{fair market value of new stock on distribution date}}{\substack{\text{sum of fair market values of new stock and old stock on} \\ \text{distribution date}}}$$

new basis of old stock =

$$\text{original basis of old stock} \quad \times \quad \frac{\text{fair market value of old stock on distribution date}}{\substack{\text{sum of fair market values of new stock and old stock on} \\ \text{distribution date[73]}}}$$

An exception applies in the case of a distribution of rights to acquire stock with a fair market value on the distribution date of less than 15% of the fair market value of the old stock on the distribution date.[74] Under this exception, the shareholder's basis in the stock rights is zero, unless the shareholder elects to allocate basis to the stock rights under the general rule.[75]

The shareholder's holding period in the stock received in a nontaxable stock distribution is determined by tacking the shareholder's holding period in the old stock.[76] Thus, for purposes of both basis and holding period, the stock received in a nontaxable distribution is treated as a continuation of the stock with respect to which the distribution was made.

> *Example 18.13.* X Corp. has 100 shares of common stock outstanding (the only class outstanding), all of which are owned by A. A's basis in her 100 shares of X Corp. common stock is $50,000, and she has held the stock for 2 years. On January 1, 2014, X Corp. distributes 100 shares of a new class of X Corp. nonconvertible preferred stock to A. As of January 1, 2014, the fair market value of the X Corp common stock is $75,000 and the fair market value of the X Corp. preferred stock is $25,000.

Applying sections 305, 307 and 1223(4) to A in Example 18.13:

---

[73] Treas. Reg. § 1.307-1(a).

[74] I.R.C. § 307(b).

[75] *Id.*

[76] I.R.C. § 1223(4).

The distribution of the X Corp. nonconvertible preferred stock is not included in A's gross income pursuant to section 305(a), because the distribution does not fall within any of the section 305(b) categories. In particular, the transaction is not a disproportionate distribution under section 305(b)(2) because A's proportionate interest in the assets or E&P of X Corp. is not increased by the distribution: although some of A's stock interest is more senior as compared to her other stock interest, A continues to have an interest in all of the assets and earnings of the corporation after the distribution.

Because A's receipt of the X Corp. nonconvertible preferred stock is nontaxable, A's basis in this stock will be determined by applying the rule provided in section 307 and its regulations:

$$\text{basis of preferred stock} = \text{original basis of common stock} \times \frac{\text{fair market value of preferred stock on distribution date}}{\text{sum of fair market values of preferred stock and common stock on distribution date}}$$

$$\$50,000 \times \frac{\$25,000}{\$25,000 + \$75,000} = \mathbf{\$12,500}$$

And A's new basis in the X Corp. common stock is equal to:

$$\text{original basis of common stock} \times \frac{\text{fair market value of common stock on distribution date}}{\text{sum of fair market values of preferred stock and common stock on distribution date}}$$

$$\$50,000 \times \frac{\$75,000}{\$25,000 + \$75,000} = \mathbf{\$37,500}$$

Under section 1223(4), A will take a tacked holding period in the X Corp. preferred stock. Accordingly, A's holding period in the preferred stock will include the two-year period that A held the X Corp. common stock.

B. Corporation Consequences

As mentioned above, a corporation recognizes no gain or loss on the distribution of its own stock, whether or not the distribution is taxable to the shareholder.[77] On a nontaxable stock distribution, a corporation does not reduce its Accumulated E&P,[78] which is consistent with the treatment at the shareholder level.

---

[77] I.R.C. § 311(a)(1).

[78] I.R.C. § 312(d)(1)(B).

§ 18.05   SECTION 306 STOCK

A.   Background: Preferred Stock Bailout

In the absence of a special rule, a corporation could effectively distribute earnings to its shareholders in a manner that allows for basis offset and capital gain treatment by distributing preferred stock to its shareholders, which is then sold to a third party for cash. The following example illustrates the so-called preferred stock bailout.

> *Example 18.14.* X Corp. has 100 shares of common stock outstanding (the only class outstanding), all of which are owned by A. A's basis in her 100 shares of X Corp. common stock is $50,000, and she has held the stock for 2 years. On January 1, 2014, X Corp. distributes 100 shares of a new class of X Corp. nonconvertible preferred stock to A. As of January 1, 2014, the fair market value of the X Corp common stock is $75,000 and the fair market value of the X Corp. preferred stock is $25,000. X Corp. has $50,000 of Current E&P for 2014 and no Accumulated E&P for prior years. On January 1, 2015, A sells the 100 shares of X Corp. nonconvertible preferred stock to Y Corp., an unrelated corporation, for $25,000.

As in Example 18.13, A's receipt of the X Corp. nonconvertible preferred stock is nontaxable, and A takes a $12,500 in the preferred stock. Without a special rule, upon the sale of the preferred stock to Y Corp., A would have a gain of $12,500 (amount realized of $25,000 minus A's basis of $12,500), which would likely be a capital gain. However, the economic effect of the transaction is similar to a $25,000 dividend, in that A has received $25,000 in cash and her proportionate interest in the corporation remains largely unchanged. While A has relinquished some interest in corporate assets and earnings by transferring the preferred stock to Y Corp., the reduction in interest is likely not significant given that a preferred shareholder typically has a limited interest in corporate assets and earnings, like that of a holder of corporate debt. Moreover, if the preferred stock were redeemed at some point, there would ultimately be no reduction in the common shareholder's proportionate interest.

To combat the preferred stock bailout, Congress enacted section 306.[79] In general, the provision (i) brands certain stock that is ripe for bailout as "section 306 stock," and (ii) imposes special treatment on the disposition of section 306 stock, which can result in all or a portion of sale (or redemption) proceeds being treated as ordinary income.

The significance of section 306 is somewhat diminished today. The traditional benefits of the preferred stock bailout are basis offset and the application of preferential capital gain rates, but because most dividends received by individuals

---

[79] Prior to the enactment of section 306, the Service unsuccessfully attempted to have the courts determine that the distribution of preferred stock in a situation similar to that in Example 18.14 should be taxable as ordinary income. *See* Chamberlin v. Commissioner, 207 F.2d 462 (6th Cir. 1953), *cert. denied*, 347 U.S. 918 (1954).

today are taxed at preferential capital gain rates,[80] only the former benefit remains in the case of individual shareholders. Consequently, there is less of an incentive under current law to use the preferred stock bailout. Nevertheless, because section 306 can prevent basis offset on the disposition of stock that is tainted under the provision, section 306 can still cause an increase in a shareholder's tax liability. These and other aspects are examined below.

B. Definition of Section 306 Stock

1. Principal Category

The principal category of section 306 stock is stock that meets the following requirements:

- The stock is distributed to the shareholder disposing of such stock,
- The distribution is nontaxable under section 305(a), and
- The stock is *other* than common stock that is distributed with respect to common stock.[81]

Stock distributions meeting the third requirement are (i) common stock distributed on preferred stock, (ii) preferred stock distributed on preferred stock, or (iii) preferred stock distributed on common stock. Of these three distributions, only the third type of distribution also meets the second requirement, as any stock distributed on preferred stock is taxable under section 305(b)(4). Therefore, section 306 stock is ordinarily preferred stock distributed on common stock. In Example 18.14, the 100 shares of X Corp. nonconvertible preferred stock sold by A is section 306 stock, because it is distributed to A in a nontaxable distribution and the distribution is other than common stock on common stock.

Preferred stock is targeted for section 306 treatment because it is ripe for bailout: preferred stock usually can be sold without reducing a shareholder's participation in corporate growth, given that such stock typically provides for limited rights to assets and earnings. In this regard, the Service focuses on whether stock has a realistic and unrestricted opportunity to participate in corporate growth in determining whether stock is common stock and thus excluded from the principal category of section 306 stock.[82]

2. Stock with Basis Determined with Reference to Section 306 Stock

Pursuant to section 306(c)(1)(C), another category of section 306 stock is stock the basis of which is determined with reference to the basis of section 306 stock. Accordingly, where the basis of the shareholder disposing of the stock is determined with reference to the basis that another person had in section 306 stock (a

---

[80] *See* Chapter 16.

[81] I.R.C. § 306(c)(1)(A).

[82] Rev. Rul. 79-163, 1979-1 C.B. 131.

transferred basis), the stock with a transferred basis is section 306 stock.[83] And where the basis of the shareholder disposing of the stock is determined with reference to the basis that the shareholder had in section 306 stock (an exchanged basis), the stock with an exchanged basis is section 306 stock.[84]

> *Example 18.15.* X Corp. has 100 shares of common stock outstanding (the only class outstanding), all of which are owned by A. A's basis in her 100 shares of X Corp. common stock is $50,000, and she has held the stock for 2 years. On January 1, 2014, X Corp. distributes 100 shares of a new class of X Corp. nonconvertible preferred stock to A. As of January 1, 2014, the fair market value of the X Corp. common stock is $75,000 and the fair market value of the X Corp. preferred stock is $25,000. X Corp. has $50,000 of Current E&P for 2014 and no Accumulated E&P for prior years. On January 1, 2015, A transfers the 100 shares of X Corp. nonconvertible preferred stock to Y Corp., in exchange for all 100 shares of Y Corp. common stock (the only class outstanding).

Applying section 306(c)(1)(C) to Example 18.15:

As in Example 18.14, the 100 shares of X Corp. nonconvertible preferred stock received by A is section 306 stock, because it is distributed to A in a nontaxable distribution and the distribution is other than common stock on common stock. And as in Example 18.14, A takes a $12,500 basis in this stock.

The transfer of the 100 shares of X Corp. nonconvertible preferred stock to Y Corp. qualifies for nonrecognition under section 351(a).[85] Under section 358(a), A takes an exchanged basis of $12,500 in the 100 shares of Y Corp. common stock received in the exchange — the same basis that A had in the X Corp. preferred stock.[86] Under section 362(a), Y Corp. takes a transferred basis of $12,500 in the X Corp. preferred stock received in the exchange — the same basis that A had in the stock.[87]

Under section 306(c)(1)(C), the Y Corp. common stock is section 306 stock in A's hands, because A takes an exchanged basis in the stock that is determined with reference to the basis of section 306 stock (the X Corp. preferred stock).[88] Thus, common stock can be section 306 stock under this provision. Under section 306(c)(1)(C), the X Corp. preferred stock is section 306 stock in Y Corp.'s hands, because Y Corp. takes a transferred basis in the stock that is determined with reference to the basis of section 306 stock (the X Corp. preferred stock).[89] As can be inferred from this example, section 306(c)(1)(C) prevents shareholders from removing the taint of section 306 by transferring the stock to controlled corpora-

---

[83] I.R.C. § 306(c)(1)(C).

[84] *Id.*

[85] *See* Chapter 14.

[86] *See id.*

[87] *See id.*

[88] Treas. Reg. § 1.306-3(e).

[89] *Id.*

tions.[90]

3. Certain Stock Received in Reorganizations

Section 306 stock also includes stock:

- Which is not common stock,

- Which is received in a reorganization[91] or section 355 transaction,[92] and

- With respect to the receipt of which, gain or loss was not recognized in whole or in part,

- "[B]ut only to the extent that either the effect of the transaction was substantially the same as a stock dividend, or the stock was received in exchange for section 306 stock."[93]

The regulations provide that a transaction has substantially the same effect of a stock dividend if cash received in lieu of stock would have resulted in a dividend in the reorganization or section 355 transaction.[94] Dividends in connection with reorganizations or section 355 transactions are examined in Chapters 21 and 22.

4. Certain Stock Received in Section 351 Transactions

A final category of section 306 stock is stock:

- Which is not common stock, and

- Which is acquired in a section 351 transaction,

- Provided money received in lieu of the stock would have been treated as a dividend to any extent.[95]

The following example demonstrates the purpose for this category of section 306 stock along with its application.

Example 18.16. A owns all 400 shares of the voting common stock of both X Corp. and Y Corp. (the only class outstanding of each corporation). A has a basis of $300,000 in both her 400 shares of X Corp. stock and her 400 shares of Y Corp. stock. On January 1, 2014, A transfers 200 shares of her X Corp. stock (with a fair market value of $200,000 and a basis of $150,000) to Y Corp. for 57 shares of Y Corp. common stock with a fair market value of $50,000 and 100 shares of a new class of Y Corp. nonconvertible preferred

---

[90] The provision would also prevent the removal of the taint where section 306 stock is transferred as a gift, because the donee would take a transferred basis in the stock under section 1015. However, on the transfer of section 306 stock upon the death of a person, the stock ceases to be section 306 stock in the hands of the transferee because the transferee takes a fair market basis in the stock under section 1014. Treas. Reg. § 1.306-3(e).

[91] *See* Chapter 21.

[92] *See* Chapter 22.

[93] I.R.C. § 306(c)(1)(B).

[94] Treas. Reg. § 1.306-3(d).

[95] I.R.C. § 306(c)(3).

stock with a fair market value of $150,000. X Corp. and Y Corp. each have no Current E&P for 2014 and $100,000 of Accumulated E&P for prior years.

Application of section 306(c)(3) to Example 18.16:

As indicated in the solution to Example 17.34, if A had received $150,000 in cash from Y Corp. in lieu of the Y Corp. preferred stock, section 304 would have applied and resulted in a $150,000 dividend to A.[96] However, on the facts of the current example, section 304 does not apply because A has received only stock of Y Corp., which is not property for purposes of section 304.[97] Instead, section 351 applies to A's receipt of the Y Corp. common and preferred stock in exchange for the X Corp. common stock, and thus A recognizes no dividend as well as no gain or loss.[98] In the absence of a special rule, A could then sell the Y Corp. preferred stock to a third party for cash, and receive basis offset and capital gain treatment even though the economic effect would be similar to a cash dividend.

Section 306(c)(3) prevents this result by branding the Y Corp. preferred stock as section 306 stock. Here this provision applies to the Y Corp. preferred stock received by A because it is (i) not common stock, (ii) acquired in a section 351 transaction, and (iii) the receipt of money in lieu of Y Corp. preferred stock would have been treated as a dividend under section 304.

5. Exception to Section 306 Stock Where No E&P

Stock falling within any of the categories of section 306 stock is, however, excepted from the definition of section 306 stock if a distribution of cash in lieu of the stock would not have been a dividend in whole or in part.[99] In other words, stock is not section 306 stock if the distributing corporation had no Current E&P for the year of the distribution and no Accumulated E&P at the time of the distribution. The rationale for this exception is that distributed stock does not have bail out potential if there are no earnings to bail out.

C. Dispositions of Section 306 Stock

On a disposition of section 306 stock, special rules apply that can result in all or a portion of the sale (or redemption) proceeds being treated as ordinary income. There are separate rules for redemptions and dispositions other than redemptions. There are also exceptions to the application of these rules.

---

[96] *See* § 17.08.

[97] I.R.C. § 317(a).

[98] A transfers property (stock in X Corp.) to Y Corp., in exchange for the stock of Y Corp., and A controls Y Corp. immediately after the exchange (A owns all of the Y Corp. stock). I.R.C. § 351(a).

[99] I.R.C. § 306(c)(2).

1. Dispositions Other than Redemptions

Subject to exceptions discussed below, on a disposition of section 306 stock that is not a redemption, e.g., a sale to a third party, section 306(a)(1) provides for the following treatment:

1. The amount realized on the disposition is treated as ordinary income to the extent of the stock's ratable share of the amount that would have been a dividend if the corporation had distributed cash equal to the fair market value of the stock at time of distribution.[100] Any ordinary income is treated as a dividend for purposes of applying the preferential capital gain rates that apply to most dividends received by individuals.[101]

2. Any remaining portion of the amount realized in excess of the adjusted basis of the stock is treated as gain from the sale of stock.[102]

3. If the adjusted basis of the stock exceeds the remaining portion of the amount realized, then no loss is recognized.[103] The unrecovered basis is allocated to the basis of the stock with respect to which the section 306 stock was distributed.[104]

Except for timing, this special treatment can place a shareholder upon a sale of section 306 stock in the same position as if cash instead of the section 306 stock had been distributed.

> *Example 18.17.* X Corp. has 100 shares of common stock outstanding (the only class outstanding), all of which are owned by A. A's basis in her 100 shares of X Corp. common stock is $50,000, and she has held the stock for 2 years. On January 1, 2014, X Corp. distributes 100 shares of a new class of X Corp. nonconvertible preferred stock to A. As of January 1, 2014, the fair market value of the X Corp common stock is $75,000 and the fair market value of the X Corp. preferred stock is $25,000. X Corp. has $50,000 of Current E&P for 2014 and no Accumulated E&P for prior years. On January 1, 2015, A sells the 100 shares of X Corp. nonconvertible preferred stock to Y Corp., an unrelated corporation, for $25,000. X Corp. has $10,000 of Current E&P for 2015 and no Accumulated E&P for prior years.

Applying the section 306(a)(1) to A in Example 18.17:

As in Example 18.14, the 100 shares of X Corp. nonconvertible preferred stock sold by A is section 306 stock, and A has a $12,500 basis in this stock. Under the first part of the rule above, A's $25,000 amount realized on the sale is all ordinary income because a $25,000 cash distribution (which is equal to the fair market value of the section 306 stock at the time of distribution) would have been a dividend (X Corp.

---

[100] I.R.C. § 306(a)(1)(A).

[101] I.R.C. § 306(a)(1)(D). The amount of ordinary income is not treated as a dividend for other purposes under the Code in the absence of regulations providing for such. *Id.*

[102] I.R.C. § 306(a)(1)(B).

[103] I.R.C. § 306(a)(1)(C).

[104] Treas. Reg. § 1.306-1(b)(2), Example 2.

has $50,000 of Current E&P for 2014).[105] Because the entire amount realized is ordinary income, there is no remaining portion of the amount realized to trigger gain under the second part of the rule. Because A was not permitted to offset her $12,500 basis in the section 306 stock against the amount realized, and is not permitted to recognize a loss under the third part of the rule, she has unrecovered basis of $12,500. This amount is added to her basis in the X Corp. common stock (the stock with respect to which the section 306 stock was distributed), increasing A's basis in the X Corp. common stock from $37,500 to $50,000, which was its basis prior to the distribution of the section 306 stock.

Except for timing (2015 v. 2014), A's consequences are the same as if X Corp. had distributed $25,000 of cash to A instead of preferred stock.[106] And even though the ordinary income here would likely be taxed using the preferential capital gain rates,[107] section 306 increases A's tax liability by denying A the ability to offset her basis in the preferred stock.

> *Example 18.18.* X Corp. has 100 shares of common stock outstanding (the only class outstanding), all of which are owned by A. A's basis in her 100 shares of X Corp. common stock is $50,000, and she has held the stock for 2 years. On January 1, 2014, X Corp. distributes 100 shares of a new class of X Corp. nonconvertible preferred stock to A. As of January 1, 2014, the fair market value of the X Corp common stock is $75,000 and the fair market value of the X Corp. preferred stock is $25,000. For 2014, X Corp. has $50,000 of Current E&P and no Accumulated E&P for prior years. On January 1, 2016, A sells the 100 shares of X Corp. nonconvertible preferred stock to Y Corp., an unrelated corporation, for *$40,000*.

Applying the section 306(a)(1) to A in Example 18.18:

Under the first part of the rule, $25,000 of A's $40,000 amount realized on the sale is ordinary income because a $25,000 cash distribution (which is equal to the fair market value of the section 306 stock at the time of distribution) would have been a dividend (X Corp. has $50,000 of Current E&P for 2014). A has $2,500 of gain (presumably capital gain) from the sale of the stock under the second part of the rule: the excess of A's remaining portion of the amount realized, $15,000, over A's adjusted basis in the section 306 stock, $12,500. And A has no unrecovered basis for purposes of the third part of the rule.

Assuming that the $25,000 of ordinary income is subject to the preferential capital gain rates,[108] the results to A would be substantially the same whether or not section 306 applies: $27,500 of gross income that is subject to preferential capital

---

[105] Note that the amount of the corporation's E&P for the year of the disposition is irrelevant in applying the special section 306 treatment to non-redemption dispositions. As will be seen below, this is not the case for redemptions of section 306 stock.

[106] X Corp. does not reduce its Accumulated E&P by the amount of ordinary income under section 306. This is because this amount is not a dividend for purposes other than the application of preferential capital gain rates (in the absence of regulations, which currently do not exist). I.R.C. § 306(a)(1)(D).

[107] *See* Chapter 16.

[108] As discussed in Chapter 16, some dividends received by individuals are excluded from the application of preferential capital gain rates.

gain rates.[109] Thus, in this situation section 306 has little effect on A's tax liability on the sale.[110]

2. Redemptions

Subject to exceptions discussed below,[111] under section 306(a)(2) the amount realized on a redemption of section 306 stock is treated as a section 301 distribution of property.[112] Here, section 301 distribution treatment is "automatic," i.e., without regard to whether the section 302(b) tests are failed. The apparent rationale for this treatment is that because the parties have used two transactions — a distribution and redemption — to accomplish a cash distribution, the transactions are collapsed and treated as a single event.[113] Because the section 301 distribution is occurring in the year of the redemption, the relevant E&P for characterizing the distribution as a dividend is the E&P for the year of the redemption, not the E&P for year that the section 306 stock was distributed.

> *Example 18.19.* X Corp. has 100 shares of common stock outstanding (the only class outstanding), all of which are owned by A. A's basis in her 100 shares of X Corp. common stock is $50,000, and she has held the stock for 2 years. On January 1, 2014, X Corp. distributes 100 shares of a new class of X Corp. nonconvertible preferred stock to A. As of January 1, 2014, the fair market value of the X Corp common stock is $75,000 and the fair market value of the X Corp. preferred stock is $25,000. X Corp. has $1,000 of Current E&P for 2014 and no Accumulated E&P for prior years. On January 1, 2016, X Corp. redeems A's 100 shares of preferred stock for $40,000. X Corp. has $50,000 of Current E&P for 2016 and no Accumulated E&P for prior years.

Applying section 306(a)(2) to A in Example 18.19:

As in prior examples, the 100 shares of X Corp. nonconvertible preferred stock is section 306 stock, and A has a $12,500 basis in this stock. The redemption of the stock is treated as a section 301 distribution of $40,000. The entire distribution is a dividend, as X Corp. has $50,000 of E&P for 2016, the year of the cash distribution. Note that the $1,000 of E&P for 2014, the year that the section 306 stock was distributed, is not relevant to the result here.

---

[109] Without section 306, on the sale A would have a gain of $27,500 ($40,000 amount realized minus $12,500 basis), which presumably would be a long-term capital gain taxed at preferential rates.

[110] In this situation, section 306 could still have some effect if A's capital losses for the year exceeded the limitation under section 1211(b), which generally provides that an individual's capital losses for a year are deductible to the extent of the capital gains for the year plus $3,000. With section 306 applying, $25,000 of the income on the transaction is ordinary income, which does not increase the amount of capital losses that are deductible under section 1211(b). Without section 306, the $25,000 would presumably be capital gain, and thereby allow for a larger limitation under section 1211(b).

[111] *See* § 18.05[C][3}.

[112] I.R.C. § 306(a)(2).

[113] *See* Stephen Schwarz and Daniel J. Lathrope, Fundamentals of Corporate Taxation 308 (2012).

3. Dispositions Exempt from Section 306 Treatment

Under section 306(b), certain dispositions of section 306 stock are exempt from the application of the special rules contained in section 306(a):

- A disposition other than a redemption that completely terminates a shareholder's stock interest in the corporation. The section 318 constructive stock ownership rules apply for this purpose.[114]

- A redemption that satisfies either the section 302(b)(3) complete termination test or the section 302(b)(4) partial liquidation test.[115]

- A disposition in the complete liquidation of the corporation under section 331.[116]

- A disposition in which gain or loss is not recognized.[117]

- If it is established that the following was not pursuant to a plan having tax avoidance as one of its principal purposes:

    - The distribution of the section 306 stock, and its disposition or redemption; or

    - In the case of a prior or simultaneous disposition (or redemption) of stock with respect to which the section 306 stock was distributed, the disposition or redemption of the section 306 stock.[118]

The rationale for exempting these dispositions is that they do not provide for opportunities to bail out earnings. For example, where a shareholder has completely terminated her interest in a corporation, the receipt of cash upon the disposition of section 306 stock does not resemble a dividend, and likewise in the case of a complete liquidation. Partial liquidations are excluded from section 306 treatment because Congress concluded that contractions of corporate business are not considered means for bailing out earnings.[119]

---

[114] I.R.C. § 306(b)(1)(A).

[115] I.R.C. § 306(b)(1)(B). For a discussion of the section 302(b)(3) complete termination test, see § 17.03[B]. For a discussion of the section 302(b)(4) partial liquidation test, see § 17.03[C].

[116] I.R.C. § 306(b)(2). Complete liquidations under section 331 are discussed in Chapter 19.

[117] I.R.C. § 306(b)(3).

[118] I.R.C. § 306(b)(4).

[119] *See* S. Rep. No. 1622, 83d Cong., 2d Sess. 243 (1954).

Chapter 19

COMPLETE LIQUIDATIONS AND TAXABLE ACQUISITIONS

BASIC OVERVIEW

This chapter examines the tax treatment to the shareholders and corporation upon a complete liquidation of a corporation, and in particular, the two categories of complete liquidations: taxable liquidations and nontaxable parent-subsidiary liquidations. The chapter also discusses the related topic of taxable acquisitions, including elections under section 338.

A. Taxable Liquidations

1. Shareholder Consequences

Under section 331(a), the amount received by a shareholder upon the liquidation of a corporation is treated as payment in full in exchange for the shareholder's stock. Accordingly, on a complete liquidation, the shareholder offsets her basis in the stock against the amounts distributed and, except as provided in section 332,[1] the resulting gain or loss is recognized and likely is capital gain or loss.[2] Liquidations in which the shareholder realizes and recognizes gain or loss under section 331 can be referred to as taxable liquidations. Under section 334(a), a shareholder's basis in property distributed in a taxable liquidation is the property's fair market value at the time of the distribution.

2. Corporation Consequences

Subject to a few exceptions, under section 336(a) a liquidating corporation recognizes gain or loss on a distribution of property in a complete liquidation as if the corporation sold the property to the shareholder for its fair market value. The section 336(a) recognition rule does not apply to nontaxable parent-subsidiary liquidations,[3] discussed below. In addition, there are two limitations on the recognition of losses, described below.

First, under section 336(d)(1) a corporation does not recognize a loss on a liquidating distribution of property to a "related person" if:

- The distribution is not pro rata, or

---

[1] Section 332, which provides nonrecognition treatment for parent-subsidiary liquidations, is discussed below.

[2] The stock is likely to be a capital asset in the shareholder's hands. I.R.C. § 1221.

[3] I.R.C. § 337.

- The distributed property is "disqualified property."[4]

A "related person" is within the meaning of section 267, and includes (among other persons) a shareholder who owns (actually or constructively) more than 50% in value of the outstanding stock of the liquidating corporation.[5] A distribution is not pro rata where a shareholder receives an interest in the distributed property that is disproportionate to the shareholder's stock interest — for example, a shareholder with a 30% stock interest receives the entire interest in particular asset. "Disqualified property" is property acquired by the distributing corporation either in a section 351 transaction or as a contribution to capital during the five-year period ending on the date of the distribution.[6]

Second, section 336(d)(2) provides that for purposes of determining the amount of recognized loss by a liquidating corporation on a distribution, sale or exchange of certain property, the corporation must reduce its basis in the property by the excess of:

- The adjusted basis of the property in the hands of the corporation immediately after its acquisition, over

- The fair market value of the property at that time.[7]

The section 336(d)(2) basis reduction rule applies to property:

- That is acquired by the liquidating corporation in a section 351 transaction or as contribution to capital, and

- The acquisition was part of a plan a principal purpose of which was to recognize a loss by the corporation in connection with the liquidation.

B. Nontaxable Parent-Subsidiary Liquidations

1. Shareholder Consequences

Under section 332, a parent corporation recognizes no gain or loss on receipt of property distributed in the complete liquidation of a subsidiary corporation, provided:

- The parent corporation owns at least 80% of the voting power and total value of the subsidiary corporation's stock from the date of adoption of the liquidation plan until the final distribution, and

- The subsidiary corporation distributes all of its assets within:

  - One taxable year, pursuant to a plan, or

  - Three years after the close of the first taxable year in which a liquidating distribution is made, pursuant to a plan calling for the

---

[4] I.R.C. § 336(d)(1)(A).

[5] *See* I.R.C. § 267(b)(2).

[6] I.R.C. § 336(d)(1)(B).

[7] I.R.C. § 336(d)(2)(A).

completion of the liquidation within such three-year period.[8]

Under section 334(b), the parent corporation's basis in the property received in a section 332 liquidation is generally the same as the subsidiary corporation's basis in the property.[9] Under section 381, the parent corporation in a section 332 liquidation inherits the E&P of the subsidiary corporation (along with other corporate attributes).[10]

Because a parent corporation in a section 332 liquidation does not need to own all of the stock of the subsidiary corporation, it is possible that the subsidiary will have other shareholders, which can be referred to as minority shareholders. Minority shareholders in a section 332 liquidation are treated the same as shareholders in a taxable section 331 liquidation. Thus, under section 331(a), the amount received by a minority shareholder in the liquidation is treated as payment in full in exchange for the shareholder's stock, and the minority shareholder recognizes the resulting gain or loss. Under section 334(a), a minority shareholder's basis in the property received in the liquidation is the property's fair market value at the time of the distribution.

2. Subsidiary Corporation Consequences

Under section 337, the subsidiary corporation in a section 332 liquidation generally recognizes no gain or loss on distributions to the parent corporation.[11] Because the section 337 nonrecognition rule only applies to distributions to a parent corporation meeting the 80% stock ownership requirements, distributions to minority shareholders in a section 332 liquidation are generally subject to the section 336 gain/loss recognition rule. However, under section 336(d)(3), a subsidiary corporation in a section 332 liquidation cannot recognize a loss on a distribution of depreciated property to a minority shareholder.

C. Taxable Acquisitions

1. Taxable Asset Acquisition

A taxable asset acquisition occurs when the acquiring corporation acquires all of the assets of the target corporation for cash, debt instruments and/or other consideration, and following the sale of its assets, the target generally liquidates, distributing the proceeds of the sale to its shareholders in exchange for all of their stock. Or the target corporation can first distribute its assets to its shareholders in a complete liquidation, followed by a sale of the assets by the shareholders to the acquiring corporation. In either case, the asset acquisition will be a taxable event to both the target corporation and its shareholders, and the acquiring corporation will take the former target assets with cost bases equal to their fair market value at the time of the acquisition.

---

[8] *See* I.R.C. §§ 332(a), (b), 1504(a)(2).

[9] I.R.C. § 334(b).

[10] I.R.C. § 381(a), (c)(2). Section 381 is more fully examined in § 23.01.

[11] I.R.C. § 337(a), (c).

2. Taxable Stock Acquisition

A taxable stock acquisition occurs when the acquiring corporation acquires all of the stock of the target corporation for cash, debt instruments and/or other consideration. The stock acquisition is a taxable event to the shareholders of the target corporation but not the target itself. Following the stock acquisition, the acquiring corporation can either keep the target alive or liquidate the target. Where the target is kept alive, the target corporation will continue to hold its assets with the same bases that it had before the transaction; the target will also generally retain its other corporate attributes, such as its E&P accounts.

If the acquiring corporation liquidates the target corporation following a stock acquisition, the liquidation would be tax-free under section 332, and the acquiring corporation would take a transferred basis in the former target assets — the same basis that the target had in these assets, as well as inherit certain tax attributes of the target (discussed in § 23.02).

3. Section 338

In general terms, section 338 allows an acquiring corporation that purchases a controlling stock interest in a target corporation an election to treat the transaction as an asset acquisition for tax purposes. If section 338 applies and is elected, the target corporation will generally take a basis in its assets that equals their fair market value at the time of the stock purchase, and the target corporation's tax attributes are wiped clean. The price for this treatment is that the target corporation has to recognize any gain or loss as if it had sold its assets for their fair market value.

Section 338 is generally applicable where a purchasing corporation acquires at least an 80 percent stock interest in the target corporation within a 12-month period in transactions that are taxable to the sellers.[12] Once section 338 is applicable, a purchasing corporation is then eligible to receive the section's treatment by making a section 338 election. The effect of a section 338 election is as follows:

- The target corporation is treated as having sold all of its assets for their fair market value in a single transaction that is deemed to occur on the date that at least 80% of the target stock is acquired, and

- The target corporation is treated as a new corporation that purchased all of these assets at the beginning of the day after the deemed sale.[13]

The tax consequences from the deemed transactions are twofold. First, the target corporation realizes and recognizes gain or loss on the deemed sale of its assets. Second, after the deemed sale, the target corporation is treated as a new corporation (for tax purposes) that has a fair market value basis in its assets and a clean slate of corporate attributes (e.g., no E&P).

Under section 338(h)(10) and its regulations, a special election is available where the target corporation is at least 80 percent owned by a parent corporation, and the

---

[12] *See* Stephen Schwarz and Daniel J. Lathrope, Fundamentals of Corporate Taxation 362 (2012).

[13] *See* I.R.C. § 338(a).

purchasing corporation acquires at least 80 percent of the stock of the target corporation from the parent corporation. The general effect of a section 338(h)(10) election is that (i) the target corporation is treated as if it had sold all of its assets to an unrelated person for an amount equal to the assets' fair market value and (ii) following the deemed asset sale, the target corporation distributed the proceeds of the sale to its parent corporation in a liquidation.[14] The deemed liquidation should qualify for nonrecognition treatment to both the target corporation and the parent corporation under sections 337 and 332, respectively. Thus, the overall consequences of a section 338(h)(10) election are that the parent corporation does not recognize any gain or loss on the sale of stock in the target corporation, but instead the target corporation realizes and recognizes gain or loss on the deemed asset sale, and the target corporation takes a new basis in its assets equal to their fair market value as of the acquisition date.

DETAILED ANALYSIS

§ 19.01 GENERAL FRAMEWORK FOR COMPLETE LIQUIDATIONS

A complete liquidation occurs "when a corporation ceases to be a going concern and its activities are merely for the purpose of winding up its affairs, paying its debts, and distributing any remaining balance to its shareholders."[15] Under section 346(a), a complete liquidation can include a series of distributions pursuant to a plan calling for the redemption of all of the stock of the corporation.

The Code provides for two distinct categories of complete liquidations: taxable liquidations and nontaxable parent-subsidiary liquidations. For each category, there are rules governing shareholder and corporation consequences.

§ 19.02 TAXABLE LIQUIDATIONS

A. Shareholder Consequences

1. Gain or Loss Recognized

Under section 331(a), the amount received by a shareholder upon the liquidation of corporation is treated as payment in full in exchange for the shareholder's stock. In this regard, section 331(b) makes it clear that distributions received by shareholders in complete liquidations are not section 301 distributions.[16] Accordingly, on a complete liquidation, the shareholder offsets her basis in the stock

---

[14] Treas. Reg. § 1.338(h)(10)-1(d).

[15] Treas. Reg. § 1.332-2(c). Legal dissolution is not required for a complete liquidation to occur. *Id.* Although this definition is contained in the regulations addressing nontaxable parent-subsidiary liquidations, it probably applies for purposes of taxable liquidations as well. *See* Boris I. Bittker & James S. Eustice, Federal Income Taxation of Corporations and Shareholders 10-9 (2000).

[16] This is subject to a limited exception for certain liquidations of personal holding companies. Chapter 20 addresses the taxation of personal holding companies.

against the amounts distributed, and except as provided in section 332,[17] the resulting gain or loss is recognized and likely is capital gain or loss.[18] Liquidations in which the shareholder realizes and recognizes gain or loss under section 331 can be referred to as taxable liquidations.

Exchange treatment, as opposed to dividend treatment, is appropriate for a complete liquidation because the shareholders have terminated their entire stock interests in the corporation. Exchange treatment for complete liquidations is also consistent with the same treatment for complete termination redemptions under section 302(b)(3).

> *Example 19.1.* Individual A owns all 100 shares of X Corp, which she has held since 2000. A's basis in the stock is $100,000. On January 1, 2014, X Corp. completely liquidates and distributes its remaining assets to A, which consists of $200,000 in cash and real estate with a fair market value of $800,000. X Corp. has $300,000 of Current E&P for 2014 and $600,000 of Accumulated E&P for prior years.

Applying section 331(a) to A in Example 19.1:

The distribution received by A is treated as a payment in exchange for A's stock. Thus, A has a realized and recognized gain on the liquidation equal to the difference between the amount realized of $1,000,000 (the sum of the amount of cash and fair market value of the real estate) and A's basis in the stock of $100,000, which is $900,000. This would likely be a capital gain. Note that X Corp.'s E&P plays no role in A's consequences and disappears following the liquidation.

In determining a shareholder's amount realized on a liquidating distribution, the *net* value of property is taken into account. Thus, if in Example 19.1 the real estate distributed by X Corp. to A had been subject to a liability of $300,000, and A took the property subject to the liability, then A's amount realized would be $700,000: $200,000 of cash plus the $500,000 net fair market value of the real estate ($800,000 gross value reduced by the $300,000 liability).

The gain or loss consequences under section 331(a) are determined on a per share basis. Consequently, where a shareholder had acquired two or more blocks of stock at different times and prices, the gain or loss consequences on a liquidation need to be determined separately with respect to each block of stock.[19]

> *Example 19.2.* Individual A owns all 100 shares of X Corp. A had acquired 50 shares on January 1, 2000 at a cost of $50,000, and the other 50 shares on July 1, 2013 at a cost of $600,000. On January 1, 2014, X Corp. completely liquidates and distributes its remaining assets to A, which consists of $1,000,000 in cash.

Applying section 331(a) to A in Example 19.2:

---

[17] Section 332, which provides nonrecognition treatment for parent-subsidiary liquidations, is discussed in § 19.03[A].

[18] The stock is likely to be a capital asset in the shareholder's hands. *See* I.R.C. § 1221.

[19] *See* Treas. Reg. § 1.331-1(e), Example.

The $1,000,000 liquidating distribution to A is allocated proportionally to each block of stock — which amounts to $500,000 on each block of 50 shares. On the 50 shares acquired in 2000, A recognizes a gain of $450,000 (amount realized of $500,000 minus A's basis of $50,000); assuming the X Corp. stock is a capital asset in A's hands, this would be a long-term capital gain. On the 50 shares acquired in 2013, A recognizes a loss of $100,000 (amount realized of $500,000 minus A's basis of $600,000), which is a short-term capital loss under the previous assumption.

2. Basis in Distributed Property

Under section 334(a), a shareholder's basis in property distributed in a liquidation in which gain or loss is recognized by the shareholder is the property's fair market value at the time of the distribution.

> *Example 19.3.* Individual A owns all 100 shares of X Corp, which she has held since 2000. A's basis in the stock is $100,000. On January 1, 2014, X Corp. completely liquidates and distributes its remaining assets to A, which consists of equipment with a fair market value of $1,000,000.

Applying section 334(a) to A in Example 19.3:

Because A recognizes gain[20] on the liquidation under section 331(a), A takes a $1,000,000 basis in the equipment, the property's fair market value at the time of the distribution.

If in Example 19.3 the equipment distributed by X Corp. to A had been subject to a liability of $200,000, and A took the property subject to the liability, A's basis in the equipment would still be $1,000,000 under section 334(a), its fair market value at the time of the distribution. Even though A only recognizes $700,000 of gain on the liquidation in this situation ($800,000 net fair market value of the equipment minus $100,000 stock basis) versus $900,000 of recognized gain in Example 19.3, a $1,000,000 basis in the equipment is appropriate because A now has a liability of $200,000.

B. Corporation Consequences: Recognition of Gain or Loss

1. In General

Subject to a few exceptions, under section 336(a) a liquidating corporation recognizes gain or loss on a distribution of property in a complete liquidation as if the corporation sold the property to the shareholder for its fair market value. As mentioned in connection with nonliquidating distributions,[21] at one time under the so-called *General Utilities* doctrine distributions of property, whether in the nonliquidating or liquidating context, did not give rise to corporate-level gain or loss. The current rule for liquidating distributions represents a near-repeal of the *General Utilities* doctrine. The recognition rule for liquidating distributions differs

---

[20] The amount of the gain is $900,000, which is equal to A's amount realized of $1,000,000 minus A's stock basis of $100,000.

[21] *See* Chapter 16.

from the rule for nonliquidating distributions, in that the latter only calls for the recognition of gain on distributions of appreciated property.

> *Example 19.4.* Individual A owns all 100 shares of X Corp, which she has held since 2000. A's basis in the stock is $100,000. On January 1, 2014, X Corp. completely liquidates and distributes its remaining assets to A, which consist of equipment with a fair market value of $300,000 and a basis of $50,000, and real estate with a fair market of $700,000 and a basis of $600,000.

Applying section 336(a) to X Corp. in Example 19.4:

On the liquidating distributions, X Corp. recognizes an amount of gain or loss that is equal to the difference between the fair market value of the distributed property and its basis in the property. Accordingly, X Corp. recognizes $250,000 of gain on the equipment ($300,000 fair market value minus $50,000 basis) and $100,000 of gain on the real estate ($700,000 fair market value minus $600,000 basis). Note that A also recognizes $900,000 of gain on the liquidation, so that there are two levels of tax on the liquidation.

The section 336(a) recognition rule does not apply to nontaxable parent-subsidiary liquidations,[22] discussed in § 19.03. There are also limitations on the recognition of losses, which are examined below.

2.   Limitations on Recognizing Losses

The ability of a corporation to recognize a loss on a liquidating distribution creates the possibility that either losses may be recognized in inappropriate situations or that shareholders would contribute property with built-in losses to the corporation in order to inflate the losses recognized on the liquidation.[23] To address these concerns, Congress enacted two provisions that limit a liquidating corporation's recognition of losses.

a.   Certain Distributions to Related Persons

Under section 336(d)(1), a corporation does not recognize a loss on a liquidating distribution of property to a "related person" if:

- The distribution is not pro rata, or
- The distributed property is "disqualified property."[24]

A "related person" is within the meaning of section 267, and includes (among other persons) a shareholder who owns (actually or constructively) more than 50% in value of the outstanding stock of the liquidating corporation.[25] A distribution is not pro rata where a shareholder receives an interest in the distributed property that is disproportionate to the shareholder's stock interest — for example, a

---

[22] *See* I.R.C. § 337.

[23] *See* H.R. Conf. Rep. No. 841, 99th Cong., 2d Sess. II-200 (1986).

[24] I.R.C. § 336(d)(1)(A).

[25] *See* I.R.C. § 267(b)(2).

shareholder with a 30 percent stock interest receives the entire interest in a particular asset. "Disqualified property" is property acquired by the distributing corporation either in a section 351 transaction or as a contribution to capital during the five-year period ending on the date of the distribution.[26]

> *Example 19.5.* X Corp. has 100 shares of voting common stock outstanding (its only class). A owns 70 shares of the X Corp. stock, and B owns 30 shares of the X Corp. stock. On January 1, 2014, X Corp. completely liquidates and distributes its remaining assets to A and B as follows: to A, real estate with a fair market value of $700,000 and adjusted basis of $900,000; to B, equipment with a fair market value of $300,000 and adjusted basis of $50,000.

Applying section 336(d)(1) to X Corp. in Example 19.5:

On the distribution of the real estate to A, X Corp. has a realized loss of $200,000 ($700,000 fair market value minus $900,000 basis), but this loss is not recognized because the distribution is to a related person — A is a more than 50% shareholder, and the distribution is not pro rata — A, a 70% shareholder, receives the entire interest in the real estate. Note that under section 334(a), A will take a $700,000 basis in the real estate, the property's fair market value at the time of the distribution. Thus, the $200,000 realized loss is not preserved in A's hands. Note also that under section 336(a), X Corp. recognizes a $250,000 gain on the equipment ($300,000 fair market value minus $50,000 basis).

> *Example 19.6.* X Corp. has 100 shares of voting common stock outstanding (its only class). A owns 70 shares of the X Corp. stock, and B owns 30 shares of the X Corp. stock. On January 1, 2014, X Corp. completely liquidates and distributes its remaining asset, real estate with a fair market value of $1,000,000 and adjusted basis of $1,200,000, to A and B as tenants in common, with A taking a 70% interest in the property and B taking a 30% interest. X Corp. had acquired the real estate from A in a section 351 transaction on January 1, 2010.

Applying section 336(d)(1) to X Corp. in Example 19.6:

On the 70% portion of the real estate that is distributed to A, X Corp. has a realized loss of $140,000 ($700,000 fair market value minus $840,000 basis),[27] but this loss is not recognized because the distribution is to a related person — A is a more than 50% shareholder, and the distribution consists of disqualified property — X Corp. had acquired the real estate within the past five years in a section 351 transaction.[28] On the 30% portion of the real estate that is distributed to B, X Corp.'s realized loss of $60,000 ($300,000 fair market value minus $360,000 basis)[29] is recognized because the distribution is not to a related person — B is not a more than 50% shareholder.

---

[26] I.R.C. § 336(d)(1)(B).

[27] This is determined by taking 70% of the real estate's fair market value and adjusted basis.

[28] Note that because A takes an interest in the real estate that is proportionate to her stock interest, the distribution is pro rata.

[29] This is determined by taking 30% of the real estate's fair market value and adjusted basis.

b.   Distributions or Dispositions of Transferred Basis Property with a Tax Avoidance Purpose

Under section 336(d)(2), for purposes of determining the amount of recognized loss by a liquidating corporation on a distribution, sale or exchange of certain property described below, the corporation must reduce its basis in the property by the excess of:

- The adjusted basis of the property in the hands of the corporation immediately after its acquisition, over

- The fair market value of the property at that time.[30]

Thus, for property subject to section 336(d)(2), the provision requires that a liquidating corporation reduce its basis for determining a loss by the property's built-in loss at the time of acquisition.

The section 336(d)(2) basis reduction rule applies to property:

- That is acquired by the liquidating corporation in a section 351 transaction or as contribution to capital, and

- The acquisition was part of a plan a principal purpose of which was to recognize a loss by the corporation in connection with the liquidation.

The statute provides that property acquired by the corporation after the date that is two years before the adoption of a plan for complete liquidation is treated as acquired with the proscribed purpose, except as provided in regulations (which to date do not exist).[31] According to the legislative history, acquisitions before this date would be treated as made with such a purpose "only in the most rare and unusual cases."[32]

The aim of section 336(d)(2) is to prevent the tactic of stuffing the corporation with property containing built-in losses that are to be recognized in connection with the liquidation. Compared to section 336(d)(1), the provision is narrower in that it requires a tax avoidance motive, but broader because it applies to sales or exchanges in connection with the liquidation as well as to liquidating distributions to any shareholder.

> *Example 19.7.* X Corp. has 100 shares of voting common stock outstanding (its only class). A owns 70 shares of the X Corp. stock, and B owns 30 shares of the X Corp. stock. On January 1, 2014, X Corp. completely liquidates pursuant to a plan of liquidation adopted on July 1, 2013, and distributes its remaining assets to A and B as follows: to A, equipment with a fair market value of $700,000 and adjusted basis of $100,000; to B, land with a fair market value of $300,000 and adjusted basis of $400,000. X Corp. had acquired the land from B in a section 351 transaction on January 1, 2013. Immediately after its acquisition by X Corp., the land had a fair market value of $375,000 and an adjusted basis in X Corp.'s hands of $400,000.

---

[30] I.R.C. § 336(d)(2)(A).

[31] I.R.C. § 336(d)(2)(B)(ii).

[32] H.R. Conf. Rep. No. 841, 99th Cong., 2d Sess. II-200 (1986).

Applying section 336(d)(2) to X Corp. in Example 19.7:

Section 336(d)(2) should apply to X Corp.'s distribution of the land to B because (i) X Corp. had acquired the land in a section 351 transaction and (ii) the acquisition should be treated as having a tax avoidance purpose given that it occurred after the date that is two years before the plan of liquidation was adopted — the liquidation plan was adopted on July 1, 2013, the "two years before date" is July 1, 2011, and the land was acquired on January 1, 2013. Consequently, the loss on the distribution of the land is determined by reducing X Corp.'s basis in the land by the land's built-in loss of $25,000 — the difference between X Corp.'s $400,000 basis upon acquisition and the $375,000 fair market value at that time. X Corp.'s basis in the land is therefore reduced to $375,000 ($400,000 minus $25,000), resulting in a recognized loss on the distribution of $75,000 ($300,000 fair market value minus $375,000 basis). Thus, of the $100,000 realized loss on the distribution of the land ($400,000 *normal* basis minus $300,000 fair market value), section 336(d)(2) prevents the recognition of the built-in loss of $25,000 but does not affect the recognition of the post-contribution loss of $75,000.[33]

The current significance of section 336(d)(2) is reduced by section 362(e)(2),[34] which, as discussed in Chapter 14, generally limits a corporation's aggregate basis of properties acquired in a section 351 transaction to the properties' aggregate fair market value in situations in which the properties had an aggregate built-in loss at the time of their acquisition. If section 362(e)(2) applies to eliminate the built-in loss on the corporation's acquisition of property, then there would be no built-in loss for section 336(d)(2) to disallow.

To illustrate this, assume that in Example 19.7 section 362(e)(2) had applied on X Corp.'s acquisition of the land, which resulted in X Corp. taking a $375,000 basis in the land, its fair market value at the time of acquisition. Under section 336(d)(2), the basis reduction would then be zero — the difference between X Corp.'s $375,000 basis in the land upon acquisition and the land's $375,000 fair market value at that time. Consequently, section 336(d)(2) would have no effect on determining X Corp.'s recognized loss on the distribution.

Section 336(d)(2) still retains some significance because section 362(e)(2) does not always apply to eliminate a built-in loss on property acquired in a section 351 transaction. One such situation is where one of properties that is transferred by a shareholder in a section 351 transaction has a built-in loss, but in the aggregate the properties transferred by the shareholder do not have a built-in loss. As an illustration, assume that in Example 19.7 B transferred appreciated property along with the land to X Corp. in a section 351 transaction, so that in the aggregate the properties transferred by B did not have a built-in loss. If this had occurred, X Corp.'s basis in the land would not be reduced to its fair market value, and there would be a built-in loss in the land for section 336(d)(2) to disallow on the liquidating distribution. In addition, a corporation's basis in property is not reduced under

---

[33] Note that section 336(d)(1) does not apply to the distribution because B is not a related person — B is not a more than 50% shareholder. If section 336(d)(1) along with section 336(d)(2) applied to the distribution, the entire loss on the property would not be recognized.

[34] Section 362(e)(2) was enacted in 2004, several years after Congress had enacted section 336(d)(2).

section 362(e)(2) where the shareholder in the section 351 transaction and the corporation jointly elect to limit the shareholder's basis in the stock received to its fair market value at the time of receipt.[35]

§ 19.03   NONTAXABLE PARENT-SUBSIDIARY LIQUIDATIONS

A.   Shareholder Consequences

1.   Parent Corporation Consequences

a.   Nonrecognition of Gain or Loss

Under section 332, a parent corporation recognizes no gain or loss on receipt of property distributed in the complete liquidation of a subsidiary corporation provided:

- The parent corporation owns at least 80% of the voting power and total value of the subsidiary corporation's stock from the date of adoption of the liquidation plan until the final distribution, and

- The subsidiary corporation distributes all of its assets within:

  ○ One taxable year, pursuant to a plan, or

  ○ Three years after the close of the first taxable year in which a liquidating distribution is made, pursuant to a plan calling for the completion of the liquidation within such three-year period.[36]

The apparent rationale for nonrecognition treatment is that the liquidation can be viewed as a change in the form of the parent corporation's holdings — the parent goes from having a substantial indirect interest in the assets of the subsidiary corporation to having a direct interest in these assets, and the assets remain in corporate solution after the liquidation. Also, from the standpoint of the shareholders of the parent corporation, they go from using two corporations to hold assets indirectly to using one corporation to do so. In addition, the preservation principle, which is a corollary to nonrecognition treatment, can be adhered to by preserving in the parent the tax attributes of the subsidiary (discussed below).

> *Example 19.8.* Y Corp. owns all 100 shares of X Corp, which it has held since 2000. Y Corp.'s basis in the stock is $100,000. On January 1, 2014, pursuant to a plan of liquidation, X Corp. completely liquidates and distributes its remaining assets to Y Corp., which consist of equipment with a fair market value of $300,000 and a basis of $50,000, and real estate with a fair market value of $700,000 and a basis of $600,000. X Corp. has $300,000 of Current E&P for 2014 and $600,000 of Accumulated E&P for prior years.

---

[35] I.R.C. § 362(e)(2)(C).

[36] *See* I.R.C. §§ 332(a), (b), 1504(a)(2).

Applying section 332 to X Corp. in Example 19.8:

Y Corp. will not recognize its realized gain of $900,000 ($1,000,000 amount realized minus $100,000 basis in the X Corp. stock) because Y Corp. owns at least 80% of the vote and value of the X Corp. stock — it owns 100% of the stock, and the liquidation was completed in a single taxable year — all assets were distributed on January 1, 2014.

b.   Basis in Distributed Property

Under section 334(b), the parent corporation's basis in the property received in a section 332 liquidation is generally the same as the subsidiary corporation's basis in the property.[37] This type of basis is generally referred to as a transferred basis.[38] Accordingly, in Example 19.8, Y Corp. will take a $50,000 basis in the equipment and a $600,000 basis in the real estate.

Note that providing the parent corporation with a transferred basis does *not* preserve the parent's realized gain or loss that was not recognized on the liquidation: in Example 19.8, $350,000 of gain is preserved in the assets distributed to Y Corp.,[39] which does not equal Y Corp.'s $900,000 of realized yet unrecognized gain on the liquidation. But a transferred basis for the parent does preserve the gain or loss realized by the subsidiary, which, as discussed below, is also not recognized in a section 332 liquidation (with a limited exception).

c.   Effect on E&P

Under section 381, the parent corporation in a section 332 liquidation inherits the E&P of the subsidiary corporation (along with other corporate attributes).[40] Accordingly, in Example 19.8, Y Corp. will include in its E&P the $900,000 of X Corp. E&P.

2.   Minority Shareholder Consequences

Because a parent corporation in a section 332 liquidation does not need to own all of the stock of the subsidiary corporation, it is possible that the subsidiary will have other shareholders, which can be referred to as minority shareholders. Minority shareholders in a section 332 liquidation are treated the same as shareholders in a taxable section 331 liquidation. Thus, under section 331(a), the amount received by

---

[37] I.R.C. § 334(b). One exception is where gain or loss is recognized by the subsidiary on the section 332 liquidation (discussed below), in which case the parent takes a fair market value basis in the property distributed. I.R.C. § 334(b)(1)(A). The parent also takes a fair market value basis in the distributed property where the property has an aggregate built-in loss and is received from a corporation that would not be subject to tax on any gain or loss with respect to the property (*e.g.*, a foreign corporation). I.R.C. § 334(b)(1)(B).

[38] I.R.C. § 7701(a)(43).

[39] $250,000 of gain is preserved in the equipment ($300,000 fair market value minus $50,000 basis), and $100,000 of gain is preserved in the real estate ($700,000 fair market value minus $600,000 basis).

[40] I.R.C. § 381(a), (c)(2). A deficit in E&P of the subsidiary can only be used to offset the parent's E&P that accumulated after the liquidation. I.R.C. § 381(c)(2)(B). Section 381 is more fully examined in § 23.01.

a minority shareholder in the liquidation is treated as payment in full in exchange for the shareholder's stock, and the minority shareholder recognizes the resulting gain or loss. Under section 334(a), a minority shareholder's basis in the property received in the liquidation is the property's fair market value at the time of the distribution.

> *Example 19.9.* X Corp. has 100 shares of voting common stock outstanding (its only class of stock). Y Corp owns 80 shares of the X Corp. stock, with a basis of $80,000. A owns 20 shares of the X Corp. stock, with a basis of $20,000. On January 1, 2014, pursuant to a plan of liquidation, X Corp. completely liquidates and distributes its remaining assets to Y Corp. and A as follows: to Y Corp., real estate with a fair market value of $800,000 and an adjusted basis of $700,000; to A, equipment with a fair market value of $200,000 and adjusted basis of $50,000.

Applying sections 331, 332 and 334 to Y Corp. and A in Example 19.9:

Under section 332, Y Corp. will not recognize its realized gain of $720,000 ($800,000 amount realized minus $80,000 basis in the X Corp. stock) because Y Corp. owns at least 80% of the vote and value of the X Corp. stock — it owns 80% of the stock, and the liquidation was completed in a single taxable year — all assets were distributed on January 1, 2014. Under 334(b), Y Corp. will take a $700,000 basis in the real estate, the same basis that X Corp. had in the real estate.

Under section 331(a), A has a realized and recognized gain of $180,000 on the liquidation — the difference between the amount realized of $200,000 (the fair market value of the equipment) and A's basis in the stock of $20,000. Under section 334(a), A takes a fair market value basis in the equipment of $200,000.

B. Subsidiary Corporation Consequences: Recognition of Gain or Loss

1. Distributions to the Parent Corporation

Under section 337, the subsidiary corporation in a section 332 liquidation generally recognizes no gain or loss on distributions to the parent corporation.[41] Thus, a section 332 liquidation is generally nontaxable to both the parent and subsidiary (with a few exceptions described below). Accordingly, in Example 19.9, X Corp. does not recognize its realized gain of $100,000[42] on the distribution of the real estate to Y Corp. As mentioned previously, the unrecognized gain or loss on the distributed assets is preserved in the hands of the parent corporation via the transferred basis that the parent takes in these assets under section 334(b). In example 19.9, the $700,000 transferred basis that Y Corp. takes in the real estate preserves the $100,000 of unrecognized gain on the liquidation.

---

[41] I.R.C. § 337(a), (c).

[42] This is the difference between the $800,000 fair market value of the real estate and X Corp.'s basis in the real estate of $700,000.

The section 337 nonrecognition rule generally does not apply to a distribution of property to a parent corporation that is a tax-exempt organization.[43] This rule prevents the subsidiary's realized gain (or loss) on the distributed property from being permanently excluded (or disallowed), given that a tax-exempt parent's disposition of the property would generally not result in taxable gain or loss.[44]

For purposes of the section 337 nonrecognition rule, transfers of property by the subsidiary corporation to the parent corporation to satisfy the subsidiary's indebtedness to the parent are treated as liquidating distributions.[45] Thus, a subsidiary in a section 332 liquidation generally recognizes no gain or loss on property that is distributed to the parent to satisfy debt owed to the parent. The purpose of this rule is to prevent a subsidiary from taking advantage of the section 337 nonrecognition rule by not recognizing gains on distributions of appreciated property in exchange for parent stock, but recognizing losses on transfers of depreciated property to satisfy indebtedness to the parent.

2. Distributions to Minority Shareholders

The section 337 nonrecognition rule only applies to distributions to a parent corporation meeting the 80% stock ownership requirements specified in section 332.[46] Thus, distributions to minority shareholders in a section 332 liquidation are generally subject to the section 336 gain/loss recognition rule. However, under section 336(d)(3), a subsidiary corporation in a section 332 liquidation cannot recognize a loss on a distribution of depreciated property to a minority shareholder. This rule prevents a subsidiary corporation from recognizing losses by distributing depreciated property to minority shareholders, while not recognizing gains by distributing appreciated property to the parent corporation. Consequently, a subsidiary corporation recognizes gains but not losses on distributions to minority shareholders.

> *Example 19.10.* X Corp. has 100 shares of voting common stock outstanding (its only class of stock). Y Corp owns 80 shares of the X Corp. stock, with a basis of $80,000. A owns 20 shares of the X Corp. stock, with a basis of $20,000. On January 1, 2014, pursuant to a plan of liquidation, X Corp. completely liquidates and distributes its remaining assets to Y Corp. and A as follows: to Y Corp., $800,000 of cash; to A, equipment with a fair market value of $50,000 and adjusted basis of $0, and land with a fair market value of $150,000 and adjusted basis of $200,000.

Applying section 336 to A in Example 19.10:

On the distribution of the equipment to A, X Corp. recognizes $50,000 of gain under section 336(a) ($50,000 fair market value minus $0 basis). On the distribution

---

[43] I.R.C. § 337(b)(2)(A).

[44] The section 337 nonrecognition rule does apply to distributions to a tax-exempt parent corporation where the distributed property is used in an unrelated trade or business. I.R.C. § 337(b)(2)(B). This is because in this circumstance the tax-exempt parent will be taxable on a disposition of the distributed property.

[45] I.R.C. § 337(b)(1).

[46] I.R.C. § 337(a), (c).

of the land to A, X Corp. has a realized loss of $50,000 ($150,000 fair market value minus $200,000 basis), but this loss is not recognized under section 336(d)(3). Note that under section 334(a), A will take a $150,000 basis in the land, the property's fair market value at the time of the distribution. Thus, the $50,000 realized loss is not preserved in A's hands.

§ 19.04   TAXABLE ACQUISITIONS

A.   In General

When one corporation (acquiring corporation) wants to acquire another corporation (target corporation), there are a few options to consider. First, the acquiring corporation could acquire the stock or the assets of the target corporation in a transaction qualifying as a corporate reorganization, which would generally allow for the nonrecognition of any realized gain or loss on the transaction, along with exchanged and transferred bases in the assets and stock received by the parties. Corporate reorganizations are examined in Chapter 21.

Alternatively, the acquiring corporation could acquire the target corporation in a taxable acquisition. A taxable acquisition can take two possible forms: an asset acquisition or a stock acquisition.

1.   Taxable Asset Acquisition

A taxable asset acquisition is where the acquiring corporation acquires all of the assets of the target corporation for cash, debt instruments and/or other consideration, and following the sale of its assets, the target generally liquidates, distributing the proceeds of the sale to its shareholders in exchange for all of their stock. Or the target corporation can first distribute its assets to its shareholders in a complete liquidation, followed by a sale of the assets by the shareholders to the acquiring corporation. In either case, the asset acquisition will be a taxable event to both the target corporation and its shareholders, and the acquiring corporation will take the former target assets with cost bases equal to their fair market value at the time of the acquisition.

> *Example 19.11.* Individual A owns all 100 shares of T Corp., having a total basis in the stock of $100,000. T Corp.'s only asset is equipment with a fair market value of $600,000 and an adjusted basis of $50,000, and T Corp. has no liabilities. On January 1, 2014, P Corp. acquires T Corp.'s equipment for $600,000 of cash, and following the sale, T Corp. completely liquidates, distributing the $600,000 (less any corporate taxes resulting from the sale) to A.

Determining the tax consequences to the parties in Example 19.11:

On the sale of the equipment, under section 1001, T Corp. has a realized and recognized gain of $550,000 ($600,000 amount realized minus $50,000 adjusted basis). On the liquidation, under section 331(a) A has a realized and recognized gain equal to the difference between the amounts received on the liquidation ($600,000 proceeds of the sale minus corporate taxes resulting from the sale) and A's $100,000 basis in the T Corp. stock. P Corp. will take a cost basis of $600,000 in the purchased equipment.[47]

2. Taxable Stock Acquisition

A taxable stock acquisition occurs when the acquiring corporation acquires all of the stock of the target corporation for cash, debt instruments and/or other consideration. The stock acquisition is a taxable event to the shareholders of the target corporation, but not the target itself. Following the stock acquisition, the acquiring corporation can either keep the target alive or liquidate the target. Where the target is kept alive, the target corporation will continue to hold its assets with the same bases that it had before the transaction; the target will also generally retain its other corporate attributes, such as its E&P accounts.[48]

> *Example 19.12.* Individual A owns all 100 shares of T Corp., having a total basis in the stock of $100,000. T Corp.'s only asset is equipment with a fair market value of $600,000 and a basis of $50,000, and T Corp. has no liabilities. On January 1, 2014, P Corp. acquires from A all 100 shares of T Corp. stock for $600,000 of cash.[49] Following the stock acquisition, P Corp. keeps T Corp. alive as a wholly-owned subsidiary.

Determining the tax consequences to the parties in Example 19.12:

On the sale of her stock, under section 1001, A has a realized and recognized gain of $500,000 ($600,000 amount realized minus $100,000 adjusted basis). Following the transaction, T Corp. will continue to hold its equipment with a $50,000 basis.

If the acquiring corporation liquidates the target corporation following a stock acquisition, the liquidation would be tax-free under section 332, and the acquiring corporation would take a transferred basis in the former target assets — the same basis that the target had in these assets,[50] as well as inherit certain tax attributes of the target (discussed in § 23.02), *provided* the stock acquisition and the liquidation are respected for tax purposes as separate transactions. However, in *Kimbell-Diamond Mill. Co. v. Commissioner*,[51] the court applied the step-transaction doctrine in the situation where the acquiring corporation's intention in purchasing the target corporation's stock was to acquire the target's assets through a liquidation of the target. The court thus treated the stock purchase and liquidation

---

[47] If T Corp. had first distributed the equipment to A in the liquidation of T Corp. before P Corp.'s purchase of the equipment, T Corp. would have recognized $550,000 of gain on the distribution of the equipment under section 336(a) ($600,000 fair market value minus $50,000 adjusted basis). On A's subsequent sale of the equipment to P Corp. for $600,000, A would realize and recognize no gain or loss, because under section 334(a) her basis in the equipment would equal its fair market value of $600,000. The other tax consequences to the parties would be the same as in Example 19.11.

[48] Following a stock acquisition, the target's use of certain corporate tax attributes may be limited. *See* §§ 23.02, 23.03.

[49] Note that P Corp. would likely not pay $600,000 for the T Corp. stock even though T Corp. holds an asset with a fair market value of $600,000 and has no liabilities, because of the unrealized gain on T Corp.'s asset and resulting future corporate tax liability. *See* Bittker & Eustice, *supra* note 15 at 10-106 – 10-107.

[50] *See* I.R.C. § 334(b).

[51] 14 T.C. 74 (1950).

as an acquisition of the target's assets, which provided the acquiring corporation with a cost basis in the acquired assets.

In former section 334(b)(2), Congress codified the essence of the *Kimbell-Diamond* doctrine but provided an objective approach that included a rule for when the target's liquidation had to occur in order for the transaction to be treated as an asset acquisition for tax purposes.[52] Thus, an acquiring corporation making a stock acquisition had a choice of whether to receive asset acquisition treatment (cost basis and elimination of the target's corporate tax attributes) or stock acquisition treatment (transferred basis and inheritance of certain corporate attributes) by liquidating the target within the prescribed time frame or not doing so. However, former section 334(b)(2) generated a good deal of criticism, which included that the rule applied automatically if a timely (per the statute) liquidation occurred, even if the acquiring corporation had not intended to buy assets, and that in order to receive asset acquisition treatment, a liquidation of the target was required.[53] As a result of these and other concerns, Congress replaced former section 334(b)(2) with section 338.[54]

B. Section 338

In general terms, section 338 allows an acquiring corporation that purchases a controlling stock interest in a target corporation an election to treat the transaction as an asset acquisition for tax purposes, without the need for the liquidation of the target corporation. If section 338 applies and is elected, the target corporation will generally take a basis in its assets that equals their fair market value at the time of the stock purchase, and the target corporation's tax attributes are wiped clean. The price for this treatment is that the target corporation has to recognize any gain or loss as if it had sold its assets for their fair market value.

1. Application of Section 338

The application of section 338 is triggered by a "qualified stock purchase,"[55] which is generally a "purchase" by the acquiring corporation (referred to as the "purchasing corporation"[56]) of at least 80 percent of the vote and value of the target corporation's stock within the "12-month acquisition period."[57] "Purchase" excludes acquisitions in which the purchasing corporation takes either a transferred, exchanged, or section 1014 date of death basis, as well as acquisitions from certain

---

[52] *See* Bittker & Eustice, *supra* note 15 at 10-103 – 10-104 (discussing former section 334(b)(2)).

[53] *See id.* at 10-104.

[54] *See id.* Section 338 also replaces the *Kimball-Diamond* doctrine. Thus, if there is a qualified stock purchase under section 338 (discussed below), a section 338 election (discussed below) is not made, and the target is liquidated, the transaction will not be treated as an asset acquisition for tax purposes under the step-transaction doctrine even if the liquidation was planned at the time of the stock acquisition. *See id.* at n. 472 (referring to Rev. Rul. 90-95, 1990-2 C.B. 67).; Treas. Reg. § 1.338-3(c)(1)(i).

[55] *See* I.R.C. § 338(a).

[56] A "purchasing corporation" is a corporation that makes a qualified stock purchase of another corporation. I.R.C. § 338(d)(1).

[57] *See* I.R.C. §§ 338(d)(3), 1504(a)(2).

related persons.[58] The 12-month acquisition period is basically the 12-month period beginning with the first purchase of stock included in the qualified stock purchase.[59] In short, section 338 is generally applicable where a purchasing corporation acquires at least an 80 percent stock interest in the target corporation within a 12-month period in transactions that are taxable to the sellers.[60]

2. The Section 338 Election and Its Consequences

Once section 338 is applicable, a purchasing corporation is then eligible to receive the section's treatment by making a section 338 election.[61] The election must be made no later than the fifteenth day of the ninth month that begins after the month in which the "acquisition date" occurs.[62] The "acquisition date" is the first date on which there is a qualified stock purchase (i.e., the purchase of at least 80 percent of the target in a 12-month period).[63]

The effect of a section 338 election is as follows:

- The target corporation is treated as having sold all of its assets at the close of the acquisition date for their fair market value in a single transaction, and

- The target corporation is treated as a new corporation that purchased all of these assets at the beginning of the day after the acquisition date.[64]

The tax consequences from the deemed transactions are twofold. First, the target corporation realizes and recognizes gain or loss on the deemed sale of its assets. Second, the day after the acquisition date, the target corporation is treated as a new corporation (for tax purposes) that has a fair market value basis in its assets and a clean slate of corporate attributes (e.g., no E&P).

---

[58] *See* I.R.C. § 338(h)(3).

[59] *See* I.R.C. § 338(h)(1).

[60] *See* Schwarz & Lathrope, *supra* note 12 at 362.

[61] Subject to several exceptions, including exceptions provided by the regulations, section 338(e) provides that a section 338 election is deemed to have occurred if the purchasing corporation acquires an asset from the target corporation (or a target affiliate) during the "consistency period," which includes the (i) 12-month acquisition period, (ii) the one year period before the 12-month acquisition period, and (iii) the one year period after the acquisition date. *See* I.R.C. § 338(h)(4). In addition, subject to exceptions, section 338(f) requires consistent treatment (elections or no elections) if the purchasing corporation makes qualified stock purchases with respect to the target corporation and one or more target affiliates during any consistency periods relating to these qualified stock purchases. These consistency rules were aimed at preventing a purchasing corporation from selectively receiving a fair market basis in some target (or target affiliate) assets while retaining a transferred basis in other target (or target affiliate) assets. *See* Bittker & Eustice, *supra* note 15 at 10-121 – 10-122. The consistency rules were enacted before the repeal of the *General Utilities* doctrine, and thus at a time when a section 338 election did not include the cost of gain recognition by the target corporation. Because of the current high cost of a deemed section 338 election, the regulations have substantially limited the application of the consistency rules, and further provide that they no longer will result in a deemed section 338 election; instead, the corporation acquiring an asset may have a carryover basis in the asset. *See* Treas. Reg. § 1.338-8; Bittker & Eustice, *supra* note 15 at 10-122 – 10-123.

[62] I.R.C. § 338(g)(1).

[63] I.R.C. § 338(h)(2). Once made, a section 338 election is irrevocable. I.R.C. § 338(g)(3).

[64] *See* I.R.C. § 338(a).

Example 19.13. Individual A owns all 100 shares of T Corp., having a total basis in the stock of $100,000. T Corp.'s only asset is equipment with a fair market value of $600,000 and a basis of $50,000, and T Corp. has no liabilities. On January 1, 2014, P Corp. acquires from A all 100 shares of T Corp. stock for $600,000 of cash.[65] Following the stock acquisition, P Corp. makes a timely section 338 election. P Corp. keeps T Corp. alive as a wholly-owned subsidiary.

Determining the tax consequences to the parties in Example 19.13:

As in Example 19.12, on the sale of her stock, A has a recognized gain of $500,000 ($600,000 amount realized minus $100,000 adjusted basis). P Corp.'s acquisition of the T Corp. stock is a qualified stock purchase because P Corp. has acquired at least 80 percent of the vote and value of the T Corp. stock in a 12-month period (here 100 percent of the stock was acquired in one day). As a result of P Corp.'s timely section 338 election, T Corp. is treated as having sold the equipment, its only asset, for its fair market value of $600,000 on January 1, 2014 (the acquisition date), thereby realizing and recognizing $550,000 of gain ($600,000 amount realized minus $50,000 adjusted basis).[66] In addition, as of January 2, 2014, T Corp. is treated as new corporation for tax purposes that has acquired the equipment in the deemed sale for $600,000; consequently, T Corp. takes a fair market value basis in the equipment of $600,000, and its corporate attributes (e.g., E&P) begin anew.

Notice that like an actual asset acquisition, a stock acquisition coupled with a section 338 election results in two levels of taxation — both the selling shareholders and the target corporation are taxable. The section 338 election does give the target corporation a fair market value basis in its assets, which if higher than the target's original basis, should produce future tax savings in the form of higher depreciation deductions and less gain or more loss on subsequent asset sales. However, in light of the time value of money, these future tax savings may not be worth incurring an immediate tax on the deemed sale of the target's assets.[67] Consequently, a section 338 election may be beneficial only where the target corporation has either net operating losses or built-in losses to offset or reduce the gains on the deemed sale.[68]

---

[65] As noted earlier, P Corp. would likely not pay $600,000 for the T Corp. stock because of the corporate tax liability attributable to the unrealized gain on T Corp.'s assets, especially if a section 338 election is planned.

[66] As discussed below, the sales price on the deemed sale of the target corporation's assets will be increased by liabilities of the target corporation, including liabilities for the tax consequences resulting from the deemed sale. For purposes of this example, this adjustment is ignored.

[67] *See* Lederman, Understanding Corporate Taxation 206 (2006).

[68] *See* Bittker & Eustice, *supra* note 15 at 10-106.

3.   Deemed Sales Price and Target's New Basis in Assets

a.   Aggregate Deemed Sales Price

The regulations provide detailed rules for determining the fair market price at which the target corporation is deemed to have sold its assets,[69] referred to in the regulations as the aggregate deemed sales price (ADSP).[70] If the purchasing corporation had acquired 100 percent of the target corporation's stock in the 12-month acquisition period and the target has no liabilities as of the close of the acquisition date, then the ADSP would simply equal the amount paid by the purchasing corporation for the stock.[71] However, if this is not the case, then the ADSP would need to be computed under the following formula provided in the regulations:[72]

- The "grossed-up amount realized" on the sale to the purchasing corporation of the purchasing corporation's "recently purchased stock," plus

- The liabilities of the target corporation as of the beginning of the day after the acquisition date (including liabilities for the tax consequences resulting from the deemed sale).[73]

"Recently purchased stock" is stock in the target corporation that is purchased by the purchasing corporation within the 12-month acquisition period and held by the purchasing corporation on the acquisition date.[74] The "grossed-up amount realized" in the first part of the formula is basically (i) the amount realized on the sale to the purchasing corporation of recently purchased stock, divided by (ii) the percentage of the target stock attributable to recently purchased stock.[75] For example, if in Example 19.13 the T Corp. stock that P Corp. had purchased during the 12-month acquisition period constituted 80 percent of the T Corp. stock (rather than 100 percent), the grossed-up amount realized would be: (i) $600,000 (the amount realized on the sale to P Corp. of recently purchased stock) divided by (ii) 80 percent (percentage of T Corp. stock attributable to recently purchased stock), which equals $750,000. This amount would also be the ADSP here.[76]

---

[69] *See* Treas. Reg. § 1.338-4.

[70] Treas. Reg. § 1.338-4(a).

[71] Because the target's liabilities for this purpose include tax liabilities resulting from the deemed sale (discussed below), this situation is not likely to occur; thus, in determining ADSP in this situation, it would typically be necessary to add such tax liabilities to the amount paid by the purchasing corporation for the target stock.

[72] Treas. Reg. § 1.338-4(b)(1).

[73] Treas. Reg. § 1.338-4(d)(1).

[74] I.R.C. § 338(b)(6)(A).

[75] Treas. Reg. § 1.338-4(c)(1).

[76] The example assumes that T Corp. has no liabilities; therefore, there is no adjustment to ADSP for target liabilities.

b.   Adjusted Grossed-Up Basis

The target corporation's new basis in its assets, referred to in the regulations as the adjusted grossed-up basis (AGUB),[77] is determined in a manner similar to that for determining ADSP. Thus, if the purchasing corporation had acquired 100 percent of the target corporation stock in the 12-month acquisition period and the target has no liabilities, then AGUB would simply equal the amount paid by the purchasing corporation for the stock.[78] For other situations, the following formula would generally need to be used to determine AGUB:[79]

- The "grossed-up basis in the purchasing corporation's recently purchased stock," plus

- The purchasing corporation's basis in "nonrecently purchased stock," plus

- The liabilities of the target corporation as of the beginning of the day after the acquisition date (including liabilities for the tax consequences resulting from the deemed sale).[80]

"Nonrecently purchased stock" is stock in the target corporation that is held on the acquisition date and is not recently purchased stock.[81] Thus, this is target stock that was purchased by the purchasing corporation prior to the 12-month acquisition period. The "grossed-up basis in the purchasing corporation's recently purchased stock" is basically the purchasing corporation's basis in recently purchased stock, multiplied by the following fraction:

$$\frac{100 \text{ minus the percentage attributable to nonrecently purchased stock}}{\text{the percentage of the target stock attributable to recently purchased stock.}[82]}$$

For example, if in Example 19.13, (i) the T Corp. stock that P Corp. had purchased during the 12-month acquisition period constituted 80 percent of the T Corp. stock (rather than 100 percent) and (ii) P Corp. had acquired 10 percent of the T Corp. stock before the 12-month acquisition period for $50,000, then the grossed-up basis in P Corp.'s recently purchased T Corp. stock would be:

$$\$600,000 \text{ (the purchasing corporation's basis in recently purchased stock)}$$
$$\times$$
$$\frac{100 \text{ minus } 10 \text{ (the percentage attributable to nonrecently purchased stock)}}{80 \text{ (the percentage of the target stock attributable to recently purchased stock)}}$$

---

[77] Treas. Reg. § 1.338-5(a).

[78] Because the target's liabilities for this purpose include tax liabilities resulting from the deemed sale (discussed below), this situation is not likely to occur; thus, in determining AGUB in this situation, it would typically be necessary to add such tax liabilities to the amount paid by the purchasing corporation for the target stock.

[79] I.R.C. § 338(b)(1), (2); Treas. Reg. § 1.338-5(b)(1).

[80] Treas. Reg. § 1.338-(e)(1).

[81] I.R.C. § 338(b)(6)(B).

[82] Treas. Reg. § 1.338-5(c).

or $600,000 $\times$ $\dfrac{90}{80}$ which equals $675,000,

and adding the $50,000 basis in the nonrecently purchased stock, the AGUB would be $725,000.[83]

c. Allocating ADSP and AGUB to Individual Target Corporation Assets

Both ADSP and AGUB are allocated to the target corporation's assets for purposes of computing gain or loss on each asset and the deemed purchase price of each asset, respectively.[84] The regulations provide the following method for allocating ADSP and AGUB to individual assets. First, the target's cash and general deposit accounts (referred to as Class I assets) generally reduce ADSP and AGUB.[85] The remaining amount of ADSP and AGUB is then allocated to several prescribed classes of assets in a certain order.[86] The amount of ADSP and AGUB that is allocated to each class is then allocated among the assets within a class in proportion to the fair market values of these assets.[87] In general, the amount of ADSP or AGUB that is allocated to an asset cannot exceed the fair market value of the asset.[88] The prescribed assets classes and their order is as follows: Class II assets — generally, actively traded personal property;[89] Class III assets — generally, assets that are subject to federal market-to-market taxation and debt instruments;[90] Class IV assets – inventory and other property held primarily for sale to customers in the ordinary course of business;[91] Class V assets — assets other than assets in classes I, II, III, IV, VI, and VII;[92] Class VI assets — section 197 intangibles, except for goodwill and going concern value;[93] Class VII assets — goodwill and going concern value.[94]

4. Section 338(h)(10) Election

Under section 338(h)(10) and its regulations, a special election is available where, prior to a qualified stock purchase by a purchasing corporation, the target corporation is a member of an "affiliated group" of corporations, other than the parent corporation of the group (whether or not the group files a consolidated

---

[83] The example assumes that T Corp. has no liabilities; therefore, there is no adjustment to AGUB for target liabilities.

[84] See I.R.C. § § 338(b)(5). Treas. Reg. § 1.338-4(e), -5(a).

[85] See Treas. Reg. § 1.338-6(b)(1).

[86] Treas. Reg. § 1.338-6(b)(2)(i).

[87] See id.

[88] Treas. Reg. § 1.338-6(c)(1).

[89] See Treas. Reg. § 1.338-6(b)(2)(ii).

[90] See Treas. Reg. § 1.338-6(b)(2)(iii).

[91] Treas. Reg. § 1.338-6(b)(2)(iv).

[92] Treas. Reg. § 1.338-6(b)(2)(v).

[93] Treas. Reg. § 1.338-6(b)(2)(vi).

[94] Treas. Reg. § 1.338-6(b)(2)(vii).

return[95]).[96] In general terms, an "affiliated group" of corporations is defined as one or more chains of corporations with a common parent, which are connected through stock ownership that consists of at least 80 percent of the vote and value of a corporation's stock.[97] Thus, in general, a section 338(h)(10) election is available where the target corporation is at least 80 percent owned by a parent corporation, and the purchasing corporation acquires (in a qualified stock purchase) stock of the target corporation from the parent corporation.

The effect of a section 338(h)(10) election[98] is that (i) the target corporation is treated as if it had sold all of its assets to an unrelated person for an amount equal to the ADSP (basically the assets' fair market value)[99] and (ii) following the deemed asset sale, the target corporation distributed the proceeds of the sale to its parent corporation in a liquidation.[100] The deemed liquidation should qualify for nonrecognition treatment to both the target corporation and the parent corporation under sections 337 and 332, respectively.[101] Thus, the overall consequences of the election are that the parent corporation does not recognize any gain or loss on the sale of stock in the target corporation, but instead the target corporation realizes and recognizes gain or loss on the deemed asset sale, and the target corporation takes a new basis in its assets equal to the AGUB (basically their market value as of the acquisition date).

> *Example 19.14.* X Corp. owns all 100 shares of T Corp., having a total basis in the stock of $100,000. T Corp.'s only asset is equipment with a fair market value of $600,000 and a basis of $150,000, and T Corp. has no liabilities. On January 1, 2014, P Corp. acquires from X Corp. all 100 shares of T Corp. stock for $600,000 of cash. Following the stock acquisition, P Corp. and X Corp. make a timely section 338(h)(10) election. P Corp. keeps T Corp. alive as a wholly-owned subsidiary.

Determining the tax consequences to the parties in Example 19.14:

P Corp.'s acquisition of the T Corp. stock is a qualified stock purchase because P Corp. has acquired at least 80 percent of the vote and value of the T Corp. stock in a 12-month period (here 100 percent of the stock was acquired in one day). As a result of P Corp. and X Corp.'s timely section 338(h)(10) election: (i) X Corp. does not recognize any gain or loss on the sale of the T Corp. stock; (ii) T Corp. is treated as having sold the equipment, its only asset, for its fair market value of $600,000 on January 1, 2014 (the acquisition date), thereby realizing and recognizing $450,000 of

---

[95] The filing of a consolidated return by an affiliated group of corporations is briefly discussed in Chapter 13.

[96] *See* I.R.C. § 338(h)(10); Treas. Reg. § 1.338(h)(10)-1(b), (c)(1).

[97] *See* I.R.C. § 1504.

[98] A section 338(h)(10) election is required to be made jointly by the purchasing corporation and the parent corporation of the target corporation (or in the case where the target's affiliated group files a consolidated return, the consolidated group of corporations of which the target is a member). Treas. Reg. § 1.338(h)(10)-1(c)(3).

[99] Treas. Reg. § 1.338(h)(10)-1(d)(3).

[100] Treas. Reg. § 1.338(h)(10)-1(d)(4).

[101] *See* § 19.03.

gain ($600,000 amount realized minus $150,000 adjusted basis);[102] (iii) following the deemed sale, T Corp. is treated as having liquidated in a section 332 parent-subsidiary liquidation, in which neither T Corp. nor X Corp. recognizes any gain or loss (and X Corp. inherits T Corp.'s corporate attributes under section 381[103]); and (iv) as of January 2, 2014, T Corp. is treated as new corporation for tax purposes that has acquired the equipment in the deemed sale for $600,000, thus taking a fair market value basis in the equipment of $600,000 (and its corporate attributes begin anew). Notice that in this situation the section 338(h)(10) election produces two benefits for the parties: it provides T Corp. with a higher fair market value basis in its assets (which typically would be the case), and it results in a lower amount of gain recognized by the parties because T Corp.'s original basis in its assets ($150,000) is greater than X Corp.'s basis in its T Corp. stock ($100,000); this latter advantage may not always be present.

---

[102] As discussed above, the sales price on the deemed sale of the target corporation's assets will be increased by liabilities of the target corporation, including liabilities for the tax consequences resulting from the deemed sale. For purposes of this example, this adjustment is ignored.

[103] *See* § 23.01

Chapter 20

CORPORATE PENALTY TAXES

BASIC OVERVIEW

The Code contains two penalty taxes that can be imposed on a corporation: the accumulated earnings tax and the personal holding company tax. In general terms, both taxes penalize corporations where they improperly accumulate earnings as opposed to paying them out as dividends. This chapter provides a primer on these penalty taxes.

A. Accumulated Earnings Tax

C corporations and their shareholders have traditionally tried to avoid the sting of the double tax on distributed corporate earnings by employing strategies that involve the accumulation and bailout of earnings by the corporation.[1] The aim of the accumulated earnings tax is to deter such strategies by penalizing a C corporation that tries to avoid the shareholder tax by unreasonably accumulating earnings.[2] Under section 531, a corporation formed or availed of for a certain tax avoidance purpose is generally subject to an annual accumulated earnings tax that is equal to 20 percent of the corporation's "accumulated taxable income." When imposed, the accumulated earnings tax is in addition to a corporation's regular income tax.

1. Corporations Subject to Accumulated Earnings Tax

Under section 532(a), the accumulated earnings tax is generally imposed on a corporation that is formed or availed of for the purpose of avoiding the income tax with respect to its shareholders by permitting E&P to accumulate instead of being distributed.

Under section 533(a), accumulating E&P beyond the reasonable needs of the business is determinative of a purpose to avoid the income tax with respect to shareholders, unless the corporation proves otherwise. As a result of this provision, whether E&P has been accumulated beyond the reasonable business needs is almost always the key issue in whether the tax will be imposed.[3] Regarding what qualifies as a reasonable business need, section 537(a) lists a few items, including the

---

[1] *See* Boris I. Bittker & James S. Eustice, Federal Income Taxation of Corporations and Shareholders 7-2 – 7-3 (2000); Stephen Schwarz and Daniel J. Lathrope, Fundamentals of Corporate Taxation 626 (2012).

[2] *See* Schwarz & Lathrope, *supra* note 1 at 626.

[3] *See id* at 630.

"reasonably anticipated needs of the business."[4] The regulations expand on this and provide that reasonable accumulations are those that are "appropriate for present business purposes and the reasonably anticipated needs of the business."[5] The Detailed Analysis examines a list of grounds provided in the regulations that may indicate that accumulations of E&P are either for reasonable business needs[6] or are unreasonable.[7]

2. Accumulated Taxable Income

When imposed for a taxable year, the accumulated earnings tax is equal to 20 percent of a corporation's "accumulated taxable income."[8] In general terms, accumulated taxable income roughly represents the corporation's economic income for the particular year that has been retained for reasons other than reasonable business needs. More specifically, section 535(a) defines "accumulated taxable income" as taxable income, with certain adjustments, minus the sum of (i) the dividends paid deduction and (ii) the accumulated earnings credit. In general, the adjustments to taxable income (examined in the Detailed Analysis) are somewhat similar to those made in determining E&P. Under section 561(a), a corporation's dividends paid deduction is equal to the sum of the dividends paid during the taxable year plus the "consent dividends" for the taxable year. A "consent dividend" occurs where a shareholder holding consent stock (basically common stock) on the last day of a corporation's taxable year agrees to treat a certain amount as a dividend by filing a consent with the corporation's tax return.[9] In general, the accumulated earnings credit under section 535(c) is equal to such part of the E&P for the year that is retained for the reasonable needs of the business, minus a deduction for net capital gains (as adjusted for taxes).[10] Under section 535(c)(2), a corporation is generally entitled to a minimum credit that is equal to the excess of $250,000 over the corporation's accumulated E&P at the close of the preceding tax year.[11] The effect of the minimum credit is that a corporation can generally accumulate up to $250,000 of E&P during its lifetime without regard to business needs.[12]

---

[4] I.R.C. § 537(a)(1).

[5] Treas. Reg. § 1.537-1(a).

[6] Treas. Reg. § 1.537-2(b).

[7] Treas. Reg. § 1.537-2(c).

[8] I.R.C. § 531.

[9] I.R.C. § 565(a).

[10] I.R.C. § 535(c)(1).

[11] I.R.C. § 535(c)(2)(A).

[12] *See* Schwarz & Lathrope, supra note 1 at 644.

B. Personal Holding Company Tax

Throughout most of U.S. income tax history, the corporate income tax rates have been lower than the individual income tax rates.[13] This led to strategies where the corporation was used as a refuge from the higher individual rates. One such strategy was the so-called incorporated pocketbook, where individuals would transfer investment assets to a corporation in order to have the interest and dividend income taxable at the then lower corporate income tax rates, rather than the steeper individual rates.[14]

The personal holding company tax was enacted to target these abusive strategies by providing an automatic penalty if certain objective criteria are met. Under section 541, a corporation that is a "personal holding company" is subject to an annual personal holding company tax that is equal to 20 percent of the corporation's "undistributed personal holding company income." Like the accumulated earnings tax, the personal holding company tax, when imposed, is in addition to a corporation's regular income tax.

1. Definition of Personal Holding Company

In general terms, a personal holding company is a closely held corporation with a high proportion of its income being passive income or certain personal service income. Specifically, section 542(a) generally defines a "personal holding company" as a corporation that satisfies both an adjusted ordinary income requirement and a stock ownership requirement. Under section 542(a)(1), the adjusted ordinary income requirement is satisfied for a taxable year if at least 60 percent of the corporation's "adjusted ordinary gross income" for the year consists of "personal holding company income."[15] "Adjusted ordinary gross income" is generally defined as gross income, excluding capital gains and section 1231 gains, reduced by expenses relating to rent as well as mineral, oil, and gas royalties.[16] In general terms, "personal holding company income" is passive investment income such as dividends, interest, annuities, certain rents, and certain royalties, as well as certain personal service income; the Detailed Analysis examines personal holding company income more closely. Under section 542(a)(2), the stock ownership requirement is satisfied if more than 50 percent in value of the corporation's stock is owned (directly or indirectly) by five or fewer individuals at any time during the last half of the taxable year. For purposes of determining stock ownership, the constructive ownership rules contained in section 544 apply.

---

[13] As discussed in Chapter 13, the highest individual rate is currently only slightly higher than the highest corporate rate.

[14] *See* Bittker and Eustice, *supra* note 1 at 7-42.

[15] I.R.C. § 542(a)(1).

[16] *See* I.R.C. § 543(b)(1), (2).

2. Undistributed Personal Holding Company Income

When imposed for a taxable year, the personal holding company tax is equal to 20 percent of a corporation's "undistributed personal holding company income."[17] In general terms, undistributed personal holding company income roughly represents the corporation's economic income for the particular year that has been retained. More specifically, section 545(a) defines "undistributed personal holding company income" as taxable income, with certain adjustments, minus the dividends paid deduction. In general, the adjustments to taxable income under section 545(b) (examined in the Detailed Analysis) are somewhat similar to those made in determining E&P. Under section 561(a), the dividends paid deduction is equal to the sum of the dividends paid during taxable the year, the "consent dividends" for the taxable year, and the dividend carryover for the taxable year. The definition of consent dividends is the same as for purposes of the accumulated earnings tax. Under section 564, the dividend carryover for a taxable year is basically the extent to which the dividends paid by the corporation in the preceding two years exceed the taxable income (as adjusted under section 545(b)) of the corporation for these years.[18] Section 547 provides a procedure (discussed in the Detailed Analysis) under which a corporation can reduce or eliminate its personal holding company tax liability after it has been established by distributing a "deficiency dividend."[19]

DETAILED ANALYSIS

§ 20.01 ACCUMULATED EARNINGS TAX

A. Overview

C corporations and their shareholders have traditionally tried to avoid the sting of the double tax on distributed corporate earnings by employing strategies that involve the accumulation of earnings by the corporation.[20] By accumulating earnings, as opposed to distributing them, a shareholder tax on dividends can be avoided. Subsequently, the earnings could be "bailed out" with basis offset and preferential capital gain rates, through a redemption or sale of stock, or a liquidation of the corporation. If the shareholder were to die before the bailout, then her heirs would take a stepped-up basis in the stock under section 1014, in which case a subsequent sale, redemption or liquidation could be tax-free to the shareholders. The aim of the accumulated earnings tax is to deter such strategies by penalizing a C corporation that tries to avoid the shareholder tax by unreasonably accumulating earnings.[21]

Under section 531, a corporation formed or availed of for a certain tax avoidance purpose is generally subject to an annual accumulated earnings tax that is equal to

---

[17] I.R.C. § 541.

[18] I.R.C. § 564(a), (b).

[19] *See* I.R.C. § 547(a).

[20] *See* Bittker & Eustice, *supra* note 1 at 7-3; Schwarz & Lathrope, *supra* note 1 at 626.

[21] *See* Schwarz & Lathrope, *supra* note 1 at 626.

20 percent of the corporation's "accumulated taxable income." When imposed, the accumulated earnings tax is in addition to a corporation's regular income tax. The following sections of this part examine (i) the corporations that are subject to the accumulated earnings tax, in particular, the prohibited tax avoidance purpose that triggers the tax and (ii) accumulated taxable income — the base of the accumulated earnings tax.

B.   Corporations Subject to Accumulated Earnings Tax

1.   In General

Under section 532(a), the accumulated earnings tax is generally imposed on a corporation that is formed or availed of for the purpose of avoiding the income tax with respect to its shareholders by permitting E&P to accumulate instead of being distributed. A few types of corporations are exempt from the imposition of the tax, including a personal holding company (which is examined in § 20.02).[22] In addition, while section 532(c) does not prevent a publicly traded corporation from being subject to the tax, the legislative history to this provision indicates that, practically speaking, it may be difficult to establish the prohibited purpose in the case of a widely held company.[23]

2.   Prohibited Tax Avoidance Purpose

a.   In General

Under section 533(a), accumulating E&P beyond the reasonable needs of the business is determinative of a purpose to avoid the income tax with respect to shareholders, unless the corporation proves otherwise. As a result of this provision, whether E&P has been accumulated beyond the reasonable business needs is almost always the key issue in whether the tax will be imposed.[24] If an unreasonable accumulation is established, corporations are rarely able to prove that the accumulation was not motivated by tax avoidance.[25] And while it is theoretically possible to establish the prohibited purpose where an accumulation is found to be reasonable,[26] the tax would not be imposed in any event in this situation because of the accumulated earnings credit,[27] which reduces the base of the accumulated earnings tax by the amount of E&P that is accumulated for

---

[22] Also excluded are tax-exempt organizations and passive foreign investment companies. *See* I.R.C. § 532(b). In addition, S corporations are exempt from the accumulated earnings tax as a result of section 1363(a), which exempts an S corporation from taxation except as otherwise provided in subchapter S. *See* Chapter 24.

[23] *See* H.R. Rep. No. 861, 98th Cong., 2d Sess. 829 (1984), reprinted in 1984-3 C.B. (vol. 2) 1, 84.

[24] *See* Schwarz & Lathrope, supra note 1 at 630.

[25] *See* Bittker & Eustice, *supra* note 1 at 7-14.

[26] In this regard, the regulations state that the prohibited purpose may be indicated by circumstances other than unreasonable accumulations. Treas. Reg. § 1.533-1(a)(2).

[27] *See* Schwarz & Lathrope, supra note 1 at 630, n. 15.

reasonable needs.[28]

Section 533(b) also provides that where a corporation is a holding or investment company, this is prima facie evidence of the prohibited purpose. According to the regulations, a holding company is a "corporation having practically no activities except holding property and collecting the income therefrom or investing therein;" if the activities of such a company further include the buying and selling of investment property, so that the income is also derived from market fluctuations, the corporation is an investment company.[29] Section 533(b) may not have much effect, however, given that most holding or investment companies are probably also personal holding companies or passive foreign investment companies, which are exempt from the accumulated earnings tax.[30]

b.   Reasonable Needs of the Business

As mentioned above, the key issue with regard to imposing the accumulated earnings tax is whether E&P has accumulated beyond the reasonable needs of the business. Regarding what qualifies as a reasonable business need, section 537(a) lists a few items, including the "reasonably anticipated needs of the business."[31] The regulations expand on this and provide that reasonable accumulations are those that are "appropriate for present business purposes and the reasonably anticipated needs of the business."[32] After pointing out the facts and circumstances nature of the inquiry,[33] the regulations provide a non-exclusive list of grounds that may indicate that accumulations of E&P are for reasonable business needs (if supported by sufficient facts):[34]

- To provide for the bona fide expansion of business or replacement of plant;

- To acquire a business enterprise through purchasing stock or assets;

- To provide for the retirement of bona fide indebtedness created in connection with a trade or business;

- To provide necessary working capital for the business;[35]

- To provide for investments or loans to suppliers or customers if necessary in order to maintain the business of the corporation; or

- To provide for the payment of reasonably anticipated "product liability losses."[36]

---

[28] See I.R.C. § 535(c). The accumulated earnings credit is discussed at § 20.01[C][3].

[29] Treas. Reg. § 1.533-1(c).

[30] See Bittker & Eustice, supra note 1 at 7-36.

[31] I.R.C. § 537(a)(1).

[32] Treas. Reg. § 1.537-1(a).

[33] Treas. Reg. § 1.537-2(a).

[34] Treas. Reg. § 1.537-2(b).

[35] In this regard, the courts have used as a guideline a formula for determining the working capital needs of a corporation, which calculates the funds needed for one operating cycle of a corporation's business. See Bardahl Manufacturing Corp. v. Commissioner, 24 T.C.M. 1030 (1965).

[36] These are defined in section 172(f), Treas. Reg. § 1.172-13(b)(1), and Treas. Reg. § 1.537-1(f).

The regulations also contain a non-exclusive list of objectives that may indicate that accumulations of E&P are unreasonable:[37]

- Loans to shareholders, or the expenditure of the corporation's funds for the personal benefit of shareholders;

- Loans having no reasonable relation to the conduct of the business made to relatives or friends of shareholders, or to other persons;

- Loan to another corporation whose business is different from that of the corporation, if the other corporation is owned (directly or indirectly) by one or more shareholders of the corporation and such shareholder or shareholders control both corporations;

- Investments that are unrelated to the corporation's business activities;

- Retention of E&P to provide against unrealistic hazards.

For purposes of the inquiry, the regulations provide that the business of a corporation is not just the business that it has been engaged in, but also includes any line of business that it may undertake.[38] In addition, the business of a corporation may, depending on the circumstances, include the business of that corporation's subsidiary, so that a parent corporation's investment of its E&P in the stock or securities of its subsidiary may be treated as if the parent employed the E&P in its own business.[39]

With regard to accumulating E&P for reasonably anticipated future needs, the regulations caution that there must be an indication that business's future needs require such an accumulation, and that "the corporation must have specific, definite, and feasible plans for the use of such accumulation."[40] The regulations further state that there is no requirement that the accumulated funds be used immediately or within a short time after the close of the particular year in which the accumulation occurs, provided that the accumulated E&P "will be used within a reasonable time depending upon all of the facts and circumstances relating to the future needs of the business;" but the execution of the plans must not be postponed indefinitely.[41]

In this regard, a good illustration is *Myron's Enterprises v. United States*,[42] where a corporation accumulated E&P in order to purchase the corporation's operating premises (a ballroom and lounge), which the corporation had been leasing from the owner. Although the corporation had attempted unsuccessfully to buy the premises for several years, and no purchase had occurred at the time of the trial, the court determined that the accumulation was for reasonably anticipated future needs. The court found that the corporation had been extremely diligent in its attempts to purchase the facility by agreeing to all of the owner's stated terms,

---

[37] Treas. Reg. § 1.537-2(c).

[38] Treas. Reg. § 1.537-3(a).

[39] Treas. Reg. § 1.537-3(b).

[40] Treas. Reg. § 1.537-1(b)(1).

[41] *Id.*

[42] 548 F.2d 331 (9th Cir. 1977).

and the owner might have decided to accept the corporation's offer at any time during the taxable years at issue.

C. Accumulated Taxable Income

When imposed for a taxable year, the accumulated earnings tax is equal to 20 percent of a corporation's "accumulated taxable income."[43] In general terms, accumulated taxable income roughly represents the corporation's economic income for the particular year that has been retained for reasons other than reasonable business needs. More specifically, section 535(a) defines "accumulated taxable income" as taxable income, with certain adjustments, minus the sum of (i) the dividends paid deduction and (ii) the accumulated earnings credit.

1. Adjustments to Taxable Income

In general, the adjustments to taxable income for purposes of determining accumulated taxable income are somewhat similar to those made in determining E&P[44]; in both cases the goal is to reflect more closely economic income and thus the corporation's dividend-paying capacity.[45] These adjustments include deductions for federal income taxes,[46] charitable contributions in excess of the limit contained in section 170(b)(2),[47] and excess capital losses disallowed under section 1211 (but subject to a possible reduction).[48] Conversely, certain deductions for taxable income purposes are disallowed in determining accumulated taxable income and thus must be added back to taxable income; these include the dividends-received deduction,[49] the net operating loss deduction,[50] and the capital loss carryover.[51] In addition, in computing accumulated taxable income, a corporation receives a deduction for net capital gain reduced by the taxes attributable to such gain.[52]

2. Dividends Paid Deduction

Under section 561(a), a corporation's dividends paid deduction is equal to the sum of the dividends paid during the taxable year plus the "consent dividends" (described below) for the taxable year. For this purpose, dividends that are paid within two and one-half months after the close of a taxable year are treated as paid

---

[43] I.R.C. § 531.

[44] *See* Chapter 16.

[45] *See* Bittker & Eustice, *supra* note 1 at 7-37.

[46] I.R.C. § 535(b)(1). The adjustment also includes a deduction for nondeductible foreign taxes, but no deduction is permitted for the accumulated earnings tax or the personal holding company tax. *Id.*

[47] I.R.C. § 535(b)(2).

[48] I.R.C. § 535(b)(5).

[49] I.R.C. § 535(b)(3).

[50] I.R.C. § 535(b)(4).

[51] I.R.C. § 535(b)(7)(B).

[52] I.R.C. § 535(b)(6). There are also some special rules for holding or investment companies. I.R.C. § 535(b)(8).

during such taxable year.[53] In general, the regular meaning of dividend[54] is used for purposes of the dividends paid deduction,[55] except that dividends generally have to be pro rata in order to qualify,[56] and a portion of the distributions on the liquidation of the corporation or redemption of stock may be treated as a deductible dividend.[57]

Under section 565(a), a "consent dividend" occurs where a shareholder holding consent stock (basically common stock[58]) on the last day of a corporation's taxable year agrees to treat a certain amount as a dividend by filing a consent with the corporation's tax return. To qualify as a consent dividend, the agreed-to amount, if distributed, would have to have constituted a dividend under its regular meaning,[59] and generally must be pro-rata.[60] A consent dividend is treated as if it were distributed to the shareholder and then contributed to the capital of the corporation, all on the last day of the corporation's taxable year.[61] The consent dividend procedure allows a corporation to reduce or eliminate its accumulated earnings tax liability without distributing an actual dividend.

3. Accumulated Earnings Credit

As mentioned above, a corporation deducts the accumulated earnings credit in determining its accumulated taxable income.[62] In general, the accumulated earnings credit under section 535(c) is equal to such part of the E&P for the year that is retained for the reasonable needs of the business, minus the deduction for net capital gains (as adjusted for taxes).[63] Thus, even though a corporation may be subject to the accumulated earnings tax because of some unreasonable accumulations, the portion of the accumulations that are reasonable reduce the tax base. Under section 535(c)(2), a corporation is generally entitled to a minimum credit that is equal to the excess of $250,000 over the corporation's accumulated E&P at the close of the preceding tax year.[64] The effect of the minimum credit is that a corporation can generally accumulate up to $250,000 of E&P during its lifetime without regard to business needs.[65]

---

[53] I.R.C. § 563(a).

[54] *See* Chapter 16.

[55] I.R.C. § 562(a).

[56] I.R.C. § 562(c).

[57] I.R.C. § 562(b)(1).

[58] I.R.C. § 565(f).

[59] I.R.C. § 565(b)(2).

[60] I.R.C. § 565(b)(1).

[61] I.R.C. § 565(c).

[62] The credit label is misleading, as the accumulated earnings credit reduces the base of the accumulated earnings tax, not the tax itself.

[63] I.R.C. § 535(c)(1). Holding or investment companies are not entitled to an accumulated earnings credit for reasonable accumulations, but are entitled to a credit equal to the excess of $250,000 over the corporation's accumulated E&P at the close of the preceding tax year. I.R.C. § 535(c)(3).

[64] I.R.C. § 535(c)(2)(A). In the case of certain service corporations, $150,000 is substituted for $250,000 in determining the minimum credit. I.R.C. § 535(c)(2)(B).

[65] *See* Schwarz & Lathrope, *supra* note 1 at 644.

§ 20.02 PERSONAL HOLDING COMPANY TAX

A. Overview

Throughout most of U.S. income tax history, the corporate income tax rates have been lower than the individual income tax rates.[66] This led to strategies where the corporation was used as a refuge from the higher individual rates. One such strategy was the so-called incorporated pocketbook, where individuals would transfer investment assets to a corporation in order to have the interest and dividend income taxable at the then-lower corporate income tax rates, rather than the steeper individual rates.[67] The parties could then employ bailout techniques to reduce or eliminate the shareholder tax on the ultimate distribution of the corporate income to the shareholders.[68] Another strategy was the incorporated talent, where most of the service income generated by a highly compensated individual would be shifted to a corporation by having the corporation perform the services through the employment of the individual at a low salary.[69]

The personal holding company tax was enacted to target these abusive strategies by providing an automatic penalty if certain objective criteria are met.[70] Under section 541, a corporation that is a "personal holding company" is subject to an annual personal holding company tax that is equal to 20 percent of the corporation's "undistributed personal holding company income." Like the accumulated earnings tax, the personal holding company tax, when imposed, is in addition to a corporation's regular income tax. While the above strategies are likely a thing of the past given the current parity in corporate and individual rates, the tax can still apply in unexpected circumstances.[71]

The following parts of this section examine (i) the definition of a "personal holding company," which determines the corporations subject to the personal holding company tax, and (ii) "undistributed personal holding company income — the base of the personal holding company tax.

---

[66] As discussed in Chapter 13, the highest individual rate is currently only slightly higher than the highest corporate rate.

[67] *See* Bittker & Eustice, *supra* note 1 at 7-42.

[68] *See* § 20.01[A].

[69] *See* Bittker & Eustice, *supra* note 1 at 7-42. There was also the strategy of the incorporated yacht or similar property, where a yacht or similar luxury property would be transferred to a corporation along with investment assets, with the aim of deducting depreciation and operating expenses on the property against the investment income, while allowing the shareholders to still benefit from the luxury property. *See id.*

[70] While the accumulated earnings tax may have been used to combat these strategies, Congress preferred a targeted, objective approach that did not rely on detecting and proving a tax avoidance purpose. *See id.*

[71] *See id* at 7-60 – 7-61 (providing as an example a corporation that has sold all of its business assets and is holding investment assets while awaiting the death of the principal shareholders, so that the shareholder's heirs can benefit from a stepped-up stock basis on the liquidation of the corporation).

B. Definition of Personal Holding Company

In general terms, a personal holding company is a closely held corporation with a high proportion of its income being passive income or certain personal service income. Specifically, section 542(a) generally defines a "personal holding company" as a corporation that satisfies both an adjusted ordinary income requirement and a stock ownership requirement, both of which are examined below. Several types of corporations are excluded from being a personal holding company, including tax-exempt organizations, banks, savings and loans, life insurance companies, foreign corporations, and certain lending or finance companies.[72]

1. Adjusted Ordinary Income Requirement

Under section 542(a)(1), the adjusted ordinary income requirement is satisfied for a taxable year if at least 60 percent of the corporation's "adjusted ordinary gross income" for the year consists of "personal holding company income."[73] "Adjusted ordinary gross income" is generally defined as gross income, excluding capital gains and section 1231 gains, reduced by expenses relating to rent as well as mineral, oil, and gas royalties.[74] The exclusion for capital gains and 1231 gains is to prevent a corporation from increasing adjusted ordinary gross income (and thereby reducing the percentage of such income that is personal holding company income) by timing the recognition of such gains.[75] The reductions for expenses relating to rental and mineral royalty income similarly prevent a corporation from diluting the percentage of personal holding company income by increasing ordinary income through leveraged investments in such property;[76] these reductions also result in a better reflection of the economic income associated with rent and mineral royalties in determining both adjusted ordinary gross income and personal holding company income.[77]

In general terms, "personal holding company income" is passive investment income and certain personal service income. More specifically, section 543(a) defines "personal holding company income" as including the following:

- Gross income from dividends, interest, annuities, and royalties — excluded are: mineral, oil, or gas royalties or copyright royalties; certain computer software royalties derived from business activities; and certain types of

---

[72] *See* I.R.C. § 542(c). In addition, S corporations are exempt from the personal holding company tax as a result of section 1363(a), which exempts an S corporation from taxation except as otherwise provided in subchapter S. *See* Chapter 24.

[73] I.R.C. § 542(a)(1).

[74] *See* I.R.C. § 543(b)(1), (2). These expenses include depreciation (generally), depletion, interest and property taxes. *See* I.R.C. § 543(b)(2)(A), (B). Also excluded in determining adjusted ordinary gross income is interest on condemnation awards, judgments and tax refunds, as well as interest received on U.S. obligations held by regular dealers in such obligations. I.R.C. § 543(b)(2)(C).

[75] *See* Schwarz & Lathrope, *supra* note 1 at 647 (referring to the legislative history of the 1964 amendments to section 543).

[76] *See id.*

[77] *See* Bittker & Eustice, *supra* note 1 at 7-46.

interest.[78]

- Adjusted income from certain rents — in general terms, this is gross income from rent, reduced by related expenses,[79] which, based on an objective standard, is not considered to have been derived from a business of leasing property.[80]

- Adjusted income from certain mineral, oil or gas royalties — in general terms, this is gross income from mineral, oil, or gas royalties, reduced by related expenses[81] that, based on an objective standard, is not considered to have been derived from a business involving mineral property.[82]

- Gross income from certain copyright royalties — in general terms, this is gross income from copyright royalties that, based on an objective standard, is not considered to have been derived from a business of licensing copyrighted works.[83]

- Gross income from produced film rents — in general terms, this is gross income from rents arising from an interest in a film acquired before the production of the film was substantially complete that, based on an objective standard, is not considered to have been derived from a business of producing films.[84]

- Gross income from the use of tangible property of the corporation by individual shareholders in certain circumstances — these circumstances occur when (i) the individual shareholder entitled to use the property owns actually or constructively[85] (directly or indirectly) 25 percent or more in value of the corporation's stock at any time during the taxable year and (ii) personal holding company income, apart from income in this category and rent (along with a few other adjustments) exceeds 10 percent of ordinary

---

[78] I.R.C. § 543(a)(1), 543(d). The interest excluded from personal holding company income includes the types of interest excluded from adjusted ordinary gross income (*see* supra note 74), along with certain interest received by dealers in securities and money market instruments and a few specialized types of interest. *See* I.R.C. § 543(a)(1).

[79] These are the same expenses that reduce gross income from rents for purposes of determining adjusted ordinary gross income. I.R.C. § 543(b)(3).

[80] I.R.C. § 543(a)(2). Under this objective standard, adjusted income from rent is excluded from personal holding company income if (i) such adjusted income constitutes at least 50 percent of adjusted ordinary income and (ii) basically, personal holding company income, apart from rent and reduced by dividends paid or deemed paid during the year, does not exceed 10 percent of ordinary gross income (which is gross income excluding capital gains and section 1231 gains). *See id.* The statute employs similar schemes for distinguishing between business and nonbusiness income for computer software royalties (mentioned above), and mineral royalties, copyright royalties, and produced film rents (discussed below).

[81] These are the same expenses that reduce gross income from such royalties for purposes of determining adjusted ordinary gross income. I.R.C. § 543(b)(4).

[82] I.R.C. § 543(a)(3).

[83] I.R.C. § 543(a)(4).

[84] I.R.C. § 543(a)(5).

[85] The section 544 constructive ownership rules apply for this purpose. I.R.C. § 544(a). *See* § 20.02[B][2] for a brief description of these rules.

gross income (which is gross income excluding capital gains and section 1231 gains).[86]

- Gross income from certain personal service contracts — this occurs when the corporation is to provide personal services under a contract if (i) some person other than the corporation can designate the individual who is to perform the services, or such individual is designated (by name or description) in the contract and (ii) the designated person owns actually or constructively[87] (directly or indirectly) 25 percent or more in value of the corporation's stock at any time during the taxable year.[88]

- Income that is includible as a result of being a beneficiary of an estate or trust.[89]

Example 20.1. For 2014, X Corp. has $300,000 of gross income from manufacturing widgets, $500,000 of capital gains from selling publicly-traded stock, and $700,000 of dividend income from its holdings of stock in publicly-traded corporations.

Determining whether the adjusted ordinary gross income requirement is satisfied in Example 20.1:

X Corp.'s adjusted ordinary gross income for 2014 is $1,000,000, its gross income from manufacturing and dividends; the capital gains are excluded. The $700,000 of dividends are personal holding company income. Therefore, for 2014 the adjusted ordinary gross income requirement is satisfied because the personal holding company income of $700,000 is at least 60 percent of the adjusted ordinary gross income of $1,000,000.

2. Stock Ownership Requirement

Under section 542(a)(2), the stock ownership requirement is satisfied if more than 50 percent in value of the corporation's stock is owned (directly or indirectly) by five or fewer individuals at any time during the last half of the taxable year. For purposes of determining stock ownership, the constructive ownership rules contained in section 544 apply. Somewhat similar to section 318,[90] these rules contain entity-to-owner (or beneficiary) attribution, family attribution (with a slightly different definition of family than that for section 318 purposes), partner attribution, and option attribution, plus a few types of chain attribution.[91]

Example 20.2. During all of 2014, the 100 shares of voting common stock (the only class outstanding) of X Corp. is owned as follows: individuals A, B, C, and D each own 15 shares, and the remaining 40 shares are owned two

---

[86] I.R.C. § 543(a)(6).

[87] The section 544 constructive ownership rules apply for this purpose. I.R.C. § 544(a). *See* § 20.03[B][2] for a brief description of these rules.

[88] I.R.C. § 543(a)(7).

[89] I.R.C. § 543(a)(8).

[90] *See* Chapter 17.

[91] I.R.C. § 544(a). For a discussion of these types of attribution in the context of section 318, see Chapter 17.

shares each by 20 individuals; all of the shareholders are unrelated for purposes of the constructive ownership rules.

Determining whether the stock ownership requirement is satisfied in Example 20.2:

During all of 2014, individuals A, B, C and D own a total of 60 out of 100 shares, or 60 percent, of the only class of X Corp. stock outstanding. Therefore, for 2014 the stock ownership requirement is satisfied because five or fewer individuals (here four individuals) own more than 50 percent in value of the X Corp. stock at any time during the last half of the year.

C. Undistributed Personal Holding Company Income

When imposed for a taxable year, the personal holding company tax is equal to 20 percent of a corporation's "undistributed personal holding company income."[92] In general terms, undistributed personal holding company income roughly represents the corporation's economic income for the particular year that has been retained. More specifically, section 545(a) defines "undistributed personal holding company income" as taxable income, with certain adjustments, minus the dividends paid deduction. Importantly, while the label may suggest otherwise, undistributed personal holding company income is not simply personal holding company income, as described above, that has been retained.[93]

1. Adjustments to Taxable Income

In general, the adjustments to taxable income under section 545(b) for purposes of determining undistributed personal holding company income are somewhat similar to those made in determining E&P, and similar to the adjustments made in computing accumulated taxable income for purposes of the accumulated earnings tax;[94] in all three cases, the goal is to reflect more closely economic income and thus the corporation's dividend-paying capacity.[95] These adjustments include a deduction for federal income taxes[96] and a revised deduction for charitable contributions that generally uses the percentage limitations for individuals contained in section 170.[97] The dividends-received deduction is disallowed and thus must be added back to taxable income.[98] Also, the regular net operating loss deduction is replaced with a deduction for the net operating loss for the preceding year (computed with certain adjustments).[99] In addition, a corporation receives a deduction for net capital gain reduced by the taxes attributable to such gain.[100] Finally, the deduction for

[92] I.R.C. § 541.

[93] See Bittker & Eustice, *supra* note 1 at 7-57 – 7-58.

[94] See § 20.01[C][1].

[95] See Bittker & Eustice, *supra* note 1 at 7-37, 7-58.

[96] I.R.C. § 545(b)(1). The adjustment also includes a deduction for nondeductible foreign taxes, but no deduction is permitted for the accumulated earnings tax or the personal holding company tax. *Id.*

[97] I.R.C. § 545(b)(2).

[98] I.R.C. § 545(b)(3).

[99] I.R.C. § 545(b)(4).

[100] I.R.C. § 545(b)(5).

depreciation and operating expenses on property owned or operated by the corporation is limited to the rent received by the corporation for the use of such property, unless the corporation establishes that (i) the rent received was the highest obtainable (or none was obtainable), (ii) the property was held in a bona fide business for profit, and (iii) either it was reasonably expected that operating the property would result in profit, or the property was necessary for conducting the business.[101]

2. Dividends Paid Deduction

The dividends paid deduction for purposes of computing undistributed personal holding company income is similar to the dividends paid deduction used for determining accumulated taxable income under the accumulated earnings tax.[102] Under section 561(a), this deduction is equal to the sum of the dividends paid during taxable the year, the "consent dividends" for the taxable year, and the dividend carryover (described below) for the taxable year. The definition of consent dividends is the same as for purposes of the accumulated earnings tax.[103] For purposes of determining the dividends paid during a taxable year, section 563(b) provides that dividends paid within three and one-half months after the close of a taxable year are treated as paid during such taxable year if the corporation elects such treatment; however, the amount treated as paid for a taxable year under section 563(b) cannot exceed either (i) the undistributed personal holding company income for the taxable year or (ii) 20 percent of the dividends paid for the taxable year, in both cases determined without regard to this provision. In general, the regular meaning of dividend[104] is used for purposes of the dividends paid deduction,[105] except that dividends generally have to be pro rata in order to qualify,[106] and a portion of the distributions on the liquidation of the corporation may be treated as a deductible dividend.[107]

Under section 564, the dividend carryover for a taxable year is basically the extent to which the dividends paid by the corporation in the preceding two years exceed the taxable income of the corporation, as adjusted under section 545(b), for these years.[108] Thus, section 564 effectively permits a corporation, which has overdistributed (vis à vis its adjusted taxable income) in the previous two years, to credit the overdistribution against its undistributed personal holding company income for the current year.[109]

Section 547 provides a procedure under which a corporation can reduce or eliminate its personal holding company tax liability after it has been established by

---

[101] I.R.C. § 545(b)(6).

[102] *See* § 20.01[C][2].

[103] *See id.*

[104] *See* Chapter 16.

[105] I.R.C. § 562(a).

[106] I.R.C. § 562(c).

[107] *See* I.R.C. § 562(b)(2), 316(b)(2).

[108] I.R.C. § 564(a), (b).

[109] *See* Schwarz & Lathrope, *supra* note 1 at 657.

distributing a "deficiency dividend."[110] A deficiency dividend is a dividend paid by the corporation within 90 days after liability for the personal holding company tax is determined (by way of a court decision or certain agreement with the Service[111]), provided the dividend would have given rise to a dividends paid deduction for the year that the personal holding company liability is determined if distributed in such year.[112] To receive a deficiency dividend deduction for purposes of determining its personal holding company tax liability, the corporation must file a claim within 120 days after the tax is determined.[113]

---

[110] *See* I.R.C. § 547(a).

[111] *See* I.R.C. § 547(c).

[112] I.R.C. § 547(d)(1).

[113] *See* I.R.C. § 547(e). No deficiency dividend deduction is allowed where the determination includes a finding of fraud with intent to evade tax or willful failure to file a timely return. I.R.C. § 547(g).

Chapter 21

CORPORATE REORGANIZATIONS

BASIC OVERVIEW

This chapter examines the tax treatment of shareholders and corporations that engage in corporate reorganizations. In very general terms, a corporate reorganization occurs when two corporations merge or otherwise come together in some fashion — i.e., an acquiring corporation acquires the assets or stock of a target corporation; or a corporate reorganization can be the restructuring of a single corporation. This chapter provides a primer on corporate reorganizations, which includes the types of reorganizations, including their requirements, and the treatment of the corporations and shareholders that are parties to a reorganization.

A. Types of Reorganizations and Requirements

Section 368(a) provides for several types of reorganizations, which include the following more basic types:

- "A" reorganizations: statutory mergers and consolidations,
- "B" reorganizations: stock-for-stock acquisitions, and
- "C" reorganizations: asset-for-stock acquisitions.

These types of reorganizations are discussed below. The Detailed Analysis examines them more fully, and also discusses several other types of reorganizations.

1. Non-Statutory Requirements for Reorganizations

To qualify as a reorganization, besides satisfying the statutory tests, a transaction must also meet certain non-statutory requirements. First, a reorganization is required to have a business purpose.[1] In addition, a reorganization must satisfy the continuity of business enterprise requirement set forth in the regulations, under which the acquiring corporation is required to either:

- Continue the target corporation's historic business, or
- Use a significant portion of the target's historic business assets in a business.[2]

The final non-statutory requirement is the continuity of interest requirement, which

---

[1] Treas. Reg. § 1.368-1(c).

[2] Treas. Reg. § 1.368-1(d)(1).

basically provides that, in the aggregate, a sufficient portion of the target corporation shareholders' interest in the target must continue in the stock of the acquiring corporation after the reorganization.[3] While the requisite percentage of qualifying consideration is not completely clear, the Service will ordinarily issue a favorable ruling where at least 50 percent of the total consideration received by the target shareholders is stock in the acquiring corporation.[4] Examples in the regulations are more lenient and provide that 40 percent continuity is sufficient to satisfy the requirement,[5] a view that is supported by case law.[6]

2. "A" Reorganizations: Statutory Mergers and Consolidations

Under section 368(a)(1)(A), an "A" reorganization is a statutory merger or consolidation.[7] A statutory merger is a transaction effected pursuant to a state or foreign statute whereby the assets and liabilities of the target corporation are transferred to the acquiring corporation and the target corporation ceases its legal existence.[8] A statutory consolidation is similar, except that the assets and liabilities of two corporations are transferred to a newly created corporation and the transferor corporations cease their legal existence. In a statutory merger or consolidation, the shareholders of the merged or consolidated corporations will exchange their stock for stock or debt instruments of the acquiring corporation, cash, or some combination thereof. Unlike the other types of reorganizations, section 368(a) does not prescribe the permissible consideration for an "A" reorganization. Nevertheless, pursuant to the continuity of interest requirement (discussed above), a sufficient portion of the consideration received by the shareholders of the merged or consolidated corporations must be stock in the acquiring corporation.

3. "B" Reorganizations: Stock-for-Stock Acquisitions

Under section 368(a)(1)(B), a "B" reorganization has the following requirements:

- An acquiring corporation acquires stock in a target corporation,
- The acquisition is *solely* in exchange for voting stock of the acquiring corporation, and
- The acquiring corporation "controls" the target corporation immediately after the acquisition.[9]

Under section 368(c), "control" is defined as the ownership of at least 80 percent of (i) the total combined voting power of all classes of stock entitled to vote and (ii) the total number of shares of all other classes of stock. Following a "B" reorganization,

---

[3] *See* Treas. Reg. § 1.368-1(e)(1)(i).

[4] Rev. Proc. 77-37, 1977-2 C.B. 568.

[5] Treas. Reg. § 1.368-1(e)(2)(v), Examples 1, 2(ii).

[6] *See* Stephen Schwarz and Daniel J. Lathrope, Fundamentals of Corporate Taxation 402 (2012).

[7] I.R.C. § 368(a)(1)(A).

[8] Treas. Reg. § 1.368-2(b)(1)(ii).

[9] I.R.C. § 368(a)(1)(B).

the target corporation is a controlled subsidiary of the acquiring corporation, and the former shareholders of the target corporation are shareholders of the acquiring corporation.

Importantly, according to the statute the only consideration permitted to be received by the target shareholders in a "B" reorganization is voting stock of the acquiring corporation (whether common or preferred stock).

4. "C" Reorganizations: Asset-for-Stock Acquisitions

Under section 368(a)(1)(C), a "C" reorganization has the following requirements:

- An acquiring corporation acquires "substantially all of the properties" of a target corporation;

- The acquisition is solely in exchange for voting stock of the acquiring corporation (subject to a modification discussed below);[10] and

- The target corporation liquidates pursuant to the plan of reorganization, unless the Service waives this requirement.[11]

The end result of a "C" reorganization is typically the same as a statutory merger qualifying as an "A" reorganization: the acquiring corporation generally acquires all of the target corporation's assets and liabilities, the target ceases its legal existence, and the former shareholders of the target corporation are shareholders of the acquiring corporation. However, the permissible consideration in an "A" reorganization is governed by the continuity of interest requirement, whereas a "C" reorganization requires sole use of the acquiring corporation's voting stock, subject to the following modifications. First, the acquiring corporation's assumption of liabilities of the target corporation is disregarded.[12] Absent this rule, the assumption of a target's liabilities would violate the solely for stock requirement, because assumed liabilities are additional consideration paid for target assets. In addition, a "boot relaxation rule" pulls back on the solely for stock requirement and permits the acquiring corporation to acquire up to 20 percent of the gross fair market value of the target's assets for consideration other than the acquiring corporation's voting stock, such as money or property.[13] However, for purposes of the boot relaxation rule, liabilities of the target corporation that are assumed by the acquiring corporation are treated as money paid for target assets.[14]

B. Tax Treatment of Parties to a Reorganization

If the transaction qualifies as a reorganization, then a set of operative rules apply to determine the tax consequences of the parties to the reorganization. In general, these rules provide for nonrecognition (full or partial) of gain or loss, exchanged and transferred bases, and tacked holding periods — concepts that

---

[10] I.R.C. § 368(a)(1)(C).

[11] I.R.C. § 368(a)(2)(G).

[12] I.R.C. § 368(a)(1)(C).

[13] I.R.C. § 368(a)(2)(B).

[14] *Id.*

were explored in connection with section 351 transactions.[15]

1. Tax Consequences to Shareholders and Security Holders

Under section 354(a)(1), the shareholders and security holders of the target corporation will not recognize any gain or loss if they exchange stock or securities in the target corporation solely for stock or securities in the acquiring corporation. While section 354's nonrecognition rule covers exchanges of stock as well as securities, there are limitations on exchanges involving securities that are discussed in the Detailed Analysis. "Securities," while not defined in the Code, are relatively long-term debt instruments issued by a corporation.[16] Section 356(a)(1) pulls back on the solely stock or securities requirement in section 354(a)(1) and provides that if the exchange otherwise would have qualified under section 354 but for fact that, in addition to stock or securities, the shareholder (or security holder) received money or other property, i.e., "boot," then any realized gain is recognized by the shareholder (or security holder) to the extent of boot.[17] Under section 356(c), if the exchange otherwise would have qualified under section 354(a) but for the fact that shareholder (or security holder) received boot, the shareholder (or security holder) still cannot recognize any realized loss.

Under section 358(a)(1), a shareholder's basis in the stock received in a reorganization is:

- The same as the shareholder's basis in stock and securities surrendered,

- Plus the amount treated as a dividend on the exchange,

- Plus the gain recognized by the shareholder on the exchange (excluding the portion of the gain treated as a dividend),

- Minus the money received by the shareholder on the exchange,

- Minus the fair market value of other property received by the shareholder on the exchange.

Under section 1223(1), a shareholder's holding period in the stock received in a reorganization will ordinarily include the period of time that the shareholder held the stock surrendered, referred to as a tacked holding period. The Detailed Analysis discusses the basis and holding period consequences for securities received in a reorganization.

2. Tax Consequences to Target Corporation

Under section 361(a), the target corporation will not recognize any gain or loss where it exchanges its property solely for stock or securities of the acquiring corporation. If the target corporation receives in a reorganization money or other property in addition to stock or securities, then the "solely" requirement contained

---

[15] *See* Chapter 14.

[16] *See* Boris I. Bittker & James S. Eustice, Federal Income Taxation of Corporations and Shareholders 12-88 (2000).

[17] As discussed in the Detailed Analysis, all or a portion of any recognized gain under section 356(a) may be treated as a dividend.

in section 361(a) is violated. Nevertheless, under section 361(b)(1), the target corporation still receives nonrecognition of gain treatment provided that the money or other property is distributed to the target's shareholders pursuant to the plan of reorganization.[18]

Following the target corporation's transfer of its assets to the acquiring corporation in exchange for stock in the acquiring corporation and possibly other consideration, there is generally an actual or deemed distribution of the stock and other consideration to the target's shareholders and creditors. Section 361(c) provides that a target corporation will not recognize any gain or loss on the distribution of "qualified property" to its shareholders pursuant to a plan of reorganization.[19] "Qualified property" generally includes stock (or stock rights) in the acquiring corporation or obligations of the acquiring corporation that were received by the target corporation in the reorganization exchange.[20] Thus, section 361(c) protects the target from recognizing gain on the distribution to its shareholders of stock or securities in the acquiring corporation (along with such corporation's stock rights and non-security obligations) that are received in the reorganization.

3. Tax Consequences to Acquiring Corporation

Under section 1032(a), an acquiring corporation recognizes no gain or loss on the transfer of its stock in exchange for the assets or stock of the target corporation. Under section 362(b), the acquiring corporation's basis in the property acquired in a reorganization is generally the same basis that the transferor had in the property, increased by any gain recognized by the transferor on the transfer. Under section 1223(2), the acquiring corporation's holding period in the property acquired in the reorganization will include the period that the transferor held the property, referred to as a tacked holding period.

DETAILED ANALYSIS

§ 21.01 INTRODUCTION

The Code contains a set of complex provisions that provide for complete or partial nonrecognition at both the corporate and shareholder level on corporate reorganizations. In very general terms, a corporate reorganization is where two corporations merge or otherwise come together in some fashion (referred to as an acquisitive reorganization), or the restructuring of a single corporation. A corporate reorganization may also take place in connection with a corporate division, which is examined in the next chapter.

As with corporate formations, nonrecognition treatment for corporate reorganizations seems to be based on the view that because a corporate reorganization

---

[18] I.R.C. § 361(b)(1)(B). In general, transfers of boot to creditors in connection with a reorganization are treated as transfers to shareholders for purposes of section 361(b). I.R.C. § 361(b)(3).

[19] I.R.C. § 361(c)(1), (2).

[20] I.R.C. § 361(c)(2)(B).

arguably changes the form rather than the substance of the parties' holdings and therefore may lack significance, taxing such transactions may impede them from happening. There may also be valuation and liquidity concerns in taxing such transactions, although these concerns are always present where a taxpayer disposes of property for other property rather than cash, and nonrecognition is not afforded for all in-kind transactions.

The tax regime for corporate reorganizations first requires a determination of whether a given transaction constitutes a reorganization as defined in section 368. If the transaction qualifies as a reorganization, then a set of rules apply to determine the tax consequences of the parties to the reorganization, which include, in the case of an acquisitive reorganization, the acquiring corporation, the target corporation, and the shareholders of both corporations. The primary tax consequences for the parties involved relate to the gain or loss that is recognized in the transaction and the basis of the property (including stock) received in the transaction.

§ 21.02 TYPES OF REORGANIZATIONS AND REQUIREMENTS

A. Overview

Section 368(a) provides for several types of reorganizations:

- "A" reorganizations: statutory mergers and consolidations
- "B" reorganizations: stock-for-stock acquisitions
- "C" reorganizations: asset-for-stock acquisitions
- Triangular "A", "B", "C" reorganizations and drop downs
- "D" reorganizations: transfers of assets to controlled corporations
- "E" reorganizations: recapitalizations
- "F" reorganizations: changes in identity, form or place of organization
- "G" reorganizations: insolvency reorganizations

"A", "B" and "C" reorganizations are types of acquisitive reorganizations, i.e., transactions where two corporations come together by an acquiring corporation's acquisition of a target corporation's assets (in the case of "A" and "C" reorganizations) or stock (in the case of "B" reorganizations). Triangular versions of these types of reorganizations are where the stock of the acquiring corporation's parent corporation is used to acquire the assets or stock of the target corporation, and drop downs of target assets or stock have a similar effect. "D" and "G" reorganizations may be either acquisitive or divisive, the latter being where the business activities of a single corporation are divided among two or more corporations. "E" and "F" reorganizations involve certain changes to a single corporation and thus are neither acquisitive nor divisive. Section 368 provides detailed terms that need to be satisfied for each of these types of reorganizations.

To qualify as a reorganization, a transaction must also meet certain non-statutory requirements. These are the business purpose requirement, the continuity of business enterprise requirement, and the continuity of interest requirement. The next section discusses these non-statutory requirements, and following this, the requirements for each type of reorganization is examined.

B. Non-Statutory Requirements for Reorganizations

1. Business Purpose Requirement

A reorganization is required to have a business purpose. This requirement was first imposed by the courts[21] and now is contained in the regulations.[22]

2. Continuity of Business Enterprise Requirement

Under the continuity of business enterprise requirement set forth in the regulations, the acquiring corporation is required to either:

- Continue the target corporation's historic business, or

- Use a significant portion of the target's historic business assets in a business.[23]

The underlying policy is to ensure that qualifying reorganizations "are limited to readjustments of continuing interests in property under the modified corporate form."[24]

a.   Continuing Target's Historic Business

In determining whether the acquiring corporation continues the target's historic business, the fact that the acquiring corporation and target corporation are in the same line of business tends to establish continuity, but this alone does not suffice.[25] Where the target has more than one line of business, the acquiring corporation need only continue a significant line of business to satisfy the continuity requirement.[26] The target corporation's historic business is the business conducted most recently, but it is not a business that the corporation enters into as a part of the plan of reorganization.[27]

---

[21] *See, e.g.,* Gregory v. Helvering, 293 U.S. 465 (1935).

[22] Treas. Reg. § 1.368-1(c).

[23] Treas. Reg. § 1.368-1(d)(1). For purposes of this rule, an acquiring corporation is treated as holding the businesses and assets of certain affiliated corporations and partnerships. *See* Treas. Reg. § 1.368-1(d)(4). For transactions occurring after February 25, 2005, a continuity of business enterprise is not required for "E" and "F" reorganizations. Treas. Reg. § 1.368-1(b).

[24] Treas. Reg. § 1.368-1(d)(1).

[25] Treas. Reg. § 1.368-1(d)(2)(i).

[26] Treas. Reg. § 1.368-1(d)(2)(ii).

[27] Treas. Reg. § 1.368-1(d)(2)(iii).

Example 21.1.[28] T Corp. conducts three lines of business of approximately equal value — product A manufacturing, product B manufacturing, and product C manufacturing. On January 1, 2014, T Corp. sells its product A manufacturing and product B manufacturing businesses for cash. On January 15, 2014, for business reasons T Corp. transfers all of its assets to P Corp. solely for P Corp. voting stock; following the transfer, T Corp. liquidates. P Corp. continues the product C manufacturing business without interruption.

Applying the continuity of business enterprise requirement in Example 21.1:

The continuity of business enterprise requirement is satisfied because P Corp. continues one of T Corp.'s three significant lines of business. The transaction will qualify as a "C" reorganization (to be discussed below).

b.   Using a Significant Portion of Target's Historic Business Assets

A target corporation's historic business assets are the assets used in the target's historic business.[29] Whether the portion of such assets that the acquiring corporation uses is significant generally depends on the relative importance of the assets to operating the business, but also considered are all other facts and circumstances, such as the net fair market value of the assets.[30]

Example 21.2.[31] P Corp. manufactures product A, and T Corp. manufactures components for product A. T Corp. sells all its manufactured components to P Corp. On January 1, 2014, P Corp. decides to buy all of its components for manufacturing product A from another supplier. On January 1, 2014, for business reasons T Corp. merges into P Corp pursuant to a State M merger statute. After the merger, P Corp. continues to buy components from another supplier but retains the component manufacturing equipment previously used by T Corp. as a backup source of supply.

Applying the continuity of business enterprise requirement in Example 21.2:

The continuity of business enterprise requirement is satisfied because P Corp.'s use of the component manufacturing equipment as a backup source of supply constitutes the use of a significant portion of T Corp.'s historic business assets.[32] The transaction will qualify as an "A" reorganization provided the continuity of interest requirement is satisfied (to be discussed below).

---

[28] This example is based on Treas. 1.368-1(d)(5), Example 1.

[29] Treas. Reg. § 1.368-1(d)(3)(ii).

[30] Treas. Reg. § 1.368-1(d)(3)(iii).

[31] This example is based on Treas. Reg. § 1.368-1(d)(5), Example 2.

[32] *See* Treas. Reg. § 1.368-1(d)(5), Example 2.

3. Continuity of Interest Requirement

a.   In General

The continuity of interest requirement basically requires that, in the aggregate, a sufficient portion of the target corporation shareholders' interest in the target continues in the stock of the acquiring corporation after the reorganization. Unlike the continuity of business enterprise requirement, which applies at the corporate level, continuity of interest is a shareholder-level requirement. The purpose of this requirement "is to prevent transactions that resemble sales from qualifying for nonrecognition of gain or loss available to corporate reorganizations."[33]

Under the continuity of interest requirement contained in the regulations, a *substantial part* of the value of shareholder interests in the target corporation[34] must be preserved after the reorganization.[35] A primary way in which a shareholder interest in the target corporation is preserved is where it is exchanged for a *proprietary* interest in the acquiring corporation.[36] Thus, there are two aspects to measuring continuity of interest: (i) the type of consideration received by target shareholders and (ii) the portion of the consideration received by target shareholders that is qualifying consideration.

b.   Type of Consideration Received

The primary type of qualifying consideration for continuity of interest purposes, i.e., a proprietary interest in the acquiring corporation, consists of either common stock or preferred stock in the acquiring corporation, whether voting or nonvoting.[37] On the other hand, cash, debt obligations (whether long or short term), and assumption of liabilities are not qualifying consideration for purposes of determining requisite continuity.[38] The regulations also provide that stock of the acquiring corporation that is redeemed in connection with the purported reorganization does not qualify.[39]

---

[33] Treas. Reg. § 1.368-1(e)(1)(i).

[34] In situations where the target corporation is in bankruptcy proceedings or is insolvent, creditor claims against a target corporation may be taken into account in determining continuity of interest, in addition to shareholder interests in the target corporation. Treas. Reg. § 1.368-1(e)(1)(i), (e)(6).

[35] Treas. Reg. § 1.368-1(e)(1)(i). For transactions occurring after February 25, 2005, a continuity of interest is not required for "E" and "F" reorganizations. Treas. Reg. § 1.368-1(b).

[36] Treas. Reg. § 1.368-1(e)(1)(i). Alternatively, a stock interest in the target corporation is preserved if the acquiring corporation exchanges a stock interest in the target corporation for a direct interest in the target corporation enterprise. *Id.* This can occur where prior to a purported reorganization, an acquiring corporation owns stock in the target corporation, and the target corporation is merged into the acquiring corporation so that the acquiring corporation takes a direct interest in the former assets of the target corporation. *See* Treas. Reg. § 1.368-1(e)(8), Example 7. Another way in which a stock interest in the target corporation is preserved is where it otherwise continues as a stock interest in the target corporation. Treas. Reg. § 1.368-1(e)(1)(i).

[37] *See* Bittker & Eustice, *supra* note 16 at 12-30.

[38] *See id;* Treas. Reg. § 1.368-1(e)(1)(i) (a proprietary interest in the target is not preserved if it is acquired for consideration other than stock of the acquiring corporation).

[39] Treas. Reg. § 1.368-1(e)(1)(i); Treas. Reg. § 1.368-1(e)(8), Example 4(i).

In addition to stock in the acquiring corporation, stock in a corporation that controls the acquiring corporation is also qualifying consideration for continuity purposes in situations involving triangular reorganizations[40] and reorganizations with a drop down of assets or stock to a controlled subsidiary of the acquiring corporation.[41] These types of transactions are discussed below.

c. Portion of Qualifying Consideration Received

To satisfy the continuity of interest requirement, a sufficient portion of the total consideration received by the shareholders of the target corporation as a group must consist of qualifying consideration. While the requisite percentage of qualifying consideration is not completely clear, the Service will ordinarily issue a favorable ruling where at least 50 percent of the total consideration received by the target shareholders is stock in the acquiring corporation.[42] Examples in the regulations are more lenient and provide that 40 percent continuity is sufficient to satisfy the requirement,[43] a view that is supported by case law.[44]

Importantly, overall continuity is what matters, as opposed to the continuity of individual shareholders of the target corporation. Thus, some target shareholders may receive entirely cash consideration, yet the transaction can still qualify if the target shareholders as a group satisfy the percentage test for qualifying consideration. It is also worth emphasizing that the test goes to the percentage of the total consideration received by the target shareholders that constitutes equity in the acquiring corporation, not the percentage of stock in the acquiring corporation that is owned by the former target shareholders after the transaction.

> *Example 21.3.* On January 1, 2014, for business reasons T Corp. merges into P Corp. pursuant to a State M merger statute. In the merger, the shareholders of T Corp. receive total consideration that consists of common stock in P Corp. (the only class outstanding) worth $4,000,000 and $6,000,000 of cash. Following the merger, the former shareholders of T Corp. own 10% of the common stock of P Corp.

Applying the continuity of interest requirement in Example 21.3:

The continuity of interest requirement should be satisfied because 40% of the total consideration received by the shareholders of T Corp. consists of stock in P Corp. ($4,000,000 of P Corp. stock out of total consideration of $10,000,000).[45] The fact that the former shareholders of T Corp. own only 10% of P Corp. common stock after the merger is irrelevant. The transaction should qualify as an "A" reorganization provided the continuity of business enterprise requirement is satisfied.

---

[40] Treas. Reg. § 1.368-1(e)(1)(i), (b) (in effect providing this).

[41] I.R.C. § 368(a)(2)(C) (permitting drop downs in connection with certain reorganizations).

[42] Rev. Proc. 77-37, 1977-2 C.B. 568.

[43] Treas. Reg. § 1.368-1(e)(2)(v), Examples 1, 2(ii).

[44] *See* Schwarz & Lathrope, *supra* note 6 at 402.

[45] *See* Treas. Reg. § 1.368-1(e)(2)(v), Examples 1, 2(ii).

d.   Effect of Stock Dispositions Before or After a Potential Reorganization

i.   Dispositions of Target Corporation Stock Prior to Potential Reorganization

It may be the case that some shareholders of the target corporation will sell their stock prior to a potential reorganization but in connection with it. In light of the step-transaction doctrine, it could be contended that such dispositions should be taken into account in determining requisite continuity of interest: that is, the shareholders who disposed of target stock before the purported reorganization, rather than the persons acquiring such stock, should be included for purposes of determining whether a sufficient portion of the target corporation shareholders' interest continues in the stock of the acquiring corporation.

The current regulations generally do away with the application of the step-transaction doctrine in these circumstances for purposes of determining requisite continuity of interest. Under the regulations, dispositions of target corporation stock prior to a potential reorganization to persons unrelated to the target or acquiring corporation are disregarded for continuity purposes.[46] However, purchases of target corporation stock by the acquiring corporation that are prior to and in connection with a potential reorganization are taken into account.[47]

ii.   Dispositions of Acquiring Corporation Stock After Potential Reorganization

It could also be contended that the step-transaction doctrine should apply to dispositions of stock in the acquiring corporation by former target corporation shareholders that are in connection with the potential reorganization. If so, then the acquiring corporation stock that is temporarily held by the former target corporation shareholders will not count for continuity of interest purposes.

The regulations generally eliminate the application of the step-transaction doctrine in this situation as well, as they provide that dispositions of acquiring corporation stock received in a potential reorganization to persons unrelated to the acquiring corporation are disregarded.[48] This is the case even if the disposition is pursuant to a binding commitment that existed at the time of the potential reorganization.[49] However, subsequent dispositions of acquiring corporation stock to the acquiring corporation or persons related to the acquiring corporation that are in connection with the potential reorganization are taken into account for

---

[46] Treas. Reg. § 1.368-1(e(1))(i).

[47] Treas. Reg. § 1.368-1(e)(8), Example 4(ii). It should be noted that if the acquiring corporation's acquisition of the target corporation stock constitutes a qualified stock purchase under section 338 and a section 338 election is not made, continuity of interest is automatically satisfied for the parties involved in the potential reorganization, other than minority shareholders of the target corporation. Treas. Reg. § 1.338-3(d). Section 338 is examined in § 19.04[B].

[48] Treas. Reg. § 1.368-1(e)(1)(i).

[49] Treas. Reg. § 1.368-1(e)(8), Example 1(i)

purposes of determining continuity of interest.[50]

C. "A" Reorganizations: Statutory Mergers and Consolidations

Under section 368(a)(1)(A), an "A" reorganization is a statutory merger or consolidation.[51] A statutory merger is a transaction effected pursuant to a state or foreign statute,[52] whereby the assets and liabilities of the target corporation are transferred to the acquiring corporation and the target corporation ceases its legal existence.[53] A statutory consolidation is similar, except that the assets and liabilities of two corporations are transferred to a newly created corporation and the transferor corporations cease their legal existence. Importantly, an "A' reorganization must be an acquisitive transaction — i.e., two corporations coming together and one (or both, in the case of a consolidation) ceasing to exist after the transaction. A divisive transaction — the assets of one corporation being divided among two or more corporations — cannot qualify as an "A" reorganization even if pursuant to a merger statute.[54]

In a statutory merger or consolidation, the shareholders of the merged or consolidated corporations will exchange their stock for stock or debt instruments of the acquiring corporation, cash, or some combination thereof. Unlike the other types of reorganizations, section 368(a) does not prescribe the permissible consideration for an "A" reorganization. Nevertheless, pursuant to the continuity of interest requirement (discussed above), a sufficient portion of the consideration received by the shareholders of the merged or consolidated corporations must be stock in the acquiring corporation.

> *Example 21.4.* On January 1, 2014, for business reasons T Corp. merges into P Corp pursuant to a State M merger statute. As a result of the merger, all of the assets and liabilities of T Corp. are transferred to P Corp., and T Corp. dissolves by operation of law. In the merger, the shareholders of T Corp. receive total consideration that consists of common stock in P Corp. (the only class outstanding) worth $10,000,000 and $10,000,000 of cash. T Corp. had conducted one line of business, which P Corp. continues after the merger without interruption.

Determining whether the transaction in Example 21.4 qualifies as an "A" reorganization:

---

[50] Treas. Reg. § 1.368-1(e)(8), Example 4(i) (redemption by acquiring corporation in connection with merger); Treas. Reg. § 1.368-1(e)(8), Example 4(iii) (purchase of acquiring corporation stock by person related to acquiring corporation).

[51] I.R.C. § 368(a)(1)(A).

[52] Treas. Reg. § 1.368-2(b)(1)(iii), Examples 13 and 14, provide examples of statutory mergers or consolidation effected pursuant to foreign law.

[53] Treas. Reg. § 1.368-2(b)(1)(ii). In general, all of the target corporation's assets and liabilities must be transferred to the acquiring corporation. There are exceptions for assets that are distributed in the transaction, and liabilities that are discharged or satisfied in the transaction, or nonrecourse liabilities that encumber assets distributed in the transaction. *Id.*

[54] Treas. Reg. § 1.368-2(b)(1)(iii), Example 1.

The merger of T Corp. into P Corp. qualifies as an "A" reorganization. The merger satisfies section 368(a)(1)(A) because it is effected pursuant to a state statute, and results in the transfer of all of T Corp.'s assets and liabilities to P Corp. and the dissolution of T Corp. The merger also satisfies the non-statutory requirements of (i) continuity of interest (50% of the total consideration received by the shareholders of T Corp. consists of stock in P Corp.) and (ii) the continuity of business enterprise (P Corp. continues T Corp.'s historic business).

D. "B" Reorganizations: Stock-for-Stock Acquisitions

Under section 368(a)(1)(B), a "B" reorganization has the following requirements:

- An acquiring corporation acquires stock in a target corporation,

- The acquisition is solely in exchange for voting stock of the acquiring corporation, and

- The acquiring corporation "controls" the target corporation immediately after the acquisition.[55]

Under section 368(c), "control" is defined as the ownership of at least 80 percent of (i) the total combined voting power of all classes of stock entitled to vote and (ii) the total number of shares of all other classes of stock.[56] Following a "B" reorganization, the target corporation is a controlled subsidiary of the acquiring corporation, and the former shareholders of the target corporation are shareholders of the acquiring corporation.

Importantly, according to the statute the only consideration permitted to be received by the target shareholders in a "B" reorganization is voting stock of the acquiring corporation (whether common or preferred stock). Thus, any other types of consideration — nonvoting stock, debt instruments or cash — will disqualify the transaction as a "B" reorganization (with a few limited exceptions[57]). This has led to the maxim "there is no boot in a B." Because of this strict consideration requirement, the non-statutory continuity of interest requirement typically has no relevance in qualifying a transaction as a "B" reorganization: the 100 percent voting stock requirement generally supersedes the 40 percent (or so) continuity of interest requirement (previously discussed).

For a transaction to qualify as a "B" reorganization, it is not necessary that the acquiring corporation acquire an 80 percent controlling interest in the particular transaction. Thus, it is permissible for the acquiring corporation to already own some of the stock of the target corporation.[58] An acquisition of target stock that occurs after the acquiring corporation has 80 percent control can also qualify as a "B" reorganization.[59] The key is that the acquiring corporation must have at least

---

[55] I.R.C. § 368(a)(1)(B).

[56] This is the same definition of control that is used for purposes of section 351.

[57] For example, the acquiring corporation may pay cash in lieu of issuing fractional shares to target shareholders in a "B" reorganization. Rev. Rul. 66-365, 1966-2 C.B. 116. Mills v. Commissioner, 331 F. 2d 321 (5th Cir. 1964).

[58] Treas. Reg. § 1.368-2(c).

[59] Id.

80 percent control following the transaction. Consequently, the statute permits so-called creeping "B" reorganizations where control is acquired in more than one transaction.

> *Example 21.5.* On January 1, 2014, for business reasons P Corp. acquires all of the voting common stock of T Corp. (the only class outstanding) from the shareholders of T Corp. solely in exchange for voting stock of P Corp. Following the transaction, P Corp. owns all of the stock of T Corp. Prior to the transaction, T Corp. had conducted one line of business, which T Corp. continues to conduct after the transaction without interruption.

Determining whether the transaction in Example 21.5 qualifies as an "B" reorganization:

Section 368(a)(1)(B) is satisfied because P Corp. acquires the stock of T Corp. solely in exchange for voting stock of P Corp., and after the acquisition, P Corp. owns at least 80% of the stock of T Corp. (P Corp owns 100% of the T Corp. stock). The transaction also satisfies the continuity of business enterprise requirement (T Corp. continues its historic business). Therefore, the transaction qualifies as a "B" reorganization.

E.   "C" Reorganizations: Asset-for-Stock Acquisitions

1.   In General

Under section 368(a)(1)(C), a "C" reorganization has the following requirements:

- An acquiring corporation acquires "substantially all of the properties" of a target corporation;

- The acquisition is solely in exchange for voting stock of the acquiring corporation (subject to a modification discussed below);[60] and

- The target corporation liquidates pursuant to the plan of reorganization, unless the Service waives this requirement.[61]

The end result of a "C" reorganization is typically the same as a statutory merger qualifying as an "A" reorganization: the acquiring corporation generally acquires all of the target corporation's assets and liabilities, the target ceases its legal existence, and the former shareholders of the target corporation are shareholders of the acquiring corporation. However, the permissible consideration in an "A" reorganization is governed by the continuity of interest requirement, whereas a "C" reorganization requires sole use of the acquiring corporation's voting stock, subject to a few modifications discussed below.

In determining whether the acquiring corporation acquires "substantially all of the properties" of the target corporation, the Service will issue a favorable ruling where the acquiring corporation acquires 90 percent of the fair market value of the net assets and 70 percent of the fair market value of the gross assets that were held

---

[60]   I.R.C. § 368(a)(1)(C).

[61]   I.R.C. § 368(a)(2)(G).

by the target corporation immediately before the transaction.[62] The cases and Service revenue rulings are less stringent, focusing on both the type and amount of assets transferred. For example, a transfer of 86 percent of the target's net assets, which included all essential business assets, was found by a court to be sufficient.[63] And a revenue ruling provides that rather than a particular percentage, what constitutes substantially all of the assets depends on the facts and circumstances of each case, including the nature and amount of the assets retained by the target as well as the purpose for the retention.[64]

2. Modifications to the Solely for Stock Requirement

In determining whether the exchange is solely for voting stock, the acquiring corporation's assumption of liabilities[65] of the target corporation is disregarded.[66] Absent this rule, the assumption of a target's liabilities would violate the solely for stock requirement, because assumed liabilities are additional consideration paid for target assets, and thus qualifying as a "C" reorganization would prove difficult given that assets may typically be encumbered with liabilities.

In addition, a "boot relaxation rule" pulls back on the solely for stock requirement and permits the acquiring corporation to acquire up to 20 percent of the gross fair market value of the target's assets for consideration other than the acquiring corporation's voting stock, such as money or property.[67] Thus, the consideration given by the acquiring corporation can be 80 percent voting stock and 20 percent boot. However, for purposes of the boot relaxation rule, liabilities of the target corporation that are assumed by the acquiring corporation are treated as money paid for target assets.[68] As with "B" reorganizations, the non-statutory continuity of interest requirement typically has no relevance in qualifying a transaction as a "C" reorganization because of the relatively strict consideration requirement.[69]

---

[62] Rev. Proc. 77-37, 1977-2 C.B. 586. In determining the assets held by the target immediately prior to transaction, payments to dissenting shareholders and redemptions and distributions (other than regular, normal distributions) made by the target immediately before the transfer and as part of the reorganization plan are taken into account. *Id.*

[63] *See* Commissioner v. First Nat'l Bank of Altoona, 104 F.2d 865 (3d Cir. 1939), *cert dismissed*, 309 U.S. 691 (1940).

[64] Rev. Rul. 57-518, 1957-2 C.B. 253.

[65] For this purpose, whether a liability is assumed is determined under section 357(d). Under this rule, a recourse liability is treated as having been assumed if, on the basis of all the facts and circumstances, the transferee corporation has agreed to, and is expected to, satisfy the liability, regardless of whether the transferor corporation has been relieved of the liability. I.R.C. § 357(d)(1)(A). A nonrecourse liability is generally treated as having been assumed where the transferee corporation takes an asset subject to the liability. I.R.C. § 357(d)(1)(B), (2).

[66] I.R.C. § 368(a)(1)(C).

[67] I.R.C. § 368(a)(2)(B).

[68] *Id.*

[69] However, if the amount of liabilities assumed is so large relative to the assets acquired so that the assumed liabilities, rather than voting stock, are the primary consideration given by the acquiring corporation for the target assets, then the C reorganization may fail due to a lack of continuity of interest. *See* Bittker & Eustice, supra note 16 at 12-85 – 12-86; Treas. Reg. § 1.368-2(d)(1).

Example 21.6. On January 1, 2014, for business reasons T Corp. transfers all of its assets and liabilities to P Corp in exchange solely for voting stock of P Corp. Following the transfer, T Corp. liquidates pursuant to the plan of reorganization. T Corp. had conducted one line of business, which P Corp. continues after the transaction without interruption.

Determining whether the transaction in Example 21.6 qualifies as a "C" reorganization:

Section 368(a)(1)(C) is satisfied because P Corp. acquires all of the assets of T Corp.; the acquisition is solely in exchange for voting stock of P Corp., disregarding the assumed liabilities; and T Corp. liquidates pursuant to the plan of reorganization. The transaction also satisfies the continuity of business enterprise requirement (P Corp. continues T Corp.'s historic business). Therefore, the transaction qualifies as a "C" reorganization.

Example 21.7. On January 1, 2014, for business reasons T Corp. transfers all of its assets worth $10,000,000 (but no liabilities) to P Corp in exchange for voting stock of P Corp worth $8,000,000 and $2,000,000 of cash. Following the transfer, T Corp. liquidates pursuant to the plan of reorganization. T Corp. had conducted one line of business, which P Corp. continues after the transaction without interruption.

Determining whether the transaction in Example 21.7 qualifies as a "C" reorganization:

Section 368(a)(1)(C) is again satisfied. Even though the acquisition of T Corp.'s assets is not solely for voting stock of P Corp., it still qualifies under the boot relaxation rule because 80% of T Corp.'s assets are acquired for voting stock ($8,000,000 out of $10,000,000 of T Corp.'s assets are acquired for voting stock); or in another words, the percentage of T Corp.'s assets that are acquired for boot does not exceed 20%. Therefore, the transaction qualifies as a "C" reorganization.

Example 21.8. On January 1, 2014, for business reasons T Corp. transfers all of its assets worth $12,000,000 along with $2,000,000 of liabilities to P Corp. in exchange for voting stock of P Corp worth $8,000,000 and $2,000,000 of cash (and P Corp. assumes the $2,000,000 of liabilities). Following the transfer, T Corp. liquidates pursuant to the plan of reorganization. T Corp. had conducted one line of business, which P Corp. continues after the transaction without interruption.

Determining whether the transaction in Example 21.8 qualifies as a "C" reorganization:

Section 368(a)(1)(C) is *not* satisfied. For purposes of the boot relaxation rule, the $2,000,000 of liabilities assumed are treated as money paid for assets of T Corp. Consequently, only 66.7% of T Corp.'s assets are acquired for voting stock ($8,000,000 out of $12,000,000 of T Corp.'s assets are acquired for voting stock); or in another words, the percentage of T Corp.'s assets that are acquired for boot exceeds 20% (it is 33.3%). Therefore, the transaction fails to qualify as a "C" reorganization.

F. Triangular Reorganizations and Drop Downs

In general terms, a triangular reorganization is where the stock of the acquiring corporation's parent corporation is used to acquire the assets or stock of the target corporation. As described below, triangular reorganizations are permitted for "A," "B," and "C" reorganizations. A related transaction that is also permitted is a drop down where, following a qualifying reorganization, the acquiring corporation drops down the acquired assets or stock to a controlled subsidiary.

1. Triangular "A" Reorganizations

a.   Forward Triangular Mergers

Section 368(a)(2)(D) allows for forward triangular mergers by permitting the acquiring corporation to use stock of its controlling parent corporation,[70] rather than its stock, in a statutory merger of the target corporation into the acquiring corporation, provided the following requirements are met:

- The acquiring corporation acquires substantially all of the properties of the target corporation[71] (which has the same meaning as in the "C" reorganization context[72]),

- The acquiring corporation is not permitted to use its stock in the transaction,[73] and

- The transaction would have qualified under section 368(a)(1)(A) if the target corporation had been merged into the acquiring corporation's parent corporation,[74] which, per the regulations, means that the transaction must satisfy the continuity of interest requirement (as well as the business purpose and continuity of business enterprise requirements).[75]

The result of a forward triangular merger is that the acquiring corporation generally acquires all of the target corporation's assets and liabilities, the target ceases its legal existence, and the former shareholders of the target corporation are shareholders of the acquiring corporation's parent corporation.

> *Example 21.9.* As of January 1, 2014, P Corp. owns all the stock of S Corp. On January 1, 2014, for business reasons T Corp. merges into S Corp pursuant to a State M merger statute. As a result of the merger, all of the assets and liabilities of T Corp. are transferred to S Corp., and T Corp. dissolves by operation of law. In the merger, the shareholders of T Corp. receive total consideration that consists of common stock in P Corp. (the

---

[70] The 80 percent tests contained in section 368(c) are used for purposes of determining whether the parent corporation controls the acquiring corporation. *See* § 21.02[D].

[71] I.R.C. § 368(a)(2)(D).

[72] Treas. Reg. § 1.368-2(b)(2).

[73] I.R.C. § 368(a)(2)(D)(i).

[74] I.R.C. § 368(a)(2)(D)(ii).

[75] Treas. Reg. § 1.368-2(b)(2).

only class outstanding) worth $10,000,000 and $10,000,000 of cash. T Corp. had conducted one line of business, which S Corp. continues after the merger without interruption.

Determining whether the transaction in Example 21.9 qualifies as a forward triangular merger:

The merger of T Corp. into S Corp. qualifies as a forward triangular merger. The merger satisfies section 368(a)(1)(A) because it is effected pursuant to a state statute, and results in the transfer of all of T Corp.'s assets and liabilities to S Corp. and the dissolution of T Corp. Under section 368(a)(2)(D), stock of P Corp. rather than S Corp. is permitted to be used because S Corp. acquires all of the properties of T Corp. (meeting the "substantially all" requirement), no stock of S Corp. is used in the transaction, and the transaction would have qualified as an "A" reorganization if T Corp. had been merged into P Corp. — that is, the transaction satisfies the non-statutory requirements of (i) business purpose, (ii) continuity of interest (50% of the total consideration received by the shareholders of T Corp. consists of stock in P Corp.) and (iii) the continuity of business enterprise (S Corp. continues T Corp.'s historic business).

b.   Reverse Triangular Mergers

Provided its requirements are met, section 368(a)(2)(E) allows for reverse triangular mergers — a transaction in which a controlled subsidiary of a parent corporation statutorily merges into the target corporation and the former shareholders of the target corporation receive stock in the parent corporation. The form of a reverse triangular merger is like that of a forward triangular merger except that the target corporation is the surviving corporation in the merger. Section 368(a)(2)(E) imposes the following requirements for a reverse triangular merger:

- After the transaction, the surviving target corporation holds substantially all of its properties *and* substantially all of the properties of the merged subsidiary (which has the same meaning as in the "C" reorganization context[76]),[77] and

- The former shareholders of the surviving target corporation exchange a controlling stock interest in the target corporation for voting stock in the parent corporation;[78] the 80 percent tests contained in section 368(c)[79] are used for purposes of determining a controlling stock interest in the target.

The overall effect of a reverse triangular merger is that the parent corporation acquires control of the target corporation, and the former shareholders of the target corporation become shareholders of the parent corporation. Thus, the transaction has the same effect as a "B" reorganization. However, unlike a "B"

---

[76] Treas. Reg. § 1.368-2(j)(3)(iii).

[77] I.R.C. § 368(a)(2)(E)(i). The "substantially all" test is applied separately to the surviving target corporation and the merged subsidiary. Treas. Reg. § 1.368-2(j)(3)(iii).

[78] I.R.C. § 368(a)(2)(E)(ii).

[79] *See* § 21.02[D].

reorganization where no boot is permitted, the parent corporation need only acquire an 80 percent (controlling) interest in the target corporation for its voting stock, thereby allowing for up to 20 percent boot in the transaction.

> *Example 21.10.* As of January 1, 2014, P Corp. owns all the stock of S Corp. On January 1, 2014, for business reasons S Corp. merges into T Corp pursuant to a State M merger statute. As a result of the merger, all of the assets and liabilities of S Corp. are transferred to T Corp., and S Corp. dissolves by operation of law. In the merger, the shareholders of T Corp. exchange all of the voting common stock of T Corp. (the only class outstanding) for voting stock of P Corp. Following the transaction, P Corp. owns all of the stock of T Corp., and T Corp. holds all of the assets that it had prior to the merger. Prior to the transaction, T Corp. had conducted one line of business, which T Corp. continues to conduct after the transaction without interruption.

Determining whether the transaction in Example 21.10 qualifies as a reverse triangular merger:

> The merger of S Corp. into T Corp. qualifies as a reverse triangular merger. The merger satisfies section 368(a)(1)(A) because it is effected pursuant to a state statute, and results in the transfer of all of S Corp.'s assets and liabilities to T Corp. and the dissolution of S Corp. Under section 368(a)(2)(E), stock of P Corp. is permitted to be used because after the transaction, T Corp. holds all of its and S Corp.'s properties, and shareholders of T Corp. exchange a controlling (at least 80%) interest in T Corp. for voting stock in P Corp. (they exchange 100% of their T Corp. stock). The transaction also satisfies the continuity of business enterprise requirement (T Corp. continues its historic business).

2. Triangular "B" Reorganizations

Section 368(a)(1)(B) allows for triangular "B" reorganizations by permitting the acquiring corporation to use voting stock of its controlling parent corporation,[80] rather than its voting stock, to acquire control of the target corporation. The acquiring corporation is not permitted to use both its stock and its parent corporation's stock to make the acquisition.[81] Following a triangular "B" reorganization, the target corporation is a controlled subsidiary of the acquiring corporation, and the former shareholders of the target corporation are shareholders of the acquiring corporation's parent corporation.

> *Example 21.11.* As of January 1, 2014, P Corp. owns all the stock of S Corp. On January 1, 2014, for business reasons S Corp. acquires all of the voting common stock of T Corp. (the only class outstanding) from the shareholders of T Corp. solely in exchange for voting stock of P Corp. Following the transaction, S Corp. owns all of the stock of T Corp. Prior to the

---

[80] The 80 percent tests contained in section 368(c) are used for purposes of determining whether the parent corporation controls the acquiring corporation. *See* § 21.02[D].

[81] Treas. Reg. § 1.368-2(c).

transaction, T Corp. had conducted one line of business, which T Corp. continues to conduct after the transaction without interruption.

Determining whether the transaction in Example 21.11 qualifies as a triangular "B" reorganization:

Section 368(a)(1)(B) is satisfied because S Corp. acquires the stock of T Corp. solely in exchange for voting stock of P Corp., a corporation that controls S Corp. (P Corp. owns 100% of the S Corp. stock, satisfying the 80% of the stock requirement for control), and after the acquisition, S Corp. has control of T Corp. (S Corp. owns 100% of the T Corp. stock). The transaction also satisfies the continuity of business enterprise requirement (T Corp. continues its historic business). Therefore, the transaction qualifies as a triangular "B" reorganization.

3. Triangular "C" Reorganizations

Similar to triangular "B" reorganizations, section 368(a)(1)(C) allows for triangular "C" reorganizations by permitting the acquiring corporation to use voting stock of its controlling parent corporation, rather than its voting stock, to acquire substantially all of the properties of the target corporation. Like a triangular "B" reorganization, an acquiring corporation is not permitted to use both its stock and its parent corporation's stock to make the acquisition.[82] The end result of a triangular "C" reorganization is typically the same as a forward triangular merger: that is, the acquiring corporation acquires at least substantially all of the target corporation's assets, the target ceases its existence, and the former shareholders of the target corporation are shareholders of the acquiring corporation's parent corporation.

Example 21.12. As of January 1, 2014, P Corp. owns all the stock of S Corp. On January 1, 2014, for business reasons T Corp. transfers all of its assets and liabilities to S Corp. in exchange solely for voting stock of P Corp. Following the transfer, T Corp. liquidates pursuant to the plan of reorganization. T Corp. had conducted one line of business, which S Corp. continues after the transaction without interruption.

Determining whether the transaction in Example 21.12 qualifies as a triangular "C" reorganization:

Section 368(a)(1)(C) is satisfied because: S Corp. acquires all of the assets of T Corp.; disregarding the assumed liabilities, the acquisition is solely in exchange for voting stock of P Corp., a corporation that controls S Corp.; and T Corp. liquidates pursuant to the plan of reorganization. The transaction also satisfies the continuity of business enterprise requirement (S Corp. continues T Corp.'s historic business). Therefore, the transaction qualifies as a triangular "C" reorganization.

[82] Treas. Reg. § 1.368-2(d).

4. Drop Downs of Assets or Stock

Section 368(a)(2)(C) provides that a transaction otherwise qualifying as an "A", "B" or "C" reorganization will not be disqualified by the acquiring corporation's drop down of all or part of the acquired assets or stock into a controlled subsidiary.[83] Note that the end result of an "A", "B" or "C" reorganization followed by a drop down is the same as a forward triangular merger, triangular "B" reorganization, or triangular "C" reorganization, as the case may be: the former shareholders of the target corporation become shareholders of the parent corporation of the corporation that ultimately acquires the target's assets or stock. The regulations extend the use of drop downs to all types of reorganizations, and also permit transfers beyond a first-tier subsidiary to certain affiliated corporations and partnerships.[84]

> *Example 21.13.* On January 1, 2014, for business reasons T Corp. transfers all of its assets and liabilities to P Corp in exchange solely for voting stock of P Corp. Following the transfer, T Corp. liquidates pursuant to the plan of reorganization. Also pursuant to the plan, P Corp. then transfers all of T Corp.'s former assets and liabilities to S Corp., a wholly owned subsidiary of P. Corp. T Corp. had conducted one line of business, which S Corp. continues after the transaction without interruption.

Determining whether the transaction in Example 21.13 qualifies as a "C" reorganization:

Section 368(a)(1)(C) is satisfied because: P Corp. acquires all of the assets of T Corp.; disregarding the assumed liabilities, the acquisition is solely in exchange for voting stock of P Corp.; T Corp. liquidates pursuant to the plan of reorganization; and the drop down of T Corp.'s former assets to S Corp., a controlled subsidiary of P Corp. (at least 80% owned), does not affect qualification under section 368(a)(1)(C). The transaction also satisfies the continuity of business enterprise requirement (S Corp. continues T Corp.'s historic business). Therefore, the transaction qualifies as a "C" reorganization.

G. "D" Reorganizations: Transfers of Assets to Controlled Corporations

Under section 368(a)(1)(D) and related provisions, a "D" reorganization can be acquisitive or divisive.[85]

1. Acquisitive "D' Reorganizations

An acquisitive "D" reorganization has the following requirements:

- A transfer by one corporation ("transferor corporation") of substantially all of its assets to another corporation ("transferee corporation");

---

[83] The 80 percent tests contained in section 368(c) are used to determine whether the subsidiary is controlled by the acquiring corporation. *See* § 21.02[D].

[84] Treas. Reg. § 1.368-2(k).

[85] *See* I.R.C. §§ 368(a)(1)(D), 354(b)(1)(A), 355.

- The transferor corporation, one or more of its shareholders (including persons who were shareholders immediately before the transfer), or any combination thereof, is in "control" of the transferee corporation immediately after the transfer; and

- Pursuant to the plan of reorganization, the transferor corporation liquidates, distributing stock or securities of the transferee corporation along with any other of its assets.[86]

In determining whether the transferor corporation transfers substantially all of its assets, the Service has the same ruling policy that it has for the "substantially all of the properties" standard for "C" reorganizations: the transfer by the transferor corporation of 90 percent of its net assets and 70 percent of its gross assets.[87] Nonetheless, the courts have interpreted the "substantially all" standard for D reorganizations more flexibly than the analogous standard for C reorganizations, with the focus on the transferor corporation's operating assets as opposed to total assets.[88]

For acquisitive D reorganizations, "control" is defined as having at least 50 percent of the voting power of the stock of a corporation or at least 50 percent of the value of the stock of a corporation.[89] For purposes of determining control, stock ownership is determined by using the constructive ownership rules contained in section 318, with some modifications.[90] The regulations provide that the continuity of interest embodied in the "D" reorganization control requirement supersedes the regular continuity of interest requirement contained in the regulations.[91]

> *Example 21.14.* As of January 1, 2014, A owns all 100 shares of the voting common stock of both X Corp. and Y Corp. (the only class outstanding). On January 1, 2014, for business reasons X Corp. transfers all of its assets and liabilities to Y Corp in exchange for 50 shares Y Corp. voting common stock. Following the transfer, X Corp. liquidates pursuant to the plan of reorganization, and distributes all of its assets, including the 50 shares of Y Corp. voting common stock, to A. X Corp. had conducted one line of business, which Y Corp. continues after the transaction without interruption.

Determining whether the transaction in Example 21.14 qualifies as an acquisitive "D" reorganization:

Section 368(a)(1)(D) is satisfied because X Corp. transfers all of its assets to Y Corp.; A, the shareholder of X Corp. immediately before the transfer, controls Y Corp. immediately after the transfer (A owns 100% of the stock of Y Corp.); and X Corp. liquidates pursuant to the plan of reorganization, distributing the Y Corp.

---

[86] I.R.C. §§ 368(a)(1)(D), 354(b)(1). In limited circumstances, an acquisitive "D" reorganization can be accomplished without the transferor corporation's distribution of stock or securities in the transferee corporation. Treas. Reg. § 1.368-2(l)(2)(i).

[87] Rev. Proc. 77-37, 1977-2 C.B. 586.

[88] *See* Bittker & Eustice, *supra* note 16 at 12-114.

[89] I.R.C. §§ 368(a)(2)(H)(i), 304(c)(1).

[90] I.R.C. §§ 368(a)(2)(H)(i), 304(c)(3).

[91] Treas. Reg. § 1.368-1(b).

stock and its other assets. The transaction also satisfies the continuity of business enterprise requirement (Y Corp. continues X Corp.'s historic business). Therefore, the transaction qualifies as a "D" reorganization.

2.   Divisive "D" Reorganizations

A divisive "D" reorganization has the following requirements:

- A transfer by one corporation ("transferor corporation") of *part* of its assets to another corporation ("transferee corporation");

- The transferor corporation, one or more of its shareholders (including persons who were shareholders immediately before the transfer), or any combination thereof, is in "control" of the transferee corporation immediately after the transfer; and

- Pursuant to the plan of reorganization, the transferor corporation distributes stock or securities of the transferee corporation in a transaction qualifying under section 355.[92]

For divisive "D" reorganizations, "control" is defined as the ownership of at least 80 percent of (i) the total combined voting power of all classes of stock entitled to vote and (ii) the total number of shares of all other classes of stock.[93] Regarding the distribution requirement, section 355 provides detailed rules for qualifying certain corporate divisions for nonrecognition treatment, which will be examined in the next chapter. The regulations provide that the continuity of interest embodied in the "D" reorganization control requirement, along with a special continuity of interest requirement under section 355 (contained in Treas. Reg. § 1.355-2(c)), supersede the regular continuity of interest requirement contained in the regulations.[94]

> *Example 21.15.* As of January 1, 2014, A owns all 100 shares of the voting common stock of X Corp. (the only class outstanding). X Corp. has two businesses — business A and business B. On January 1, 2014, for business reasons X Corp. transfers the assets of business B to a new corporation, Y Corp., in exchange for all 100 shares of Y Corp. voting common stock (the only class outstanding). Following the transfer and pursuant to the plan of reorganization, X Corp. distributes the 100 shares of Y Corp. voting common stock to A. Following the transaction, X Corp. continues to conduct business A, and Y Corp. conducts business B.

Determining whether the transaction in Example 21.15 qualifies as a divisive "D" reorganization:

Provided that X Corp.'s distribution of Y Corp. stock qualifies under section 355, section 368(a)(1)(D) would be satisfied because X Corp. transfers part of its assets to Y Corp., and A, the shareholder of X Corp., controls Y Corp. immediately after the transfer (A owns 100% of the stock of Y Corp.). The transaction also satisfies the

---

[92] I.R.C. § 368(a)(1)(D).

[93] I.R.C. § 368(c). This is the same definition of control that is used for purposes of section 351 and section 368(a)(1)(B). Note that a different definition of control is used for acquisitive "D" reorganizations.

[94] Treas. Reg. § 1.368-1(b).

continuity of business enterprise requirement (X Corp.'s historic businesses, business A and business B, are continued by X Corp. and Y Corp., respectively.)

H. "E" Reorganizations: Recapitalizations

Under section 368(a)(1)(E), an "E" reorganization is a recapitalization, which is basically a reshuffling of the capital structure of a *single* corporation. A corporation's capital structure consists of the mix of stock and debt instruments held by corporate investors — e.g., common stock, preferred stock and bonds. Thus, a recapitalization involves situations where investors exchange stock or debt in a corporation for stock or debt in the same corporation. In this regard, there are four permutations that form the categories of recapitalizations, which are described below.[95]

1. Stock for Stock

One category of recapitalization is an exchange by shareholders of one type of stock in the corporation for another type of stock. For example, this could be common stock for preferred stock,[96] or preferred stock for common stock.[97]

> *Example 21.16.* X Corp. has 100 shares of voting common stock outstanding, all of which are owned by A. X Corp. also has outstanding 100 shares of nonvoting preferred stock, all of which are owned by B. On January 1, 2014, for business reasons, B exchanges her 100 shares of X Corp. nonvoting preferred stock for 100 shares of X Corp. voting common stock.

The transaction qualifies as a recapitalization and thus an "E" reorganization because B has exchanged preferred stock for common stock.

As a reorganization, a recapitalization will generally be tax-free to the shareholders involved, as discussed in the next section. However, in certain circumstances a stock-for-stock recapitalization may constitute a constructive stock distribution under section 305(c),[98] which could then result in a taxable dividend to the particular shareholders. Under the regulations, a recapitalization will result in a constructive stock distribution if:

- It is pursuant to a plan to periodically increase a shareholder's proportionate interest in assets or E&P of the corporation, or

- A preferred shareholder with dividend arrearages exchanges her preferred stock for other stock and, as a result, increases her proportionate interest in the assets or E&P of the corporation.[99]

---

[95] As mentioned previously, for transactions occurring after February 25, 2005, neither the continuity of business enterprise requirement nor the continuity of interest requirement apply to "E" reorganizations. Treas. Reg. § 1.368-1(b).

[96] Treas. Reg. § 1.368-2(e)(3).

[97] Treas. Reg. § 1.368-2(e)(4).

[98] *See* § 18.02[F].

[99] Treas. Reg. § 1.305-7(c). A stock-for-stock recapitalization can also result in the receipt of section 306 stock. This can occur where a shareholder holding common stock exchanges some common shares for preferred shares, provided that the receipt of cash in lieu of the preferred stock would have been a

2. Holders' Exchange of Corporate Debt Instruments for Stock

Another category of recapitalization qualifying as an "E" reorganization is an exchange by a holder of a debt instrument issued by the corporation for stock of the corporation.[100] This is illustrated by the following example.

> *Example 21.17.* X Corp. has a 20-year bond outstanding, which is held by A. On January 1, 2014, for business reasons, A exchanges the X Corp. bond for X Corp. nonvoting preferred stock.

3. Corporate Debt Instruments for Corporate Debt Instruments

A third category of recapitalization qualifying as an "E" reorganization is an exchange of a debt instrument issued by a corporation for another debt instrument issued by the corporation.[101] This is illustrated by the following example.

> *Example 21.18.* X Corp. has bonds outstanding, which are held by A. On January 1, 2014, for business reasons, A exchanges her X Corp. bonds for newly issued X Corp. bonds.

4. Shareholders' Exchange of Stock for Corporate Debt Instruments

A final category of transactions that may constitute a recapitalization qualifying as an "E" reorganization is an exchange by shareholders of stock in the corporation for a debt instrument issued by the corporation. This is illustrated by the following example.

> *Example 21.19.* X Corp. has 100 shares of voting common stock outstanding. A and B each own 50 shares of the stock. On January 1, 2014, for business reasons, B exchanges her 50 shares of X Corp. voting common stock for a twenty-year bond issued by X Corp.

Even if this exchange is a recapitalization, the relevant nonrecognition provision, section 354 (to be discussed later), does not apply because the transaction is in effect a redemption subject to section 302[102] — a corporation's acquisition of its stock for property[103] (which includes a corporation's debt instrument[104]).

Moreover, in certain situations a shareholder's exchange of stock for debt may be treated as section 301 distribution of property, as illustrated by the following

---

dividend under section 356(a)(2). *See* Treas. Reg. § 1.306-3(d); see also § 18.03 for a discussion of receiving section 306 stock in connection with reorganizations. Dividends in connection with reorganizations under section 356(a)(2) are examined in § 21.03.

[100] Treas. Reg. § 1.368-2(e)(1).

[101] Rev. Rul. 77-415, 1977-2 C.B. 311.

[102] *See* Treas. Reg. § 1.354-1(d), Example 3.

[103] I.R.C. § 317(b).

[104] I.R.C. § 317(a).

example.

> *Example 21.20.* X Corp. has 100 shares of voting common stock outstanding. A and B each own 50 shares of the stock. On January 1, 2014, for business reasons, A and B each exchange their 50 shares of X Corp. voting common stock for 50 shares of newly issued X Corp. voting common stock and a twenty-year bond issued by X Corp.

The section 301 regulations treat the shareholders' receipt of the bonds as a distribution of property subject to section 301, even though the stock-for-stock portion of the exchange may be a recapitalization qualifying for nonrecognition treatment.[105] The underlying rationale is that the substance of the transaction is a distribution of corporate bonds.[106]

I. "F" Reorganizations: Changes in Identity, Form or Place of Organization

Under section 368(a)(1)(F), an "F" reorganization is "a mere change in identity, form, or place of incorporation of one corporation, however effected."[107] A typical "F" reorganization is the reincorporation of an existing operating company in a different state. The following example provides an illustration.

> *Example 21.21.* X Corp. is a corporation that is incorporated in State S, which operates a business that develops computer software. On January 1, 2014, for business reasons X Corp. changes its place of incorporation to State T by merging into Y Corp., a newly organized corporation incorporated in State T; prior to the merger, Y Corp. conducted no business activities. Pursuant to the merger, all of the assets and liabilities of X Corp. are transferred to Y Corp., X Corp. dissolves by operation of law, and the shares in X Corp. are converted into an equal number of shares in Y Corp.

Even though the transaction in Example 21.21 involves two corporations, it qualifies as an "F" reorganization because it involves a single operating company; this is made clear by the legislative history to the amendment that added the "one corporation" limitation to section 368(a)(1)(F).[108]

J. "G" Reorganizations: Insolvency Reorganizations

In general terms, a "G" reorganization is the transfer of assets by one corporation to another corporation in a bankruptcy or similar proceeding. Under section 368(a)(1)(G) and related provisions, a "G" reorganization, like a "D"

---

[105] Treas. Reg. § 1.301-1(l).

[106] Treas. Reg. § 1.301-1(l) is based on a principle announced in *Bazely v. Commissioner*, 331 U.S. 737 (1947).

[107] As mentioned previously, for transactions occurring after February 25, 2005, neither the continuity of business enterprise requirement nor the continuity of interest requirement apply to "F" reorganizations. Treas. Reg. § 1.368-1(b).

[108] *See* H.R. Rep. No. 97-760, 97th Cong., 2d Sess. 540-41 (1982), *reprinted in* 1982-2 C.B. 634-35.

reorganization, can be acquisitive or divisive.[109]

1. Acquisitive "G' Reorganizations

An acquisitive "G" reorganization has the following requirements:

- A transfer by one corporation ("debtor corporation") of substantially all of its assets to another corporation ("acquiring corporation") pursuant to a court-approved reorganization plan in a title 11 bankruptcy case or in a receivership, foreclosure, or similar proceeding in a federal or state court; and

- Pursuant to the plan of reorganization, the debtor corporation liquidates, distributing stock or securities of the acquiring corporation along with any other of its assets.[110]

In determining whether the debtor corporation transfers substantially all of its assets, the need of the debtor corporation to pay off its creditors by selling assets to raise cash is taken into account.[111] Thus, a transaction should not fail the "substantially all" test merely because prior to the transfer to the acquiring corporation, the debtor corporation sold assets and made payments to creditors in order to provide the acquiring corporation with a more manageable situation in which to continue the debtor's business.[112]

As with an "A" reorganization, section 368(a) does not prescribe the permissible consideration for a "G" reorganization. Nevertheless, pursuant to the continuity of interest requirement,[113] a sufficient portion of the consideration received by the holders of proprietary interests in the debtor corporation must be stock in the acquiring corporation. For "G' reorganizations, proprietary interest holders in the debtor corporation can include creditors of the debtor corporation. Specifically, the following persons are included: (i) creditors of the debtor corporation that receive stock in the acquiring corporation; (i) creditors of the debtor corporation that are in the same class as creditors receiving stock in the acquiring corporation; (iii) creditors of the debtor corporation that are in a class equal to the class of creditors receiving stock in the acquiring corporation; (iv) creditors of the debtor corporation that are in a class junior to the class of creditors receiving stock in the acquiring corporation; and (v) shareholders of the debtor corporation that receive consideration in the potential reorganization.[114]

> *Example 21.22.* On January 1, 2014, for business reasons D Corp. transfers all of its assets to P Corp. pursuant to a court-approved reorganization plan in a title 11 bankruptcy case, in exchange for 100 shares of P Corp. voting common stock. Following the transfer, D Corp. liquidates pursuant to the plan of reorganization, and distributes all of its assets, which consists of the

---

[109] *See* I.R.C. §§ 368(a)(1)(G), 354(b)(1)(A), 355.

[110] I.R.C. §§ 368(a)(1)(G), 368(a)(3)(A), (B), 354(b)(1).

[111] *See* S. Rep. No. 96-1035, 96th Cong., 2d Sess. 34-38, *reprinted in* 1980-2 C.B. 620, 637.

[112] *See id.*

[113] *See* § 21.02[B].

[114] Treas. Reg. § 1.368-1(e)(6).

100 shares of P Corp. voting common stock, to its creditors; the shareholders of D Corp. receive nothing. D Corp. had conducted one line of business, which P Corp. continues after the transaction without interruption.

Determining whether the transaction in Example 21.22 qualifies as an acquisitive "G" reorganization:

Section 368(a)(1)(G) is satisfied because D Corp. transfers all of its assets to P Corp. pursuant to a court-approved plan of reorganization in a title 11 case, and D Corp. liquidates pursuant to the plan of reorganization, distributing all of its assets, which consists of the P Corp. stock. The transaction satisfies the continuity of interest requirement because 100% of the consideration received by the creditors of D Corp. is stock in P Corp. (here, the D Corp. creditors are taken into account for continuity of interest purposes, and the D Corp. shareholders are not because they received no consideration in the transaction). The transaction also satisfies the continuity of business enterprise requirement (P Corp. continues D Corp.'s historic business), and thus qualifies as a "G" reorganization.

Section 368(a)(2)(D) also permits triangular acquisitive "G" reorganizations.[115] And section 368(a)(3)(E) allows for a reverse triangular merger[116] in a bankruptcy or similar proceeding provided that in lieu of the consideration requirement contained in section 368(a)(2)(E),[117] (i) no former shareholder of the surviving debtor corporation receives any consideration for her stock and (ii) former creditors of the surviving debtor corporation exchange an 80 percent or more interest (by fair market value) in the debt of the debtor corporation for voting stock in the parent corporation. In addition, section 368(a)(2)(C) permits an acquisitive "G" reorganization followed by a drop down of all or part of the acquired assets into a controlled subsidiary.

2. Divisive "G' Reorganizations

A divisive "G" reorganization has requirements that are similar to those of the acquisitive version, except that the debtor corporation only transfers part of its assets to the acquiring corporation, and the debtor corporation is required to distribute stock or securities of the acquiring corporation in a transaction qualifying under section 355.[118]

As noted previously, section 355 provides detailed rules for qualifying certain corporate divisions for nonrecognition treatment, which will be examined in the next chapter.

---

[115] As described § 21.02[F], this is a transaction in which an acquiring corporation acquires the assets of a target corporation in exchange for stock in the controlling parent corporation of the acquiring corporation.

[116] As described in § 21.02[F][1][b], this is a transaction in which a controlled subsidiary of a parent corporation statutorily merges into the target corporation and the former shareholders of the target corporation receive stock in the parent corporation.

[117] This consideration requirement is that the former shareholders of the surviving target corporation exchange a controlling stock interest in the target corporation for voting stock in the parent corporation. *See* § 21.02[F][1][b].

[118] I.R.C. § 368(a)(1)(G).

Example 21.23. D Corp. has two businesses — business A and business B. On January 1, 2014, for business reasons D Corp. transfers the assets of business B to a new corporation, P Corp., pursuant to a court-approved reorganization plan in a title 11 bankruptcy case, in exchange for all 100 shares P Corp. voting common stock (the only class outstanding). Following the transfer and pursuant to the plan of reorganization, D Corp. distributes the 100 shares of P Corp. voting common stock to its creditors. Following the transaction, D Corp. continues to conduct business A, and P Corp. conducts business B.

Determining whether the transaction in Example 21.23 qualifies as an divisive "G" reorganization:

Provided that D Corp.'s distribution of P Corp. stock qualifies under section 355, section 368(a)(1)(G) would be satisfied because D Corp. transfers part of its assets to P Corp. pursuant to a court-approved plan of reorganization in a title 11 case. The transaction also satisfies the continuity of business enterprise requirement (D Corp.'s historic businesses, business A and business B, are continued by D Corp. and P Corp., respectively.)

§ 21.03   TAX TREATMENT OF PARTIES TO A REORGANIZATION

A.   Introduction

If the transaction qualifies as a reorganization, then a set of operative rules applies to determine the tax consequences of the parties to the reorganization. In general, these rules provide for nonrecognition (full or partial) of gain or loss, exchanged and transferred bases, and tacked holding periods — concepts that were explored in connection with section 351 transactions.[119]

The operative rules govern the tax consequences of the corporations that are "a party to a reorganization" along with their shareholders and security holders. Under section 368(b), "a party to a reorganization" includes (i) both corporations, in the case of the acquisition by one corporation of the assets or stock of another corporation (e.g., the acquiring and target corporations in an acquisitive reorganization), (ii) a corporation resulting from a reorganization (e.g., the surviving corporation in a consolidation), and (iii) the acquiring corporation's controlling parent in triangular reorganizations and drop downs.

The remainder of this chapter examines the rules for determining the tax consequences of the shareholders, holders of securities, and corporations involved in a reorganization.

---

[119] *See* Chapter 14.

B.   Tax Consequences to Shareholders and Security Holders

1.   Recognition of Gain or Loss

a.   In General

The main benefit provided to shareholders and security holders in a reorganization is nonrecognition treatment under section 354. Absent such treatment, a shareholder's exchange of stock in the target corporation for stock in the acquiring corporation (or a similar exchange of securities) would be a taxable event, as illustrated by the following example.

> *Example 21.24:* T Corp. has 100 shares of voting common stock outstanding, all of which is owned by A. A's basis in the 100 shares of T Corp. stock is $100,000. On January 1, 2014, T Corp. is merged into P Corp. in a transaction qualifying as an "A" reorganization. Pursuant to the plan of reorganization, A exchanges her 100 shares of T Corp. stock for 10,000 shares of P Corp. voting common stock. The 10,000 shares of P Corp. stock have a fair market value of $500,000.

Under section 1001(a), A has realized gain on the exchange equal to $400,000:

- the fair market value of the property received (10,000 shares of P Corp. stock), which is $500,000, minus

- A's $100,000 adjusted basis in the T Corp. exchanged.

Under section 1001(c), except as otherwise provided in the Code, realized gain or loss is recognized — i.e., included in gross income (absent an exclusion provision) or potentially allowed as a deduction. Therefore, absent the application of a nonrecognition rule, A would include the $400,000 of gain in her gross income for 2014.

Section 354 comes to A's aid and results in the nonrecognition of A's $400,000 of realized gain. Specifically, section 354(a)(1) provides that no gain or loss is recognized if stock or securities in a corporation that is a party to a reorganization are exchanged *solely* for stock or securities of another corporation that is a party to a reorganization, provided the exchange is pursuant to the plan of reorganization. Because T Corp. and P Corp. are parties to a reorganization,[120] A's exchange of T Corp. stock solely for P Corp. stock meets the requirements for nonrecognition treatment under section 354.

Section 354's nonrecognition rule covers exchanges of stock as well as "securities," although there are limitations on exchanges involving securities that will be examined below. "Securities," while not defined in the Code, are relatively long-term debt instruments issued by a corporation; corporate debt instruments with terms of 10 or more years appear to be generally classified as securities.[121]

---

[120] *See* § 21.03[A].

[121] See Bittker & Eustice, supra note 16 at 12-188. While earlier court decisions focused on the term of the debt instruments, some later decisions state that the term alone is not controlling and instead adopt an approach that looks at the nature of the debt, degree of the creditor's participation and interest in the corporation, and the purpose of the loan, among other factors. *See id.*

b.   Receipt of Boot

If a shareholder receives in a reorganization money or other property in addition to stock or securities, then the "solely" requirement contained in section 354(a)(1) is violated. Does this mean that the shareholder in this situation would have to recognize all of her realized gain?

The answer is no. Pursuant to section 356(a)(1), if the exchange otherwise would have qualified under section 354(a) but for fact that in addition to stock or securities, the shareholder (or security holder) received money or other property, commonly referred to as "boot," then any realized gain is recognized by the shareholder (or security holder) to the extent of the money plus the fair market of the other property.[122] In other words, in this situation the shareholder's (or security holder's) recognized gain equals the lesser of:

- Realized gain, or

- Money and fair market value of other property.

Example 21.25: T Corp. has 100 shares of voting common stock outstanding, all of which is owned by A. A's basis in the 100 shares of T Corp. stock is $100,000. On January 1, 2014, T Corp. is merged into P Corp. in a transaction qualifying as an "A" reorganization. Pursuant to the plan of reorganization, A exchanges her 100 shares of T Corp. stock for 7,000 shares of P Corp. voting common stock and $150,000 of cash. The 7,000 shares of P Corp. stock have a fair market value of $350,000.

Applying section 356(a)(1) to A in Example 21.25:

Because A receives P Corp. stock and boot, A qualifies under section 354(a)(1) except for the solely stock requirement. A recognizes the lesser of $400,000 (realized gain)[123] or $150,000 (money received), or $150,000 of gain.[124]

For purposes of recognizing gain under section 356(a)(1), all or a portion of the securities received may constitute boot. Specifically, section 356(d) provides that if the principal amount of the securities received exceeds the principal amount of the securities surrendered, the fair market value of the excess principal amount is

---

[122] A similar rule applied in the context of section 351 transactions. *See* Chapter 14.

[123] This is the difference between A's amount realized of $500,000 ($350,000 fair market value of P Corp. stock plus $150,000 of cash) and A's basis in the T Corp. stock of $100,000.

[124] The character of this gain is explored below. In situations where a shareholder surrenders shares of stock (or securities) that have different adjusted bases and acquisition dates, there would need to be an allocation of the stock, securities and boot received for purposes of recognizing gain under section 356(a)(1). This is analogous to the recognition of gain under section 351(b) where a transferor in a section 351 transaction transfers multiple properties to a corporation in exchange for stock and boot. *See* Chapter 14. Treas. Reg. § 1.356-1(b) provides that if the terms of the exchange specify the stock, securities and boot that are received for particular shares of stock or securities, these terms will control the allocation of these items to the stock and securities surrendered, provided that the terms are economically reasonable. Otherwise, a pro rata portion of the stock, securities, and boot received is treated as received for each share of stock and security surrendered, based on the relative fair market value of the share of stock or security surrendered. The latter approach is the same that is used in the section 351(b) context. *See* Chapter 14.

treated as "other property" for purposes of section 356(a)(1).[125] Where securities are received but no securities are surrendered, the fair market value of the securities received is other property.[126]

> *Example 21.26:* T Corp. has 100 shares of voting common stock outstanding, all of which is owned by A. A's basis in the 100 shares of T Corp. stock is $100,000. On January 1, 2014, T Corp. is merged into P Corp. in a transaction qualifying as an "A" reorganization. Pursuant to the plan of reorganization, A exchanges her 100 shares of T Corp. stock for 7,000 shares of P Corp. voting common stock and P Corp. securities. The 7,000 shares of P Corp. stock have a fair market value of $350,000, and the P Corp. securities have a principal amount and fair market value of $150,000.

Applying section 356(a)(1), (d) to A in Example 21.26:

Because A receives P Corp. securities but does not surrender any T Corp. securities, the fair market value of the P Corp. securities is boot for purposes of sections 354 and 356. Because A receives P Corp. stock and boot, A qualifies under section 354(a)(1) except for the solely stock requirement. A recognizes the lesser of $400,000 (realized gain)[127] or $150,000 (fair market value of the P Corp. securities), or $150,000 of gain.

Under section 356(c), if an exchange otherwise would have qualified under section 354(a) but for fact that the shareholder (or security holder) received money or other property, the shareholder (or security holder) still cannot recognize any realized loss.[128] Accordingly, if in Example 21.25 A's basis in the T Corp. stock had been $600,000, and A thus had a $100,000 realized loss on the exchange, then none of that loss would be recognized.

c.   Dividend Treatment of Recognized Gain

Section 356(a)(2) provides that all or a portion of the section 356(a)(1) gain recognized by a shareholder will be treated as a dividend if the *effect* of the exchange is a *distribution of a dividend*. In that case, the gain will be treated as a dividend to the extent of the shareholder's ratable share of the Accumulated E&P of the target corporation. Any remaining gain is treated as gain from the sale of property.

To determine whether an exchange has the effect of a dividend, the U.S. Supreme Court in *Commissioner v. Clark*[129] adopted a post-reorganization hypothetical redemption test. Under this test, the shareholder is treated as if (i) she received in the exchange only stock in the acquiring corporation and (ii)

---

[125] I.R.C. § 356(d)(2)(B).

[126] *Id.* In addition, nonqualified preferred stock is also treated as boot for purposes of sections 354 and 356, unless it is received in exchange for stock that is nonqualified preferred stock. I.R.C. §§ 354(a)(2)(C), 356(e). Nonqualified preferred stock is discussed in Chapter 14.

[127] This is the difference between A's amount realized of $500,000 ($350,000 fair market value of P Corp. stock plus $150,000 of P Corp. securities) and A's basis in the T Corp. stock of $100,000.

[128] A similar rule applied in the context of section 351 transactions. *See* Chapter 14.

[129] 489 U.S. 726 (1989).

following the exchange, the acquiring corporation redeemed, for the amount of boot received by the shareholder, the portion of the stock in the acquiring corporation that the shareholder did not actually receive. The section 302(b) redemption tests are then applied to this hypothetical redemption, and if they are all failed, the exchange has the effect of a dividend.

> *Example 21.27:* T Corp. has 100 shares of voting common stock outstanding, all of which is owned by A. A's basis in the 100 shares of T Corp. stock is $100,000. On January 1, 2014, T Corp. is merged into P Corp. in a transaction qualifying as an "A" reorganization. Pursuant to the plan of reorganization, A exchanges her 100 shares of T Corp. stock for 7,000 shares of P Corp. voting common stock (the only class outstanding) and $150,000 of cash. The 7,000 shares of P Corp. voting common stock have a fair market value of $350,000 ($50 per share). The 7,000 shares of P Corp. voting common stock represent .07% of the P Corp. voting common stock. 10,000 shares of P Corp. voting common stock represent .10% of the P Corp. voting common stock.

Applying section 356(a)(1), (2) to A in Example 21.27:

As in Example 21.25, A recognizes the lesser of $400,000 (realized gain)[130] or $150,000 (money received), or $150,000 of gain. Applying the post-reorganization hypothetical redemption test, A is treated as if she received only P Corp. voting common stock in the exchange, in which case she would have received 10,000 shares of P Corp. voting common stock.[131] A hypothetical redemption of the 3,000 shares of P Corp. voting common shares that A did not actually receive would have caused A's interest in P Corp. voting common stock to go from 10,000 shares (.10%) to 7,000 shares (.07%). Such a redemption would satisfy the substantially disproportionate redemption test contained in section 302(b)(2), because after the redemption, A has less than 50% of the voting power of P Corp., and the redemption causes her percentage of the P Corp. voting and common stock to decrease by more than 20%.[132] Therefore, because a hypothetical redemption satisfies one of the section 302(b) tests, the exchange does not have the effect of a dividend, and all of the gain is from an exchange of property and therefore likely capital gain.

If in Example 21.27 A had received 8,000 shares of P Corp. voting common stock and $100,000 of cash, then a hypothetical redemption would result in A's interest in P Corp. voting common stock going from 10,000 shares (.10%) to 8,000 shares (.08%). While this redemption would not satisfy the substantially disproportionate redemption test (because A's percentage of voting and common stock has not decreased by more than 20%), it should satisfy the "not essentially equivalent to a dividend" test contained in section 302(b)(1), because insignificant reductions in voting stock can satisfy this test where the shareholder does not have either control

---

[130] This is the difference between A's amount realized of $500,000 ($350,000 fair market value of P Corp. stock plus $150,000 of cash) and A's basis in the T Corp. stock of $100,000.

[131] At a price of $50 per share, 10,000 shares of P Corp. voting common stock have a value of $500,000, which is equal to the value of the consideration actually received by A in the exchange: sum of the value of the 7,000 shares of P Corp. common stock (worth $350,000) and $150,000 of cash.

[132] *See* Chapter 17.

or potential for group control before the redemption.[133] Thus, the exchange again would not have the effect of a dividend. Where the acquiring corporation is much larger than the target corporation (which seems typical), so that the shareholder's percentage of the acquiring corporation's stock is quite small, capital gain rather than dividend treatment should be the normal result.

The significance of section 356(a)(2) today is reduced because most dividends received by individuals are taxed at preferential capital gain rates.[134] For individuals, even if a portion of the gain is treated as a dividend, the entire amount of the gain will likely be taxed at preferential rates (assuming that the stock is a capital asset, which is very likely). However, dividend treatment under section 356(a)(2) still matters for corporate shareholders, because of the dividends-received deduction,[135] and for the acquiring corporation, due to the reduction in the target corporation's E&P that the acquiring corporation inherits under section 381.[136]

2. Basis in Property Received

Under section 358(a)(1), a shareholder's basis in the stock received in a reorganization is the same as the shareholder's basis in the stock surrendered, with certain adjustments that are described below. This is the same basis rule that applied to determine a shareholder's stock basis in the section 351 context.[137] As in the case of section 351 transactions, the purpose of this rule is to preserve in the stock received the gain or loss that went unrecognized in the exchange.

Stating the section 358(a)(1) basis rule fully, a shareholder's basis in stock received in a reorganization is:

- The same as the shareholder's basis in stock and securities surrendered,

- Plus the amount treated as a dividend on the exchange,

- Plus the gain recognized by the shareholder on the exchange (excluding the portion of the gain treated as a dividend),

- Minus the money received by the shareholder on the exchange,

- Minus the fair market value of other property received by the shareholder on the exchange.

The section 358(a)(1) basis rule would also apply to determine the basis of securities received to the extent that their principal amount does not exceed the principal amount of the securities surrendered.[138] The shareholder's basis in other property received in the exchange is its fair market value at the time of receipt.[139]

---

[133] *See* Chapter 17.

[134] *See* Chapter 16.

[135] *See id.*

[136] *See* Chapter 23.

[137] *See* Chapter 14.

[138] *See* Treas. Reg. § 1.358-2(a)(1); I.R.C. § 356(d).

[139] I.R.C. § 358(a)(2).

The application of section 358(a)(1) in the reorganizations context is illustrated by applying the provision to Example 21.25:

A's total basis in the 7,000 shares of P Corp. voting common stock received is:

- A's adjusted basis in the 100 shares of T Corp. voting common stock surrendered ($100,000),
- Plus the amount treated as a dividend on the transaction ($0),
- Plus gain recognized by A on the exchange ($150,000),
- Minus money received by A on the exchange ($150,000),
- Minus fair market value of other property received by A on the exchange ($0),

Which equals $100,000.

Treas. Reg. § 1.358-2(a) provides detailed rules for allocating the total basis determined under section 358(a)(1) to particular shares or securities received. These allocation rules are applicable (i) where the stock or securities surrendered were acquired at different prices and acquisition dates,[140] and (ii) where the stock or securities received are of different classes, or where money or other property are received.[141] Very generally, the regulations use a tracing approach, which permits shareholders to identify, through the terms of the exchange, the particular stock, securities, or boot that are received for particular stock or securities surrendered.[142] Where the terms of the exchange do not so specify, the regulations generally allocate the items received to those surrendered in a pro rata manner based on the relative fair market values of the stock or securities surrendered.[143]

3. Holding Period in Stock or Securities Received

A shareholder's holding period in the stock received in a reorganization will ordinarily include the period of time that the shareholder held the stock surrendered, referred to as a tacked holding period. This is a result of section 1223(1), which provides a tacked holding period if:

- The taxpayer's basis in property received in an exchange is the same in whole or part as the basis of the property exchanged ("exchanged basis"), and
- The property exchanged is either a capital asset or a section 1231 asset.

Because a shareholder in a reorganization takes an exchanged basis under section 358(a)(1) in the stock received, and assuming that the stock surrendered is a capital asset in the shareholder's hands, the shareholder has a tacked holding period in the stock received. Accordingly, in Example 21.25, A's holding period in the P Corp. stock received in the exchange will include her holding period in the T Corp. stock surrendered.

---

[140] *See* Treas. Reg. § 1.358-2(a)(2)(i), (c), Example 1.

[141] Treas. Reg. § 1.358-2(a)(2)(ii).

[142] *See* Treas. Reg. § 1.358-2(a).

[143] Treas. Reg. § 1.358-2(a)(2)(ii), (vii).

Securities that are received in a reorganization will also have a tacked holding period under section 1223(1) if the securities take an exchanged basis under section 358(a)(1), i.e., if the principal amount of the securities received does not exceed the principal amount of the securities surrendered.[144] As previously discussed, section 1223(1) also can apply to give a shareholder a tacked holding period in the stock received in a section 351 transaction.[145]

B.   Tax Consequences to Target Corporation

1.   Recognition of Gain or Loss on Transfer of Assets to Acquiring Corporation

a.   In General

In several of the types of reorganizations, the target corporation is transferring its assets to the acquiring corporation for stock in the acquiring corporation and possibly other consideration (including the assumption of target liabilities).[146] This occurs in "A", "C", "D", "F", and "G" reorganizations, along with their triangular versions. In the absence of a nonrecognition rule, the target corporation's transfer of assets would be a taxable event, as illustrated by the following example.

> *Example 21.28:* T Corp. has business assets with a fair market value of $1,000,000 and adjusted basis of $100,000. On January 1, 2014, T Corp. transfers all of its assets to P Corp in exchange solely for 10,000 shares of voting stock of P Corp, which have a fair market value of $1,000,000. Following the transfer, T Corp. liquidates pursuant to the plan of reorganization. The transaction qualifies as a "C" reorganization.

Under 1001(a), T Corp. has a total realized gain on the exchange equal to $900,000:

- the fair market value of the property received (10,000 shares of P Corp. voting stock), which is $1,000,000, minus
- T Corp.'s $100,000 adjusted basis in the assets transferred.

Absent the application of a nonrecognition rule, T Corp. would have to recognize the $900,000 of realized gain and include this amount in its gross income for 2014.

Pursuant to section 361(a), T Corp does not recognize the $900,000 of realized gain. Specifically, section 361(a) provides that no gain or loss is recognized by a corporation that is a party to a reorganization on an exchange of property *solely* for stock or securities of another corporation that is a party to a reorganization, provided the exchange is pursuant to the plan of reorganization. Because T Corp.

---

[144] *See* Treas. Reg. § 1.358-2(a)(1); I.R.C. § 356(d). This assumes that the securities surrendered are capital assets.

[145] *See* Chapter 14.

[146] In the case of a statutory merger qualifying as an "A" reorganization, there is a constructive receipt of stock and other consideration by the target corporation.

and P Corp. are parties to a reorganization,[147] T Corp.'s exchange of its assets solely for P Corp. stock meets the requirements for nonrecognition treatment under section 361(a).

b.   Receipt of Boot

If the target corporation receives in a reorganization money or other property in addition to stock or securities, then the "solely" requirement contained in section 361(a) is violated. Nevertheless, under section 361(b)(1), the target corporation still receives nonrecognition of gain treatment provided that the money or other property is distributed to the target's shareholders pursuant to the plan of reorganization.[148] Because the target corporation is required to liquidate in the context of "A", "C",[149] acquisitive "D," and acquisitive "G" reorganizations, it is rare for boot to be retained by the target and thus gain recognized.[150] If boot is retained, the target corporation would recognize any realized gain to the extent of the amount of boot retained.[151] Even if boot is received and retained, the target corporation is still not permitted to recognize any realized loss on the transfer of assets to the acquiring corporation.[152]

> *Example 21.29:* T Corp. has business assets with a fair market value of $1,000,000 and adjusted basis of $100,000. On January 1, 2014, T Corp. transfers all of its assets to P Corp in exchange for 10,000 shares of voting stock of P Corp, which have a fair market value of $800,000, and $200,000 of cash. Following the transfer, T Corp. liquidates pursuant to the plan of reorganization, and transfers the P Corp. stock and cash received to its shareholders. The transaction qualifies as a "C" reorganization.

Applying section 361(a), (b) to T Corp. in Example 21.29:

T Corp. recognizes none of its $900,000 of realized gain on the transfer of its assets. Although T Corp. received boot in addition to stock on the transfer, the boot was distributed to its shareholders, allowing for the nonrecognition of gain under section 361(b)(1).

In general, the assumption of liabilities of the target corporation by the acquiring corporation is not considered boot received by the target corporation, as provided in section 357(a). As an exception, section 357(b) treats the assumption of liabilities as the receipt of money if the target corporation's principal purpose with respect to the assumption either was a purpose to avoid federal income tax or was not a bona

---

[147] *See* § 21.03[A].

[148] I.R.C. § 361(b)(1)(A). In general, transfers of boot to creditors in connection with a reorganization are treated as transfers to shareholders for purposes of section 361(b). I.R.C. § 361(b)(3).

[149] As mentioned previously, the Service can waive the liquidation requirement for a "C" reorganization. I.R.C. § 368(a)(2)(G). However, if such a waiver were to occur, the target corporation is treated for tax purposes as if it had liquidated and the shareholders then contributed the deemed distributed property back to the corporation. H.R. Rep. No. 98-861, 98th Cong., 2d Sess. 845-846.

[150] Retention of boot is possible in divisive "D" and divisive "G" reorganizations.

[151] I.R.C. § 361(b)(1).

[152] I.R.C. § 361(b)(2).

fide business purpose.[153] In addition, the recognition of section 357(c) gain,[154] which occurs where assumed liabilities exceed the aggregate basis of transferred assets, can occur in a divisive "D" reorganization but not in other types of reorganizations. As discussed previously, these provisions are also applicable to section 351 transactions.[155]

2. Recognition of Gain or Loss on Distribution of Property to Shareholders and Creditors

Following the target corporation's transfer of its assets to the acquiring corporation in exchange for stock in the acquiring corporation and possibly other consideration, there is generally an actual or deemed distribution of the stock and other consideration to the target's shareholders and creditors; in most reorganizations involving asset acquisitions, the distribution is mandatory in light of the liquidation requirement for "A", "C", acquisitive "D," and acquisitive "G" reorganizations. In the absence of a nonrecognition rule, the target corporation would recognize gain (and possibly loss) under sections 336[156] or 311[157] on the distribution of the stock and other items, in an amount equal to the difference between the fair market value of the distributed items and the items' adjusted basis in the target's hands.[158]

Section 361(c) overrides sections 336 and 311[159] and provides that a target corporation will not recognize any gain or loss on the distribution of "qualified property" to its shareholders pursuant to a plan of reorganization.[160] "Qualified property" generally includes (i) stock (or stock rights) in the acquiring corporation or obligations of the acquiring corporation that were received by the target corporation in the reorganization exchange or (ii) stock (or stock rights) in the target corporation or obligations of the target corporation.[161] Thus, section 361(c) protects the target from recognizing gain on the distribution to its shareholders of stock or securities in the acquiring corporation (along with such corporation's stock rights and non-security obligations) that are received in the reorganization. The target corporation's transfer of qualified property to its creditors in connection with

[153] Apparently, no case has applied section 357(b) to a reorganization. *See* Bittker & Eustice, *supra* note 16 at 12-202. Even if the provision was applied to create the receipt of boot by the target in a reorganization, arguably such boot could be treated as distributed to the target's creditors in connection with the reorganization for purposes of the section 361(b) nonrecognition rule. *See id.*

[154] *See* Chapter 14.

[155] *See id.*

[156] *See* Chapter 19.

[157] *See* Chapter 16.

[158] In this regard, the target's basis in the stock or securities in the acquiring corporation is an exchanged basis determined under section 358(a)(1), which is generally the same basis that the target had in the assets transferred to the acquiring corporation in exchange for the stock or securities.

[159] I.R.C. § 361(c)(4).

[160] I.R.C. § 361(c)(1), (2).

[161] I.R.C. § 361(c)(2)(B). For divisive D reorganizations, there are two situations where stock or securities in the acquiring corporation (or using section 355 terminology, the controlled corporation) are not treated as qualified property. These are mentioned in Chapter 22.

a reorganization is also covered by the nonrecognition rule, as such transfers are treated as distributions to the target's shareholders for purposes of section 361(c).[162]

> *Example 21.30:* T Corp. has business assets with a fair market value of $1,000,000 and adjusted basis of $100,000. On January 1, 2014, T Corp. transfers all of its assets to P Corp in exchange for 10,000 shares of voting stock of P Corp, which have a fair market value of $1,000,000. Following the transfer, T Corp. liquidates pursuant to the plan of reorganization, and transfers the P Corp. stock received to its shareholders. The transaction qualifies as a "C" reorganization.

Applying section 361(c) to T Corp. in Example 21.30:

T Corp. recognizes no gain or loss on the distribution of the P Corp. stock to its shareholders. The P Corp. stock is qualified property for purposes of section 361(c) because it is stock in the acquiring corporation that is received by T Corp. in the reorganization exchange.

On a target corporation's distribution of property that is *not* qualified property, the target corporation is required to recognize gain if the property's fair market value exceeds its adjusted basis in the target's hands, with the amount of the recognized gain equal to the difference between the property's fair market value and adjusted basis.[163] This rule would apply, for example, where the target corporation distributes to its shareholders appreciated property that was not transferred to the acquiring corporation in the reorganization. A distributing corporation is not permitted to recognize a loss on a distribution of property, whether or not the property is qualified property.[164] The recognition rules for distributions of property other than qualified property are in effect the same as those provided in section 311 for nonliquidating distributions.[165]

C. Tax Consequences to Acquiring Corporation

1. Recognition of Gain or Loss

An acquiring corporation recognizes no gain or loss on the transfer of its stock in exchange for the assets or stock of the target corporation. This is a result of section 1032(a) (also applicable in the section 351 context[166]), which provides that no gain or loss is recognized to a corporation on the receipt of money or other property in exchange for its stock.[167] Section 1032(a) also provides a corporation with

---

[162] I.R.C. § 361(c)(3).

[163] I.R.C. § 361(c)(2)(A).

[164] I.R.C. § 361(c)(1), (2).

[165] *See* Chapter 16.

[166] *See* Chapter 14.

[167] Note that the applicability of section 1032 is *not* dependent on there being a reorganization under section 368. In the case of triangular reorganizations, section 1032(a) also provides tax-free treatment to both the controlling parent and the controlled acquiring corporation (generally) on the acquiring corporation's use of the parent stock to make the acquisition. Treas. Reg. § 1.1032-2(b), (c).

nonrecognition treatment where it exchanges shares of its own stock for other shares of its own stock in a recapitalization under section 368(a)(1)(E).[168] To the extent that an acquiring corporation uses its own debt instruments, including securities, to acquire assets or stock, the acquiring corporation also does not recognize gain or loss because it is simply purchasing property by issuing its own debt instrument.[169] However, if the acquiring corporation uses consideration other than its stock or debt to make an acquisition, it has to recognize any realized gain or loss according to general tax principles.[170]

2. Basis in Property Received

Under section 362(b), the acquiring corporation's basis in the property acquired in a reorganization is generally the same basis that the transferor had in the property, increased by any gain recognized by the transferor on the transfer,[171] referred to generally as a transferred basis.[172] Thus, in the case of a reorganization involving an asset acquisition (e.g., an "A", "C" or "D" reorganization), the acquiring corporation takes a basis in the former assets of the target corporation that is the same as the target's basis in the assets, plus any gain recognized by the target in the reorganization; because it is rare for the target to recognize gain,[173] the acquiring corporation's basis in the acquired assets will generally be the same as the target's.

> *Example 21.31:* T Corp. has business assets with a fair market value of $1,000,000 and adjusted basis of $100,000. On January 1, 2014, T Corp. transfers all of its assets to P Corp in exchange solely for 10,000 shares of voting stock of P Corp., which have a fair market value of $1,000,000. Following the transfer, T Corp. liquidates pursuant to the plan of reorganization. The transaction qualifies as a "C" reorganization.

Applying section 362(b) to P Corp. in Example 21.31:

P Corp.'s basis in the assets acquired is $100,000 — the same as T Corp.'s basis in the assets ($100,000) plus gain recognized ($0) (T Corp. recognizes no gain under section 361(a)).

In the case of a "B" reorganization, the acquiring corporation's basis in the stock of the target is the same as the target shareholders' basis in the stock; this is because the target shareholders cannot recognize gain in a "B" reorganization as no boot is permitted.[174]

---

[168] *Id.*

[169] *See* Bitker & Eustice, *supra* note 16 at 12-210.

[170] *See id.*

[171] An exception applies where property with a built-in loss (i.e., adjusted basis in excess of fair market value) is transferred by a person not subject to U.S. tax (e.g., a foreign corporation) to a corporation subject to U.S. tax (e.g., a domestic corporation). I.R.C. § 362(e)(1). Where this occurs, the transferee takes a fair market value basis in the transferred property. *Id.*

[172] I.R.C. § 7701(a)(43).

[173] *See* § 21.03[B][1].

[174] *See* § 21.02[D].

Example 21.32. A owns all of the voting common stock of T Corp. (the only class outstanding), which has a fair market value of $1,000,000 and a basis in A's hands of $100,000. On January 1, 2014, P Corp. acquires all of the voting common stock of T Corp. from A solely in exchange for voting stock of P Corp. The transaction qualifies as a "B" reorganization.

Applying section 362(b) to P Corp. in Example 21.32:

P Corp.'s basis in the stock acquired is $100,000 — the same as A's basis in the stock ($100,000) plus gain recognized ($0) (A recognizes no gain under section 354(a)).

3. Holding Period in Property Received

The acquiring corporation's holding period in the property acquired in the reorganization will include the period of time that the transferor held the property, referred to as a tacked holding period. This is a result of section 1223(2), which provides:

- If a taxpayer's basis in property received in an exchange is the same in whole or part as the basis of the property in the hands of another person ("transferred basis"),

- Then the taxpayer's holding period in the property received in the exchange includes the other person's holding period in that property ("tacked holding period").

Because the acquiring corporation in a reorganization takes a transferred basis under section 362(b) in the property acquired, the acquiring corporation has a tacked holding period in this property. Accordingly, in Example 21.31, P Corp.'s holding period in the assets acquired in the reorganization will include T Corp.'s holding period in these assets. Likewise, in Example 21.32, P Corp.'s holding period in the T Corp. stock acquired in the reorganization will include A's holding period in this stock. As previously discussed, section 1223(2) also applies to give a corporation a tacked holding period in the property received in a section 351 transaction.[175]

---

[175] *See* Chapter 14.

Chapter 22

CORPORATE DIVISIONS

BASIC OVERVIEW

This chapter examines the tax treatment of shareholders and corporations that engage in corporate divisions. In very general terms, a corporate division is a where the business enterprise of a corporation (and possibly its subsidiaries) is divided among two or more separate corporations that are then owned by shareholders of the original corporation. This chapter provides a primer on corporate divisions, which includes the general types of corporate divisions, the tax stakes involved, the requirements for obtaining full or partial nonrecognition under section 355, and the tax treatment of the shareholders and corporations that are involved in qualifying corporate divisions.

A. Types of Corporate Divisions

There are three types of corporate divisions, commonly called spin-offs, split-offs and split-ups.[1] All three types involve transactions where one corporation (referred to in section 355 as the "distributing corporation") distributes to its shareholders stock in a corporation that the distributing corporation controls immediately before the distribution (referred to in section 355 as the "controlled corporation"). The types differ with regard to the form of the distribution. A spin-off is a distribution by the distributing corporation of stock in the controlled corporation to shareholders of the distributing corporation where the shareholders do not surrender any of their stock in the distributing corporation. A spin-off takes the form of a dividend of the stock in the controlled corporation. A split-off is a distribution by the distributing corporation of stock in the controlled corporation to shareholders of the distributing corporation where the shareholders surrender some or all of their stock in the distributing corporation. A split-off takes the form of a redemption of stock in the distributing corporation. A split-up is a distribution of stock in two or more controlled corporations in the complete liquidation of the distributing corporation. A split-up takes the form of a complete liquidation of the distributing corporation.

B. Tax Stakes Involved

If not for full or partial nonrecognition under section 355, a corporate division would be a taxable event at both the shareholder and corporation levels. Specifically, in the absence of section 355, the shareholder consequences would be

---

[1] As discussed in the Detailed Analysis, a corporate division can occur either with or without a divisive "D" reorganization.

as follows:

- A spin-off is a section 301 distribution of property that would be treated as a dividend to the extent of the distributing corporation's E&P; [2]
- A split-off is a redemption of stock that would be tested under section 302 for treatment as either a taxable exchange or a section 301 distribution;[3]
- A split-up is a liquidating distribution that would be a taxable exchange under section 331.[4]

Without section 355, the distributing corporation in a spin-off or split-off would recognize any gain (but not any loss) on the distribution of the stock in the controlled corporation under section 311.[5] Similarly, the distributing corporation in a split-up would recognize any gain and generally recognize any loss on the distribution of the controlled corporation's stock under section 336.[6]

C. Requirements for Nonrecognition Treatment

To qualify for nonrecognition treatment, a corporate division needs to satisfy all of the detailed requirements of section 355, along with certain non-statutory requirements, as follows:

- Control requirement
- Distribution requirement
- Active business requirement
- Corporate business purpose requirement
- No device requirement
- Continuity of interest requirement

1. Control Requirement

Under section 355(a)(1)(A), the distributing corporation is required to distribute to its shareholders and security holders stock or securities of a controlled corporation. A controlled corporation is a corporation that the distributing corporation controls immediately before the distribution.[7] Under section 368(c), "control" is defined as the ownership of at least 80% of (i) the total combined voting power of all classes of stock entitled to vote and (ii) the total number of shares of all other classes of stock.[8]

---

[2] *See* Chapter 16.
[3] *See* Chapter 17.
[4] *See* Chapter 19.
[5] *See* Chapter 16.
[6] *See* Chapter 19.
[7] I.R.C. § 355(a)(1)(A).
[8] This is the same definition of control that is used for purposes of section 351 and the reorganization provisions in general.

2.   Distribution Requirement

Under section 355(a)(1)(D), the distributing corporation is required to distribute either:

- All of the stock and securities that it holds in the controlled corporation immediately before the distribution, or

- An amount of stock in the controlled corporation that constitutes control (per section 368(c)), provided the distributing corporation can establish that its retention of stock or securities in the controlled corporation was not pursuant to a plan having the avoidance of federal income tax as one of its principal purposes.

3.   Active Business Requirement

Under section 355(a)(1)(C), the transaction must satisfy the active business requirement contained in section 355(b). To satisfy this requirement, either:

- The distributing corporation and the controlled corporation[9] are each "engaged in the active conduct of a trade or business" immediately after the distribution, or

- Immediately before the distribution, the distributing corporation's only assets were stock or securities in the controlled corporations, and each controlled corporation is "engaged in the active conduct of a trade or business" immediately after the distribution.[10]

Several requirements must be met in order for a corporation to be treated as "engaged in the active conduct of a trade or business." A corporation must be "engaged in a trade or business,"[11] and the trade or business must be "actively conducted," which, under the regulations, generally requires that the corporation itself perform active and substantial management functions.[12] In addition, section 355(b)(2)(B) provides that the trade or business must have been actively conducted throughout the five-year period ending on the date of the distribution. Moreover, section 355(b)(2)(C) requires that the trade or business was not acquired by the corporation within the aforementioned five-year period in a transaction in which gain or loss was recognized.[13] Finally, section 355(b)(2)(D) prevents the distributing corporation from acquiring control of a corporation conducting the trade or

---

[9] Where the stock of more than one controlled corporation is distributed, each of such controlled corporations must be engaged in the active conduct of a trade or business immediately after the distribution. I.R.C. § 355(b)(1)(A).

[10] I.R.C. § 355(b)(1).

[11] The Detailed Analysis examines the specific meaning of "engaged in a trade or business," as provided in the regulations.

[12] Treas. Reg. § 1.355-3(b)(2)(iii).

[13] While the statute is not clear, it must be referring to gain or loss recognized by the seller, since the purchaser would not recognize any gain or loss on the acquisition of a business. *See* Boris I. Bittker & James S. Eustice, Federal Income Taxation of Corporations and Shareholders 11-33 (2000).

business in a taxable transaction within the five-year period.[14]

4. Corporate Business Purpose Requirement

Under Treas. Reg. § 1.355-2(b)(1), the transaction must be carried out for one or more corporate business purposes. According to the regulations, '[a] corporate business purpose is a real and substantial non-Federal tax purpose germane to the business of the distributing corporation, the controlled corporation, or the affiliated group . . . to which the distributing corporation belongs."[15]

5. No Device Requirement

Under section 355(a)(1)(B), the transaction must not be used principally as a device for distributing the E&P of the distributing corporation, the controlled corporation, or both corporations. The regulations state that the device determination is generally made from all of the facts and circumstances.[16] In this regard, the regulations provide certain factors that are either evidence of a device or evidence of a nondevice,[17] as well as types of distributions that are ordinarily not considered to have been used principally as a device; the Detailed Analysis examines these factors and types of distributions.

6. Continuity of Interest Requirement

As is the case with corporate reorganizations, a corporate division must satisfy a continuity of interest requirement. Specifically, Treas. Reg. § 1.355-2(c)(1) requires that the historic shareholders of the distributing corporation own, in the aggregate, an amount of stock establishing a continuity of interest in *each* of the corporations after the separation. Using the Service's benchmark for ruling purposes, the historic shareholders of the distributing corporation would generally need at least a 50% equity interest in both the distributing corporation and controlled corporation after the transaction in order to satisfy this requirement.[18]

D. Tax Treatment of Parties to a Section 355 Transaction

If a transaction qualifies under section 355, then the rules generally provide for nonrecognition treatment for the shareholders, security holders and corporations involved in the corporate division, along with exchanged bases and tacked holding periods — concepts that were explored in connection with both section 351 transactions and corporate reorganizations.[19]

---

[14] Control is defined using the 80% tests contained in section 368(c), which is addressed in Chapter 14 and Chapter 21.

[15] Treas. Reg. § 1.355-2(b)(2).

[16] Treas. Reg. § 1.355-2(d)(1).

[17] *Id.*

[18] *See* Chapter 21.

[19] *See* Chapter 14; Chapter 21.

1. Tax Consequences to Shareholders and Security Holders

In a transaction qualifying under section 355, shareholders receiving solely stock do not recognize any gain or loss, and do not include any amounts in income, pursuant to section 355(a)(1).[20] Similarly, security holders receiving solely stock or securities[21] in a qualifying section 355 transaction do not recognize any gain, loss or income (subject to limitations on transactions involving the receipt of securities that are discussed in the Detailed Analysis). If a shareholder or securities holder receives money or other property, i.e., boot, in a transaction otherwise qualifying under section 355, then nonrecognition treatment is not completely lost. Specifically, in the case of a split-off or split-up, where a shareholder relinquishes stock in the distributing corporation, under section 356(a)(1) the shareholder recognizes any realized gain to the extent of the money plus the fair market value of the other property received;[22] however, the shareholder is not permitted to recognize any realized loss under section 356(c).[23] In the case of a spin-off, where a shareholder relinquishes no stock in the distributing corporation, the boot received is treated as a section 301 distribution of property, and thus is a taxable dividend to the extent of the E&P of the distributing corporation.[24]

Under section 358, a shareholder's basis in the stock received and retained in a section 355 transaction is determined under a two-step process. First, under section 358(a)(1) there is a determination of the aggregate basis in (i) the stock of the controlled corporation that is received and (ii) any stock of the distributing corporation that is retained.[25] Second, this aggregate basis is then allocated between the stock of the controlled corporation and the stock of the distributing corporation, in proportion to their fair market values.[26] The aggregate stock basis in the stock of the controlled and distributing corporations is:

- The same as the shareholder's original basis in the stock and securities of the distributing corporation,

- Plus the amount treated as a dividend on the transaction,

- Plus the gain recognized by the shareholder on the transaction (excluding the portion of the gain treated as a dividend),

- Minus the money received by the shareholder in the transaction,

- Minus the fair market value of other property received by the shareholder in the transaction.

---

[20] I.R.C. § 355(a)(1).

[21] *See* Chapter 21 for a definition of securities.

[22] As discussed in the Detailed Analysis, all or a portion of any recognized gain under section 356(a) may be treated as a dividend.

[23] The same rule would apply where a security holder exchanges securities for stock or securities and boot.

[24] I.R.C. § 356(b).

[25] *See* I.R.C. § 358(b)(2), (c). In the case of a split-up, no stock in the distributing corporation is retained, but stock in two or more controlled corporations is received. Accordingly, in this situation, there is a determination of the aggregate basis in the stock of the controlling corporations that is received.

[26] *See* I.R.C. § 358(b)(2); Treas. Reg. § 1.358-2(a)(2)(iv). In the case of a split-up, the aggregate basis is allocated between the stock in the two or more controlled corporations that is received.

Under section 1223(1), a shareholder takes a tacked holding period in the stock received in a section 355 transaction, assuming that the stock in the distributing corporation is capital asset. The Detailed Analysis discusses the basis and holding period consequences for securities received in a section 355 transaction.

2. Tax Consequences to the Distributing Corporation

Section 355(c) provides that a distributing corporation will not recognize any gain or loss on the distribution of "qualified property" to its shareholders in a section 355 transaction that is not pursuant to a plan of reorganization.[27] Subject to two exceptions (discussed in the Detailed Analysis), "qualified property" is stock or securities in the controlled corporation.[28] Thus, section 355(c) generally protects the distributing corporation from recognizing gain on the distribution to its shareholders of stock or securities in the controlled corporation.

DETAILED ANALYSIS

§ 22.01 INTRODUCTION

The Code contains a complex provision, section 355, that provides for complete or partial nonrecognition at both the corporate and shareholder levels on qualifying corporate divisions. In very general terms, a corporate division occurs when the business enterprise of a corporation (and possibly its subsidiaries) is divided among two or more separate corporations that are then owned by shareholders of the original corporation. Corporate divisions are of three general types — "spin-offs," "split-offs," and "split-ups", which are described below. A qualifying corporate division can occur either with or without a divisive "D" reorganization (discussed in Chapter 21). As with corporate formations and corporate reorganizations, the main rationale for nonrecognition treatment seems to be that because a corporate division arguably changes the form rather than the substance of the parties' holdings and therefore may lack significance, taxing such transactions may impede them from happening.

§ 22.02 TYPES OF CORPORATE DIVISIONS

A. Overview

As mentioned above, there are three types of corporate divisions, commonly called spin-offs, split-offs and split-ups. All three types involve transactions in which one corporation (referred to in section 355 as the "distributing corporation") distributes to its shareholders stock in a corporation that the distributing corporation controls immediately before the distribution (referred to in section 355 as the "controlled corporation"). The types differ with regard to the form of the distribution, as explained below.

---

[27] I.R.C. § 355(c)(1), (2).
[28] I.R.C. § 355(c)(2)(B).

As noted above, a corporate division can occur either with or without a divisive "D" reorganization. To explain, if part of the distributing corporation's business enterprise is not already in one or more controlled corporations, then the corporate division would be accomplished by first having the distributing corporation transfer part of its enterprise to one or more controlled corporations, followed then by a distribution of the stock or securities in the controlled corporation(s). If the requirements of sections 368(a)(1)(D)[29] and 355 are satisfied, the first step would constitute a divisive "D" reorganization. In the alternative, if part of the distributing corporation's business enterprise had already been in one or more controlled corporations, then there is no need for the first step divisive "D" reorganization in order to accomplish a corporate division — only a distribution of stock or securities in the controlled corporation is necessary.

B.　Spin-off

A spin-off is a distribution by the distributing corporation of stock in the controlled corporation to shareholders of the distributing corporation where the shareholders do not surrender any of their stock in the distributing corporation. A spin-off takes the form of a dividend of the stock in the controlled corporation.[30] The following example illustrates a spin-off.

> *Example 22.1.* A and B each own 50 shares of the voting common stock of D Corp. (the only class outstanding), which operates business P. D Corp. owns all 100 shares of the voting common stock of C Corp. (the only class outstanding), which operates business Q. On January 1, 2014, D Corp. distributes 50 shares of the C Corp. voting common stock to A and 50 shares of the C Corp. voting common stock to B. After the distribution, A and B each own 50 shares of the voting common stock of D Corp. and C Corp.

C.　Split-off

A split-off is a distribution by the distributing corporation of stock in the controlled corporation to shareholders of the distributing corporation where the shareholders surrender some or all of their stock in the distributing corporation. A split-off takes the form of a redemption of stock in the distributing corporation. The following example illustrates a split-off.

> *Example 22.2.* A and B each own 50 shares of the voting common stock of D Corp. (the only class outstanding), which operates business P. D Corp. owns all 100 shares of the voting common stock of C Corp. (the only class outstanding), which operates business Q. On January 1, 2014, D Corp. distributes all 100 shares of the C Corp. voting common stock to A in redemption of her 50 shares of D Corp. voting common stock. After the

---

[29] *See* Chapter 21.

[30] More precisely, a spin-off takes the form of a section 301 distribution of property that would be a dividend to the extent of the distributing corporation's E&P in the absence of section 355.

distribution, A owns all 100 shares of the C Corp. voting common stock, and B owns all 50 shares of the D Corp. voting common stock.

D. Split-up

A split-up is a distribution of stock in two or more controlled corporations in the complete liquidation of the distributing corporation. A split-up takes the form of a complete liquidation of the distributing corporation. The following example illustrates a split-up.

> *Example 22.3.* A and B each own 50 shares of the voting common stock of D Corp. (the only class outstanding). D Corp.'s only assets are all 100 shares of the voting common stock (the only class outstanding) of both C1 Corp. and C2 Corp. C1 Corp. and C2 Corp. operate business P and business Q, respectively. On January 1, 2014, D Corp. completely liquidates, and distributes all 100 shares of the C1 Corp. voting common stock to A and all 100 shares of C2 voting common stock to B. After the liquidation, A owns all 100 shares of the C1 Corp. voting common stock, and B owns all 100 shares of the C2 Corp. voting common stock.

§ 22.03 TAX STAKES INVOLVED

If not for full or partial nonrecognition under section 355, a corporate division would be a taxable event at both the shareholder and corporation levels. Specifically, in the absence of section 355, the shareholder consequences would be as follows:

- A spin-off is a section 301 distribution of property that would be treated as a dividend to the extent of the distributing corporation's E&P;[31]

- A split-off is a redemption of stock that would be tested under section 302 for treatment as either a taxable exchange or a section 301 distribution;[32]

- A split-up is a liquidating distribution that would be a taxable exchange under section 331.[33]

Without section 355, the distributing corporation in a spin-off or split-off would recognize any gain (but not any loss) on the distribution of the stock in the controlled corporation under section 311.[34] Similarly, the distributing corporation in a split-up would recognize any gain and generally recognize any loss on the distribution of the controlled corporation's stock under section 336.[35] If a corporate division includes a first step transfer of assets by the distributing corporation to the controlled corporation, then absent section 355, the distributing corporation's transfer of assets would be a taxable exchange under section 1001.[36]

---

[31] *See* Chapter 16.

[32] *See* Chapter 17.

[33] *See* Chapter 19.

[34] *See* Chapter 16.

[35] *See* Chapter 19.

[36] This is because a divisive "D" reorganization, which would provide the distributing corporation with

§ 22.04   REQUIREMENTS FOR NONRECOGNITION TREATMENT

To qualify for nonrecognition treatment, a corporate division needs to satisfy all of the detailed requirements of section 355, along with certain non-statutory requirements, as follows:

- Control requirement
- Distribution requirement
- Active business requirement
- Corporate business purpose requirement
- No device requirement
- Continuity of interest requirement

Each of these requirements is examined below.[37]

A.   Control Requirement

Under section 355(a)(1)(A), the distributing corporation is required to distribute to its shareholders and security holders stock or securities of a controlled corporation. A controlled corporation is a corporation that the distributing corporation controls immediately before the distribution.[38] Under section 368(c), "control" is defined as the ownership of at least 80% of (i) the total combined voting power of all classes of stock entitled to vote and (ii) the total number of shares of all other classes of stock.[39]

B.   Distribution Requirement

Under section 355(a)(1)(D), the distributing corporation is required to distribute either:

- All of the stock and securities that it holds in the controlled corporation immediately before the distribution, or
- An amount of stock in the controlled corporation that constitutes control (per section 368(c)), provided the distributing corporation can establish that its retention of stock or securities in the controlled corporation was not pursuant to a plan having the avoidance of federal income tax as one of its principal purposes.

---

nonrecognition treatment on the transfer, requires a distribution of stock or securities in the controlled corporation that satisfies section 355. *See* § 21.02.

[37] As apparently an additional requirement, the regulations provide that "[s]ection 355 contemplates the continued operation of the business or businesses existing prior to the separation." Treas. Reg. § 1.355-1(b). Presumably, this would be violated if a business in a spun-off corporation had been sold shortly after the separation. *See* Bittker & Eustice, *supra* note 13 at 11-62.

[38] I.R.C. § 355(a)(1)(A).

[39] This is the same definition of control that is used for purposes of section 351 and the reorganization provisions in general. *See* Chapters 14 and Chapter 21.

C. Active Business Requirement

1. In General

Under section 355(a)(1)(C), the transaction must satisfy the active business requirement contained in section 355(b). To satisfy this requirement, either:

- The distributing corporation and the controlled corporation[40] are each "engaged in the active conduct of a trade or business" immediately after the distribution, or

- Immediately before the distribution, the distributing corporation's only assets were stock or securities in the controlled corporations, and each controlled corporation is "engaged in the active conduct of a trade or business" immediately after the distribution.[41]

The active business requirement is aimed at preventing a corporation from making a tax-free distribution that has the effect of separating liquid assets as a substitute for paying a taxable dividend in cash or liquid property.[42]

2. Active Conduct of a Trade or Business

a. "Trade or Business" and "Actively Conducted"

Several requirements must be met in order for a corporation to be treated as "engaged in the active conduct of a trade or business."[43] First, a corporation must be "engaged in a trade or business," which, according to the regulations, is where "a specific group of activities are being carried on by the corporation for the purpose of earning income or profit, and the activities included in such group include every operation that forms a part of, or a step in, the process of earning income or profits. Such group of activities ordinarily must include the collection of income and payment of expenses."[44] Second, the trade or business must be "actively conducted," which, under the regulations, generally requires that the corporation itself perform active and substantial management functions.[45] Generally, the corporation itself is not considered to have performed activities that are performed by persons outside the corporation, such as independent

---

[40] Where the stock of more than one controlled corporation is distributed, each of such controlled corporations must be engaged in the active conduct of a trade or business immediately after the distribution. I.R.C. § 355(b)(1)(A).

[41] I.R.C. § 355(b)(1).

[42] *See* Bittker & Eusstice, *supra* note 13 at 11-32.

[43] For purposes of determining whether a corporation meets this requirement, all members of the corporation's "separate affiliated group" are treated as one corporation. I.R.C. § 355(b)(3)(A). A corporation's "separate affiliated group" is the affiliated group that would be determined under section 1504(a) (basically corporations that are connected through 80% vote and value stock ownership) if the particular corporation were the common parent. I.R.C. § 355(b)(3)(B). Essentially this means that in determining whether the distributing or controlled corporation is engaged in the active conduct of a trade or business, the activities of that corporation's 80%-owned affiliates are taken into account.

[44] Treas. Reg. § 1.355-3(b)(2)(ii).

[45] Treas. Reg. § 1.355-3(b)(2)(iii).

contractors.[46] The regulations go on to treat two activities as not within the active conduct of a trade or business: (i) the holding of property for investment purposes or (ii) the ownership and operation (including leasing) of real or personal property used in a trade or business, absent significant owner-performed services with respect to the property's operation and management.[47]

b.   Five-Year Requirements

In addition, section 355(b)(2)(B) provides that the trade or business must have been actively conducted throughout the five-year period ending on the date of the distribution. For this purpose, the regulations provide that changes to a trade or business within the five-year period will be disregarded, as long as the changes do not constitute the acquisition of a new or different business.[48] For example, a corporation that acquires a trade or business in the same line of business as the corporation's existing business is ordinarily treated as having expanded its original business, unless the acquisition causes "a change of such a character as to constitute the acquisition of a new or different business."[49] Moreover, section 355(b)(2)(C) requires that the trade or business was not acquired within the aforementioned five-year period in a transaction in which gain or loss was recognized.[50] Thus, it is permissible for either the distributing or controlled corporation to acquire an existing business within the five-year period in a tax-free reorganization or parent-subsidiary liquidation, but a violation would occur if the business had been acquired in a taxable purchase for cash or debt. Finally, section 355(b)(2)(D) prevents the distributing corporation from acquiring control of a corporation conducting the trade or business in a taxable transaction within the five-year period.[51] The purpose of the five-year history requirement and the prohibition on taxable acquisitions within the five-year period is to prevent a corporation from temporarily investing liquid assets in a new business as a prelude to a tax-free separation under section 355.[52]

> *Example 22.4.* As of January 1, 2014, S owns all 100 shares of the voting common stock of D Corp. (the only class outstanding). For the past 10 years, D Corp. has been actively conducting business A. For the past 10 years, D Corp. has owned all 100 shares of the voting common stock (the only class outstanding) of C Corp., and C Corp. has actively conducted business B during this period. On January 1, 2014, D Corp. distributes the 100 shares of C Corp. voting common stock to S. Following the transaction, D Corp. continues to actively conduct business A, and C Corp. continues to actively conduct business B.

---

[46] *Id.*

[47] Treas. Reg. § 1.355-3(b)(2)(iv).

[48] Treas. Reg. § 1.355-3(b)(3)(ii).

[49] *Id.*

[50] While the statute is not clear, it must be referring to gain or loss recognized by the seller, since the purchaser would not recognize any gain or loss on the acquisition of a business. *See* Bittker & Eustice, *supra* note 13 at 11-33.

[51] Control is defined using the 80% tests contained in section 368(c). *See* Chapter 14 and Chapter 21.

[52] *See* Bittker and Eustice, *supra* note 13 at 11-32.

Determining whether the transaction in Example 22.4 satisfies the active business requirement:

The active business requirement is satisfied because D Corp. and C Corp., the distributing corporation and controlled corporation, respectively, are each engaged in the active conduct of a trade or business immediately after the distribution. Through D Corp.'s active conduct of business A, D Corp. is treated as engaged in the active conduct of a trade or business, because D Corp. has been actively conducting business A for at least five years, D Corp. did not acquire business A in a taxable transaction within the past five years, and D Corp. did not acquire control of a corporation conducting business A in a taxable transaction within the past five years. Similarly, through C Corp.'s active conduct of business B, C Corp. is treated as engaged in the active conduct of a trade or business, because C Corp. has been actively conducting business B for at least five years, C Corp. did not acquire business B in a taxable transaction within the past five years, and D Corp. did not acquire control of C Corp. in a taxable transaction within the past five years. The above analysis assumes that the corporations' conduct of businesses A and B constitutes being "engaged in a trade or business" as defined in the regulations, and that the businesses are "actively conducted" by the corporations according to the regulations.

D. Corporate Business Purpose Requirement

Under Treas. Reg. § 1.355-2(b)(1), the transaction must be "carried out for one or more corporate business purposes. According to the regulations, "[a] corporate business purpose is a real and substantial non-Federal tax purpose germane to the business of the distributing corporation, the controlled corporation, or the affiliated group . . . to which the distributing corporation belongs."[53]

The regulations provide the following examples of corporate business purposes that satisfy the requirement:

- A separation pursuant to an order under antitrust law to divest a corporation of certain properties.[54]

- A separation of a corporation's unregulated business from a regulated business to allow the unregulated business to charge higher rates to customers.[55]

- A separation substantially motivated by the need to issue stock to a key employee.[56]

- A separation to allow shareholders to split up the corporation's businesses and go their separate ways, where it is anticipated that the separation will enhance the businesses because each shareholder will be able to devote

---

[53] Treas. Reg. § 1.355-2(b)(2).

[54] Treas. Reg. § 1.355-2(b)(5), Example 1.

[55] Treas. Reg. § 1.355-2(b)(5), Example 5.

[56] Treas. Reg. § 1.355-2(b)(5), Example 8.

her attention to the business in which she is more interested and proficient.[57]

The last example demonstrates that the corporate business purpose requirement is satisfied even though there is also a shareholder purpose for the separation; in this case, the corporate and shareholder purposes are so nearly coextensive as to preclude any distinction between the two purposes.[58] However, a shareholder purpose that is not so nearly coextensive with a corporate business purpose is not considered a valid corporate business purpose — e.g., a shareholder's personal planning purposes.[59] The regulations also provide that a reduction in non-federal taxes is not a corporate business purpose if (i) there will also be a reduction in federal taxes because of similarities between the federal and non-federal tax law and (ii) the federal tax reduction is greater than, or substantially coextensive with, the non-federal tax reduction.[60]

The regulations make it clear that the *distribution of stock in a controlled corporation* must be carried out for a corporate business purpose.[61] That is, a separation is not treated as carried out for a particular business purpose if there is a tax-free way of accomplishing the particular corporate business purpose without a distribution, provided that this alternative is neither impractical nor unduly expensive.[62] For example, where a corporation wants to protect one of its businesses from the potential liabilities of another of its businesses, the corporation's transfer of the risky business to a controlled subsidiary is all that is needed to achieve that business purpose; a distribution of the stock in the controlled subsidiary is not necessary and therefore is not carried out for that corporate business purpose.[63]

E. No Device Requirement

Under section 355(a)(1)(B), the transaction must not be used principally as a device for distributing the E&P of the distributing corporation, the controlled corporation, or both corporations. The underlying concern is that a distributing corporation and its shareholders can avoid the dividend provisions through a tax-free distribution of stock in the controlled corporation followed by a sale of the distributed stock.[64] The economic effect would be similar to a dividend in that assets have left the distributing corporation and its shareholders end up with the proceeds of the sale, but if the distribution were tax-free under section 355, the only tax would be a capital gains tax on the sale. With most dividends received by

---

[57] Treas. Reg. § 1.355-2(b)(5), Example 2.

[58] *See* Treas. Reg. § 1.355-2(b)(5), Example 2; Treas. Reg. § 1.355-2(b)(2).

[59] Treas. Reg. § 1.355-2(b)(2).

[60] *Id; see* Treas. Reg. § 1.355-2(b)(5), Example 7.

[61] Treas. Reg. § 1.355-2(b)(3).

[62] *Id.*

[63] Treas. Reg. § 1.355-2(b)(5), Example 3.

[64] *See* Treas. Reg. § 1.355-2(d)(1).

non-corporate taxpayers now taxable at preferential capital gain rates,[65] the concern is not as important as it once was, but there is still the ability to recover basis in a transaction taxed as an exchange as opposed to a dividend.[66]

The regulations state that the device determination is generally made from all of the facts and circumstances.[67] In this regard, the regulations provide certain factors, described below, that are either evidence of a device or evidence of a nondevice.[68]

The regulations also specify three types of distributions that are ordinarily not considered to have been used principally as a device:

- The distributing corporation and the controlled corporation have neither (i) accumulated E&P at the beginning of the taxable year; (ii) current E&P on the date of the distribution; nor (iii) immediately before the distribution, property, the distribution of which would require the recognition of gain resulting in current E&P for the taxable year of the distribution.[69]

- For each shareholder distributee, the distribution would have qualified for exchange treatment under section 303(a) (applying to certain redemptions to pay death taxes and expenses[70]).[71]

- For each shareholder distributee, the distribution would have qualified for exchange treatment under section 302(a).[72]

However, the second and third type of distribution are not protected from being a device if the distribution involves the stock of two or more controlled corporations and facilitates avoiding the dividend provisions through the subsequent sale or exchange of the stock in one corporation and the retention of the stock in the other corporation(s).[73]

1. Device Factors

The regulations provide that the following factors are evidence of device:

- A distribution that is pro rata or substantially pro rata among shareholders.[74]

---

[65] *See* Chapter 16.

[66] *See* Treas. Reg. § 1.355-2(d)(1) (stating that a "device can include a transaction that effects a recovery of basis").

[67] Treas. Reg. § 1.355-2(d)(1).

[68] *Id.*

[69] Treas. Reg. § 1.355-2(d)(5)(ii).

[70] *See* Chapter 17.

[71] Treas. Reg. § 1.355-2(d)(5)(iii).

[72] Treas. Reg. § 1.355-2(d)(5)(iv). For this purpose, the waiver of family attribution under section 302(c)(2) is applied without regard to the prohibition against acquiring certain interests and the requirement that the shareholder file an agreement with the Service. *Id. See* Chapter 17.

[73] Treas. Reg. § § 1.355-2(d)(5)(i); 1.355-2(d)(5)(v), Example 2.

[74] Treas. Reg. § 1.355-2(d)(2)(ii).

- A sale or exchange of stock of the distributing corporation or the controlled corporation after the distribution — the greater the percentage of the stock sold or exchanged, or the shorter the period between the distribution and sale or exchange, the stronger the evidence of device; a sale or exchange negotiated or agreed upon before the distribution is *substantial* evidence of a device.[75]

- Either the distributing corporation or the controlled corporation has assets that are *not* used in a trade or business that satisfies the active business requirement (discussed above) — for example, cash and other liquid assets not related to the reasonable needs of an active trade or business.[76]

- Either the distributing corporation or the controlled corporation has a "secondary business" that continues for a significant period after the distribution and can be sold without adversely affecting the other corporation's business; a "secondary business" is a business of one of the corporations that has a principal function of serving the business of the other corporation.[77]

2. Nondevice Factors

The regulations provide that the following factors are evidence of nondevice:

- The corporate business purpose for the transaction[78] — the stronger the evidence of device, the stronger the corporate business purpose required to determine that the transaction was not used principally as a device; examples of factors considered in assessing the strength of the corporate business purpose are (i) the importance of achieving the purpose to the business's success, (ii) the extent to which the transaction is prompted by non-shareholders of either corporation or by other factors beyond the distributing corporation's control, and (iii) the immediacy of conditions prompting the transaction.[79]

- The distributing corporation is publicly traded and has no shareholder owning beneficially (directly or indirectly) more than five percent of any class of stock.[80]

- The stock of the controlled corporation is distributed to a domestic corporation that (absent section 355) would be entitled to an 80% or 100% dividends-received deduction[81].[82]

---

[75] Treas. Reg. § 1.355-2(d)(2)(iii).

[76] Treas. Reg. § 1.355-2(d)(2)(iv)(B).

[77] Treas. Reg. § 1.355-2(d)(2)(iv)(C).

[78] As discussed above, having a corporate business purpose is also an independent requirement for satisfying section 355.

[79] Treas. Reg. § 1.355-2(d)(3)(ii).

[80] Treas. Reg. § 1.355-2(d)(3)(iii).

[81] *See* Chapter 16.

[82] Treas. Reg. § 1.355-2(d)(3)(iv).

3. Applying the Device and Nondevice Factors

The following example contained in the regulations demonstrates an application of the device and nondevice factors:[83]

> Corporation X owns and operates a fast food restaurant in State M and owns all of the stock of corporation Y, which owns and operates a fast food restaurant in State N. X and Y operate their businesses under franchises granted by D and E, respectively. X owns cash and marketable securities that exceed the reasonable needs of its business but whose value is small relative to the value of its business. E has recently changed its franchise policy and will no longer grant or renew franchises to subsidiaries (or other members of the same affiliated group) of corporations operating businesses under franchises granted by its competitors. Thus, Y will lose its franchise if it remains a subsidiary of X. The franchise is about to expire. Accordingly, X distributes the stock of Y pro rata among X's shareholders. X retains its business and transfers cash and marketable securities to Y in an amount proportional to the value of Y's business. There is no other evidence of device or evidence of nondevice. The transfer by X to Y and the retention by X of cash and marketable securities is relatively weak evidence of device because after the transfer X and Y hold cash and marketable securities in amounts proportional to the values of their businesses. The fact that the distribution is pro rata is evidence of device. A strong corporate business purpose is relatively strong evidence of nondevice. Accordingly, the transaction is considered not to have been used principally as a device.

F. Continuity of Interest Requirement

As is the case with corporate reorganizations, a corporate division must satisfy a continuity of interest requirement. Specifically, Treas. Reg. § 1.355-2(c)(1) requires that the historic shareholders of the distributing corporation own, in the aggregate, an amount of stock establishing a continuity of interest in *each* of the corporations after the separation. Using the Service's benchmark for ruling purposes,[84] the historic shareholders of the distributing corporation would generally need at least a 50 percent equity interest[85] in both the distributing corporation and controlled corporation after the transaction in order to satisfy this requirement.[86] Notice that this is different from the formulation of the continuity of interest requirement in the corporate reorganization context, which requires that in the aggregate, a sufficient portion of the target corporation shareholders' interest in the target

---

[83] Treas. Reg. § 1.355-2(d)(4), Example 2. The regulations contain a few other examples as well. *See* Treas. Reg. § 1.355-2(d)(4), Examples 1, 3 and 4.

[84] *See* Chapter 21.

[85] In addition to being the Service's benchmark for ruling purposes, examples in the section 355 regulations use a 50 percent threshold for the continuity of interest requirement (*see* Treas. Reg. § 1.355-2(c)(2), Examples 2, 3), although 40 percent continuity may be sufficient for corporate divisions given its sufficiency for corporate reorganizations. *See* Chapter 21.

[86] In the case of a split-up where the distributing corporation liquidates, there would need to be at least a 50 percent interest in each of the controlled corporations after the transaction (using the Service's standard for ruling purposes).

continues in the stock of the acquiring corporation after the reorganization. This difference is due to the nature of corporate divisions, where it is necessary (given section 355's underlying policy[87]) to have the requisite continuity in each of the corporations following the transaction.

> *Example 22.5.*[88] For the past several years, the voting common stock (the only class outstanding) of D Corp. has been owned by A and B, who each own 50 shares. For the past 10 years, D Corp. has been actively conducting business P. For the past 10 years, D Corp. has owned all 100 shares of the voting common stock (the only class outstanding) of C Corp., and C Corp. has actively conducted business Q during this period. Business P and business Q are of equal value. Pursuant to a plan to acquire a stock interest in D Corp. without acquiring an interest in C Corp., P purchases A's 50 shares of stock in D Corp. and immediately thereafter, D Corp. distributes its 100 shares in C Corp. to B in exchange for B's 50 shares of stock in D Corp. As a result, after the transaction neither A nor B owns any stock in D Corp., and B owns all of the stock of C Corp. Following the transaction, D Corp. continues to actively conduct business P, and C Corp. continues to actively conduct business Q.

Determining whether the transaction in Example 22.5 satisfies the continuity of interest requirement:

The transaction fails the continuity of interest requirement because the historic shareholders of D Corp., A and B, have not, in the aggregate, maintained the requisite continuity in each of D Corp. and C Corp. after the distribution — neither A nor B owns any stock in D Corp. after the transaction.[89] This is the case even though A and B retain 50 percent of their equity interest in the former combined enterprise through B's 100 percent ownership of C Corp., which constitutes 50 percent of the value of D Corp. before the distribution.[90]

§ 22.05   TAX TREATMENT OF PARTIES TO A SECTION 355 TRANSACTION

If a transaction qualifies under section 355, then the rules generally provide for nonrecognition treatment for the shareholders, security holders and corporations involved in the corporate division, along with exchanged bases and tacked holding periods — concepts that were explored in connection with both section 351 transactions and corporate reorganizations.[91] The remainder of this chapter examines these consequences.

---

[87] According to the regulations, "[s]ection 355 applies to a separation that effects only a readjustment of continuing interests in the property of the distributing and controlled corporations." Treas. Reg. § 1.355-2(c)(1).

[88] This example is based on Treas. Reg. § 1.355-2(c)(2), Examples 1, 3.

[89] *See* Treas. Reg. § 1.355-2(c)(2), Example 3.

[90] *See id.*

[91] *See* Chapters 14 and 21.

A. Tax Consequences to Shareholders and Security Holders

1. Recognition of Gain, Loss or Income

a. In General

As mentioned previously, in the absence of nonrecognition treatment, shareholders who receive stock in a controlled corporation on a distribution by a distributing corporation would either have a section 301 distribution of property (that would be a taxable dividend to the extent of the distributing corporation's E&P) or a taxable exchange.[92] In a transaction qualifying under section 355, shareholders receiving solely stock do not recognize any gain or loss, and do not include any amounts in income, pursuant to section 355(a)(1).[93] Similarly, security holders receiving solely stock or securities[94] in a qualifying section 355 transaction do not recognize any gain, loss or income (unless the securities received have an excess principal amount, as discussed below). The section 355(a)(1) nonrecognition rule is very similar to the nonrecognition rule applying to corporate reorganizations under section 354(a).[95]

> *Example 22.6.* As of January 1, 2014, S owns all 100 shares of the voting common stock of D Corp. (the only class outstanding). For the past 10 years, D Corp. has been actively conducting business A. For the past 10 years, D Corp. has owned all 100 shares of the voting common stock (the only class outstanding) of C Corp., and C Corp. has actively conducted business B during this period. On January 1, 2014, D Corp. distributes the 100 shares of C Corp. voting common stock (having a fair market value of $1,000,000) to S. Following the transaction, D Corp. continues to actively conduct business A, and C Corp. continues to actively conduct business B. The transaction qualifies under section 355.

Applying section 355(a)(1) to S in Example 22.6:

Because S receives solely stock in a qualifying section 355 transaction, she includes no income on the distribution.

b. Receipt of Boot

As is the case with corporate formations and reorganizations, if a shareholder or securities holder receives money or other property, i.e., boot, in a transaction otherwise qualifying under section 355, then nonrecognition treatment is not completely lost. Specifically, in the case of a split-off or split-up, where a shareholder relinquishes stock in the distributing corporation, under section 356(a)(1) the shareholder recognizes any realized gain to the extent of the money plus the fair market value of the other property received; however, the shareholder

---

[92] *See* § 22.03.

[93] I.R.C. § 355(a)(1).

[94] *See* Chapter 21 for a definition of securities.

[95] *See id.*

is not permitted to recognize any realized loss under section 356(c).[96] In the case of a spin-off, where a shareholder relinquishes no stock in the distributing corporation, the boot received is treated as a section 301 distribution of property, and thus is a taxable dividend to the extent of the E&P of the distributing corporation.[97]

> *Example 22.7.* As of January 1, 2014, S and T each own 50 out of 100 shares of the voting common stock of D Corp. (the only class outstanding); each shareholder has a total basis of $100,000 in her 50 shares of D Corp. stock. For the past 10 years, D Corp. has been actively conducting business A. For the past 10 years, D Corp. has owned all 100 shares of the voting common stock (the only class outstanding) of C Corp., and C Corp. has actively conducted business B during this period. On January 1, 2014, D Corp. distributes the 100 shares of C Corp. voting common stock (having a fair market value of $800,000) and $200,000 of cash to S in exchange for her 50 shares of D Corp. voting common stock, which have a fair market value of $1,000,000. Following the transaction, D Corp. continues to actively conduct business A, and C Corp. continues to actively conduct business B. The transaction qualifies under section 355.

Applying section 356(a)(1) to S in Example 22.7:

Because S receives C Corp. stock and boot in a split-off, S recognizes her realized gain of $900,000[98] to the extent of the $200,000 of money received, resulting in $200,000 of recognized gain.[99]

> *Example 22.8.* As of January 1, 2014, S owns all 100 shares of the voting common stock of D Corp. (the only class outstanding), having a total basis of $100,000 in these shares. For the past 10 years, D Corp. has been actively conducting business A. For the past 10 years, D Corp. has owned all 100 shares of the voting common stock (the only class outstanding) of C Corp., and C Corp. has actively conducted business B during this period. On January 1, 2014, D Corp. distributes the 100 shares of C Corp. voting common stock, having a fair market value of $1,000,000, and $200,000 of

---

[96] The same rule would apply where a security holder exchanges securities for stock or securities and boot.

[97] I.R.C. § 356(b).

[98] This is the difference between A's amount realized of $1,000,000 ($800,000 fair market value of C Corp. stock plus $200,000 of cash) and S's basis in the D Corp. stock of $100,000.

[99] The character of this gain is explored below. In situations where a shareholder surrenders shares of stock (or securities) that have different adjusted bases and acquisition dates, there would need to be an allocation of the stock, securities and boot received for purposes of recognizing gain under section 356(a)(1). This is analogous to the recognition of gain under section 351(b) where a transferor in a section 351 transaction transfers multiple properties to a corporation in exchange for stock and boot. *See* Chapter 14. As with corporate reorganizations, Treas. Reg. § 1.356-1(b) provides that if the terms of the exchange specify the stock, securities and boot that are received for particular shares of stock or securities, these terms will control the allocation of these items to the stock and securities surrendered, provided that the terms are economically reasonable. Otherwise, a pro rata portion of the stock, securities, and boot received is treated as received for each share of stock and security surrendered, based on the relative fair market value of the share of stock or security surrendered. The latter approach is the same that is used in the section 351(b) context. *See* Chapter 14.

cash to S. Following the transaction, D Corp. continues to actively conduct business A, and C Corp. continues to actively conduct business B. The transaction qualifies under section 355. D Corp. has $1,000,000 of Current E&P for 2014 and no Accumulated E&P for prior years.

Applying section 356(b) to S in Example 22.8:

Because S receives C Corp. stock and boot in a spin-off, the $200,000 of money received by S is treated as a section 301 distribution of property that would be a taxable dividend to the extent of D Corp.'s E&P.[100] Because D Corp. has ample E&P, the $200,000 is a dividend.[101]

As with corporate reorganizations, for purposes of recognizing gain and income under section 356 in a section 355 transaction, all or a portion of the securities received may constitute boot. Specifically, section 356(d)(2)(C) provides that if the principal amount of the securities in the controlled corporation that are received exceeds the principal amount of the securities in the distributing corporation that are surrendered, the fair market value of the excess principal amount is treated as "other property" for purposes of section 356.[102] In addition, so-called "hot stock"[103] is treated as boot for purposes of sections 355 and 356. Generally, this is stock in the controlled corporation that was acquired by the distributing corporation within five years of the distribution in a transaction in which gain or loss was recognized.[104] However, the regulations provide that hot stock does not include stock in the controlled corporation if the controlled corporation becomes part of the distributing corporation's "separate affiliated group"[105] at any time after the acquisition of the stock and before the distribution.[106]

c. Dividend Treatment of Recognized Gain

As with corporate reorganizations, section 356(a)(2) provides that all or a portion of the gain recognized by a shareholder in a section 355 split-off or split-up will be treated as a dividend if the *effect* of the exchange is a *distribution of a dividend*. In that case, the gain will be treated as a dividend to the extent of the shareholder's ratable share of the Accumulated E&P of the distributing corporation. Any remaining gain is treated as gain from the sale of property.

---

[100] *See* Chapter 16.

[101] *See id.*

[102] Similar to its treatment in corporate reorganizations, nonqualified preferred stock is also treated as boot for purposes of sections 355 and 356 if it is received in a distribution with respect to stock that is not nonqualified preferred stock. I.R.C. §§ 355(a)(3)(D), 356(e). Nonqualified preferred stock is discussed in Chapter 14.

[103] *See* Bittker & Eustice, *supra* note 13 at 11-64.

[104] I.R.C. § 355(a)(3)(B).

[105] The distributing corporation's "separate affiliated group" is the affiliated group that would be determined under section 1504(a) (basically corporations that are connected through 80% vote and value stock ownership) if the distributing corporation were the common parent. *See* I.R.C. § 355(b)(3)(B).

[106] Treas. Reg. § 1.355-2(g)(2)(i). Generally, hot stock also excludes stock in the controlled corporation that is acquired by the distributing corporation from another member of the distributing corporation's affiliated group. Treas. Reg. § 1.355-2(g)(2)(ii); Treas. Reg. § 1.355-3(b)(4)(iii); Treas. Reg. § 1.355-2(g)(5), Example 4.

As is done with corporate reorganizations, a hypothetical redemption test is used to determine whether a section 355 exchange has the effect of a dividend. However, unlike the *post*-reorganization hypothetical redemption that is used in the acquisitive reorganization context, for section 355 transactions the redemption is deemed to occur *before* the stock in the distributing corporation is exchanged for the stock in the controlled corporation.[107] Accordingly, a section 355 exchange is tested for dividend effect by treating the shareholder as if there was, before the exchange, a redemption of stock in the distributing corporation equal in value to the boot received. The section 302(b) redemption tests are then applied to this hypothetical redemption, and if they are all failed, the exchange has the effect of a dividend.[108]

2. Basis and Holding Period in Property Received

Under section 358, a shareholder's basis in the stock received and retained in a section 355 transaction is determined under a two-step process. First, under section 358(a)(1) there is a determination of the aggregate basis in (i) the stock of the controlled corporation that is received and (ii) any stock of the distributing corporation that is retained.[109] Second, this aggregate basis is then allocated between the stock of the controlled corporation and the stock of the distributing corporation, in proportion to their fair market values.[110]

The determination of the aggregate stock basis under section 358(a)(1) is done in the same manner as the determination of stock basis in the corporate reorganization and section 351 contexts, except that the shareholder is treated as if she surrendered in the transaction all of her stock or securities in the distributing corporation.[111] Accordingly, the aggregate stock basis in the stock of the controlled and distributing corporations is:

- The same as the shareholder's original basis in the stock and securities of the distributing corporation,
- Plus the amount treated as a dividend on the transaction,
- Plus the gain recognized by the shareholder on the transaction (excluding the portion of the gain treated as a dividend),
- Minus the money received by the shareholder in the transaction,
- Minus the fair market value of other property received by the shareholder in the transaction.

---

[107] Rev. Rul. 93-62, 1993-2 C.B. 118.

[108] As mentioned previously, the significance of section 356(a)(2) today is reduced because most dividends received by individuals are taxed at preferential capital gain rates. *See* Chapter 16.

[109] *See* I.R.C. § 358(b)(2), (c). In the case of a split-up, no stock in the distributing corporation is retained, but stock in two or more controlled corporations is received. Accordingly, in this situation, there is a determination of the aggregate basis in the stock of the controlling corporations that is received.

[110] *See* I.R.C. § 358(b)(2); Treas. Reg. § 1.358-2(a)(2)(iv). In the case of a split-up, the aggregate basis is allocated between the stock in the two or more controlled corporations that is received.

[111] *See* I.R.C. § 358(c).

The same process would also apply to determine the basis of securities received to the extent that their principal amount does not exceed the principal amount of the securities surrendered.[112] The shareholder's basis in other property received in the exchange is its fair market value at the time of receipt.[113]

> *Example 22.9.* As of January 1, 2014, S owns all 100 shares of the voting common stock of D Corp. (the only class outstanding), having a total basis of $100,000 in these shares. For the past 10 years, D Corp. has been actively conducting business A. For the past 10 years, D Corp. has owned all 100 shares of the voting common stock (the only class outstanding) of C Corp., and C Corp. has actively conducted business B during this period. On January 1, 2014, D Corp. distributes the 100 shares of C Corp. voting common stock, having a fair market value of $1,000,000, and $200,000 of cash to S. Following the transaction, D Corp. continues to actively conduct business A, and C Corp. continues to actively conduct business B. The transaction qualifies under section 355. Immediately after the distribution, S's 100 shares of D Corp. voting common stock have a fair market value of $3,000,000. D Corp. has $1,000,000 of Current E&P for 2014 and no Accumulated E&P for prior years.

Determining S's stock basis under section 358 in Example 22.9:

As in Example 22.8, S has a $200,000 dividend on the transaction. Under section 358(a)(1), S's aggregate basis in the C Corp. voting common stock received and the D Corp. voting common stock retained is equal to:

- S's original adjusted basis in the 100 shares of D Corp. voting common stock ($100,000),

- Plus the amount treated as a dividend on the transaction ($200,000),

- Plus the gain recognized by the shareholder on the transaction (excluding the portion of the gain treated as a dividend) ($0),

- Minus money received by S on the exchange ($200,000),

- Minus the fair market value of other property received by S on the exchange ($0),

Which equals $100,000. The $100,000 of aggregate basis is then allocated between the D Corp. stock and C Corp. stock in proportion to their fair market values. Because the fair market value of the 100 shares of D Corp. voting stock constitutes 75 percent of the combined fair market values of the 100 shares of D Corp. stock and the 100 shares of C Corp. stock ($3,000,000 for the D Corp. stock out of $4,000,000 for the D Corp. stock and C Corp. stock together), the 100 shares of D Corp. voting common stock take a basis of $75,000. The remaining $25,000 of basis goes to the 100 shares of C Corp. voting common stock.

As in the case of corporate reorganizations, Treas. Reg. § 1.358-2(a) provides detailed rules for allocating the total bases determined under section 358 to particular shares or securities received or retained. These allocation rules are

---

[112] *See* Treas. Reg. § 1.358-2(a)(1); I.R.C. § 356(d).

[113] I.R.C. § 358(a)(2).

applicable (i) where the stock or securities of the distributing corporation were acquired at different prices and acquisition dates[114] and (ii) where the stock or securities received are of different classes, or where money or other property are received.[115] Very generally, the regulations use a tracing approach, which permits shareholders to identify, through the terms of the exchange, the particular stock, securities, or boot that are received for, or distributed with respect to, particular stock or securities.[116] Where the terms of the transaction do not so specify, the regulations generally allocate the items received to the stock or securities of the distributing corporation in a pro rata manner based on the relative fair market values of such stock or securities.[117]

Under section 1223(1), a shareholder takes a tacked holding period in the stock received in a section 355 transaction, assuming that the stock in the distributing corporation is a capital asset; this is because the shareholder takes an exchanged basis in such stock under section 358. Securities that are received in a section 355 transaction will also have a tacked holding period under section 1223(1) if the securities take an exchanged basis under section 358(a), i.e., if the principal amount of the securities received does not exceed the principal amount of the securities surrendered.[118]

B. Tax Consequences to the Distributing Corporation

As mentioned previously, in the absence of nonrecognition treatment, a distributing corporation would recognize gain (and possibly loss) on a distribution of stock in the controlled corporation under either section 311 or section 336. Similar to section 361(c) in the reorganization context,[119] section 355(c) overrides sections 336 and 311[120] and provides that a distributing corporation will not recognize any gain or loss on the distribution of "qualified property" to its shareholders in a section 355 transaction that is *not* pursuant to a plan of reorganization.[121] Subject to two exceptions mentioned below, "qualified property" is stock or securities in the controlled corporation.[122] Thus, section 355(c) generally protects the distributing corporation from recognizing gain on the distribution to its shareholders of stock or securities in the controlled corporation. For example, in Example 22.9 D Corp. will not recognize any gain or loss on the distribution of the 100 shares of C Corp. voting common stock (assuming that sections 355(d) and 355(e) — mentioned below — do not apply to the distribution).

---

[114] *See* Treas. Reg. § 1.358-2(a)(2)(i), (iv).

[115] Treas. Reg. § 1.358-2(a)(2)(v).

[116] *See* Treas. Reg. § 1.358-2(a).

[117] Treas. Reg. § 1.358-2(a)(2)(v), (vii).

[118] *See* Treas. Reg. § 1.358-2(a)(1); I.R.C. § 56(d). This assumes that the securities surrendered are capital assets.

[119] *See* Chapter 21.

[120] I.R.C. § 355(c)(3).

[121] I.R.C. § 355(c)(1), (2). If the section 355 transaction is pursuant to a reorganization, then nonrecognition treatment will be provided by section 361(c), as described below.

[122] I.R.C. § 355(c)(2)(B). Note that there is a somewhat broader definition of qualified property for purposes of section 361(c). *See* Chapter 21.

On a distributing corporation's distribution of property that is *not* qualified property, the distributing corporation is required to recognize gain if the property's fair market value exceeds its adjusted basis in the distributing corporation's hands, with the amount of the recognized gain equal to the difference between the property's fair market value and adjusted basis.[123] A distributing corporation is not permitted to recognize a loss on a distribution of property, whether or not the property is qualified property.[124] The recognition rules for distributions of property other than qualified property are in effect the same as those provided in section 311 for nonliquidating distributions,[125] as well as those provided in section 361(c) for corporate reorganizations.[126]

In two situations, stock or securities of the controlled corporation are *not* treated as qualified property. Section 355(d) provides this result in the case of a "disqualified distribution."[127] In general, a "disqualified distribution" is a section 355 distribution where, immediately after the distribution, any person holds "disqualified stock" in either the distributing corporation or the controlled corporation that constitutes a 50% or greater interest in such corporation.[128] "Disqualified stock" is generally stock acquired by purchase during the five-year period ending on the date of the distribution.[129] In addition, section 355(e) generally treats stock or securities of the controlled corporation as other than qualified property where a section 355 distribution is a part of a plan pursuant to which one or more persons acquire a 50% or greater interest in either the distributing corporation or any controlled corporation.[130] Both sections 355(d) and 355(e) are aimed at preventing the avoidance of a corporate-level tax through the use of section 355 on disguised sales of businesses.[131] Note that by not treating stock or securities of the controlled corporation as qualified property for purposes of section 355(c), the provisions only result in corporate-level gain on a distribution, and have no effect on the section 355 consequences at the shareholder level.

If a section 355 transaction occurs in connection with a divisive "D" reorganization, then section 355(c) does not apply. However, in this case section 361(c) will generally protect the distributing corporation from recognizing gain on the distribution of stock or securities in the controlled corporation (along with a few other items). As noted above and described in Chapter 21, the rules of section 361(c) are very similar to those contained in section 355(c). The exceptions to qualified property contained in sections 355(d) and 355(e) also apply for purposes of

[123] I.R.C. § 355(c)(2)(A).

[124] I.R.C. § 355(c)(1), (2).

[125] *See* Chapter 16.

[126] *See* Chapter 21.

[127] I.R.C. § 355(d)(1).

[128] I.R.C. § 355(d)(2).

[129] I.R.C. § 355(d)(3).

[130] I.R.C. § 355(e)(1), (2).

[131] *See* Bittker & Eustice, supra note 13 at 11-72; Stephen Schwarz and Daniel J. Lathrope, Fundamentals of Corporate Taxation 514 (2012).

applying section 361(c) to divisive "D" reorganizations.[132]

---

[132] I.R.C. § 355(d)(1), (e)(1).

Chapter 23

CORPORATE TAX ATTRIBUTES

BASIC OVERVIEW

The Code contains rules that permit the carryover of corporate attributes, such as net operating losses (NOLs) and E&P, from one corporation to another upon the occurrence of asset acquisitions qualifying for nonrecognition treatment. There also are rules that limit the use of NOLs and other items in certain situations. This chapter briefly examines the carryover of corporate attributes and the limits on using certain corporate attributes.

A. Carryover of Corporate Attributes in Certain Acquisitions Under Section 381

Section 381(a) generally allows for the carryover of certain corporate attributes where one corporation ("acquiring corporation") acquires the assets of another corporation ("transferor corporation") in certain nonrecognition transactions. Where this occurs, the acquiring corporation succeeds to and takes into account certain attributes (described below) of the transferor corporation. Section 381(a) applies to parent-subsidiary liquidations under section 332, "A" and "C" reorganizations, along with a few other types of reorganizations that are mentioned in the Detailed Analysis. Section 381(c) lists 22 items that can be carried from the transferor corporation to the acquiring corporation. Some of the more significant items include:

- NOL carryovers,[1]
- E&P,[2]
- capital loss carryovers,[3]
- accounting methods,[4]
- inventory methods,[5]

---

[1] I.R.C. § 381(c)(1). Basically, an NOL is the excess of a taxpayer's allowable business deductions over the taxpayer's gross income for a taxable year. *See* I.R.C. § 172(c), (d). A taxpayer is generally permitted an NOL carryback to each of the two years preceding the year of the NOL, and an NOL carryover to each of the 20 years following the year of the NOL. *See* I.R.C. § 172(b)(1). The NOL carryback or carryover, as a deduction, can be used to reduce taxable income for the year to which it is carried.

[2] I.R.C. § 381(c)(2).

[3] I.R.C. § 381(c)(3).

[4] I.R.C. § 381(c)(4).

[5] I.R.C. § 381(c)(5).

- depreciation methods,[6] and

- installment method[7]

Section 381 provides some limits on using corporate tax attributes, which are described in the Detailed Analysis. In addition, other provisions impose limitations on a corporation's use of tax attributes, whether inherited from another corporation or generated by the corporation itself, which are discussed below.

B. Limitations on Using NOLs Under Section 382

Section 382 is a complex provision that limits the use of NOL carryovers that a corporation possesses upon undergoing a significant change in ownership ("ownership change").[8] When section 382 is triggered by a corporation's ownership change, the amount of the corporation's taxable income for any post-change year that can be offset by NOL carryovers cannot exceed the "section 382 limitation" for the year. In general terms, the "section 382 limitation" for a year is equal to the corporation's value prior to the ownership change multiplied by a certain prescribed interest rate.

More specifically, under section 382(g) an "ownership change" is generally a change in the ownership of the stock of a corporation that has a NOL carryover, which in the aggregate is more than 50 percentage points over a three-year period.[9] The change in ownership can come about through a variety of means, including taxable and nontaxable stock acquisitions, redemptions, new issuances, and reorganizations. Once triggered by an ownership change, section 382(a) imposes a limit on the amount of the new loss corporation's[10] taxable income for any post-change year[11] that can be offset by NOL carryovers, which is referred to as the "section 382 limitation." In general, under section 382(b)(1) the section 382 limitation for any post-change year is an amount equal to:

- The fair market value of the "old loss corporation," multiplied by

- "Long-term tax-exempt rate" (described in the Detailed Analysis).

The term "old loss corporation" refers to the corporation that was entitled to use the NOL carryovers before the ownership change.[12] The fair market value of the old loss corporation is generally the fair market value of all the stock of such corporation immediately before the ownership change.[13] The section 382 limitation is generally zero if the new loss corporation does not continue the business

---

[6] I.R.C. § 381(c)(6).

[7] I.R.C. § 381(c)(8).

[8] Section 382 can also apply to limit the use of a corporation's built-in losses. See I.R.C. § 382(h). This aspect of section 382 is not discussed in this book.

[9] See Boris I. Bittker & James S. Eustice, Federal Income Taxation of Corporations and Shareholders 14-68 (2000).

[10] The "new loss corporation" is the corporation that is entitled to use the NOL carryovers after the ownership change. I.R.C. § 382(k)(3).

[11] A "post-change year" is any taxable year ending after the ownership change. I.R.C. § 382(d)(2).

[12] I.R.C. § 382(k)(2).

[13] I.R.C. § 382(e)(1).

enterprise of the old loss corporation for at least two years after the ownership change.[14]

C. Other Limitations on Using Corporate Tax Attributes

1. Limitation on Using Certain Credits and Net Capital Losses under Section 383

In general terms, section 383 provides Treasury with the authority to promulgate regulations using the principles of section 382 to limit, in a post-ownership change year, a corporation's use of net capital losses and certain credits that arise in pre-change years.[15] The section 383 regulations impose the section 382 limitation on a new loss corporation's use of pre-change capital loss carryovers.[16] The regulations also impose the "section 383 credit limitation" (described in the Detailed Analysis) on the corporation's use of certain credits covered by the provision.[17]

2. Limitation on Using Preacquisition Losses to Offset Built-In Gains Under Section 384

In general terms, section 384 applies to the situation in which a corporation with net operating loss carryovers combines with a corporation having built-in gains, and prevents recognized built-in gains from being offset by the loss carryovers for a five-year period after the combination. More details are provided in the Detailed Analysis.

3. Authority Under 269 to Disallow Tax Benefits in Connection with Tax-Avoidance Acquisitions

Section 269(a) empowers the Service to disallow deductions, credits or other allowances where certain acquisitions of the stock or assets of a corporation are made for the principal purpose of "evading or avoiding Federal income tax by securing the benefit of a deduction, credit, or other allowance" that would otherwise not be enjoyed.[18] The Detailed Analysis discusses this provision in more detail.

---

[14] I.R.C. § 382(c).

[15] *See* I.R.C. § 383(a), (b), (c).

[16] Treas. Reg. § 1.383-1(b).

[17] *Id.*

[18] I.R.C. § 269(a).

DETAILED ANALYSIS

§ 23.01 CARRYOVER OF CORPORATE ATTRIBUTES IN CERTAIN ACQUISITIONS UNDER SECTION 381

A. In General

Section 381(a) generally allows for the carryover of certain corporate attributes where one corporation ("acquiring corporation") acquires the assets of another corporation ("transferor corporation") in certain nonrecognition transactions (described below). Where this occurs, the acquiring corporation succeeds to and takes into account certain attributes (described below) of the transferor corporation. The basic idea is that the acquiring corporation is a continuation of the transferor corporation for tax purposes, which is also reflected in the other tax consequences for these nonrecognition transactions (i.e., nonrecognition of gain or loss, exchanged and transferred bases, tacked holding periods).

B. Transactions Covered

Section 381(a) applies to the following nonrecognition transactions:

- Parent-subsidiary liquidation under section 332
- "A," "C", and "F" reorganizations
- Acquisitive "D" and "G" reorganizations.

"B" and "E" reorganizations are left out of the reorganizations covered by section 381(a). For "B" reorganizations, the corporation that generated the tax attributes continues to exist after the transaction,[19] so there is no need for another corporation to succeed to its tax attributes. For "E" reorganizations, only one corporation is involved,[20] so there is no other corporation to inherit tax attributes. Section 355 transactions and divisive "D" reorganizations are also omitted from section 381(a)'s coverage. The allowance of carryovers in these situations is governed by the common law rules that applied prior to the enactment of section 381.[21]

C. Corporate Attributes Covered

Section 381(c) lists 22 items that can be carried from the transferor corporation to the acquiring corporation. Some of the more significant items include:

- NOL carryovers,[22]

---

[19] *See* Chapter 21.

[20] *See id.*

[21] See Bittker & Eustice, supra note 9 at 14-23.

[22] I.R.C. § 381(c)(1). Basically, an NOL is the excess of a taxpayer's allowable business deductions over the taxpayer's gross income for a taxable year. *See* I.R.C. § 172(c), (d). A taxpayer is generally permitted an NOL carryback to each of the two years preceding the year of the NOL, and an NOL

- E&P,[23]
- capital loss carryovers,[24]
- accounting methods,[25]
- inventory methods,[26]
- depreciation methods,[27] and
- installment method.[28]

D. Section 381 Limits on Using Corporate Tax Attributes

Section 381 provides some limits on using corporate tax attributes. For example, section 381(c)(2)(B) provides that a deficit in E&P of the transferor corporation that is inherited by the acquiring corporation can only be used to offset E&P of the acquiring corporation that accumulated after the transaction giving rise to the carryover. Thus, an acquiring corporation is prevented from using an accumulated E&P deficit that it inherited to reduce its accumulated E&P surplus that existed before the acquisition. As another limitation, section 381(b)(3) generally prevents an acquiring corporation from carrying back an NOL or net capital loss that it generated after the acquisition to a taxable year of the transferor corporation.

Aside from section 381, other provisions impose limitations on a corporation's use of tax attributes, whether inherited from another corporation or generated by the corporation itself. The remainder of this Chapter examines the basics of these limitation rules.

§ 23.02 LIMITATIONS ON USING NOLS UNDER SECTION 382

A. In General

Section 382 is a complex provision that limits the use of NOL carryovers that a corporation possesses upon undergoing a significant change in ownership ("ownership change").[29] When section 382 is triggered by a corporation's ownership change, the amount of the corporation's taxable income for any post-change year that can be offset by NOL carryovers cannot exceed the "section 382 limitation" for the year. In general terms, the "section 382 limitation" for a year is

---

carryover to each of the 20 years following the year of the NOL. *See* I.R.C. § 172(b)(1). The NOL carryback or carryover, as a deduction, can be used to reduce taxable income for the year to which it is carried.

[23] I.R.C. § 381(c)(2).

[24] I.R.C. § 381(c)(3).

[25] I.R.C. § 381(c)(4).

[26] I.R.C. § 381(c)(5).

[27] I.R.C. § 381(c)(6).

[28] I.R.C. § 381(c)(8)

[29] Section 382 can also apply to limit the use of a corporation's built-in losses. *See* I.R.C. § 382(h). This aspect of section 382 is not discussed in this book.

equal to the corporation's value prior to the ownership change multiplied by a certain prescribed interest rate.[30]

Section 382 can apply to limit the NOL carryovers of a corporation that undergoes a significant change in ownership; for example, where a current shareholder sells a large portion of stock to a new shareholder. The provision can also apply where the assets of a corporation with NOL carryovers are acquired by another corporation in a reorganization. While the acquiring corporation will inherit the NOL carryovers and other corporate attributes of the target corporation under section 381, the acquiring corporation's use of the inherited NOLs can be limited by section 382.

The basic purpose of section 382 is to restrict trafficking in net operating losses, i.e., the tax-motivated acquisitions of corporations with NOLs. Absent section 382, a profitable company would have an incentive to acquire a company with NOL carryovers in order to use these losses to offset future income. Section 382 aims to achieve tax neutrality on the disposition of loss corporations by not eliminating the use of the acquired NOL carryovers entirely, but instead essentially permitting the use of the NOLs to the extent that the loss corporation could have used them without the ownership change.[31]

The remainder of this section provides a general description of an ownership change — the section 382 triggering event, and the operation of the section 382 limitation.

B. Ownership Change

Under section 382(g), an "ownership change" is generally a change in the ownership of the stock of a corporation that has a NOL carryover, which in the aggregate is more than 50 percentage points over a three-year period.[32] The change in ownership can come about through a variety of means, including taxable and nontaxable stock acquisitions, redemptions, new issuances, and reorganizations.

More technically, section 382(g)(1) provides that an ownership change occurs if, immediately after any "owner shift involving a 5-percent shareholder" or any "equity structure shift," the percentage of stock of the "loss corporation" owned by one or more "5-percent shareholders" increases by more than 50 percentage points during the "testing period." Most of these terms have straightforward meanings. The "loss corporation" is basically the corporation that is entitled to use the NOL carryover.[33] A "5-percent shareholder" is a person holding five percent or more of the stock of the corporation at any time during the testing period.[34] The "testing

---

[30] See I.R.C. § 382(b).

[31] See Bittker & Eustice, *supra* note 9 at 14-61; Leandra Lederman, Understanding Corporate Taxation, 351 (2006).

[32] See Bittker & Eustice, *supra* note 9 at 14-68.

[33] I.R.C. § 382(k)(1).

[34] I.R.C. § 382(k)(7). A special rule generally treats all stock owned by less than 5-percent shareholders as owned by one 5-percent shareholder. I.R.C. § 382(g)(4)(A).

period" is generally the three-year period ending on the day of any "owner shift involving a 5-percent shareholder" or "equity structure shift."[35]

This brings us to the final two terms. An "owner shift involving a 5-percent shareholder" (hereinafter "owner shift") is a change in the ownership of stock of the loss corporation that affects the percentage of such stock owned by any person who is a 5-percent shareholder.[36] An owner shift can occur by almost any means, including a stock purchase, redemption, section 351 transaction, corporate reorganization or corporate division.[37] An "equity structure shift" is any corporate reorganization, except divisive "D", divisive "G", and "F" reorganizations.[38]

The percentage of stock that a person owns is determined on the basis of fair market value.[39] For purposes of determining stock ownership, the section 318 constructive ownership rules[40] apply, with some modifications.[41]

To sum up, a loss corporation is required to determine whether an ownership change has occurred upon either (i) a change in stock ownership affecting a person who owns five percent or more of the stock at any time in the past three years or (ii) a reorganization (other than an "F", divisive "D" or divisive "G"); the regulations refer to the date of such event as the "testing date."[42] Once either event takes place, a loss corporation then (i) determines, as of the testing date, the percentage of stock (by value) owned (actually and constructively) by one or more persons who own five percent or more of the corporation's stock at any time in the past three years and (ii) compares this to the lowest percentage of stock owned by such persons at any time within the past three years. Taking into account only those persons whose stock ownership has increased as of the testing date, if the total increase is more than 50 percentage points, then an ownership change has occurred.

Example 23.1.[43] For more than three years, A has owned all 100 shares of the voting common stock (the only class outstanding) of L Corp. On January 1, 2013, A sells 40 shares of L Corp. voting common stock to B.

Determining whether an ownership change has occurred in Example 23.1:

The transaction is an owner shift, because it affects the stock ownership of any person who owns five percent or more of the L Corp. stock within the past three years — in this case both A and B. As of the testing date (January 1, 2013, the date

---

[35] I.R.C. § 382(i).

[36] I.R.C. § 382(g)(2).

[37] Treas. Reg. § 1.382-2T(e)(1)(i). However, owner shifts effectively do not include stock transfers by reason of death, gift or divorce. I.R.C. § 382(l)(3)(B).

[38] I.R.C. § 382(g)(3). The statute also grants regulatory authority to treat taxable reorganization-type transactions and public offerings as equity shifts, but to date no such regulations have been issued. Treas. Reg. § 1.382-2T(e)(2)(ii).

[39] I.R.C. § 382(k)(6)(C), (k)(5).

[40] *See* Chapter 17.

[41] I.R.C. § 382(l)(3)(A).

[42] Treas. Reg. § 1.382-2(a)(4)(i).

[43] This example is based on Treas. Reg. § 1.382-2T(e)(1)(iii), Example 1.

of the transaction), B is a 5-percent shareholder who owns 40 percent of the L Corp. stock (40 out of 100 shares). B's lowest percentage of stock ownership of L Corp. during the three-year testing period is 0%. Therefore, B has increased her percentage of stock ownership of L Corp. by 40% during the three-year testing period. No other 5-percent shareholder has increased her percentage ownership of L Corp. stock during the testing period. Therefore, the 5-percent shareholders whose stock ownership percentage in L Corp. has increased have a total increase of 40%, and consequently, the transaction does not result in an ownership change.

> *Example 23.2.* For more than three years, A has owned all 100 shares of the voting common stock (the only class outstanding) of L Corp. On January 1, 2013, A sells 40 shares of L Corp. voting common stock to B. On July 1, 2013, A sells 20 shares of L Corp. voting common stock to C.

Determining whether an ownership change has occurred in Example 23.2:

While the January 1, 2013, sale is not an ownership change (as determined in Example 23.1), the July 1, 2013, sale needs to be evaluated. The July 1, 2013, sale is an owner shift, because it affects the stock ownership of any person who owns five percent or more of the L Corp. stock within the past three years — in this case both A and C. As of the testing date (July 1, 2013, the date of the transaction), C is a 5-percent shareholder who owns 20 percent of the L Corp. stock (20 out of 100 shares). C's lowest percentage of stock ownership of L Corp. during the three-year testing period is 0%. Therefore, C has increased her percentage of stock ownership of L Corp. by 20% during the three-year testing period. Based on the analysis of Example 23.1, B has increased her percentage of stock ownership of L Corp. by 40% during the three-year testing period. Therefore, the 5-percent shareholders whose stock ownership percentage in L Corp. has increased have a total increase of 60%, and consequently, the July 1, 2013, sale results in an ownership change.

> *Example 23.3.*[44] For more than three years, A has owned all 100 shares of the voting common stock (the only class outstanding) of L Corp., and B has owned all 100 shares of the voting common stock (the only class outstanding) of P Corp. On January 1, 2014, L Corp. is merged into P Corp., in a transaction qualifying as an "A" reorganization. As a result of the merger, A and B own 40% and 60% of the stock of P Corp., respectively. L Corp. has NOL carryovers that P Corp. inherits under section 381.

Determining whether an ownership change has occurred in Example 23.3:

Before proceeding with the analysis, it should be pointed out that for purposes of section 382, both L Corp. and P Corp. are loss corporations for the periods in which they are entitled to the loss — for L Corp., before the merger, and for P Corp., after the merger.[45] Accordingly, in determining whether an ownership change has occurred in this type of situation, a 5-percent shareholder's stock ownership in the acquiring corporation must be compared to the shareholder's stock ownership in the target corporation.[46]

---

[44] This example is based on Treas. Reg. § 1.382-2T(e)(2)(iv), Example 1.

[45] *See* Treas. Reg. § 1.382-2(a)(1)(ii); Bittker & Eustice, *supra* note 9 at 14-71.

[46] Bittker & Eustice, *supra* note 9 at 14-71.

The transaction is an equity shift because it is an "A" reorganization. It is also an owner shift, because it affects the stock ownership of any person who owns five percent or more of the loss corporation's stock within the past three years — in this case both A and B. As of the testing date (January 1, 2014, the date of the transaction), B is a 5-percent shareholder who owns 60% of the P Corp. stock. B's lowest percentage of stock ownership of L Corp. during the three-year testing period is 0%. Therefore, B has increased her percentage of stock ownership by 60% during the three-year testing period. Thus, the 5-percent shareholders whose stock ownership percentage has increased have a total increase of 60%, and consequently, an ownership change has occurred as a result of the merger. As a result, the NOLs inherited by P Corp. from L Corp. are subject to the section 382 limitation.

C.   Operation of the Section 382 Limitation

Before proceeding with an examination of the limitation under section 382, some more terminology is needed. The term "old loss corporation" refers to the corporation that was entitled to use the NOL carryovers before the ownership change.[47] The "new loss corporation" is the corporation that is entitled to use the NOL carryovers after the ownership change.[48] As the statute points out, the same corporation may be both the old loss corporation and the new loss corporation,[49] which occurs when a corporation undergoes an ownership change without ceasing its existence.

Once triggered by an ownership change, section 382(a) imposes a limit on the amount of the new loss corporation's taxable income for any post-change year[50] that can be offset by NOL carryovers. This is referred to as the "section 382 limitation."

1.   In General

In general, under section 382(b)(1) the section 382 limitation for any post-change year is an amount equal to:

- The fair market value of the old loss corporation, multiplied by
- The "long-term tax-exempt rate."

Accordingly, for each post-change year, a new loss corporation can generally use its NOL carryover only to the extent of this amount. The general section 382 limitation is subject to a few modifications as well as a continuity of business enterprise requirement, which are discussed below.

The fair market value of the old loss corporation is generally the fair market value of all the stock of such corporation immediately before the ownership change.[51] For purposes of this determination, the statute contains special rules that

---

[47]   I.R.C. § 382(k)(2).

[48]   I.R.C. § 382(k)(3).

[49]   *Id.*

[50]   A "post-change year" is any taxable year ending after the ownership change. I.R.C. § 382(d)(2).

[51]   I.R.C. § 382(e)(1).

are aimed at perceived abuses, such as stuffing the corporation with assets to increase its value (and therefore the limitation),[52] and redeeming stock in connection with the ownership change in order to reduce the revenue of the new loss corporation while retaining the NOL carryovers.[53] The "long-term tax-exempt rate" is the highest federal long-term rate determined under section 1274(d) that is in effect for any month in the three-month period that ends with the month in which the ownership change occurs, with adjustments for differences between the rates for taxable and tax-exempt obligations.[54]

> *Example 23.4.* On January 1, 2014, L Corp., which has NOL carryovers of $1,000,000, undergoes an ownership change for purposes of section 382. Immediately before the ownership change, the fair market value of all of the stock of L corp. is $10,000,000. The long-term tax-exempt rate is 3% compounded annually.

Determining the general section 382 limitation in Example 23.4:

The section 382 limitation under section 382(b)(1) is $10,000,000 (the fair market value of L Corp.) multiplied by 3% (the long-term tax-exempt rate), which is $300,000. Therefore, for each post-change year, L Corp.'s deduction for NOL carryovers generally cannot exceed $300,000.

2. Increases in Limitation: Carryforward of Unused Limitation and Built-In Gains

The section 382 limitation amount is increased for a year where, for the preceding year, the taxable income that was offset by the NOL carryovers was less than the section 382 limitation amount.[55] Where this occurs, the corporation's section 382 limitation for the year is increased by the excess of (i) the section 382 limitation for the previous year over (ii) the taxable income for the previous year that was offset by the NOL carryover.[56] In addition, the section 382 limitation is increased by certain recognized built-in gains.[57]

3. Continuity of Business Enterprise Requirement

Under section 382(c), the section 382 limitation is generally zero if the new loss corporation does not continue the business enterprise of the old loss corporation for at least two years after the ownership change.[58] Thus, all of the NOL carryovers are generally disallowed where this continuity of business enterprise requirement is

---

[52] *See* I.R.C. § 382(l)(1), (l)(4).

[53] *See* I.R.C. § 382(e)(2); Stephen Schwarz and Daniel J. Lathrope, Fundamentals of Corporate Taxation 577 (2012).

[54] I.R.C. § 382(f).

[55] This can occur when a corporation has insufficient taxable income to use its NOL carryover to the extent of its full limitation amount.

[56] I.R.C. § 382(b)(2).

[57] *See* I.R.C. § 382(h)(1)(A).

[58] However, the limitation in this situation will not be less than the sum of certain recognized built-in gains and gain recognized by reason of an election under section 338. *See* I.R.C. § 382(c)(2).

failed. According to section 382's legislative history, the standard used to determine whether the business enterprise is continued is the same as that used under the continuity of business requirement for corporate reorganizations (discussed in Chapter 21).[59]

§ 23.03   OTHER LIMITATIONS ON USING CORPORATE TAX ATTRIBUTES

A.   Limitation on Using Certain Credits and Net Capital Losses under Section 383

In general terms, section 383 provides Treasury with the authority to promulgate regulations using the principles of section 382 to limit, in a post-ownership change year, a corporation's use of net capital losses and certain credits that arise in pre-change years.[60] The credits covered under section 383 are the unused general business credit (under section 39),[61] the unused minimum tax credit (under section 53),[62] and foreign tax credit carryovers (under section 904(c)).[63]

The section 383 regulations impose the section 382 limitation[64] on a new loss corporation's use of pre-change capital loss carryovers.[65] The regulations also impose the "section 383 credit limitation" on the corporation's use of the credits covered by the provision.[66] The "section 383 credit limitation" is generally the tax liability of the corporation for the post-change year that is attributable to a portion of the corporation's taxable income; this portion is equal to the corporation's section 382 limitation that remains after accounting for the use of net operating loss and capital loss carryovers.[67] Thus, the section 382 limitation is first absorbed by pre-change losses, and any remaining limitation effectively serves as a cap on the corporation's ability to use certain pre-change credits. The regulations provide ordering rules for using net operating losses and capital losses under the section 382 limitation, as well as for using the different credits under the section 383 credit limitation.[68]

---

[59]   H.R. Rep. No. 841, 99th Cong., 2d Sess. II-189.

[60]   *See* I.R.C. § 383(a), (b), (c).

[61]   I.R.C. § 383(a)(2)(A).

[62]   I.R.C. § 383(a)(2)(B).

[63]   I.R.C. § 383(c).

[64]   *See* § 23.02[C].

[65]   Treas. Reg. § 1.383-1(b). Also subject to the limitation is a portion of a net capital loss of the old loss corporation for the year in which the ownership changes occurs, and certain recognized built-in losses. *See* Treas. Reg. § 1.383-1(c)(2).

[66]   Treas. Reg. § 1.383-1(b).

[67]   *Id.*

[68]   Treas. Reg. § 1.383-1(d)(2).

B. Limitation on Using Preacquisition Losses to Offset Built-In Gains Under Section 384

In general terms, section 384 applies to the situation in which a corporation with net operating loss carryovers combines with a corporation having built-in gains, and prevents recognized built-in gains from being offset by the loss carryovers for a five-year period after the combination. By restricting the sheltering of a profitable corporation's recognized built-in gains through a combination with a loss corporation, the primary aim of section 384 is to protect the repeal of the *General Utilities* doctrine.[69]

More specifically, section 384 is generally triggered when:

- One corporation acquires either:

    o "Control" of another corporation, or

    o The assets of another corporation in an "A", "C", or "D" reorganization, and

- Either corporation has a "net unrealized built-in gain."[70]

For this purpose, the section 1504(a)(2) definition of "control" is used, which is basically 80 percent stock ownership by both vote and value.[71] A "net unrealized built-in gain" is generally the amount by which (i) the fair market value of a corporation's assets immediately before the acquisition date exceeds (ii) the aggregate adjusted basis of the assets at that time.[72] Pursuant to an exception contained in section 384(b), the provision does not apply if both corporations were members of the same controlled group at all times during the five-year period ending on the acquisition date.[73]

Once triggered, section 384(a) prevents "recognized built-in gains" during the five-year period beginning on the acquisition date from being offset by "preacquisition losses," other than a preacquisition loss of the corporation with a net unrealized built-in gain. A "recognized built-in gain" is any gain recognized during the five-year period, except to the extent that it is established that (i) the corporation with a net unrealized built-in gain did not hold the asset on the acquisition date or (ii) the gain exceeds the unrealized gain on that date.[74] However, the amount of recognized built-in gains for any year in the five-year period cannot exceed the difference between (i) the net unrealized built-in gain and (ii) the recognized built-in gains for prior years in the five-year period that would

---

[69] *See* Bittker & Eustice, *supra* note 9 at 14-117.

[70] I.R.C. § 384(a).

[71] I.R.C. § 384(c)(5).

[72] I.R.C. §§ 384(c)(8), 382(h)(3).

[73] I.R.C. § 384(b). Basically, a controlled group for this purpose is corporations connected through 50 percent stock ownership (by both vote and value). *See* I.R.C. §§ 384(b)(2), 1563(a).

[74] I.R.C. § 384(c)(1)(A). Income items attributable to periods before the acquisition date are also taken into account for purposes of determining recognized built-in gains and net unrealized built-in gain. I.R.C. § 384(c)(1)(B).

have been offset by preacquisition losses if not for section 384.[75] A "preacquisition loss" is any net operating loss carryover to the year in which the acquisition date occurs,[76] along with a portion of a net operating loss for that year[77] and certain recognized built-in losses.[78]

C.   Authority Under 269 to Disallow Tax Benefits in Connection with Tax-Avoidance Acquisitions

Section 269(a) empowers the Service to disallow deductions, credits or other allowances where certain acquisitions are made for the principal purpose of "evading or avoiding Federal income tax by securing the benefit of a deduction, credit, or other allowance" that would otherwise not be enjoyed.[79] The acquisitions subject to section 269(a)'s tax avoidance rule are:

- Any person's acquisition (directly or indirectly) of control of a corporation,[80] or

- One corporation's acquisition (directly or indirectly) of the property of another corporation, provided the acquiring corporation takes a transferred basis[81] in the acquired property and neither the acquiring corporation nor its shareholders controlled (directly or indirectly) the transferor corporation immediately before the acquisition.[82]

For this purpose, "control" is the ownership of at least 50 percent of the stock by vote and value.[83] Under section 269(b), the Service has the same authority to disallow deductions and the like if (i) there is a qualified stock purchase by a corporation,[84] (ii) a section 338 election is not made,[85] and (iii) the acquired corporation is liquidated pursuant to a plan that is adopted within two years of the acquisition.

Section 269 differs from the other provisions limiting the use of corporate attributes in that its application is triggered by a bad motive on the part of the taxpayer, in addition to meeting fairly broad objective requirements. The provision also is not limited to the disallowance of certain deductions or credits. Consequently, section 269 can potentially be applied to a broad range of transactions[86] and tax attributes.[87]

---

[75] I.R.C. § 384(c)(1)(C).

[76] I.R.C. § 384(c)(3)(A)(i).

[77] I.R.C. § 384(c)(3)(A)(ii).

[78] I.R.C. § 384(c)(3)(B).

[79] I.R.C. § 269(a).

[80] I.R.C. § 269(a)(1).

[81] *See* Chapter 14.

[82] I.R.C. § 269(a)(2).

[83] I.R.C. § 269(a).

[84] *See* Chapter 19.

[85] *See id.*

[86] *See* Bittker & Eustice, *supra* note 9 at 14-45; Lederman, *supra* note 30 at 369; Treas. Reg.

§ 1.269-3(b), (c) (describing several types of transactions that ordinarily indicate the requisite tax avoidance purpose).

[87] *See* Bittker & Eustice, *supra* note 9 at 14-46.

PART III:
S CORPORATIONS

Chapter 24

TAXATION OF S CORPORATIONS AND SHAREHOLDERS

BASIC OVERVIEW

As addressed in previous chapters of this book, under subchapter C the earnings of a corporation are subject to two levels of taxation — first in the hands of the corporation and a second time when distributed as dividends to the shareholders. Under subchapter S, a different regime applies to eligible corporations that elect to become S corporations. Under this regime, the taxable income of an S corporation is generally subject to a single level of tax that applies at the shareholder level. More specifically, the taxable income of an S corporation passes through to the shareholders, who then include this taxable income on their individual returns. This chapter explores the details of subchapter S, which include the following: the eligibility requirements for electing S corporation status; making and terminating the S election; the treatment of S corporation shareholders, the few situations where the S corporation is taxable; and the application of subchapter C to S corporations.

A. Eligibility for Electing S Corporation Status

Under section 1361(a)(1), a corporation is an S corporation for a particular taxable year if the corporation:

- Is a "small business corporation,"
- For which an election is in effect for the particular taxable year.

To be a "small business corporation," a corporation must satisfy the following requirements:

- It is a domestic corporation (i.e., incorporated in the United States),
- It is not an "ineligible corporation,"[1]
- It meets the number of shareholders limit,
- It meets the permitted shareholder requirement, and
- It meets the one class of stock requirement.[2]

---

[1] The term "ineligible corporation" includes a few specialized types of corporations that are mentioned in the Detailed Analysis.

[2] I.R.C. § 1361(b)(1).

In general, an S corporation cannot have more than 100 shareholders.[3] The 100-shareholder limit is extended in two ways. First, a husband and wife count as one shareholder for purposes of the limit.[4] In addition, "members of a family" (and their estates) are treated as one shareholder.[5] "Members of a family" is defined broadly as a common ancestor and any lineal descendant of the common ancestor, including spouses and former spouses thereof, provided that the common ancestor is no more than six generations removed from the youngest generation of shareholders.[6]

An S corporation is permitted to have only certain types of shareholders:

- Individuals (other than nonresident aliens),

- Estates,

- Qualified pension or profit-sharing trusts under section 401, or non-profit organizations under section 501(c)(3), and

- Certain types of trusts (described in the Detailed Analysis).[7]

Thus, an S corporation cannot have other types of shareholders, such as corporations or partnerships.

An S corporation cannot have more than one class of stock.[8] For purposes of this requirement, differences in voting rights are disregarded.[9] Thus, each share of stock must have identical rights to distributions and liquidation proceeds, but the voting rights of shares may vary.[10] To reduce the risk that corporate debt instruments will be reclassified as a second class of stock, the statute provides a "straight debt" safe harbor for avoiding such reclassification, which is discussed in the Detailed Analysis.[11]

B. Electing S Corporation Status

A corporation that qualifies as a small business corporation may elect to be an S corporation under section 1362(a). To do so, all of the shareholders of the corporation on the day that the election is made must consent to the election.[12] The Detailed Analysis discusses rules for determining the effective date of the election.

---

[3] I.R.C. § 1361(b)(1)(A).

[4] I.R.C. § 1361(c)(1)(A)(i).

[5] I.R.C. § 1361(c)(1)(A)(ii).

[6] I.R.C. § 1361(c)(1)(B).

[7] I.R.C. § 1361(b)(1)(B), (C).

[8] I.R.C. § 1361(b)(1)(D).

[9] I.R.C. § 1361(c)(4).

[10] Treas. Reg. § 1.1361-1(l)(1).

[11] I.R.C. § 1361(c)(5).

[12] I.R.C. § 1362(a)(2).

C. Terminating S Corporation Status

An election to be an S corporation remains in effect until it is terminated.[13] Under section 1362(d), there are three ways in which an election is terminated. An S corporation election is terminated by revocation, provided shareholders holding more than one-half of the shares on the day of the revocation consent to the revocation.[14] In addition, an S corporation election is terminated whenever a corporation ceases to be a small business corporation.[15] Finally, an S corporation election is terminated if for three consecutive taxable years, the corporation has:

- An amount of passive investment income for the year that is in excess of 25% of its gross receipts for the year, and

- Accumulated E&P at the close of the year.[16]

Because an S corporation cannot create E&P from its operations,[17] the only S corporations that can have Accumulated E&P for purposes of this termination rule are corporations that were once C corporations or had inherited E&P from a C corporation in a corporate reorganization or similar transaction under section 381.[18] As discussed in the Detailed Analysis, the Service can disregard a termination that it determines to be inadvertent.[19]

D. Treatment of S Corporation Shareholders

1. Pass-Through Taxation of S Corporation Income or Loss

The key feature of the tax regime for S corporations is that the taxable income of an S corporation passes through to its shareholders, who then include this taxable income on their individual returns. Except for a few situations (discussed below), an S corporation is not subject to federal income taxation.[20] An S corporation generally computes its taxable income in the same manner as an individual. In reporting its taxable income, an S corporation is required to separately state income, deduction and loss items the separate treatment of which could affect the tax liability of the shareholders.[21] Under section 1366(a), the shareholders of an S corporation then take into account their pro rata shares of the corporation's (i) separately stated income, loss, deduction, or credit and (ii) nonseparately computed income or loss. As far as timing, a shareholder takes into

---

[13] I.R.C. § 1362(c).

[14] I.R.C. § 1362(d)(1)(A), (B). The shares taken into account include both voting and nonvoting stock. Treas. Reg. § 1.1362-2(a)(1).

[15] I.R.C. § 1362(d)(2).

[16] I.R.C. § 1362(d)(3)(A).

[17] I.R.C. § 1371(c)(1).

[18] See I.R.C. § 1371(c)(2).

[19] See I.R.C. § 1362(f).

[20] I.R.C. § 1363(a).

[21] I.R.C. §§ 1363(b)(1), 1366(a)(1)(A).

account her share of items during the shareholder's taxable year in which the corporation's taxable year ends.[22] Under section 1366(d), the amount of losses and deductions that pass through to a shareholder for a taxable year is limited to the sum of:

- The shareholder's adjusted basis in the stock of the corporation, plus
- The shareholder's adjusted basis in any indebtedness of the corporation to the shareholder.[23]

Losses and deductions that are disallowed for a taxable year as a result of the limitation are generally carried forward by the shareholder indefinitely.[24]

2. Adjustments to Basis

Under section 1367(a)(1), a shareholder's basis in the stock of an S corporation is increased by the shareholder's pro rata share of:

- Separately stated income items, including tax-exempt income, and
- Nonseparately computed income.[25]

Under section 1367(a)(2), a shareholder's basis in the stock of an S corporation is decreased, but not below zero,

- By the shareholder's pro rata share of:
  - o Separately stated items of loss and deduction,
  - o Nonseparately computed loss, and
  - o Nondeductible, non-capital expenses, and
- By distributions received by the shareholder that were not includable in income under section 1368.[26]

3. Treatment of Distributions

Under section 1368(b), a distribution made by an S corporation without Accumulated E&P is excluded from the shareholder's gross income to the extent that the distribution does not exceed the shareholder's adjusted basis in the stock of the corporation.[27] To the extent that the amount of the distribution exceeds the shareholder's stock basis, the excess is treated as gain from the sale of the stock.[28] There is also a rule for the treatment of distributions by S corporations that have Accumulated E&P, which is discussed in the Detailed Analysis. As mentioned

---

[22] I.R.C. § 1366(a)(1).

[23] I.R.C. § 1366(d)(1).

[24] I.R.C. § 1366(d)(2)(A).

[25] A shareholder's stock basis is also increased by the excess of depletion deductions over the basis of the property subject to depletion. I.R.C. § 1367(a)(1)(C).

[26] The treatment of distributions by an S corporation to its shareholders is discussed below. A shareholder's stock basis is also decreased by the shareholder's deduction for depletion for any oil or gas property held by the corporation, subject to a certain limitation. I.R.C. § 1367(a)(2)(E).

[27] I.R.C. § 1368(b)(1).

[28] I.R.C. § 1368(b)(2).

earlier, because an S corporation cannot create E&P from its operations, it is unusual for an S corporation to have Accumulated E&P.

E.　Taxing the S Corporation

Except for two situations, an S corporation is not subject to a corporate-level federal income tax.[29] The exceptions are the tax on built-in gains and the tax on excess net passive income. In very general terms, section 1374 taxes an S corporation on the recognition of net gains that accrued while the corporation was a C corporation if the gains are recognized during the 10-year period beginning on the first day that the corporation is an S corporation. The section 1374 tax generally does not apply to a corporation that has always been an S corporation.[30] In addition, section 1375 imposes a tax on an S corporation for a taxable year in which the corporation has excessive passive income along with Accumulated E&P at the close of the year. Again, because an S corporation cannot create E&P from its operations,[31] the only S corporations that can have Accumulated E&P for purposes of the section 1375 tax are corporations that were once C corporations or had inherited E&P from a C corporation in a corporate reorganization or similar transaction. The Detailed Analysis provides a closer examination of these S corporation taxes.

F.　Application of Subchapter C to S Corporations

A large part of subchapter C still applies to S corporations. That is, except for the provisions implementing the shareholder tax on dividends (sections 301 and 316), the other parts of subchapter C apply with equal force to S corporations. These include, among others, the provisions addressing corporate formations, redemptions, liquidations, and reorganizations.

DETAILED ANALYSIS

§ 24.01　INTRODUCTION

As addressed in previous chapters of this book, under Subchapter C the earnings of a corporation are subject to two levels of taxation — first in the hands of the corporation and a second time when distributed as dividends to the shareholders. Under subchapter S, a different regime applies to eligible corporations that elect to become S corporations. Under this regime, the taxable income of an S corporation is generally subject to a single level of tax that applies at the shareholder level. More specifically, the taxable income of an S corporation passes through to the shareholders, who then include this taxable income on their individual returns. This is similar to the way in which the income of a partnership passes through to the partners, but simpler because unlike the pass-through regime of subchapter K, which allows for special allocations and other complicating features, the taxable

---

[29]　I.R.C. § 1363(a).

[30]　I.R.C. § 1374(c)(1).

[31]　I.R.C. § 1371(c)(1).

income of an S corporation passes through to the shareholders on a pro-rata basis according to the shareholders' percentage of stock ownership.

It should be emphasized at the outset that a large part of subchapter C still applies to S corporations. That is, except for the provisions implementing the shareholder tax on dividends (sections 301 and 316), the other parts of subchapter C apply with equal force to S corporations. These include, among others, the provisions addressing corporate formations, redemptions, liquidations, and reorganizations. The last part of this chapter discusses in more detail the application of subchapter C to S corporations.

§ 24.02 ELIGIBILITY FOR ELECTING S CORPORATION STATUS

A. Definition of an S Corporation

Under section 1361(a)(1), a corporation is an S corporation for particular taxable year if the corporation:

- Is a "small business corporation,"
- For which an election is in effect for the particular taxable year.

Thus, to be eligible to elect S corporation status, a corporation must meet the requirements for being a "small business corporation," which are described below.

B. Small Business Corporation

To be a "small business corporation," a corporation must satisfy the following requirements:

- It is a domestic corporation (i.e., incorporated in the United States),
- It is not an "ineligible corporation,"
- It meets the number of shareholders limit,
- It meets the permitted shareholder requirement, and
- It meets the one class of stock requirement.[32]

1. Ineligible Corporation

An "ineligible corporation" for purposes of the above requirements is a corporation that is:

- A financial institution that uses the reserve method for bad debts,
- An insurance company subject to tax under subchapter L,
- A corporation that has an election under section 936 in effect, or
- A Domestic International Sales Corporation (DISC) or former DISC.[33]

---

[32] I.R.C. § 1361(b)(1).
[33] I.R.C. § 1361(b)(2).

These types of corporations are not eligible to elect S corporation status.

2.   Number of Shareholders

In general, an S corporation cannot have more than 100 shareholders.[34] A corporation that exceeds the maximum number of shareholders is ineligible to elect S corporation status. The apparent rationale for this requirement is to limit the size of S corporation operations as well as avoid the administrative difficulty of applying pass-through taxation to entities with thousands of owners, although subchapter K allows for pass-through taxation for partnerships without any limit.

The 100-shareholder limit is extended in two ways. First, a husband and wife count as one shareholder for purposes of the limit.[35] In addition, "members of a family" (and their estates) are treated as one shareholder.[36] "Members of a family" is defined broadly as a common ancestor and any lineal descendant of the common ancestor, including spouses and former spouses thereof, provided that the common ancestor is no more than six generations removed from the youngest generation of shareholders.[37]

> *Example 24.1.* X Corp. has 1,000 shares of common stock outstanding (the only class outstanding). The shareholders of X Corp. consist of 99 unrelated individual shareholders, along with A and B, who are husband and wife, respectively.

Applying the number of shareholders limit to X Corp. in Example 24.1.

X Corp. satisfies the number of shareholders limit because A and B, as husband and wife, are treated as one shareholder, and therefore the corporation has 100 shareholders.

> *Example 24.2.* X Corp. has 1,000 shares of common stock outstanding (the only class outstanding). The shareholders of X Corp. consist of 98 unrelated individual shareholders, along with A and her two children, B and C.

Applying the number of shareholders limit to X Corp. in Example 24.2.

A, B and C are members of a family for purposes of the number of shareholders limit, because they entail a common ancestor (A) and her lineal descendants (B and C) who are not separated by more than six generations (only one generation here). Therefore, A, B and C are treated as one shareholder, and thus the number of shareholders limit is satisfied because X Corp. has 99 shareholders.

---

[34] I.R.C. § 1361(b)(1)(A).

[35] I.R.C. § 1361(c)(1)(A)(i).

[36] I.R.C. § 1361(c)(1)(A)(ii).

[37] I.R.C. § 1361(c)(1)(B).

3. Permitted Shareholders

a.   In General

An S corporation is permitted to have only certain types of shareholders:

- Individuals (other than nonresident aliens),
- Estates,
- Qualified pension or profit-sharing trusts under section 401, or non-profit organizations under section 501(c)(3), and
- Certain types of trusts (described below).[38]

Thus, an S corporation cannot have other types of shareholders, such as corporations or partnerships. A corporation that has shareholders other than those permitted is ineligible to elect S corporation status.

> *Example 24.3.* X Corp. has 1000 shares of common stock outstanding (the only class outstanding). The shareholders of X Corp. are A, a U.S. citizen, and the estate of B.

Applying the permitted shareholder requirement to X Corp. in Example 24.3:

X Corp. satisfies the permitted shareholder requirement because its shareholders are an individual who is not a nonresident alien (A) and an estate (B's estate).

> *Example 24.4.* X Corp. has 1000 shares of common stock outstanding (the only class outstanding). The shareholders of X Corp. are A, a U.S. citizen, the estate of B, and Y Corp.

Applying the permitted shareholder requirement to X Corp. in Example 24.4:

X Corp. fails the permitted shareholder requirement because one of its shareholders, Y Corp., is a corporation, which is not permitted. Therefore, X Corp. is not eligible to elect S corporation status.

b.   Permitted Trusts

The following types of trusts are permitted shareholders of an S corporation:[39]

- Grantor trusts of U.S. citizens or residents — trusts considered as owned by such persons under the Code.[40]
- Former grantor trusts of U.S. citizens or residents — trusts that exist after the deemed owner's death, for two years thereafter.[41]
- Testamentary trusts — trusts holding stock transferred to it by will, for two years after the transfer.[42]

---

[38] I.R.C. § 1361(b)(1)(B), (C).

[39] Foreign trusts are excluded as permitted shareholders. I.R.C. § 1361(c)(2)(A).

[40] I.R.C. § 1361(c)(2)(A)(i).

[41] I.R.C. § 1361(c)(2)(A)(ii).

[42] I.R.C. § 1361(c)(2)(A)(iii).

- Voting trusts — trusts created to exercise the voting power of stock transferred to it.[43]

- Qualified Subchapter S trusts (QSST) — generally a trust with a single beneficiary who (i) is a U.S. citizen or resident, (ii) who is entitled to all of the income and any corpus distributions during that beneficiary's life, and (iii) who is entitled to all of the assets of the trust if the trust were to terminate during the life of the beneficiary, provided that the beneficiary elects to treat the trust as a QSST.[44]

- Electing small business trusts (ESBT) — generally a trust (i) that has as its only beneficiaries individuals, estates, certain non-profit organizations, or governmental bodies that only hold contingent remainder interests in the trust; (ii) none of whose interests were acquired by purchase; and (iii) that makes an election to be treated as an ESBT.[45]

Rules are provided for applying the number of shareholders limit in connection with trusts — e.g., for an ESBT, each potential current beneficiary is treated as a shareholder for purposes of the 100-shareholder limit.[46]

> *Example 24.5.* X Corp. has 1000 shares of common stock outstanding (the only class outstanding). The shareholders of X Corp. are A, a U.S. citizen, and a voting trust that has five beneficial owners.

Applying the permitted shareholder requirement to X Corp. in Example 24.5:

X Corp. satisfies the permitted shareholder requirement because its shareholders are A, an individual who is not a nonresident alien, and a voting trust, which is a permitted trust.

4. One Class of Stock

a.   In General

An S corporation cannot have more than one class of stock.[47] A corporation that violates the one class of stock requirement is ineligible to elect S corporation status. For purposes of this requirement, differences in voting rights are disregarded.[48] Thus, each share of stock must have identical rights to distributions and liquidation proceeds, but the voting rights of shares may vary.[49] The one class of stock requirement simplifies the pass-through of income and expense items to

---

[43] I.R.C. § 1361(c)(2)(A)(iv).

[44] I.R.C. § 1361(d).

[45] I.R.C. § 1361(c)(2)(A)(v), (e). Certain trusts are excluded from being an ESBT — e.g., a trust that is tax exempt. I.R.C. § 1361(e)(1)(B). In addition to the trusts described above, also permitted are IRA trusts that hold certain stock in banks or depository institution holding companies. I.R.C. § 1361(c)(2)(A)(vi).

[46] I.R.C. § 1361(c)(2)(B).

[47] I.R.C. § 1361(b)(1)(D).

[48] I.R.C. § 1361(c)(4).

[49] Treas. Reg. § 1.1361-1(l)(1).

shareholders and prevents the special allocations that can occur under subchapter K.[50]

> *Example 24.6.* X Corp. has outstanding 100 shares of voting common stock and 100 shares of nonvoting preferred stock. Shareholders holding preferred stock only have prior rights to receive $10 of dividends per share each year and $1,000 per share on the liquidation of the corporation. Shareholders holding common stock have rights to unlimited dividends and liquidation proceeds, subject to the prior rights of the preferred shareholders.

Applying the one class of stock requirement to X Corp. in Example 24.6:

X Corp. fails the requirement because it has two classes of stock with different rights to distributions and liquidation proceeds. Therefore, X Corp. is not eligible to elect S corporation status.

> *Example 24.7.* X Corp. has outstanding 100 shares of voting common stock and 100 shares of nonvoting common stock. The stock of each class has identical rights to distributions and liquidation proceeds.

Applying the one class of stock requirement to X Corp. in Example 24.7:

X Corp. satisfies the requirement because it has two classes of stock with identical economic rights, and the differences in voting rights are disregarded.

b.   Straight Debt Safe Harbor

As discussed in Chapter 15, purported debt of a corporation can sometimes be reclassified as stock for tax purposes. In the context of S corporations, reclassifying corporate debt as a second class of stock could result in a violation of the one class of stock requirement.[51] Section 1361(c)(5) reduces this risk with a safe harbor that provides that "straight debt" is not treated as a second class of stock.

"Straight debt" is a written unconditional promise to pay a sum certain in money on a specified date or on demand if:

- The interest rate and payment dates are not contingent on profits, borrower's discretion, or similar factors;
- The instrument is not convertible into stock (either directly or indirectly); and
- The creditor is an individual (other than a nonresident alien), an estate, a trust that would be an eligible S corporation shareholder, or a person who is actively and regularly engaged in a money lending business.[52]

The rationale for the straight debt safe harbor is that the debt falling within the

---

[50] *See* Stephen Schwarz and Daniel J. Lathrope, Fundamentals of Corporate Taxation 667 (2012).

[51] In this regard, Treas. Reg. § 1.1361-1(l)(4) generally provides that any instrument issued by a corporation, even if designated as debt, is treated as a second class of stock if (i) the instrument constitutes equity under general tax law principles and (ii) a principal purpose of issuing the instrument is to circumvent the economic rights of outstanding shares or the limitations on permitted shareholders.

[52] I.R.C. § 1361(c)(5)(B).

safe harbor is not being used either to allocate corporate profits or to avoid the permitted shareholder limitations.[53]

> *Example 24.8.* A and B, both U.S. citizens, form X Corp. by each transferring $50,000 in cash to X Corp. in exchange for 50 shares of X Corp. voting common stock (the only class outstanding). In addition, A loans X Corp. $1,000,000 and takes back X Corp.'s note to repay $1,000,000 plus interest payable at a fixed rate that is twice the prime rate, in equal annual installments over the next 10 years, with payments to occur on December 31 of each year; the note is not convertible into X Corp. stock. X Corp.'s obligation to A on the note is subordinated to any claims of non-shareholder creditors.

Applying the straight debt safe harbor to X Corp. in Example 24.8:

The X Corp. note held by A is straight debt under the safe harbor and thus is not a second class of stock, because the note is an unconditional promise to pay a sum certain in money, neither the interest rate nor interest payment dates are contingent, the note is not convertible into stock, and the creditor is an individual who is not a nonresident alien (A is a U.S. citizen). According to the regulations, the fact that the note is subordinated to other debt does not prevent it from qualifying as straight debt.[54]

Note that absent protection from being treated as a second class of stock under the straight debt safe harbor, there is a significant risk that the X Corp. note would be reclassified as equity under general tax law principles because of the following equity factors:[55] questionable form (apparently high interest rate), high debt/equity ratio (10 to 1[56]), and subordination. The regulations make it clear that obligations satisfying the safe harbor are not treated as a second class of stock even if they would be treated as equity under general principles.[57]

§ 24.03   ELECTING, REVOKING AND TERMINATING S CORPORATION STATUS

A.   Electing S Corporation Status

A corporation that qualifies as a small business corporation by satisfying the above requirements may elect to be an S corporation under section 1362(a). To do so, all of the shareholders of the corporation on the day that the election is made

---

[53] Besides the straight debt safe harbor, the regulations contain other safe harbors for certain short-term unwritten advances and proportionately held obligations. Treas. Reg. § 1.1361-1(l)(4)(ii)(B).

[54] Treas. Reg. § 1.1361-1(l)(5)(ii).

[55] *See* Chapter 15.

[56]

Total debt-equity ratio is $\dfrac{\$1,000,000 \text{ (total liabilities)}}{\$100,000 \text{ (assets minus liabilities)}} = \dfrac{10}{1}$

[57] Treas. Reg. § 1.1361-1(l)(5)(iv).

must consent to the election.[58]

In general, an election is effective at the beginning of a particular taxable year if it is made:

- At any time during the preceding taxable year, or

- During the particular taxable year and on or before the fifteenth day of the third month of such taxable year.[59]

However, an election made during the first two and one-half months of a particular taxable year will be effective for the following taxable year if:

- The corporation was not a small business corporation during the entire portion of the particular taxable that occurs before the date of the election, or

- Any person who was a shareholder during the particular taxable year and before the date of the election did not consent to the election.[60]

Example 24.9. X Corp. has 100 shares of voting common stock outstanding (the only class outstanding). A and B, both U.S. citizens, each own 50 shares of the X Corp. stock. X Corp. is a small business corporation and uses the calendar year. On March 1, 2014, with the consent of A and B, X Corp. makes an election to be an S corporation, indicating that the election is to be effective for 2014.

Applying the election rule to X Corp. in Example 24.9:

X Corp. has made a valid election to be an S corporation because it is a small business corporation on the day of the election, and all of its shareholders on that day have consented to the election. The election is effective as of January 1, 2014 because the election was made on or before the fifteenth day of the third month of calendar year 2014 (which is March 15, 2014).

Example 24.10. X Corp. has 100 shares of voting common stock outstanding (the only class outstanding). As of January 1, 2014, A (a U.S. citizen) owns 50 shares of the X Corp. stock, and Y Corp. owns 50 shares of the X Corp. stock. X Corp. uses the calendar year. On February 1, 2014, Y Corp. sells its 50 shares of X Corp. stock to B (a U.S. citizen); as of that date, X Corp. is a small business corporation. On March 1, 2014, with the consent of A, B, and Y Corp., X Corp. makes an election to be an S corporation, indicating that the election is to be effective for 2014.

Applying the election rule to X Corp. in Example 24.10:

---

[58] I.R.C. § 1362(a)(2). In the case of an invalid election that is determined by the Service to be inadvertent, section 1362(f) permits a waiver of the defect if certain requirements are met. Section 1362(f) also applies to inadvertent terminations of S corporation elections, and is addressed in more detail in connection with terminations below.

[59] I.R.C. § 1361(b)(1). The Service has authority to excuse a late election where there was reasonable cause for a failure to make a timely election. I.R.C. § 1362(b)(5).

[60] I.R.C. § 1362(b)(2).

X Corp. has made a valid election to be an S corporation because it is a small business corporation on the day of the election, and all of its shareholders on that day have consented to the election. Even though the election is intended to be effective for 2014, it is not effective until 2015 because X Corp. was not a small business corporation for the entire portion of 2014 that occurred before the election was made — up until February 1, 2014, X Corp. failed the permitted shareholder requirement because it had a corporate shareholder (Y Corp.).

B. Terminating S Corporation Status

An election to be an S corporation remains in effect until it is terminated.[61] Under section 1362(d), there are three ways in which an election is terminated: by shareholder revocation; by the corporation ceasing to be a small business corporation; or by the corporation having both excess passive investment income and E&P for a certain period.

1. Shareholder Revocation

Under section 1362(d)(1), an S corporation election is terminated by revocation, provided shareholders holding more than one-half of the shares on the day of the revocation consent to the revocation.[62] The corporation may specify an effective date for the revocation that is on or after the date that the revocation is made. If no such date is specified, a revocation made during a particular taxable year and on or before the fifteenth day of the third month of such year is effective at the beginning of that year,[63] and a revocation made after such date is effective at the beginning of the following taxable year.[64]

> *Example 24.11.* X Corp. has 100 shares of voting common stock outstanding (the only class outstanding). A owns 60 shares of the X Corp. stock, and B owns 40 shares of the X Corp. stock. As of January 1, 2010, X Corp. is an S corporation. On February 1, 2014, X Corp. files a revocation of its S corporation election, with A consenting to the revocation. The revocation specifies that it will be effective as of January 1, 2015.

Applying the revocation rule to X Corp. in Example 24.11:

X Corp.'s S corporation election is terminated by revocation because A, who holds more than one-half of the shares, has consented to the revocation. Because X Corp. specifies a prospective effective date for the revocation, the corporation's S corporation status is terminated as of that date, January 1, 2015.

> *Example 24.12.* X Corp. has 100 shares of voting common stock outstanding (the only class outstanding). A owns 60 shares of the X Corp. stock, and B owns 40 shares of the X Corp. stock. As of January 1, 2010, X Corp. is an

---

[61] I.R.C. § 1362(c).

[62] I.R.C. § 1362(d)(1)(A), (B). The shares taken into account include both voting and nonvoting stock. Treas. Reg. § 1.1362-2(a)(1).

[63] I.R.C. § 1362(d)(1)(C)(i).

[64] I.R.C. § 1362(d)(1)(C)(ii).

S corporation; X Corp. uses the calendar year. On February 1, 2014, X Corp. files a revocation of its S corporation election, with A consenting to the revocation. The revocation does not specify an effective date.

Applying the revocation rule to X Corp. in Example 24.12:

Again, X Corp.'s S corporation election is terminated by revocation because A, who holds more than one-half of the shares, has consented to the revocation. Because X Corp. does not specify a prospective effective date for the revocation, X Corp.'s S corporation status is terminated as of January 1, 2014 because the election was made on or before the fifteenth day of the third month of calendar year 2014 (which is March 15, 2014).

2.   Ceasing to be a Small Business Corporation

Under section 1362(d)(2)(A), an S corporation election is terminated whenever a corporation ceases to be a small business corporation. The termination of S corporation status is effective as of the date of cessation.[65]

Example 24.13. X Corp. has 100 shares of voting common stock outstanding (the only class outstanding). A and B, both U.S. citizens, each own 50 shares of the X Corp. stock. As of January 1, 2010, X Corp. is an S corporation. On April 1, 2014, B sells her 50 shares of X Corp. stock to Y Corp.

Applying the small business corporation cessation rule to X Corp. in Example 24.13:

Upon the sale of B's 50 shares of X Corp. to Y Corp., X Corp. is no longer a small business corporation because by having a corporate shareholder, it fails the permitted shareholder requirement. Consequently, X Corp.'s status as an S corporation terminates as of the date of the sale, April 1, 2014.[66]

3.   Having Excess Passive Income and E&P

Under section 1362(d)(3), an S corporation election is terminated if for three consecutive taxable years, the corporation has:

- An amount of "passive investment income" for the year that is in excess of 25% of its gross receipts for the year, and

- Accumulated E&P at the close of the year.[67]

"Passive investment income" generally includes royalties, rents, dividends, interest and annuities.[68] For purposes of the rule, gross receipts from the sale or exchange of stocks or securities are taken into account only to the extent of the gains from

---

[65] I.R.C. § 1362(d)(2)(B).

[66] To guard against such terminations, it is prudent for S corporations to have restrictions on transferring stock. As discussed below, it is possible that the Service could determine that a termination of this type is inadvertent, thus allowing for a waiver of the termination under section 1362(f).

[67] I.R.C. § 1362(d)(3)(A).

[68] I.R.C. § 1362(d)(3)(C)(i). Exceptions are provided for certain situations. I.R.C. § 1362(d)(3)(C)(ii) – (v).

such dispositions;[69] in the case of a sale or exchange of other capital assets, gross receipts from such dispositions are taken into account only to the extent of the excess of capital gains over capital losses.[70] The termination of S corporation status under this rule is effective as of the first day of the first taxable year beginning after the third consecutive year.[71]

Because an S corporation cannot create E&P from its operations,[72] the only S corporations that can have Accumulated E&P for purposes of this termination rule are corporations that were once C corporations or had inherited E&P from a C corporation in a corporate reorganization or similar transaction under section 381.[73] The purpose of this termination rule is to restrict C corporations with E&P from converting to S corporations in order to have a single level of tax on the investment income earned on retained earnings, while delaying indefinitely a second level of tax on the E&P.

> *Example 24.14.* X Corp. was formed on January 1, 2005, and operated for several years as C corporation, accumulating E&P of $1,000,000. As of January 1, 2012, X Corp. is an S corporation. X Corp. uses the calendar year. For each of 2012, 2013, and 2014, X Corp. has (i) interest and dividends from investments in the amount of $100,000, (ii) gross receipts of $300,000, and (iii) Accumulated E&P at the close of the year of $1,000,000.

Applying the excess passive income termination rule to X Corp. in Example 24.14:

The $100,000 of interest and dividends is passive investment income. Therefore, X Corp.'s S corporation election is terminated because for three consecutive years (2012, 2013 and 2014), X Corp. has (i) passive investment income of $100,000 that is in excess of 25% of its gross receipts of $300,000, or $75,000;[74] and (ii) Accumulated E&P at the close of each year.[75] The termination of S corporation status is effective as of January 1, 2015 — the beginning of the first taxable year following the third consecutive year.

4. Inadvertent Terminations

Under section 1362(f), a termination (other than by way of revocation) will be disregarded if:

- The Service determines that the termination was inadvertent,
- Within a reasonable period of time after discovery, steps were taken so that the corporation is a small business corporation (if the failure to be such was the cause of the termination), and

---

[69] I.R.C. § 1362(d)(3)(B)(ii).

[70] I.R.C. § 1362(d)(3)(B)(i).

[71] I.R.C. § 1362(d)(3)(A)(ii).

[72] I.R.C. § 1371(c)(1).

[73] *See* I.R.C. § 1371(c)(2).

[74] 25% of $300,000 is $75,000.

[75] As discussed below, it is possible that the Service could determine that a termination of this type is inadvertent, thus allowing for a waiver of the termination under section 1362(f).

- The corporation and each shareholder agree to make adjustments that are required by the Service.[76]

According to the regulations, an inadvertent termination tends to be established by demonstrating (i) that the terminating event was not reasonably within the control of the corporation and not part of a plan to terminate the S corporation election, or (ii) that the terminating event took place without the corporation's knowledge despite the corporation's due diligence to prevent such an event.[77]

Having the termination disregarded under section 1362(f) takes on added significance in light of section 1362(g). This section provides that if an S corporation election is terminated, the corporation is not eligible to make another S corporation election until the fifth taxable year following the taxable year of termination, unless the Service consents to an earlier election.[78]

§ 24.04   TREATMENT OF S CORPORATION SHAREHOLDERS

A.   Pass-Through Taxation of S Corporation Income or Loss

1.   In General

The key feature of the tax regime for S corporations is that the taxable income of an S corporation passes through to its shareholders, who then include this taxable income on their individual returns. Except for a few situations (discussed in § 24.05), an S corporation is not subject to federal income taxation.[79] Thus, for the most part, the taxable income of an S corporation is subject to a single level of tax that applies at the shareholder level.

2.   Computing an S Corporation's Taxable Income

Under section 1363(b), an S corporation generally computes its taxable income in the same manner as an individual. Accordingly, an S corporation, like an individual, is not entitled to a dividends-received deduction. As exceptions, an S corporation is not entitled to certain personal deductions, such as the deduction for personal exemptions and certain itemized deductions (e.g., deductions for medical expenses, alimony and moving expenses).[80] In addition, an S corporation can elect to deduct organizational expenses under section 248.[81]

---

[76] As noted previously, section 1362(f) also applies to invalid elections to be an S corporation. In the case of an invalid election, the Service must determine that the event causing the invalid election was inadvertent, and the second section 1362(f) requirement (mentioned above) also includes taking steps to acquire the required shareholder consents.

[77] Treas. Reg. § 1.1362-4(b).

[78] I.R.C. § 1362(g).

[79] I.R.C. § 1363(a).

[80] I.R.C. § 1363(b)(2) (referring to the deductions mentioned in section 703(a)(2)).

[81] I.R.C. § 1363(b)(3).

While an S corporation is generally not a taxable entity, it is generally required to make elections that affect the computation of items derived from the corporation.[82] For example, elections of accounting methods and depreciation methods are made by the S corporation and not by the shareholders individually.[83]

Under section 1378, an S corporation generally must use the calendar year as its taxable year.[84] An S corporation can use a fiscal year as its taxable year if it can establish a business purpose for its use; in this regard, a desire to defer income to shareholders is not a business purpose.[85] An S corporation can also select a taxable year that ends on either September 30, October 31, or November 30 without establishing a business purpose by making an election under section 444.[86] If this election is made, the S corporation is required to make the payments required by section 7519.[87] Although the manner of computing the payments required by section 7519 is rather complex, the effect of these payments is that the S corporation is prepaying the tax applicable to the income deferred by reason of making the election under section 444.

In reporting its taxable income, an S corporation is required to separately state income, deduction and loss items the separate treatment of which could affect the tax liability of the shareholders.[88] For example, an S corporation needs to separately state its net capital gains and losses grouped by holding period and category under section 1(h), as opposed to lumping these items together with other taxable income;[89] this is because separate treatment of these gains and losses will affect the shareholders' tax liability in light of the preferential capital gain rates and capital loss limitations. As another example, an S corporation's charitable contributions must be separately stated given the deduction limitations under section 170.[90]

3.   Pass-Through of Items to Shareholders

a.   In General

Under section 1366(a), the shareholders of an S corporation take into account their pro rata shares of the corporation's (i) separately stated income, loss, deduction, or credit and (ii) nonseparately computed income or loss. The shareholder's pro rata share of an item for a particular taxable year is generally determined under a three step process: (i) apportion the item in equal amounts to each day during the taxable year (ii) divide the apportioned amounts by the shares

---

[82] I.R.C. § 1363(c)(1). A few elections with respect to S corporation items are made at the shareholder level, including whether to credit foreign taxes under section 901. I.R.C. § 1363(c)(2).

[83] Treas. Reg. § 1.1363-1(c)(1).

[84] *See* I.R.C. § 1378(a), (b).

[85] *See* I.R.C. § 1378(b).

[86] *See* I.R.C. § 444(a), (b), (e).

[87] I.R.C. § 444(c)(1).

[88] I.R.C. §§ 1363(b)(1), 1366(a)(1)(A).

[89] Treas. Reg. § 1.1366-1(a)(2)(i).

[90] Treas. Reg. § 1.1366-1(a)(2)(iii).

outstanding on each day, and (iii) add up the per share, per day amounts for each shareholder based on the shareholder's stock ownership throughout the year.[91] Where the shareholders' stock ownership percentage remains constant throughout the year, this percentage is used to determine the shareholders' pro rata share of items.

As far as timing, a shareholder takes into account her pro rata share of items during the shareholder's taxable year in which the corporation's taxable year ends.[92] The character of income and deductions is generally determined at the corporate level.[93]

> *Example 24.15.* X Corp., an S corporation, has 100 shares of voting common stock outstanding (the only class outstanding). During all of 2014, A owns 60 shares of the X Corp. stock, and B owns 40 shares of the X Corp. stock. X Corp., A and B use the calendar year. For 2014, X Corp. has $10,000 of long term capital gain from selling publicly traded stock, $100,000 of ordinary income from business operations, and $50,000 of deductible business expenses.

Applying section 1366(a) to A and B in Example 24.15:

Because A and B's stock ownership percentage remains constant throughout 2014, these percentages are used to determine their pro rata shares of X Corp.'s items. The $10,000 of long-term capital gain is a separately stated item, and the $50,000 of net ordinary business income is nonseparately computed income. A and B will take their pro rata shares of these items into account for 2014, the taxable year in which the 2014 taxable year of X Corp. ends. Therefore, A will take into account on her 2014 tax return $6,000 of long term capital gain and $30,000 of ordinary business income, based on her 60% stock interest; B will take into account on her 2014 return $4,000 of long term capital gain and $20,000 of ordinary business income, based on her 40% stock interest.

b.   Limitations on the Pass-Through of Losses and Deductions

Under section 1366(d), the amount of losses and deductions that pass through to a shareholder for a taxable year is limited to the sum of:

- The shareholder's adjusted basis in the stock of the corporation, plus

---

[91] I.R.C. § 1377(a)(1). If a shareholder's entire interest is terminated during a taxable year, and the terminated shareholder, all persons to whom such shareholder transferred shares, and the corporation agree, then the pro rata shares of the terminated shareholder and the persons to whom such shareholder transferred shares is determined as if the taxable year consisted of two taxable years, with the first taxable year ending on the date that the shareholder's interest terminates. I.R.C. § 1377(a)(2).

[92] I.R.C. § 1366(a)(1).

[93] I.R.C. § 1366(b). Where the corporation is being used by the shareholders for the principal purpose of converting, with respect to contributed property, ordinary income to capital gain or capital loss to ordinary loss, then the gain or loss is treated as ordinary income or capital loss, as the case may be. Treas. Reg. § 1.1366-1(b)(2), (3).

- The shareholder's adjusted basis in any indebtedness of the corporation to the shareholder.[94]

The purpose is to limit the pass-through of losses and deductions to the shareholder's economic investment in the corporation, similar to a taxpayer's depreciation deductions with respect to property being limited by the taxpayer's basis in the property. Losses and deductions that are disallowed for a taxable year as a result of the limitation are generally carried forward by the shareholder indefinitely, and can be passed through to the shareholder in a subsequent year if, and to the extent that, the shareholder acquires additional basis in the corporation's stock or debt.[95]

> *Example 24.16.* X Corp., an S corporation, has 100 shares of voting common stock outstanding (the only class outstanding). During all of 2014, A owns 60 shares of the X Corp. stock, and B owns 40 shares of the X Corp. stock. A has a $50,000 basis in her stock, and B has a $10,000 basis in her stock. In 2012, B made a $5,000 loan to X Corp., which is to be repaid in 2017. X Corp., A and B use the calendar year. For 2014, X Corp. has $100,000 of ordinary income from business operations, and $150,000 of deductible business expenses.

Applying section 1366(a) and (d) to A and B in Example 24.16:

Based on her 60% stock interest, A's pro rata share of X Corp.'s net ordinary loss of $50,000 is $30,000. Because A's share of the loss does not exceed A's stock basis of $50,000, A will take into account on her 2014 tax return $30,000 of ordinary loss. Based on her 40% stock interest, B's pro rata share of X Corp.'s net ordinary loss is $20,000. However, because B's share of the loss exceeds the sum of B's $10,000 basis in her stock and B's $5,000 basis in X Corp.'s debt to B, which totals $15,000, B is limited to taking into account only $15,000 of ordinary loss on her 2014 tax return. B can carry forward indefinitely the remaining $5,000 of the loss.

B. Adjustments to Basis

Under section 1367(a)(1), a shareholder's basis in the stock of an S corporation is increased by the shareholder's pro rata share of:

- Separately stated income items, including tax-exempt income, and
- Nonseparately computed income.[96]

---

[94] I.R.C. § 1366(d)(1). An issue that has generated considerable litigation is whether a shareholder receives basis for loss limitation purposes for guaranteeing a debt of an S corporation. All but one case have decided against the taxpayer on this issue. *See, e.g.,* Harris v. United States, 902 F.2d 439 (5th Cir. 1990). Note that even if the losses pass through to the shareholder, the losses may be restricted by the at-risk rules (section 465) and the passive loss rules (section 469).

[95] I.R.C. § 1366(d)(2)(A). Where stock in an S corporation is transferred to a spouse or former spouse in a transaction subject to section 1041(a), any suspended losses with respect to the transferred stock are carried forward by the transferee. I.R.C. § 1366(d)(2)(B).

[96] A shareholder's stock basis is also increased by the excess of depletion deductions over the basis of the property subject to depletion. I.R.C. § 1367(a)(1)(C).

By increasing the shareholders' stock basis by the amount of income that has been passed through to shareholders, the statute prevents the shareholders from being taxed a second time on this income if they were to sell the stock at a price reflecting the retained income.[97] The shareholders also increase their stock basis by their share of tax-exempt income; otherwise, the shareholders would be effectively taxed on such income upon a sale of their stock.

> *Example 24.17.* X Corp., an S corporation, has 100 shares of voting common stock outstanding (the only class outstanding). During all of 2014, A owns 60 shares of the X Corp. stock, and B owns 40 shares of the X Corp. stock. A has a $12,000 basis in her stock, and B has a $8,000 basis in her stock. X Corp., A and B use the calendar year. For 2014, X Corp. has $10,000 of long-term capital gain from selling publicly traded stock, $100,000 of ordinary income from business operations, and $50,000 of deductible business expenses.

Applying section 1367(a)(1) to A and B in Example 24.17:

As in Example 24.15, A will take into account on her 2014 tax return $6,000 of long-term capital gain and $30,000 of ordinary business income, and B will take into account on her tax 2014 return $4,000 of long-term capital gain and $20,000 of ordinary business income. A's basis in the stock of X Corp. will be increased by the amount of her income from the corporation, $36,000, which will result in a basis of $48,000 ($12,000 original basis plus $36,000 increase). Likewise, B's basis in the stock of X Corp. will be increased by the amount of her income from the corporation, $24,000, which will result in a basis of $32,000 ($8,000 original basis plus $24,000 increase).

Under section 1367(a)(2), a shareholder's basis in the stock of an S corporation is decreased, but not below zero,

- By the shareholder's pro rata share of:
    - ○ Separately stated items of loss and deduction,
    - ○ Nonseparately computed loss,
    - ○ Nondeductible, non-capital expenses, and
- By distributions received by the shareholder that were not includable in income under section 1368.[98]

Similar to increasing stock basis for income, the reduction in stock basis for passed-through losses and deductions prevents the shareholders from also using these items to increase the loss or reduce the gain upon a sale of the stock.[99] Nondeductible, non-capital expenses also reduce the shareholders' stock basis so that such items are not effectively deductible by the shareholders upon selling the

---

[97] *See* Boris I. Bittker & James S. Eustice, Federal Income Taxation of Corporations and Shareholders 6-30 – 6-31 (2000).

[98] The treatment of distributions by an S corporation to its shareholder is discussed below. A shareholder's stock basis in also decreased by the shareholder's deduction for depletion for any oil or gas property held by the corporation, subject to a certain limitation. I.R.C. § 1367(a)(2)(E).

[99] *See* Bittker & Eustice, *supra* note 97 at 6-31.

stock. And it is necessary to reduce stock basis by the amount of tax-free distributions received by the shareholders, lest there would be an inappropriate decrease in the gain (or increase in the loss) upon the shareholders' sale of the stock.

Based on the limitation for passing through losses and deductions (discussed above), a shareholder can take into account an amount of S corporation losses and deductions that exceed the shareholder's stock basis, to the extent of the shareholder's basis in indebtedness of the corporation to the shareholder. Where this occurs, section 1367(b)(2)(A) reduces the shareholder's basis in the corporate indebtedness (but not below zero) by the amount of passed-through losses and deductions in excess of the shareholder's stock basis. Following such a reduction, any subsequent net upward adjustments under section 1367(a) are first applied to increase the shareholder's basis in corporate indebtedness before increasing the shareholder's stock basis.[100]

> *Example 24.18.* X Corp., an S corporation, has 100 shares of voting common stock outstanding (the only class outstanding). During all of 2014, A owns 60 shares of the X Corp. stock, and B owns 40 shares of the X Corp. stock. A has a $50,000 basis in her stock, and B has a $10,000 basis in her stock. In 2012, B made a $5,000 loan to X Corp., which is to be repaid in 2017. X Corp., A and B use the calendar year. For 2014, X Corp. has $100,000 of ordinary income from business operations, and $150,000 of deductible business expenses.

Applying section 1367(a)(2) and (b) to A and B in Example 24.18:

As in Example 24.16, A will take into account on her 2014 tax return $30,000 of ordinary loss, and B will take into account on her 2014 tax return $15,000 of ordinary loss. A's basis in the stock of X Corp. will be decreased by the amount of her loss from the corporation, $30,000, which will result in a basis of $20,000 ($50,000 original basis minus $30,000 decrease). B's basis in the stock of X Corp. will be decreased, but not below zero, by the amount of her loss from the corporation, $15,000, which will result in a basis of $0 ($10,000 original basis minus $15,000 decrease). In addition, B's basis in X Corp.'s indebtedness to her will be decreased by the excess of her loss from the corporation, $15,000, over her original stock basis, $10,000, which equals $5,000; this will reduce B's basis in the X Corp. indebtedness to $0 ($5,000 original basis minus $5,000 decrease).

The regulations provide ordering rules for making stock basis adjustments, which generally provide that basis (i) is first increased by income items, (ii) is then decreased by tax-free distributions, and (iii) is finally decreased by loss and deduction items.[101] Basis adjustments are determined and generally effective as of the close of the S corporation's taxable year; however, if a shareholder disposes of stock during a taxable year, the basis adjustments with respect to the transferred stock are effective immediately prior to the disposition.[102]

---

[100] I.R.C. § 1367(b)(2)(B).

[101] Treas. Reg. § 1.1367-1(f).

[102] Treas. Reg. § 1.1367-1(d)(1).

C.   Treatment of Distributions

The tax treatment of distributions of property by an S corporation to its shareholders is governed by section 1368. More specifically, this section applies to distributions of property by an S corporation with respect to its stock that would otherwise be subject to section 301(c) if made by a C corporation.[103]

As described below, the tax treatment of distributions under section 1368 depends on whether or not the S corporation has Accumulated E&P. In this connection, it is worth repeating that since an S corporation cannot create E&P from its operations,[104] the only S corporations that can have Accumulated E&P are corporations that were once C corporations or had inherited E&P from a C corporation in a corporate reorganization or similar transaction under section 381.[105] Consequently, the vast majority of S corporation distributions should be subject to the rule for S corporations without Accumulated E&P.

1.   S Corporations with No E&P

Under section 1368(b), a distribution made by an S corporation without Accumulated E&P is excluded from the shareholder's gross income to the extent that the distribution does not exceed the shareholder's adjusted basis in the stock of the corporation.[106] To the extent that the amount of the distribution exceeds the shareholder's stock basis, the excess is treated as gain from the sale of the stock.[107] Thus, a distribution by an S corporation with no Accumulated E&P is treated as a tax-free return of capital up to the shareholder's stock basis and gain from the sale of stock thereafter. The general tax-free treatment of S corporation distributions carries out the general policy of imposing a single tax on the income of an S corporation.

> *Example 24.19.* A owns all 100 shares of X Corp., an S corporation. X Corp. has no Accumulated E&P. A's adjusted basis in the X Corp. stock is $4,000. During 2014, X Corp. distributes $5,000 to A.

Applying section 1368(b) to A in Example 24.19:

$4,000 of the distribution is not included in A's gross income, as this amount does not exceed A's $4,000 adjusted basis in the X Corp. stock. The excess of the $5,000 distribution over A's $4,000 stock basis, or $1,000, is treated as gain from the sale of X Corp. stock. Note that under section 1367(a)(2), A's stock basis is reduced to $0 — original basis of $4,000 minus the tax-free distribution of $4,000.

---

[103]   I.R.C. § 1368(a). Accordingly, in addition to applying to nonliquidating distributions of property, section 1368 also applies to other transactions treated as section 301 distributions, such as redemptions under section 302(d) and stock distributions under section 305(b).

[104]   I.R.C. § 1371(c)(1).

[105]   *See* I.R.C. § 1371(c)(2).

[106]   I.R.C. § 1368(b)(1).

[107]   I.R.C. § 1368(b)(2).

2. S Corporations with E&P

Under section 1368(c), a distribution made by an S corporation with Accumulated E&P is subject to the following three-part rule:

- To the extent that the distribution does not exceed the corporation's accumulated adjustments account ("AAA"), the distribution is treated under section 1368(b), that is, the distribution is:

  - Not included in gross income to the extent of the shareholder's adjusted basis in the stock, and

  - Treated as gain from sale of stock to the extent that the distribution exceeds the shareholder's adjusted basis in the stock.[108]

- Any portion of the distribution that is in excess of the corporation's AAA is treated as a dividend to the extent of the corporation's Accumulated E&P.[109]

- Any remaining portion of the distribution (after exhausting both the corporation's AAA and Accumulated E&P) is treated under part 1 of the rule, that is, it is:

  - Not included in gross income to the extent of the shareholder's adjusted basis in the stock, and

  - Treated as gain from sale of stock to the extent that the remaining portion of the distribution exceeds the shareholder's adjusted basis in the stock.[110]

An S corporation's AAA essentially represents the corporation's net undistributed income that accumulated while the corporation was an S corporation. The AAA is determined by (i) starting at zero, (ii) generally adding S corporation income items, and (iii) generally subtracting S corporation deduction and loss items (including nondeductible, non-capital expenses) as well as S corporation distributions.[111] The AAA does not include tax-exempt income and related expenses.[112] Also, there is no adjustment for Federal taxes attributable to a year in which the corporation was a C corporation.[113] The adjustments can result in a negative AAA,[114] but the AAA cannot be reduced below zero by distributions.[115]

The distribution rule for an S corporation with E&P prevents a C corporation with Accumulated E&P from converting to an S corporation and then distributing its E&P to the shareholders as either tax-free returns of capital or capital gains.[116]

---

[108] I.R.C. § 1368(c)(1).

[109] I.R.C. § 1368(c)(2).

[110] I.R.C. § 1368(c)(3).

[111] I.R.C. § 1368(e)(1)(A); *see* Treas. Reg. § 1.1368-2.

[112] I.R.C. § 1368(e)(1)(A).

[113] *Id.*

[114] *Id.*

[115] Treas. Reg. § 1.1368-2(a)(3)(iii).

[116] *See* Bittker & Eustice, *supra* note 97 at 6-47.

The rule permits such tax-free or capital gain treatment only to the extent of the corporation's AAA, which as previously mentioned, represents net income accumulated while the corporation was an S corporation.

> *Example 24.20.* X Corp. was formed on January 1, 2005, and operated for several years as a C corporation, accumulating E&P of $1,000,000. As of January 1, 2012, X Corp. becomes an S corporation. Since X Corp.'s formation, A has owned all 100 shares of X Corp. For the period consisting of 2012, 2013 and 2014, X Corp. has $400,000 of net ordinary business income and made no distributions to its shareholder, A, until December 31, 2014 when X Corp. distributed $600,000 to A. A's adjusted basis in the X Corp. stock is $500,000.

Applying section 1368(c) to A in Example 24.20:

As of the close of 2014, X Corp.'s AAA is $400,000, based on the positive adjustment for X Corp.'s $400,000 of net ordinary business income while X Corp. is an S corporation. Consequently, the results under section 1368(c) are as follows:

- $400,000 of the distribution does not exceed the corporation's AAA, and this amount is not included in gross income because it does not exceed A's basis in the X Corp. stock (which is $500,000).

- The $200,000 portion of the distribution that is in excess of X Corp.'s AAA of $400,000 is treated as a dividend because X Corp. has Accumulated E&P of $1,000,000.[117]

- There is no remaining portion of the distribution for applying the third part of the rule.

Therefore, of the $600,000 distribution, $400,000 is tax-free and $200,000 is a dividend.

An S corporation can elect to not apply the first part of the distribution rule and instead treat distributions as first coming out of Accumulated E&P, provided that all shareholders receiving distributions during a taxable year consent to this election.[118] A reason for doing this would be to eliminate Accumulated E&P (via the charge to E&P[119]), in order to avoid the section 1375 tax on excess net passive income for S corporations with E&P (discussed below), as well as the termination of the S election under section 1362(d)(3) for S corporations with excess passive income and E&P.

§ 24.05   TAXING THE S CORPORATION

Except for the two situations described in this section, an S corporation is not subject to a corporate-level federal income tax.[120] The exceptions are the tax on built-in gains and the tax on excess net passive income.

---

[117] I.R.C. § 1368(c)(2).

[118] I.R.C. § 1368(e)(3).

[119] I.R.C. §§ 312(a), 1371(c)(3).

[120] I.R.C. § 1363(a).

A.   Tax on Built-In Gains

In very general terms, section 1374 taxes an S corporation on the recognition of net gains that accrued while the corporation was a C corporation if the gains are recognized during the ten-year period beginning on the first day that the corporation is an S corporation. Section 1374 was enacted in order to prevent a C corporation holding appreciated property from converting to S corporation status in order to avoid a corporate-level tax on a sale of the property.[121]

Under section 1374, an S corporation is generally taxed on any "net recognized built-in gain" that it has during the "recognition period."[122] The tax is computed by applying the highest tax rate specified in section 11(b).[123]

Several terms need to be defined:

- Subject to a limitation described below, with respect to a particular taxable year, a "net recognized built-in gain" is defined as the lesser of (i) "recognized built-in gains" reduced by "recognized built-in losses" for the year or (ii) the corporation's taxable income for the year.[124]

- A "recognized built-in gain" is any gain recognized during the recognition period, *except* to the extent that the corporation establishes either (i) that the asset giving rise to the gain was not held by the corporation when it became an S corporation or (ii) the amount of the gain is in excess of the unrealized gain on the asset[125] when the corporation became an S corporation.[126]

- A "recognized built-in loss" is any loss recognized during the recognition period to the extent that the corporation establishes (i) that the asset giving rise to the loss was held by the corporation when it became an S corporation and (ii) the amount of the loss is not in excess of the unrealized loss on the asset[127] when the corporation became an S corporation.[128]

- The "recognition period" is generally the ten-year period beginning on the first day that the corporation is an S corporation.[129]

The amount of net recognized built-in gain that is taken into account for any taxable year is *limited* to excess of:

- The "net unrealized built-in gain," over

---

[121] See Schwarz & Lathrope, *supra* note 50 at 693-694.

[122] I.R.C. § 1374(a).

[123] I.R.C. § 1374(b)(1).

[124] I.R.C. § 1374(d)(2)(A).

[125] This is the difference between the asset's fair market value and adjusted basis.

[126] I.R.C. § 1374(d)(3).

[127] This is the difference between the asset's adjusted basis and fair market value.

[128] I.R.C. § 1374(d)(4).

[129] I.R.C. § 1374(d)(7)(A). For taxable years beginning in 2009 or 2010, the recognition period was reduced to seven years. I.R.C. § 1374(d)(7)(B). For taxable years beginning in 2011, 2012 or 2013, the recognition period was reduced to five years. I.R.C. § 1374(d)(7)(B), (C).

- The amount of net recognized built-in gains that were subject to the section 1374 tax in prior years.[130]

"Net unrealized built-in gain" is the amount by which the fair market value of the corporation's assets on the first day it is an S corporation exceeds the aggregate adjusted basis of such assets at such time.[131] This amount serves as the overall ceiling on the S corporation's gain that is subject to the section 1374 tax.

The section 1374 tax generally does not apply to a corporation that has always been an S corporation.[132] An exception is where an S corporation acquires an asset with a built-in gain from a C corporation in a transaction in which the S corporation's basis in the asset is determined with reference to the asset's basis in the hands of the C corporation (e.g., in a tax free reorganization).[133] In this situation, the recognition period for taxing any net recognized built-in gain attributable to the acquired asset begins on the day that the asset was acquired by the S corporation.[134]

> *Example 24.21.* X Corp. was formed on January 1, 2005, and operated for several years as a C corporation. As of January 1, 2014, X Corp. becomes an S corporation. On January 1, 2014, X Corp. held the following assets: equipment with a fair market value of $600,000 and adjusted basis of $0, and real estate with a fair market value of $1,000,000 and adjusted basis of $1,200,000. In 2014, X Corp. sells the equipment for $600,000 and the real estate for $1,050,000. For 2014, X Corp. has taxable income of $500,000.

Applying section 1374 to X Corp. in Example 24.21:

On the sale of the equipment, there is a recognized gain of $600,000 ($600,000 amount realized minus $0 adjusted basis); on the sale of the real estate, there is a recognized loss of $150,000 ($1,050,000 amount realized minus $1,200,000 adjusted basis). The $600,000 recognized gain and $150,000 recognized loss in 2014 are within the 10-year recognition period. The $600,000 recognized gain and $150,000 recognized loss are recognized built-in gain and recognized built-in loss, respectively, because the items are attributable to assets held by X Corp. when it became an S corporation, and the amounts of gain and loss do not exceed the unrealized gain and loss at that time. Subject to the net unrealized built-in gain limitation, X Corp.'s net recognized built-in gain for 2014 is the lesser of (i) $450,000 ($600,000 recognized built-in gain reduced by the $150,000 recognized built-in loss) or (ii) $500,000 (X Corp.'s taxable income for the year), which is $450,000. The net recognized built-in gain for 2014, however, is limited to the net unrealized built-in gain less the amounts subject to the section 1374 tax in prior years (which is zero), with the former equal to the fair market value of X Corp.'s assets when it became an S corporation, $1,600,000, minus the aggregate adjusted basis of such assets, $1,200,000, which equals $400,000. Therefore, the net recognized built-in gain for 2014 that is subject

---

[130] I.R.C. § 1374(c)(2); *see* Schwarcz & Lathrope, *supra* note 50 at 695.

[131] I.R.C. § 1374(d)(1).

[132] I.R.C. § 1374(c)(1).

[133] I.R.C. § 1374(d)(8)(A).

[134] I.R.C. § 1374(d)(8)(B)(i).

to the section 1374 tax is limited to $400,000.

B. Tax on Excess Net Passive Income

Section 1375 imposes a tax on an S corporation for a taxable year in which the corporation has:

- An amount of "passive investment income" for the year that is in excess of 25% of its gross receipts for the year, and
- Accumulated E&P at the close of the year.

The section 1375 tax is computed by applying the highest tax rate specified in section 11(b) to the corporation's "excess net passive income" for the year.

As with the rule contained in section 1362(d)(3) that terminates the S corporation election where the above conditions persist for three consecutive years, the purpose of the section 1375 tax is to restrict a C corporation with E&P from converting to an S corporation in order to have a single level of tax on the investment income earned on retained earnings, while delaying indefinitely a second level of tax on the E&P.

"Passive investment income" and "gross receipts" have the same meanings as for the section 1362(d)(3) termination rule.[135] "Passive investment income" generally includes royalties, rents, dividends, interest and annuities.[136] Gross receipts from the sale or exchange of stocks or securities are taken into account only to the extent of the gains from such dispositions;[137] in the case of a sale or exchange of other capital assets, gross receipts from such dispositions are taken into account only to the extent of the excess of capital gains over capital losses.[138]

Subject to a limitation, "excess net passive income" for a year is defined as:

$$\text{"net passive income" for the year} \times \frac{\text{amount of passive investment income for the year in excess of 25\% of gross receipts for the year}}{\text{passive investment income for the year.}^{139}}$$

The amount of excess net passive income for a year cannot exceed the corporation's taxable income for the year.[140] "Net passive income" is generally passive investment income reduced by deductions that are directly connected with the production of such income.[141]

---

[135] I.R.C. § 1375(b)(3).

[136] I.R.C. § 1362(d)(3)(C)(i). Exceptions are provided for certain situations. I.R.C. § 1362(d)(3)(C)(ii) – (v).

[137] I.R.C. § 1362(d)(3)(B)(ii).

[138] I.R.C. § 1362(d)(3)(B)(i).

[139] I.R.C. § 1375(b)(1)(A).

[140] I.R.C. § 1375(b)(1)(B).

[141] I.R.C. § 1375(b)(2).

Since an S corporation cannot create E&P from its operations,[142] the only S corporations that can have Accumulated E&P for purposes of the section 1375 tax are corporations that were once C corporations or had inherited E&P from a C corporation in a corporate reorganization or similar transaction under section 381.[143] The same is true for purposes of the section 1362(d)(3) termination rule, as mentioned previously.

> *Example 24.22.* X Corp. was formed on January 1, 2005, and operated for several years as C corporation, accumulating E&P of $1,000,000. As of January 1, 2014, X Corp. is an S corporation. X Corp. uses the calendar year. For 2014, X Corp. has (i) interest and dividends from investments in the amount of $100,000, (ii) gross receipts of $300,000, (iii) taxable income of $250,000 and (iii) Accumulated E&P at the close of the year of $1,000,000. X Corp. has no deductions that are allocable to its interest and dividends.

Applying the section 1375 tax to X Corp. in Example 24.22:

The $100,000 of interest and dividends is passive investment income. Therefore, X Corp. is subject to the section 1375 tax for 2014 because X Corp. has (i) passive investment income of $100,000 that is in excess of 25% of its gross receipts of $300,000, which is $75,000;[144] and (ii) Accumulated E&P at the close of the year. The amount of the tax is equal to the highest tax specified in section 11(b), currently 35%, multiplied by X Corp.'s excess net passive income for the year. With no deductions allocable to the $100,000 of passive investment income, the net passive income is also $100,000. The amount of the net passive income in excess of 25% of gross receipts is $100,000 minus $75,000, or $25,000. Therefore, X Corp.'s excess net passive income for 2014 is:

$$\text{net passive income for the year (\$100,000)} \times \frac{\text{amount of passive investment income for the year in excess of 25\% of gross receipts for the year (\$25,000)}}{\text{passive investment income for the year (\$100,000)}},$$

which equals $25,000. Because X Corp.'s taxable income for 2014 is $250,000, the taxable income limitation does not apply.

The Service has the authority to waive the section 1375 tax if the S corporation establishes (i) that the corporation had determined in good faith that it did not have Accumulated E&P at the close of a year and (ii) that the corporation had distributed its E&P within a reasonable period of time after a determination that it did in fact have Accumulated E&P at the close of such year.[145]

---

[142] I.R.C. § 1371(c)(1).

[143] *See* I.R.C. § 1371(c)(2).

[144] 25% of $300,000 is $75,000.

[145] I.R.C. § 1375(d).

§ 24.06   APPLICATION OF SUBCHAPTER C TO S CORPORATIONS

A large part of subchapter C still applies to S corporations. This is a result of section 1371(a), which provides that subchapter C applies to an S corporation and its shareholders, except as otherwise provided in the Code and except to the extent inconsistent with subchapter S.

Accordingly, the subchapter C provisions for implementing the shareholder tax on dividends (sections 301 and 316) are superseded by the section 1368 rules for distributions by S corporations.[146] On the other hand, the following subchapter C provisions apply to S corporations:

- Corporate formation — Section 351 and related provisions apply in the same manner on the formation of an S corporation.

- Corporate-level consequences of nonliquidating distributions — On an S corporation's nonliquidating distribution of property, section 311 applies in the same manner except that any gain recognized at the corporate level is not subject to a corporate tax (unless section 1374 applies) but instead passes through to the shareholders.

- Redemptions — Section 302 applies to an S corporation's distribution of money or property in the redemption of its stock. If the redemption is treated as a section 301 distribution of property under section 302(d), the section 1368 rules for distributions by S corporations would apply to the amount distributed.

- Stock distributions — Section 305 applies to an S corporation's distribution of its own stock. If the stock distribution is treated as a section 301 distribution of property under section 305(b), the section 1368 rules would apply to the amount distributed.

- Liquidations — On the liquidation of an S corporation, sections 331 and 336 apply in the same manner, except that any gain recognized at the corporate level is not subject to a corporate tax (unless section 1374 applies) but instead passes through to the shareholders. An S corporation cannot be the subsidiary in a nontaxable liquidation under section 332, because an S corporation is not permitted to have a corporate shareholder. An S corporation can be the parent in a section 332 liquidation, because an S corporation is permitted to have subsidiaries.

- Corporate reorganizations and divisions — Section 368 and other provisions related to tax-free corporate reorganizations apply the same to S corporations. Section 355 and related provisions applying to tax-free divisions apply the same to S corporations.

---

[146] Section 306 also should not apply to an S corporation because an S corporation is not permitted to issue preferred stock. Schwarcz & Lathrope, *supra* note 50 at 701, n. 9. Its application also appears to be inconsistent with subchapter S.

TABLE OF CASES

[References are to pages]

[References are to pages]

TABLE OF STATUTES

[References are to pages]

[References are to pages]

[References are to pages]

TS-6 TABLE OF STATUTES

[References are to pages]

[References are to pages]

[References are to pages]

[References are to pages]

[References are to pages]

[References are to pages]

[References are to pages]

[References are to pages]

TAX SOURCES

Proposed Treasury Regulations

TABLE OF AGENCY DECISIONS

[References are to pages]

[References are to pages]

INDEX

[References are to pages.]

[References are to pages.]

[References are to pages.]

[References are to pages.]

[References are to pages.]

[References are to pages.]

[References are to pages.]

R

RECAPITALIZATIONS
"E" reorganizations (See REORGANIZATIONS, CORPORATE, subhead: "E" reorganizations: recapitalizations)
Property to partnership, transfer of . . . 29

RECAPTURE PROPERTY
Property to partnership, transfer of . . . 29

RECEIPT OF BOOT
Corporate formation (See CORPORATE FORMATION, subhead: Receipt of boot, shareholders')
Gain/loss recognition
  Corporate divisions . . . 498
  Shareholders and security holders, tax consequences to . . . 469
  Transfer of assets to acquiring corporation, on . . . 475
Partnership, effect in . . . 31

RECOURSE LIABILITY
Allocation of . . . 51
Defined . . . 47; 48

REORGANIZATIONS, CORPORATE
Generally . . . 443
Acquiring corporation, tax consequences to
  Generally . . . 443
  Gain/loss, recognition of . . . 477
  Property received
    Basis in . . . 478
    Holding period in . . . 479
"A" reorganization: statutory merger/consolidation . . . 440; 450
"B" reorganizations: stock-for-stock acquisitions . . . 440; 451
Business enterprise requirement, continuity of
  Generally . . . 445
  Target's historic business
    Assets, use of . . . 446
    Continuing . . . 445
"C" reorganizations: asset-for-stock acquisitions
  Generally . . . 441; 452
  Solely for stock requirement, modifications to . . . 453
"D" reorganizations: asset-for-stock acquisitions
  Acquisitive . . . 459
  Divisive . . . 461
"E" reorganizations: recapitalizations
  Generally . . . 462
  Corporate debt instruments
    Corporate debt instruments for . . . 463
    Holders' exchange of corporate debt instruments for stock . . . 463
    Shareholders' exchange of stock for . . . 463
  Holders' exchange of corporate debt instruments for stock . . . 463
  Shareholders' exchange of stock for corporate debt instruments . . . 463
  Stock for stock . . . 462
"F" reorganizations: changes in identity, form or place of organization . . . 464

REORGANIZATIONS, CORPORATE—Cont.
Gain/loss recognition
  Acquiring corporation . . . 477
  Distribution of property to shareholders and creditors, on . . . 476
  Transfer of assets to acquiring corporation, on
    Generally . . . 474
    Receipt of boot . . . 475
"G" reorganizations: insolvency reorganizations
  Generally . . . 464
  Acquisitive . . . 465
  Divisive . . . 466
Interest requirement, continuity of
  Generally . . . 447
  Consideration received, type of . . . 447
  Qualifying consideration received, portion of . . . 448
  Stock dispositions before/after potential reorganization, effect of . . . 449
Non-statutory requirements for reorganizations
  Generally . . . 439
  Business enterprise requirement, continuity of (See subhead: Business enterprise requirement, continuity of)
  Business purpose requirement . . . 445
  Interest requirement, continuity of (See subhead: Interest requirement, continuity of)
Shareholders and security holders, tax consequences to
  Generally . . . 442
  Basis in property received . . . 472
  Gain/loss, recognition of
    Generally . . . 468
    Dividend treatment of recognized gain . . . 470
    Receipt of boot . . . 469
  Holding period in stock/securities received . . . 473
Target corporation, tax consequences to
  Generally . . . 442
  Gain/loss recognition (See subhead: Gain/loss recognition)
Tax treatment of parties to reorganization
  Generally . . . 441; 444; 467
  Acquiring corporation (See subhead: Acquiring corporation, tax consequences to)
  Shareholders and security holders (See subhead: Shareholders and security holders, tax consequences to)
  Target corporation
    Generally . . . 442
    Gain/loss recognition (See subhead: Gain/loss recognition)
Triangular reorganizations and drop downs
  "A" reorganizations
    Forward triangular mergers . . . 455
    Reverse triangular mergers . . . 456
  Assets/stock, drop downs of . . . 459
  "B" reorganizations . . . 457
  "C" reorganizations . . . 458
Types
  Generally . . . 439

[References are to pages.]

[References are to pages.]